NIXON

[NIXON, RICHARD MILHOUS]

The Fourth Year of His Presidency

CONGRESSIONAL QUARTERLY

1735 K STREET, N. W., WASHINGTON, D. C.

Congressional Quarterly Inc.

Congressional Quarterly Inc., an editorial research service and publishing company, serves clients in the fields of news, education, business and government. It combines specific coverage of Congress, government and politics by Congressional Quarterly with the more general subject range of an affiliated service, Editorial Research Reports.

Congressional Quarterly was founded in 1945 by Nelson and Henrietta Poynter. Its basic periodical publication was and still is the CQ *Weekly Report,* mailed to clients every Saturday. A cumulative index is published quarterly.

The CQ *Almanac,* a compendium of legislation for one session of Congress, is published every spring. *Congress and the Nation* is published every four years as a record of government for one presidential term.

Congressional Quarterly also publishes paperback books on public affairs. These include the twice-yearly *Guide to Current American Government* and such recent titles as *The Power of the Pentagon, Education for a Nation* and *The U.S. Economy.*

CQ Direct Research is a consulting service which performs contract research and maintains a reference library and query desk for the convenience of clients.

Editorial Research Reports covers subjects beyond the specialized scope of Congressional Quarterly. It publishes reference material on foreign affairs, business, education, cultural affairs, national security, science and other topics of news interest. Service to clients includes a 6,000-word report four times a month bound and indexed semi-annually. Editorial Research Reports publishes paperback books in its fields of coverage. Founded in 1923, the service merged with Congressional Quarterly in 1956.

Nixon: the Fourth Year of His Presidency was edited by Robert A. Diamond, Book Service Editor.

Contributors: Janice L. Goldstein, Peter A. Harkness, Andrea W. Loewenstein, August Maffry Jr., Wayne Walker. Index: Janet Sims.

Library of Congress Catalog No. 72-94077
International Standard Book No. 0-87187-039-8

Copyright 1973 by Congressional Quarterly Inc.
1735 K Street, N.W., Washington, D.C. 20006

TABLE OF CONTENTS

Messages and Statements

NIXON'S RECORD: A SWEEPING ENDORSEMENT BY THE VOTERS

For Richard Nixon, 1972 was the year to put it all together to accelerate the economy, slow down inflation, seek an "honorable peace" in Vietnam, open up a dialogue with Communist China and cool off the arms race with the Russians.

Finally, it was the year to face the voters in his fifth national campaign, to seek a "new American majority" that would grant him four more years in the White House. The Nixon sweep of every state except Massachusetts and the District of Columbia—achieved by a politician who never before had commanded the trust or affection of the American electorate—was a testament to the President's political skill, his keen sense of timing and his mastery of events.

In the year it counted most, he looked his best. He had eased tensions abroad and brought some semblance of stability to the nation. In a pre-election analysis, television commentator David Brinkley sought to put the 1972 campaign in some perspective by listing all the traumatic events the nation had endured since the end of the Korean war. "No other democratic country has put up with so much," he concluded. "A people with that history must hunger for some calm and order. How that translated into votes everyone can decide for himself. But seeing the election as a sequel to all that might help explain whatever happens" on election day.

What seemed important to the voters in 1972 was the prospect of peace in Vietnam, an upsurge in the economy, a leveling off of unemployment and a slowdown of inflation. It appeared that the President's hard line on the war, his diplomatic initiatives with the largest communist nations and his continuance of economic controls all were decisions that contributed to his lopsided victory in the polls.

In a sense, then, his fourth year in office marked the grand finale of a four-year campaign for re-election, which with only one exception went without a hitch.

The exception was the Watergate incident. Although the President maintained a lofty, presidential demeanor throughout the campaign, revelations of political dirtywork being conducted by his lieutenants cast a pall over the White House, conjuring up for many the apparition of the old "Tricky Dick." While reports that the Republicans had conducted an unprecedented espionage and sabotage opeation against the Democrats inflicted only limited damage to the GOP campaign, most observers felt its repercussions would be evident well into the second Nixon administration

Relations With Congress

1969. The Nixon administration and lieutenants on Capitol Hill have faced a political situation in Washington unique in this century. Not since the inauguration of Zachary Taylor in 1849 had a President entered office facing opposition majorities in both houses of Congress.

The President won on 74 percent of the 119 congressional roll-call votes that presented clear-cut tests of support for his views in 1969. Mr. Nixon ranked lower in over-all support than any other President since 1953, when Congressional Quarterly's support studies began.

In 1969, the President frequently called on Democratic leaders in the House and Senate to push his legislative programs. But at times, he had trouble keeping members of his own party in line. Particularly in the Senate, Republicans opposed him on a number of issues. These included the President's narrowest victory of the year (a 50-50 vote) on an amendment to delete the Safeguard ABM system and his major defeat—the rejection of Federal Judge Clement F. Haynsworth Jr. as a Supreme Court justice.

The main issue separating the White House and Congress was national priorities. Moderates and liberals on Capitol Hill wanted to spend less for defense and more on education, health and pollution control than the President had requested.

Throughout the year, Nixon had difficulty establishing effective liaison with Congress, especially with Senate Republican liberals. All three of the Senate Republican leaders, for instance, voted against the Haynsworth nomination.

The sentiments of the Republican liberals probably were best expressed by Sen. Charles McC. Mathias Jr. (Md.), who referred to the President's advisers as "Prussians," and added: "I suppose they're bright in their way. But they just don't understand this body (the Senate). They just haven't found any way to communicate effectively."

1970. Congress in 1970 spent most of its time disputing the President over spending priorities. It sliced funds from his military, foreign aid and space requests and added money to numerous domestic programs, primarily education, health, manpower training and pollution control.

Nixon met with greatest resistance from Congress on his military and foreign policy stands concerning Vietnam and Cambodia.

The President's Senate spokesman, Minority Leader Hugh Scott (R Pa.), charged that Congress had "dawdled, postured, delayed" for two years, leading to "confusion and loss of confidence in government" and to "embarrassment" of the Congress.

But presidential vetoes had contributed partly to the slow legislative pace. Four of the President's six vetoes during the year were sustained. Two of the four were appropriation bills which had to be rewritten. Despite the unusual length of the 1970 session—the longest since 1950—Congress did not complete action on some of the President's major requests: welfare reform, revenue sharing, consumer protection and Social Security increases.

Of the 210 specific requests made by Nixon for legislation, 97—or about 46 percent—were enacted into law. The President won 77 percent of the 156 roll-call votes that presented clear-cut tests of support for his views.

Among proposals enacted into law, there were some major victories: postal reform, environmental measures and crime legislation. For the second time, Congress approved further deployment of the controversial anti-ballistic missile system (ABM), but only after Nixon's request was cut back substantially.

1971. Nixon began his third year of the presidency with a pledge to restructure government and turn power "back to the people." In his state of the union message, he introduced "six great goals" of his administration: welfare reform, revenue sharing, health insurance reform, environmental initiatives, government reorganization and full employment. All but the last required legislation. Achievement of all six, Nixon said, would bring about "a new American revolution."

By the end of the year, none of the first five goals had been enacted. They were bogged down in what the President called a lagging Congress controlled by Democrats. His two major domestic proposals—welfare reform and revenue sharing—were locked in committee, partly because the President himself had asked that they be delayed.

Nixon had other difficulties with Congress. It spent more for domestic programs than he wanted, resulting in three vetoes of legislation the administration considered too costly. It also turned down his requests for funding of the supersonic transport (SST) and the foreign aid program.

In all, Congress approved one-fifth of the administration's legislative proposals. Of the 202 specific requests for legislation made by the President, 40 were enacted into law. The President won 75 percent of the 139 recorded congressional votes that presented clear-cut tests of support for his views. But much of what the administration proposed never came to a vote in the House or Senate.

This reflected the detailed nature of Nixon's proposals as well as congressional inaction. Proceedings were not completed—or even begun, in some cases—on many specific proposals on natural resources, taxes, small business, health and government operations.

1972. The 92nd Congress adjourned Oct. 18 after two acrimonious encounters with the White House. By lopsided margins, Congress overrode a Nixon veto of a Democratic-inspired $24.7-billion water pollution control bill. And House acquiescence to a Senate vote rejecting a $250-billion ceiling on federal spending in fiscal 1973 killed the President's proposal that Congress grant him the authority to slash whatever he wanted from any congressional appropriation.

To the President, the issue was spending, and votes to override his midnight veto of the "staggering, budget-wrecking" anti-pollution measure were votes for "higher prices and higher taxes." In his veto message, the President noted: "I have nailed my colors to the mast on this issue; the political winds may blow where they may."

Only one of Nixon's "great goals" *(above)* was enacted by the 92nd—general revenue sharing. But the blame for inaction rested with the administration as well as Capitol Hill since the White House had been unwilling to work very hard for some of its proposals (government reorganization) and to accept congressional substitutes for others (environmental legislation).

Generally, the administration received what it wanted in foreign affairs and national security, while the Democratic-controlled Congress was successful in bolstering some domestic and social welfare programs. In a sense, then, it was a standoff, with Nixon having the final word: after Congress adjourned, he pocket vetoed nine bills on grounds that they spent too much.

During the year, the President won 66 percent of the 83 congressional recorded votes that presented a clear-cut test of support for his views.

The Economy

1969. The Nixon administration's drive to slow down the pace of the economy's inflationary growth met with little tangible success in 1969. The President and his financial advisers pursued a policy of "gradualism" in an attempt to halt inflation without bringing on a recession. Unlike some previous administrations, President Nixon maintained an official hands-off policy toward labor and industry concerning wage and price increases.

But by the end of the year, the administration's actions showed—at best—limited success in holding down government expenditures and the wage-price spiral.

When he submitted his revised budget to Congress in April, Mr. Nixon promised to hold federal spending to $192.9-billion and to produce an anti-inflationary surplus for fiscal 1970 of nearly $6-billion. But actions and inactions of Congress, coupled with increases in uncontrollable spending, quickly made those goals illusory.

In a move initiated on Capitol Hill instead of by the White House, Congress in 1969 passed legislation providing the most comprehensive reform of the nation's tax statutes in history and the largest tax cut since 1964. The measure, passed over the threat of a presidential veto, resulted in a net annual loss to the Treasury of $2.5-billion.

1970. The economy, which reached the trillion-dollar level in its annual output of goods and services on Dec. 15, continued to be plagued with inflation. The Nixon administration, its critics charged, had achieved recession, unemployment and inflation simultaneously.

The outcome of the Nov. 3 off-year elections, which left Congress under firm Democratic control, was widely attributed to the state of the economy. By the end of the year, Democratic leaders in Congress were calling for stringent controls. (Congress had passed legislation over the President's opposition authorizing credit controls and a wage-price freeze.)

Late in the year, Nixon appeared to shift more positively from previous policy in three broad areas: federal expenditures, monetary policy and private wage and price decisions. In a major economic speech Dec. 4, he confirmed a widespread expection of new tactics.

The President announced he would use deficit spending to stimulate economic growth. He said he was planning the new budget "on the basis that it would be balanced if we were at full employment and the economy were producing full revenues." He announced measures taken to offset oil price increases and plans to intervene in wage negotiations in the construction industry if strikes and rising costs were not limited.

1971. After two and a half years of unsuccessful attempts to curb inflation, the President Aug. 15 imposed wage and price controls on the economy and sought to reverse growing deficits in the U.S. balance of trade. Under authority voted by Congress in 1970 (despite opposition from the White House), Nixon froze wages, prices and rents for 90 days and then set up mechanisms for continued limitations during the post-freeze "Phase Two."

The President also called for tax reductions to stimulate economic growth and reduce unemployment, a tax credit for business investment, a step-up in scheduled increases in personal tax exemptions and a repeal of the excise taxes on cars. He suspended the $35-an-ounce fixed price for gold, which had pegged the value of the dollar in international exchange for nearly 40 years, and imposed an indefinite 10-percent surcharge on imports. He established a Cost of Living Council to oversee the program.

In addition to new tax laws, he asked Congress to extend his authority to control wages, prices and rents and to add powers to regulate interest rates and dividends. Congress cleared such a bill Dec. 14.

The President established his Phase Two program by executive order under existing authority. He established a Pay Board of five members each from the public, labor and management and a seven-member Price Commission to devise guidelines to take effect after the freeze ended.

The imposition of the freeze and subsequent actions of the Pay Board widened a rift between the Nixon administration and organized labor. Labor objected chiefly to the Pay Board's action limiting wage increases scheduled by existing contracts.

In keeping with his state of the union pledge, the President Jan. 29 had sent Congress a record $229.2-billion budget with an $11.6-billion deficit for fiscal 1972. "By operating as if we were at full employment," Nixon predicted in his budget message, "we will help to bring about that full employment."

1972. The economic news in 1972 generally was favorable. The gross national product was increasing at the rate of $100-billion a year. Wages were increasing faster than prices, thereby bolstering the real income of workers. Farmers were making profits. And, according to the Census Bureau, for the first time, more than half the families in the country had incomes of more than $10,000. The bureau noted, however, that because of inflation, the increase in 1971 income over 1970 was illusory.

On the other hand, unemployment was still high (5.5 percent in September), and the administration had decided to abandon its goal of 4-percent unemployment. On election day, 4.8 million Americans did not have jobs, 2 million more than when President Nixon took office. Prices also continued to rise (.5 percent in September, or at an annual rate of 6 percent). And the deficit in the federal budget was looking larger than had been expected. (One report claimed the Nixon experts predicted a deficit of at least $34-billion for fiscal 1973, or $8.5-billion more than had been expected in January. The cumulative deficit for Nixon's four years in office was expected to reach $75-billion.)

So, even as it appeared that the economy was emerging from the doldrums, the President still faced serious problems.

Vietnam and Foreign Policy

1969. The Nixon administration in 1969 attempted to shape a policy on Vietnam which would gradually shift responsibility for fighting the ground war from Washington to Saigon.

In an address to the nation Nov. 3, the President reported that virtually no progress had been made at the Paris peace talks. U.S. policy, he said, would stress "Vietnamization" of the war, whereby American combat troops would be withdrawn according to an "orderly scheduled timetable."

Nixon restated earlier peace proposals, and—for the first time—put on record his so-called Asian Doctrine. The doctrine maintained that the United States should continue its alliances in the Pacific but should not become involved in future wars on the Asian mainland. Greater stress would be placed on self-help and on economic development of the region, he said.

On March 13, the Senate ratified a treaty banning the spread of nuclear weapons. By the end of the year, 24 of the 40 countries required to effect the treaty had ratified it, including the major sponsors—Britain, the Soviet Union and the United States.

1970. Despite the President's efforts in Vietnam, the apparent extension of the war to neighboring Laos and Cambodia gave rise to the fear that the United States would become further bogged down in Southeast Asia.

When Nixon ordered U.S. combat troops into Cambodia April 30, he claimed his move did not constitute a widening of the war or an invasion of Cambodia. U.S. troops, he said, would only enter border areas held by the North Vietnamese and Viet Cong. He claimed the incursion was necessary to protect U.S. forces during the prolonged withdrawal process from Vietnam.

In the Senate, the President's decision precipitated a seven-week debate which ended June 30 with the passage (58-37 roll-call vote) of an amendment sponsored by Senators John Sherman Cooper (R Ky.) and Frank Church (D Idaho) prohibiting re-entry of U.S. ground forces in Cambodia. A revised version of the amendment was included as part of the supplemental foreign aid authorization bill, which cleared Congress Dec. 31. The substitute still contained a clause prohibiting U.S. ground troops from participating in combat operations in Cambodia.

Aside from Vietnam, the President had set forth a new policy (termed the Nixon Doctrine) which had as its goal avoiding direct U.S. military involvement in remote corners of the globe. The Nixon Doctrine was formally stated by the President Feb. 18 in a 40,000-word message to Congress entitled "United States Foreign Policy for the 1970s: A New Strategy for Peace." In the document, widely described as a "state of the world" message, the President said that the Nixon Doctrine's "central thesis is that the United States will participate in the defense and development of allies and friends, but that America cannot—and will not—conceive all the plans, design all the programs, execute all the decisions and undertake all the defense of the free nations of the world."

The President tread a cautious path in the tense Middle East arms race during 1970. In March, he announced that Israel's request to purchase additional combat aircraft had been turned down on an "interim basis," but he emphasized that the decision would be "constantly reappraised" if the Arab-Israeli arms balance shifted.

When the Soviet Union began deploying military personnel, aircraft and surface-to-air missiles in Egypt, pressure built up on the President, particularly from Congress, to supply Israel with additional aircraft.

In the closing days of the 1970 session, Congress approved an administration request for $500-million to finance credit sales of arms to Israel.

1971. President Nixon, who made his early political reputation as a strong anti-Communist, jolted the world in 1971 with announcements that he would visit both Peking and Moscow the following year. After two decades of hostility and non-recognition of the People's Republic of China, the administration made three dramatic shifts in U.S. policy toward the Peking regime:

• On June 10, the President ended a 21-year embargo on trade with Mainland China.

• On July 15, Nixon announced he would visit Peking in 1972.

• On Aug. 2, Secretary of State William P. Rogers announced that the United States would support the seating of Communist China in the United Nations.

In thus abandoning the long-standing policy of non-recognition of the communist regime in Peking, the President cast himself in the role of a statesman seeking new roads to world peace. Reaction in Congress and the nation generally was favorable, although the move did arouse fears among some conservatives that the United States would abandon its alliance with the Chinese communists' bitter enemy, the Nationalist Chinese government on Taiwan.

Dissent over the Vietnam war—which seemed on the rise in the spring of 1971—had waned by mid-year following further troop withdrawal announcements by Nixon. At year's end, 45,000 additional troops were scheduled for withdrawal, practically bringing to an end the offensive combat involvement of U.S. ground forces.

But in Congress, total U.S. withdrawal from Southeast Asia remained a major issue. For the first time, Congress in 1971 called for an end to the Indochina war. Yet, Nixon, when signing the bill containing the withdrawal amendment, told reporters the measure was not binding and would not change his policies.

In keeping with the Nixon Doctrine, the President proposed increased military aid for Southeast Asia in his foreign aid request. But in the Senate, doubts about the doctrine were among a variety of conflicting ideas and positions that endangered the future of the foreign aid program. For the first time in the program's history, a foreign aid bill was defeated as the Senate rejected the legislation authorizing fiscal 1972 funds.

The Senate revived the authorization legislation in a two-bill package in reduced form, and Senate and House conferees engaged in a bitter struggle to resolve differences over a Senate amendment setting a policy of complete withdrawal of troops from Vietnam within six months. The amendment finally was deleted.

After war broke out between Pakistan and India, members of Congress criticized the President for not making more vigorous efforts to settle differences over East Pakistan and for blaming India as the aggressor. The

administration countered that India had started the open fighting as behind-the-scenes U.S. efforts to persuade Pakistan to grant East Pakistan autonomy were about to be successful.

1972. By late in 1972, it appeared that a settlement of the Vietnam war, or at least a cease-fire and return of U.S. prisoners, was imminent. Presidential aide Henry Kissinger and North Vietnamese officials had hammered out a nine-point agreement, but the Saigon government balked, and the elusive peace still had not been attained.

If successful in negotiating an end to the war, the administration would cap off a year in foreign policy that was at times spectacular. Nixon made successful trips to Peking in February and the Soviet Union in May. Both were historic; both were widely praised throughout the nation. And together they contributed to the President's stature among the voters.

The first American President to visit Moscow, Nixon returned to Washington June 1 with seven agreements he had signed with Soviet leaders. They included pacts on joint space missions, technology, the environment, medical research, trade, incidents at sea and the limitation of strategic arms.

There were two elements to the arms agreement: a treaty that would limit the deployment of anti-ballistic missiles (ABMs) and an executive agreement limiting the number of offensive weapons to those already under construction or deployed when the agreement was signed. The executive agreement also placed limitations on the number of missile-carrying submarines that could be constructed.

Congress approved the offensive arms agreement, and the Senate ratified the ABM treaty.

The arms agreements were quickly followed by trade pacts, the United States purchasing a reported $45.6-billion in natural gas from the Soviet Union, while both Russia and China bought wheat, feed grain and corn.

National Security

1969. The Nixon administration and Congress engaged in a protracted debate in 1969 over priorities: whether increased weight should be given to national security needs or domestic programs. In the end, Congress cut $5.6-billion from budget requests for defense spending.

The most dramatic fight came in the Senate over the administration's Safeguard anti-ballistic missile system (ABM). Senators debated the issue for two months before defeating by a 50-50 vote a proposal to block any work on the Safeguard system. The Aug. 6 vote was a central, if shaky, victory for the administration, which had extensively revised former President Johnson's Sentinel ABM system.

In an attempt to shave funds from defense spending, the administration dropped requests for the Manned Orbiting Laboratory (MOL), the Cheyenne helicopters and the controversial F-111 fighter-bomber. Responding to mounting criticism from Congress and the public, the President announced near the end of the year a halt to military biological aspects of chemical-biological warfare (CBW).

1970. Congress in 1970 cut $2-billion from the President's $68.7-billion budget request for the military in fiscal 1971. Final action on the $66.6-billion defense appropriations bill came late in the session after months of debate on the ABM, the Indochina war and procurement of new weapons systems.

Nixon asked congressional approval of plans to enlarge the ABM system and add five additional sites as anti-Chinese defenses. A total of $1-billion for non-construction costs and $357-million in construction appropriations was finally allocated by Congress, but only after cutting out the anti-Chinese portion of the President's request.

Late in the year, Defense Secretary Melvin R. Laird indicated that defense spending would have to increase in the near future "in order to meet urgent requirements, many of them too long deferred."

1971. The President asked Congress for a $73.5-billion defense appropriations bill which would cover all Defense Department expenses during fiscal 1972 except building programs. Congress cut $3-billion from the administration request with more than half the cuts coming from the weapons procurement budget. On two different occasions, the White House mounted lobby efforts to defeat attempts in the Senate to reduce the number of U.S. troops stationed in Europe. Both times, the administration was successful.

The administration also succeeded in thwarting all efforts in Congress to shorten the two-year draft extension requested by the Pentagon, although the House turned back a one-year extension amendment to the draft bill by just a two-vote margin.

1972. The Nixon administration's request for military spending shot up to $82.3-billion in 1972, due, in some part, to the escalation of fighting in Vietnam. Congress approved $74.4-billion in defense appropriations and $2.3-billion for military construction during the year.

The Defense Department accelerated its plans for development of weapons systems not covered by the U.S.-Soviet arms accords, including the B-1 bomber and the Trident submarine.

In mid-July, the General Accounting Office reported that cost overruns on 77 weapons systems had increased by $28.7-billion despite "measurable progress" in the Pentagon's arms-purchasing procedures.

Domestic Programs

1969

During his first year in office, Nixon proposed few new domestic programs. Unlike President Johnson, whose Great Society programs focused chiefly on urban blight and poor city dwellers, President Nixon stressed a balance between urban and non-urban needs and greater emphasis on state and local action instead of an expanded federal role. Rather than stressing the needs of the poor, he emphasized "the quality of life" for all Americans.

The administration's most dramatic new proposal was a complete overhaul of the federal welfare system. Along with welfare reform, Nixon recommended change in two other areas: manpower training and revenue shar-

ing. Together, the President said, they represented "a new federalism, in which power, funds and responsibility will flow from Washington to the states and to the people."

The House Ways and Means Committee held hearings on the welfare proposal late in the year, but took no further action.

Social Security. Congress enacted a 15-percent increase in basic Social Security payments but adopted none of the other reforms requested by Nixon. The President had asked for a 10-percent increase, automatic cost-of-living adjustment, changes in the Medicare tax rates and provisions for recipients with outside earnings, widows and aging parents of retired and disabled workers.

Hunger. The administration proposed a $270-million increase in spending for fiscal 1970 for the food stamp program, bringing the total authorization to $610-million. For fiscal 1971, he requested a $1-billion increase in the authorization, and asked that families with incomes of less than $30 a month receive free food stamps. Congress passed legislation raising the fiscal 1970 authorization but did not complete action on broad reforms in the program.

Consumer Affairs. On Oct. 30, the President sent to Congress a message calling for a "buyer's bill of rights." He requested legislation establishing a statutory office of consumer affairs in the White House and a consumer protection division in the Justice Department. He also asked for legislation allowing class action suits in which consumers could sue in groups for damages resulting from certain fraudulent trade practices. Some Democrats criticized the legislation on grounds that it did not go far enough in protecting consumers.

In October, Robert H. Finch, secretary of the Department of Health, Education and Welfare, banned the use of cyclamates, low-calorie artificial sweeteners used widely in diet foods and soft drinks, because laboratory animals given large daily doses showed a high incidence of tumors. In November, Finch rescinded the order for all products except soft drinks.

In November, Secretary of Agriculture Clifford M. Hardin announced limitations on the use of the pesticide DDT. A total ban on the widely-used chemical would be forthcoming, he said.

Environment. Congress substantially increased the President's $214-million budget request for sewage treatment—the same amount President Johnson had requested. As cleared, the public works appropriation bill contained $800-million for the program.

1970

Environment. The President won passage of both air and water pollution bills, although the legislation was stronger than what the administration had requested. Congress took no action on a presidential proposal to help communities in building sewage treatment plants.

Presidential plans to create an independent Environmental Protection Agency and a National Oceanic and Atmospheric Administration in the Commerce Department became law Oct. 2 despite attempts by some members of Congress to block the move.

Welfare and Urban Affairs. The administration's welfare reforms and Social Security increase proposals were left for the 92nd Congress. The Family Assistance

Plan died in the Senate and the Social Security legislation in the House.

Crime. Nixon in 1970 saw Congress fulfill one of his key campaign promises—enactment of four major pieces of legislation to combat rising crime rates. The bills were aimed at strengthening the federal attack on organized crime, reducing the crime rate in the District of Columbia, halting illegal traffic in dangerous drugs and narcotics, curbing obscenity in the mails and increasing funds available for local, state and federal law enforcement agencies.

Health and Education. The President suffered defeats on both his elementary and higher education programs. Although it passed the House, a $1.5-billion authorization bill giving aid to schools undergoing desegregation or trying to overcome racial imbalance was defeated in the Senate when a coalition of southern conservatives and northern liberals succeeded in delaying it until adjournment.

The only proposals Congress approved in the health field were the Family Planning Services Act and the Health Services Improvement Act to consolidate four existing health care programs.

Congress defeated two amendments to the Hill-Burton hospital construction program proposed by Nixon when he vetoed the bill June 22. The President requested repeal of the hospital construction grants and elimination of the requirement that funds be spent in the same fiscal year they were appropriated. Congress overrode the President's veto, making none of the requested changes in the bill.

Agriculture and Labor. Congress approved three proposals submitted by the President to provide free food stamps to the neediest of the poor, expand the unemployment insurance system and establish a comprehensive federal occupational health and safety program.

Defeats for the President were failure to act on revisions in the procedures for dealing with national emergency strikes in the transportation industry and failure to approve the Employee Benefits Protection Act.

Post Office. The President won a major victory with passage of his proposal to convert the Post Office Department into a government-owned corporation and eliminate patronage in the selection of postmasters. However, Congress did not act on proposals for a postal rate increase.

1971

Agriculture. After a short but bitter floor fight, the Senate Dec. 2 confirmed Nixon's nomination of Earl L. Butz to be secretary of agriculture. The roll-call vote was 51-44. Opponents of the nomination charged that Butz was tied too closely to farming corporations and was unsympathetic to the family farmer.

Labor and Manpower. The administration's manpower revenue-sharing program was rejected by the House Education and Labor Committee, and the Senate Labor and Public Welfare Committee conducted one day of hearings on the proposal but reported no legislation.

Although Nixon originally opposed a public service job program to ease unemployment, he eventually signed a Democratic-sponsored $2.25-billion authorization to provide public service jobs at the state and local levels. However, another Democratic move to provide $2-billion

for hiring persons in public service jobs was vetoed by the President.

Election Reform. After some delay on the issue of political campaign spending reform, the administration formed ranks behind the Federal Election Campaign Practices Act passed by the Senate in December. Nixon reportedly was "very pleased" with the bill. As approved by the Senate, the bill did not contain limitations on contributions and did not repeal the equal broadcast time requirement—two provisions opposed by the administration.

Cancer Research. In December, Congress cleared legislation expanding cancer research efforts of the National Cancer Institute within the National Institutes of Health and authorizing $1.59-billion over fiscal 1972-1974.

Anti-Poverty. Because of a section authorizing $2.1-billion for a comprehensive child development program, President Nixon Dec. 9 vetoed legislation providing for a two-year extension of the Office of Economic Opportunity. The Senate, in a 51-36 vote, was seven votes short of the two-thirds majority needed to override the veto.

SST. In a major setback for the administration, Congress in 1971 voted not to spend $134-million for construction of two prototypes of the supersonic transport aircraft.

Education. Once again there was a White House-Congress tug-of-war over federal funds for education. Although the Senate approved a measure containing $5.6-billion, House-Senate conferees—fearing a third presidential veto of education funds in three years—reported out a bill providing $5.1-billion. The President signed it July 11.

Both the House and Senate rejected the major thrusts of the President's student aid proposals for higher education during the year.

Environment. In February and June, Nixon sent Congress messages detailing a number of administration proposals on the environment. In November, the Senate passed water pollution legislation that was considered far stronger than what the administration had requested. The White House announced that it opposed the Senate version of the bill and called on the House to make changes.

Consumers. In a message to Congress, Nixon recommended one new program—federal authority to set new safety standards on all consumer products—and reminded Congress of all the holdover proposals on consumer affairs from the 91st Congress.

1972

General Revenue Sharing. The only one of the President's "six great goals" to be enacted was a bill establishing a five-year program to share $30-billion in federal revenues with state and local governments.

Social Security. In June, Congress increased Social Security benefits by 20 percent and provided for an automatic increase in benefits whenever the cost of living increased by more than 3 percent in a calendar year. The President charged that the measure threatened to "escalate the rate of inflation." In October, certain benefits were increased more, as were the Social Security taxes to pay for them.

Women's Rights. Although the administration did not request one, it supported a constitutional amendment passed by Congress guaranteeing equal rights for women.

Higher Education. On June 23, the President signed into law legislation authorizing $19-billion for higher education through fiscal 1975, incorporating a restructuring of federal higher education programs and providing $2-billion in emergency aid for school desegregation. The bill also contained compromise anti-busing provisions. (*Civil Rights action, below*)

Drug Abuse. On March 17, Congress completed action on an administration measure establishing an office in the Executive Office of the President to coordinate all federal drug abuse programs except law enforcement.

Heart and Lung Research. Congress authorized an additional $1.38-billion in fiscal 1973-75 to expand programs of the National Heart and Lung Institute to combat heart, blood vessel, lung and blood diseases.

Civil Rights

1969. President Nixon was elected to office with little support from Negroes and other non-white minorities. Although he promised early in his presidency "to rectify" his reputation of indifference to black aspirations, the new administration took few public actions in 1969 to back up the promise.

The administration's policy statement on school desegregation guidelines, made public July 3, stated that plans for dismantling dual school systems must be carried out by September unless "bona fide educational and administrative problems" warrant delay. But in late August, HEW Secretary Finch asked a federal court to delay implementation of HEW plans scheduled to go into effect in September. Later, the Justice Department aligned itself with southern school officials and against civil rights advocates in defending the delay before the Supreme Court. This marked the first split in the Justice Department-civil rights partnership since the 1954 Supreme Court decision which declared that segregated schools were illegal. The court refused to delay the desegregation plans.

In June, the Labor Department drew up what became known as the "Philadelphia Plan," a scheme for increasing the employment of black laborers in the highly segregated construction industry unions. The plan survived a strong move in Congress late in the session to kill it.

1970. The Nixon administration's second year was marked by continued evolution of a more cautious federal stance in regard to school desegregation enforcement. The President made it clear that he saw the nation's schools primarily as instruments of education, not integration. Nixon went on record as opposing busing and favoring neighborhood schools. Many of the more activist officials with desegregation responsibilities left the administration during the year.

In a defeat related to civil rights, Congress passed over the President's objections a bill extending the Voting Rights Act of 1965 and allowing 18-year-olds to vote in elections. The administration had proposed a revision of the voting rights legislation in what civil rights advocates called an attempt to water down the act to take some of the burden of the legislation off the South. The 18-year-old vote provisions, tacked onto the bill in the Senate, was opposed by the President on grounds that the change should be made by constitutional amendment rather than by statute. But Nixon signed the bill into law on June 22 and called for an early court test of its constitutionality.

1971. After the Supreme Court decision in April sanctioned the use of busing and other methods of pupil assignment to desegregate schools, the administration moved quickly to carry out such a policy. By midsummer, HEW had warned 64 school districts that they should move to increase the desegregation of their schools when sessions started in the fall. But in a statement issued in August, the President reiterated his opposition to busing.

On June 11, in a long-awaited statement on equal opportunity in housing, President Nixon said he would enforce federal laws barring racial discrimination in the sale, rental or construction of housing—but that he would not approve a federal policy of forcing cities and neighborhoods to accept low-income housing.

1972. In March, Congress passed and the President signed legislation providing court enforcement powers for the Equal Employment Opportunity Commission. The measure authorized the EEOC to institute suits in federal court to enforce U.S. laws against job discrimination.

Nixon also signed the higher education bill containing compromise busing provisions which postponed the effective date of court orders requiring busing until 1974 and limited the use of federal funds for busing intended to overcome racial imbalance or to desegregate schools.

The President, responding to strong anti-busing sentiment throughout the country, had proposed (1) that a moratorium be established on new, court-ordered busing orders until July 1, 1973, or until Congress legislated limits on busing, whichever came first, and (2) that busing be made a last resort and strictly limited means of achieving school desegregation.

Supreme Court

Because of three retirements and one resignation, the President was given the opportunity to reshape the Supreme Court in a more conservative image—as he had promised in 1968. Reshaping the court, however, gave him his two most embarrassing defeats in Congress.

The Senate Nov. 21, 1969, by a 45-55 roll-call vote refused to confirm Clement F. Haynsworth Jr. of South Carolina and chief justice of the 4th Circuit Court of Appeals to be an associate justice. Opponents questioned his sensitivity to the appearance of ethical impropriety.

On April 8, 1970, the Senate on a 45-51 roll call, turned down the nomination of G. Harrold Carswell of Florida. Carswell, a judge on the 5th Circuit Court of Appeals, was opposed by key senators who did not like his record on civil rights.

The four men who were confirmed made it with little difficulty. They were Warren Earl Burger of Minnesota, who became chief justice, and Associate Justices Harry A. Blackmun of Minnesota, Lewis F. Powell Jr. of Virginia and William H. Rehnquist of Arizona.

NIXON LANDSLIDE VICTORY OF HISTORIC PROPORTIONS

Richard M. Nixon, a man who once had the image of a political loser, swept back into the White House Nov. 7 with a devastating landslide victory over Sen. George McGovern (D S.D.).

Nixon, who barely lost and then barely won in his two previous bids for the presidency, carried a record of 49 states for 521 electoral votes. Only Massachusetts and the District of Columbia went for McGovern, for a meager total of 17 electoral votes.

The margin of Nixon's electoral vote victory was the third largest in the nation's history, eclipsed only by the elections of 1820, when James Monroe rolled up 231 electoral votes to 1 for John Quincy Adams, and 1936, when Franklin D. Roosevelt outdistanced Alfred M. Landon by 523 to 8.

With only scattered precincts still to be counted, Nixon's popular vote was running at 60.8 percent, slightly behind the 61.1 percent recorded by Lyndon B. Johnson in his 1964 landslide over Barry Goldwater. (McGovern was receiving 37.8 percent of the vote, with about 1.4 percent going to American Independent Party candidate John G. Schmitz and less than 1 percent to People's Party candidate Dr. Benjamin Spock.) Only two other presidential candidates have taken 60 percent or more of the popular vote: Warren G. Harding in 1920 (60.3 percent) and Franklin D. Roosevelt in 1936 (60.8 percent).

Another feature of the Nixon landslide was the first Republican sweep since Reconstruction of the once solid Democratic South. (And it was the first time since 1944 that the South had gone solidly for anybody.) By runaway margins, Nixon took all 11 states of the old Confederacy, plus all the border states. His victory in Arkansas marked the first presidential race since 1872 in which the state had gone Republican.

Outcome of the race appeared so certain after a few sample returns that television networks projected Nixon the winner before the polls even closed in a number of western states. NBC projected the outcome at 8:30 p.m. (EST), 20 minutes before CBS' announcement. But the timing of these projections was behind that of the 1964 election, when NBC projected Johnson the winner at 6:44 p.m.

Nixon, describing his landslide as "one of the great political victories of all time," promised to make lasting peace the priority goal of his second term in office. "We are on the eve of what could be the greatest generation of peace, true peace, for the whole world that man has ever known," Nixon said in his victory statement. "This is a great goal, bigger than whether we're Democrats or Republicans...." In a nationwide radio hookup Nov. 5, Nixon had cited the peace theme among 10 major goals for his next term. Among the others were elimination of racial and sex discrimination, better health care and upgrading of the environment.

For his part, McGovern promised to support any efforts by Nixon to achieve "peace abroad and justice at home" but indicated that Nixon had not gone far enough in those directions during his first term. Democrats would "not rally," he said, "to the support of policies that we deplore. But we do love this country and we will continue to beckon it to a higher standard."

As in 1968, the nation's two major voter preference polls forcast the outcome of the election almost to perfection. The final Gallup Poll projected 61 percent of the vote for Nixon, 35 percent for McGovern, 3 percent undecided and 1 percent for minor party candidates. The last Harris Survey called the race 59-35 for Nixon, with 6 percent undecided. On the eve of the election, McGovern sought to downplay his showing in the polls and predicted that he would upset Nixon.

A key ingredient of McGovern's defeat was the crumbling of the old Roosevelt coalition of blacks, Jews and Catholic voters. A survey taken by CBS on election day showed Nixon taking the Catholic vote by 59 to 33 percent, in contrast to the 55 to 70 percent of that vote that Democrats have carried in recent elections. The CBS poll, compiled from a random sample of 15,000 voters as they left the polls, also revealed other surprises: Nixon taking 59 percent of the blue-collar vote, 47 percent of the vote of unemployed persons and 48 percent of the youth vote—three categories of voters that McGovern strategists had considered solidly in their column.

According to NBC, which sampled 1,500 strategically located precincts, Nixon corralled 39 percent of the Jewish vote, compared to 17 percent in 1968. The NBC poll also showed Nixon winning 58 percent of the vote in the nation's cities—another traditional bastion of Democratic strength.

The final days of campaigning were marked by vigorous efforts by McGovern to provoke Nixon into partisan rhetoric—something that had proved damaging to Nixon in previous campaigns. To the end, McGovern discounted reports that Nixon's peace efforts were on the verge of success. He said they were a "cynical effort" to win the election. "Peace is not at hand," McGovern said Nov. 5. "It is not even in sight."

Nixon countered that a vote for him was a "message to those with whom we are negotiating and to the leaders of the world that you back the President of the United States as he insists that we seek peace with honor and never peace with surrender."

Vote Breakdown

	Popular Votes	Percent	Electoral Votes
Nixon	45,631,189	60.8	521
McGovern	28,422,015	37.8	17
Minor Parties	1,063,400	1.5	0

(Nearly complete figures compiled by CQ. Final official results will be carried in 1973 CQ Weekly Reports.)

1972 Presidential Election Results

Based on nearly complete, unofficial returns as compiled by the News Election Service and reported by United Press International

270 Electoral Votes Needed to Win

STATE	POPULAR VOTE		ELECTORAL VOTE		PLURALITY	PERCENTAGE OF MAJOR-PARTY VOTE	
	Nixon	McGovern	Nixon	McGovern		Nixon	McGovern
Alabama	661,525	205,343	9		456,182 R	76	24
Alaska	41,809	24,362	3		17,447 R	63	37
Arizona	369,068	181,651	6		187,417 R	67	33
Arkansas	427,014	190,598	6		236,416 R	69	31
California	4,544,134	3,431,824	45		1,112,310 R	57	43
Colorado	568,426	305,522	7		262,904 R	65	35
Connecticut	763,880	507,331	8		256,549 R	60	40
Delaware	139,796	91,907	3		47,889 R	60	40
District of Columbia	29,697	109,974		3	80,277 D	21	79
Florida	1,751,210	690,565	17		1,060,645 R	72	28
Georgia	766,899	330,607	12		436,292 R	70	30
Hawaii	167,414	100,617	4		66,797 R	62	38
Idaho	197,589	80,558	4		117,031 R	71	29
Illinois	2,613,162	1,794,765	26		818,397 R	59	41
Indiana	1,397,748	703,202	13		694,546 R	67	33
Iowa	702,398	492,642	8		209,756 R	59	41
Kansas	605,632	265,158	7		340,474 R	70	30
Kentucky	670,937	369,082	9		301,855 R	65	35
Louisiana	679,944	305,836	10		374,108 R	69	31
Maine	251,327	160,845	4		90,482 R	61	39
Maryland	795,358	486,195	10		309,163 R	62	38
Massachusetts	1,104,310	1,323,843		14	219,533 D	45	55
Michigan	1,860,186	1,467,562	21		392,624 R	56	44
Minnesota	881,326	789,473	10		91,853 R	53	47
Mississippi	498,680	125,756	7		372,924 R	80	20
Missouri	1,132,111	682,030	12		450,081 R	62	38
Montana	177,926	116,490	4		61,436 R	60	40
Nebraska	384,157	162,600	5		221,557 R	70	30
Nevada	114,593	65,258	3		49,335 R	64	36
New Hampshire	212,232	115,474	4		96,758 R	65	35
New Jersey	1,769,458	1,058,451	17		711,007 R	63	37
New Mexico	233,036	138,756	4		94,280 R	63	37
New York	4,149,761	2,884,949	41		1,264,812 R	59	41
North Carolina	1,051,583	437,299	13		614,284 R	71	29
North Dakota	166,131	94,927	3		71,204 R	64	36
Ohio	2,361,238	1,524,118	25		837,120 R	61	39
Oklahoma	745,910	243,338	8		502,572 R	75	25
Oregon	483,229	390,867	6		92,362 R	55	45
Pennsylvania	2,703,975	1,788,034	27		915,941 R	60	40
Rhode Island	209,166	185,239	4		23,927 R	53	47
South Carolina	468,036	184,958	8		283,078 R	72	28
South Dakota	163,746	137,432	4		26,314 R	54	46
Tennessee	812,484	355,817	10		456,667 R	70	30
Texas	2,147,970	1,091,800	26		1,056,170 R	66	34
Utah	318,407	124,430	4		193,977 R	72	28
Vermont	115,453	67,508	3		47,945 R	63	37
Virginia	982,792	439,546	12		543,246 R	69	31
Washington	679,156	475,553	9		203,603 R	59	41
West Virginia	471,858	271,856	6		200,002 R	63	37
Wisconsin	986,751	805,726	11		181,025 R	55	45
Wyoming	100,561	44,341	3		56,220 R	69	31
TOTALS	**45,631,189**	**28,422,015**	**521**	**17**	**17,209,174**	**61**	**39**

NIXON TRAVELS TO TWO COMMUNIST NATIONS IN 1972

In major foreign policy initiatives, President Nixon in 1972 paid visits to the communist world's two major capitals—Moscow and Peking. The trips were the first state visits by a U.S. President to either country.

The President's conferences with leaders of the Soviet Union and the People's Republic of China had a common goal: stabilization of U.S. relations with the two vast countries vying for power and influence as leader in the communist world.

In terms of substantial results, the President's journeys were vastly different. Returning from China after his February visit, the President brought home only the prospect of formal relations with Peking—by itself a significant departure from U.S. policy followed since 1949.

Returning from Moscow on June 1, however, the President brought seven agreements with the Soviet government, including two nuclear arms control accords. Both accords—a treaty limiting anti-ballistic missile sites and an agreement limiting offensive missiles—received Senate approval in early August.

The Moscow agreements brought formal recognition by the two superpowers of their mutual interests in arms control, trade, scientific development and preservation of the environment. The Peking discussions brought only recognition by estranged rivals of the need for better understanding of each other, with the specific issues dividing them left for future resolution.

China

Nixon's Feb. 21-28 visit to mainland China ended more than 20 years of official U.S. hostility toward the People's Republic, which was proclaimed in 1949 after the communists drove the Nationalist Chinese government of Chiang Kai-shek from the mainland to Taiwan.

Led by Premier Chou En-lai, Chinese officials gave Nixon a restrained welcome upon his arrival in Peking. Later that day, however, the President met four hours with Communist Party Chairman Mao Tse-tung—an indication of the importance the Chinese leadership assigned Nixon's visit.

After a week of private conferences, public banquets and sightseeing tours, Nixon and Chou Feb. 27 issued a joint communique indicating agreement on the need for increased contacts between their nations.

The communique's most controversial part gave U.S. acceptance to Peking's contention that Taiwan was part of China, Conceding that Taiwan's fate should be determined only by the Chinese, the United States pledged ultimate withdrawal of its military forces from Taiwan.

For its part, the Chinese government in the communique repeated its claim to sovereignty over Taiwan, governed by the Nationalist Chinese since 1949 with U.S. military and diplomatic support. Settlement of the Taiwan question, Peking maintained, was crucial to normal relations with the United States.

Nixon returned triumphant Feb. 28 and was met by a rising chorus of praise for establishing contacts with the Chinese communist government.

The praise was not unanimous, however. Nixon's agreement that Taiwan was a part of China and that its future was a matter to be determined by the Chinese, evoked bitter criticism from some sources.

The statement was interpreted by some conservatives as meaning the abandonment of the Nationalist Chinese government. Criticism came from such disparate candidates for president as Rep. John M. Ashbrook (R Ohio), Nixon's conservative opponent for the Republican nomination, and Sen. Hubert H. Humphrey (D Minn.), the Senate's most articulate liberal in the years when U.S. policy on China was dominated in Congress by pro-Chiang forces, which included Nixon as a representative, as a senator and as vice president.

"For over two decades," Ashbrook said, "it is we who have fostered and supported, both by words and deeds, the concept of an independent Republic of China on Taiwan. Now, in a single week, we have abandoned that position—and in so doing we have set up the framework to abandon 15 million people to the tender mercies of a regime that during its tenure in office—its 23 years of enlightenment and progress—has managed to slay, at conservative estimate, 34 million of its own citizens."

Humphrey's concern was more for the native Taiwanese, as distinct from the Nationalist Chinese who came from the mainland.

"It is now clear," he said, "that the rug has been pulled out from under the Taiwanese, though the people of the island of Formosa once aspired to determine their own destiny."

Humphrey also took issue with Nixon's statement (in his arrival speech) that no other nation's fate was negotiating behind its back in the talks with Chou and that no American commitment to another country was given up.

"It is apparent from the communique as I read it," Humphrey said, "that concessions were made by the President and by Dr. (Henry A.) Kissinger (Nixon's national security adviser), but not any, insofar as I have been able to interpret, were made by the Chinese."

Ashbrook's view was echoed by four House conservatives, Representatives Philip M. Crane (R Ill.), John R. Rarick (D La.), John G. Schmitz (R Calif.) and Robert L. Sikes (D Fla.).

Further criticism came from two other candidates for the presidency, Rep. Paul N. McCloskey Jr. (R Calif.) and Sen. Henry M. Jackson (D Wash.). McCloskey welcomed the limited renewal of relations with China but said that, despite Nixon's trip, "we did not progress one inch toward settling the major problem of today, ending the Vietnam war." Jackson expressed disappointment that Nixon had not gained concessions on Vietnam from the Chinese government.

from April 19 to May 3, and House Majority Leader Hale Boggs (D La.) and Minority Leader Gerald R. Ford (R Mich.) followed June 23-July 8.

Nuclear Pacts and Congress

Congressional approval was required on both the offensive and defensive aspects of agreements on nuclear arms reached by the President with the Soviets.

A provision in the 1961 law establishing the Arms Control and Disarmament Agency, which negotiated the pacts, specifies that any agreement to limit U.S. armed forces or armaments must be approved by legislation or treaty.

President Nixon June 13 submitted the two accords to Congress together with documents explaining U.S.-Soviet agreements and disagreements on interpretations of the accords.

The disagreements concerned mainly the ultimate size of nuclear submarine fleets and the size of certain offensive weapons. The explanation of the differences was designed to head off reservations on the part of the Senate to the treaty.

The President urged approval "without delay" promising that U.S. defense capabilities would remain "second to none." He called for "a sound strategic modernization program" as the nation moved to negotiate further arms accords.

The explanatory statements, drawn up in Moscow by U.S.-Soviet negotiators, emphasized U.S. concern over development of large Soviet missiles and envisaged future negotiations on nuclear limitations.

The document recorded a unilateral Soviet statement, not agreed to by the United States, that the Soviet Union increase the number of its nuclear submarines, if Washington's NATO allies increase theirs.

The President said the two Moscow agreements were "a significant step into a new era of mutually agreed restraint and arms limitation between the two principal nuclear powers." The agreements did not, he said, "close off all avenues of strategic competition." They "open(ed) up the opportunity for a new and more constructive U.S.-Soviet relationship, characterized by negotiated settlement of differences, rather than by the hostility and confrontation of decades past."

Sen. James L. Buckley (Cons-R N.Y.), said that relaxation of the U.S. commitment to defend Taiwan would "vastly diminish" his regard for Nixon. But he said he still would support Nixon for re-election.

Sen. George McGovern (D S.D.), the eventual Democratic nominee for President, praised the Nixon trip, as did Sen. Edward M. Kennedy (D Mass.). Chairman J.W. Fulbright of the Senate Foreign Relations Committee, a persistent critic of Nixon's Vietnam policy, indicated he was satisfied with the results of the trip. So did Sen. Barry Goldwater (R Ariz.), the unsuccessful Republican presidential candidate in 1964. Goldwater said he was satisfied that "we have not given away one single thing to the Red Chinese" and that "we will uphold our treaty commitments to the Taiwan government."

During Nixon's visit, U.S. officials arranged for high-level visits to China by congressional leaders. Senate Majority Leader Mike Mansfield (D Mont.) and Minority Leader Hugh Scott (R Pa.) visited six Chinese cities,

Soviet Union

Back in the United States for less than half an hour from his mission to Moscow, the President reported June 1, 1972, to Congress and the American people on the results of his agreements with the Soviet leaders.

The President had been in the Soviet Union from May 22-30. On May 26, he and Soviet Communist Party General Secretary Leonid I. Brezhnev signed a treaty limiting construction of antiballistic missile sites to two and an agreement limiting the number of offensive strategic missiles each side would have.

He urged the assembled lawmakers to "seize the moment so that our children and the world's children live free of the fears and free of the hatreds that have been the lot of mankind through the centuries."

He assured them that "the present and planned strategic forces of the United States are without question sufficient for the maintenance of our security and the protection of our vital interests."

"No power on earth is stronger than the United States of America today," he said. "None will be stronger than the United States of America in the future."

He added: "It is clear the agreements forestall a major spiraling of the arms race—one which would have worked to our disadvantage."

The President encouraged "the fullest scrutiny of these accords," and said he was confident that "such examination will underscore...that this is an agreement in the interest of both nations."

As the President urged Congress to approve the accords, the Soviet news agency, Tass, reported that the Soviet Politburo, the Council of Ministers and the Presidium of the Supreme Soviet all had "entirely approved" the summit pacts. U.S. endorsement required action by Congress. *(Below)*

Partisan feelings were evident in the House chamber as the President spoke. The American success in the strategic arms and other negotiations, the President said, "came about because, over the past three years we have consistently refused proposals for unilaterally abandoning the ABM (antiballistic missile), unilaterally pulling back our forces from Europe and drastically cutting the defense budget."

Nixon said Congress deserved "the appreciation of the American people for having the courage to vote such proposals down and to maintain the strength America needs to protect its interests."

Past Summits. The President alluded to past meetings of Soviet leaders and American Presidents. "One meeting after another," he said, "produced a short-lived euphoric mood—the spirit of Geneva, the spirit of Camp David, the spirit of Vienna, the spirit of Glassboro—without producing significant progress on the really difficult issues."

But this summit was different, he said. "This was a working summit. We sought to establish not a superficial spirit of Moscow, but a solid record of progress on solving the difficult issues which for so long have divided our two nations and the world." That goal was accomplished, the President added.

Seven Agreements. The first American President to visit Moscow, Nixon returned to Washington June 1 with seven agreements he had signed with Soviet leaders.

They included pacts on joint space missions, technology, the environment, medical research, trade, incidents at sea and the limitation of strategic arms.

But it was the arms accord that overshadowed every other aspect of the dramatic week in Moscow. The agreement was based on three premises:

• That development of offensive weaponry clearly was more advanced than the development of defensive weapons systems. Therefore, the freeze on both offensive and defensive weapons would leave both nations naked to a first attack.

• That both powers were confident they could survive a first strike to the extent they could retaliate with enough force to totally destroy the opposing nation.

• That the threat of nuclear obliteration—the "balance of terror" that had prevailed for almost a quarter century—was an adequate deterrent to all-out war.

Two Arms Agreements

There were two elements to the arms agreement worked out by the American and Soviet leaders: a treaty that would limit the deployment of antiballistic missiles (ABMs) and an executive agreement limiting the number of offensive weapons to those already under construction or deployed when the agreement was signed. The executive agreement also placed limitations on the number of missile-carrying submarines that could be constructed.

Under the defensive arms treaty, both the United States and Soviet Union would be limited to one ABM site for the defense of their capital cities, plus one additional site each for the defense of an ICBM (Intercontinental Ballistic Missile) field.

Defense critic Senator William Proxmire (D Wis.) argued that the treaty did not require construction of the two ABM sites.

Under the offensive arms agreement, the Soviet Union would be permitted to field about 300 of its new giant SS-9 missiles in silos occupied by older models. But the total number of the larger variety could not be increased.

Both sides would be able to construct new submarine-launched ballistic missiles (SLBMs) of the Polaris or Poseidon variety if they dismantled an equal number of land-based ICBM launchers or older submarine launchers. Thus, while the number of submarines could increase, the total of warheads would not.

Although the Russians were left with more land- and sea-based missiles in their arsenal, the United States—because it had developed systems whereby one missile delivers a number of independently targeted warheads—would have more than three times the Soviet number of deliverable warheads.

The Soviets had not yet tested a multiple warhead weapons system, although the treaty would allow them to do so.

The agreement did not provide for any on-site inspection. Both sides apparently were satisfied that satellite reconnaissance was adequate for monitoring the other's activities. But there was an unusual agreement whereby each side pledged not to interfere with the other's gathering of technical data. Both promised not to try and conceal their missile deployments or tests.

Fact Sheet on Agreements

Following is the text of a White House fact sheet, released May 26, 1972, on the strategic arms limitation agreement.

The Current Agreements

The ABM Treaty

• Limits each side to one ABM site for defense of their national capital (Moscow and Washington) and one site for each side for the defense of an ICBM field.

• There will be a total of 200 ABM interceptors permitted each side, 100 at each site.

• Radars will be limited to Modern ABM Radar Complexes (called MARCs) six for each side within a circle of a 150 kilometer radius around the national capitals; (MARCs are a circle of 3 km diameter, in which radars can be deployed; in practice they can accommodate about one large radar or a few smaller ones).

• For the ICBM defense fields there will be a total of twenty radars permitted; two of them can be about the size of the two larger radars deployed at Grand Forks; the other eighteen radars will be much smaller.

• The Soviet ICBM protection site will be at least 1300 km from Moscow. Our comparable site will be at Grand Forks, North Dakota.

• Other large non-ABM radars that may be built in the future will be restricted to space tracking or early warning and limited in size so as not to create a clandestine ABM potential.

• The treaty will be of unlimited duration with withdrawal rights if supreme interests are jeopardized, and on six months notice.

The Interim Offensive Agreement

• Limits ICBMs to those under construction or deployed at the time of signing the treaty or July 1. (This will mean about 1618 ICBMs for the USSR and 1054 for the United States. The USSR will field about 300 large SS-9s, but they will be prohibited from converting other ICBM silos to accommodate the large SS-9 types. Other silos can be modified, but not to a significant degree. Modernization is permitted.

• Construction of submarine launched ballistic missiles on all nuclear submarines will be frozen at current levels. The further construction of SLBMs on either side, can only be accomplished by dismantling of an equal number of older land based ICBMs or older submarine launchers.

• The Interim Agreement will run for five years (compared to the original Soviet proposal of 18 months), and both sides are committed to negotiating a permanent and more comprehensive agreement.

• Both sides will abide by the obligations of the agreement once it is signed, though formal implementation will await ratification of the ABM treaty.

Debate in Congress

For both President Nixon and his Soviet counterparts, the road from the conference table promised a few more obstacles. Communist Party chief Brezhnev had to contend with some of the more reluctant members of the Soviet hierarchy.

President Nixon had to face the Congress.

The ABM treaty had to be ratified by a two-thirds majority in the Senate and did not require consideration by the House. The offensive arms agreement—while not requiring congressional action—was submitted June 13 by the President to the House and Senate as a presidential courtesy to Congress. A resolution formally approving the accord would take a majority vote of both chambers.

President Nixon had several advantages going into congressional hearings in the summer of 1972 on the nuclear arms pacts he negotiated with the Soviet Union. Though sentiment was mixed, the President hoped to avert an all-out battle like the one when the Senate ratified the 1963 nuclear test ban treaty.

By contrast with 1963, the 1972 agreements:

• Were produced by a President with a long record of anti-communism.

• Received early approval of the Joint Chiefs of Staff. In 1963 the joint chiefs qualified their endorsement with insistence on four safeguards eventually incorporated. In 1972 they insisted on weapons progress.

• **Were** supported by a secretary of defense (Melvin R. Laird) with a congressional record of backing a strong military posture. In 1963 Secretary of Defense Robert S. McNamara was widely criticized by defense-oriented sources.

• Were negotiated in a period of comparatively relaxed tensions between the United States and Soviet Union. In 1963 the memory of the 1962 Cuban missile crisis was fresh in congressional minds.

On the other hand, Congress had not abandoned support for a strong military defense. Proxmire and others succeeded in trimming military funds by several billion dollars in 1969, but Congress in 1971 resisted defense-cutting attempts.

Many members of Congress who voiced basic approval of the 1972 pacts, as well as some who criticized them, emphasized they would be influenced by disclosures at committee hearings. A chief complaint by early critics was the lack of details and lack of clarification of complex technical questions affecting U.S. security.

Senate Approval

The Senate Aug. 3 gave its approval to ratification of the ABM treaty by an 88-2 vote.

But approval of the offensive arms agreement was harder in coming. After six weeks of debate and adoption of several modifications, action finally was completed on the accord Sept. 25. Final action came when the House, by a 308-4 vote, approved a resolution concurring with amendments that had been added to the pact by the Senate Sept. 14.

The most significant of the amendments, sponsored by Sen. Henry M. Jackson (D Wash.), a leading congressional proponent of a hard line vis-a-vis the Soviets, specified that any future permanent treaty on offensive arms must assure each country of rough numerical superiority in intercontinental strategic forces. It was deliberation over the Jackson amendment that had prevented quick Senate acceptance of the accord.

The White House Aug. 7 had given public endorsement to Jackson's effort after he modified his proposal by dropping a stipulation that any Soviet action or deployment that threatened the U.S. deterrent capability would be grounds for repudiating the interim agreement.

The Jackson and other amendments added to the bill had no effect on the accord itself as signed in Moscow. But they served to emphasize the disquiet of many members of Congress—and a majority of the Senate, which must ratify any permanent treaty to emerge from the second round of the SALT talks—concerning the terms of the interim agreement.

In approving the resolution, Congress merely was seconding the President's earlier decision to agree to the accord. No further action had been necessary to consummate the agreement with the Soviets, although the Nixon administration presumably would have dropped the agreement had Congress disapproved. Nixon Sept. 30 signed the congressional resolution upholding his approval.

The Jackson amendment was adopted by a 56-35 roll vote Sept. 14 after its supporters had beaten back several attempts to weaken it. In a key test of sentiment on the amendment, the Senate rejected by a 38-48 vote language sponsored by J. W. Fulbright (D Ark.), chairman of the Senate Foreign Relations Committee, which would have directed the United States to seek "over-all equality, parity and sufficiency" with the Soviets in nuclear weapons. Twenty-five Democrats and 13 Republicans voted for the Fulbright amendment, while 22 Democrats and 26 Republicans opposed it.

Trade Mission

Following up on Nixon's Moscow visit, the administration and the Soviet leaders sought agreements to broaden trade between the two nations.

The first major result was an agreement by the Soviet Union to buy at least $750-million in American grains over a three-year period.

Secretary of Commerce Peter G. Peterson in July led a delegation of American officials to Moscow to discuss further trade accommodations. The discussions were the first formal meeting of the U.S.-Soviet commercial commission created as a result of the Moscow summit.

A major stumbling block at issue in the bargaining was settlement of the Soviet Union's World War II Lend-Lease debts to the United States. Administration officials were insisting on settlement of the debts as part of any broad trade arrangement.

Soviet officials were seeking trade credits and "most favored nation" trade status with the United States—a status allowing Russian imports to the United States at the lowest tariff levels made available to other nations.

Japan

U.S. relations with Japan, since World War II a staunch U.S. ally, were strained in 1971 by Nixon's announcement that he would visit Mainland China.

The Japanese government of Premier Eisaku Sato was stunned by Nixon's secret dealings with China, undertaken without advance notice to Tokyo.

A new premier, Kakuei Tanaka, took office in 1972 committed to establishing formal relations with the People's Republic. Shortly after Tanaka assumed power, he and Nixon agreed to confer in Hawaii in an effort to repair strained relations between the two nations.

BUDGET: $246.3-BILLION SPENDING, $25.5-BILLION DEFICIT

President Nixon Jan. 24 sent to Congress a record quarter-trillion-dollar budget with a $25.5-billion deficit for the government's fiscal year 1973.

It was Nixon's third budget (former President Johnson submitted the budget for fiscal year 1970, as required by law, before leaving office in January 1969). It also was the third deficit budget of the Nixon administration: The 1971 budget was designed to produce a small surplus but ended deeply in deficit; the 1972 and 1973 budgets called for deliberate deficit spending to stimulate the economy.

Budget totals for the four fiscal years were:

(Billions of dollars)

	1970	1971	1972	1973
	(actual)	(actual)	(est.)	(est.)
Receipts	193.7	188.4	197.8	220.8
Outlays	196.6	211.4	236.6	246.3
Deficit	—2.8	—23.0	—38.8	—25.5
Budget authority	213.0	236.4	249.8	270.9

When submitted in January 1971, the budget for fiscal 1972 called for a much smaller deficit—$11.6-billion. The $38.8-billion deficit estimated for fiscal 1972 in the new budget, if it occurred as expected, would be the largest since World War II.

References. *President's budget message, p. 25-A, President's economic report p. 66-A; budget authority and outlays by function, table p. 18; budget authority and outlays by agency, table p. 20.*

For the second year, the budget as presented was called, in an economist's term, a full-employment budget. That meant that, while in actual deficit, the budget would have been in balance or surplus if the economy had been at full production and employment, which would have entailed slightly reduced spending and much larger receipts.

The 1970 budget was at a $3.1-billion surplus on a full-employment basis. Figures for the new budget and the intervening fiscal years were:

(Billions of dollars)

	1971	1972	1973
	(actual)	(est.)	(est.)
Full-employment receipts	214.1	225.0	245.0
Full-employment outlays	209.2	233.1	244.3
Surplus/deficit	4.9	—8.1	.7

In his budget message, Nixon said the economy was able to absorb the full-employment deficit for fiscal 1972. But he said the continued deficits on a full-employment basis which occurred in fiscal 1966, 1967 and 1968, during the Vietnam war escalation, led to the inflation which the economy was still experiencing.

Holding the increase in outlays to $9.7-billion in fiscal 1973 while receipts were expected to rise by $23-billion reduced the actual deficit from 1972 to 1973 and kept the 1973 budget just above balance on a full-employment basis. The spending plan also provided less stimulation during fiscal 1973, when the administration forecast that the economy would be expanding vigorously.

Later Developments. Final fiscal 1973 budget totals for the year ending June 30, 1973, depended on the President's efforts to hold spending to $250-billion—an increase of $4-billion over the budget projected in January 1972. Spending could go even higher making the deficit $29-billion, according to an estimate in October made by the Joint Committee on the Reduction of Federal Expenditures.

Major Initiatives

The President renewed his call for congressional approval and funding of his welfare reform and revenue sharing programs, both of which he originally proposed in his first year in office. He requested budget authority of

(Continued on p. 16)

Federal Budget 1954-1973

(in millions of dollars)

Fiscal Year	Receipts	Outlays	Surplus/ Deficit
1954	69,719	70,890	—1,170
1955	65,469	68,509	—,041
1956	74,547	70,460	+4,087
1957	79,990	76,741	+3,249
1958	79,636	82,575	—2,939
1959	79,249	92,104	—12,855
1960	92,492	92,223	+269
1961	94,389	97,795	—3,406
1962	99,676	106,813	—7,137
1963	106,560	111,311	—4,751
1964	112,662	118,584	—5,922
1965	116,833	118,430	—1,596
1966	130,856	134,652	—3,796
1967	149,552	158,254	—8,702
1968	153,671	178,833	—25,161
1969	187,784	184,548	+3,236
1970	193,743	196,588	—2,845
1971	188,392	211,425	—23,033
1972 est.	197,827	236,610	—38,783
1973 est.	220,785	246,257	—25,472

Note: Figures for years before fiscal year 1969 adjusted to conform to unified budget concept adopted in fiscal 1969.

APPROPRIATIONS IN 2nd SESSION, 92nd CONGRESS

For fiscal year 1973 unless otherwise noted; in millions of dollars

Budget authority in this type. *Outlays in this type.*

Budget authority: authority to commit funds. *Outlays: funds spent or obligated.* [1]

C—Committtee   F—Floor

BILL	NIXON REQUEST [2]	HOUSE	SENATE	CONFERENCE and FINAL	PAGE
Agriculture-Environmental (HR 15690)	$12,952.2	C-$12,897.0 F-$12,897.0 (June 29)	C-$13,394.9 F-$13,561.1 (July 27)	$13,434.0 *$12,520.4* (Aug. 22, PL 92-399)	345
Defense (HR 16593)	$79,237.8	C-$74,577.5 F-$74,577.5 (Sept. 14)	C-$74,604.7 F-$74,571.7 (Oct. 2)	$74,373.0 *$72,054.3* (Oct. 13, PL 92-570)	801
District of Columbia [3] (HR 15259)	$343.3	C-$332.3 F-$332.3 (June 7)	C-$313.7 F-$313.7 (June 14)	$316.4 *$344.1* (June 30, PL 92-344)	432
Foreign Assistance (HR 16705)	$5,163.0	C-$4,195.2 F-$4,195.2 (Sept. 21)	C-$2,823.9 F-$2,823.9 (Sept. 28)	Killed, passed continuing resolution	833
HUD-NASA-Veterans (HR 15093)	$20,258.2	C-$19,718.5 F-$19,718.5 (May 23)	C-$20,583.4 F-$20,583.4 (June 14)	$20,126.0 *$19,117.0* (Aug. 14, PL 92-383)	281
Interior-Related Agencies (HR 15418)	$2,527.2	C-$2,529.6 F-$2,529.6 (June 13)	C-$2,550.9 F-$2,550.9 (June 28)	$2,548.9 *$2,543.7* (Aug. 10, PL 92-369)	516
Labor-HEW [4] (HR 16654)	$33,426.2	C-$29,603.4 F-$29,603.4 (Sept. 19)	C-$30,538.9 F-$30,538.9 (Oct. 3)	$30,538.9 *$30,111.3* (Oct. 14)	865
Legislative Branch (HR 13955)	$519.3	C-$427.6 F-$427.6 (March 23)	C-$514.7 F-$514.7 (March 28)	$513.8 *$517.9* (June 29, PL 92-342)	310
Military Construction (HR 16754)	$3,017.8	C-$2,278.7 F-$2,280.8 (Sept. 25)	C-$2,337.7 F-$2,337.7 (Oct. 3)	$2,323.4 *$1,971.7* (Oct. 12, PL 92-547)	747
Public Works (HR 15586)	$5,489.1	C-$5,437 F-$5,437.7 (June 26)	C-$5,571.6 F-$5,571.7 (June 30)	$5,504.9 *$5,737.5* (Aug. 25, PL 92-405)	295
State-Justice-Commerce (HR 14989)	$4,704.3	C-$4,585.1 F-$4,587.1 (May 18)	C-$4,819.3 F-$4,820.7 (June 15)	$4,681.0 *$4,260.1* (Oct. 13, PL 92-544)	301
Transportation Department (HR 15097)	$2,946.5	C-$2,759.9 F-$2,791.6 (May 24)	C-$2,903.0 F-$2,907.0 (June 16)	$2,867.9 *$8,456.5* [5] (Aug. 22, PL 92-398)	340
Treasury-Postal-Executive Office (HR 15585)	$5,066.6	C-$5,057.1 F-$5,057.1 (June 22)	C-$5,055.2 F-$5,057.2 (June 23)	$5,057.8 *$5,147.7* (June 30, PL 92-351)	263
Supplemental First, FY 1973 (HR 17034)	$5,016.5	C-$3,565.0 F-$3,565.0 (Oct. 11)	C-$5,204.7 F-$5,266.7 (Oct. 12)	$4,933.4 *$2,988.0* (Oct. 14, PL 92-607)	135
Disaster Relief Supplemental (HR 16254)	$1,569.8	C-$1,587.3 F-$1,587.3 (Aug. 15)	C-$1,587.3 F-$1,587.3 (Aug. 16)	$1,587.3 *$1,406.0* (Aug. 16, PL 92-393)	294
Foreign Assistance FY 1972 (HR 12067)	$4,342.6	C-$2,845.5 F-$3,003.5 (Dec. 8, 1971)	C-$2,888.6 F-$3,076.5 (Feb. 4)	$3,189.4 *$3,428.2* (March 8, PL 92-242)	227
Supplemental, Urgent, FY 1972 (H J Res 1097)	$957.5	C-$957.5 F-$957.5 (March 14)	C-$957.5 F-$957.5 (March 15)	$957.5 *$957.5* (March 21, PL 92-256)	194
Supplemental, Second, FY 1972 (HR 14582)	$4,881.9	C-$4,124.1 F-$3,954.5 (April 26)	C-$5,063.4 F-$5,063.5 (May 1)	$4,347.7 *$4,458.4* (May 27, PL 92-306)	174
Supplemental, Special, FY 1972 (H J Res 1174)	$1,600.0	C-$1,600.0 F-$1,600.0 (May 4)	C-$1,600.0 F-$1,600.0 (May 5)	$1,600.0 *0* (May 18, PL 92-301)	240

1 Outlay estimates, provided by the Joint Committee on Reduction of Federal Expenditures, of total fiscal 1973 spending from funds appropriated by fiscal 1973 bills and from unspent funds appropriated by Congress for previous fiscal years.
2 Nixon requests include amendment submitted after original budget.

3 House bill also included $543.4 million in funds generated by District of Columbia; Senate bill, $511.2-million; conference bill, $518.4-million.
4 President vetoed first bill; HR 16654 permits him to impound $1,238,919,000.
5 Includes substantially greater funds appropriated to liquidate contract authority.

$5.3-billion for revenue sharing with state and local governments for general purposes and $12.3-billion in

special revenue-sharing funds for six broad purposes: education, urban community development, rural community development, manpower training, law enforcement and transportation.

Nixon proposed that Congress make general revenue sharing effective Jan. 1, 1972, granting $2.25-billion to state and local governments during the remainder of fiscal year 1972 and $5-billion in fiscal 1973. He had proposed both general and special revenue sharing in the budget submitted to Congress in January 1971.

The President renewed major proposals made previously in health, Social Security and education. He urged new initiatives and increased funding for:

- Defense
- Health
- Education
- Assistance to the elderly
- Community development and housing
- Veterans' benefits
- International affairs and finance
- Research and development

Priorities

As he had in the budgets for fiscal 1971 and 1972, Nixon stressed that spending for human resources exceeded expenditures for national defense. The new budget showed spending for human resources as 45 percent of the total; defense spending was 31.8 percent of the total. This was almost exactly the reverse, the President said, of the proportions allocated in fiscal 1968.

Also as in previous years, the new budget stressed the growing proportion of relatively uncontrollable expenditures. These include expenditures for open-ended programs, such as Social Security, unemployment compensation, farm price supports and veterans' benefits, under which the government is committed to pay all legitimate claims. Also included are interest on the public debt and contract obligations undertaken in previous years.

Together they totaled $174.6-billion, or 71 percent of total outlays. The budget provided a total of $79.8-billion in relatively controllable outlays—those over which the government exercises year-to-year discretion. Almost two-thirds of that amount was in national defense expenditures.

Of the $110.8-billion in estimated outlays for human resources programs for fiscal 1973, $91.4-billion was for programs shown by the budget as relatively uncontrollable. Social Security, unemployment compensation and similar trust fund expenditures accounted for $68.1-billion of the human resources total; veterans' benefits, medicaid, public assistance and the food stamp program were included in the remainder.

The relative uncontrollability of most of the human resources expenditures showed that the shift taking place in proportionate spending for human resources and defense since fiscal 1968 was due primarily to the inexorable growth in commitments under human resource programs, some of long standing, and not to initiatives of the Nixon administration, although the administration claimed credit for the change.

Budget Terminology

The federal budget is a plan of expected receipts and expenditures, a statement of priorities, an accounting of how funds have been and will be spent and a request for authority to spend public money.

The 1973 budget covers the government's fiscal year beginning July 1, 1972, and ending June 30, 1973.

The federal expenditures reported are most frequently outlays: amounts spent, obligated or committed during the year. Examples are funds spent to buy equipment or property, to meet the government's liability under a contract or to pay the salary of an employee. Outlays also include net lending—the difference between disbursements and repayments under government lending programs.

The administration's request to Congress, presented in the form of the budget, is for authority to obligate or lend funds: New Obligational Authority (abbreviated NOA) and Loan Authority (LA).

Budget authority determines the scope of operations of the government. Congress confers budget authority on a federal agency in general in the form of appropriations.

Appropriations may be for a single year, a specified period of years, or an indefinite number of years, according to the restrictions Congress wishes to place on spending for particular purposes.

Congress also restricts itself in the appropriation process by requiring that an appropriation be preceded by an authorization to appropriate a certain or an indefinite amount of money for a certain purpose over a period of time. These authorizations, which in practice are often larger than the actual appropriations, are self-imposed limits on Congress, distinct from budget authority.

Usually an authorization establishes the scope of a particular program, and Congress appropriates funds within the limits it has previously approved. In the case of authority to enter contract obligations, however, Congress authorizes the administration to make firm commitments for which funds must be appropriated later. Congress also occasionally includes mandatory spending requirements in an authorization, designed to ensure spending at a certain level.

Budget authority, either NOA or LA, often differs from actual outlays. This is because, in practice, funds actually spent or obligated during a year are drawn partly from the budget authority conferred in the year in question and partly from budget authority conferred in previous years.

Similarly, part of the budget authority granted for the current year will not be spent or obligated until succeeding years. Delays, first in appropriating and then in making expenditures under federal programs, produce the lag. Consequently a change in budget authority is not necessarily reflected immediately in a change of the same amount and direction in outlays.

Revenues

The sources of federal government receipts in fiscal 1973 and the two previous fiscal years, according to the new budget, were:

(Billions of dollars)

	1971	1972	1973
	(actual)	(estimate)	(estimate)
Individual income taxes	86.2	86.5	93.9
Corporation income taxes	26.8	30.1	35.7
Social insurance taxes	48.6	54.1	63.7
Excise taxes	16.6	15.2	16.3
Estate and gift taxes	3.7	5.2	4.3
Customs duties	2.6	3.2	2.8
Miscellaneous receipts	3.9	3.5	4.1
TOTAL	188.4	197.8	220.8

NOTE: Includes both federal funds and trust funds.

Receipts were expected to increase $9.4-billion in fiscal 1972 and $23-billion in fiscal 1973. The Revenue Act of 1971 (PL 92-178), proposed by the President as a part of his new economic policy, was expected to reduce revenues by $4.4-billion in fiscal 1972 and $6.9-billion in fiscal 1973.

Trust Funds

The unified budget, the budget form used since fiscal 1969, combines federal funds and trust funds and deducts the transactions that occur between them. Federal funds are those which are not earmarked at the source for specific purposes. They are raised chiefly from taxes and borrowing and are available for all legitimate government purposes.

Trust funds are those collected and segregated for specific purposes, such as the Social Security and unemployment compensation funds, which are raised from payroll taxes. Both the trust funds and payments from them are included in the unified budget.

Federal funds were expected to be in deficit by $36.2-billion in fiscal 1973, and the trust funds in surplus by $10.7-billion. In effect, the federal funds borrowed the trust fund surplus, increasing both the total public debt and the amount of debt held by the trust funds.

A separate accounting for the two types of funds showed:

(Billions of dollars, fiscal years)

	1971	1972	1973
	(actual)	(est.)	(est.)
Federal funds transactions:			
With the public	—$18.5	—$31.8	—$23.3
With trust funds	— 11.4	— 12.9	—12.8
Total	— 29.9	— 44.7	—36.2
Trust funds transactions:			
With the public	— 4.6	— 7.0	—2.2
With federal funds	11.4	12.9	12.8
Total	6.8	5.9	10.7
Budget total:			
Federal funds	— 29.9	— 44.7	—36.2
Trust funds	6.8	5.9	10.7
Unified budget deficit	— 23.0	— 38.8	—25.5

Public Debt

Total public debt was expected to rise $37.4-billion in fiscal 1973, to $493.2-billion. Debt held by the public, including the Federal Reserve System, was to rise $27.5-billion, to $371.3-billion. The remainder was to be held by the trust funds and certain federal agencies— $121.9-billion; these would absorb a net $9.9-billion of the increase. The $1.2-billion difference between the federal funds deficit and the increase in the total public debt was the net total of a number of transactions and adjustments in non-debt financing.

Economic Basis

The President said progress had been recorded in 1971 in moderating inflation and expanding economic output before his new economic policy went into effect. But he said inflation and unemployment remained unacceptably high. Together with deterioration in the balance of international payments, they required a decisive change in policy.

On Aug. 15, 1971, Nixon imposed a wage-price freeze. He proposed a major tax reduction and cuts in federal spending. Further, he imposed a 10-percent surtax on imports and suspended convertibility of the dollar into gold. In mid-November, he inaugurated Phase Two of his new economic policy, under which more limited controls have been exercised on economic activity. (1971 Almanac p. 58)

Since then, Nixon said, inflation had abated further and economic activity appeared to have accelerated. For calendar year 1972, the budget included a forecast of gross national product (total economic output) of $1.1-trillion ($1,145-billion), an increase of $98-billion over the estimate for 1971. Corresponding increases were forecast for personal income, corporate profits and government revenues. (Economic Report of the President, p. 66-A)

Long-range Forecast

In a forecast five years ahead, the budget for fiscal 1972 estimated there would be a surplus in fiscal 1976 of $30-billion on the basis of existing government programs and revenues from the existing tax structure at full employment.

The new budget found that action during the year, adding to programs and reducing taxes, had virtually eliminated the future budget margin. Assuming passage of Social Security tax proposals pending before Congress, there would be a $5-billion surplus in fiscal 1976 and a $23-billion surplus in fiscal 1977.

This calculation, an innovation of the Nixon administration based on an assumed 4.3-percent annual growth of gross national product, projections of population changes and predictable growth in existing program costs, showed that the margin was small for additions to existing programs and inauguration of new programs.

(Continued on p. 20)

FISCAL 1973 BUDGET BY FUNCTION: $246.3 BILLION IN

(in millions of dollars)†

	BUDGET AUTHORITY†			EXPENDITURES		
	1971	1972 est.	1973 est.	1971	1972 est.	1973 est.
NATIONAL DEFENSE						
Military Defense	$ 71,159	$ 75,320	$ 81,568	$ 74,471	$ 74,920	$ 75,818
Loan Authority and Net Lending, Military Defense •	0	0	0	*	—*	—3
Civil Defense	73	78	88	75	80	85
Military Assistance	1,655	1,746	1,722	999	800	600
Atomic Energy	2,308	2,316	2,563	2,275	2,358	2,422
Defense Related Activities	113	119	115	—69	91	80
Loan Authority and Net Lending, Defense Related Activities•	—1	—1	—1	—1	—1	—1
Deductions for Offsetting Receipts	—89	—218	—692	—89	—218	—692
TOTAL	$ 75,218	$ 79,360	$ 85,363	$ 77,661	$ 78,030	$ 78,309
INTERNATIONAL AFFAIRS AND FINANCE						
Conduct of Foreign Affairs	$ 422	$ 464	$ 496	$ 405	$ 459	$ 487
Economic and Financial Assistance	2,252	2,896	3,769	1,856	2,328	2,479
Loan Authority and Net Lending, Economic and Financial Assistance •	54	0	0	—49	48	16
Foreign Information and Exchange	233	276	297	242	277	292
Food for Peace	702	1,320	895	918	1,114	839
Deductions for Offsetting Receipts	—276	—266	—268	—276	—266	—268
TOTAL	$ 3,387	$ 4,690	$ 5,189	$ 3,096	$ 3,960	$ 3,845
SPACE RESEARCH AND TECHNOLOGY	$ 3,322	$ 3,308	$ 3,389	$ 3,392	$ 3,193	$ 3,202
Deductions for Offsetting Receipts	—11	—13	—11	—11	—13	—11
TOTAL	$ 3,311	$ 3,295	$ 3,378	$ 3,381	$ 3,180	$ 3,191
AGRICULTURE AND RURAL DEVELOPMENT						
Farm Income Stabilization	$ 3,218	$ 5,775	$ 5,624	$ 3,561	$5,483	$ 5,445
Loan Authority and Net Lending, Farm Income Stabilization •	263	174	115	91	18	—434
Financing Rural Housing and Public Facilities	212	242	181	66	262	266
Loan Authority and Net Lending, Financing Rural Housing and Public Facilities •	292	793	580	261	347	352
Agricultural Land and Water Resources	372	411	341	346	375	388
Research and Other Services	831	890	946	813	901	915
Deductions for Offsetting Receipts	—42	—41	—41	—42	—41	—41
TOTAL	$ 5,146	$ 8,243	$ 7,746	$ 5,096	$ 7,345	$ 6,890
NATURAL RESOURCES AND ENVIRONMENT						
Water Resources and Power	$ 5,302	$ 2,462	$ 2,715	$ 2,384	$ 2,990	$ 3,192
Loan Authority and Net Lending, Water Resources and Power •	7	10	16	5	15	15
Land Management	895	936	869	837	935	918
Mineral Resources	117	130	110	130	121	103
Pollution Control and Abatement	1,289	2,448	2,478	701	1,287	1,541
Recreational Resources	667	806	709	479	642	640
Other Natural Resources Programs	137	158	182	136	149	176
Deductions for Offsetting Receipts	—1,957	—1,763	—4,135	—1,957	—1,763	—4,135
TOTAL	$ 6,457	$ 5,187	$ 2,944	$ 2,715	$ 4,376	$ 2,450
COMMERCE AND TRANSPORTATION						
Air Transportation	$ 1,675	$ 1,676	$ 1,536	$ 1,602	$ 1,742	$ 1,688
Water Transportation	1,154	1,242	1,358	1,050	1,208	1,233
Loan Authority and Net Lending, Water Transportation •	—8	—7	—6	—10	—8	—8
Ground Transportation	8,810	6,262	6,187	5,037	5,361	5,665
Loan Authority and Net Lending, Ground Transportation	149	0	0	33	51	55
Postal Service	12,577	1,418	1,424	2,183	1,943	1,409
Advancement of Business	593	692	836	515	490	529
Loan Authority and Net Lending, Advancement of Business •	625	516	475	223	253	113
Area and Regional Development	826	848	774	664	764	809
Loan Authority and Net Lending, Area and Regional Development •	61	67	57	53	52	48
Regulation of Business	1,139	153	157	136	146	153
Loan Authority and Net Lending, Regulation of Business •	46	28	—*	46	28	—*
Deductions for Offsetting Receipts	—221	—159	—143	—221	—159	—143
TOTAL	$ 27,426	$ 12,736	$ 12,655	$ 11,311	$ 11,871	$ 11,551
COMMUNITY DEVELOPMENT AND HOUSING						
Community Planning, Management and Development	$ 3,309	$ 3,070	$ 2,757	$ 2,488	$ 2,720	$ 2,988
Loan Authority and Net Lending, Community Planning, Management and Development •	2	1	*	—2	25	21

EXPENDITURES, $270.9 BILLION IN SPENDING AUTHORITY

(in millions of dollars)†

	BUDGET AUTHORITY			EXPENDITURES		
	1971	1972 est.	1973 est.	1971	1972 est.	1973 est.
Urban Community Development Revenue Sharing	0	0	490	0	0	490
Low and Moderate Income Housing Aids	890	1,425	2,040	792	1,406	1,941
Loan Authority and Net Lending, Low and Moderate Income Housing Aids •	45	90	0	451	268	124
Maintenance of Housing Mortgage Market	99	78	265	—276	—248	—288
Loan Authority and Net Lending, Maintenance of Housing Mortgage Market •	0	149	95	—43	—132	—432
Deductions for Offsetting Receipts	—53	—*	—*	—53	—*	—*
TOTAL	$ 4,292	$ 4,813	$ 5,647	$ 3,357	$ 4,039	$ 4,844
EDUCATION AND MANPOWER						
Elementary and Secondary Education	$ 3,300	$ 3,999	$ 4,102	$ 3,164	$ 3,383	$ 3,619
Loan Authority and Net Lending, Elementary and Secondary Education •	*	—*	—*	—*	—*	—*
Higher Education	1,059	1,692	1,372	1,294	1,356	1,305
Loan Authority and Net Lending, Higher Education •	16	30	34	134	85	65
Vocational Education	527	584	554	415	531	568
Education Revenue Sharing	0	0	224	0	0	110
Manpower Training and Employment Services	2,564	3,800	4,084	2,380	3,318	3,918
General Science	506	622	653	522	538	596
Other Education Aids	531	631	1,029	534	632	745
Other Manpower Aids	253	334	397	223	325	387
Deductions for Offsetting Receipts	—12	—29	—32	—12	—29	—32
TOTAL	$ 8,744	$ 11,663	$ 12,417	$ 8,654	$ 10,140	$ 11,281
HEALTH						
Development of Health Resources	$ 2,293	$ 2,965	$ 2,851	$ 2,199	$ 2,430	$ 2,770
Loan Authority and Net Lending, Development of Health Resources •	40	85	—*	2	17	17
Providing or Financing Medical Services	12,657	15,633	20,115	11,946	14,214	14,733
Prevention and Control of Health Problems	360	571	738	319	382	619
Deductions for Offsetting Receipts	—3	—18	—22	—3	—18	—22
TOTAL	$ 15,347	$ 19,236	$ 23,682	$ 14,463	$ 17,025	$ 18,117
INCOME SECURITY						
Retirement and Social Insurance	$ 50,174	$ 55,598	$ 60,795	$ 46,321	$ 52,654	$ 57,047
Public Assistance	8,035	9,745	11,030	7,773	10,109	10,333
Loan Authority and Net Lending, Public Assistance •	3	3	2	2	2	2
Social and Individual Services	1,742	2,483	2,514	1,617	2,477	2,297
Deductions for Offsetting Receipts	—1	—18	—21	—1	—18	—21
TOTAL	$ 59,953	$ 67,811	$ 74,320	$ 55,712	$ 65,224	$ 69,658
VETERANS BENEFITS AND SERVICES						
Income Security	$ 6,601	$ 6,899	$ 7,366	$ 6,409	$ 6,926	$ 7,036
Loan Authority and Net Lending, Income Security •	39	24	14	39	24	14
Education, Training and Rehabilitation	1,696	2,119	2,443	1,659	2,240	2,437
Loan Authority and Net Lending, Education, Training and Rehabilitation •	*	0	0	*	0	0
Housing	98	6	5	—16	—17	20
Loan Authority and Net Lending, Housing •	—92	0	0	—162	—289	—309
Hospital and Medical Care	2,096	2,503	2,758	2,038	2,422	2,693
Other Veterans Benefits and Services	297	355	351	294	322	349
Deductions for Offsetting Receipts	—484	—500	—495	—484	—500	—495
TOTAL	$ 10,251	$ 11,406	$ 12,442	$ 9,777	$ 11,128	$ 11,745
INTEREST	$ 21,097	$ 21,563	$22,864	$ 21,097	$ 21,563	$ 22,864
Deductions for Offsetting Receipts	—1,488	—1,496	—1,703	—1,488	—1,496	—1,703
TOTAL	$ 19,609	$ 20,067	$ 21,161	$ 19,609	$ 20,067	$ 21,161
GENERAL GOVERNMENT	$ 4,905	$ 6,065	$ 5,981	$ 4,186	$ 5,400	$ 5,736
Loan Authority and Net Lending, General Government •	—5	133	111	44	209	139
Deductions for Offsetting Receipts	—261	—307	—344	—261	—307	—344
TOTAL	$ 4,639	$ 5,891	$ 5,748	$ 3,969	$ 5,302	$ 5,531
GENERAL REVENUE SHARING	0	$ 2,500	$ 5,300	0	$ 2,250	$ 5,000
CIVILIAN PAY INCREASES	0	$ 260	$ 800	0	$ 250	$ 775
CONTINGENCIES	0	$ 500	$ 700	0	$ 300	$ 500
UNDISTRIBUTED INTRAGOVERNMENTAL PAYMENTS	$—7,376	$—7,877	$—8,590	$—7,376	$—7,877	$—8,590
GRAND TOTAL	$236,405	$249,779	$270,897	$211,425	$236,610	$246,257

† *Figures may not add to totals due to rounding.*
‡ *Primarily appropriations.*
SOURCE: Office of Management and Budget

* *Less than $500 thousand.*
• *Figures in the first three columns are Loan Authority; figures in remaining columns are Net Lending.*

Budget Authority and Outlays by Agency

(Fiscal years, in millions of dollars)

Agency	Budget authority			Outlays		
	1971 actual	1972 estimate	1973 estimate	1971 actual	1972 estimate	1973 estimate
Legislative Branch	$ 436	$ 567	$ 492	$ 384	$ 477	$ 505
The Judiciary	152	174	192	142	171	189
Executive Office of the President	50	68	67	47	63	71
Funds appropriated to the President	5,426	5,610	6,476	4,454	4,433	4,131
Agriculture	8,591	12,799	11,877	8,560	11,610	11,005
Commerce	1,274	1,485	1,533	1,188	1,289	1,425
Defense—Military *	71,232	75,398	81,656	74,546	75,000	75,900
Defense—Civil	1,343	1,620	1,838	1,376	1,655	1,822
Health, Education & Welfare	65,829	76,533	86,887	61,866	71,911	78,953
Housing & Urban Development	3,355	3,974	4,755	2,890	3,462	4,214
Interior	524	1,208	—1,106	225	1,053	—1,138
Justice	1,248	1,563	1,739	916	1,230	1,476
Labor	6,559	9,414	9,523	7,923	10,466	9,589
State	488	573	602	468	545	576
Transportation	11,262	8,650	8,558	7,247	7,851	8,155
Treasury	21,007	24,404	28,057	20,990	24,124	27,737
Atomic Energy Commission	2,308	2,316	2,563	2,275	2,358	2,422
Environmental Protection Agency	1,289	2,448	2,478	701	1,287	1,541
General Services Administration	651	619	77	501	511	110
National Aeronautics & Space Administration	3,311	3,295	3,378	3,381	3,180	3,191
U.S. Postal Service	12,577	1,418	1,424	2,183	1,943	1,409
Veterans Administration	10,219	11,367	12,397	9,756	11,101	11,715
Other Independent Agencies	14,653	11,393	12,525	6,785	8,216	8,572
Allowances for:						
Pay raises **	—	260	800	—	250	775
Contingencies	—	500	700	—	300	500
Undistributed intergovernmental transactions:						
Employer share, employee retirement	—2,611	—2,687	—2,893	—2,611	—2,687	—2,893
Interest received by trust funds	—4,765	—5,190	—5,697	—4,765	—5,190	—5,697
Total budget authority and outlays	$236,406	$249,777	$270,898	$211,425	$236,610	$246,257

Includes Defense Department civilian and military pay raises and military retirement system reform.
**Excludes Defense Department.*

SOURCE: 1973 Budget.

(Continued from p. 17)

Additional revenues or offsetting reductions in existing programs would be required for most new initiatives.

Budget Trends

The budget recommended $270.9-billion in budget authority for outlays in fiscal 1973 and future years:

- $269.4-billion in new obligational authority for expenditures.
- $1.5-billion in loan authority.

Of the total, $185.3-billion required action by Congress; the remainder was available from permanent authority.

The budget contemplated outlays of $148-billion from the 1973 authority. Outlays of $98.3-billion from authority enacted in previous years made up the rest of the $246.3-billion total outlays.

The draw-down of new authority would leave $122.9-billion in authority for future years. Together with $166.9-billion in previously enacted authority left over after fiscal 1973, there would be $289.8-billion in unused budget authority for future years.

The relatively small growth in outlays contemplated for fiscal 1973 was reflected in outlay growth trends as shown by the budget. From 1965 to 1968—the period of build-up in the Vietnam war—outlays increased an average of 17 percent per year. From 1969 to 1972, outlays grew by slightly more than 9 per cent per year, on the average.

The increase of fiscal 1973 over 1972 was only 4.1 percent. The small increase was strongly influenced by reduced revenues springing from Congressional changes in the tax structure since 1969.

PRESIDENT OUTLINES GOALS AND CONCEPT OF GOVERNMENT

On the eve of his expected landslide re-election victory, President Nixon was interviewed by the *Washington Star-News* on what the nation could expect from his second term.

The interview was instructive not only for what programs the President would follow, but also for his conception of government and the American people.

The President promised no new spending programs or taxes, but reform in many areas to more efficiently use the money available. His foreign policy would be a continuation of the first four years, with less emphasis on the spectacular such as the Peking and Moscow visits, and hoped for progress on strategic arms limitation and international monetary stability.

Nixon described his political philosophy as that of a "Disraeli conservative—a strong foreign policy, strong adherence to basic values that the nation believes in...to conserving those values..." and combining them with effective reform.

Nixon said many of the solutions of the 1960s were failures because the government "threw money at the problems." The next Nixon administration would cut back those programs that have failed, he said.

The President said the people needed more responsibility and self-discipline, and his reforms would attempt to give it to them. He described the average American as "just like a child in the family" who needed more responsibility to amount to something, but who had been pampered in previous decades by a federal government that tried to do everything for him.

The interview was given on Nov. 5, two days before the election, to the *Star-News'* reporter Garnett Horner with the stipulation that it would not be published until after the election. Following is a transcript of the interview as published by the *Star-News* Nov. 9:

Text of Interview

FOREIGN POLICY

The first year will be a very busy one. We are going to move on SALT II. We, of course, will be moving on the European Security Conference, and in a parallel channel we will be moving on the M.B.F.R., mutual balanced force reduction. We will continue the dialogue with the P.R.C. (People's Republic of China), although that is a long-range process. Nothing sudden is going to happen. There will be no change, no change whatever, in our policy toward Cuba, unless and until—and I do not anticipate this will happen—Castro changes his policy toward Latin America and the United States. The Middle East will have a very high priority because while the Mideast has been, over the past couple of years, in a period of uneasy truce or armistice, or whatever you want to call it, it can explode at any time.

Now, as far as the other parts of the world are concerned, I wouldn't want to leave the impression that Latin America and Africa will not get attention. They will, because none of our present policies are going to be sacred cows. I am going to look at the Latin-American policy and African policy to see how our programs can be improved in those areas.

TRADE POLICY CITED

In the international field we must move to get a more stable monetary system, and we must move in the trade field so that the United States can continue to get a proper break in our trading relations with other countries.

So I would say that while the next four years will not be as spectacular as the year 1972, where we had the opening to Peking, the first summit with the Russians and the Aug. 15th international monetary moves, that the next four years will build on those and will really accomplish more, because those were basically the first steps which opened the way for much bigger steps in the future.

For example, SALT-II will be more important than SALT-I. It is going to have more of a limitation, the European Security Conference, the Mideast, all of these areas. Let me tell you this on Vietnam—when I tell you I am completely confident that we are going to have a settlement, you can bank on it.

Assuming there is a Vietnam settlement, the President was asked about Southeast Asia's future for the next four years.

Well, it will have to be a future in which we continue to provide economic assistance, and some military assistance, as well, to our friends in that area, because the Communist nations are going to provide the same kind of assistance to North Vietnam. We will, as we have said, provide some assistance also to North Vietnam on an economic basis.

Our interest is not only to bring an agreement that ends the war now, but to have an influence on the events in the future, and it is much better to have a relationship with the North Vietnamese than not to have it.

DOMESTIC POLICY

I seldom recommend any speech, and particularly my own, for others to read, but I think in terms of setting of a candidate, setting forth his views, perhaps the most extensive exercise in that respect were the 15 radio and television speeches where I went into my philosophy, and I was also specific. All of that sets forth my views in general in the foreign and domestic fields.

Being more specific, as far as what the agenda will be on the domestic front, we are going to start with what I said in the 1972 State of the Union, where of the six goals we had action only on revenue sharing. I don't mean that some of those programs that I laid forth will not now require modification, because after a year's experience, and because of some fiscal restraints, we are going to have to modify some. But the philosophical approach that I set forth in that State of the Union, and these 15 radio television speeches is the one that I will follow now.

So that you have something more direct I have noted that the suggestion has been made that this is on the assumption that I will win the election, which may prove to be untrue—but not facing the problem of re-election, I will now be more free to advocate some massive new social programs. Nothing could be further from the mark.

This country has enough on its plate in the way of new spending programs, social programs, throwing dollars at problems. What we need is, basically, reform of existing institutions and not the destruction of our tried values in this country. Consequently, the next administration will be one of reform, not just adding more dollars—reform in the field of education, reform in the field of health; reform in Federal-state relations; reform in all fields. Reform using money more effectively will be the mark of this Administration, rather than simply coming up with huge new bundles of money to throw at the problems. I don't believe that the answer to the nation's problems is simply massive new programs in terms of dollars and in terms of people.

I haven't answered...simply in terms of philosophy in general. When we talk about philosophy. I am not saying we are going to be more conservative, more liberal. Maybe I can describe it this way: I think if you would look at it in terms of the great debates in the British system in the 19th century, I would say that my views, my approach, is probably that of a Disraeli conservative—a strong foreign policy, strong adherence to basic values that the nation believes in and the people believe in, and to conserving those values, and not being destructive of them, but combined with reform, reform that will work, not reform that destroys.

The President was asked how he would solve domestic problems in the cities such as housing, education and health care.

We start with this: I feel very strong—you can't take an extreme right position, that if you ignore them the problems will go away. First you must start with an honest awareness of the fact that the problems are basically there. The debate, really, is not whether we do something about problems, not whether they exist, but what we do. That is what it's really about. What we have to realize is that many of the solutions of the 60's were massive failures. They threw money at the problems and for the most part they have failed and we are going to shuck off those programs and trim down those programs that have proved simply to be failures.

Now, how do you solve some of these problems? As we go into this next year, this is receiving the most intensive study within the Domestic Council, and we will be presenting to the Congress, in addition to what I have already presented in 1972, we are going to present to the Congress solutions to these problems that we think can more effectively deal with them.

But let me begin with some restraints that we have. First, there will be no solutions of problems that require a tax increase. Now, therefore, even if we wanted to go down the line or felt to solve a problem it was best to go down the line of more spending, huge new spending programs, we can't do it because more important than more money to solve a problem is to avoid a tax increase. I am convinced that the total tax burden of the American people, Federal state and local, has reached the breaking point. It can not go higher. If it does go higher I believe that we will do much to destroy the incentives which produce the progress we want.

So therefore, this gets back to our reforms. The reforms have to be ones which will make Government run better at less cost. The reforms also, insofar as any new programs are concerned, must be ones that are within our budget limitations.

...We have had very little success in getting action on our reorganization plans, as you know. We have had very little success in getting our special revenue sharing through, which, of course, also involves reorganization. In other words, our reorganization of the Cabinet, special revenue sharing—no action.

Now, what I have determined to do, and I am having this now studied within the Domestic Council and the Bureau of the Budget, is to accomplish as much as I can of that reorganization through executive action, obviously not doing anything which would be in violation of the law, but I am convinced that the thrust of our reorganization plan, the thrust of our special revenue sharing, is right, that it is needed, and I intend to accomplish it, as much as I can, through action at the executive level unless and until the Congress acts.

BIG GOVERNMENT

I honestly believe that Government in Washington is too big and it is too expensive. I realize that it is difficult to thin it down in terms of the number of people, but you can be sure that we are going to make an effort. We can do the job better with fewer people.

And incidentally, that is going to cut across the board, including the White House staff. We can do a better job with fewer people. We have got to set the example on the White House staff. No agencies are going to be exempt in this respect.

There are certain areas, for example, like in the field of narcotics, crime, law enforcement, Social Security, et cetera, where you cannot make cuts because as the population grows, the need for more people goes up.

But there are other areas where you can. That includes the new agencies—HUD, HEW, Transportation are all too fat, too bloated. They came in and they did some good things, but we have to look at not only what they are doing right but at some of the things that they are doing that haven't proved out.

I instituted three months ago, through the Domestic Council, an examination of what we can reform in these areas; and second, in those things that we continue, we are going to find ways to do them with less people.

But also, may I emphasize the old agencies are not going to be exempt—Interior, Agriculture, Defense, et cetera. Let's look at Defense just a moment.

MINIMAL DEFENSE CUTS POSSIBLE

When I speak of Defense, in terms of the hardware of Defense, in terms of the military personnel in Defense, the cuts that can be made certainly are minimal, except when we get mutual agreement with other countries. But in terms of the masses of civilian employes who are getting in the way of each other over in the Pentagon and around the country, they are going to have to take a thinning down.

When we talk about thinning down, we naturally want to accomplish that goal with the least possible human dislocation. Generally speaking you will find that attrition—there is a huge turnover in government, to begin with. There are many people in government as we begin a new term—who perhaps will feel that they should leave, that they would like to leave. We are going to try to do it in a way that will consider the individual, but we have to accomplish the objective.

Now, let me say, as far as Presidential appointees are concerned, and all of those subject to appointments by the departments, as far as they are concerned, they have had their four years and I will expect all of them to submit their resignations. If it is found that any of them no longer are needed or that their jobs are no longer needed, then their resignations will be accepted. So, at that level we have no problem. When we get down into the other levels there is a problem.

CONSERVATISM

The President was asked his views about what some consider a strong conservative swing in the country.

Well, let me begin by saying that the liberal establishment, during the four years I have been in office, thought that I was out of touch with the country. That is not true. What this election will demonstrate is that out across the country, and including, incidentally up in the Northeast, which is considered to be the playground of the limousine liberal set, you will find that a solid majority of the American people do not want to go to the far left. What this election will demonstrate is that when a candidate takes basically an extreme position on issues, he inevitably splits his party and assures his defeat, even when it is a majority party; always when it is a minority party, but even when it is a majority party, as is the Democratic party.

What happened here it that Senator McGovern's views, even though he won the nomination, probably did not represent even a majority of Democrats. They certainly represented a minority of the country.

Now, the Eagleton matter and the way McGovern conducted his campaign may have affected this election, by five points, no more. This election was decided the day he was nominated. The issue in this election was his views. Oh, it is true, the issue is also the man, one man against another. But in this election his views were clearly the issue and his views simply turned off the solid majority of the American people, most of the Republicans, a great number of Democrats, and a very solid majority of the independents.

PRESS REPORTED HONESTLY

So, I would respectfully suggest, and incidentally, let me say in all respect, too, that the great majority of the members of the press and the media tried to report this honestly. I understand that, I am not complaining about the reporting. They went after me. They went after McGovern. That isn't what is in issue.

What we have to realize is that what was on the line here was my position of a strong national defense, my position of peace with honor in Vietnam, my position of opposing, for example, busing for racial balance, my position against permissiveness, amnesty being part of that, against legalizing marijuana, being part of that. All of these things were involved.

Now, having said this, however, this does not mean that my position is over on the far right. Basically it means my position is simply in the center. In the field of foreign policy, I think most people would describe my position as being that of a centrist. In domestic policy, if you look at the Nixon proposals in the first four years —and I can assure you, Jack, that when you look at them over the next four years, this will be known as an Administration which advocated—and if we get proper support in the Congress after the election, was able to accomplish—more significant reform than any Administration since Franklin Roosevelt's in 1932; but reform in a different direction. Roosevelt's reforms led to bigger and bigger power in Washington. It was perhaps needed then. The country's problems were so massive they couldn't be handled otherwise.

The reforms that we are instituting are ones which will diffuse the power throughout the country and which will make government leaner, but in a sense will make it stronger. After all, fat government is weak, weak in handling the problems.

CAMPAIGNS

The President was reminded that he had mentioned recently that the British system of limiting election campaigns to three weeks is better than our prolonged campaigns, and was asked if he thought anything could be done about it.

The trouble is that it would require mutual agreement, and you are never going to get either side to agree. I think what is involved here is that with the advent of television we have to realize that campaigns now bore the people to death, because they are simply too long and they see them on the tube a lot. Then you can read about it in the newspaper or put it aside, but when the evening news comes on, month after month—it isn't just two of the regular campaigns: you hear of the convention; you hear it between the conventions; but then the campaign begins two years before when they start speculating about who is going to run in the primaries and then the polls are taken. Then you have the primary campaigns.

By the time you get to the election, the people say, "Oh no; not more politics."

The other point is this: You have to realize that with the advent of television combined with radio, a candidate goes on, he has a massive audience, and they hear his speech and there are not very many speeches to be made. My own view, therefore, is that while many can say America is too big a country to have the British kind of approach, they overlook the fact that television makes this a country in which the candidates can communicate with the whole nation through television.

BETTER COMMUNICATION

And I don't mean to underestimate what the press does, too. Press communication in this country is infinitely better than it used to be. It goes out on the wires and every newspaper—the P.M., and A.M., and so forth, radio gets it.

But the point I make is that it would be better for both parties, and certainly better for the candidates and particularly better where a Presidential candidate is concerned—because we don't want to wear our people down to a frazzle before they take on the awesome responsibilities of this position—to shorten these campaigns.

I must say, I am very pessimistic whether or not it can be done. It is competitive, and being as competitive as it is, I think we are still going to find that all the television does, instead of shortening the campaign, is add one other burden you didn't have previously.

For example, as I did these radio addresses, I thought how good it would have been to have been President during the period Franklin Roosevelt was President. I mean, doing a radio speech is infinitely less taxing than having to do it on television.

OFFICIAL FAMILY

With regard to appointments, I think I will stay away from that, due to the fact that if I answer it with regard to Kissinger, then I would have to answer with regard to others.

The problem of the relationship between the President's international affairs adviser and the State Department has always been a difficult one. It is particularly at this time because we have had so many initiatives that had to be undertaken at the Presidential level. But I think Bill Rogers put it very well. He said, "When the team is winning, you don't complain because the second baseman may be getting more publicity than the short-stop, because it may be that he has a chance to be up at better times, and so be it."

But what I am getting at is that there is going to continue to be some friction, competition, and I think it is not unhealthy, between departments and major White House advisers. Kissinger on the one hand in the foreign field, Ehrlichman in the domestic field. But that is the way it is going to have to be with them or their successors.

THE PRESS

Even though you didn't ask the question, let me say with regard to this whole business of press relations and so forth, you may want to carry something in this respect.

We want to have good relations with the press. We expect to. When people talk about numbers of press conferences, though, I respectfully suggest that you go back and look over this year. It was my view that it would not have been in the best interest of the country to have held press conferences during periods of delicate negotiations.

On the other hand as we go into the next year, we are going to have an open Administration, contact with the press, and so forth, but only when it serves the public interest. Whenever I find that we are engaged in very sensitive negotiations where it wouldn't be useful to have a press conference, I won't have one. Where we are not, I will. That is the way it is going to be.

The other point I should make is this: I thrive on the idea that I always gain from criticism, and was never

short of it, but there should not be a double standard for the press. On both sides, give us hell.

A SUMMING UP

The President has often indicated he would like to be remembered on the world scene as a President who brought in a new era of peace, and he was asked how he would like to be remembered on domestic affairs as well.

Let me say on the world scene I would change it just a little. Whether the United States, as the only nation powerful enough in the free world to play this role, steps up to its responsibility and leads the way to this new period of peace, this is the real issue: Whether we step up to it or turn isolationist.

That is why I thought that was one of the great issues of this campaign. A weaker America, turned inward, in my view wouldn't have been good for the people in this country at home. But that is debatable. It would have been a disaster for the world, because without the United States on the world scene, smaller nations would be living in terror, because where there is a power vacuum, that vacuum is filled.

The United States now has a relationship with the Soviet Union and the Chinese, one of whom is a super-power, the other who has the potential in the future, which is a healthy relationship, but it is one in which our strength must always be maintained until we have mutual agreement to reduce.

Now, on the domestic scene: I think that the tragedy of the 60's is that so many Americans, and particularly so many young Americans, lost faith in their country, in the American system, in their country's foreign policy. Many were influenced to believe that they should be ashamed of our country's record in foreign policy and what we were doing in the world; that we should be ashamed of what America did, and all.

Many Americans got the impression that this was an ugly country, racist, not compassionate, and part of the reason for this was the tendency of some to take every mole that we had and to make it look like a cancer.

Now, let us understand: This is not a perfect country. There is much that needs to be corrected. But I don't say this in any jingoistic sense—I have seen the world, and I don't know any young person abroad, if he had the chance, who wouldn't rather be here than someplace else.

RESTORE PRIDE

What I think we have to do is not simply to rein-still in Americans a pride in country, a majority of the Americans do have a pride in country. You see how they respond.

But they must not do it on blind faith, "My country, right or wrong but my country." We want them to know why this country is right. Now, taking the foreign field, we want to make the American people feel proud of their country's role in the foreign field. I think the trips to Peking and Moscow helped in that respect. I think the people saw that the United States was leading the world in peace and that we were the only ones who could do it. They were proud of our country.

We are going to continue to exert that kind of leadership.

At home, as we move toward equality of opportunity and it will not come overnight, but as we move toward equality of opportunity, as we move toward dealing with the problems of the environment, whether it is clean, air, or a better health system, or improvement in education, as we make progress in all of these fields, I think that we will reinstill some of the faith that has been lost in the 60's.

I think we have somewhat digressed from your question, but I think what we are talking about here is that we have passed through a very great spiritual crisis in this country—during the late 60's, the war in Vietnam by many was blamed for it totally. It was only part of the problem and in many cases it was only an excuse rather than a reason. But we saw a breakdown in frankly what I could call the leadership class of this country.

I am not saying that critically because many lost faith in many of our institutions. For example, the enormous movement toward permissiveness which led to the escalation in crime, the escalation in drugs in this country, all of this came as a result of those of us who basically have a responsibility of leadership not recognizing that above everything else you must not weaken a people's character.

CONSERVATIVE JUDGES

Now, let's try to get at it another way. One issue you haven't touched on is the whole area of the courts. I said several times that I intend to continue to appoint conservative judges to the court. I do. The courts need them and they need men like Rehnquist and Burger and Blackman and Powell on their court, not reactionary judges but men who are constitutional conservatives because the trend had gone too far in the other direction. I don't mean that there weren't well-intentioned judges calling them as they see them. But I don't believe that that was the right trend for this country and I think we have got to continue to reverse that trend in the whole field of law enforcement.

Drugs, etc. We are going to continue a very strong program here because the whole era of permissiveness has left its mark.

Now, having said that, I do not mean that we turn to reaction. I do not mean that we turn to an attitude which does not have compassion for those who cannot be blamed for some of the problems that they have. But I feel very strongly that this country wants and this election will demonstrate that the American people want and the American people will thrive upon a new feeling of responsibility, a new feeling of self-discipline, rather than go back to the thoughts of the sixties that it was government's job every time there was a problem, to make people more and more dependent upon it to give way to their whims.

'WELFARE MESS'

The welfare mess is an example. This escalation of the numbers on welfare, much of it is a result simply of running down what I call the work ethnic. Now, I understand that is considered to be reactionary, to suggest people ought to work rather than go on welfare. And I do know there are some who can't work and must go on welfare. But on the other hand, another thing this election is about is whether we should move toward more massive handouts to people, making the people more and more dependent, looking to Government, or whether we say, no, it is up to you. The people are going to have to carry their share of the load.

The average American is just like the child in the family. You give him some responsibility and he is going to amount to something. He is going to do something. If, on the other hand, you make him completely dependent and pamper him and cater to him too much, you are going to make him soft, spoiled and eventually a very weak individual.

So, I would simply sum it up by saying that when you are looking in the next four years at the domestic front and the international front, it will be an exciting period. Internationally, because of instead of withdrawing from the world, as our opponents advocated in so many areas, we are going to continue to play a great role in the world because that is the only way you can have the peace we talk about.

On the domestic front, it will be exciting because it is going to be a different approach. The approach that has always been considered to be the most certain vote-getter in the past has been who is going to promise the most to get the votes. In others, it was a question of how much you were going to promise, how much money were you going to promise to pay out for this program or that program. This is the first campaign in history, I think you see probably the first campaign of a candidate who didn't go out with a whole bag full of goodies.

'STUCK BY THE PROGRAM'

I have stuck by the program I have and I haven't laid out a lot of new goodies. This is a case where the American people were confronted with a choice of one candidate who promised to spend billions more of their money, basically, as they put it, to help them, and the other candidate said, "No, we are not going to promise to do that; we are going to promise to give you the chance to help yourself."

The American people will speak on that issue. It is our responsibility to find a way to reform our government institutions so that this new spirit of independence, self-reliance, pride, that I sense in the American people can be nurtured. I think it is out there.

Now, I realize what I have just said in many quarters in Washington in which we live, and the Georgetown cocktail set that will be tuttutted by those who are living in another era. They honestly believe that the answer to the problem is always some new massive government program. I totally disagree with that. Sometimes a new program is needed. But what we need now, rather than more Government, is better Government. I realize that is a cliché, but rather than more it is better and many times the better is not the fatter, but the leaner.

We are going to change the way we are going to do this and rather than Government doing more for people and making people more dependent upon it, what I am standing for is Government finding ways through the Government programs to allow people to do more for themselves, to encourage them to do more for themselves; not only to encourage them, but to give them incentive to do more for themselves on their own without Government assistance.

PRESIDENT NIXON MADE THREE CABINET CHANGES IN 1972

President Nixon made three Cabinet changes in 1972. George P. Shultz was named Secretary of the Treasury, Peter G. Peterson was appointed Secretary of Commerce and Richard G. Kleindienst was confirmed as Attorney General.

In addition, Nixon filled the posts of Chairman of the Joint Chiefs of Staff and Army Chief of Staff.

One former representative was confirmed as an ambassador. Rep. Frank T. Bow (R Ohio 1951-73) announced he would retire from the House at the end of the 92nd Congress. He was confirmed by the Senate Sept. 8 to be ambassador to Panama. But he died Nov. 14.

Kleindienst. On June 8, the Senate by a 64-19 roll-call vote, confirmed the nomination of Richard G. Kleindienst, 49, as Attorney General of the United States. Kleindienst, who was Deputy Attorney General for the first three years of the Nixon administration, was the subject of seven days of Senate debate. A motion to recommit the nomination to the Judiciary Committee failed by a vote of 20-63.

The Kleindienst confirmation came almost four months after Nixon nominated him to the post. Hearings on his nomination lasted 24 days—what one senator called "the longest confirmation hearings" in the history of the Senate. Kleindienst was nominated on Feb. 15 and had been acting attorney general since the resignation of John N. Mitchell on March 1.

Shultz. President Nixon nominated George P. Shultz May 17 to replace John B. Connally as Secretary of the Treasury. Shultz, 52, President Nixon's third treasury secretary, was confirmed by the Senate June 8 by a unanimous vote of 83-0. Shultz had been director of the Office of Management and Budget and Secretary of Labor under Nixon.

Peterson. Peter G. Peterson, 46, was nominated by President Nixon Jan. 27 as Secretary of Commerce. Peterson succeeded Maurice H. Stans, who resigned Jan. 27 to head the Republican finance committee.

Peterson was confirmed Feb. 21 by voice vote. He had been the first Assistant to the President for International Economic Affairs, as well as Executive Director of the new Council on International Economic Policy.

President Nixon reappointed Admiral Thomas Hinman Moorer as chairman of the Joint Chiefs of Staff. Moorer was confirmed June 30 by voice vote. Gen. Creighton W. Abrams was confirmed as Army Chief of Staff on Oct. 12. Abrams had served as commanding general for the U.S. Army in Vietnam.

Judicial Nominations

The Senate in 1972 confirmed President Nixon's nomination to 25 federal circuit and district judgeships. At the end of October, 1972, there were 10 vacancies in federal courts. There were three in the circuit courts and seven in the district courts.

Total Nominations

In the second session of the 92nd Congress, the Senate received 66,536 nominations and confirmed 66,054. President Nixon withdrew five nominations which had been submitted to the Senate and 477 nominations remained unconfirmed at the end of the 92nd Congress.

Regulatory Agencies

President Nixon made 14 appointments in 1972 to the federal regulatory agencies. He had made 16 appointments to the agencies in 1971.

By the end of his first term in early 1973, President Nixon would have, through his appointment, nominal control over 9 of 11 independent agencies and commissions that exercise regulatory powers over a broad range of public interests.

Only the Federal Reserve System Board of Governors and the Federal Trade Commission would retain through 1972 a majority membership, appointed by previous Presidents.

Confirmations of 1972 Nominations

Listed below are the names of 98 persons named to major federal posts by President Nixon and confirmed by the Senate in 1972. Information is given in the following order: name of office, salary, appointee, voting residence, occupation before appointment, date and place of birth, party affiliation (if known) and date of Senate confirmation. Ambassadorial confirmations are listed only if the appointment was of more than routine interest.

Executive Office of the President

Office of Economic Opportunity

Assistant Director and General Counsel, $38,000—**Bert A. Gallegos;** Denver, Colo.; attorney; Sept. 19, 1922, in Santa Fe, N.M.; Rep.; March 8.

Council of Economic Advisors

Member, $38,000—**Marina von Neumann Whitman;** Pittsburgh, Pa.; member of the Price Commission, on leave from the University of Pittsburgh; March 6, 1935, in New York City; Rep.; Feb. 18.

Departments

State Department

Under Secretary (Coordinating Security Assistance Programs), $40,000—**Curtis W. Tarr;** Appleton, Wis.; director, U.S. Selective Service System; Sept. 18, 1924, in Stockton, Calif.; Rep.; April 27.

Assistant Secretary (Economic Affairs), $38,000—**Willis C. Armstrong;** Princeton, N.J.; president, U.S. Council of the

U.S. Chamber of Commerce; April 2, 1972, in New York City; Rep.; Feb. 14.

Assistant Secretary (European Affairs), $38,000—**Walter J. Stoessel Jr.;** Santa Monica, Calif.; U.S. Ambassador to Poland; Jan. 24, 1920, in Manhattan, Kan.; July 21.

Agency for International Development

Assistant Administrator (Program and Policy), $38,000—**Philip Birnbaum;** Teaneck, N.J.; Deputy Assistant Administrator (African Bureau), AID; Oct. 3, 1928, in Union City, N.J.; March 14.

Assistant Administrator (Population and Humanitarian Assistance), $38,000—**Jarold A. Kieffer;** Fairfax, Va.; director, Office of International Training, AID; May 5, 1923, in Minneapolis, Minn.; Rep.; April 27.

Ambassadors

Salaries for Ambassadors depend upon seniority and station, and range between $36,000 and $42,500 per year. Only those appointments which are of more than routine interest are listed.

Belgium, **Robert Strausz-Hupe;** Newton Square, Pa.; U.S. Ambassador to Ceylon; March 25, 1903, in Vienna, Austria; Rep.; Feb. 14.

Fiji, **Kenneth Franzheim II;** Houston, Texas; to serve concurrently with present post of ambassador to New Zealand, and Western Samoa; Sept. 12, 1925, in New York City; Rep.; Feb. 14.

Iran, **Joseph S. Farland;** Morgantown, W. Va.; U.S. Ambassador to Pakistan; Aug. 11, 1914, in Clarksburg, W. Va.; April 27.

Japan, **Robert Stephen Ingersoll;** Winnetka, Ill.; chief executive officer, Borg-Warner Corp.; Jan. 28, 1914, in Galesburg, Ill.; Feb. 25.

NATO, **David M. Kennedy;** Northfield, Ill.; to serve concurrently with present post of ambassador at-large; July 21, 1905, in Randolph, Utah; Rep.; March 14.

Panama, **Frank T. Bow;** Canton, Ohio; U.S. representative; Feb. 20, 1901, in Canton, Ohio; Rep.; Sept. 8.

Tonga, **Kenneth Franzheim II,** Houston, Texas; to serve concurrently with present post of ambassador to New Zealand, Western Samoa and Fiji; Sept. 12, 1925, in New York City; Rep.; Oct. 3.

Trinidad and Tobago, **Anthony D. Marshall;** New York City; U.S. ambassador to Malagasy Republic; May 30, 1924, in New York City; Feb. 14.

Treasury Department

Secretary, $60,000—**George P. Shultz;** Arlington, Va.; director, Office of Management and Budget; Dec. 13, 1920, in New York City; Rep.; June 8.

Deputy Secretary, $42,500—**Charls E. Walker;** Riverside, Conn.; Under Secretary of the Treasury; Dec. 24, 1923, in Graham, Texas; Rep.; June 8.

Under Secretary, $40,000—**Edwin S. Cohen;** Charlottesville, Va.; Assistant Secretary of the Treasury (Tax Policy); Sept. 27, 1914, in Richmond, Va.; Rep.; June 8.

Comptroller of the Currency, $40,000—**William B. Camp;** Rockville, Md.; First Deputy Comptroller of the Currency; Nov. 25, 1913, in Greenville, Texas; Dem.; Feb. 18.

Assistant Secretary (International Affairs), $38,000—**John Michael Hennessy;** Boston, Mass.; Deputy Assistant Secretary of the Treasury (Development Finance); May 5, 1936, in Massachusetts; Rep.; June 8.

Assistant Secretary (Administration), $38,000—**Warren F. Brecht;** Darien, Conn.; Deputy Assistant Secretary (Management and Budget) for the Interior Department; May 21, 1932, in Detroit, Mich.; Rep.; Aug. 17.

Assistant Secretary (Tax Policy), $38,000—**Frederic W. Hickman;** Chicago, Ill.; partner in the law firm of Hopkins, Sutter, Owen, Mulroy & Davis; June 30, 1927, in Sioux City, Iowa; Aug. 17.

Internal Revenue Service

Chief Counsel, $36,000—**Lee H. Henkel Jr.;** Columbus, Ga.; partner in the law firm of Swift, Page, Henkel & Chapman; Sept. 16, 1928, in Charleston, W.Va.; Rep.; June 8.

Defense Department

Deputy Secretary, $42,500—**Kenneth Rush;** Rye, N.Y.; U.S. Ambassador to West Germany; Jan. 17, 1910, in Walla Walla, Wash.; Rep.; Feb. 3.

Assistant Secretary (Telecommunications), $38,000—**Eberhardt Rechtin;** Rockville, Md.; Principal Deputy Director of Defense (Research and Engineering); Jan. 16, 1926, in Orange, N.J.; Rep.; Feb. 3.

Navy

Secretary, $42,500—**John W. Warner;** White Post, Va.; Under Secretary of the Navy; Feb. 8, 1927, in Washington, D.C.; Rep.; April 25.

Under Secretary, $38,000—**Frank P. Sanders;** Bethesda, Md.; Assistant Secretary of the Navy (Installations and Logistics); July 30, 1919, in Tarboro, N.C.; Rep.; April 25.

Assistant Secretary (Financial Management), $38,000—**Robert D. Nesen;** Oxnard, Calif.; president, Nesen Oldsmobile; Jan. 22, 1918, in St. Louis, Mich.; Rep.; April 25.

Joint Chiefs of Staff

Chairman for an additional term of 2 years ending July, 1974, $38,844—**Admiral Thomas Hinman Moorer;** Eufala, Ala.; reappointment; Feb. 9, 1912, in Mt. Willing, Ala.; June 30.

Army Chief of Staff, $36,000—**Gen. Creighton W. Abrams;** Springfield, Mass.; commanding general, U.S. Army, Vietnam; Sept. 15, 1914, in Springfield, Mass.; Oct. 12.

Justice Department

Attorney General, $60,000—**Richard G. Kleindienst;** McLean, Va.; Deputy Attorney General; Aug. 5, 1923, in Winslow, Ariz.; Rep.; June 8.

Deputy Attorney General, $42,500—**Ralph E. Erickson;** Los Angeles, Calif.; Assistant Attorney General (Office of Legal Counsel); Oct. 3, 1928, in Jamestown, N.Y.; Rep.; June 28.

Assistant Attorney General (Land and Natural Resources), $38,000—**Dale Kent Frizzell;** Topeka, Kan.; partner in the law firm of Sabatini & Harrison; Feb. 11, 1929, in Wichita, Kan.; Rep.; Feb. 3.

Assistant Attorney General (Anti-trust), $38,000—**Thomas E. Kauper;** Ann Arbor, Mich.; executive director, National Institute for Consumer Justice; Sept. 25, 1935, in Brooklyn, N.Y.; June 28.

Assistant Attorney General (Internal Security), $38,000—**A. William Olson Jr.;** McLean, Va.; Deputy Assistant Attorney General (Internal Security); July 3, 1922, in Portland, Ore.; Rep.; June 28.

Assistant Attorney General (Criminal), $38,000—**Henry E. Petersen;** Silver Spring, Md.; Deputy Assistant Attorney General (Criminal); March 26, 1921, in Philadelphia, Pa.; Feb. 3.

Assistant Attorney General (Civil), $38,000—**Harlington Wood Jr.;** Springfield, Ill.; Associate Deputy Attorney General (Civil); April 17, 1920, in Springfield, Ill.; Rep.; June 28.

Assistant Attorney General (Office of Legal Counsel), $38,000—Roger C. Cramton; Ann Arbor, Mich.; chairman, Administrative Conference of the United States; May 18, 1929, in Pittsfield, Mass.; Aug. 8.

Agriculture Department

Assistant Secretary (International Affairs and Commodity Programs), $38,000—**Carroll G. Brunthaver;** Alexandria, Va.; Assoc. Administrator Agricultural Stabilization and Conservation Service; March 27, 1932, in Fremont, Ohio; Rep.; June 22.

Commerce Department

Secretary, $60,000—**Peter G. Peterson;** Washington, D.C.; Assistant to the President for International Economic Affairs; June 5, 1926, in Kearney, Neb.; Rep.; Feb. 21.

Assistant Secretary (Maritime Affairs), $38,000—**Robert J. Blackwell;** McLean, Va.; Deputy Assistant Secretary of

Commerce (Maritime Affairs); Feb. 26, 1925, in Brooklyn, N.Y.; June 30.

Assistant Secretary (Domestic and International Business), $38,000—**Andrew E. Gibson;** Rockville, Md.; Assistant Secretary of Commerce (Maritime Affairs); Feb. 19, 1922, in New York City; Rep.; June 30.

Labor Department

Assistant Secretary (Policy, Evaluation and Research), $38,000—**Michael H. Moskow;** Paterson, N.J.; Deputy Under Secretary of Labor; Jan. 7, 1938, in Paterson, N.J.; Rep.; March 20.

Transportation Department

Assistant Secretary (Policy and International Affairs), $38,000—**John L. Hazard;** E. Lansing, Mich.; Professor, Michigan State University; June 10, 1923 in Sioux City, Iowa; April 17.

Assistant Secretary (Environment and Urban Affairs), $38,000—**John E. Hirten;** San Diego, Calif.; Deputy Assistant Secretary of Transportation Environment and Urban Affairs); Nov. 2, 1925, in New York City; Rep.; Aug. 10.

Health, Education and Welfare Department

Assistant Secretary (Education), $38,000—**Sidney P. Marland Jr.;** Hampton, Conn.; Commissioner of Education at HEW; Aug. 19, 1914, in Danielson, Conn.; Ind.; Oct. 14.

Independent Agencies

ACTION

Deputy Director, $38,000—**Walter Charles Howe;** Olympia, Wash.; director, Office of Program Planning and Fiscal Management, state of Washington; March 2, 1934, in Portland, Ore.; Rep.; April 10.

Associate Director (Office of Policy and Program Development), $36,000—**Charles W. Ervin;** Los Angeles, Calif.; on leave of absence as vice president (investment division) of Security Pacific National Bank; Nov. 20, 1932, in Oxnard, Calif.; Rep.; Oct. 14.

Associate Director (International Operations), $36,000—**Donald Kready Hess;** Bethesda, Md.; Peace Corps director, Korea; Nov. 18, 1930, in Lancaster County, Pa.; Aug. 10.

Associate Director (Domestic and Anti-poverty Operations), $36,000—**Christopher M. Mould;** Washington, D.C.; Acting Associate Director (Domestic and Anti-poverty Operations); Dec. 12, 1936, in Erie, Pa.; Dem.; Sept. 26.

Associate Director (International Operations), $36,000—**Kevin O'Donnell;** Potomac, Md.; acting deputy director, Peace Corps; June 9, 1925, in Cleveland, Ohio; Feb. 25.

Atomic Energy Commission

Member for the term expiring June 30, 1977, $40,000—**Dixy Lee Ray;** Seattle, Wash.; director, Pacific Science Center; Sept. 3, 1914, in Tacoma, Wash.; Ind.; Aug. 2.

Civil Aeronautics Board

Member for the term expiring Dec. 31, 1977, $38,000—**Whitney Gillilland;** Glenwood, Iowa; reappointment; Jan. 13, 1904, in Glenwood, Iowa; Rep.; Feb. 29.

Environmental Protection Agency

Assistant Administrator (Air and Water Programs), $38,000—**Robert Lewis Sansom;** Arlington, Va.; Deputy Assistant Administrator (Planning and Evaluation); July 17, 1941, in Knoxville, Tenn.; June 14.

Equal Employment Opportunity Commission

Member for the term expiring July 1, 1977, $38,000—**Colston A. Lewis,** Richmond, Va.; attorney; Jan. 23, 1912, in Lynchburg, Va.; Rep.; Sept. 26.

General Counsel, $36,000—**William A. Carey;** Evanston, Ill.; attorney; May 16, 1932, in Chicago, Ill.; Rep.; June 8.

Federal Communications Commission

Member for the term expiring July 1, 1979, $38,000—**Benjamin L. Hooks;** Memphis, Tenn.; attorney; Jan. 31, 1925, in Memphis, Tenn.; Dem.; May 30.

Member for the remainder of the term expiring July 1, 1977, $38,000—**Richard E. Wiley;** Northbrook, Ill.; General Counsel, FCC; July 20, 1934, in Peoria, Ill.; Rep.; May 30.

Federal Maritime Commission

Commissioner for the term expiring June 30, 1977, $38,000—**Ashton C. Barrett;** Biloxi, Miss.; reappointment; March 4, 1901, in Hinds County, Miss.; Dem.; June 30.

Federal Reserve System

Member of Board of Governors for the term expiring Jan. 31, 1986, $40,000—**Jeffrey M. Bucher;** Los Angeles, Calif.; senior vice president, United California Bank (trust department); Feb. 9, 1933, in Los Angeles, Calif.; May 31.

Member of Board of Governors for the term expiring Jan. 31, 1982, $40,000—**John Eugene Sheehan;** Louisville, Ky.; president and chief executive officer, Corhart Refractories Co.; Dec. 11, 1929, in Johnstown, Pa.; Rep.; Feb. 7.

Interstate Commerce Commission

Commissioner for the term expiring Dec. 31, 1978, $38,000—**Rupert L. Murphy;** Atlanta, Ga.; reappointment, July 27, 1909, in Byronville, Ga.; Dem.; Oct. 5.

Commissioner for the remainder of the term expiring Dec. 31, 1973, $38,000—**Chester M. Wiggin Jr.;** Hopkinton, N.H.; federal cochairman, New England Regional Commission (Commerce Department); June 4, 1917, in Conway, N.H.; Rep.; Oct. 5.

National Labor Relations Board

Member for the term expiring Aug. 27, 1976, $38,000—**John A. Penello;** Linstead on the Severn, Md.; regional director Region 5, NLRB; Aug. 27, 1909, Norfolk, Va., Dem.; Feb. 9.

National Mediation Board

Member for the term expiring July 1, 1975, $38,000—**George S. Ives;** Bethesda, Md.; reappointment; Jan. 10, 1922, in Brooklyn, N.J.; Rep.; June 22.

Member for the remainder of the term expiring July 1, 1974—$38,000—**Kay McMurray;** Hinsdale, Ill.; consultant on government affairs, United Airlines; March 18, 1918, in Boise, Idaho; Rep.; Sept. 26.

U.S. Tariff Commission

Member for the term expiring June 16, 1978, $36,000—**Italo H. Ablondi;** New York City; lawyer with the firm of Milbank, Tweed, Hope, Hadley & McCloy; Aug. 25, 1929, in Parma, Italy; Dem.; June 29.

U.S. Tax Court

Judge for the term expiring Aug. 30, 1987, $40,000—**Cynthia Holcomb Hall;** Los Angeles, Calif.; member of Brawerman & Holcomb Professional Corporation; Feb. 19, 1929, in Los Angeles, Calif.; Aug. 18.

Judge for the term expiring June 30, 1987, $40,000—**William H. Quealy;** Arlington, Va.; reappointment; March 11, 1913, in New Orleans, La.; Rep.; May 30.

Judge for the term expiring June 30, 1987, $40,000—**Arnold Raum;** Swampscott, Mass.; reappointment; born in Swampscott, Mass.; May 30.

Judge for the term expiring June 30, 1987, $40,000—**Irene Feagin Scott;** Montgomery, Ala.; reappointment; Oct. 6, 1912, in Union Springs, Ala.; May 30.

Judge for the term expiring Oct. 24, 1987, $40,000—**Darrell D. Wiles;** St. Louis, Mo.; member of the law firm of Wiles & Giljum; Sept. 14, 1914, in Fraser, Iowa; Sept. 25.

Judiciary

Judges' party affiliations were compiled from entries in *Who's Who in American Politics* and from the senators of the states involved.

U.S. Circuit Courts of Appeal

Judge for the First Circuit, $42,500—**Levin H. Campbell;** Cambridge, Mass.; U.S. District Judge, District of Massachusetts; Jan. 2, 1927, in Summit, N.J.; Rep.; June 28.

Judge for the Fourth Circuit, $42,500—**H. Emory Widener Jr.;** Bristol, Va.; U.S. District Judge, Western District of Virginia; April 30, 1923, in Abingdon, Va.; Rep.; Oct. 12.

Judge for the Sixth Circuit, $42,500—**Frederick Pierce Lively;** Danville, Ky.; partner in the law firm of Lively & Rodes; Aug. 17, 1921, in Louisville, Ky.; Rep.; Oct. 3.

Judge for the Ninth Circuit, $42,500—**J. Clifford Wallace;** La Mesa, Calif.; U.S. District Judge, Southern District of California; Dec. 11, 1928, in San Diego, Calif.; Rep.; June 28.

U.S. Court of Customs and Patent Appeals

Chief Judge, $42,500—**Howard T. Markey;** Chicago, Ill.; attorney; Nov. 10, 1920, in Chicago, Ill.; June 21.

U.S. District Courts

Judge for the Southern District of California, $40,000—**William B. Enright;** La Mesa, Calif.; partner in the law firm of Enright, Knutson, Tobin & Meyer; July 12, 1925, in Long Island, N.Y.; Dem.; June 28.

Judge for the Southern District of Florida, $40,000—**Norman C. Roettger Jr.;** Ft. Lauderdale, Fla.; partner in the law firm of Fleming, O'Bryan & Fleming; Nov. 3, 1930, in Lucasville, Ohio; Rep.; May 31.

Judge for the Middle District of Georgia, $40,000—**Wilbur D. Owens Jr.;** Macon, Ga.; partner in the law firm of Block, Hall, Hawkins & Owens; Feb. 1, 1930, in Albany, Ga.; Rep.; Feb. 17.

Judge for the District of Hawaii, $40,000—**Samuel P. King;** Honolulu, Hawaii; attorney; April 13, 1916, in Hankow, China; Rep.; June 28.

Judge for the District of Massachusetts, $40,000—**Frank H. Freedman;** Springfield, Mass.; mayor of Springfield, Mass.; Dec. 15, 1924, in Springfield, Mass.; Rep.; Oct. 12.

Judge for the District of Massachusetts, $40,000—**Joseph L. Tauro;** Marblehead, Mass.; partner in the law firm of Jaffe & Tauro; Sept. 26, 1931, in Winchester, Mass.; Rep.; Oct. 12.

Judge for the Eastern District of Michigan, $40,000—**Charles W. Joiner;** Ann Arbor, Mich.; dean and professor of law, Wayne State University Law School; Jan. 14, 1916, in Maquoketa, Iowa; Rep.; June 8.

Judge for the Southern District of New York, $40,000—**Robert L. Carter;** New York City; partner in the law firm of Poletti, Freidin, Parshker, Feldman & Gartner; March 11, 1917, in Caryville, Fla.; Dem.; July 21.

Judge for the Southern District of New York, $40,000—**Kevin Thomas Duffy;** Bronxville, N.Y.; regional administrator, Securities and Exchange Commission; Jan. 10, 1933, in New York City; Rep.; Oct. 12.

Judge for the Southern District of New York, $40,000—**Thomas P. Griesa;** New York City; partner in the law firm of Davis, Polk & Wardwell; Oct. 11, 1930, in Kansas City, Mo.; Rep.; June 28.

Judge for the Southern District of New York, $40,000—**Whitman Knapp;** New York City; partner in the law firm of Barrett, Knapp, Smith, Schapiro & Simon; Feb. 24, 1909, in New York City; Rep.; June 28.

Judge for the Southern District of New York, $40,000—**Charles E. Stewart Jr.;** Ardsley-On-Hudson, N.Y.; member of the law firm of Dewey, Ballantine, Bushby, Palmer & Wood; Sept. 1, 1916, in Glen Ridge, N.J.; Rep.; June 28.

Judge for the Southern District of New York, $40,000—**Robert J. Ward;** New York City; partner in the law firm of Aranow, Brodsky, Bohlinger, Benetar, Einhorn & Dann; Jan. 31, 1926, in New York City; Rep.; Oct. 12.

Judge for the Middle District of North Carolina, $40,000—**Hiram H. Ward;** Denton, N.C.; partner in the law firm of DeLapp & Ward; April 29, 1923, in Thomasville, N.C.; Rep.; June 28.

Judgeships as Patronage

The prestige of a federal judgeship is high, and appointment to the judiciary is considered by most attorneys and politicians to be the apex of a legal and public career.

Federal judgeships are lifetime appointments and pay $42,500 in the circuit court and $40,000 in the district court annually. There is no mandatory retirement age, but judges may retire at full salary at age 65 after 15 years or at 70 after 10 years on the bench.

The following list gives the number of confirmed federal circuit and district court judges appointed by President Nixon during his first four years in office and by his five immediate predecessors.

	Democrats	Republicans
Roosevelt	188	6
Truman	116	9
Eisenhower	9	165
Kennedy	111†	11
Johnson	159	9
Nixon (1969)	2	24
Nixon (1970)	1	62*
Nixon (1971)	6	55
Nixon (1972)	3‡	21‡

†One New York Liberal also was appointed.
*One judge was appointed from the New Progressive Party of Puerto Rico.
‡Party affiliation was not available for a judge from Puerto Rico.

Judge for the District of Oregon, $40,000—**Otto R. Skopil Jr.;** Salem, Ore.; senior partner in the law firm of Williams & Skopil; June 3, 1919, in Portland, Ore.; Rep.; May 25.

Judge for the District of Oregon, $40,000—**James M. Burns;** Portland, Ore.; Judge, circuit court of Oregon; Nov. 24, 1924, in Portland, Ore.; Rep.; May 25.

Judge for the District of Puerto Rico, $40,000—**Hernan G. Pesquera;** Santurce, Puerto Rico; partner in the law firm of Geigel, Silva & Pesquera; May 25, 1924, in Santurce, Puerto Rico; Oct. 12.

Judge for the Northern District of Texas, $40,000—**Eldon B. Mahon;** Fort Worth, Texas; U.S. Attorney, northern district of Texas; April 9, 1918, in Loraine, Texas; Dem.; June 28.

Judge for the District of Vermont, $40,000—**Albert W. Coffrin;** Burlington, Vt.; partner in the law firm of Coffrin, Pierson & Affolter; Dec. 21, 1919, in Burlington, Vt.; Rep.; June 8.

Judge for the Western District of Virginia, $40,000—**James C. Turk;** Radford, Va.; senior partner in the law firm of Dalton, Turk & Stone; May 3, 1923, in Roanoke County, Va.; Rep.; Oct. 12.

Judge for the Eastern District of Washington, $40,000—**Marshall A. Neill;** Olympia, Wash.; associate justice, Washington Supreme Court; Aug. 23, 1914, in Pullman, Wash.; Rep.; Aug. 2.

Membership of Federal Regulatory Agencies 1972

Atomic Energy Commission

(Five members appointed for five-year terms; no statutory limitation on political party membership)

Member	Party	Term Expires	Nominated By Nixon	Confirmed By Senate
*James R. Schlesinger (C)	R	6/30/75	7/21/71	8/6/71
*William Offutt Doub	R	6/30/76	7/21/71	8/6/71
*Dixy Lee Ray	I	6/30/77	7/17/72	8/2/72
James T. Ramey	D	6/30/73		
*Clarence E. Larson	R	6/30/74	6/30/69	8/8/69

Civil Aeronautics Board

(Five members appointed for six-year terms; not more than three members from one political party)

Member	Party	Term Expires	Nominated By Nixon	Confirmed By Senate
*Robert D. Timm	R	12/31/76	12/14/70	12/16/70
**Whitney Gillilland	R	12/31/77	12/13/71	2/29/72
Robert T. Murphy	D	12/31/72		
Joseph G. Minetti	D	12/31/73		
*Secor D. Browne (C)	R	12/31/74	9/12/69	10/3/69

Federal Communications Commission

(Seven members appointed for seven-year terms; not more than four members from one political party)

Member	Party	Term Expires	Nominated By Nixon	Confirmed By Senate
*Charlotte T. Reid	R	6/30/78	7/6/71	7/29/71
*Richard E. Wiley	R	6/30/77	1/24/72	5/30/72
*Benjamin L. Hooks	D	6/30/79	4/12/72	8/2/72
Nicholas Johnson	D	6/30/73		
Robert E. Lee	R	6/30/74		
H. Rex Lee	D	6/30/75		
*Dean Burch (C)	R	6/30/76	9/17/69	10/30/69

Federal Maritime Commission

(Five members appointed for five-year term; not more than three members from one political party)

Member	Party	Term Expires	Nominated By Nixon	Confirmed By Senate
*Clarence Morse	R	6/30/76	8/7/71	10/7/71
Helen D. Bentley (C)	R	6/30/75	5/5/70	6/3/70
**Ashton C. Barrett	D	6/30/77	5/11/72	6/30/72
George H. Hearn	D	6/30/73		
**James V. Day	R	6/30/74	9/17/69	10/23/69

Federal Power Commission

(Five members appointed for five-year terms; not more than three members from one political party)

Member	Party	Term Expires	Nominated By Nixon	Confirmed By Senate
*Rush Moody Jr.	D	6/22/76	7/20/71	10/8/71
*John N. Nassikas (C)	R	6/22/75	3/23/70	4/30/70
*Pinkney Calvin Walker	R	6/22/72‡	4/25/72	
**Albert B. Brooke Jr.	R	6/22/74	6/23/69	10/23/69
Vacancy				

Federal Reserve System, Board of Governors

(Seven members appointed for fourteen-year terms; no statutory limitation on political party membership, but not more than one member may be appointed from each Federal Reserve District. No member may be appointed to serve more than one full term.)

Member	Party	Term Expires	Nominated By Nixon	Confirmed By Senate
*John E. Sheehan	R	1/31/82	1/24/72	2/7/72
*Arthur F. Burns (C)	R	1/31/84	10/22/69	12/18/69
*Jeffrey M. Bucher	NA	1/31/86	4/27/72	5/31/72
J. Dewey Daane	NA	1/31/74		
George W. Mitchell	D	1/31/76		
J. L. Robertson	NA	1/31/78		
Andrew F. Brimmer	D	1/31/80		

Federal Trade Commission

(Five members appointed for seven-year terms; not more than three members from one political party)

Member	Party	Term Expires	Nominated By Nixon	Confirmed By Senate
*David S. Dennison Jr.	R	9/25/77	9/22/70	10/13/70
Mary G. Jones	R	9/25/73		
Paul Rand Dixon	D	9/25/74		
A. Everette MacIntyre	D	9/25/75		
*Miles W. Kirkpatrick (C)	R	9/25/76	8/12/70	8/24/70

Interstate Commerce Commission

(Eleven members appointed for seven-year terms; not more than six members from one political party)

Member	Party	Term Expires	Nominated By Nixon	Confirmed By Senate
*Virginia Mae Brown	D	12/31/77	4/14/71	6/30/71
**Dale W. Hardin	R	12/31/77	4/14/71	6/30/71
*William Donald Brewer	R	12/31/76	5/18/70	7/14/70
**Rupert I. Murphy	D	12/31/78	3/23/72	10/5/72
Willard Deason	D	12/31/72		
*Chester M. Wiggin Jr.	R	12/31/73	6/19/72	10/5/72
George M. Stafford (C)	R	12/31/73		
*Robert C. Gresham	R	12/31/74	9/25/69	11/19/69
Kenneth H. Tuggle	R	12/31/75		
*Alfred Towson MacFarland	D		recess appointment	
*Rodolfo Montejano	D		recess appointment	

National Labor Relations Board

(Five members appointed for five-year terms; no statutory limitation on political party membership)

Member	Party	Term Expires	Nominated By Nixon	Confirmed By Senate
*Ralph E. Kennedy	R	8/27/75	9/21/70	12/2/70
John H. Fanning	D	12/16/72		
Howard Jenkins Jr.	R	8/27/73		
Edward B. Miller (C)	R	12/16/74	2/20/70	5/21/70
*John A. Penello	D	8/27/76	1/24/72	2/7/72

National Mediation Board

(Three members appointed for three-year terms; not more than two members from one political party)

Member	Party	Term Expires	Nominated By Nixon	Confirmed By Senate
*Kay McMurray	R	7/1/74	9/11/72	9/26/72
David H. Stowe (C)	D	7/1/73	9/22/70	12/2/70
*George S. Ives	R	7/1/75	6/22/72	6/22/72

Securities and Exchange Commission

(Five members appointed for five-year terms; not more than three members from one political party)

Member	Party	Term Expires	Nominated By Nixon	Confirmed By Senate
*William J. Casey (C)	R	6/5/74	2/4/71	3/25/71
**Hugh F. Owens	D	6/5/75	5/13/70	5/20/70
*A. Sydney Herlong Jr.	D	6/5/76	6/3/71	6/17/71
*Philip A. Loomis Jr.	R	6/5/72†	9/10/71	9/23/71
Vacancy				

(C) chairman.
* Nixon appointment.
**Reappointed by Nixon; first appointed in a previous Administration.
‡Renominated but not yet confirmed; still serving.
†Has not been renominated; can serve till successor is appointed.

PRESIDENTIAL SUPPORT: CONGRESS LOWERS NIXON'S SCORE

President Nixon in 1972 won 66 percent of the 83 congressional recorded votes that represented a clearcut test of support for his views. This was a four-year low for the President and the lowest score since 1960 when President Dwight D. Eisenhower won 65 percent of the congressional votes on which he took a position.

Nixon's 1972 percentage was nine points below his 1971 figure of 75 percent and 11 points under his best score—77 percent recorded in 1970. In 1969, the first year of his administration, the President won 74 percent of all congressional votes on which he took a position.

Compared with past years, the Nixon White House in 1972 was hard to pin down on many of the major pieces of legislation considered by Congress. Congressional Quarterly's tabulation showed that Nixon took a clear position on only 83 recorded votes in the House and Senate during 1972. In 1971, by comparison, Nixon took a position on 139 recorded congressional votes.

The 83 votes on which the President took a position in 1972 equals the lowest number since Congressional Quarterly began its study of presidential support in 1953. In that year President Eisenhower took positions on 83 votes (49 in the Senate and 34 in the House).

Nixon's 1972 drop in announced presidential positions came despite a record number of 861 recorded votes cast in both the House and Senate. (In comparison, Eisenhower's announced position on 83 recorded votes in 1953 accounted for more than half of the 160 House and Senate votes taken.)

Of the 81 votes on which he took a position in 1972, Nixon won 30 of 37 votes in the House (81 percent) and 25 of 46 votes in the Senate (54 percent).

Ground Rules. Congressional Quarterly's 1972 presidential support study was based on those votes on which there was a clear indication of the President's preference, revealed before each vote in his own messages and public statements. *(List p. 33; rules, p. 35)*

Support Breakdowns

Party Differences. In both the House and Senate, the average Republican backed the President on a majority of the test votes. Composite scores showed that Republicans in 1972 voted with the President 66 percent of the time in the Senate and 64 percent in the House.

The average Democrat, on the other hand, supported the President 44 percent of the time in the Senate and 47 percent of the time in the House.

Regional Averages. Consistent with previous years, southerners composed the regional bloc most likely to go along with the President's legislative wishes. Among Republicans, the average southerner supported the President 73 percent of the time in the Senate and 58 percent of the time in the House.

The average House Republican from other regions topped the southerners in 1972, however. The President won support among Republican House members from the East 70 percent of the time and from the West and Midwest 63 percent of the time.

Southern Democrats supported the President 60 percent of the time in the Senate and 48 percent of the time in the House.

Nixon got his lowest composite support scores from Senate Democrats representing the Midwest (29 percent) and the East (36 percent).

Individual Scores. The President's most consistent Senate supporters were seven Republicans led by Roman L. Hruska (Neb.) who backed Nixon 91 percent of the time. The next six senators in line were Republicans—Edward J. Gurney (Fla.) and Wallace F. Bennett (Utah), both 89 percent; Robert Dole (Kan.), 87 percent; Paul J. Fannin (Ariz.), Norris Cotton (N.H.) and Milton R. Young (N.D.), all with 85 percent.

Harry F. Byrd Jr., an independent from Virginia who caucuses with the Democrats, voted with Nixon 83 percent of the time. Leading Nixon supporters among the Senate Democrats were James B. Allen (Ala.) and John C. Stennis (Miss.), both with 78 percent.

Six southern Democrats who head important Senate committees rank high on the list of Democrats who sided with the President most of the time. They are Stennis (Miss.), chairman of the Armed Services Committee, 78 percent; John Sparkman (Ala.), chairman of the Banking, Housing and Urban Affairs Committee, 70 percent; James O. Eastland (Miss.), chairman of the Judiciary Committee, 70 percent; Sam J. Ervin Jr. (N.C.), chairman of the Government Operations Committee, 70 percent; Herman E. Talmadge (Ga.), chairman of the Agriculture and Forestry Committee, 67 percent; and Russell B. Long (La.), chairman of the Finance Committee, 67 percent.

At the top of the list of Senate Democrats who voted against Nixon most often were Gaylord Nelson (Wis.) who opposed the President 70 percent of the time, and Philip A. Hart (Mich.) and Quentin N. Burdick (N.D.) who both opposed him 65 percent of the time.

Chief Republican opponents of the President's position on Senate votes were Clifford P. Case (N.J.) and Jacob K. Javits (N.Y.), both with 54 percent opposition scores.

The two most loyal Nixon supporters in the House were Republicans Barber B. Conable Jr. (N.Y.) and Clifford D. Carlson (Ill.) who backed the President 89 percent of the time. Among House Democrats, Samuel S. Stratton (N.Y.) supported the President's position 78 percent of the time, followed by Clement J. Zablocki (Wis.) at 73 percent.

Most consistent opponents of the President's position in the House were Andrew Jacobs Jr. (D Ind.) and Ken Hechler (D W.Va.), each with 62 percent opposition scores. Among Republicans, conservative representatives scored highest on the opposition tally. John M. Ashbrook (Ohio), who opposed Nixon for the party's presidential nomination in 1972, opposed the President's position 51 percent of the time. Ashbrook was followed by Philip Crane (Ill.), M.G. (Gene) Snyder (Ky.) and Durward G. Hall (Mo.), who opposed the President 46 percent of the time.

Key Nixon Wins and Losses

Federal spending and the Vietnam war were central to both President Nixon's wins and losses in 1972. Congress passed the President's general revenue-sharing bill, one of the "six great goals" first proposed by the President in 1971, sharing $30,236,400,000 in federal revenues with states and local governments over five years. *(Votes and 1972 CQ Almanac page references, p. 33)*

At the same time, the Congress rejected Nixon's request late in the session for the power to cut federal department and agency budgets to hold total federal outlays to $250-billion. The debt-ceiling bill was passed by both houses but the conference report on the bill was killed by the Senate.

Two bills vetoed by the President with the claim he found them too costly were passed over the President's objections, while a third veto was sustained.

The House and Senate overrode a veto on a bill authorizing $24.7-billion for a program to fight water pollution. Both chambers also overrode a veto on a bill increasing pensions for retired railroad workers.

The House sustained the veto of the fiscal 1973 appropriations bill for the Health, Education and Welfare Department and the Labor Department.

Congressional opposition to the Vietnam war sparked six key votes in the Senate and three in the House on ending the war. The House backed the President's position on all three; the Senate rejected the President's position on five of the six votes. The Senate anti-war votes represented the strongest stand it has taken to date, but the House prevented any troop-withdrawal requirements from becoming law.

Domestic Issues. On domestic issues, the House supported the President's position on school busing while the Senate rejected three times the motion to cut off debate and vote on the equal educational opportunities bill which would have limited school busing.

In considering new powers for the Equal Employment Opportunities Commission, the Senate at first rejected and then accepted the President's position that the EEOC should seek action in federal courts for its complaints rather than have cease-and-desist enforcement powers.

Average Scores

Composites of Republican and Democratic scores for presidential support and opposition in 1972 and the 92nd Congress (1971-72):

	1972		92nd Congress	
	Dems.	Reps.	Dems.	Reps.
SUPPORT				
Senate	44%	66%	42%	65%
House	47	64	47	69
OPPOSITION				
Senate	41%	20%	43%	20%
House	37	22	40	20

Breakdown by Regions

Regional presidential support scores for 1972:

	East	West	South	Midwest
DEMOCRATS				
Senate	36%	40%	60%	29%
House	48	44	48	45
REPUBLICANS				
Senate	63%	66%	73%	64%
House	70	63	58	63

Regional presidential opposition scores for 1972:

	East	West	South	Midwest
DEMOCRATS				
Senate	45%	42%	25%	57%
House	39	39	33	40
REPUBLICANS				
Senate	30%	16%	11%	16%
House	19	17	28	23

High Scorers—Support

Highest individual scorers in Nixon support—those who voted with the President most often in 1972:

SENATE

Democrats		Republicans	
Byrd (Va.)	83%	Hruska (Neb.)	91%
Allen (Ala.)	78	Gurney (Fla.)	89
Stennis (Miss.)	78	Bennett (Utah)	89
Sparkman (Ala.)	70	Dole (Kan.)	87
Eastland (Miss.)	70	Fannin (Ariz.)	85
Ervin (N.C.)	70	Cotton (N.H.)	85
Talmadge (Ga.)	67	Young (N.D.)	85
Long (La.)	67	Roth (Del.)	83
Byrd (W.Va.)	67	Smith (Maine)	83
		Griffin (Mich.)	83
		Thurmond (S.C.)	83

HOUSE

Democrats		Republicans	
Stratton (N.Y.)	78%	Conable (N.Y.)	89%
Zablocki (Wis.)	73	Carlson (Ill.)	89*
Price (Ill.)	70	Quie (Minn.)	86
Hanley (N.Y.)	70	Cleveland (N.H.)	86
Taylor (N.C.)	70	Ware (Pa.)	86
Wilson (Calif.)	68	Conover (Pa.)	85*
Stephens (Ga.)	68	Hogan (Md.)	84
Johnson (Calif.)	68	Brown (Mich.)	84
Hamilton (Ind.)	68	Keating (Ohio)	84
Colmer (Miss.)	68	Mallary (Vt.)	84
Fountain (N.C.)	68	Poff (Va.)	83*
Preyer (N.C.)	68	Teague (Calif.)	81
Jarman (Okla.)	68	Hosmer (Calif.)	81
Flood (Pa.)	68	Brotzman (Colo.)	81
Foley (Wash.)	68	Arends (Ill.)	81
		Cederberg (Mich.)	81
		Lent (N.Y.)	81
		Pirnie (N.Y.)	81
		Williams (Pa.)	81

*Not eligible for all recorded votes in 1972.

High Scorers—Opposition

Highest individual scorers in Nixon opposition—those who voted against the President most often in 1972:

SENATE

Democrats		Republicans	
Nelson (Wis.)	70%	Case (N.J.)	54%
Hart (Mich.)	65	Javits (N.Y.)	54
Burdick (N.D.)	65	Brooke (Mass.)	52
Church (Idaho)	63	Mathias (Md.)	50
Mondale (Minn.)	63	Percy (Ill.)	48
Cranston (Calif.)	61	Schweiker (Pa.)	48
Symington (Mo.)	61	Stevens (Alaska)	43
Proxmire (Wis.)	61	Hatfield (Ore.)	41
		Stafford (Vt.)	41

HOUSE

Democrats		Republicans	
Jacobs (Ind.)	62%	Ashbrook (Ohio)	51%
Hechler (W.Va.)	62	Crane (Ill.)	46
Long (Md.)	59	Snyder (Ky.)	46
Roy (Kan.)	57	Hall (Mo.)	46
Hicks (Mass.)	57	Landgrebe (Ind.)	43
Slack (W.Va.)	57	Gude (Md.)	43
Burton (Calif.)	54	Whalen (Ohio)	43
Roybal (Calif.)	54	Myers (Ind.)	41
Brademas (Ind.)	54	Scherle (Iowa)	41
Dent (Pa.)	54	Camp (Okla.)	41
Denholm (S.D.)	54	Heinz (Pa.)	41
Reuss (Wis.)	54	Robinson (Va.)	41

House Presidential Votes

(Numbers refer to CQ House and Senate vote numbers. An "N" means a nay vote supported the President; a "Y" means a yea vote supported him. An asterisk (*) preceding a vote number indicates a vote on which the President was defeated. All page references are to the vote charts in the 1972 CQ *Almanac*.)

2. Federal Election Campaign Act. Adoption of the conference report. Nixon—Y. Adopted 334-20. (*p. 2-H*)

9. Inter-American Development Bank Authorization. Nixon—Y. Passed 285-102. (*p. 4-H*)

10. Asian Development Bank Authorization. Nixon—Y. Passed 257-132. (*p. 4-H*)

12. International Development Association Authorization. Nixon—Y. Passed 208-165. (*p. 4-H*)

25. West Coast Dock Strike Settlement. Adoption of the rule for consideration of the bill. Nixon—Y. Adopted 203-170. (*p. 8-H*)

26. West Coast Dock Strike Settlement. Nixon—Y. Passed 214-139. (*p. 8-H*)

*27. Office of Economic Opportunity Extension. Amendment providing a straight two-year extension of existing OEO programs. Nixon—Y. Rejected 159-206. (*p. 10-H*)

40. Equal Employment Opportunities Enforcement Act. Adoption of the conference report. Nixon—Y. Adopted 303-110. (*p. 14-H*)

52. Dollar Devaluation. Nixon—Y. Passed 343-43. (*p. 16-H*)

*105. State, Justice, Commerce Appropriations, Fiscal 1973. Amendment restoring funds for the United Nations and deleting a provision limiting U.S. contributions to the UN. Nixon—Y. Rejected 156-202. (*p. 32-H*)

146. Revenue Sharing. Motion to recommit the bill with instructions to delete retroactive payment provision. Nixon—N. Rejected 157-241. (*p. 46-H*)

147. Revenue Sharing. Nixon—Y. Passed 275-122. (*p. 46-H*)

153. Washington, D.C., Area Subway System Bond Guarantees. Nixon—Y. Passed 282-75. (*p. 48-H*)

155. Defense Procurement Authorization. Amendment reducing the authorization for Safeguard antiballistic missile (ABM) system. Nixon—N. Rejected 116-258. (*p. 48-H*)

156. Defense Procurement Authorization. Amendment deleting authorization for research and development of the B-1 bomber. Nixon—N. Rejected 94-279. (*p. 48-H*)

157. Defense Procurement Authorization. Amendment continuing the prohibition against building a Safeguard ABM site around Washington, D.C. Nixon—N. Rejected 128-261. (*p. 48-H*)

158. Defense Procurement Authorization. Amendment to cut off all funds in the bill as of Sept. 1, 1972, for U.S. military activity in Southeast Asia, subject only to the release of U.S. prisoners of war, and an accounting of those persons missing in action. Nixon—N. Rejected 152-244. (*p. 48-H*)

181. Control of Predator Animals. Nixon—Y. Passed 279-73. (*p. 56-H*)

206. Canal Zone Management Policy and Program. Nixon—Y. Passed 376-6. (*p. 62-H*)

223. Foreign Military Aid Authorizations. Amendment deleting provision terminating U.S. involvement in the Indochina war by Oct. 1, 1972. Nixon—Y. Adopted 229-177. (*p. 68-H*)

236. Labor-HEW Appropriations, Fiscal 1973. Reconsideration and passage of the bill over the President's veto. Nixon—N. Rejected 203-171. A two-thirds majority (250 in this case) of members present and voting is necessary to override a veto. (*p. 72-H*)

241. School Busing. Amendment permitting the reopening of cases involving court desegregation orders to bring them into conformity with the provisions of the bill. Nixon—Y. Adopted 245-141. (*p. 72-H*)

246. SALT Agreement. Resolution authorizing the President to approve the interim agreement between the U.S. and the USSR. Nixon—Y. Adopted 330-7. (*p. 74-H*)

262. Defense Department Appropriations, Fiscal 1973. Amendment calling for a cutoff of all funds appropriated in the bill to support U.S. involvement in Indochina. Nixon—N. Rejected 160-208. (*p. 80-H*)

*265. Labor-HEW Appropriations, Fiscal 1973. Amendment prohibiting funds in the bill from being used to inspect firms employing 15 persons or fewer for compliance with the Occupational Safety and Health Act. Nixon—N. Adopted 191-182. (*p. 80-H*)

*268. Consumer Product Safety Commission. Nixon—N. Passed 319-50. (*p. 82-H*)

274. SALT Agreement. Adoption of the resolution concurring in Senate amendments, including the Jackson reservation. Nixon—Y. Adopted 308-4. *(p. 82-H)*

*289. Railroad Retirement Act Amendments. Reconsideration and passage of the bill over the President's veto. Nixon—N. Passed 353-29. *(p. 88-H)*

*294. Federal Highway Authorization. Motion to move the previous question (end debate and preclude amendments) on the rule for consideration of the bill. Nixon—N. Agreed to 200-168. *(p. 88-H)*

298. Debt Ceiling. Amendment requiring the President to inform Congress by Jan. 2, 1973, what spending cuts he would make to reduce budget expenditures to $250-billion. Nixon—N. Rejected 167-216. *(p. 90-H)*

299. Debt Ceiling. Nixon—Y. Passed 221-163. *(p. 90-H)*

303. Military Incentive Pay and Bonuses. Nixon—Y. Passed 337-35. *(p. 92-H)*

307. Maritime Authorization. Nixon—Y. Passed 353-3. *(p. 72-H)*

308. Revenue Sharing. Adoption of the conference report. Nixon—Y. Adopted 265-110. *(p. 92-H)*

320. Longshoremen-Harbor Workers Disability and Survivors Benefits. Nixon—Y. Passed 198-71. *(p. 96-H)*

326. Debt Ceiling. Adoption of the conference report. Nixon—Y. Adopted 166-137. *(p. 98-H)*

*328. Water Pollution Control. Reconsideration and passage of the bill over the President's veto. Nixon—N. Passed 247-23. *(p. 98-H)*

Senate Presidential Votes

*3. Equal Employment Opportunities Enforcement Act. Amendment substituting for the cease-and-desist powers in the bill an alternative procedure permitting employment discrimination cases to be taken into federal court. Nixon—Y. Rejected 41-43. *(p. 2-S)*

*8. Equal Employment Opportunities Enforcement Act. Amendment allowing the EEOC to take recalcitrant discriminatory employers to federal district courts for enforcement of equal job opportunity. Nixon—Y. Rejected 46-48. *(p. 3-S)*

*13. Equal Employment Opportunities Enforcement Act. Motion to table an amendment substituting the provisions of the House-passed bill for the Senate committee version. Nixon—N. Agreed to 45-32. *(p. 3-S)*

16. Equal Employment Opportunities Enforcement Act. Amendment deleting language extending EEOC jurisdiction to employees of state and local governments. Nixon—N. Rejected 16-59. *(p. 4-S)*

*31. West Coast Dock Strike Settlement. Motion to table an amendment providing a permanent procedure for settling labor-management disputes in transportation industries. Nixon—N. Agreed to 42-39. *(p. 6-S)*

32. West Coast Dock Strike Settlement. Nixon—Y. Passed 79-3. *(p. 6-S)*

37. Seabed Weapons Treaty. Nixon—Y. Ratified 83-0. *(p. 7-S)*

39. Equal Employment Opportunities Enforcement Act. Amendment providing that the EEOC general counsel would seek enforcement of equal job opportunities against recalcitrant employers by bringing suit in federal district court; cases against state or local governments would be handled by the U.S. attorney general. Nixon—Y. Adopted 45-39. *(p. 7-S)*

40. Equal Employment Opportunities Enforcement Act. (Same as vote 39, above). Nixon—Y. Adopted 82-3. *(p. 7-S)*

49. Equal Employment Opportunities Enforcement Act. Nixon—Y. Passed 73-16. *(p. 9-S)*

74. Increase in the Price of Gold. Nixon—Y. Passed 86-1. *(p. 12-S)*

110. Equal Rights Constitutional Amendment. Nixon—Y. Passed 84-8. *(p. 18-S)*

*135. Definition of War Powers. Nixon—N. Passed 68-16. *(p. 22-S)*

150. State Department-USIA Authorization. Amendment increasing the authorization for USIA salaries and expenses to the amount of the budget request. Nixon—Y. Adopted 57-15. *(p. 24-S)*

161. NASA Authorization. Amendment deleting the authorizations for the space shuttle program. Nixon—N. Rejected 21-61. *(p. 26-S)*

162. State-Department-USIA Authorizations. Amendment making an internationally supervised cease-fire a condition for withdrawal of U.S. forces from Indochina. Nixon—Y. Adopted 47-43. *(p. 26-S)*

*174. State Department-USIA Authorizations. Amendment deleting a provision repealing a 1971 law forbidding the President to prohibit the importation of strategic goods from a non-communist nation if such goods were imported from a communist country. Nixon—N. Adopted 40-36. *(p. 29-S)*

180. Kleindienst Nomination. Nixon—Y. Confirmed 64-19. *(p. 30-S)*

181. Shultz Nomination. Nixon—Y. Confirmed 83-0. *(p. 30-S)*

190. Foreign Military Aid Authorizations. Amendment extending to 20 years the period for repayment for U.S. military equipment sold to other nations on credit under the Foreign Military Sales Act of 1962. Nixon—Y. Adopted 41-36. *(p. 32-S)*

*206. Foreign Military Aid Authorizations. Amendment increasing the authorization for foreign military credit sales and increasing the annual ceiling on all types of military credit sales. Nixon—Y. Rejected 32-47. *(p. 34-S)*

*219. Corporation for Public Broadcasting. Amendment providing a one-year, rather than a two-year authorization. Nixon—Y. Rejected 26-58. *(p. 36-S)*

*277. Foreign Military Aid Authorizations. Amendment stating it to be the sense of Congress that all U.S. forces be withdrawn from Vietnam four months after an internationally supervised cease-fire throughout Indochina went into effect. Nixon—Y. Rejected 45-50. *(p. 37-S)*

*279. Foreign Military Aid Authorizations. Amendment deleting an amendment forbidding use of funds for U.S. participation in the Indochina war except for withdrawal of troops. Nixon—Y. Rejected 46-49. *(p. 44-S)*

295. Defense Procurement Authorization. Amendment reducing authorization for accelerated development and procurement of the Navy's Trident submarine-missile system. Nixon—N. Rejected 39-47. *(p. 47-S)*

299. Defense Procurement Authorization. Amendment reducing to the amount of fiscal 1972 requests, the fiscal 1973 funds for new obligational authority for the Defense Department. Nixon—N. Rejected 33-59. *(p. 47-S)*

Ground Rules for CQ Presidential Support-Opposition

● **Presidential Issues**—CQ analyzes all messages, press conference remarks and other public statements of the President to determine what he personally, as distinct from other administration spokesmen, does or does not want in the way of legislative action.

● **Borderline Cases**—By the time an issue reaches a vote, it may differ from the original form on which the President expressed himself. In such cases, CQ analyzes the measure to determine whether, on balance, the features favored by the President outweigh those he opposed or vice versa. Only then is the vote classified.

● **Some Votes Excluded**—Occasionally, important measures are so extensively amended on the floor that it is impossible to characterize final passage as a victory or defeat for the President.

● **Motions**—Roll calls on motions to recommit, to reconsider or to table often are key tests that govern the legislative outcome. Such votes are necessarily included in the Nixon support tabulations.

● **Rules**—In the House, debate on most significant bills is governed by rules that restrict time and may bar floor amendments. These rules must be adopted by the House before the bills in question may be considered. Members may vote for the rule, in order to permit debate, although they intend to vote against the bill. Generally, however, a vote against a rule is a vote against the bill, and vice versa, since rejection of the rule prevents consideration of the bill. CQ assumes that if the President favored a bill, he favored the rule unless it was a closed rule that would prevent amendments he wanted.

● **Appropriations**—Generally, roll calls on passage of appropriation bills are not included in this tabulation, since it is rarely possible to determine the President's position on the over-all revisions Congress almost invariably makes in the sums allowed. Votes to cut or increase specific funds requested in the President's budget, however, are included.

● **Failures to Vote**—In tabulating the Support or Opposition scores of members on the selected Nixon-issue votes, CQ counts only "yea" and "nay" votes on the ground that only these affect the outcome. Most failures to vote reflect absences because of illness or official business.

● **Weighting**—All Nixon-issue roll calls have equal statistical weight in the analysis.

● **Changed Position**—Presidential Support is determined by the position of the President at the time of a vote even though that position may be different from an earlier position, or may have been reversed after the vote was taken.

---

300. Defense Procurement Authorization. Amendment terminating the draft on Dec. 31, 1972, instead of July 1, 1973. Nixon—N. Rejected 25-64. *(p. 47-S)*

*307. Defense Procurement Authorization. Motion to table an amendment requiring a cutoff of funds for support of U.S. troops in Indochina. Nixon—Y. Rejected 46-51. *(p. 48-S)*

*308. Defense Procurement Authorization. Amendment requiring a cutoff of funds for support of U.S. troops in Indochina. Nixon—N. Adopted 49-47. *(p. 48-S)*

*310. Defense Procurement Authorization. Motion to table amendment requiring a cutoff of funds for support of U.S. troops in Indochina. Nixon—Y. Rejected 46-50. *(p. 49-S)*

*312. Defense Procurement Authorization. Amendment requiring a cutoff of funds for support of U.S. troops in Indochina. Nixon—N. Adopted 50-47. *(p. 49-S)*

319. ABM Treaty. Nixon—Y. Ratified 88-2. *(p. 50-S)*

363. Narcotics Addicts Methadone Treatment. Nixon—Y. Passed 81-0. *(p. 57-S)*

373. SALT Agreement. Amendment endorsing the second agreement of the Declaration of Basic Principles of Mutual Relations, stating that neither the U.S. nor the USSR would try to achieve a unilateral advantage in nuclear arms at the expense of the other. Nixon—Y. Adopted 84-1. *(p. 58-S)*

401. SALT Agreement. Jackson reservation. Nixon—Y. Adopted 56-35. *(p. 62-S)*

402. SALT Agreement. Nixon—Y. Passed 88-2. *(p. 63-S)*

438. Foreign Military Aid Authorizations. Amendment deleting provision forbidding use of funds for U.S. forces in Indochina for any purpose except a troop withdrawal. Nixon—Y. Adopted 45-42. *(p. 68-S)*

*483. Railroad Retirement Act Amendments. Reconsideration and passage of the bill over the President's veto. Nixon—N. Passed 76-5. *(p. 74-S)*

*502. Equal Educational Opportunities. Motion to invoke cloture (end debate) on the bill. Nixon—Y. Rejected 45-37. A two-thirds majority of those senators present and voting is needed to invoke cloture. *(p. 77-S)*

*503. Equal Educational Opportunities. Motion to invoke cloture (end debate) on the bill. Nixon—Y. Rejected 49-37. A two-thirds majority (58 in this case) of those senators present and voting is needed to invoke cloture. *(p. 77-S)*

*504. Equal Educational Opportunities. Motion to invoke cloture (end debate) on the bill. Nixon—Y. Rejected 49-38. A two-thirds majority (58 in this case) of those senators present and voting is needed to invoke cloture. *(p. 77-S)*

505. Abrams Nomination. Nixon—Y. Confirmed 84-2. *(p. 77-S)*

516. Revenue Sharing. Adoption of the conference report. Nixon—Y. Adopted 59-19. *(p. 79-S)*

*518. Debt Ceiling. Amendment providing a proportional reduction for all reducible items in the budget sufficient to bring spending within a $250-billion limitation. Nixon—N. Adopted 46-28. *(p. 79-S)*

*529. Debt Ceiling. Adoption of the conference report. Nixon—Y. Rejected 27-39. *(p. 81-S)*

*532. Water Pollution Control. Reconsideration and passage of the bill over the President's veto. Nixon—N. Passed 52-12. *(p. 81-S)*

- KEY -

†Not eligible for all recorded votes in 1972.

*Not eligible for all recorded votes in 92nd Congress.

•Speaker Albert votes only on recorded teller votes.

	1	2	3	4
ALABAMA				
1 Edwards	59	22	69	17
2 Dickinson	43	24	62	21
3 Andrews, E.[1]	57†	32†	57*	32*
4 Nichols	35	22	53	20
5 Flowers	59	24	69	19
6 Buchanan	76	19	82	14
7 Bevill	54	24	61	24
8 Jones	54	35	57	31
ALASKA				
AL Begich	43	46	34	62
ARIZONA				
1 Rhodes	73	11	81	9
2 Udall	43	41	31	54
3 Steiger	51	27	59	24
ARKANSAS				
1 Alexander	41	38	43	34
2 Mills	57	22	57	23
3 Hammerschmidt	68	30	73	23
4 Pryor	24	19	31	40
CALIFORNIA				
1 Clausen	76	22	80	16
2 Johnson	68	32	66	30
3 Moss	43	38	32	49
4 Leggett	43	38	41	45
5 Burton	43	54	30	66
6 Mailliard	73	11	83	9
7 Dellums	49	49	28	64
8 Miller	49	24	62	15
9 Edwards	49	49	35	63
10 Gubser	76	5	70	3
11 McCloskey	49	27	47	35
12 Talcott	65	11	73	14
13 Teague	81	14	87	9
14 Waldie	41	30	31	50
15 McFall	54	41	65	28
16 Sisk	54	35	55	34
17 Anderson	49	38	46	47
18 Mathias	76	11	70	11
19 Holifield	38	38	56	29
20 Smith	57	38	60	27
21 Hawkins	35	32	32	45
22 Corman	27	51	36	46
23 Clawson	54	24	60	18
24 Rousselot	35	38	46	32
25 Wiggins	73	14	76	9
26 Rees	41	51	34	54
27 Goldwater	59	22	63	17
28 Bell	35	5	62	10
29 Danielson	51	41	50	46
30 Roybal	41	54	32	60
31 Wilson	68	27	49	28
32 Hosmer	81	8	85	5
33 Pettis	65	16	79	13
34 Hanna	49	35	48	30
35 Schmitz	19	30	43	37
36 Wilson	70	11	74	9
37 Van Deerlin	41	46	43	44
38 Veysey	68	22	74	12
COLORADO				
1 McKevitt	76	16	76	15
2 Brotzman	81	8	82	14
3 Evans	30	35	35	46
4 Aspinall	46	41	61	29
CONNECTICUT				
1 Cotter	51	38	48	43
2 Steele	62	22	60	26
3 Giaimo	46	27	49	31

	1	2	3	4
4 McKinney	57	16	63	23
5 Monagan	51	27	54	36
6 Grasso	59	35	44	38
DELAWARE				
AL DuPont	76	16	78	19
FLORIDA				
1 Sikes	54	35	59	24
2 Fuqua	54	35	59	30
3 Bennett	57	43	54	46
4 Chappell	51	38	59	29
5 Frey	68	24	71	16
6 Gibbons	49	38	47	45
7 Haley	43	32	56	34
8 Young	65	32	74	22
9 Rogers	62	32	65	33
10 Burke	46	24	62	23
11 Pepper	65	27	63	30
12 Fascell	62	32	53	41
GEORGIA				
1 Hagan	24	24	52	21
2 Mathis	57	41	63	33
3 Brinkley	51	46	65	34
4 Blackburn	49	22	59	22
5 Thompson	49	27	69	20
6 Flynt	43	32	43	26
7 Davis	57	27	63	20
8 Stuckey	35	46	38	30
9 Landrum	65	24	51	24
10 Stephens	68	22	65	21
HAWAII				
1 Matsunaga	46	30	41	47
2 Mink	51	46	34	60
IDAHO				
1 McClure	38	16	47	10
2 Hansen	73	11	80	6
ILLINOIS				
1 Metcalfe	35	30	30	34
2 Mikva	38	35	29*	54*
3 Murphy, M.	49	38	45	40
4 Derwinski	54	19	51	15
5 Kluczynski	49	30	55	28
6 Collins	38	41	29	51
7 Annunzio	46	35	52	33
8 Rostenkowski	54	30	51	33
9 Yates	46	49	36	62
10 Collier	62	22	74	15
11 Pucinski	43	19	45	38
12 McClory	70	16	74	16
13 Crane	35	46	50	38
14 Erlenborn	68	5	79	6
15 Carlson[2]	89†	11†	89*	11*
16 Anderson	78	11	84	9
17 Arends	81	8	82	6
18 Michel	51	24	66	19
19 Railsback	76	8	65	18
20 Findley	65	11	67	16
21 Gray	51	32	54	33
22 Springer	73	5	79	9
23 Shipley	46	38	50	37
24 Price	70	30	71	24
INDIANA				
1 Madden	57	41	43	53
2 Landgrebe	49	43	62	33
3 Brademas	41	54	38	57
4 Roush	49	49	38	57
5 Hillis	65	14	81	9
6 Bray	59	35	74	18
7 Myers	54	41	71	26
8 Zion	70	27	77	17
9 Hamilton	68	30	52	45
10 Dennis	65	32	67	28
11 Jacobs	30	62	30	65
IOWA				
1 Schwengel	54	30	61	32
2 Culver	43	43	32	55
3 Gross	35	38	43	46
4 Kyl	62	24	73	18
5 Smith	41	43	43	48
6 Mayne	70	19	72	18
7 Scherle	49	41	56	33

	1	2	3	4
KANSAS				
1 Sebelius	68	30	73	19
2 Roy	38	57	36	60
3 Winn	76	16	78	13
4 Shriver	73	27	83	17
5 Skubitz	59	27	70	16
KENTUCKY				
1 Stubblefield	51	30	56	32
2 Natcher	54	46	60	40
3 Mazzoli	49	51	46	53
4 Snyder	43	46	50	44
5 Carter	62	19	74	15
6 Curlin	49	32	51*	31*
7 Perkins	51	43	54	44
LOUISIANA				
1 Hebert	32	5	47	7
2 Boggs	41	22	52	24
3 Caffery	22	22	51	23
4 Waggonner	54	32	66	23
5 Passman	41	32	54	24
6 Rarick	30	51	46	43
7 Breaux[3]	60†	20†	60*	20*
8 Long	30	30	18	14
MAINE				
1 Kyros	38	46	37	55
2 Hathaway	49	41	38	55
MARYLAND				
1 Mills	62	27	73*	21*
2 Long	38	59	32	65
3 Garmatz	59	27	59	28
4 Sarbanes	54	43	38	57
5 Hogan	84	16	80	17
6 Byron	65	27	77	20
7 Mitchell	41	46	30	62
8 Gude	46	43	47	48
MASSACHUSETTS				
1 Conte	54	32	51	41
2 Boland	54	41	52	45
3 Drinan	54	46	38	62
4 Donohue	46	43	29	44
5 Morse[4]	67†	33†	55*	42*
6 Harrington	57	41	43	56
7 Macdonald	41	41	37	48

	1	2	3	4
8 O'Neill	49	38	47	46
9 Hicks	65	35	59	37
10 Heckler	51	27	44	40
11 Burke	54	46	46	54
12 Keith	76	3	84	3
MICHIGAN				
1 Conyers	41	43	28	54
2 Esch	49	22	50	30
3 Brown	84	14	81	16
4 Hutchinson	59	35	65	33
5 Ford	70	8	82	7
6 Chamberlain	78	16	85	11
7 Riegle	38	35	34	47
8 Harvey	57	24	66	26
9 Vander Jagt	78	14	68	18
10 Cederberg	81	16	87	10
11 Ruppe	54	30	50	26
12 O'Hara	51	35	39	50
13 Diggs	38	35	22	33
14 Nedzi	51	46	41	55
15 Ford	46	35	33	51
16 Dingell	46	41	46	47
17 Griffiths	46	22	45	28
18 Broomfield	54	11	65	20
19 McDonald	49	5	50	29
MINNESOTA				
1 Quie	86	14	78	21
2 Nelsen	76	16	84	10
3 Frenzel	68	27	61	29
4 Karth	51	46	41	53
5 Fraser	43	46	34	60
6 Zwach	65	27	62	31
7 Bergland	59	32	47	50
8 Blatnik	35	32	29	46
MISSISSIPPI				
1 Abernethy	24	32	54	24
2 Whitten	49	51	61	36
3 Griffin	51	27	62	23
4 Montgomery	57	41	65	27
5 Colmer	68	27	65	23
MISSOURI				
1 Clay	22	30	16	43
2 Symington	46	35	40	49

Presidential Support And Opposition: House

1. Support Score, 1972. Percentage of 37 Nixon-issue roll calls in 1972 on which representative voted "yea" or "nay" *in agreement* with the President's position. Failures to vote lower both Support and Opposition scores.

2. Opposition Score, 1972. Percentage of 37 Nixon-issue roll calls in 1972 on which representative voted "yea" or "nay" *in disagreement* with the President's position. Failures to vote lower both Support and Opposition scores.

1 Rep. Elizabeth Andrews (D Ala.) sworn in in April 10, 1972, to replace Rep. George W. Andrews (D), deceased.
2 Rep. Clifford D. Carlson (R Ill.) sworn in April 11, 1972, to replace Rep. Charlotte T. Reid (R), resigned.
3 Rep. Edwin W. Edwards (D La.) resigned May 9, 1972. His scores for 1972 were 0 percent support and 0 percent opposition. Rep. John B. Breaux (D) sworn in Oct. 12, 1972, to replace Edwards.
4 Rep. Bradford Morse (R Mass.) resigned May 1, 1972.

Democrats   *Republicans*

	1	2	3	4
3 Sullivan	49	32	41	38
4 Randall	59	35	61	30
5 Bolling	46	41	50	44
6 Hull	43	43	64	30
7 Hall	49	46	54	37
8 Ichord	54	30	65	21
9 Hungate	30	49	32	54
10 Burlison	43	46	46	50
MONTANA				
1 Shoup	59	30	67	20
2 Melcher	51	27	43	44
NEBRASKA				
1 Thone	70	19	72	23
2 McCollister	73	27	77	23
3 Martin	49	27	63	19
NEVADA				
AL Baring	16	27	46	21
NEW HAMPSHIRE				
1 Wyman	76	22	81	16
2 Cleveland	86	11	79	19
NEW JERSEY				
1 Hunt	68	22	70	20
2 Sandman	68	27	78	16
3 Howard	49	38	34	55
4 Thompson	35	38	31	53
5 Frelinghuysen	78	5	78	5
6 Forsythe	68	16	70	23
7 Widnall	73	16	70	16
8 Roe	54	43	48	48
9 Helstoski	49	41	36	51
10 Rodino	54	46	41	49
11 Minish	57	41	46	50
12 Dwyer	27	5	43	21
13 Gallagher	16	5	39	20
14 Daniels	46	43	52	41
15 Patten	57	38	52	45
NEW MEXICO				
1 Lujan	57	14	54	15
2 Runnels	32	49	32	32
NEW YORK				
1 Pike	49	51	52	48
2 Grover	76	19	79	16
3 Wolff	38	41	38	48
4 Wydler	73	19	71	19
5 Lent	81	11	76	16
6 Halpern	59	22	39	36
7 Addabbo	43	51	40	55
8 Rosenthal	43	49	34	63
9 Delaney	49	30	61	27
10 Celler	46	46	33	50
11 Brasco	51	43	40	52
12 Chisholm	32	35	26	56
13 Podell	46	43	39	52
14 Rooney	41	11	51	26
15 Carey	49	32	37	50
16 Murphy	51	19	56	17
17 Koch	54	43	38	52
18 Rangel	49	46	30	56
19 Abzug	46	49	33	65
20 Ryan5	42†	33†	31*	62*
21 Badillo	51	41	29	63
22 Scheuer	43	41	35	55
23 Bingham	51	46	36	61
24 Biaggi	49	38	44	45
25 Peyser	68	14	73	15
26 Reid	41	32	43	46
27 Dow	35	32	28	55
28 Fish	76	14	71	19
29 Stratton	78	16	71	21
30 King	68	22	74*	17*
31 McEwen	70	16	71	15
32 Pirnie	81	11	78	9
33 Robison	70	22	67	28
34 Terry	57	24	69	19
35 Hanley	70	24	61	35
36 Horton	68	16	66	24
37 Conable	89	11	85	9
38 Hastings	78	8	74	13
39 Kemp	76	22	79	17
40 Smith	73	14	80	11
41 Dulski	46	49	44	49
NORTH CAROLINA				
1 Jones	49	46	60	35
2 Fountain	68	30	77	21
3 Henderson	54	41	67	30
4 Galifianakis	38	16	47	29
5 Mizell	70	24	81	16
6 Preyer	68	27	64	34
7 Lennon	43	32	60	22
8 Ruth	70	27	78	21
9 Jonas	62	30	69	18
10 Broyhill	78	19	76	18
11 Taylor	70	30	65	26
NORTH DAKOTA				
1 Andrews	59	24	68	23
2 Link	35	24	36	47
OHIO				
1 Keating	84	11	86	12
2 Clancy	51	38	71	22
3 Whalen	51	43	52	45
4 McCulloch	54	22	33	11
5 Latta	70	30	72	23
6 Harsha	73	24	71	22
7 Brown	76	14	82	9
8 Betts	62	16	80	10
9 Ashley	51	49	50	34
10 Miller	68	32	69	31
11 Stanton	76	14	74	16
12 Devine	59	22	69	18
13 Mosher	54	24	50	41
14 Seiberling	43	46	32	60
15 Wylie	70	22	73	20
16 Bow	70	11	77	9
17 Ashbrook	35	51	52	34
18 Hays	41	49	44	49
19 Carney	46	38	46	41
20 Stanton	54	38	47	46
21 Stokes	32	46	26	53
22 Vanik	51	49	41	57
23 Minshall	62	14	63	17
24 Powell	54	24	70	19
OKLAHOMA				
1 Belcher	78	11	81	7
2 Edmondson	35	22	49	24
3 Albert	9•	18•	47•	32•
4 Steed	57	38	60	32
5 Jarman	68	27	63	20
6 Camp	59	41	66	28
OREGON				
1 Wyatt	76	16	69	15
2 Ullman	54	32	46	44
3 Green	41	19	38	39
4 Dellenback	73	27	76	23
PENNSYLVANIA				
1 Barrett	43	49	37	43
2 Nix	43	49	41	53
3 Byrne	43	24	44	35
4 Eilberg	54	46	39	54
5 Green	54	46	36	51
6 Yatron	32	49	33	53
7 Williams	81	16	84	15
8 Biester	70	30	62	37
9 Ware	86	14	90	9
10 McDade	57	22	63	28
11 Flood	68	27	69	28
12 Whalley	78	16	80	10
13 Coughlin	68	22	64	31
14 Moorhead	41	46	40	49
15 Rooney	51	46	50	46
16 Eshleman	78	14	66	15
17 Schneebeli	59	19	67	20
18 Heinz	59	41	60*	36*
19 Goodling	68	27	69	27
20 Gaydos	46	49	41	52
21 Dent	32	54	21	40
22 Saylor	51	38	53	28
23 Johnson	76	16	72	13
24 Vigorito	59	30	60	36
25 Clark	38	32	45	19
26 Morgan	62	32	65	26
27 Conover6	85†	15†	85*	15*
RHODE ISLAND				
1 St Germain	49	38	44	49
2 Tiernan	51	38	40	47
SOUTH CAROLINA				
1 Davis	27	24	48*	27*
2 Spence	62	35	68	26
3 Dorn	57	35	62	26
4 Mann	62	24	68	22
5 Gettys	57	24	54	27
6 McMillan	32	16	52	16
SOUTH DAKOTA				
1 Denholm	24	54	20	61
2 Abourezk	30	24	26	52
TENNESSEE				
1 Quillen	59	30	72	16
2 Duncan	68	32	71	29
3 Baker	43	32	62	19
4 Evins	38	30	39	22
5 Fulton	35	32	34	45
6 Anderson	32	22	28	34
7 Blanton	22	14	41	16
8 Jones	43	35	48	27
9 Kuykendall	43	22	64	13
TEXAS				
1 Patman	51	38	50	30
2 Dowdy	5	8	29	13
3 Collins	68	24	68	28
4 Roberts	43	49	60	26
5 Cabell	51	27	62	24
6 Teague	41	49	53	29
7 Archer	62	27	70	24
8 Eckhardt	43	51	38	55
9 Brooks	54	38	54	37
10 Pickle	51	41	57	33
11 Poage	57	41	50	34
12 Wright	57	38	63	27
13 Purcell	54	19	56	18
14 Young	46	43	57	34
15 de la Garza	57	41	50	41
16 White	54	43	66	30
17 Burleson	57	35	66	29
18 Price	46	35	65	22
19 Mahon	62	35	71	28
20 Gonzalez	49	51	55	44
21 Fisher	51	32	63	26
22 Casey	59	38	67	29
23 Kazen	49	46	59	39
UTAH				
1 McKay	54	35	60	36
2 Lloyd	62	5	74	7
VERMONT				
AL Mallary	84	16	84*	16*
VIRGINIA				
1 Downing	57	35	69	27
2 Whitehurst	73	24	81	18
3 Satterfield	43	49	64	32
4 Abbitt	59	32	67	22
5 Daniel	57	41	69	30
6 Poff7	83†	9†	76*	10*
7 Robinson	57	41	72	26
8 Scott	43	30	63	26
9 Wampler	68	27	73	22
10 Broyhill	57	38	65	27
WASHINGTON				
1 Pelly	54	5	70	4
2 Meeds	43	43	46	44
3 Hansen	32	19	48	26
4 McCormack	30	30	39	40
5 Foley	68	32	59	36
6 Hicks	41	57	48	50
7 Adams	43	51	45	48
WEST VIRGINIA				
1 Mollohan	46	16	56	18
2 Staggers	49	35	55	29
3 Slack	43	57	50	45
4 Hechler	38	62	34	66
5 Kee	49	24	54	23
WISCONSIN				
1 Aspin	46	43	39	52
2 Kastenmeier	49	51	35	64
3 Thomson	65	22	73	20
4 Zablocki	73	27	74	26
5 Reuss	46	54	38	60
6 Steiger	78	14	76	18
7 Obey	46	49	38	60
8 Byrnes	68	14	71	14
9 Davis	54	24	72	14
10 O'Konski	46	27	64	26
WYOMING				
AL Roncalio	30	41	29	57

Presidential Support And Opposition: House

3. Support Score, 92nd Congress. Percentage of 94 Nixon-issue roll calls in 1971 and 1972 on which representative voted "yea" or "nay" *in agreement* with the President's position. Failures to vote lower both Support and Opposition scores.

4. Opposition Score, 92nd Congress. Percentage of 94 Nixon-issue roll calls in 1971 and 1972 on which representative voted "yea" or "nay" *in disagreement* with the President's position. Failures to vote lower both Support and Opposition scores.

5 Rep. William F. Ryan (D N.Y.) died Sept. 17, 1972.
6 Rep. William S. Conover (R Pa.) sworn in May 24, 1972, to replace Rep. James G. Fulton (R), deceased.
7 Rep. Richard H. Poff (R Va.) resigned Aug. 29, 1972.

Presidential Support and Opposition: Senate

1. Support Score, 1972. Percentage of 46 Nixon-issue roll calls in 1972 on which senator voted "yea" or "nay" in *agreement* with the President's position. Failures to vote lower both Support and Opposition scores.

2. Opposition Score, 1972. Percentage of 46 Nixon-issue roll calls in 1972 on which senator votes "yea" or "nay" *in disagreement* with the President's position. Failures to vote lower both Support and Opposition scores.

3. Support Score, 92nd Congress. Percentage of 128 Nixon-issue roll calls in 1971 and 1972 on which senator voted "yea" or "nay" *in agreement* with the President's position. Failures to vote lower both Support and Opposition scores.

4. Opposition Score, 92nd Congress. Percentage of 128 Nixon-issue roll calls in 1971 and 1972 on which senator voted "yea" or "nay" *in disagreement* with the President's position. Failures to vote lower both Support and Opposition scores.

	1	2	3	4
ALABAMA				
Allen	78	20	66	31
Sparkman	70	11	59	16
ALASKA				
Gravel	26	50	20	54
Stevens	43	43	54	31
ARIZONA				
Fannin	85	9	81	12
Goldwater	59	9	56	9
ARKANSAS				
Fulbright	33	59	29	59
McClellan	61	13	53	34
CALIFORNIA				
Cranston	35	61	35	60
Tunney	35	54	37	52
COLORADO				
Allott	72	7	73	6
Dominick	78	4	67	9
CONNECTICUT				
Ribicoff	35	54	32	56
Weicker	65	24	66	21
DELAWARE				
Boggs	70	20	80	13
Roth	83	17	84	16
FLORIDA				
Chiles	61	33	51	40
Gurney	89	7	86	13
GEORGIA				
Gambrell	50	13	48	30
Talmadge	67	22	61	34
HAWAII				
Inouye	33	54	31	47
Fong	70	13	71	12
IDAHO				
Church	28	63	31	55
Jordan	76	20	64	20
ILLINOIS				
Stevenson	30	59	37	55
Percy	46	48	48	37
INDIANA				
Bayh	30	54	25	50
Hartke	22	46	20	41

	1	2	3	4
IOWA				
Hughes	28	59	29	63
Miller	70	11	59	15
KANSAS				
Dole	87	4	83	10
Pearson	48	39	57	32
KENTUCKY				
Cook	48	30	56	28
Cooper	70	26	67	23
LOUISIANA				
Edwards[1]	64†	7†	64*	7*
Long	67	20	59	23
MAINE				
Muskie	15	46	19	42
Smith	83	17	78	15
MARYLAND				
Beall	76	17	77	17
Mathias	41	50	43	44
MASSACHUSETTS				
Kennedy	22	52	27	51
Brooke	46	52	44	48
MICHIGAN				
Hart	33	65	32	59
Griffin	83	7	84	8
MINNESOTA				
Humphrey	24	46	32	45
Mondale	35	63	33	63
MISSISSIPPI				
Eastland	70	9	65	16
Stennis	78	22	72	24
MISSOURI				
Eagleton	28	59	37	52
Symington	39	61	40	56
MONTANA				
Mansfield	33	54	30	55
Metcalf	24	39	26	46
NEBRASKA				
Curtis	70	9	70	13
Hruska	91	7	84	10
NEVADA				
Bible	57	37	54	34
Cannon	54	17	55	26

	1	2	3	4
NEW HAMPSHIRE				
McIntyre	46	24	42	37
Cotton	85	7	74	14
NEW JERSEY				
Williams	28	57	32	59
Case	35	54	44	50
NEW MEXICO				
Anderson	54	28	48	33
Montoya	37	54	41	49
NEW YORK				
Buckley[2]	74	11	78	13
Javits	43	54	46	39
NORTH CAROLINA				
Ervin	70	22	65	28
Jordan	59	20	45	41
NORTH DAKOTA				
Burdick	35	65	35	58
Young	85	13	72	19
OHIO				
Saxbe	61	17	63	14
Taft	62†	24†	70*	13*
OKLAHOMA				
Harris	13	46	17	36
Bellmon	80	7	70	10
OREGON				
Hatfield	15	41	27	50
Packwood	65	15	63	18
PENNSYLVANIA				
Schweiker	52	48	50	48
Scott	70	22	75	9
RHODE ISLAND				
Pastore	43	52	43	49
Pell	26	48	31	48
SOUTH CAROLINA				
Hollings	57	35	48	31
Thurmond	83	7	77	16
SOUTH DAKOTA				
McGovern	9	35	12	39
Mundt	0	0	0	0
TENNESSEE				
Baker	63	4	66	13
Brock	83	7	71	13

- KEY -

†Not eligible for all roll calls in 1972.

*Not eligible for all roll calls in 92nd Congress.

	1	2	3	4
TEXAS				
Bentsen	57	35	59	36
Tower	72	4	70	9
UTAH				
Moss	37	57	30	49
Bennett	89	7	69	12
VERMONT				
Aiken	74	20	66	26
Stafford	43	41	49*	35*
VIRGINIA				
Byrd, Jr.[3]	83	17	72	26
Spong	59	30	50	41
WASHINGTON				
Jackson	61	15	48	20
Magnuson	35	39	39	40
WEST VIRGINIA				
Byrd	67	30	59	34
Randolph	46	46	46	44
WISCONSIN				
Nelson	30	70	29	66
Proxmire	39	61	38	62
WYOMING				
McGee	50	11	56	17
Hansen	78	4	70	13

Democrats   *Republicans*

1 *Sen. Allen J. Ellender (D La.) died July 27, 1972. His scores for 1972 were 52 percent support and 32 percent opposition. Sen. Elaine Edwards was sworn in Aug. 7, 1972, to replace Ellender.*
2 *Buckley elected as Conservative.*
3 *Byrd elected as independent.*

CONGRESS APPROVES 44 PERCENT OF NIXON'S 1972 REQUESTS

The second session of the 92nd Congress adjourned Oct. 18 after having approved fewer than half of President Nixon's 1972 legislative proposals.

Foreign affairs, which dominated much of the President's time in 1972, provided him with a number of legislative victories during the year. Congress gave its approval to a five-year agreement with the Soviet Union limiting the deployment of all offensive nuclear weapons and the Senate ratified a companion treaty limiting anti-ballistic missile (ABM) sites. Also granted were presidential requests for almost $2-billion in contributions to various international development funds and more than $42-million for support of international narcotics control activities.

Other Nixon proposals to clear Congress included a bill establishing a consumer product safety agency, a program to encourage rural growth and appropriations increases for the school lunch program and cancer research.

The President suffered major defeats on his requests for a $250-billion spending ceiling in fiscal 1973 and for a tough, anti-busing bill.

As measured by Congressional Quarterly's annual Boxscore, Nixon made 116 specific requests for legislation (including treaties submitted for ratification) in 24 messages to Congress and other public statements. Of these, 51—or about 44 percent—were enacted into law or ratified.

The Nixon score represents a significant improvement over his 20-percent mark in 1971. *(1971 Almanac p. 111-H)*

The Boxscore is a survey of specific presidential legislative requests during a calendar year and their fate during that year's session of Congress. It is not a comprehensive review of an administration's legislative accomplishments. Issues are not reflected in the Boxscore unless they were the subject of public statements or messages to Congress by the President himself in 1972. Success in legislative struggles spanning more than one session of a Congress is not recorded in the Boxscore. For example, the passage of general revenue sharing, though a significant victory of the President, is not included in the 1972 study because the presidential request and major legislative action occurred prior to 1972.

Similarly, ocean dumping regulation, which became law in early 1972, was excluded because it had been requested in 1971 and was in conference at the end of the first session of the 92nd Congress.

Nor does the Boxscore differentiate between major legislation and less significant proposals. (In District of Columbia affairs, however, some minor requests of purely local interest are omitted.) The individual requests are itemized as they were presented in the messages.

MAJOR PROPOSALS. Following is a summary of congressional action on the major aspects of President Nixon's program during 1972:

Foreign Policy. The President submitted to Congress two agreements produced by the Strategic Arms Limitation Treaty (SALT) talks, which were signed by the President and Soviet Communist Party General Secretary Leonid I. Brezhnev during the President's visit to Moscow in May.

The Senate approved ratification of the first, a treaty with the Soviet Union limiting each nation to two anti-ballistic missile (ABM) sites. The second agreement, an interim agreement on strategic offensive arms, was endorsed by the Senate Sept. 14 and the House Sept. 25.

Congress appropriated the full amounts authorized for contributions to three multilateral development institutions: the Inter-American Development Bank, the International Development Association, and the Asian Development Bank. It also appropriated $42.5 million for the control of international narcotics traffic.

How the Boxscore Works

The items tabulated in the Boxscore include only the specific legislative requests contained in the President's messages to Congress and other public statements during a calendar year.

Excluded from the Boxscore are proposals advocated by executive branch officials but not specifically by the President; measures endorsed by the President but not specifically requested by him; nominations, and suggestions that Congress consider or study particular topics when legislative action is not requested.

Except for major proposals, presidential requests for District of Columbia legislation also are excluded from the Boxscore tabulation.

Routine appropriation requests, which provide funds for regular, continuing government operations, are excluded. Appropriation requests for specific programs, or requests for substantial budget increases, are included if the President indicated in special messages or other communications that they were important in his overall legislative program.

Because the Boxscore fundamentally is a tabular checklist of the President's program, presented in neither greater nor less detail than is found in presidential messages, the individual requests necessarily differ considerably from one another in their scope and importance.

Because Congress does not always vote "yes" or "no" on a proposal, CQ evaluates legislative action to determine whether compromises amount to approval or rejection of the President's requests.

Legislative activity on an item must occur in the same year as the presidential request in order to be credited in the Boxscore.

Symbols in the Final Outcome column indicate whether Congress took favorable or unfavorable action on the proposal. *(Chart, p. 41-46)*

The Senate in July rejected the foreign assistance authorization bill (S 3390). An almost identical bill (HR 16029) died in conference at the end of the session.

Taxes and Economic Policy. Congress passed the Small Business Investment Act Amendments, but omitted in it specific provisions, requested by the President, which would have increased government support of Small Business Investment Companies (SBIC's) and increased the ownership limits of SBIC's by federally regulated commercial banks.

Congress denied the President the $250-billion spending ceiling he first requested in his budget message and asked for again in July in an "urgent appeal." The President said he would not let "reckless spending destroy the tax reductions we have secured and the hard-won successes we have earned in the battle against inflation."

National Security. Much of the President's proposal to improve benefits for military retirees and family survivors was accepted by Congress and enacted into law. A bill to offer incentive pay to attract and retain servicemen with special skills passed the House, but died when the Senate took no action in 1972.

Congress granted the President most of the funds he requested for "sea-based deterrent forces." But it sharply cut back his request for military research and development funds.

Natural Resources. Congress considered several of President Nixon's environmental proposals, but only his request for regulation of toxic waste disposal passed both houses. Certain provisions of this proposal were also contained in the water pollution bill (S 2770), which cleared Congress Oct. 18 over Nixon's veto. The President described the $24-billion measure as "budget wrecking."

General Welfare. In 1972 Congress passed bills appropriating a total of $200-million to be spent by the Administration on Aging, as requested by the President. Legislation recommended by the President which would have extended the Older Americans Act and expanded person-to-person volunteer service programs for older Americans passed Congress, but was then pocket-vetoed by the President. In his Oct. 30 veto message, the President said that Congress had added "narrow, categorical service programs which would seriously interfere with our effort to develop coordinated services for older persons."

Civil Rights. Congress approved two of the President's requests in the civil rights area during the 1972 session. It extended the operations and expanded the jurisdiction of the Civil Rights Commission. Congress also approved a constitutional amendment to guarantee equal rights for men and women, 49 years after it was first introduced.

Consumer Protection. Congress passed a bill intended to protect consumers against hazardous products by creating an independent agency which would promulgate mandatory safety standards. The President had advocated a product safety commission within the Department of Health, Education and Welfare, rather than an independent agency.

The Senate Labor and Public Welfare Committee took no action in 1972 on legislation aimed at establishing safety standards for medical devices or on a bill to simplify identification of pills and tablets.

Labor. Congress responded favorably to the President's request for legislation to end the West Coast dock strike.

In March a House subcommittee rejected permanent anti-strike legislation which the President had sought. In April the Senate held hearings on similar transportation dispute legislation. In July the President withdrew his support for legislation to prevent strikes in the transportation industry.

Agriculture. In amending the Consolidated Farmers Home Administration Act of 1961, Congress in 1972 fulfilled many of the provisions outlined in President Nixon's rural development plan. But Congress did not act on the President's request for a $1.3-billion authorization for a new rural development credit-sharing program.

Source Key: Nixon's 1972 Legislative Requests

The sources of President Nixon's 1972 legislative requests are listed below, preceded by a letter-symbol. Messages asking Senate consent to treaty ratifications are excluded from this compilation. Page numbers refer to those requests appearing in the text section of this book.

	Source, Message	Date	Page
A	State of the Union	Jan. 20	5-A
B	West Coast Dock Strike	Jan. 21	—
C	Rural Development	Feb. 1	37-A
D	Emergency Transportation Disputes	Feb. 2	59-A
E	District of Columbia's Bicentennial Observance	Feb. 4	61-A
F	Environmental Program	Feb. 8	18-A
G	Health Care	March 2	41-A
H	Multilateral Development Institutions	March 10	—
I	Foreign Assistance	March 14	47-A
J	Science and Technology	March 15	—
K	Educational Opportunity and Busing	March 17	50-A
L	Equal Rights for Women	March 18	—
M	Minority Enterprise	March 20	46-A
N	Older Americans	March 23	64-A
O	Campaign Against Cancer	April 26	—
P	School Nutrition	May 6	—
Q	Letter to Senate Majority and Minority Leaders on Foreign Assistance	June 10	—
R	Message to the Senate and Letter to the Speaker of the House on Strategic Arms Limitation	June 13	—
S	Government Spending	July 26	75-A
T	Disaster Recovery	Aug. 2	—
U	Historic Monuments	Aug. 4	—
V	Letter to Rep. Peyser (R N.Y.) Opposing Heroin Maintenance Programs	Aug. 18	—
W	All-Volunteer Armed Forces	Aug. 28	—
X	Wilderness Areas	Sept. 21	78-A

PRESIDENTIAL BOXSCORE FOR 1972

Following is a list of President Nixon's specific legislative requests to Congress in 1972 and a summary in tabular form of the action taken on each. A letter in parentheses following each item indicates the presidential statement or message which was the most definitive source of the request. A key to the sources appears on the preceding page. Each treaty ratification request made during the Nixon Administration and pending in 1972 is followed by the date the treaty was originally sent to the Senate.

STATUS KEY

√ Favorable Action.
X Unfavorable Action.
  No Action Taken.
H Hearings Held.
\# Congressional Inaction Constitutes Favorable Action.
* Request Previously Submitted, But Denied or Not Acted Upon.

Foreign Policy

FOREIGN AID

	HOUSE COMMITTEE ACTION (1)	HOUSE FLOOR ACTION (2)	SENATE COMMITTEE ACTION (3)	SENATE FLOOR ACTION (4)	FINAL OUTCOME (5)	PUBLIC LAW NUMBER (6)
1. Increase substantially the budget for the United States Travel Service. (A)	√	√	√	√	√	544
2. Commit the United States to provide a "fair share" contribution to a United Nations Fund for the Environment, should such a fund be established, on a matching basis over the first five years of the fund's existence. (F)			√	√	X	
3. Fund in full the recommended levels of foreign assistance for fiscal 1972 before the interim funding arrangement expires in late February, 1972. (A)	X	X	X	X	X	
4.*Act upon the fundamental aid reform proposals first submitted by the administration in 1971. (A)					X	
5. Appropriate full amount authorized for U.S. contribution to the Asian Development Bank. (H)	√	√	√	√	√	245
6. Appropriate full amount authorized for U.S. contribution to the Inter-American Development Bank. (H)	√	√	√	√	√	246
7. Appropriate full amount authorized for U.S. contribution to the International Development Association. (H)	√	√	√	√	√	247
8. Pass the Foreign Assistance Authorization Bill without reduction or restriction in order to provide adequate security assistance and back up U.S. commitments abroad. (Q)						
9. Authorize $2,151-million in fiscal 1973 for security assistance. (I)	√	√	X	X	X	
10. Appropriate $42.5-million for support of international narcotics control activities. (I)	√	√	√	√	√	352
11. Authorize an additional $100-million in fiscal 1973 for refugee relief and humanitarian assistance in South Asia. (I)	√	√	X	√	X	

TREATIES

Consent to the ratification of:

	HOUSE COMMITTEE ACTION (1)	HOUSE FLOOR ACTION (2)	SENATE COMMITTEE ACTION (3)	SENATE FLOOR ACTION (4)	FINAL OUTCOME (5)	PUBLIC LAW NUMBER (6)
1. Renewal of request for convention on prevention and punishment of the crime of genocide. 6/16/49						
2. Protocol for the Prohibition of the Use in War of Asphyxiating, Poisonous or Other Gases, and of Bacteriological Methods of Warfare. 8/19/70						
3. Convention on Psychotropic Substances. 6/29/71						
4. Convention on the Law of Treaties. 11/22/71						
5. Convention on the Taking of Evidence Abroad in Civil or Commercial Matters. 2/1/72			√	√	√	—

	1	2	3	4	5	6
6. Convention on the Means of Prohibiting and Preventing the Illicit Import, Export and Transfer of Ownership of Cultural Property. 2/3/72			√	√	√	—
7. Amendment to paragraphs A, B, C, and D of Article VI of the Statute of the International Atomic Energy Agency, expanding the size of the Board of Governors. 2/3/72			√	√	√	—
8. Convention with Norway for the avoidance of double taxation. 2/3/72			√	√	√	—
9. Partial revision of the 1959 Radio Regulations on space telecommunications, with a final protocol relating to the use of radio space techniques. 2/16/72			√	√	√	—
10. Treaty with Argentina updating extradition relations and adding to the list of extraditable offenses both narcotics violations and aircraft hijacking. 3/8/72			√	√	√	—
11. Convention and two protocols intended to help developing countries gain ready access to educational, scientific and technical works without weakening present copyright protection. 3/15/72			√	√	√	—
12. Treaty with Honduras on the Swan Islands, recognizing Honduran sovereignty over the islands and providing for cooperation in meteorology and telecommunications. 3/28/72			√	√	√	—
13. Convention establishing an International Organization of Legal Metrology, concerning standards for legal determination of quantity and quality. 4/11/72			√	√	√	—
14. Protocol amending the Single Convention on Narcotic Drugs. 5/4/72			√	√	√	—
15. International Convention on the Establishment of an International Fund for Compensation for Oil Pollution Damage, and an amendment to the 1954 Convention for the Prevention of Pollution of the Sea. 5/5/72						
16. Treaty with the Soviet Union on the limitation of anti-ballistic missile systems. 6/13/72			√	√	√	—
17. Convention on International Liability for Damage Caused by Space Objects. 6/15/72			√	√	√	—
18. International Convention on Tonnage Measurement of Ships. 6/15/72						
19. Amendments to the 1960 Convention for the Safety of Life at Sea, requiring specified navigational and personal safety equipment aboard vessels. 7/24/72			√	√	√	—
20. Agreement with Brazil for the regulation of shrimp fisheries off the Brazilian coast and the solution of jurisdictional questions involving coastal fisheries. 7/28/72			√	√	√	—
21. Convention on the Prohibition of the Development, Production and Stockpiling of Bacteriological (Biological) and Toxin Weapons, and on their Destruction. 8/10/72						
22. Convention with Japan for the Protection of Migratory Birds and Birds in Danger of Extinction, and their Environment. 8/18/72						
23. Treaty simplifying the process of filing and examining patent applications on the same invention in member countries. 9/12/72						
24. Convention for the Suppression of Unlawful Acts Against the Safety of Civil Aviation. 9/15/72			√	√	√	—
25. Convention with Poland establishing consular relations. 9/19/72						
26. Convention with Romania establishing consular relations. 9/19/72						
27. Convention with Hungary establishing consular relations. 9/19/72						

Taxes and Economic Policy

SMALL BUSINESS

	1	2	3	4	5	6
1. Provide additional means for the Small Business Investment Companies (SBIC's) to improve the availability of venture capital to small, high technology firms. (J)					X	
2. Increase ratio of government support to SBIC's, to be channelled to small business concerns principally engaged in the development or exploitation of technological improvements and new products. (J)					X	
3. Permit federally-regulated commercial banks to achieve 100-percent ownership of an SBIC, rather than the currently allowed 50-percent ownership. (J)			√	√	X	
4. Increase the current limit on Small Business Administration loans to each SBIC to $20-million to allow for growth in SBIC funds devoted to technology investments. (J)	√	√	√	√	√	595
5. Pass the small business tax bill, to enhance risk-taking and entrepreneurial ventures. (J)					X	
6. Introduce, on a cooperative, voluntary basis, the metric system of measurement in the United States in order to foster technological innovations and enhance the U.S. position in world trade. (J)			√	√	X	

	1	2	3	4	5	6
7.*Pass the Minority Enterprise Small Business Investment Act of 1972, which would reduce the level of private capital required to qualify for SBA assistance, provide increased equity to MESBICS, and lower interest rates on SBA loans to MESBICS. (M)	√	√	√	√	√	595
8. Appropriate $1,569,800,000 in supplemental funds for disaster loans. (T)	√	√	√	√	√	393

ECONOMIC POLICY

	1	2	3	4	5	6
1. Enact a spending ceiling of $250-billion. (S)	√	√	√	X	X	

National Security

	1	2	3	4	5	6
1. Allocate $900-million to improve sea-based deterrent forces. (A)	√	√	√	√	√	570
2. Step up military research and development programs through an $838-million budget increase. (A)	X	X	X	X	X	
3. Raise the level of protection for military families under military retirement and survivor benefit programs. (A)	√	√	√	√	√	425
4.*Pass the Uniformed Services Special Pay Act of 1972, to provide needed bonus authority to help fill projected shortages in critical skills and other possible shortages in the number of enlistees available under a zero draft. (W)	√	√	X	X	X	
5. Recompute military retirement pay on the basis of Jan. 1, 1971, pay scales, thus liberalizing annuities for current retirees. (N)	H				X	
6. Provide military retirees with a less expensive survivor annuity plan similar to the civil servant annuity plan. (N)	√	√	√	√	√	425
7. Approve the interim agreement with the Soviet Union on strategic offensive arms. (R)	√	√	√	√	√	448

Resources and Public Works

NATURAL RESOURCES

	1	2	3	4	5	6
1. Pass a Toxic Wastes Disposal Control Act, under which the Environmental Protection Agency would establish guidelines and requirements for state programs to regulate disposal of hazardous toxic wastes. The act would provide for enforcement action if a state should fail to establish its own program. (F)	√	√	√	√	X	
2. Require states to establish regulatory programs to control sediment affecting water quality. (F)					X	
3. Amend pending national land use policy legislation to require states to control the siting of major transportation facilities, and to impose sanctions on any state which does not establish an adequate land use program. (F)			√	X	X	
4. Limit applicability of certain federal tax benefits when development occurs in coastal wetlands. (F)					X	
5. Provide for early identification and protection of endangered species, make the taking of endangered species a federal offense and permit protective measures to be undertaken before a species is so depleted that regeneration is difficult or impossible. (F)			√		X	
6. Empower the federal government to acquire the requisite legal interest in 547,000 acres of Big Cypress Swamp, Florida, and create the Big Cypress National Fresh Water Reserve. (F)	H		H		X	
7. Pass the National Land Use Policy Act, which will help states to exercise protective controls over historic buildings and districts. (U)			√	√	X	
8. Change the Internal Revenue Code to provide tax benefits for the restoration and tax penalties for the destruction of historic structures. (U)					X	
9. Authorize the Department of Housing and Urban Development to guarantee loans for the restoration and rehabilitation of historic structures for residential purposes. (U)	√		√	√	X	
10. Pass the Agnes Recovery Act of 1972. (T)	√	√	√	√	√	385

	1	2	3	4	5	6

PARKS AND RECREATION AREAS

	1	2	3	4	5	6
1. Establish a Golden Gate National Recreation Area in and around San Francisco Bay. (F)			√		X	
2. Add 18 new areas, totalling 1.3 million acres, to the national wilderness system. (F)			H		X	
3. Add an additional 16 new areas, totalling 3.5 million acres, to the national wilderness system, plus 216,519 acres from other regions. (X)					X	

Welfare and Urban Affairs

HOUSING

	1	2	3	4	5	6
1. Increase the budget for enforcing fair housing laws by 20 percent. (A)	√	√	√	√	√	383

TRANSPORTATION

	1	2	3	4	5	6
1. Enact legislation to modernize railway equipment and operations and update regulatory practices. (A)	H				X	
2. Allow states and localities to use some of the funds now in the Highway Trust Fund to help finance their mass transit programs. (N)	X	X	√	√	X	
3. Authorize $200-million for federal highway emergency relief. (T)	√	√	√	√	√	361

GENERAL WELFARE

	1	2	3	4	5	6
1. Pass the Allied Services Act of 1972 to strengthen state and local planning and administrative capacities, allow for transfer of funds among various HEW programs, and permit the waiver of certain cumbersome federal requirements. (A)					X	
2. Appropriate $100-million in fiscal 1973 for the Administration on Aging. (A)	√	√	√	√	X ‡	
3. Appropriate an additional $100-million for nutritional and related purposes to be spent through the Administration on Aging. (N)	√	√	√	√	√	258
4. Extend the Older Americans Act for an indefinite rather than for a specified period of years. (N)	√	√	√	√	X†	
5. Authorize ACTION to expand person-to-person volunteer service programs—helping more older Americans to work both with children and with older persons who need their help. (N)	√	√	√	√	X†	
6. Broaden the Age Discrimination in Employment Act of 1967 to include state and local governments. (N)					X	

Civil Rights

	1	2	3	4	5	6
1. Increase budget for the Cabinet Committee on Opportunities for the Spanish-speaking by 42 percent. (A)	√	√	√	√	X‡	
2. Extend operations of the Civil Rights Commission for five years and broaden the commission's jurisdiction to encompass sex-based discrimination. (A)	√	√	√	√	√	496
3. Enact a constitutional amendment to guarantee equal rights for women. (L)	√	√	√	√	√•	

General Government

DISTRICT OF COLUMBIA

(Major Requests Only)

	1	2	3	4	5	6
1. Approve federal guarantees for METRO revenue bonds. (E)	√	√	√	√	√	349
2. Approve fiscal 1973 construction funds for the National Air and Space Museum. (E)	√	√	√	√	√	369

†Pocket-vetoed Oct. 30, 1972. (HR 15657)

‡Included in Labor-HEW appropriations bill (HR 16654), which President Nixon pocket-vetoed on Oct. 27, 1972.

•Sent to states for ratification on March 22, 1972.

	1	2	3	4	5	6
3. Approve the Bicentennial Outdoor Museum and authorize appropriations for planning. (E)	X		X		X	
4.*Enact Pennsylvania Avenue Bicentennial Development Corporation bill. (E)	√	√			X	

Consumer Protection

	1	2	3	4	5	6
1. Enact a consumer product safety bill, authorizing the federal government to establish and enforce new standards for product safety. (G)	√	√	√	√	√	573
2. Authorize the establishment of safety standards for medical devices and provide for premarketing scientific review when warranted. (G)					X	
3.*Enact a drug identification bill, to make possible quick and accurate identification of any pill or tablet. (G)					X	

Health and Education

EDUCATION

	1	2	3	4	5	6
1. Appropriate $200-million for predominantly black colleges. (A)	√	√	√	√	X†	
2. Pass the Equal Educational Opportunities Act of 1972. (K)	√	√		X	X	
3. Pass the Student Transportation Moratorium Act of 1972. (K)	X		X		X	
4. Enact an amendment to the Disaster Recovery Act of 1972 to make private, non-profit educational institutions eligible for disaster relief grants. (R)	√	√	√	√	√	385
5. Enact a comprehensive school nutrition bill to revise and reform the present school lunch and school breakfast program. (P)	√	√	√	√	√	433
6. Allocate an additional $25-million to feed needy city children in the summer of 1972. (P)	√	√	√	√	√	433
7. Provide an additional $19.5-million to extend the school breakfast program to some 3,000 additional schools in 1973. (P)	√	√	√	√	√	433

HEALTH

	1	2	3	4	5	6
1. Eliminate the $5.80 monthly fee now charged under part B of Medicare. (A)					X	
2. Appropriate an additional $93-million for cancer research in fiscal 1973. (G)	√	√	√	√	X†	
3. Appropriate $40-million in supplemental funds to expand the campaign against cancer. (O)	√	√	√	√	√	306
4. Appropriate $15-million for sickle cell disease research in fiscal 1973. (G)	X				X	
5. Pass a bill to prevent implementation of heroin maintenance programs. (V)					X	
6. Permit the federal government to assume the entire cost of state inspection of homes receiving payment under the Medicaid program. (N)	√	√	√	√	√	603

Agriculture and Labor

LABOR

	1	2	3	4	5	6
1. Increase appropriations for the Equal Employment Opportunity Commission by 36 percent. (A)	X	X	X	X	X	
2. Set up a three-member arbitration board, appointed by the Secretary of Labor, to hear all the issues in the West Coast dock strike dispute and issue a statement which would be binding for at least 18 months. (B)		√	√	√	√	235
3. Enact the West Coast Dock Strike Resolution. (B)		√	√	√	√	235
4. Discontinue the emergency strike provisions of the Railway Labor Act of 1926 and provide that all transportation disputes be settled under the Taft-Hartley Act. (D)	X	H			X	
5. Grant to the President three options in emergency transportation disputes when the 80-day Taft-Hartley "cooling-off" period fails to produce a settlement: a) extend the "cooling-off" period for 30 days; b) require partial operation of the troubled industry, so that those segments essential to the national health or safety could be kept in operation for an additional 180 days; c) invoke a "final offer selection" procedure whereby a neutral panel would select the most reasonable of the final offers of the disputing parties as the final and binding contract between the parties. (D)	X	H			X	

†Included in Labor-HEW appropriations bill (HR 16654), which President Nixon pocket-vetoed on Oct. 27, 1972.

	1	2	3	4	5	6
6. Establish a National Special Industries Commission to conduct a two-year study of labor relations in industries which are especially subject to national emergency disputes. (B)	X		H		X	

AGRICULTURE

	1	2	3	4	5	6
1. Establish a new Rural Development Credit Fund to provide loans, loan insurance and loan guarantees to states for their use in assisting rural development. (C)	√	√	√	√	√	419
2. Make credit available through the Farmers Home Administration for up to 80 percent of the cost of establishing or improving businesses which help create growth in rural areas. (C)	√	√	√	√	√	419
3. Require that most of the credit-sharing authorizations be divided among the states according to the same formula established for rural community development revenue sharing. (C)					X	
4. Authorize $1.3-billion in fiscal 1974 for a new rural community development credit-sharing program, including the existing Farmers Home Administration water and sewer program. (C)					X	
5. Increase the Department of Agriculture farm operating loan limit to $50,000. (C)	√	√	√	√	√	419
6. Increase the limit on new loans to be held in the agricultural credit insurance fund from $100-million to $500-million. (C)	√	√	√	√	√	419
7. Authorize Secretary of Agriculture to share costs of long-term conservation in watershed areas. (C)	√	√	√	√	√	419
8. Authorize technical and cost-sharing assistance within watershed areas for the improvement of water quality. (C)	√	√	√	√	√	419
9. Authorize Secretary of Agriculture to inventory and monitor soil water and related resources and to issue a national land inventory report at five-year intervals. (C)	√	√	√	√	√	419

Science and Technology

SPACE

	1	2	3	4	5	6
1. Approve plan for earth orbital vehicle (space shuttle). (A)	√	√	√	√	√	304

PRESIDENTIAL MESSAGES AND STATEMENTS

STATE OF UNION: DUAL PLEA FOR ACTION ON PAST REQUESTS

President Nixon broke with precedent Jan. 20 when he delivered two state-of-the-union messages to Congress—a 4,000-word speech tailored for national television and a 15,000-word document elaborating on the address.

STATE OF UNION TEXT I

Following is the text, as prepared for delivery to a joint session of Congress, of President Nixon's Jan. 20, 1972 State of the Union message.

Mr. Speaker, Mr. President, my colleagues in the Congress, our distinguished guests and my fellow Americans:

Twenty-five years ago I sat here as a freshman Congressman—along with Speaker Albert—and listened for the first time to the President address us on the State of the Union.

I shall never forget that moment. The Senate, the Diplomatic Corps, the Supreme Court, the Cabinet entered the chamber, and then the President of the United States. As all of you are aware, I had some differences with President Truman, as he did with me. But I remember that on the day he addressed that Joint Session of the newly-elected Republican Congress, he spoke not as a partisan but as President of all the people—calling upon the Congress to put aside partisan considerations in the national interest.

The Greek-Turkish aid program, the Marshall Plan, the great foreign policy initiatives which have been responsible for avoiding a world war for the past 25 years were approved by that 80th Congress, by a bipartisan majority of which I was proud to be a part.

1972 is before us. It holds precious time in which to accomplish good for this Nation. We must not waste it. I know the political pressures in this session of the Congress will be great. There are more candidates for the Presidency in this chamber today than there probably have been at any one time in the whole history of the Republic. There is an honest division of opinion, not only between the parties but within the parties, on some issues of foreign policy and domestic policy as well.

However, there are great national problems that are so vital they transcend partisanship. Let us have our debates. Let us have our honest differences. But let us join in keeping the national interest first. Let us join in making sure that legislation the Nation needs does not become hostage to the political interest of any party or any person.

There is ample precedent, in this election year, for me to present you with a huge list of new proposals, knowing full well that there could be no possibility that they could be enacted even if you worked night and day.

I shall not do that.

I have presented to the leaders of the Congress today a message of 15,000 words discussing in some detail where the Nation stands and setting forth specific legislative items on which I ask the Congress to act. Much of this is legislation which I proposed in 1969, in 1970, and to the First Session of this 92nd Congress last year, and on which I feel it is essential that action be completed this year.

I am not presenting proposals which have attractive labels but no hope of passage. I am presenting only vital programs which are within the capacity of the Congress to enact, within the capacity of the budget to finance, and which I believe should be above partisanship—programs which deal with urgent priorities for the Nation, which should and must be the subject of bipartisan action by this Congress in the interests of the country in 1972.

When I took the oath of office on the steps of this building just three years ago today, the Nation was ending one of the most tortured decades in its history.

The 1960s were a time of great progress in many areas. They were also a time of great agony—the agonies of war, of inflation, of rapidly rising crime, of deteriorating cities—of hopes raised and disappointed, and of anger and frustration that led finally to violence, and to the worst civil discord in a century.

To recall these troubles is not to point fingers of blame. The Nation was so torn in those final years of the 60s that many in both parties questioned whether America could be governed at all.

The Nation has made significant progress in these first years of the 70s.

Our cities are no longer engulfed by civil disorders.

Our colleges and universities have again become places of learning instead of battlegrounds.

A beginning has been made on preserving and protecting our environment.

The rate of increase in crime has been slowed—and here in the District of Columbia, the one city where the Federal Government has direct jurisdiction, serious crime in 1971 was actually reduced by 13 percent from the year before.

Most important—because of the beginnings that have been made, we can say today that the year 1972 can be the year in which America may make the greatest progress in 25 years toward achieving our goal of being at peace with all the nations in the world.

As our involvement in the war in Vietnam comes to an end, we must now go on to build a generation of peace.

To achieve that goal, we must face realistically the need to maintain our defenses.

In the past three years, we have reduced the burden of arms. For the first time in 20 years, spending on defense has been brought below spending on human resources.

As we look to the future, we find encouraging progress in our negotiations with the Soviet Union on limitation of strategic arms. Looking further into the future, we hope there can eventually be agreement on the mutual reduction of arms. But until there is such a mutual agreement, we must maintain the strength necessary to deter war.

Because of rising research and development costs, because of increases in military and civilian pay, and because of the need to proceed with new weapons systems, my budget for the coming fiscal year will provide for an increase in defense spending.

Strong military defenses are not the enemy of peace. They are the guardian of peace.

There could be no more misguided set of priorities than one which would tempt others by weakening America, and thereby endanger the peace of the world.

In our foreign policies, we have entered a new era. The world has changed greatly in the eleven years since President John F. Kennedy said, in his Inaugural Address, "We shall pay any price, bear any burden, meet any hardship, support any friend, oppose any foe, to assure the survival and the success of liberty."

Our policy has been carefully and deliberately adjusted to meet the new realities of the new world we now live in. We make only those commitments we are able and prepared to meet.

Our commitment to freedom remains strong and unshakable. But others must bear their share of the burden of defending freedom around the world.

This is our policy:

• We will maintain a nuclear deterrent adequate to meet any threat to the security of the United States or of our allies.

• We will help other nations develop the capability of defending themselves.

• We will faithfully honor all of our treaty commitments.

• We will act to defend our interests whenever and wherever they are threatened any place in the world.

• But where our interests or our treaty commitments are not involved our role will be limited.

• We will not intervene militarily.

• But we will use our influence to prevent war.

• If war comes we will use our influence to try to stop it.

• Once war is over we will do our share in helping to bind up the wounds of those who have participated in it.

I shall soon be visiting the Peoples Republic of China and the Soviet Union. I shall go there with no illusions. We have great differences with both powers. We will continue to have great differences. But peach depends on the ability of great powers to live together on the same planet despite their differences. We would not be true to our obligation to generations yet unborn if we failed to seize this moment to do everything in our power to insure that we will be able to talk about these differences rather than fight about them.

As we look back over this century, we can be proud of our Nation's record in foreign affairs.

America has given more generously of itself toward maintaining freedom, preserving peace and alleviating human suffering around the globe than any nation has ever done.

We have fought four wars in this century—but our power has never been used to break the peace, only to keep it; never to destroy freedom, only to defend it. We now have within our reach the goal of ensuring that the next generation can be the first generation in this century to be spared the scourges of war.

Here at home, we are making progress toward our goal of a new prosperity without war.

Industrial production, consumer spending, retail sales and personal income all have been rising. Total employment and real income are the highest in history. New home-building starts this past year reached the highest level ever. Business and consumer confidence have both been rising. Interest rates are down, and the rate of inflation is down. We can look with confidence to 1972 as the year when the back of inflation will finally be broken.

Good as this record is, it is not good enough—not when we still have an unemployment rate of six percent.

It is not enough to point out that this was the rate of the early, peacetime years of the 1960s, or that, if the more than 2 million men released from the Armed Forces and defense-related industries were still on their wartime jobs, unemployment would be far lower.

Our goal is full employment in peacetime—and we intend to meet that goal.

The Congress has helped to meet it by passing our job-creating tax program last month.

The historic monetary agreements we have reached with the major European nations, Canada and Japan will help meet it, by providing new markets for American products—and thus new jobs for American workers.

Our budget will help meet it, by being expansionary without being inflationary—a job-producing budget that will help take up the gap as the economy expands to full employment.

Our program to raise farm income will help meet it, by helping to revitalize rural America—and by giving to America's farms their fair share of America's increasing productivity.

We will also help meet our goal of full employment in peacetime with a set of major initiatives to stimulate more imaginative use of America's great capacity for technological advance, and to direct it toward improving the quality of life for every American.

In reaching the moon, we saw what miracles American technology is capable of achieving. Now the time has come to move more deliberately toward making full use of that technology here on earth, in harnessing the wonders of science to the service of man.

I shall soon send to the Congress a special message proposing a new program of Federal partnership in technological research and development—with Federal incentives to in-crease private research, and federally-supported research on projects designed to improve our everyday lives in ways that will range from improving mass transit to developing new systems of emergency health care that could save thousands of lives annually.

Historically, our superior technology and high productivity have made it possible for America's workers to be the most highly paid in the world, and for our goods still to compete in world markets.

Now that other nations are moving rapidly forward in technology, the answer to the new competition is not to build a wall around America, but rather to remain competitive by improving our own technology still further, and by increasing productivity in American industry.

Our new monetary and trade agreements will make it possible for American goods to compete fairly in the world's markets—but they still must compete. The new technology program will not only put to use the skills of many highly-trained American—skills that might otherwise be wasted. It will also help meet the growing technological challenge from abroad, and thus help to create new industries as well as creating jobs for America's workers in producing for the world's markets.

This Second Session of the 92nd Congress already has before it more than 90 major administration proposals which still await action.

I have discussed these in the written message that I delivered today.

They include our programs to improve life for the aging; to combat crime and drug abuse; to improve health services and to ensure that no one will be denied needed health care because of inability to pay; to protect workers' pension rights; to promote equal opportunity for members of minorities and others who have been left behind; to expand consumer protection; to improve the environment; to revitalize rural America; to help the cities; to launch new iniatives in education; to improve transportation, and to put an end to costly labor tie-ups in transportation.

They also include basic reforms which are essential if our structure of government is to be adequate to the needs of the decades ahead.

They include reform of our wasteful and outmoded welfare system—and substitution of a new system that provides work requirements and work incentives for those who can help themselves, income support for those who cannot help themselves, and fairness for the working poor.

They include a $17.6-billion program of Federal revenue sharing with the States and localities—as an investment in their renewal, and an investment of faith of the people.

They also include a sweeping reorganization of the Executive branch of the Federal Government, so that it will be more efficient, more responsive, and able to meet the challenges of the decades ahead.

One year ago, I laid before the opening session of this Congress six great goals.

One of these was welfare reform. That proposal has been before the Congress now for nearly two and a half years.

My proposals on revenue sharing, government reorganization, health care and the environment have now been before the Congress for nearly a year. Many of my other major proposals have been here as long or longer.

1971 was a year of consideration of these measures. Now let us join in making 1972 a year of action on them—action by the Congress, for the Nation and for the people of America.

In addition, there is one pressing need which I have not previously covered, but which must be placed on the national agenda.

We long have looked to the local property tax as the main source of financing for public primary and secondary education.

As a result, soaring school costs and soaring property tax rates now threaten both our communities and our schools. They threaten communities because property taxes—which more than doubled in the 10 years from 1960 to 1970—have become one of the most oppressive and discriminatory of all taxes, hitting most cruelly at the elderly and the retired; and they threaten schools, as hard-pressed voters understandably reject new bond issues at the polls.

The problem has been given even greater urgency by three recent court decisions, which have held the conventional method of financing schools through local property taxes discriminatory and unconstitutional.

Nearly two years ago, I named a special Presidential Commission to study the problems of school finance, and I also directed the Federal Departments to look into the same problems. We are developing comprehensive proposals to meet these problems.

This issue involves two complex and inter-related sets of problems: support of the schools, and the basic relationships of Federal, State and local governments in any tax reforms.

Under the leadership of the Secretary of the Treasury, we are carefully reviewing the tax aspects; and I have this week enlisted the Advisory Commission on Intergovernmental Relations in addressing the intergovernmental relations aspects.

I have asked this bipartisan Commission to review our proposals for Federal action to cope with the gathering crisis of school finance and property taxes. Later in the year, when both Commissions have completed their studies, I shall make my final recommendations for relieving the burden of property taxes and providing both fair and adequate financing for our children's education.

All of my recommendations, however, will be rooted in one fundamental principle with which there can be no compromise: local school boards must have control over local schools.

As we look ahead over the coming decades, vast new growth and change are not only certainties. They will be the dominant reality of our life in America.

Surveying the certainty of rapid change, we can be like a fallen rider caught in the stirrups—or we can sit high in the saddle, the masters of change, directing it on a course that we choose.

The secret of mastering change in today's world is to reach back to old and proven principles, and to adapt them, with imagination and intelligence, to the new realities of a new age.

This is what we have done in the proposals that I have laid before the Congress. They are rooted in basic principles that are as enduring as human nature and as robust as the American experience; and they are responsive to new conditions. Thus they represent a spirit of change that is really renewal.

As we look back at these old principles, we find them as timely as they are timeless.

We believe in independence, and self-reliance, and in the creative value of the competitive spirit.

We believe in full and equal opportunity for all Americans, and in the protection of individual rights and liberties.

We believe in the family as the keystone of the community, and in the community as the keystone of the Nation.

We believe in compassion toward those in need.

We believe in a system of law, justice and order as the basis of a genuinely free society.

We believe that a person should get what he works for—and those who can should work for what they get.

We believe in the capacity of people to make their own decisions, in their own lives and in their own communities—and we believe in their right to make those decisions.

In applying these principles, we have done so with a full understanding that our quest in the 70s is not merely for more, but for better—for a better quality of life for all Americans.

Thus, for example, we are giving a new measure of attention to cleaning up our air and water, and to making our surroundings more attractive. Thus we are providing broader support for the arts, and helping stimulate a deeper appreciation of what they can contribute to the Nation's activities and to our individual lives.

Nothing matters more to the quality of our lives than the way we treat one another—than our capacity to live respect-

fully together as a unified society, with a full and generous regard for the rights of others and the feelings of others.

As we recover from the turmoil and violence of recent years, as we learn once again to speak with one another instead of shouting at one another, we are regaining that capacity.

As is customary here, on this occasion, I have been talking about programs. These programs are important. But even more important than programs is what we are as a Nation—what we mean as a Nation, to ourselves and to the world.

In New York harbor stands one of the most famous statues in the world—the Statue of Liberty, the gift in 1886 of the people of France to the people of the United States. This statue is more than a landmark; it is a symbol—a symbol of what America has meant to the world.

It reminds us that what America has meant is not its wealth, not its power, but its spirit and purpose—a land that enshrines liberty and opportunity, and that has held out a hand of welcome to millions in search of a better and a fuller and above all, a freer life.

The world's hopes poured into America, along with its people—and those hopes, those dreams, that have been brought from every corner of the world, have become a part of the hope that we hold out to the world.

Four years from now, America will celebrate the 200th anniversary of its founding as a Nation.

There are some who say that the old Spirit of '76 is dead—that we no longer have the strength of character, the idealism, the faith in our founding purposes, that that spirit represents.

Those who say this do not know America.

We have been undergoing self-doubts and self-criticism. But these are the other side of our growing sensitivity to the persistence of want in the midst of plenty, and of our impatience with the slowness with which age-old ills are being overcome.

If we were indifferent to the shortcomings of our society, or complacent about our institutions, or blind to the lingering inequities—then we would have lost our way.

The fact that we have these concerns is evidence that our ideals are still strong: And indeed, they remind us that what is best about America is its compassion. They remind us that in the final analysis, America is great not because it is strong, not because it is rich, but because it is good.

Let us reject the narrow visions of those who would tell us that we are evil because we are not yet perfect, that we are corrupt because we are not yet pure, that all the sweat and toil and sacrifice that have gone into the building of America were for naught because the building is not yet done.

Let us see that the path we are traveling is wide, with room in it for all of us, and that its direction is toward a better Nation in a more peaceful world.

Never has it mattered more that we go forward together.

The leadership of America is here today, in this Chamber—the Supreme Court, the Cabinet, the Senate, the House of Representatives.

Together, we hold the future of the Nation, and the conscience of the Nation, in our hands.

Because this year is an election year, it will be a time of great pressure.

If we yield to that pressure, and fail to deal seriously with the historic challenges that we face, then we will have failed America. We will have failed the trust of millions of Americans, and shaken the confidence they have a right to place in their government.

Never has a Congress had a greater opportunity to leave a legacy of profound and constructive reform for the Nation than this Congress.

If we succeed in these tasks, there will be credit enough for all—not only for doing what is right, but for doing it the right way, by rising above partisan interest to serve the national interest.

If we fail, then more than any of us, America will be the loser.

That is why my call upon the Congress today is for a high statesmanship—so that in the years to come, Americans will look back and say that because it withstood the intense pres-

sures of a political year, and achieved such great good for the American people, and for the future of this Nation—this was truly a great Congress.

NIXON'S STATE OF UNION TEXT II

Following is the text, as made available by the White House, of President Nixon's expanded and more detailed State of the Union message sent to Congress Jan. 20, 1972.

TO THE CONGRESS OF THE UNITED STATES:

It was just 3 years ago today that I took the oath of office as President. I opened my address that day by suggesting that some moments in history stand out "as moments of beginning," when "courses are set that shape decades or centuries." I went on to say that "this can be such a moment."

Looking back 3 years later, I would suggest that it was such a moment—a time in which new courses were set on which we now are traveling. Just how profoundly these new courses will shape our decade or our century is still an unanswered question, however, as we enter the fourth year of this administration. For moments of beginning will mean very little in history unless we also have the determination to follow up on those beginnings.

Setting the course is not enough. Staying the course is an equally important challenge. Good government involves both the responsibility for making fresh starts and the responsibility for perseverance.

The responsibility for perseverance is one that is shared by the President, the public, and the Congress.

• We have come a long way, for example, on the road to ending the Vietnam war and to improving relations with our adversaries. But these initiatives will depend for their lasting meaning on our persistence in seeing them through.

• The magnificent cooperation of the American people has enabled us to make substantial progress in curbing inflation and in reinvigorating our economy. But the new prosperity we seek can be completed only if the public continues in its commitment to economic responsibility and discipline.

• Encouraging new starts have also been made over the last 3 years in treating our domestic ills. But continued progress now requires the Congress to act on its large and growing backlog of pending legislation.

America's agenda for action is already well established as we enter 1972. It will grow in the weeks ahead as we present still more initiatives. But we dare not let the emergence of new business obscure the urgency of old business. Our new agenda will be little more than an empty gesture if we abandon—or even de-emphasize—that part of the old agenda which is yet unfinished.

Getting Ourselves Together

One measure of the Nation's progress in these first years of the Seventies is the improvement in our national morale. While the 1960's were a time of great accomplishment, they were also a time of growing confusion. Our recovery from that condition is not complete, but we have made a strong beginning.

Then we were a shaken and uncertain people, but now we are recovering our confidence. Then we were divided and suspicious, but now we are renewing our sense of common purpose. Then we were surrounded by shouting and posturing, but we have been learning once again to lower our voices. And we have also been learning to listen.

A history of the 1960s' was recently published under the title, *Coming Apart*. But today we can say with confidence that we are coming apart no longer. The "center" of American life has held, and once again we are getting ourselves together.

The Spirit of Reason and Realism

Under the pressures of an election year, it would be easy to look upon the legislative program merely as a political device and not as a serious agenda. We must resist this temptation. The year ahead of us holds precious time in which to accomplish good for this Nation and we must not, we dare not, waste it. Our progress depends on a continuing spirit of partnership between the President and the Congress, between the House and the Senate, between Republicans and Democrats. That spirit does not require us always to agree with one another, but it does require us to approach our tasks, together, in a spirit of reason and realism.

Clear words are the great servant of reason. Intemperate words are the great enemy of reason. The cute slogan, the glib headline, the clever retort, the appeal to passion—these are not the way to truth or to good public policy.

To be dedicated to clear thinking, to place the interests of all above the interests of the few, to hold to ultimate values and to curb momentary passions, to think more about the next generation and less about the next election—these are now our special challenges.

Ending The War

The condition of a nation's spirit cannot be measured with precision, but some of the factors which influence that spirit can. I believe the most dramatic single measurement of the distance we have traveled in the last 36 months is found in the statistics concerning our involvement in the war in Vietnam.

On January 20, 1969 our authorized troop ceiling in Vietnam was 549,500. And there was no withdrawal plan to bring these men home. On seven occasions since that time, I have announced withdrawal decisions—involving a total of 480,500 troops. As a result, our troop ceiling will be only 69,000 by May 1. This means that in 3 years we will have cut our troop strength in Vietnam by 87 percent. As we proceed toward our goal of a South Vietnam fully able to defend itself, we will reduce that level still further.

In this same period, expenditures connected with the war have been cut drastically. There has been a drop of well over 50 percent in American air activity in all of Southeast Asia. Our ground combat role has been ended. Most importantly, there has been a reduction of 95 percent in combat deaths.

Our aim is to cut the death and casualty toll by 100 percent, to obtain the release of those who are prisoners of war, and to end the fighting altogether.

It is my hope that we can end this tragic conflict through negotiation. If we cannot, then we will end it through Vietnamization. But end it we shall—in a way which fulfills our commitment to the people of South Vietnam and which gives them the chance for which they have already sacrificed so much—the chance to choose their own future.

The Lessons of Change

The American people have learned many lessons in the wake of Vietnam—some helpful and some dangerous. One important lesson is that we can best serve our own interests in the world by setting realistic limits on what we try to accomplish unilaterally. For the peace of the world will be more secure, and its progress more rapid, as more nations come to share more fully in the responsibilities for peace and for progress.

At the same time, to conclude that the United States should now withdraw from all or most of its international responsibilities would be to make a dangerous error. There has been a tendency among some to swing from one extreme to the other in the wake of Vietnam, from wanting to do too much in the world to wanting to do too little. We must resist this temptation to over-react. We must stop the swinging pendulum before it moves to an opposite position, and forge instead an attitude toward the world which is balanced and sensible and realistic.

America has an important role to play in international affairs, a great influence to exert for good. As we have throughout this century, we must continue our profound concern for advancing peace and freedom, by the most effective means possible, even as we shift somewhat our view of what means are most effective.

This is our policy:

• We will maintain a nuclear deterrent adequate to meet any threat to the security of the United States or of our allies.

• We will help other nations develop the capability of defending themselves.

• We will faithfully honor all of our treaty commitments.

• We will act to defend our interests whenever and wherever they are threatened any place in the world.

• But where our interests or our treaty commitments are not involved our role will be limited.

• We will not intervene militarily.

• But we will use our influence to prevent war.

• If war comes we will use our influence to try to stop it.

• Once war is over we will do our share in helping to bind up the wounds of those who have participated in it.

Opening New Lines of Communication

Even as we seek to deal more realistically with our partners, so we must also deal more realistically with those who have been our adversaries. In the last year we have made a number of notable advances toward this goal.

In our dealings with the Soviet Union, for example, we have been able, together with our allies, to reach an historic agreement concerning Berlin. We have advanced the prospects for limiting strategic armaments. We have moved toward greater cooperation in space research and toward improving our economic relationships. There have been disappointments such as South Asia and uncertainties such as the Middle East. But there has also been progress we can build on.

It is to build on the progress of the past and to lay the foundations for greater progress in the future that I will soon be visiting the capitals of both the Peoples Republic of China and the Soviet Union. These visits will help to fulfill the promise I made in my Inaugural address when I said "that during this administration our lines of communication will be open," so that we can help create "an open world—open to ideas, open to the exchange of goods and people, a world in which no people, great or small, will live in angry isolation." It is in this spirit that I will undertake these journeys.

We must also be realistic, however, about the scope of our differences with these governments. My visits will mean not that our differences have disappeared or will disappear in the near future. But peace depends on the ability of great powers to live together on the same planet despite their differences. The important thing is that we talk about these differences rather than fight about them.

It would be a serious mistake to say that nothing can come of our expanded communications with Peking and Moscow. But it would also be a mistake to expect too much too quickly.

It would also be wrong to focus so much attention on these new opportunities that we neglect our old friends. That is why I have met in the last few weeks with the leaders of two of our

hemisphere neighbors, Canada and Brazil, with the leaders of three great European nations, and with the Prime Minister of Japan. I believe these meetings were extremely successful in cementing our understandings with these governments as we move forward together in a fast changing period.

Our consultations with our allies may not receive as much attention as our talks with potential adversaries. But this makes them no less important. The cornerstone of our foreign policy remains—and will remain—our close bonds with our friends around the world.

A Strong Defense: The Guardian of Peace

There are two additional elements which are critical to our efforts to strengthen the structure of peace.

The first of these is the military strength of the United States.

In the last 3 years we have been moving from a wartime to a peacetime footing, from a period of continued confrontation and arms competition to a period of negotiation and potential arms limitation, from a period when America often acted as policeman for the world to a period when other nations are assuming greater responsibility for their own defense. I was recently encouraged, for example, by the decision of our European allies to increase their share of the NATO defense budget by some $1 billion.

As a part of this process, we have ended the production of chemical and biological weaponry and have converted two of our largest facilities for such production to humanitarian research. We have been able to reduce and in some periods even to eliminate draft calls. In 1971, draft calls—which were as high as 382,000 at the peak of the Vietnam war—fell below 100,000, the lowest level since 1962. In the coming year they will be significantly lower. I am confident that by the middle of next year we can achieve our goal of reducing draft calls to zero.

As a result of all these developments, our defense spending has fallen to 7 percent of our gross national product in the current fiscal year, compared with 8.3 percent in 1964 and 9.5 percent in 1968. That figure will be down to 6.4 percent in fiscal year 1973. Without sacrificing any of our security interests, we have been able to bring defense spending below the level of human resource spending for the first time in 20 years. This condition is maintained in my new budget—which also, for the first time, allocates more money to the Department of Health, Education, and Welfare than to the Department of Defense.

But just as we avoid extreme reactions in our political attitudes toward the world, so we must avoid over-reacting as we plan for our defense. We have reversed spending priorities, but we have never compromised our national security. And we never will. For any step which weakens America's defenses will also weaken the prospects for peace.

Our plans for the next year call for an increase in defense spending. That increase is made necessary in part by rising research and development costs, in part by military pay increases—which, in turn, will help us eliminate the draft—and in part by the need to proceed with new weapon systems to maintain our security at an adequate level. Even as we seek with the greatest urgency stable controls on armaments, we cannot ignore the fact that others are going forward with major increases in their own arms programs.

In the year ahead we will be working to improve and protect, to diversify and disperse our strategic forces in ways which make them even less vulnerable to attack and more effective in deterring war. I will request a substantial budget increase to preserve the sufficiency of our strategic nuclear deterrent, including an allocation of over $900 million to improve our sea-based deterrent force. I recently directed the Department of Defense to develop a program to build additional missile launching submarines, carrying a new and far mor effective missile. We will also proceed with programs to reoutfit our Polaris submarines with the Poseidon missile system, to replace older land-based missiles with Minuteman III, and to deploy the SAFEGUARD Antiballistic Missile System.

At the same time, we must move to maintain our strength at sea. The Navy's budget was increased by $2 billion in the current fiscal year, and I will ask for a similar increase next year, with particular emphasis on our shipbuilding programs.

Our military research and development program must also be stepped up. Our budget in this area was increased by $594 million in the current fiscal year and I will recommend a further increase for next year of $838 million. I will also propose a substantial program to develop and procure more effective weapons systems for our land and tactical air forces, and to improve the National Guard and Reserves, providing more modern weapons and better training.

In addition, we will expand our strong program to attract volunteer career soldiers so that we can phase out the draft. With the cooperation of the Congress, we have been able to double the basic pay of first-time enlistees. Further substantial military pay increases are planned. I will also submit to the Congress an overall reform of our military retirement and survivor benefit programs, raising the level of protection for military families. In addition, we will expand efforts to improve race relations, to equalize promotional opportunities, to control drug abuse, and generally to improve the quality of life in the Armed Forces.

As we take all of these steps, let us remember that strong military defenses are not the enemy of peace; they are the guardians of peace. Our ability to build a stable and tranquil world—to achieve an arms control agreement, for example—depends on our ability to negotiate from a position of strength. We seek adequate power not as an end in itself but as a means for achieving our purpose. And our purpose is peace.

In my Inaugural address 3 years ago I called for cooperation to reduce the burden of arms—and I am encouraged by the progress we have been making toward that goal. But I also added this comment: "...to all those who would be tempted by weakness, let us leave no doubt that we will be as strong as we need to be for as long as we need to be." Today I repeat that reminder.

A Realistic Program of Foreign Assistance

Another important expression of America's interest and influence in the world is our foreign assistance effort. This effort has special significance at a time when we are reducing our direct military presence abroad and encouraging other countries to assume greater responsibilities. Their growing ability to undertake these responsibilities often depends on America's foreign assistance.

We have taken significant steps to reform our foreign assistance programs in recent years, to eliminate waste and to give them greater impact. Now three further imperatives rest with the Congress:

• To fund in full the levels of assistance which I have earlier recommended for the current fiscal year, before the present interim funding arrangement expires in late February;

• To act upon the fundamental aid reform proposals submitted by this administration in 1971;

• And to modify those statutes which govern our response to expropriation of American property by foreign governments, as I recommended in my recent statement on the security of overseas investments.

These actions, taken together, will constitute not an exception to the emerging pattern for a more realistic American role in the world, but rather a fully consistent and crucially important element in that pattern.

As we work to help our partners in the world community develop their economic potential and strengthen their military forces, we should also cooperate fully with them in meeting international challenges such as the menace of narcotics, the threat of pollution, the growth of population, the proper use of the seas and seabeds, and the plight of those who have been victimized by wars and natural disasters. All of these are global problems and they must be confronted on a global basis. The efforts of the United Nations to respond creatively to these challenges have been most promising, as has the work of NATO in the environmental field. Now we must build on these beginnings.

America's Influence for Good

The United States is not the world's policeman nor the keeper of its moral conscience. But—whether we like it or not—we still represent a force for stability in what has too often been an unstable world, a force for justice in a world which is too often unjust, a force for progress in a world which desperately needs to progress, a force for peace in a world that is weary of war.

We can have a great influence for good in our world—and for that reason we bear a great responsibility. Whether we fulfill that responsibility—whether we fully use our influence for good—these are questions we will be answering as we reshape our attitudes and policies toward other countries, as we determine our defensive capabilities, and as we make fundamental decisions about foreign assistance. I will soon discuss these and other concerns in greater detail in my annual report to the Congress on foreign policy.

Our influence for good in the world depends, of course, not only on decisions which touch directly on international affairs but also on our internal strength—on our sense of pride and purpose, on the vitality of our economy, on the success of our efforts to build a better life for all our people. Let us turn then from the state of the Union abroad to the state of the Union at home.

The Economy: Toward A New Prosperity

Just as the Vietnam war occasioned much of our spiritual crisis, so it lay at the root of our economic problems 3 years ago. The attempt to finance that war through budget deficits in a period of full employment had produced a wave of price inflation as dangerous and as persistent as any in our history. It was more persistent, frankly, than I expected it would be when I first took office. And it only yielded slowly to our dual efforts to cool the war and to cool inflation.

Our challenge was further compounded by the need to reabsorb more than 2 million persons who were released from the Armed Forces and from defense-related industries and by the substantial expansion of the labor force.

In short, the escalation of the Vietnam war in the late 1960's destroyed price stability. And the de-escalation of that war in the early 1970's impeded full employment.

Throughout these years, however, I have remained convinced that both price stability and full employment were realistic goals for this country. By last summer it became apparent that our efforts to eradicate inflation without wage and price controls would either take too long or—if they were to take effect quickly—would come at the cost of persistent high unemployment. This cost was unacceptable. On August 15th I therefore announced a series of new economic policies to speed our progress toward a new prosperity without inflation in peacetime.

These policies have received the strong support of the Congress and the American people, and as a result they have been effective. To carry forward these policies, three important steps were taken this past December—all within a brief 2-week period—which will also help to make the coming year a very good year for the American economy.

On December 10, I signed into law the Revenue Act of 1971, providing tax cuts over the next 3 years of some $15 billion, cuts which I requested to stimulate the economy and to provide hundreds of thousands to new jobs. On December 22, I signed into law the Economic Stabilization Act Amendments of 1971, which will allow us to continue our program of wage and price restraints to break the back of inflation.

Between these two events, on December 18, I was able to announce a major breakthrough on the international economic front—reached in cooperation with our primary economic partners. This breakthrough will mitigate the intolerable strains which were building up in the world's monetary and payments structure and will lead to a removal of trade barriers which have impeded American exports. It also sets the stage for broader reforms in the international monetary system so that we can avoid repeated monetary crises in the future. Both the monetary realignment—the first of its scope in history—and our progress in readjusting trade conditions will mean better markets for American goods abroad and more jobs for American workers at home.

A Brighter Economic Picture

As a result of all these steps, the economic picture—which has brightened steadily during the last 5 months—will, I believe, continue to grow brighter. This is not my judgment alone; it is widely shared by the American people. Virtually every survey and forecast in recent weeks shows a substantial improvement in public attitudes about the economy—which are themselves so instrumental in shaping economic realities.

The inflationary psychology which gripped our Nation so tightly for so long is on the ebb. Business and consumer confidence has been rising. Businessmen are planning a 9.1 percent increase in plant and equipment expenditures in 1972, more than four times as large as the increase in 1971. Consumer spending and retail sales are on the rise. Home building is booming—housing starts last year were up more than 40 percent from 1970, setting an all-time record. Interest rates are sharply down. Both income and production are rising. Real out put in our economy in the last 3 months of 1971 grew at a rate that was about double that of the previous two quarters.

Perhaps most importantly, total employment has moved above the 80 million mark—to a record high—and is growing rapidly. In the last 5 months of 1971, some 1.1 million additional jobs were created in our economy and only a very unusual increase in the size of our total labor force kept the unemployment rate from falling.

But whatever the reason, 6 percent unemployment is too high. I am determined to cut that percentage—through a variety of measures. The budget I present to the Congress next week will be an expansionary budget—reflecting the impact of new job-creating tax cuts and job-creating expenditures. We will also push to increase employment through our programs for manpower training and public service employment, through our efforts to expand foreign markets, and through other new initiatives.

Expanded employment in 1972 will be different, however, from many other periods of full prosperity. For it will come without the stimulus of war—and it will come without inflation. Our program of wage and price controls is working. The consumer price index, which rose at a yearly rate of slightly over 6 percent during 1969 and the first half of 1970, rose at a rate of only 1.7 percent from August through November of 1971.

I would emphasize once again, however, that our ultimate objective is lasting price stability without controls. When we achieve an end to the inflationary psychology which developed in the 1960's, we will return to our traditional policy of relying on free market forces to determine wages and prices.

I would also emphasize that while our new budget will be in deficit, the deficit will not be irresponsible. It will be less than this year's actual deficit and would disappear entirely under full employment conditions. While Federal spending continues to grow, the rate of increase in spending has been cut very sharply—to little more than half that experienced under the previous administration. The fact that our battle against inflation has led us to adopt a new policy of wage and price restraints should not obscure the continued importance of our fiscal and monetary policies in holding down the cost of living.

It is most important that the Congress join now in resisting the temptation to overspend and in accepting the discipline of a balanced full employment budget.

I will soon present a more complete discussion of all of these matters in my Budget Message and in my Economic Report.

A New Era in International Economics

Just as we have entered a new period of negotiation in world politics, so we have also moved into a new period of negotiation on the international economic front. We expect these negotiations to help us build both a new international system for the exchange of money and a new system of international trade. These accomplishments, in turn, can open a new era of fair competition and constructive interdependence in the global economy.

We have already made important strides in this direction. The realignment of exchange rates which was announced last month represents an important forward step—but now we also need basic long-range monetary reform. We have made an important beginning toward altering the conditions for international trade and investment—and we expect further substantial progress. I would emphasize that progress for some nations in these fields need not come at the expense of others. All nations will benefit from the right kind of monetary and trade reform.

Certainly the United States has a high stake in such improvements. Our international economic position has been slowly deteriorating now for some time—a condition which could have dangerous implications for both our influence abroad and our prosperity at home. It has been estimated, for example, that full employment prosperity will depend on the creation of some 20 million additional jobs in this decade. And expanding our foreign markets is a most effective way to expand domestic employment.

One of the major reasons for the weakening of our international economic position is that the ground rules for the exchange of goods and money have forced us to compete with one hand tied behind our back. One of our most important accomplishments in 1971 was our progress in changing this situation.

Competing More Effectively

Monetary and trade reforms are only one part of this story. The ability of the United States to hold its own in world competition depends not only on the fairness of the rules, but also on the competitiveness of our economy. We have made great progress in the last few months in improving the terms of competition. Now we must also do all we can to strengthen the ability of our own economy to compete.

We stand today at a turning point in the history of our country—and in the history of our planet. On the one hand, we have the opportunity to help bring a new economic order to the world, an open order in which nations eagerly face outward to build that network of interdependence which is the best foundation for prosperity and for peace. But we will also be tempted in the months ahead to take the opposite course—to withdraw from the world economically as some would have us withdraw politically, to build an economic "Fortress America" within which our growing weakness could be concealed. Like a child who will not go out to play with other children, we would probably be saved a few minor bumps and bruises in the short run if we were to adopt this course. But in the long run the world would surely pass us by.

I reject this approach. I remain committed to that open world I discussed in my Inaugural address. That is why I have worked for a more inviting climate for America's economic activity abroad. That is why I have placed so much emphasis on increasing the productivity of our economy at home. And that is also why I believe so firmly that we must stimulate more long-range investment in our economy, find more effective ways to develop and use new technology, and do a better job of training and using skilled manpower.

An acute awareness of the international economic challenge led to the creation just one year ago of the Cabinet-level Council on International Economic Policy. This new institution has helped us to understand this challenge better and to respond to it more effectively.

As our understanding deepens, we will discover additional ways of improving our ability to compete. For example, we can enhance our competitive position by moving to implement the metric system of measurement, a proposal which the Secretary of Commerce presented in detail to the Congress last year. And we should also be doing far more to gain our fair share of the international tourism market, now estimated at $17 billion annually, one of the largest factors in world trade. A substantial part of our balance of payments deficit results from the fact that American tourists abroad spend $2.5 billion more than foreign tourists spend in the United States. We can help correct this situation by attracting more foreign tourists to our shores—especially as we enter our Bicentennial era. I am therefore requesting that the budget for the United States Travel Service be nearly doubled in the coming year.

The Unfinished Agenda

Our progress toward building a new economic order at home and abroad has been made possible by the cooperation and cohesion of the American people. I am sure that many Americans had misgivings about one aspect or another of the new economic policies I introduced last summer. But most have nevertheless been ready to accept this new effort in order to build the broad support which is essential for effective change.

The time has now come for us to apply this same sense of realism and reasonability to other reform proposals which have been languishing on our domestic agenda. As was the case with our economic policies, most Americans agree that we need a change in our welfare system, in our health strategy, in our programs to improve the environment, in the way we finance State and local government, and in the organization of government at the Federal level. Most Americans are not satisfied with the status quo in education, in transportation, in law enforcement, in drug control, in community development. In each of these areas —and in others—I have put forward specific proposals which are responsive to this deep desire for change.

And yet achieving change has often been difficult. There has been progress in some areas, but for the most part, as a nation we have not shown the same sense of self-discipline in our response to social challenges that we have developed in meeting our economic needs. We have not been as ready as we should have been to compromise our differences and to build a broad coalition for change. And so we often have found ourselves in a situation of stalemate—doing essentially nothing even though most of us agree that nothing is the very worst thing we can do.

Two years ago this week, and again one year ago, my messages on the state of the Union contained broad proposals for domestic reform. I am presenting a number of new proposals in this year's message. But I also call once again, with renewed urgency, for action on our unfinished agenda.

Welfare Reform

The first item of unfinished business is welfare reform.

Since I first presented my proposals in August of 1969, some 4 million additional persons have been added to our welfare rolls. The cost of our old welfare system has grown by an additional $4.2 billion. People have not been moving as fast as they should from welfare rolls to payrolls. Too much of the traffic has been the other way.

Our antiquated welfare system is responsible for this calamity. Our new program of "workfare" would begin to end it.

Today, more than ever, we need a new program which is based on the dignity of work, which provides strong incentives for work, and which includes for those who are able to work an effective work requirement. Today, more than ever, we need a new program which helps hold families together rather than driving them apart, which provides day care services so that low income mothers can trade dependence on government for the dignity of employment, which relieves intolerable fiscal pressures on State and local governments, and which replaces 54 administrative systems with a more efficient and reliable nationwide approach.

I have now given prominent attention to this subject in three consecutive messages on the state of the Union. The House of Representatives has passed welfare reform twice. Now that the new economic legislation has been passed, I urge the Senate Finance Committee to place welfare reform at the top of its agenda. It is my earnest hope that when this Congress adjourns, welfare reform will not be an item of pending business but an accomplished reality.

Revenue Sharing: Returning Power to the People

At the same time that I introduced my welfare proposals 2-1/2 years ago, I also presented a program for sharing Federal revenues with State and local governments. Last year I greatly expanded on this concept. Yet, despite undisputed evidence of compelling needs, despite overwhelming public support, despite the endorsement of both major political parties and most of the Nation's Governors and mayors, and despite the fact that most other nations with federal systems of government already have such a program, revenue sharing still remains on the list of unfinished business.

I call again today for the enactment of revenue sharing. During its first full year of operation our proposed programs would spend $17.6 billion, both for general purposes and through six special purpose programs for law enforcement, manpower, education, transportation, rural community development, and urban community development.

As with welfare reform, the need for revenue sharing becomes more acute as time passes. The financial crisis of State and local government is deepening. The pattern of breakdown in State and municpal services grows more threatening. Inequitable tax pressures are mounting. The demand for more flexible and more responsive government—at levels closer to the problems and closer to the people—is building.

Revenue sharing can help us meet these challenges. It can help reverse what has been the flow of power and resources toward Washington by sending power and resources back to the States, to the communities, and to the people. Revenue sharing can bring a new sense of accountability, a new burst of energy and a new spirit of creativity to our federal system.

I am pleased that the House Ways and Means Committee has made revenue sharing its first order of business in the new session. I urge the Congress to enact in this session, not an empty program which bears the revenue sharing label while continuing the outworn system of categorical grants, but a bold, comprehensive program of genuine revenue sharing.

I also presented last year a $100 million program of planning and management grants to help the States and localities do a better job of analyzing their problems and carrying out solutions. I hope this program will also be quickly accepted. For only as State and local governments get a new lease on life can we hope to bring government back to the people—and with it a stronger sense that each individual can be in control of his life, that every person can make a difference.

Overhauling the Machinery of Government: Executive Reorganization

As we work to make State and local government more responsive—and more responsible—let us also seek these same goals at the Federal level. I again urge the Congress to enact my proposals for reorganizing the executive branch of the Federal Government. Here again, support from the general public—as well as from those who have served in the executive branch under several Presidents—has been most encouraging. So has the success of the important organizational reforms we have already made. These have included a restructured Executive Office of the President—with a new Domestic Council, a new Office of Management and Budget, and other units; reorganized field operations in Federal agencies; stronger mechanisms for interagency coordination, such as Federal Regional Councils; a new United States Postal Service; and new offices for such purposes as protecting the environment, coordinating communications policy, helping the consumer, and stimulating voluntary service. But the centerpiece of our efforts to streamline the executive branch still awaits approval.

How the government is put together often determines how well the government can do its job. Our Founding Fathers understood this fact—and thus gave detailed attention to the most precise structural questions. Since that time, however, and especially in recent decades, new responsibilities and new constituencies have caused the structure they established to expand enormously—and in a piecemeal and haphazard fashion.

As a result, our Federal Government today is too often a sluggish and unresponsive institution, unable to deliver a dollar's worth of service for a dollar's worth of taxes.

My answer to this problem is to streamline the executive branch by reducing the overall number of executive departments and by creating four new departments in which existing responsibilities would be refocused in a coherent and comprehensive way. The rationale which I have advanced calls for organizing these new departments around the major purposes of the government—by creating a Department of Natural Resources, a Department of Human Resources, a Department of Community Development, and a Department of Economic Affairs. I have revised my original plan so that we would not eliminate the Department of Agriculture but rather restructure that Department so it can focus more effectively on the needs of farmers.

The Congress has recently reorganized its own operations, and the Chief Justice of the United States has led a major effort to reform and restructure the judicial branch. The impulse for reorganization is strong and the need for reorganization is clear. I hope the Congress will not let this opportunity for sweeping reform of the executive branch slip away.

A New Approach to the Delivery of Social Services

As a further step to put the machinery of government in proper working order, I will also propose new legislation to reform and rationalize the way in which social services are delivered to families and individuals.

Today it often seems that our service programs are unresponsive to the recipients' needs and wasteful of the taxpayers' money. A major reason is their extreme fragmentation. Rather than pulling many services together, our present system separates them into narrow and rigid categories. The father of a family is helped by one program, his daughter by another, and his elderly parents by a third. An individual goes to one place for nutritional help, to another for health services, and to still another for educational counseling. A community finds that it cannot transfer Federal funds from one program area to another area in which needs are more pressing.

Meanwhile, officials at all levels of government find themselves wasting enormous amounts of time, energy, and the taxpayers' money untangling Federal red tape—time and energy and dollars which could better be spent in meeting people's needs.

We need a new approach to the delivery of social services—one which is built around people and not around programs. We need an approach which treats a person as a whole and which treats the family as a unit. We need to break through rigid categorical walls, to open up narrow bureaucratic compartments, to consolidate and coordinate related programs in a comprehensive approach to related problems.

The Allied Services Act which will soon be submitted to the Congress offers one set of tools for carrying out that new approach in the programs of the Department of Health, Education and Welfare. It would strengthen State and local planning and administrative capacities, allow for the transfer of funds among various HEW programs, and permit the waiver of certain cumbersome Federal requirements. By streamlining and simplifying the delivery of services, it would help more people move more rapidly from public dependency toward the dignity of being self-sufficient.

Good men and good money can be wasted on bad mechanisms. By giving those mechanisms a thorough overhaul, we can help to restore the confidence of the people in the capacities of their government.

Protecting the Environment

A central theme of both my earlier messages on the state of the Union was the state of our environment—and the importance of making "our peace with nature." The last few years have been a time in which environmental values have become firmly embedded in our attitudes—and in our institutions. At the Federal level, we have established a new Environmental Protection Agency, a new Council on Environmental Quality and a new National Oceanic and Atmospheric Administration, and we have proposed an entire new Department of Natural Resources. New air quality standards have been set, and there is evidence that the air in many cities is becoming less polluted. Under authority granted by the Refuse Act of 1899, we have instituted a new permit program which, for the first time, allows the Federal Government to inventory all significant industrial sources of water pollution and to specify required abatement actions. Under the Refuse Act, more than 160 civil actions and 320 criminal actions to stop water pollution have been filed against alleged polluters in the last 12 months. Major programs have also been launched to build new municipal waste treatment facilities, to stop pollution from Federal facilities, to expand our wilderness areas, and to leave a legacy of parks for future generations. Our outlays for inner city parks have been significantly expanded, and 62 Federal tracts have been transferred to the States and to local governments for recreational uses. In the coming year, I hope to transfer to local park use much more Federal land which is suitable for recreation but which is now underutilized. I trust the Congress will not delay this process.

The most striking fact about environmental legislation in the early 1970's is how much has been proposed and how little has been enacted. Of the major legislative proposals I made in my special message to the Congress on the environment last winter, 18 are still awaiting final action. They include measures to regulate pesticides and toxic substances, to control noise pollution, to restrict dumping in the oceans, in coastal waters, and in the Great Lakes, to create an effective policy for the use and development of land, to regulate the siting of power plants, to control strip mining, and to help achieve many other important environmental goals. The unfinished agenda also includes our National Resource Land Management Act, and other measures to improve environmental protection on federally owned lands.

The need for action in these areas is urgent. The forces which threaten our environment will not wait while we procrastinate. Nor can we afford to rest on last year's agenda in the environmental field. For as our understanding of these problems increases, so must our range of responses. Accordingly, I will soon be sending to the Congress another message on the environment that will present further administrative and legislative initiatives. Altogether our new budget will contain more than three times as much money for environmental programs in fiscal year 1973 as we spent in fiscal year 1969. To fail in meeting the environmental challenge, however, would be even more costly.

I urge the Congress to put aside narrow partisan perspectives that merely ask "whether" we should act to protect the environment and to focus instead on the more difficult question of "how" such action can most effectively be carried out.

Abundant Clean Energy

In my message to the Congress on energy policy, last June, I outlined additional steps relating to the environment which also merit renewed attention. The challenge, as I defined it, is to produce a sufficient supply of energy to fuel our industrial civilization and at the same time to protect a beautiful and healthy environment. I am convinced that we can achieve both these goals, that we can respect our good earth without turning our back on progress.

In that message last June, I presented a long list of means for assuring an ample supply of clean energy—including the liquid metal fast breeder reactor—and I again emphasize their importance. Because it often takes several years to bring new technologies into use in the energy field, there is no time for delay. According, I am including in my new budget increased funding for the most promising of these and other clean energy programs. By acting this year, we can avoid having to choose in some future year between too little energy and too much pollution.

Keeping People Healthy

The National Health Strategy I outlined last February is designed to achieve one of the Nation's most important goals for the 1970's, improving the quality and availability of medical care, while fighting the trend toward runaway costs. Important elements of that strategy have already been enacted. The Comprehensive Health Manpower Training Act and the Nurse Training Act, which I signed on November 18, represent the most far-reaching effort in our history to increase the supply of doctors, nurses, dentists and other health professionals and to attract them to areas which are experiencing manpower shortages. The National Cancer Act, which I signed on December 23, marked the climax of a year-long effort to step up our campaign against cancer. During the past year, our cancer research budget has been increased by $100 million and the full weight of my office has been given to our all-out war on this disease. We have also expanded the fight against sickle cell anemia by an additional $5 million.

I hope that action on these significant fronts during the first session of the 92nd Congress will now be matched by action in other areas during the second session. The Health Maintenance Organization Act, for example, is an essential tool for helping doctors deliver care more effectively and more efficiently with a greater emphasis on prevention and early treatment. By working to keep our people healthy instead of treating us only when we are sick, Health Maintenance Organizations can do a great deal to help us reduce medical costs.

Our National Health Insurance Partnership legislation is also essential to assure that no American is denied basic medical care because of inability to pay. Too often, present health insurance leaves critical outpatient services uncovered, distorting the way in which facilities are used. It also fails to protect adequately against catastrophic costs and to provide sufficient assistance for the poor. The answer I have suggested is a comprehensive national plan—not one that nationalizes our private health insurance industry but one that corrects the weaknesses in that system while building on its considerable strengths.

A large part of the enormous increase in the Nation's expenditures on health in recent years has gone not to additional services but merely to meet price inflation. Our efforts to balance the growing demand for care with an increased supply of services will help to change this picture. So will that part of our economic program which is designed to control medical costs. I am confident that with the continued cooperation of those who provide health services, we will succeed on this most important battlefront in our war against inflation.

Our program for the next year will also include further funding increases for health research—including substantial new sums for cancer and sickle cell anemia—as well as further increases for medical schools and for meeting special problems such as drug addiction and alcoholism. We also plan to construct new veterans hospitals and expand the staffs at existing ones.

In addition, we will be giving increased attention to the fight against diseases of the heart, blood vessels and lungs, which presently account for more than half of all the deaths in this country. It is deeply disturbing to realize that, largely because of heart disease, the mortality rate for men under the age of 55 is about twice as great in the United States as it is, for example, in some Scandinavian countries.

I will shortly assign a panel of distinguished experts to help us determine why heart disease is so prevalent and so menacing and what we can do about it. I will also recommend an expanded budget for the National Heart and Lung Institute. The young father struck down by a heart attack in the prime of life, the productive citizen crippled by a stroke, an older person tortured by breathing difficulties during his later years—these are tragedies which can be reduced in number and we must do all that is possible to reduce them.

Nutrition

One of the critical areas in which we have worked to advance the health of the Nation is that of combating hunger and improving nutrition. With the increases in our new budget, expenditures on our food stamp program will have increased ninefold since 1969, to the $2.3 billion level. Spending on school lunches for needy children will have increased more than sevenfold, from $107 million in 1969 to $770 million in 1973. Because of new regulations which will be implemented in the year ahead, we will be able to increase further both the equity of our food stamp program and the adequacy of its benefits.

Coping with Accidents— and Preventing Them

Last year, more than 115,000 Americans lost their lives in accidents. Four hundred thousand more were permanently disabled and 10 million were temporarily disabled. The loss to our economy from accidents last year is estimated at over $28 billion. These are sad and staggering figures—especially since this toll could be greatly reduced by upgrading our emergency medical services. Such improvement does not even require new scientific breakthroughs; it only requires that we apply our present knowledge more effectively.

To help in this effort, I am directing the Department of Health, Education and Welfare to develop new ways of organizing emergency medical services and of providing care to accident victims. By improving communication, transportation, and the training of emergency personnel, we can save many thousands of lives which would otherwise be lost to accidents and sudden illnesses.

One of the significant joint accomplishments of the Congress and this administration has been a vigorous new program to protect against job-related accidents and illnesses. Our occupational health and safety program will be further strengthened in the year ahead—as will our ongoing efforts to promote air traffic safety, boating safety, and safety on the highways.

In the last 3 years, the motor vehicle death rate has fallen by 13 percent, but we still lose some 50,000 lives on our highways *each year*—more than we have lost in combat in the entire Vietnam war.

Fully one-half of these deaths were directly linked to alcohol. This appalling reality is a blight on our entire Nation—and only the active concern of the entire Nation can remove it. The Federal Government will continue to help all it can, through its efforts to promote highway safety and automobile safety, and through stronger programs to help the problem drinker.

Yesterday's Goals:
Tomorrow's Accomplishments

Welfare reform, revenue sharing, executive reorganization, environmental protection, and the new national health strategy —these, along with economic improvement, constituted the six great goals I emphasized in my last State of the Union address— six major components of a New American Revolution. They remain six areas of great concern today. With the cooperation of the Congress, they can be six areas of great accomplishment tomorrow.

But the challenges we face cannot be reduced to six categories. Our problems—and our opportunities—are manifold, and action on many fronts is required. It is partly for this reason that my State of the Union address this year includes this written message to the Congress. For it gives me the chance to discuss more fully a number of programs which also belong on our list of highest priorities.

Action for the Aging

Last month, I joined with thousands of delegates to the White House Conference on Aging in a personal commitment to make 1972 a year of action on behalf of 21 million older Americans. Today I call on the Congress to join me in that pledge. For unless the American dream comes true for our older generation it cannot be complete for any generation.

We can begin to make this a year of action for the aging by acting on a number of proposals which have been pending since 1969. For older Americans, the most significant of these is the bill designated H.R. 1. This legislation, which also contains our general welfare reform measures, would place a national floor under the income of all older Americans, guarantee inflation-proof social security benefits, allow social security recipients to earn more from their own work, increase benefits for widows, and provide a 5-percent across-the-board increase in social security. Altogether, HR 1—as it now stands—would mean some $5.5 billion in increased benefits for America's older citizens. I hope the Congress will also take this opportunity to eliminate the $5.80 monthly fee now charged under Part B of Medicare— a step which would add an additional $1.5 billion to the income of the elderly. These additions would come on top of earlier social security increases totalling some $3 billion over the last 3 years.

A number of newer proposals also deserve approval. I am requesting that the budget of the Administration on Aging be increased five-fold over last year's request, to $100 million, in part so that we can expand programs which help older citizens live dignified lives in their own homes. I am recommending substantially larger budgets for those programs which give older Americans a better chance to serve their countrymen—Retired Senior Volunteers, Foster Grandparents, and others. And we

will also work to ease the burden of property taxes which so many older Americans find so inequitable and so burdensome. Other initiatives, including proposals for extending and improving the Older Americans Act, will be presented as we review the recommendations of the White House Conference on Aging. Our new Cabinet-level Domestic Council Committee on Aging has these recommendations at the top of its agenda.

We will also be following up in 1972 on one of the most important of our 1971 initiatives—the crackdown on substandard nursing homes. Our follow-through will give special attention to providing alternative arrangements for those who are victimized by such facilities.

The legislation I have submitted to provide greater financial security at retirement, both for those now covered by private pension plans and those who are not, also merits prompt action by the Congress. Only half the country's work force is now covered by tax deductible private pensions; the other half deserve a tax deduction for their retirement savings too. Those who are now covered by pension plans deserve the assurance that their plans are administered under strict fiduciary standards with full disclosure. And they should also have the security provided by prompt vesting—the assurance that even if one leaves a given job, he can still receive the pension he earned there when he retires. The legislation I have proposed would achieve these goals, and would also raise the limit on deductible pension savings for the self-employed.

The state of our Union is strong today because of what older Americans have so long been giving to their country. The state of our Union will be stronger tomorrow if we recognize how much they still can contribute. The best thing our country can give to its older citizens is the chance to be a part of it, the chance to play a continuing role in the great American adventure.

Equal Opportunity for Minorities

America cannot be at its best as it approaches its 200th birthday unless all Americans have the opportunity to be at their best. A free and open American society, one that is true to the ideals of its founders, must give each of its citizens an equal chance at the starting line and an equal opportunity to go as far and as high as his talents and energies will take him.

The Nation can be proud of the progress it has made in assuring equal opportunity for members of minority groups in recent years. There are many measures of our progress.

Since 1969, we have virtually eliminated the dual school system in the South. Three years ago, 68 percent of all black children in the South were attending all black schools; today only 9 percent are attending schools which are entirely black. Nationally, the number of 100 percent minority schools has decreased by 70 percent during the past 3 years. To further expand educational opportunity, my proposed budget for predominantly black colleges will exceed $200 million next year, more than double the level of 3 years ago.

On the economic front, overall Federal aid to minority business enterprise has increased threefold in the last 3 years, and I will propose a further increase of $90 million. Federal hiring among minorities has been intensified, despite cutbacks in Federal employment, so that one-fifth of all Federal employees are now members of minority groups. Building on strong efforts such as the Philadelphia Plan, we will work harder to ensure that Federal contractors meet fair hiring standards. Compliance reviews will be stepped up, to a level more than 300 percent higher than in 1969. Our proposed budget for the Equal Employment Opportunity Commission will be up 36 percent next year, while our proposed budget for enforcing fair housing laws will grow by 20 percent. I also support legislation to strengthen the enforcement powers of the EEOC by providing the Commission with authority to seek court enforcement of its decisions and by giving it jurisdiction over the hiring practices of State and local governments.

Overall, our proposed budget for civil rights activities is up 25 per cent for next year, an increase which will give us nearly three times as much money for advancing civil rights as we had 3 years ago. We also plan a 42 percent increase in the budget for the Cabinet Committee on Opportunities for the Spanish speaking. And I will propose that the Congress extend the operations of the Civil Rights Commission for another 5-year period.

Self-Determination for Indians

One of the major initiatives in the second year of my Presidency was designed to bring a new era in which the future for American Indians is determined by Indian acts and Indian decisions. The comprehensive program I put forward sought to avoid the twin dangers of paternalism on the one hand and the termination of trust responsibility on the other. Some parts of this program have now become effective, including a generous settlement of the Alaska Native Claims and the return to the Taos Pueblo Indians of the sacred lands around Blue Lake. Construction grants have been authorized to assist the Navajo Community College, the first Indian-managed institution of higher education.

We are also making progress toward Indian self-determination on the administrative front. A newly reorganized Bureau of Indian Affairs, with almost all-Indian leadership, will from now on be concentrating its resources on a program of reservation-by-reservation development, including redirection of employment assistance to strengthen reservation economies, creating local Indian Action Teams for manpower training, and increased contracting of education and other functions to Indian communities.

I again urge the Congress to join in helping Indians help themselves in fields such as health, education, the protection of land and water rights, and economic development. We have talked about injustice to the first Americans long enough. As Indian leaders themselves have put it, the time has come for more rain and less thunder.

Equal Rights for Women

This administration will also continue its strong efforts to open equal opportunities for women, recognizing clearly that women are often denied such opportunities today. While every woman may not want a career outside the home, every woman should have the freedom to choose whatever career she wishes—and an equal chance to pursue it.

We have already moved vigorously against job discrimination based on sex in both the private and public sectors. For the first time, guidelines have been issued to require that Government contractors in the private sector have action plans for the hiring and promotion of women. We are committed to strong enforcement of equal employment opportunity for women under Title VII of the Civil Rights Act. To help carry out these commitments I will propose to the Congress that the jurisdiction of the Commission on Civil Rights be broadened to encompass sex-based discrimination.

Within the Government, more women have been appointed to high posts than ever before. As the result of my directives issued in April 1971 the number of women appointed to high-level Federal positions has more than doubled—and the number of women in Federal middle management positions has also increased dramatically. More women than ever before have been appointed to Presidential boards and commissions. Our vigorous program to recruit more women for Federal service will be continued and intensified in the coming year.

Opportunity for Veterans

A grateful nation owes it servicemen and servicewomen every opportunity it can open to them when they return to civil-ian life. The Nation may be weary of war, but we dare not grow weary of doing right by those who have borne its heaviest burdens.

The Federal Government is carrying out this responsibility in many ways: through the G.I. Bill for education—which will spend 2-1/2 times more in 1973 than in 1969; through home loan programs and disability and pension benefits—which also have been expanded; through better medical services—including strong new drug treatment programs; through its budget for veterans hospitals, which is already many times the 1969 level and will be stepped up further next year.

We have been particularly concerned in the last 3 years with the employment of veterans—who experience higher unemployment rates than those who have not served in the Armed Forces. During this past year I announced a six-point national program to increase public awareness of this problem, to provide training and counseling to veterans seeking jobs and to help them find employment opportunities. Under the direction of the Secretary of Labor and with the help of our Jobs for Veterans Committee and the National Alliance of Businessmen, this program has been moving forward. During its first five months of operation, 122,000 Vietnam-era veterans were placed in jobs by the Federal-State Employment Service and 40,000 were enrolled in job training programs. During the next six months, we expect the Federal-State Employment Service to place some 200,000 additional veterans in jobs and to enroll nearly 200,000 more in manpower training programs.

But let us never forget, in this as in so many other areas, that the opportunity for any individual to contribute fully to his society depends in the final analysis on the response—in his own community—of other individuals.

Greater Role for American Youth

Full participation and first class citizenship—these must be our goals for America's young people. It was to help achieve these goals that I signed legislation to lower the minimum voting age to 18 in June of 1970, and moved to secure a court validation of its constitutionality. And I took special pleasure a year later in witnessing the certification of the amendment which placed this franchise guarantee in the Constitution.

But a voice at election time alone is not enough. Young people should have a hearing in government on a day-by-day basis. To this end, and at my direction, agencies throughout the Federal Government have stepped up their hiring of young people and have opened new youth advisory channels. We have also convened the first White House Youth Conference—a wide-open forum whose recommendations have been receiving a thorough review by the Executive departments.

Several other reforms also mean greater freedom and opportunity for America's young people. Draft calls have been substantially reduced, as a step toward our target of reducing them to zero by mid-1973. Already the lottery system and other new procedures, and the contributions of youth advisory councils and younger members on local boards have made the draft far more fair than it was. My educational reform proposals embody the principle that no qualified student who wants to go to college should be barred by lack of money—a guarantee that would open doors of opportunity for many thousands of deserving young people. Our new career education emphasis can also be a significant springboard to good jobs and rewarding lives.

Young America's "extra dimension" in the sixties and seventies has been a drive to help the less fortunate—an activist idealism bent on making the world a better place to live. Our new ACTION volunteer agency, building on the successful experiences of constituent units such as the Peace Corps and Vista, has already broadened service opportunities for the young—and more new programs are in prospect. The Congress can do its part in forwarding this positive momentum by assuring that the ACTION programs have sufficient funds to carry out their mission.

The American Farmer

As we face the challenge of competing more effectively abroad and of producing more efficiently at home, our entire Nation can take the American farmer as its model. While the productivity of our non-farm industries has gone up 60 percent during the last 20 years, agricultural productivity has gone up 200 percent, or nearly 3-1/2 times as much. One result has been better products and lower prices for American consumers. Another is that farmers have more than held their own in international markets. Figures for the last fiscal year show nearly a $900 million surplus for commercial agricultural trade.

The strength of American agriculture is at the heart of the strength of America. American farmers deserve a fair share in the fruits of our prosperity.

We still have much ground to cover before we arrive at that goal—but we have been moving steadily toward it. In 1950 the income of the average farmer was only 58 percent of that of his non-farm counterpart. Today that figure stands at 74 percent—not nearly high enough, but moving in the right direction.

Gross farm income reached a record high in 1971, and for 1972 a further increase of $2 billion is predicted. Because of restraints on production costs, net farm income is expected to rise in 1972 by 6.4 percent or some $1 billion. Average income per farm is expected to go up 8 percent—to an all-time high—in the next 12 months.

Still there are very serious farm problems—and we are taking strong action to meet them.

I promised 3 years ago to end the sharp skid in farm exports—and I have kept that promise. In just 2 years, farm exports climbed by 37 percent, and last year they set an all-time record. Our expanded marketing programs, the agreement to sell 2 million tons of feed grains to the Soviet Union, our massive aid to South Asia under Public Law 480, and our efforts to halt transportation strikes—by doing all we can under the old law and by proposing a new and better one—these efforts and others are moving us toward our $10 billion farm export goal.

I have also promised to expand domestic markets, to improve the management of surpluses, and to help in other ways to raise the prices received by farmers. I have kept that promise, too. A surprisingly large harvest drove corn prices down last year, but they have risen sharply since last November. Prices received by dairy farmers, at the highest level in history last year, will continue strong in 1972. Soybean prices will be at their highest level in two decades. Prices received by farmers for hogs, poultry and eggs are all expected to go higher. Expanded Government purchases and other assistance will also provide a greater boost to farm income.

With the close cooperation of the Congress, we have expanded the farmers' freedom and flexibility through the Agricultural Act of 1970. We have strengthened the Farm Credit System and substantially increased the availability of farm credit. Programs for controlling plant and animal disease and for soil and water conservation have also been expanded. All these efforts will continue, as will our efforts to improve the legal climate for cooperative bargaining—an important factor in protecting the vitality of the family farm and in resisting excessive government management.

Developing Rural America

In my address to the Congress at this time 2 years ago, I spoke of the fact that one-third of our counties had lost population in the 1960's, that many of our rural areas were slowly being emptied of their people and their promise, and that we should work to reverse this picture by including rural America in a nationwide program to foster balanced growth.

It is striking to realize that even if we had a population of one billion—nearly five times the current level—our area is so great that we would still not be as densely populated as many European nations are at present. Clearly, our problems are not so much those of numbers as they are of distribution. We must work to revitalize the American countryside.

We have begun to make progress on this front in the last 3 years. Rural housing programs have been increased by more than 450 percent from 1969 to 1973. The number of families benefiting from rural water and sewer programs is now 75 percent greater than it was in 1969. We have worked to encourage sensible growth patterns through the location of Federal facilities. The first biennial Report on National Growth, which will be released in the near future, will further describe these patterns, their policy implications and the many ways we are responding to this challenge.

But we must do more. The Congress can begin by passing my $1.1-billion program of Special Revenue Sharing for Rural Community Development. In addition, I will soon present a major proposal to expand significantly the credit authorities of the Farmers Home Administration, so that this agency—which has done so much to help individual farmers—can also help spur commercial, industrial and community development in rural America. Hopefully, the FHA will be able to undertake this work as a part of a new Department of Community Development.

In all these ways, we can help ensure that rural America will be in the years ahead what it has been from our Nation's beginning—an area which looks eagerly to the future with a sense of hope and promise.

A Commitment to Our Cities

Our commitment to balanced growth also requires a commitment to our cities—to old cities threatened by decay, to suburbs now sprawling senselessly because of inadequate planning, and to new cities not yet born but clearly needed by our growing population. I discussed these challenges in my special message to the Congress on Population Growth and the American Future in the summer of 1969—and I have often discussed them since. My recommendations for transportation, education, health, welfare, revenue sharing, planning and management assistance, executive reorganization, the environment—especially the proposed Land Use Policy Act—and my proposals in many other areas touch directly on community development.

One of the keys to better cities is better coordination of these many components. Two of my pending proposals go straight to the heart of this challenge. The first, a new Department of Community Development, would provide a single point of focus for our strategy for growth. The second, Special Revenue Sharing for Urban Community Development, would remove the rigidities of categorical project grants which now do so much to fragment planning, delay action, and discourage local responsibility. My new budget proposed a $300 million increase over the full year level which we proposed for this program a year ago.

The Department of Housing and Urban Development has been working to foster orderly growth in our cities in a number of additional ways. A Planned Variation concept has been introduced into the Model Cities program which gives localities more control over their own future. HUD's own programs have been considerably decentralized. The New Communities Program has moved forward and seven projects have received final approval. The Department's efforts to expand mortgage capital, to more than double the level of subsidized housing, and to encourage new and more efficient building techniques through programs like Operation Breakthrough have all contributed to our record level of housing starts. Still more can be done if the Congress enacts the administration's Housing Consolidation and Simplification Act, proposed in 1970.

The Federal Government is only one of many influences on development patterns across our land. Nevertheless, its influence is considerable. We must do all we can to see that its influence is good.

Improving Transportation

Although the executive branch and the Congress have been led by different parties during the last 3 years, we have cooperated with particular effectiveness in the field of transportation. Together we have shaped the Urban Mass Transportation Assistance Act of 1970—a 12-year, $10 billion effort to expand and improve our common carriers and thus make our cities more livable. We have brought into effect a 10-year, $3 billion ship construction program as well as increased research efforts and a modified program of operating subsidies to revamp our merchant marine. We have accelerated efforts to improve air travel under the new Airport and Airway Trust Fund and have been working in fresh ways to save and improve our railway passenger service. Great progress has also been made in promoting transportation safety and we have moved effectively against cargo thefts and skyjacking.

I hope this strong record will be even stronger by the time the 92nd Congress adjourns. I hope that our Special Revenue Sharing program for transportation will by then be a reality—so that cities and states can make better long-range plans with greater freedom to achieve their own proper balance among the many modes of transportation. I hope, too, that our recommendations for revitalizing surface freight transportation will by then be accepted, including measures both to modernize railway equipment and operations and to update regulatory practices. By encouraging competition, flexibility and efficiency among freight carriers, these steps could save the American people billions of dollars in freight costs every year, helping to curb inflation, expand employment and improve our balance of trade.

One of our most damaging and perplexing economic problems is that of massive and prolonged transportation strikes. There is no reason why the public should be the helpless victim of such strikes—but this is frequently what happens. The dock strike, for example, has been extremely costly for the American people, particularly for the farmer for whom a whole year's income can hinge on how promptly he can move his goods. Last year's railroad strike also dealt a severe blow to our economy.

Both of these emergencies could have been met far more effectively if the Congress had enacted my Emergency Public Interest Protection Act, which I proposed in February of 1970. By passing this legislation in this session, the Congress can give us the permanent machinery so badly needed for resolving future disputes.

Historically, our transportation systems have provided the cutting edge for our development. Now, to keep our country from falling behind the times, we must keep well ahead of events in our transportation planning. This is why we are placing more emphasis and spending more money this year on transportation research and development. For this reason, too, I will propose a 65 percent increase—to the $1-billion level—in our budget for mass transportation. Highway building has been our first priority —and our greatest success story—in the past two decades. Now we must write a similar success story for mass transportation in the 1970s.

Peace at Home: Fighting Crime

Our quest for peace abroad over the last 3 years has been accompanied by an intensive quest for peace at home. And our success in stabilizing developments on the international scene has been matched by a growing sense of stability in America. Civil disorders no longer engulf our cities. Colleges and universities have again become places of learning. And while crime is still increasing, the rate of increase has slowed to a 5-year low. In the one city for which the federal government has a special responsibility—Washington, D.C.—the picture is even brighter, for here serious crime actually fell by 13 percent in the last year. Washington was one of 52 major cities which recorded a net reduction in crime in the first nine months of 1971, compared to 23 major cities which made comparable progress a year earlier.

This encouraging beginning is not something that has just happened by itself—I believe it results directly from strong new crime fighting efforts by this administration, by the Congress, and by state and local governments.

Federal expenditures on crime have increased 200 percent since 1969 and we are proposing another 18 percent increase in our new budget. The Organized Crime Control Act of 1970, the District of Columbia Court Reform Act, and the Omnibus Crime Control Act of 1970 have all provided new instruments for this important battle. So has our effort to expand the federal strike force program as a weapon against organized crime. Late last year, we held the first National Conference on Corrections—and we will continue to move forward in this most critical field. I will also propose legislation to improve our juvenile delinquency prevention programs. And I again urge action on my Special Revenue Sharing proposal for law enforcement.

By continuing our stepped-up assistance to local law enforcement authorities through the Law Enforcement Assistance Administration, by continuing to press for improved courts and correctional institutions, by continuing our intensified war on drug abuse, and by continuing to give vigorous support to the principles of order and respect for law, I believe that what has been achieved in the Nation's capital can be achieved in a growing number of other communities throughout the Nation.

Combating Drug Abuse

A problem of modern life which is of deepest concern to most Americans—and of particular anguish to many—is that of drug abuse. For increasing dependence on drugs will surely sap our Nation's strength and destroy our Nation's character.

Meeting this challenge is not a task for government alone. I have been heartened by the efforts of millions of individual Americans from all walks of life who are trying to communicate across the barriers created by drug use, to reach out with compassion to those who have become drug dependent. The federal government will continue to lead in this effort. The last 3 years have seen an increase of nearly 600 percent in federal expenditures for treatment and rehabilitation and an increase of more than 500 percent in program levels for research, education and training. I will propose further substantial increases for these programs in the coming year.

In order to develop a national strategy for this effort and to coordinate activities which are spread through nine federal agencies, I asked Congress last June to create a Special Action Office for Drug Abuse Prevention. I also established an interim office by Executive order, and that unit is beginning to have an impact. But now we must have both the legislative authority and the funds I requested if this office is to move ahead with its critical mission.

On another front, the United States will continue to press for a strong collective effort by nations throughout the world to eliminate drugs at their source. And we will intensify the worldwide attack on drug smugglers and all who protect them. The Cabinet Committee on International Narcotics Control—which I created last September—is coordinating our diplomatic and law enforcement efforts in this area.

We will also step up our program to curb illicit drug traffic at our borders and within our country. Over the last 3 years federal expenditures for this work have more than doubled, and I will propose a further funding increase next year. In addition, I will soon initiate a major new program to drive drug traffickers and pushers off the streets of America. This program will be built around a nationwide network of investigative and prosecutive units, utilizing special grand juries established under the Organized Crime Control Act of 1970, to assist state and local agencies in detecting, arresting, and convicting those who would profit from the misery of others.

Strengthening Consumer Protection

Our plans for 1972 include further steps to protect consumers against hazardous food and drugs and other dangerous products. These efforts will carry forward the campaign I launched in 1969 to establish a "Buyer's Bill of Rights" and to strengthen consumer protection. As a part of that campaign, we have established a new Office of Consumer Affairs, directed by my Special Assistant for Consumer Affairs, to give consumers greater access to government, to promote consumer education, to encourage voluntary efforts by business, to work with state and local governments, and to help the federal government improve its consumer-related activities. We have also established a new Consumer Product Information Coordinating Center in the General Services Administration to help us share a wider range of federal research and buying expertise with the public.

But many of our plans in this field still await congressional action, including measures to insure product safety, to fight consumer fraud, to require full disclosure in warranties and guarantees, and to protect against unsafe medical devices.

Reforming and Renewing Education

It was nearly 2 years ago, in March of 1970, that I presented my major proposals for reform and renewal in education. These proposals included student assistance measures to ensure that no qualified person would be barred from college by a lack of money, a National Institute of Education to bring new energy and new direction to educational research, and a National Foundation for Higher Education to encourage innovation in learning beyond high school. These initiatives are still awaiting final action by the Congress. They deserve prompt approval.

I would also underscore my continuing confidence that Special Revenue Sharing for Education can do much to strengthen the backbone of our educational system, our public elementary and secondary schools. Special Revenue Sharing recognizes the nation's interest in their improvement without compromising the principle of local control. I also call again for the enactment of my $1.5 billion program of Emergency School Aid to help local school districts desegregate wisely and well. This program has twice been approved by the House and once by the Senate in different versions. I hope the Senate will now send the legislation promptly to the conference committee so that an agreement can be reached on this important measure at an early date.

This bill is designed to help local school districts with the problems incident to desegregation. We must have an end to the dual school system, as conscience and the Constitution both require—and we must also have good schools. In this connection, I repeat my own firm belief that educational quality—so vital to the future of all of our children—is not enhanced by unnecessary busing for the sole purpose of achieving an arbitrary racial balance.

Financing Our Schools

I particularly hope that 1972 will be a year in which we resolve one of the most critical questions we face in education today: how best to finance our schools.

In recent years the growing scope and rising costs of education have so overburdened local revenues that financial crisis has become a way of life in many school districts. As a result, neither the benefits nor the burdens of education have been equitably distributed.

The brunt of the growing pressures has fallen on the property tax—one of the most inequitable and regressive of all public levies. Property taxes in the United States represent a higher proportion of public income than in almost any other nation. They have more than doubled in the last decade and have been particularly burdensome for our lower and middle income families and for older Americans.

These intolerable pressures—on the property tax and on our schools—led me to establish the President's Commission on School Finance in March of 1970. I charged this Commission with the responsibility to review comprehensively both the revenue

needs and the revenue resources of public and non-public elementary and secondary education. The Commission will make its final report to me in March.

At the same time, the Domestic Council—and particularly the Secretaries of the Treasury and of Health, Education and Welfare—have also been studying this difficult and tangled problem. The entire question has been given even greater urgency by recent court decisions in California, Minnesota and Texas, which have held the conventional method of financing schools through local property taxes discriminatory and unconstitutional. Similar court actions are pending in more than half of our states. While these cases have not yet been reviewed by the Supreme Court, we cannot ignore the serious questions they have raised for our states, for our local school districts, and for the entire nation.

The overhaul of school finance involves two complex and interrelated sets of problems: those concerning support of the schools themselves, and also the basic relationships of Federal, State and local governments in any program of tax reform.

We have been developing a set of comprehensive proposals to deal with these questions. Under the leadership of the Secretary of the Treasury, we are carefully reviewing the tax aspects of these proposals; and I have this week enlisted the Advisory Commission on Intergovernmental Relations in addressing the intergovernmental relations aspects. Members of the Congress and of the executive branch, Governors, state legislators, local officials and private citizens comprise this group.

Later in the year, after I have received the reports of both the President's Commission on School Finance and the Advisory Council on Intergovernmental Relations, I shall make my final recommendations for relieving the burden of property taxes and providing both fair and adequate financing for our children's education—consistent with the principle of preserving the control by local school boards over local schools.

A New Emphasis on Career Education

Career Education is another area of major new emphasis, an emphasis which grows out of my belief that our schools should be doing more to build self-reliance and self-sufficiency, to prepare students for a productive and fulfilling life. Too often, this has not been happening. Too many of our students, from all income groups, have been "turning off" or "tuning out" on their educational experiences. And—whether they drop out of school or proceed on to college—too many young people find themselves unmotivated and ill equipped for a rewarding social role. Many other Americans, who have already entered the world of work, find that they are dissatisfied with their jobs but feel that it is too late to change directions, that they already are "locked in."

One reason for this situation is the inflexibility of our educational system, including the fact that it so rigidly separates academic and vocational curricula. Too often vocational education is foolishly stigmatized as being less desirable than academic preparation. And too often the academic curriculum offers very little preparation for viable careers. Most students are unable to combine the most valuable features of both vocational and academic education; once they have chosen one curriculum, it is difficult to move to the other.

The present approach serves the best interests of neither our students nor our society. The unhappy result is high numbers of able people who are unemployed, underemployed, or unhappily employed on the one hand—while many challenging jobs go begging on the other.

We need a new approach, and I believe the best new approach is to strengthen career education.

Career Education provides people of all ages with broader exposure to and better preparation for the world of work. It not only helps the young, but also provides adults with an opportunity to adapt their skills to changing needs, changing technology, and their own changing interests. It would not prematurely force an individual into a specific area of work but would expand his ability to choose wisely from a wider range of options. Neither would it result in a slighting of academic preparation, which would remain a central part of the educational blend.

Career Education is not a single specific program. It is more usefully thought of as a goal—and one that we can pursue through many methods. What we need today is a nationwide search for such methods—a search which involves every area of education and every level of government. To help spark this venture, I will propose an intensified Federal effort to develop model programs which apply and test the best ideas in this field.

There is no more disconcerting waste than the waste of human potential. And there is no better investment than an investment in human fulfillment. Career Education can help make education and training more meaningful for the student, more rewarding for the teacher, more available to the adult, more relevant for the disadvantaged, and more productive for our country.

Manpower Programs: Tapping our Full Potential

Our trillion dollar economy rests in the final analysis on our 88 million member labor force. How well that force is used today, how well that force is prepared for tomorrow—these are central questions for our country.

They are particularly important questions in a time of stiff economic challenge and burgeoning economic opportunity. At such a time, we must find better ways to tap the full potential of every citizen.

This means doing all we can to open new education and employment opportunities for members of minority groups. It means a stronger effort to help the veteran find useful and satisfying work and to tap the enormous talents of the elderly. It means helping women—in whatever role they choose—to realize their full potential. It also means caring for the unemployed—sustaining them, retraining them and helping them find new employment.

This administration has grappled directly with these assignments. We began by completely revamping the Manpower Administration in the Department of Labor. We have expanded our manpower programs to record levels. We proposed—and the Congress enacted—a massive reform of unemployment insurance, adding 9 million workers to the system and expanding the size and duration of benefits. We instituted a Job Bank to match jobs with available workers. The efforts of the National Alliance of Businessmen to train and hire the hard-core unemployed were given a new nationwide focus. That organization has also joined with our Jobs for Veterans program in finding employment for returning servicemen. We have worked to open more jobs for women. Through the Philadelphia Plan and other actions, we have expanded equal opportunity in employment for members of minority groups. Summer jobs for disadvantaged youths went up by one-third last summer. And on July 12 of last year I signed the Emergency Employment Act of 1971, providing more than 130,000 jobs in the public sector.

In the manpower field, as in others, there is also an important unfinished agenda. At the top of this list is my Special Revenue Sharing program for manpower—a bill which would provide more Federal dollars for manpower training while increasing substantially the impact of each dollar by allowing States and cities to tailor training to local labor conditions. My welfare reform proposals are also pertinent in this context, since they are built around the goal of moving people from welfare rolls to payrolls. To help in this effort, HR 1 would provide transitional opportunities in community service employment for another 200,000 persons. The Career Education program can also have an important long-range influence on the way we use our manpower. And so can a major new thrust which I am announcing today to stimulate more imaginative use of America's great strength in science and technology.

Marshalling Science and Technology

As we work to build a more productive, more competitive, more prosperous America, we will do well to remember the keys to our progress in the past. There have been many, including the competitive nature of our free enterprise system; the energy of our working men and women; and the abundant gifts of nature. One other quality which has always been a key to progress is our special bent for technology, our singular ability to harness the discoveries of science in the service of man.

At least from the time of Benjamin Franklin, American ingenuity has enjoyed a wide international reputation. We have been known as a people who could "build a better mousetrap"—and this capacity has been one important reason for both our domestic prosperity and our international strength.

In recent years, America has focused a large share of its technological energy on projects for defense and for space. These projects have had great value. Defense technology has helped us preserve our freedom and protect the peace. Space technology has enabled us to share unparalleled adventures and to lift our sights beyond earth's bounds. The daily life of the average man has also been improved by much of our defense and space research—for example, by work on radar, jet engines, nuclear reactors, communications and weather satellites, and computers. Defense and space projects have also enabled us to build and maintain our general technological capacity, which—as a result—can now be more readily applied to civilian purposes.

America must continue with strong and sensible programs of research and development for defense and for space. I have felt for some time, however, that we should also be doing more to apply our scientific and technological genius directly to domestic opportunities. Toward this end, I have already increased our civilian research and development budget by more than 40 percent since 1969 and have directed the National Science Foundation to give more attention to this area.

I have also reoriented our space program so that it will have even greater domestic benefits. As a part of this effort, I recently announced support for the development of a new earth orbital vehicle that promises to introduce a new era in space research. This vehicle, the space shuttle, is one that can be recovered and used again and again, lowering significantly both the cost and the risk of space operations. The space shuttle would also open new opportunities in fields such as weather forecasting, domestic and international communications, the monitoring of natural resources, and air traffic safety.

The space shuttle is a wise national investment. I urge the Congress to approve this plan so that we can realize these substantial economies and these substantial benefits.

Over the last several months, this administration has undertaken a major review of both the problems and the opportunities for American technology. Leading scientists and researchers from our universities and from industry have contributed to this study. One important conclusion we have reached is that much more needs to be known about the process of stimulating and applying research and development. In some cases, for example, the barriers to progress are financial. In others they are technical. In still other instances, customs, habits, laws, and regulations are the chief obstacles. We need to learn more about all these considerations—and we intend to do so. One immediate step in this effort will be the White House Conference on the Industrial World Ahead which will convene next month and will devote considerable attention to research and development questions.

But while our knowledge in this field is still modest, there are nevertheless a number of important new steps which we can take at this time. I will soon present specific recommendations for such steps in a special message to the Congress. Among these proposals will be an increase next year of $700 million in civilian research and development spending, a 15 percent increase over last year's level and a 65 percent increase over 1969. We will place new emphasis on cooperation with private research and development, including new experimental programs for cost sharing and for technology transfers from the public to the private sector. Our program will include special incentives for smaller high technology firms, which have an excellent record of cost effectiveness.

In addition, our Federal agencies which are highly oriented toward technology—such as the Atomic Energy Commission and the National Aeronautics and Space Administration—will work more closely with agencies which have a primary social mission. For example, our outstanding capabilities in space technology should be used to help the Department of Transportation develop better mass transportation systems. As has been said so often in the last 2 years, a nation that can send three people across 240,000 miles of space to the moon should also be able to send 240,000 people 3 miles across a city to work.

Finally, we will seek to set clear and intelligent targets for research and development, so that our resources can be focused on projects where an extra effort is most likely to produce a breakthrough and where the breakthrough is most likely to make a difference in our lives. Our initial efforts will include new or accelerated activities aimed at:

• Creating new sources of clean and abundant energy;
• Developing safe, fast, pollution-free transportation;
• Reducing the loss of life and property from earthquakes, hurricanes and other natural disasters;
• Developing effective emergency health care systems which could lead to the saving of as many as 30,000 lives each year;
• Finding new ways to curb drug traffic and rehabilitate drug users.

And these are only the beginning.

I cannot predict exactly where each of these new thrusts will eventually lead us in the years ahead. But I can say with assurance that the program I have outlined will open new employment opportunities for American workers, increase the productivity of the American economy, and expand foreign markets for American goods. I can also predict with confidence that this program will enhance our standard of living and improve the quality of our lives.

Science and technology represent an enormous power in our life—and a unique opportunity. It is now for us to decide whether we will waste these magnificent energies—or whether we will use them to create a better world for ourselves and for our children.

A Growing Agenda for Action

The danger in presenting any substantial statement of concerns and requests is that any subject which is omitted from the list may for that reason be regarded as unimportant. I hope the Congress will vigorously resist any such suggestions, for there are many other important proposals before the House and the Senate which also deserve attention and enactment.

I think, for example, of our program for the District of Columbia. In addition to proposals already before the Congress, I will soon submit additional legislation outlining a special balanced program of physical and social development for the nation's capital as part of our Bicentennial celebration. In this and other ways, we can make that celebration both a fitting commemoration of our revolutionary origins and a bold further step to fulfill their promise.

I think, too, of our program to help small businessmen, of our proposals concerning communications, of our recommendations involving the construction of public buildings, and of our program for the arts and humanities—where the proposed new budget is 6 times the level of 3 years ago.

In all, some 90 pieces of major legislation which I have recommended to the Congress still await action. And that list is growing longer. It is now for the Congress to decide whether this agenda represents the beginning of new progress for America —or simply another false start.

The Need for Reason and Realism

I have covered many subjects in this message. Clearly, our challenges are many and complex. But that is the way things must be for responsible government in our diverse and complicated world.

We can choose, of course, to retreat from this world, pretending that our problems can be solved merely by trusting in a new philosophy, a single personality, or a simple formula. But such a retreat can only add to our difficulties and our disillusion.

If we are to be equal to the complexity of our times we must learn to move on many fronts and to keep many commitments. We must learn to reckon our success not by how much we start but by how much we finish. We must learn to be tenacious. We must learn to persevere.

If we are to master our moment, we must first be masters of ourselves. We must respond to the call which has been a central theme of this message—the call to reason and to realism.

To meet the challenge of complexity we must also learn to disperse and decentralize power—at home and abroad—allowing more people in more places to release their creative energies. We must remember that the greatest resource for good in this world is the power of the people themselves—not moving in lockstep to the commands of the few—but providing their own discipline and discovering their own destiny.

Above all, we must not lose our capacity to dream, to see, amid the realities of today, the possibilities for tomorrow. And then—if we believe in our dreams—we also must wake up and work for them.

RICHARD NIXON

ENVIRONMENTAL MESSAGE: RENEWED CALL FOR LEGISLATION

Following is the text, as made available by the White House, of President Nixon's Feb. 8 message to Congress on the environment.

TO THE CONGRESS OF THE UNITED STATES:

From the very first, the American spirit has been one of self-reliance and confident action. Always we have been a people to say with Henley "I am the master of my fate...the captain of my soul"—a people sure that man commands his own destiny. What has dawned dramatically upon us in recent years, though, is a new recognition that to a significant extend man commands as well the very destiny of this planet where he lives, and the destiny of all life upon it. We have even begun to see that these destinies are not many and separate at all—that in fact they are indivisibly one.

This is the environmental awakening. It marks a new sensitivity of the American spirit and a new maturity of American public life. It is working a revolution in values, as commitment to responsible partnership with nature replaces cavalier assumptions that we can play God with our surroundings and survive. It is leading to broad reforms in action, as individuals, corporations, government, and civic groups mobilize to conserve resources, to control pollution, to anticipate and prevent emerging environmental problems, to manage the land more wisely, and to preserve wilderness.

In messages to the Congress during 1970 and 1971 I proposed comprehensive initiatives reflecting the earliest and most visible concerns of the environmental awakening. The new cast of the public mind had to be translated into new legislation. New insights had to have new governmental forms and processes through which to operate. Broadly-based problems—such as air pollution, water pollution and pesticide hazards—had to be dealt with first.

The necessary first steps in each of these areas have now been taken, though in all of them the work is far from completed. Now, as we press on with that work in 1972, we must also come to grips with the basic factors which underlie our more obvious environmental problems—factors like the use of land and the impact of incentives or disincentives built into our economic system. We are gaining an increasingly sophisticated understanding of the way economic, institutional, and legal forces shape our surroundings for good or ill; the next step is learning how to turn such forces to environmental benefit.

Primary responsibility for the actions that are needed to protect and enhance our environment rests with State and local government, consumers, industry, and private organizations of various kinds—but the Federal Government must provide leadership. On the first day of this decade I stated that "it is literally now or never" for true quality of life in America. Amide much encouraging evidence that it can and will be "now," we must not slacken our pace but accelerate it. Environmental concern must crystallize into permanent patterns of thought and action. What began as environmental awakening must mature finally into a new and higher environmental way of life. If we flag in our dedication and will, the problems themselves will not go away. Toward keeping the momentum of awareness and action, I pledge my full support and that of this Administration, and I urgently solicit the continuing cooperation of the Congress and the American people.

Two Years' Agenda

From Consideration to Action. In my 1971 environmental message, just one year ago today, I sent to the Congress a comprehensive program designed to clean up the problems of the past, and to deal with emerging problems before they become critical. These proposals included:

- Regulation of toxic substances
- Comprehensive improvement in pesticide control authority
- Noise control
- Preservation of historic buildings
- Power plant siting
- Regulation of environmental effects of surface and underground mining
- Ocean dumping regulation
- More effective control of water pollution through a greatly expanded waste treatment grant program and strengthened standard-setting and enforcement authorities
- A National Land Use Policy Act
- Substantial expansion of the wilderness system
- Expanded international cooperation

To date, most of the legislation on this list has been the subject of congressional hearings; most of it has attracted heartening interest and support; but none of it has yet received final congressional action. Last year was, quite properly, a year of consideration of these measures by the Congress. I urge, however, that this be a year of action on all of them, so that we can move on from intention to accomplishment in the important needs they address. Passage of these measures and creation of the unified Department of Natural Resources which I also proposed in 1971—by this 92nd Congress—will be essential if we are to have an adequate base for improving environmental quality.

Building on the Base. As that base is being established, we must move ahead to build wisely and rapidly upon it. I shall outline today a plan for doing that, with initiatives and actions in the following areas:

- Tightening pollution control: A Toxic Wastes Disposal Control Act; legislation to control sediment from construction activities; an emissions charge to reduce sulfur oxide air pollution; clean energy research and energy conservation measures.
- Making technology an environmental ally: Integrated pest management; stepped-up research on noise control; stepped-up research on air pollution effects and measurement.

- Improving land use: Expansion and strengthening of the National Land Use Policy Act; protection of wetlands.
- Protecting our natural heritage: A ban on use of poisons for predator control on public lands; a stronger law to protect endangered species of wildlife; Big Cypress National Fresh Water Reserve; National Recreation Areas around New York Harbor and the Golden Gate; conversion of 20 additional Federal properties to recreational use; 18 new Wilderness Areas; regulation of off-road vehicles on Federal lands.
- Expanding international cooperation on the environment: Establishment of a United Nations Fund for the Environment; further measures to control marine pollution.
- Protecting children from lead-based paint.
- Enlisting the young: President's Environmental Merit Awards Program for high schools; youth opportunities in the Department of Agriculture Field Scout program.

Tightening Pollution Control

The legislative framework for dealing with our major air pollution problems has become law, and I have made comprehensive recommendations regarding water pollution control. But several problems remain to be addressed which are difficult to deal with under the general pollution control authorities.

Disposal of Toxic Wastes. Increasingly strict air and water pollution control laws and their more effective enforcement have led to greater reliance on land—both surface and underground—for disposal of waste products from the toxic substances being used in ever greater volume and variety in our society. Without adequate controls, such waste disposal may cause contamination of underground and surface waters leading to direct health hazards.

I propose a Toxic Wastes Disposal Control Act, under which the Environmental Protection Agency would establish Federal guidelines and requirements for State programs to regulate disposal on or under the land of those toxic wastes which pose a hazard to health. The act would provide for Federal enforcement action if a State should fail to establish its own program.

Sediment Control. Sediment, small particles of soil which enter the water, is the most pervasive water pollution problem which does not come primarily from municipal or industrial sources. Heavy loads of sediment interfere with many beneficial uses of water, such as swimming and water supply, and can change the entire character of an aquatic environment. Many of our great waterways are afflicted with this problem. In our urban areas, a significant amount of sediment comes from construction. However, if proper construction practices are followed, sediment runoff from this source can be greatly reduced.

I propose legislation calling upon the States to establish, through appropriate local and regional agencies, regulatory programs to control sediment affecting water quality from earthmoving activities such as building and road construction.

The Environmental Protection Agency, together with other Federal agencies, would develop Federal guidelines for appropriate control measures. Federal enforcement would take place in situations where a State failed to implement such a program.

Sulfur Oxides Emissions Charge. In my 1971 Environmental Message, I announced plans to ask for imposition of a charge on sulfur oxides emissions, one of the air pollutants most damaging to human health and property, and vegetation. The Council on Environmental Quality, the Treasury Department and the Environmental Protection Agency have now completed their studies on this measure and have developed the details of an emission charge proposal.

I propose a charge on sulfur emitted into the atmosphere from combustion, refining, smelting, and other processes.

This charge would begin in 1976 and apply in all regions where the air quality does not meet national standards for sulfur oxides during 1975. The charge would be 15¢ per pound on sulfur emitted in regions where the primary standards—which are designed to be protective of public health—have not been met within the deadline for achievement prescribed in the Clean Air Act. In regions where air quality met the primary standard but exceeded the secondary national standard—designed to protect property, vegetation, and aesthetic values—a charge of $.10 per pound of sulfur emitted would apply. Areas which reduce emissions sufficiently to meet both primary and secondary air quality standards would be exempt from the emission charge.

This charge is an application of the principle that the costs of pollution should be included in the price of the product. Combined with our existing regulatory authority, it would constitute a strong economic incentive to achieve the sulfur oxides standards necessary to protect health, and then further to reduce emissions to levels which protect welfare and aesthetics.

Clean Energy Generation and Conservation. Ours is an energy-based economy, and energy resources are the basis for future economic progress. Yet the consumption of energy-producing fuels contributes to many of our most serious pollution problems. In order to have both environmental quality and an improving standard of living, we will need to develop new clean energy sources and to learn to use energy more efficiently.

Our success in meeting energy needs while preventing adverse environmental effects from energy generation and transmission will depend heavily on the state of available technology. In my message to the Congress on energy of last June, I announced a series of steps to increase research on clean and efficient energy production. But further action is needed.

As part of my new commitment to augment Federal Research and development and target it more effectively on solving domestic problems, I have requested in the 1973 budget an additional $88 million for development of a broad spectrum of new technologies for producing clean energy.

In addition to carrying forward the priority efforts I have already announced—the liquid metal fast breeder reactor, pipeline quality gas from coal, and sulfur oxide control technology—the budget provides funds for new or increased efforts on fusion power, solar energy, magnetohydrodynamics, industrial gas from coal, dry cooling towers for power plant waste heat, large energy storage batteries and advanced underground electric transmission lines. These new efforts relate to both our immediate and our future energy problems, and are needed to assure adequate supplies of clean energy.

My message on energy also announced several steps that would be taken by the Federal Government to use energy more efficiently and with less environmental harm. One of these steps was issuance by the Secretary of Housing and Urban Development of revised standards for insulation in new federally insured houses. The new standards for single-family structures, which have now been issued through the Federal Housing Administration, reduce the maximum permissible heat loss by about one-third for a typical home. The fuel savings which will result from the application of these new standards will, in an average climate, exceed in one year the cost of the additional insulation required.

I am now directing the Secretary of Housing and Urban Development to issue revised insulation standards for apartments and other multifamily structures not covered by the earlier revision. The new rules will cut maximum permissible heat loss by 40%.

The savings in fuel costs after a 5-year period will on the average more than offset the additional construction costs occasioned by these revised standards.

These stricter insulation standards are only one example of administrative actions which can be taken by the Federal Government to eliminate wasteful use of energy. The Federal Government can and must provide leadership by finding and implementing additional ways of reducing such waste.

I have therefore instructed the Council on Environmental Quality and the Office of Science and Technology, working with other Federal agencies, to conduct a survey to determine what additional actions might be taken to conserve energy in Federal activities.

This survey will look at innovative ways to reduce wasteful consumption of energy while also reducing total costs and undesirable environmental impact.

Recycling. Recycling—the technique which treats many types of solid wastes not as pollutants but as recoverable and reusable "resources out of place"—is an important part of the answer to the Nation's solid waste burden. Last year, at my direction, the General Services Administration began reorienting government procurement policies to set a strong Federal example in the use of recycled products.

Because Federal tax policy should also offer recycling incentives, the Treasury Department is clarifying the availability of tax exempt treatment industrial revenue bond financing for the construction of recycling facilities built by private concerns to recycle their own wastes.

The Environmental Transition. Many environmental problems are influenced by the way our economy operates. Conversely, efforts to improve environmental quality have an impact on the economy. Our national income accounting does not explicitly recognize the cost of pollution damages to health, materials, and aesthetics in the computation of our economic well-being. Many goods and services fail to bear the full costs of the damages they cause from pollution, and hence are underpriced.

Environmental quality requirements will affect many of our industries by imposing new costs on production. We know that these impacts fall unevenly on industries, new and old firms, and on communities, but little concrete data has been available. Contract studies have recently been performed for the Council on Environmental Quality, the Environmental Protection Agency, and the Department of Commerce, under the policy guidance of the Council of Economic Advisers. These initial studies suggest that pollution control costs will result in some price increases, competitive trade disadvantages, and employment shifts. The major impact of these costs will be on older, and usually smaller plants.

As long as we carefully set our environmental goals to assure that the benefits we achieve are greater than the social and economic costs, the changes which will occur in our economy are desirable, and we as a Nation will benefit from them.

Making Technology an Environmental Ally

The time has come to increase the technological resources allocated to the challenges of meeting high-priority domestic needs. In my State of the Union Message last month, I announced an expanded Federal research and development commitment for this purpose. There is great potential for achievement through technology in the fight against pollution and the larger drive for quality in our environment.

The temptation to cast technology in the role of ecological villain must be resisted—for to do so is to deprive ourselves of a vital tool available for enhancing environmental quality. As Peter Drucker has said, "the environment is a problem of (the) success" of technological society, by no means a proof of its failure. The difficulties which some applications of technology have engendered might indeed be rectified by turning our backs on the 20th century, but only at a price in privation which we do not want to pay and do not have to pay. There is no need to throw out the baby with the bath water. Technology can and must be wisely applied so that it becomes environmentally self-corrective. This is the standard for which we must aim.

Integrated Pest Management. Chemical pesticides are a familiar example of a technological innovation which has provided unintended and unanticipated harm. New technologies of integrated pest management must be developed so that agricultural and forest productivity can be maintained together with, rather than at the expense of, environmental quality. Integrated pest management means judicious use of selective chemical pesticides in combination with nonchemical agents and methods. It seeks to maximize reliance on such natural pest population controls as predators, sterilization, and pest diseases. The following actions are being taken:

• I have directed the Department of Agriculture, the National Science Foundation, and the Environmental Protection Agency to launch a large-scale integrated pest management research and development program. This program will be conducted by a number of our leading universities.

• I have directed the Department of Agriculture to increase field testing of promising new methods of pest detection and control. Also, other existing Federal pesticide application programs will be examined for the purpose of incorporating new pest management techniques.

• I have directed the Departments of Agriculture and of Health, Education, and Welfare to encourage the development of training and certification programs at appropriate academic institutions in order to provide the large number of crop protection specialists that will be needed as integrated pest management becomes more fully utilized.

• I have authorized the Department of Agriculture to expand its crop field scout demonstration program to cover nearly four million acres under agricultural production by the upcoming growing season.

Through this program many unnecessary pesticide applications can be eliminated, since the scouts will be used to determine when pesticide applications are actually needed.

In my message on the environment last February, I proposed a comprehensive revision of our pesticide control laws—a revision which still awaits final congressional action. Also essential to a sound national pesticide policy are measures to ensure that agricultural workers are protected from adverse exposures to these chemicals.

I am directing the Departments of Labor and Health, Education, and Welfare to develop standards under the Occupational Safety and Health Act to protect such workers from pesticide poisoning.

Noise Control Research. Scientific findings increasingly confirm what few urban dwellers or industrial workers need to be told—that excessive noise can constitute a significant threat to human well-being. The Congress already has before it a comprehensive noise control bill, which I proposed a year ago. A quieter environment cannot simply be legislated into being. We shall also need to develop better methods to achieve our goal.

I have requested in my 1973 budget a $23 million increase in research and development funds for reducing noise from airplanes. I have also requested new funds for research and development for reducing street traffic noise.

Research on Air Pollution Effects and Measurement. Our pollution control efforts are based largely on the establishment of enforceable standards of environmental quality. Initial standards have often been based on incomplete knowledge because the necessary information has not been available. Also, the lack of adequate instruments to measure pollution and of models of how pollutants are dispersed has made it difficult to know exactly how much pollution must be controlled in a particular area. We need added research and development to make more precise judgments of what standards should be set and how we can most practically achieve our goals.

I have requested in my 1973 budget an additional $12 million to increase research on the health effects of air pollution, on regional air pollution modeling, and on improved pollution instrumentation and measurement.

Improving Land Use

In recent years we have come to view our land as a limited and irreplaceable resource. No longer do we imagine that there will always be more of it over the horizon—more woodlands and shorelands and wetlands—if we neglect or overdevelop the land in view. A new maturity is giving rise to a land ethic which recognizes that improper land use affects the public interest and limits the choices that we and our descendants will have.

Now we must equip our institutions to carry out the responsibility implicit in this new outlook. We must create the administrative and regulatory mechanisms necessary to assure wise land use and to stop haphazard, wasteful, or environmentally damaging development. Some States are moving ahead on their own to develop stronger land-use institutions and controls. Federal programs can and should reinforce this encouraging trend.

National Land Use Policy Act. The National Land Use Policy Act, which I proposed to the Congress last year, would provide Federal assistance to encourage the States, in cooperation with local governments, to protect lands which are of critical environmental concern and to control major development. While not yet enacted, this measure has been the subject of much useful debate.

I propose amendments to this pending National Land Use Policy legislation which would require States to control the siting of major transportation facilities, and impose sanctions on any State which does not establish an adequate land use program.

Under these amendments, the State programs established pursuant to the act would not only have to embody methods for controlling land use around key growth-inducing developments such as highways, airports, and recreational facilities; the States would also have to provide controls over the actual siting of the major highways and airports themselves. The change recognizes the fact that these initial siting decisions, once made, can often trigger runaway growth and adverse environmental effects.

The amendments would further provide that any State that had not established an acceptable land use program by 1975 would be subject to annual reductions of certain Federal funds. Seven percent of the funds allocated under sections of the Airport and Airways Development Act, the Federal-Aid Highway Acts including the Highway Trust Fund, and the Land and Water Conservation Fund, would be withheld in the first year. An additional 7 percent would be withheld for each additional year that a State was without an approved land use program. Money thus withheld from noncomplying States would be allocated among States which did have acceptable programs.

These strong new amendments are necessary in view of the significant effect that Federal programs, particularly transportation programs, have upon land use decisions.

Protection of Wetlands. The Nation's coastal and estuarine wetlands are vital to the survival of a wide variety of fish and wildlife; they have an important function in controlling floods and tidal forces; and they contain some of the most beautiful areas left on this continent. These same lands, however, are often some of the most sought-after for development. As a consequence, wetland acreage has been declining as more and more areas are drained and filled for residential, commercial, and industrial projects.

My National Land Use Policy Act would direct State attention to these important areas by defining wetlands among the "environmentally critical areas" which it singles out for special protection, and by giving priority attention to the coastal zones. I propose to supplement these safeguards with new economic disincentives to further discourage unnecessary wetlands development.

I propose legislation to limit applicability of certain Federal tax benefits when development occurs in coastal wetlands.

Management of Public Lands. During 1971, I acted to strengthen the environmental requirements relating to management and use of the Nation's vast acreage of federally-owned public lands administered by the Department of the Interior. I proposed new legislation to establish an overall management policy for these public lands, something which we have been without for far too long. This legislation, still pending before the Congress, would direct the Secretary of the Interior to manage our public lands in a manner that would protect their environmental quality for present and future generations.

The policy which it would establish declares the retention to the public lands to be in the national interest except where disposal of particular tracts would lead to a significant improvement in their management, or where the disposal would serve important public objectives which cannot be achieved on non-public lands.

Protecting our National Heritage

Wild places and wild things constitute a treasure to be cherished and protected for all time. The pleasure and refreshment which they give man confirm their value to society. More importantly perhaps, the wonder, beauty, and elemental force in which the least of them share suggest a higher right to exist—not granted them by man and not his to take away. In environmental policy as anywhere else we cannot deal in absolutes. Yet we can at least give considerations like these more relative weight in the seventies, and become a more civilized people in a healthier land because of it.

Predator Control. Americans today set high value on the preservation of wildlife. The old notion that "the only good predator is a dead one" is no longer acceptable as we understand that even the animals and birds which sometimes prey on domesticated animals have their own value in maintaining the balance of nature.

The widespread use of highly toxic poisons to kill coyotes and other predatory animals and birds is a practice which has been a source of increasing concern to the American public and to the Federal officials responsible for the public lands.

Last year the Council on Environmental Quality and the Department of the Interior appointed an Advisory Committee on Predator Control to study the entire question of predator and related animal control activities. The Committee found that persistent poisons have been applied to range and forest lands without adequate knowledge of their effects on the ecology or their utility in preventing losses to livestock. The large-scale use of poisons for control of predators and field rodents has resulted in unintended losses of other animals and in other harmful effects on natural ecosystems. The Committee concluded that necessary control of coyotes and other predators can be accomplished by methods other than poisons.

Certainly, predators can represent a threat to sheep and some other domesticated animals. But we must use more selective methods of control that will preserve ecological values while continuing to protect livestock.

I am today issuing an Executive Order barring the use of poisons for predator control on all public lands. (Exceptions will be made only for emergency situations.) I also propose legislation to shift the emphasis of the current direct Federal predator control program to one of research and technical and financial assistance to the States to help them control predator populations by means other than poisons.

Endangered Species. It has only been in recent years that efforts have been undertaken to list and protect those species of animals whose continued existence is in jeopardy. Starting with our national symbol, the bald eagle, we have expanded our concern over the extinction of these animals to include the present list of over 100. We have already found, however, that even the most recent act to protect endangered species, which dates only from 1969, simply does not provide the kind of management tools needed to act early enough to save a vanishing species. In particular, existing laws do not generally allow the Federal Government to control shooting, trapping, or other taking of endangered species.

I propose legislation to provide for early identification and protection of endangered species. My new proposal would make the taking of endangered species a Federal offense for the first time, and would permit protective measures to be undertaken before a species is so depleted that regeneration is difficult or impossible.

Migratory Species. The protection of migratory species, besides preserving wildlife values, exemplifies cooperative environmental effort among the United States, Canada, and Mexico. By treaties entered into among these three countries, migratory species are protected. New species may be added by common agreement between the United States and Mexico.

I have authorized the Secretary of State, in conjunction with the Secretary of the Interior, to seek the agreement of the Mexican Government to add 33 new families of birds to the protected list.

Included in the proposal are eagles, hawks, falcons, owls, and many of the most attractive species of wading birds. I am hopeful that treaty protection can be accorded them in the near future.

Big Cypress National Fresh Water Reserve. After careful review of the environmental significance of the Big Cypress Swamp in Florida, particularly of the need for water from this source to maintain the unique ecology of Everglades National Park, I directed the Secretary of the Interior to prepare legislation to create the Big Cypress National Fresh Water Reserve. This legislation, which has now been submitted to the Congress, will empower the Federal Government to acquire the requisite legal interest in 547,000 acres of Big Cypress.

New Parklands at the Gateways. The need to provide breathing space and recreational opportunities in our major urban centers is a major concern of this Administration. Two of the Nation's major gateways to the world—New York City and San Francisco—have land nearby with exceptional scenic and recreational potential, and we are moving to make that land available for people to enjoy. In May of 1971, I proposed legislation to authorize a Gateway National Recreation Area in New York and New Jersey. This proposal would open to a metropolitan region of more than 14 million people a National Recreation Area offering more than 23,000 acres of prime beaches, wildlife preserves, and historical attractions including the nation's oldest operating lighthouse.

On our western shore lies another area uniquely appropriate for making recreational and scenic values more accessible to a metropolitan community.

I propose legislation to establish a Golden Gate National Area in and around San Francisco Bay.

This proposal would encompass a number of existing parks, military reservations, and private lands to provide a full range of recreation experiences. Altogether, the area would encompass some 24,000 acres of fine beaches, rugged coasts, and readily accessible urban parklands, extending approximately 30 miles along some of America's most beautiful coastline north and south of Golden Gate Bridge. Angel and Alcatraz Islands in the bay would be within the boundaries of the National Recreation Area, as would a number of properties on the mainland which afford magnificent views of the city, the bay and the ocean. As part of this plan, I am directing that the Presidio at San Francisco be opened for dual military and civilian recreational uses.

Converting Federal Properties to Parks. Among the most important legacies that we can pass on to future generations is an endowment of parklands and recreational areas that will enrich leisure opportunities and make the beauties of the earth and sea accessible to all Americans. This is the object of our Legacy of Parks program, initiated early in 1971. As part of this program, I directed the Property Review Board to give priority to potential park and recreation areas in its search for alternative uses of federally held real property. The results of this search so far have been most encouraging. To the original 40 properties which I announced in my Environmental Message of 1971 as being well suited for park use, another 111 prospects have been added. And from this total of 151 prospective parklands, 63 have already been made available.

Today I am pleased to announce that 20 more parcels of Federal land are being made available for park and recreation use.

These newest parcels, combined with those which have been announced over the past year, provide a legacy of 83 parklands for America which comprise 14,585 acres in 31 States and Puerto Rico. The estimated fair market value of these properties is over $56 million. In the months to come, every effort will be made to extend this legacy to all 50 States. The green spaces and natural retreats that we tend to take for granted will not be available for future enjoyment unless we act now to develop and protect them.

Wilderness Areas. One of the first environmental goals I set when I took office was to stimulate the program to identify and recommend to the Congress new wilderness areas. Although this program was behind a schedule at that time, I am now able to report that the September, 1974, statutory deadline for reviews can and will be met.

The Wilderness Act of 1964 set aside 54 acres, consisting of about 9.1 million acres, as the nucleus of our wilderness system. Since then, 33 new areas totalling almost 1.2 million acres within National Forests, National Parks, and National Wildlife Refuges have been added to the system. Thirty-one areas totalling about 3.6 million acres, including 18 areas submitted by this Administration, have been proposed to the Congress but have yet to be acted upon. One of the most significant elements of this process has been the active participation by the public in all of its phases. At public wilderness hearings held all across the country, fair consideration has been given to all interests and points of view, with constructive citizen involvement in the decision-making process.

I am today proposing 18 new wilderness areas which, when approved, will add another 1.3 million acres to the wilderness system.

Eight of these proposals are within the National Forests, four are within National Park areas, and six are in National Wildlife Refuges.

Of these areas, 1.2 million acres would be in the following National Forests: Blue Range National Forest, Arizona and New Mexico; Agua Tibia and Emigrant National Forests, California; Eagles Nest and Weminuche National Forests, Colorado; Mission Mountains National Forest, Montana; Aldo Leopold National Forest, New Mexico; and Glacier National Forest, Wyoming.

A total of 40,000 acres would be in our National Park system in the following locations: Black Canyon of the Gunnison National Monument, Colorado; Bryce Canyon National Park, Utah; Chiricahua National Monument, Arizona; Colorado National Monument, Colorado.

Finally, a total of 87,000 acres would be in areas administered by the Fish and Wildlife Services of the Department of the Interior in the following locations: St. Marks, National Wildlife Refuge, Florida; Wolf Island, National Wildlife Refuge, Georgia; Moosehorn National Wildlife Refuge, Maine; San Juan Islands, National Wildlife Refuge, Washington; Cape Romain, National Wildlife Refuge, South Carolina; and Bosque del Apache, National Wildlife Refuge, New Mexico.

The year 1972 can bring some of the greatest accomplishment in wilderness preservation since passage of the Wilderness Act in 1964. I urge prompt and systematic consideration by the Congress of these 18 new proposals and of the 31 currently pending before it. Approval of all 49 additions would bring the system up to a total of over 15 million acres.

Unfortunately, few of these wilderness areas are within easy access of the most populous areas of the United States. The major purpose of my Legacy of Parks program is to bring recreation opportunities closer to the people, and while wilderness is only one such opportunity, it is a very important one. A few of the areas proposed today or previously are in the eastern sections of the country, but the great majority of wilderness areas are found in the West. This of course is where

most of our pristine wild areas are. But a greater effort can still be made to see that wilderness recreation values are preserved to the maximum extent possible, in the regions where most of our people live.

I am therefore directing the Secretaries of Agriculture and the Interior to accelerate the identification of areas in the Eastern United States having wilderness potential.

Off-road Vehicles. A recent study by the Department of the Interior estimated that Americans own more than 5 million off-road recreational vehicles—motorcycles, minibikes, trail bikes, snowmobiles, dune-buggies, all-terrain vehicles, and others. The use of these vehicles is dramatically on the increase: data show a three-fold growth between 1967 and 1971 alone.

As the number of off-road vehicles has increased, so has their use on public lands. Too often the land has suffered as a result. Increasingly, Federal recreational lands have become the focus of conflict between the newer motorized recreationist and the traditional hiker, camper, and horseback rider. In the past, Federal land-management agencies have used widely varying approaches to dealing with this conflict. The time has come for a unified Federal policy toward use of off-road vehicles on Federal lands.

I have today signed an Executive Order directing the Secretaries of Agriculture, Interior, Army and the Board of Directors of the Tennessee Valley Authority to develop regulations providing for control over the use of off-road vehicles on Federal lands.

They will designate areas of use and non-use, specify operating conditions that will be necessary to minimize damage to the natural resources of the Federal lands, and ensure compatibility with other recreational uses, taking into account noise and other factors.

Expanding International Cooperation
On the Environment

We are now growing accustomed to the view of our planet as seen from space—a blue and brown disk shrouded in white patches of clouds. But we do not ponder often enough the striking lesson it teaches about the global reach of environmental imperatives. No matter what else divides men and nations, this perspective should unite them. We must work harder to foster such world environmental consciousness and shared purpose.

United Nations Conference on the Human Environment. To cope with environmental questions that are truly international, we and other nations look to the first world conference of governments ever convened on this subject: the United Nations Conference on the Human Environment, to be held in Stockholm, Sweden, in June of this year. This should be a seminal event of the international community's attempt to cope with these serious, shared problems of global concern that transcend political differences.

But efforts to improve the global environment cannot go forward without the means to act.

To help provide such means, I propose that a voluntary United Nations Fund for the Environment be established, with an initial funding goal of $100 million for the first 5 years.

This Fund would help to stimulate international cooperation on environmental problems by supporting a centralized coordination point for United Nations activities in this field. It would also help to bring new resources to bear on the increasing number of worldwide problems through activities such as monitoring and cleanup of the oceans and atmosphere.

If such a Fund is established, I will recommend to the Congress that the United States commit itself to provide its fair share of the Fund on a matching basis over the first 5 years.

This level of support would provide startup assistance under mutually agreed-upon terms. As these programs get underway, it may well be that the member nations will decide that additional resources are required. I invite other nations to join with us in this commitment to meaningful action.

Control of Marine Pollution. Ocean pollution is clearly one of our major international environmental problems. I am gratified that in the past year the Congress has taken several steps to reduce the risks of oil spills on the high seas. However, further congressional action is needed to ratify several pending international conventions and to adopt implementing legislation for the various oil-spill conventions which have been ratified or which are awaiting approval.

Action on these recommendations will complete the first round of international conventions to deal with marine pollution. We have taken initiatives in three international forums to develop a second and more sophisticated round of agreements in this area. We are preparing for a 1973 Intergovernmental Maritime Consultative Organization (IMCO) Conference to draft a convention barring intentional discharges to the sea of oil and hazardous substances from ships. In conjunction with the Law of the Sea Conference scheduled for 1973, we are examining measures to control the effects of developing undersea resources. And, in the preparatory work for the 1972 U.N. Conference on the Human Environment, progress has been made on an agreement to regulate the ocean dumping of shore-generated wastes, and further work in this area has been scheduled by IMCO. We hope to conclude conventions in each of these areas by 1973.

Protecting Children From Lead-Based Paint

To many Americans, "environment" means the city streets where they live and work. It is here that a localized but acutely dangerous type of "pollution" has appeared and stirred mounting public concern.

The victims are children: the hazard is lead-based paint. Such paint was applied to the walls of most dwellings prior to the 1950's. When the paint chips and peels from the walls in dilapidated housing, it is frequently eaten by small children. This sometimes results in lead poisoning which can cause permanent mental retardation and occasionally death. We can and must prevent unnecessary loss of life and health from this hazard, which particularly afflicts the poorest segments of our population.

To help meet the lead-paint threat, the Department of Health, Education, and Welfare will administer grants and technical assistance to initiate programs in over 50 communities to test children in high-risk areas for lead concentrations. In addition, these programs will support the development of community organization and public education to increase public awareness of this hazard. Other Federal agencies are also active in the effort to combat lead-based paint poisoning. ACTION and other volunteers will assist city governments to help alleviate lead paint hazards. The Department of Housing and Urban Development is engaged in research and other actions to detect and eliminate this hazard.

The resources of the private sector should also be utilized through local laws requiring owners of housing wherever possible to control lead paint hazards.

Enlisting the Young

The starting point of environmental quality is in the hearts and minds of the people. Unless the people have a deep commitment to the new values and a clear understanding of the new problems, all our laws and programs and spending will avail little. The young, quick to commit and used to learning, are gaining the changed outlook fastest of all. Their enthusiasm about the environment spreads with a healthy contagion: their energy in its behalf can be an impressive force for good.

Four youth participation programs of mutual benefit to the young and the Nation are now planned or underway:

Last October, I initiated the Environmental Merit Awards Program. This program, directed by the Environmental Protection Agency in cooperation with the U.S. Office of Education, awards national recognition to successful student projects leading to environmental understanding or improvement. Qualifications for the awards are determined by a local board consisting of secondary school students, faculty, and representatives of the local community. Already more than 2,000 high schools, representing all fifty States, have registered in the program.

The Department of Agriculture's expanded field scout demonstration program, designed to permit more effective pest control with less reliance on chemical pesticides, will employ thousands of high school and college students. These young people will be scouting cotton and tobacco pests in the coming growing season, and the program will be expanded to other crops in future years.

The Environmental Protection Agency has recently initiated in its Seattle regional office a pilot program using young people to assist the agency in many of its important tasks, including monitoring. EPA is working with State and local pollution control agencies to identify monitoring needs. ACTION and the youth training programs are providing the manpower. If this initial program proves successful, the concept will be expanded.

ACTION volunteers and young people employed through the Neighborhood Youth Corps, Job Corps, and college work-study programs will work with city governments to help alleviate lead paint hazards, gaining experience in community health work as they give urgently needed aid to inner-city families.

Young people working on environmental projects, learning the skills necessary for a particular job, must also understand how their work relates to the environmental process as a whole. Thus, all of these activities must be supplemented by continued improvement in many aspects of environmental education to help all of our citizens, both young and old, develop a better awareness of man's relation to his environment. In my first Environmental Quality Report, I stressed the importance of improving the Nation's "environmental literacy." This goal remains as important as ever, and our progress toward it must continue.

One Destiny

Our destiny is one: this the environmental awakening has taught America in these first years of the seventies. Let us never forget, though, that it is not a destiny of fear, but of promise. As I stated last August in transmitting the Second Annual Report of the Council on Environmental Quality: "The work of environmental improvement is a task for all our people.... The achievement of that goal will challenge the creativity of our science and technology, the enterprise and adaptability of our industry, the responsiveness and sense of balance of our political and legal institutions, and the resourcefulness and the capacity of this country to honor those human values upon which the quality of our national life must ultimately depend." We shall rise to the challenge of solving our environmental problems by enlisting the creative energy of all of our citizens in a cause truly worthy of the best that each can bring to it.

While we share our environmental problems with all the people of the world, our industrial might, which has made us the leader among nations in terms of material well-being, also gives us the responsibility of dealing with environmental problems first among the nations. We can be proud that our solutions and our performance will become the measure for others climbing the ladder of aspirations and difficulties; we can set our sights on a standard that will lift their expectations of what man can do.

The pursuit of environmental quality will require courage and patience. Problems that have been building over many years will not yield to facile solutions. But I do not doubt that Americans have the wit and the will to win—to fulfill our brightest vision of what the future can be.

RICHARD NIXON

PRESIDENT NIXON'S MESSAGE ON FISCAL 1973 BUDGET

Following is the complete text, as made available by the White House, of President Nixon's Jan. 24 budget message to Congress.

To the Congress of the United States:

The Budget of the United States for the fiscal year 1973 has as a central purpose a new prosperity for all Americans without the stimulus of war and without the drain of inflation.

To provide for the needs of our people by creating new peacetime jobs and revitalizing the economy, we are spending $38.8 billion more in the current (1972) fiscal year than our receipts.

I make that estimate fully aware that it is a large deficit, but one that is necessary in a year of reduced receipts, as we increase jobs and bring the economy back toward capacity.

I am able to project a 1973 budget, with rising revenues, that cuts this year's actual deficit by $13½ billion and brings us strongly forward toward our goal of a balanced budget in a time of full employment.

If we were to spend less, we would be "too little and too late" to stimulate greater business activity and create more jobs; if we were to spend more, we would be spending "too much, too soon" and thereby invite a renewal of inflation. Instead, we must spend "enough and on time" to keep the economy on a steadily upward peacetime course while providing jobs for all who want them and meeting the urgent needs of the American people.

The budget for fiscal 1972 reflects this Government's confidence in the American economy's ability and capacity to respond to sensible stimulation. The budget for 1973, held to full-employment balance, diminishes stimulation as the new prosperity takes hold and, by so doing, acts as a barrier against the renewal of inflationary pressure.

I strongly urge the Congress to respect the full-employment spending guideline this year, just as business and labor are expected to re-spect wage and price guidelines set forth to protect the earning and buying power of the American worker and consumer. In the long run, only the intelligent application of responsible fiscal and monetary policies, coupled with the breaking of inflationary expectations, will bring about peacetime prosperity without rising prices in a free market economy.

Deficit spending at this time, like temporary wage and price controls, is strong but necessary medicine. We take that medicine because we need it, not because we like it; as our economy successfully combats unemployment, we will stop taking the medicine well before we become addicted to it.

Preparing the Federal budget forces us to face up to the choices and challenges before us—to decide what national interests take priority.

The budget is a superb deflator of rhetoric because it calls to account the open-ended promises heard so often in an election year. Proposals, no matter how attractive, must be paid for, and when spending is proposed that takes us beyond full employment balance, that payment must either be in the form of new taxes or rising prices. As the budget submitted herewith proves, I intend to resist the kind of spending that drives up taxes or drives up prices.

One priority that most Americans will agree upon is the return of power to people, after decades of the flow of power to Washington. One good way of turning rhetoric into reality is to put that principle into practice in the tax area.

Power in its most specific sense is spending power. My own choice between Government spending and individual spending has been clear and consistent: I believe some of that power should be taken from the Federal Government and returned to the individual.

Accordingly, over the past 3 years, *the rate of increase in Government spending has been cut nearly in half* compared to the 3 comparable years before this Administration took office.

From 1965 to 1968, Federal spending increased by 51%—an annual average of 17%; over the 3-year period 1969–72, spending rose by 28%—an average of 9% per year. The increase from 1972 to the spending level proposed in this budget is only 4.1%. This slash in the momentum of Federal spending is all the more dramatic when you consider that 71% of Federal spending is "uncontrollable"—that is. locked into the budget by previous congressional decisions.

By putting the brakes on the increase in Government spending, we have been able to leave more spending power in the hands of the individual taxpayer. *In 1973, individuals will pay $22 billion less in Federal income taxes than they would if the tax rates and structure were the same as those in existence when I took office.* To a family of four that earns $7,500 a year, that means a reduction of Federal income taxes of $272 this calendar year. I believe that the members of that family can use that money more productively for their own needs than Government can use it for them.

THE BUDGET DOLLAR
Fiscal Year 1973 Estimate

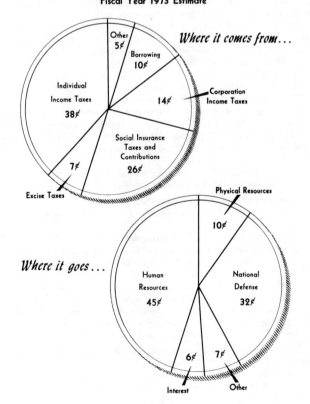

Where it comes from...

Other 5¢
Borrowing 10¢
Individual Income Taxes 38¢
Corporation Income Taxes 14¢
Social Insurance Taxes and Contributions 26¢
Excise Taxes 7¢

Where it goes...

Physical Resources 10¢
Human Resources 45¢
National Defense 32¢
Interest 6¢
Other 7¢

Wage income	Taxes paid		Reduction between 1969 and 1972	
	1969	1972	Amount	Percentage
$5,000	$290	$98	$192	66
$7,500	756	484	272	36
$10,000	1,225	905	320	26
$15,000	2,268	1,820	448	20

FEDERAL INCOME TAX REDUCTIONS FOR MARRIED COUPLE WITH 2 CHILDREN, 1969–72

[Calendar year]

The basic shift in the Government's fiscal philosophy has gone relatively unnoticed. The upward curve of Federal spending is beginning to flatten out, while the Federal income tax "bite" out of the individual paycheck is becoming measurably less. This change in direction is as remarkable as it has been unremarked. We are not only talking about returning power—economic power, real power—to people and localities, we are doing something about it.

Throughout this budget, a clear trend can be seen that is designed to return power to people—in real terms, in dollars-and-cents terms. It is a trend which is expressed by Federal income tax cuts, by more State and local participation in program administration, and by more Federal funds going to State and local governments without restrictions.

This is the right course for the American people; it reflects their will; I remind the Congress of its power and responsibility to make revenue sharing and other returns of power to people a reality in this current session.

Another priority—one upon which so much of our progress at home depends—is to create a peaceful world order. We could never fulfill our hopes for a full generation of peace from a position of weakness; we can only negotiate and maintain peace if our military power continues to be second to none.

A demagogue may find it easy enough to advocate that we simply allocate necessary defense dollars to social programs, but a responsible Congress and a responsible President cannot afford such easy answers.

Our success in reducing our involvement in Vietnam by 480,000 men before May 1, 1972, and comparable materiel reductions will help enable us—for the first time—to spend more in the Department of Health, Education, and Welfare than we spend in the Department of Defense.

But it would be foolhardy not to modernize our defense at this crucial moment. Accordingly, and still within our full-employment guideline, I propose a $6.3 billion increase in budget authority for military programs, including vitally needed additions to our strategic forces and our naval strength.

In the 1972 defense appropriation bill, which the Congress did not pass until December of 1971, the Congress cut my appropriation request by $3 billion. My 1971 defense request was cut by the Congress by $2.1 billion. These were costly cuts, especially in the field of research and development.

We must be prudent in our defense spending, making certain we get the best defense for each taxpayer dollar spent. Productivity here too must be increased, but we cannot afford to be "penny-wise and pound-foolish." *Nothing could be more wasteful than to have to pay the price of weakness.* It costs far less to maintain our strength than it would cost to fall behind and have to catch up, even if that could be done. I urge the Congress not to make the costly mistakes it has made in previous years in its defense cuts; the budget as submitted represents America's actual military needs, and offers the best means to secure peace for the coming generation.

Another priority of this budget is to direct the resources of the Federal Government toward those needs the American people most want met and to the people who are most in need.

Welfare Reform, with training and work incentives, with a new fairness toward the working poor and a minimum income for every dependent family, is a good idea whose time has come. It has been proposed and studied; it has been refined and improved upon; it is ripe for action now. Further delay in enactment would not only be unwise in fiscal terms, but cruel in human terms. The proposed program is infinitely better than the wasteful, demeaning system that now calls itself welfare. This budget proposes appropriation of $450 million to start the replacement of welfare with "workfare."

Revenue Sharing has been debated at length. Each day and each State's experience only confirms the inescapable fact that it is wanted and needed—now. The States and cities urgently require this aid; individual Americans need it for everything from improved law enforcement to tax relief. This budget allocates $2.5 billion in 1972 and $5.3 billion in 1973 to make General Revenue Sharing a reality now.

Schools need emergency assistance now to make necessary adjustments to provide equal educational opportunity. This budget allocates $500 million in 1972 and $1 billion in 1973 for this purpose.

Government reorganization is needed now, to deliver more services for each tax dollar collected. The pain this change will bring to special interests and bureaucracies is less important than the pain existing bureaucratic arrangements now cause the people. A reorganized government will be a better, more efficient government.

Health care must be improved and made available to all Americans, without driving up medical costs. This budget provides for legislative actions and necessary funding to make better health care available on the most widespread basis, to emphasize preventive medicine, and to pursue an all-out campaign to eliminate cancer and sickle cell anemia.

Drug abuse prevention must be intensified to curb narcotics trafficking and to expand Federal drug rehabilitation efforts coordinated by the White House Special Action Office. The budget allocates $594 million to these and other drug abuse prevention campaigns.

A new commitment to the aging is long overdue to add dignity and usefulness to their lives. This budget provides for total spending of $50 billion on behalf of the aging, $16 billion more than in 1969. Most importantly, $51½ billion will be added to the incomes of older Americans when proposed social security and Welfare Reform legislation is fully in effect. In addition, service initiatives will be launched that will focus on better nutrition and other services designed to help the elderly live independently in their own homes.

Scientific research and technology, so essential to our national security, also must focus more directly on solving our domestic problems, increasing our productivity, and improving our competitive position in international trade. The budget allocates $17.8 billion for this, an increase of $1.4 billion over 1972.

Veterans of the Nation will receive the special consideration they deserve, with particular emphasis on those reentering civilian life after service in Vietnam. This budget provides more than $12 billion in budget authority for veterans benefits, with an increase of over $1 billion for modernization, replacement, and record staffing of VA hospitals, higher compensation for disabled veterans, and enhanced job training opportunities, higher GI bill allowances, and other improved services.

Details on each of these proposals are given later in this Budget Message.

ECONOMIC SETTING AND FISCAL POLICY

Economic setting.—In January 1969, the Nation's chief economic problem was mounting inflation.

Anti-inflationary policies that we adopted began gradually to lower the rate of price increases. However, progress was slower than we had hoped and was accompanied by an unacceptable increase in unemployment. This increase was in part a result of the transition of 2½ million people from wartime to peacetime activities.

During 1970 and 1971, responsible economic policies provided stimulus to expand the economy. The budgets for these years had actual deficits of $2.8 billion and $23 billion, but full-employment surpluses of $3.1 billion and $4.9 billion.

As a result of these policies, progress was made in moderating inflation and in expanding real output in the first half of calendar year 1971. However, inflation and unemployment continued to be unacceptably high. Meanwhile, a deterioration in the trade and balance of payments position of the United States, caused in part by the inflationary pressures of the latter half of the 1960's and aggravated by weaknesses in international monetary and trading arrangements, required decisive corrective action.

Action was called for and action was taken.

On August 15, 1971, I announced a new economic policy that:

—imposed a 90-day freeze on wage and price increases;
—proposed a job development tax credit to increase employment by stimulating investment;
—recommended repeal of the automobile excise tax and an early increase in the personal tax exemption, which together would provide an extra $8 billion of stimulus to the economy over a 3-year period;
—reduced planned Federal spending in 1972 by $5 billion; and
—suspended the convertibility of the dollar into gold and other reserve assets and imposed a temporary 10% import surcharge, thereby laying the foundation for improved trade performance and for basic changes in the international economic system.

The public responded to the new economic policy with the widespread support essential to its success.

This policy has begun to move the economy toward full employment without inflation and without war, a condition we have not experienced in this generation. The consumer price index rose only 1.7% at an annual rate from August to November—the lowest rate of increase for a comparable period in 4½ years. From August to December, industrial wholesale prices rose only 0.5% at an annual rate, after increasing at a 4.6% annual rate during the first 8 months of the year.

Now we have moved beyond the wage and price freeze into a transitional period of flexible wage and price controls and on the way to a return to reasonable stability under free markets.

The proposed tax reductions were part of the Revenue Act of 1971, which became law on December 10. Because of the general expectation that the Congress would approve them, the economic effect of these reductions began to be felt immediately after August 15. Automobile

A Slowdown in Inflation— Percent Change in the CPI (Annual Rates)

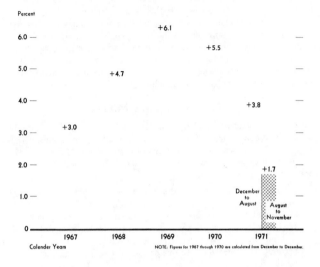

sales soared to a record rate in October, interest rates declined, and business investment plans—after some hesitation—are being revised upward. Taken together, these results will create many of the new jobs needed for full employment.

Negotiations with our international trading partners produced a major agreement in mid-December. Exchange rates were realigned through a devaluation of the dollar and revaluation of the currencies of some of our major trading partners. The 10% surcharge on imports was removed as promised. That agreement will improve the competitive position of U.S. industry and agriculture and permit us to move forward in negotiations on fundamental reform of the international monetary system and on elimination of barriers to expanded international trade.

Each element of the new economic policy has a vital role in sustaining the momentum of our economy. The 1973 budget carries out a fiscal policy that is responsive to the needs of the Nation and responsible in holding down inflation.

Budget policy.—The full-employment budget concept is central to the budget policy of this Administration. Except in emergency conditions, *expenditures should not exceed the level at which the budget would be balanced under conditions of full employment.* The 1973 budget conforms to this guideline. By doing so, it provides necessary stimulus for expansion, but is not inflationary.

We have planned the 1973 expenditures to adhere to the full-employment budget concept, even though this has required making many difficult decisions. It now appears that the 1972 full-employment budget will be $8.1 billion in deficit. While our economy can absorb such a deficit for a time, the experience of the late 1960's provides ample warning of the danger of continued, and rising, full-employment deficits. The lesson of 1966–68, when such deficits led to an intolerable inflation, is too clear and too close to permit any relaxation of control of Government spending.

Keeping the 1973 budget in full-employment balance will not be easy. The tax changes that have been made during my Administration have reduced 1973 full-employment revenue by a net total of $20 billion. This reduction has been good for the economy, and has given

Full Employment Budget —Surplus or Deficit

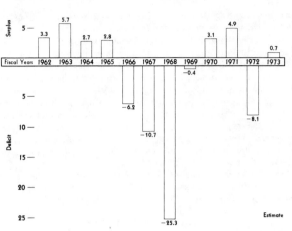

each of us more freedom to decide how he will spend his money and live his life. However, the lower receipts and the need to balance the 1973 full-employment budget require that the Congress carefully consider the Nation's priorities, as I have done in preparing this budget. The task is made harder by the fact that the growth of programs—especially, uncontrollable programs, which now account for 71% of total outlays—could easily lead to another full-employment deficit in 1973 if the Congress adds to my recommendations for domestic spending as it did last year.

The simple fact is that not all programs can or should grow. I urge the Congress to face squarely the difficult questions involved in setting priorities within the overall constraint of a full-employment balance, and not to take the dangerous course of trying to match domestic spending increases with cuts in vitally needed defense funds.

SUMMARY OF THE 1973 BUDGET

For 1973, the Federal budget at full-employment is approximately in balance.

THE BUDGET TOTALS
[Fiscal years. In billions]

Description	1971 actual	1972 estimate	1973 estimate
Budget receipts	$188.4	$197.8	$220.8
Budget outlays	211.4	236.6	246.3
Deficit (—)	—23.0	—38.8	—25.5
Full-employment receipts	214.1	225.0	245.0
Full-employment outlays [1]	209.2	233.1	244.3
Full-employment surplus or deficit (—)	4.9	—8.1	0.7
Budget authority	236.4	249.8	270.9

Outstanding debt, end of year:	1970 actual		
Gross Federal debt	$382.6	$409.5	$455.8	$493.2
Debt held by the public	284.9	304.3	343.8	371.3

Outstanding Federal and federally assisted credit, end of year:			
Direct loans [2]	51.1	53.2	50.7	51.4
Guaranteed and insured loans [3]	105.4	118.7	136.8	158.6
Direct loans by Government-sponsored agencies	37.5	38.8	54.6	65.8

[1] These estimates reflect the fact that under conditions of full employment outlays for unemployment insurance benefits and the Emergency Employment Act program would be lower. Spending under other programs are also affected by employment conditions. For example, outlays for food stamps, social security benefits, public assistance, and veterans' pensions would also be lower under conditions of full employment, and interest would be higher. If adjustments were feasible for all such items, full employment outlays probably would be lower.
[2] Including loans in expenditure account.
[3] Excluding loans held by Government or Government-sponsored agencies.

Budget receipts in 1973 are estimated to be $220.8 billion, which is $23 billion higher than in 1972. If the economy were operating at full employment throughout the year, the revenues produced would be $245 billion.

Estimated receipts for 1973 reflect a reduction of $6.9 billion as a result of the tax cuts proposed in the new economic policy and incorporated in the Revenue Act of 1971. About $5 billion of this reduction is in individuals' taxes. The resulting increase in consumers' purchasing power will be a major source of strength in the economy.

Budget outlays in the coming year are expected to be $246.3 billion, an increase of $9.6 billion over the current year. This outlay increase will also help provide jobs and business investment in the year ahead, while remaining within the limit set by full-employment budget guidelines. If the economy were operating at full employment throughout the year, outlays for unemployment insurance benefits and the Emergency Employment Act—and outlay totals—would be lower than the amounts included in the 1973 budget.

This budget requests $271 billion of *budget authority*—the right to make commitments to spend—in 1973. About $185 billion of this amount will require new action on the part of the Congress.

STRATEGY FOR PEACE

The highest priority of my Administration is to bring about an era of peace and prosperity. We are pursuing this goal through partnership with our allies, military strength adequate to deter aggression, negotiations with those with whom we differ, and foreign assistance that encourages self-sufficiency.

We seek peace to reduce the human suffering that is an inevitable part of war. With peace we can release energies and resources that can be used to improve the quality of life everywhere. We have accomplished much of this high purpose during the past 3 years—particularly as a result of the Vietnamization program.

- South Vietnamese forces have assumed the responsibility for ground combat operations. Vietnamization is moving forward in other areas as well. As a result:

  —U.S. casualties due to hostilities have been averaging less than 10 per week, as compared with 300 per week in 1968;
  —the authorized troop level in South Vietnam will have been reduced from 549,500 in January 1969 to 69,000 as of May 1, 1972; and
  —draft calls have been reduced from a Vietnam war high of 382,000 to 94,000 in calendar year 1971, as we move toward the goal of zero draft calls.

- Negotiations with the Soviet Union on strategic arms limitations are progressing.
- Agreement has been reached with NATO members on a 5-year plan to strengthen their defenses, with a substantial increase in their financial contribution.
- Security assistance programs are being planned with a view toward better coordinating them with our overall security effort. In some cases, this may permit additional reductions in U.S. manpower needs overseas.

Our efforts toward peace have not been—and will not be—at the expense of our military strength. Indeed, measures to maintain that strength are a vital part of our peace efforts. Accordingly, this budget proposes a substantial increase in defense programs to provide for the following improvements:

—additional resources for our strategic forces to increase emphasis on our sea-based strategic deterrent force and to continue modernization of present offensive and defensive forces;
—a major increase in shipbuilding, reflecting the high priority I place upon modernizing our naval forces;
—a sizable increase in research and development to assure continuation of our technological superiority;
—newer equipment, higher manning levels, and further training to improve the ability of the National Guard and Reserves to supplement the Active Forces;
—continued development and procurement of more effective weapons systems for the land and tactical air forces; and
—a major effort to achieve an all-volunteer force. Toward this end,

a career in the Armed Forces was made more attractive by doubling the basic pay of first time enlistees in November 1971. Other increases in military pay are budgeted for January 1972 and 1973.

Strong foreign assistance programs are also an essential part of our strategy for peace, serving to:

—implement the Nixon Doctrine by helping foreign nations assume a greater share of the responsibility for their defense;
—strengthen the economies of developing nations; and
—provide humanitarian assistance and relief.

We must be steadfast in our foreign assistance. We are moving from an era of confrontation to an era of negotiation and increased reliance on our allies to defend themselves. In this setting, I have carefully weighed our basic assistance requirements against our domestic priorities, and now submit a program based on a thorough assessment of what is essential. We must not undercut the efforts of developing nations to stand on their own. Nor can we shortchange the nations now shouldering the burden of their own defense after they—and we—have given so much.

MEETING HUMAN NEEDS

My Administration has begun widespread reform and has sought to take new directions in Federal human resources programs. From 1969 to 1972, outlays for these purposes grew by 63%, while total budget outlays grew by only 28%. This increase is designed to buy such real improvements as:

—greater benefits for the aged and other beneficiaries under social security;
—additional training opportunities for the disadvantaged;
—reform of the food stamp program to establish national standards and to give more help to the most needy;
—better health care for millions of low-income persons and for the aged;
—expanded and improved veterans programs;
—increased educational opportunities for students from lower income families; and
—extension of unemployment insurance coverage to more Americans.

As a result, human resources spending will be 45% of the 1973 budget, while defense programs will be 32%. Our policy of ending our involvement in the Vietnam war has helped make this possible by freeing resources to keep us strong externally as well as internally. This exactly reverses the priorities of the prior administration. In 1968, the defense share was 45% and the human resources share was 32%.

While this is a substantial record of progress, our work is far from complete.

This budget recommends new initiatives and emphasizes many reforms proposed last year—*on which the Congress has yet to complete action*. These proposals are a necessary part of my efforts to return more of the power to the people, to strengthen the capacity of State and local governments to govern, and—especially by assuring the civil rights of all our citizens—to contribute to personal freedom and human dignity.

To help overcome the fragmentation in human services, which so often loses sight of the whole person and the family, I am proposing Allied Services legislation that would assist State and local governments to respond to human needs more efficiently, more flexibly, and more comprehensively. The legislation would authorize the transfer of Federal funds between Department of Health, Education, and Welfare programs not included in revenue sharing, the waiver of cumbersome Federal program requirements, and limited funding for planning and administrative costs.

Welfare Reform.—Almost four decades of experience with the present welfare system is more than enough to teach us that the system has failed.

- It takes away the incentive to work.
- It lacks adequate job opportunities and child care services that would encourage and assist recipients to become self-supporting.

- Its benefits are inadequate to the needs of its recipients.
- It encourages families to break up so that they might qualify for assistance.
- Its 54 different systems with diverse standards defy efficient administration and create severe inequities.

I urge that the Congress approve promptly the Administration's Workfare legislative proposal. My proposal would remove the greatest evils of the present system by:

—emphasizing work incentives, work requirements, job training and public employment opportunities, child care, and reform of social service programs to encourage families to become and remain self-supporting;

—providing benefits for the first time to families with fathers who work but who do not earn enough to provide a decent standard of living for the family;

—setting a national minimum income standard for all families with children in America;

—establishing uniform national eligibility standards;

—reducing the fiscal pressure on States caused by rapidly rising welfare expenditures; and

—raising income limits to allow retired persons to earn more without loss of benefits.

Nutrition for the needy.—This Administration has taken decisive steps to feed the hungry and eliminate malnutrition in America. Most importantly, major reforms of the Food Stamp program that I proposed are now in operation. New regulations will:

—establish uniform eligibility standards that equal or exceed the present State standards in all States;

—concentrate benefits on those most in need;

—guarantee family stamp allotments for the needy large enough to purchase a nutritionally adequate diet, with increases tied to the cost of living; and

—provide a work requirement for those able to work.

As a result of these and earlier Administration actions, we have provided more benefits to more people in need than ever before. Food stamp outlays have increased ninefold from 1969 to 1973—reaching an estimated $2.3 billion in benefits for 13 million poor in 1973.

In addition, there will be nearly a threefold increase between 1969 and 1973 in the number of needy schoolchildren receiving subsidized lunches.

Food Assistance

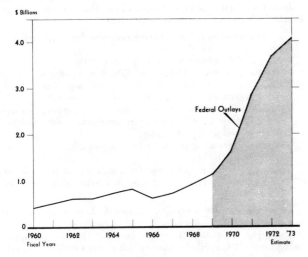

A new dignity for the aging.—Last November, I convened the White House Conference on Aging to develop proposals for improving the lives of our senior citizens. The recommendations of the Conference clearly indicate that programs to aid the aged should serve two essential purposes.

- They should provide the aged with sufficient income and necessary services to permit them to remain independent.
- They should assist aged citizens to live active and useful lives.

This budget is responsive to these recommendations. In 1973, the Federal Government will spend nearly $50 billion to assist the Nation's 21 million aged persons. This is $16 billion more than the amount spent to assist the aging in 1969.

Federal Outlays for the Elderly

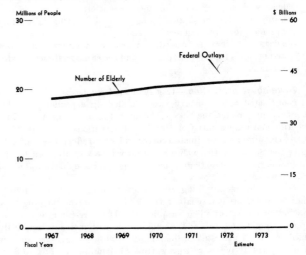

Several major proposals in this budget are responsive to the special needs of the aged:

—social security and workfare legislation that will add $5.5 billion to the income of the elderly when it is fully in effect and provide an income floor for older Americans;

—elimination of the monthly premium for supplementary medical insurance in Medicare that will save the elderly $1.5 billion in the first full year;

—$100 million, a fivefold increase over the amount budgeted last year, for the Administration on Aging to provide additional homemaker services, home health aides, transportation, and nutrition services to help older Americans remain in their homes;

—a tripling of the retired senior volunteer program, a doubling of the foster grandparents programs, and a doubling of jobs programs for older persons with low incomes from the levels budgeted last year to enable more of the aged to engage in useful community projects; and

—tax incentives that will broaden the coverage of private pension plans.

The Congress has not yet acted on the major reform in the social security system that I proposed last year—providing automatic adjustments for increases in the cost of living. The older Americans who depend on their social security checks have waited long enough. I urge the Congress to act promptly on this reform and, in addition to:

—raise benefits by 5%, effective July 1, 1972, making the cumulative increase more than one-third in less than 3 years;

—allow recipients to earn more money from wages without losing their benefits; and

—increase widows' benefits up to the level their deceased husbands would have received.

Improving health care.—Almost a year ago, I submitted a health message to the Congress establishing a National Health Strategy for the 1970's. This strategy was directed toward three objectives: prevention of health problems, assured access to medical care, and greater efficiency within the health care system.

To achieve these objectives, I urge the Congress to act promptly on the pending National Health Insurance Standards Act, the proposed Family Health Insurance Plan, and legislation to support the development of health maintenance organizations.

In addition, in 1973, I propose further actions that are essential to my national health strategy, including:

—a substantial increase in funds for the attacks on cancer and sickle cell anemia;

—continued financial support to our health manpower training institutions and to their students;

—expanded efforts to develop health maintenance organizations as a model of improved health care delivery;

—significant increases for protecting consumers from hazardous food and products;

—expanded community programs to deal with special health problems, such as drug addiction and alcoholism;

—improvement of the Medicare program by eliminating the monthly premium for physician services; and

—substantial increases in medical personnel at veterans' hospitals and in funds for constructing new and better hospital facilities for veterans.

Drug abuse prevention.—Last summer, I emphasized the need for a coordinated attack on drug abuse and drug dependency in this country and created the Special Action Office for Drug Abuse Prevention and the Cabinet Committee on International Narcotics Control to monitor and coordinate a concerted Federal effort. Legislation to give the Special Action Office a statutory base was proposed by the Administration more than 7 months ago and should be approved promptly.

In 1973, I am proposing an increase in program levels of $120 million for treatment, rehabilitation, and law enforcement programs, including control of illicit supplies. Funds for research, education, prevention, treatment, and rehabilitation will increase from $310 million in 1972 to $365 million in 1973 while obligations for law enforcement activities will grow from $164 million in 1972 to $229 million in 1973. Under the direction of a Special Consultant to the President, we are mounting a coordinated attack on dope sellers in 24 cities throughout the country.

Guaranteeing civil rights.—All of our citizens should expect a first priority of government to be protection of their civil rights. My Administration is committed to a course of action to insure that people can share fully in the benefits of our society regardless of race, sex, religion, or national origin. Significant accomplishments have been made. Much remains to be done:

• We will continue the increase in minority hirings in the Federal service, especially in professional and supervisory positions, despite cutbacks in Federal employment. More than 13,000 minority employees were hired between November 1969 and May 1971, and minority increases in upper and middle grade levels occurred at much faster rates than for nonminorities. Minorities now constitute approximately one-fifth of all Federal employees.

• We will continue to press efforts to assure that women will hold more jobs with greater responsibilities than ever before. Between October 31, 1970 and October 31, 1971, women holding Federal positions at levels GS–13 and above increased by 7%.

• We will continue the upgrading of efforts to open opportunities for Spanish-speaking Americans. The budget of the Cabinet Committee on the Spanish-Speaking will be increased by 42%.

• We will step up our efforts to promote self-determination for Indians on reservations and to assist them in their economic development. For example, legislation to establish an Indian Trust Counsel Authority has been proposed to guarantee that the rights of the Indian people in natural resources are—at last—effectively defended. Outlays for programs benefiting Indians on reservations will reach $1.2 billion in 1973.

• We will double our resources and our efforts to assure that Federal contractors meet the commitments of their affirmative minority hiring plans. Compliance reviews will increase to 52,000 compared to 12,300 in 1969.

• We will continue to accelerate Federal financial aid and technical assistance to increase minority business opportunities in America. Outlays for these programs have grown from $213 million in 1969 to $716 million in 1973.

• We will continue our efforts to help with the problems of school desegregation and upgrade our assistance to black colleges and other developing institutions of higher education. The Emergency School Act will provide $1.5 billion over a two-year period to assist in school desegregation.

• We will add to our efforts to eradicate unlawful discrimination in the sale, rental, or financing of housing. Expenditures for these programs will increase 20% in 1973 to $11 million.

• We will increase the outlays of the Equal Employment Opportunity Commission from $22 million to $30 million to enhance their capability to end discrimination in the private sector.

To carry out these plans, I have recommended total expenditures of $2.6 billion for Federal civil rights activities in 1973. This compares with $911 million in 1969. Outlays will increase by 25% between 1972 and 1973.

Veterans benefits.—In moving toward a generation of peace, we will provide improved benefits for the men and women who have helped obtain that peace through military service and great sacrifice. For the returning veteran, this budget demonstrates our concern by providing greater opportunities for entry into jobs, education, and training. For those who have been disabled in service, this budget provides medical care of high quality that is better tailored to their needs—together with greater benefits for rehabilitation and compensation. For the widows and children of those who did not return, this budget provides additional dependents' compensation, education, and training. Budget authority for these and other benefits and services will be increased by $1 billion in 1973—to $12.4 billion.

Marked benefit improvements will include:

—an increase of 10,000 in average employment in VA medical facilities, raising the staff to patient ratio for VA hospital care to a record 1.5 to 1;

—a 66% increase in budget authority for construction of new and better hospital facilities, including seven new replacement hospitals;

—improvements in the structure and levels of veterans compensation benefits, to insure more adequate benefits for the most seriously disabled; and

—an increase in the monthly individual benefit payment for the GI bill from $175 to $190, linked with other program improvements I have proposed.

Education and manpower training.—The need for reform in Federal education and manpower training programs has not diminished since last year, but the reforms I recommended then are *still awaiting action by the Congress.*

We must reform these programs so that people can achieve their potential intellectual and occupational skills. For this reason, I again emphasize the need for action on proposals to:

—substitute special revenue sharing programs for categorical grant programs in both of these areas;

—assist school districts in desegregation efforts;

—establish a National Institute of Education to support research and experimentation and a National Foundation on Higher Education to promote reforms in our colleges and universities;

—provide additional training opportunities and strong incentives under Welfare Reform for welfare recipients to undertake suitable employment or job training;

—assure the returning veteran greater opportunities for jobs, education, and training; and

—reform student aid programs for higher education to increase their effectiveness and direct more aid to students from lower income families.

Let me use that last proposal as an example. I believe that no qualified student should be denied a college education because he cannot afford to pay for it. Most Americans and most Congressmen agree. I have proposed the legislation that will make this a reality. I am ready to sign that legislation. But there it sits, in Congress, while thousands of young people miss their chance.

FIGHTING CRIME

When I took office, the safety and health of our citizens were menaced by rising crime. Violent crimes and illegal traffic in narcotics and dangerous drugs were threatening to get out of control. A crisis existed, and prompt action was called for. I directed that a national strategy to combat crime be developed and promptly put into effect.

Any successful strategy to combat crime must recognize that State and local governments are responsible for most law enforcement in the United States. Such a strategy must also provide for the prevention of crime and for the rehabilitation of criminals.

I took action early to strengthen the hand of State and local government law enforcement agencies.

- Outlays for law enforcement assistance were increased substantially. They will total $595 million in 1973, nearly 18 times the $33½ million of 1969.
- Law enforcement special revenue sharing was proposed to give State and local governments increased flexibility to use Federal funds in ways that are best suited to solving local crime problems. *The Congress should act on this proposal.*

Federal law enforcement activities are also an essential part of our efforts to combat crime—especially organized crime and traffic in narcotics and dangerous drugs. In 1973, we will:

—step up our attack against the criminal systems that import and distribute narcotics and dangerous drugs; and
—continue to enforce vigorously the Organized Crime Control Act of 1970.

Outlays for law enforcement activities will be $2.3 billion in 1973, an increase of $1.7 billion over 1969.

Federal Outlays for Crime Reduction

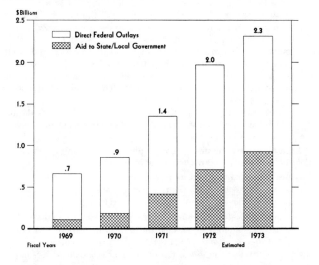

My Administration has given priority to combating crime in our Nation's Capital, where the Federal Government has a special responsibility. These efforts have been successful. Serious crime in the District of Columbia in 1971 was approximately 14% below the level of the previous calendar year.

IMPROVING THE ENVIRONMENT

Protecting and improving our environment is a never-ending job. The basic responsibility rests with States and local governments, industry, and the public. However, the Federal Government must provide leadership.

In 1970, the Environmental Protection Agency was established to improve our pollution control efforts, and the Council on Environmental Quality was established to advise on problems and policies related to environmental quality.

Now, new initiatives are being undertaken.

- To clean our air, we have:
  —set national standards for the six major air pollutants and guidelines for State implementation plans to meet these standards;

—set pollution abatement standards for new facilities in five industrial categories;
—recommended a sulfur emissions tax to encourage reductions in this major source of pollution; and
—supported research and development to provide a low-pollution alternative to the conventional internal combustion engine and to provide means to reduce pollution from burning coal and oil.

- To clean our water, we have:
  —required permits under the Refuse Act to control discharges of industrial pollutants into our waterways;
  —proposed legislation to control dumping into oceans, coastal waters, and the Great Lakes; and
  —initiated a 3-year, $6 billion program to assist State and local governments in building sewage treatment facilities.
- To reduce noise pollution, we have proposed legislation to regulate and to set labeling requirements for major sources of noise.
- To improve and protect health, we have proposed new legislation on pesticides to regulate their use and to strengthen and coordinate Federal and State control efforts.
- To use our lands more wisely, we have proposed legislation on powerplant siting, mined area protection, and land use regulation.

Many of the proposals that I have submitted to the Congress have not yet been enacted. Our Nation cannot make the major efforts that are needed to protect and improve the environment unless Congress will respond to the urgent need for this legislation. *I urge rapid approval by the Congress of these pending environmental proposals.* With the passage of this legislation—and the additional proposals that I will submit to Congress in a special environmental message in February—we will be able to move forward vigorously in all areas of environmental quality.

Pollution Control and Abatement Programs

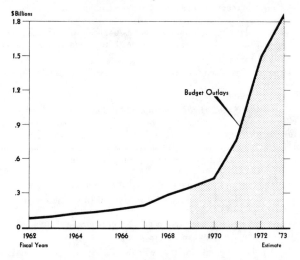

The outlays requested for major environmental programs in 1973 are $2.5 billion, *more than three times the 1969 level.* These funds will support expanded efforts in all major environmental programs. For example, Federal programs have assisted in increasing the population served by secondary sewage treatment from 91 million in 1969 to 115 million in 1973, and in removing 27% more pollution from municipal sewage effluent than was removed in 1968.

Parks and open spaces.—As our expanding economy provides higher standards of living and increased opportunity for leisure, our citizens will want additional parks and other recreational facilities, especially in and near cities. We also want to assure the preservation of nationally important natural and historic areas. This budget provides for meeting these future needs.

I am proposing that the Land and Water Conservation Fund annual authorization be fully funded to provide:

—$197 million in grants for State and local governments to assist them to acquire and develop lands for recreation and parks; and

—$98 million for the acquisition of nationally significant natural or historic areas by Federal agencies.

In the period 1970–73, this program will have provided over $1.1 billion, compared to $535 million provided for this purpose in 1966–69.

The budget also proposes to continue, under the Legacy of Parks program, the transfer of surplus Federal property to State and local governments for recreation facilities, parks, and historic sites. In 1973, over 20,000 acres, with a market value of $120 million, will be transferred under this program. For the period 1969–73, a total of 47,000 acres of land with a market value of $245 million will have been provided to State and local governments.

Community development and housing.—During the past 3 years, solid progress has been made toward providing decent, safe, and sanitary housing for every American. In calendar year 1971, the volume of new housing construction—more than 2 million new starts—was the highest in the history of this country. The construction of Government-assisted housing for low- and moderate-income families has also been increased to record high levels over the past 3 years.

This Administration has taken steps to decentralize Federal programs that assist community development and housing activities to make them more responsive to local needs and preferences.

Our efforts to aid community development and to provide better housing are still not as productive as they can be. I have proposed major reforms that would make them more so:

—a program of urban community development revenue sharing that would replace five categorical grant programs and provide State and local governments $2.3 billion in 1973;

—a Department of Community Development that would consolidate in one organization the many programs and activities that are essential to community development;

—legislation that would simplify and consolidate housing programs; and

—a new planning and management assistance program that would help States and localities improve their executive management capabilities.

These reforms, pending before the Congress, should be enacted promptly.

Agriculture and rural development.—This Administration has made major improvements in programs to help farmers share equitably in the Nation's progress. In addition, I have proposed a new program for rural community development through revenue sharing. I urge the Congress to enact this program in time to be effective on July 1, 1973.

I will shortly recommend further legislation to:

—improve the availability of credit for both farmers and rural residents; and

—give greater emphasis to our efforts to encourage community and industrial development in rural areas.

My budget proposals for 1973 will also further our goal of making all rural residents first-class citizens living in first-class communities. Specifically, we will:

—expand the availability of rural housing;

—strengthen farm incomes through orderly handling of the bumper 1971 grain crop; and

—help finance critically needed waste disposal and water supply systems for nearly 500,000 rural families.

SCIENCE AND TECHNOLOGY IN THE SERVICE OF MAN

In this year's budget, and subsequently, I shall propose how we can accelerate the effort I began 3 years ago to turn science and technology to the service of man.

Research and development have been critical elements of our national life since World War II. They have been the key to our national security and health and instrumental in the solution of many important civilian problems. Research and development also have made significant contributions to our economy in terms of jobs, productivity, and foreign trade.

This Administration has continuously searched for more effective ways to turn science and technology to the service of man. Since 1969, funds for civilian R & D have increased 65%. We have started new programs and strengthened others to help focus R & D on priority human needs.

We have been reordering our research and development investments in defense and space. We have reassessed the space program and placed it on a firm future footing with increased attention to practical and economical applications of space and reductions in the cost of manned space flight.

At the same time we have strengthened our defense research and development capability to insure that the country will not face the possibility of technological surprise or lack the deterrent power necessary to protect our national security. To provide this assurance, budget authority for Department of Defense research, development, test, and evaluation is being increased $838 million to an all-time high of $8.5 billion in 1973.

To emphasize this Administration's strong belief that science and technology can make significant contributions to the quality of American life and to economic growth, I propose additional steps in 1973 to:

—secure the contributions that science and technology can make to our national life;

—initiate a series of experiments to find better ways to encourage private investment in R & D, including investment by small entrepreneurial R & D firms, which have made significant contributions to the generation and exploitation of innovative ideas;

—draw more directly on the capabilities of those agencies which have created the technologies that harnessed the atom and conquered space. AEC and NASA will increasingly use their talents on such problems as clean, economical energy, and clean, safe, and fast transportation systems. For example, this year we shall have the agency which sent men to the moon and back begin to assist the Department of Transportation in finding better ways to send people downtown and back; and

—review carefully our policies in areas of economic regulation, which may unnecessarily restrict wider utilization or development of new technical advances.

I am also initiating new programs and strengthening research and development aimed at three important objectives:

—protecting man and nature from each other;

—using the resources of nature to serve mankind's needs; and

—pioneering new and improved human services.

The overall result of our efforts to strengthen science and technology in the national interest is reflected in the 1973 increase of $1.4 billion in obligations to a total of $17.8 billion. I firmly believe this large increase is vital to the security, welfare, and economic well-being of our country.

IMPROVING GOVERNMENT

Improved efficiency and responsiveness at all levels of government is a major objective of this Administration. One of my first acts as President was to direct that an intensive review be made of our Federal system of government. We found that the executive branch was badly organized to accomplish domestic objectives. We found that State and local governments were often unable to meet the needs of their citizens because of a fiscal crisis that was steadily worsening. And we also found that Federal programs to assist State and local governments had become a maze of separate programs, understood only by members of a new profession—grantsmanship specialists.

The Administration has developed a comprehensive strategy for dealing with these problems. This strategy includes:

• *Revenue sharing*—an important element of the strategy—to provide fiscal relief and to strengthen State and local governments;

• *Reorganization of the executive branch* to create four new departments structured around the basic domestic activities of government;

- *Federal Assistance Review (FAR)* to strengthen delivery of Federal assistance to State and local governments;
- *Regional councils* to help in our program of returning power to the people;
- *Technical assistance* to help State and local governments improve their organizational structures and management processes; and
- *Budget reform* to enable the executive branch and the Congress better to serve the people.

Revenue sharing.—A year ago I proposed to the Congress a General Revenue Sharing program and six special revenue sharing programs to relieve the fiscal crisis of State and local governments and to eliminate some of the problems of the present categorical grant system. No action has yet been taken on these proposals. I *again* urge that Congress enact these proposals.

If enacted to become effective January 1, 1972, as I am proposing, the General Revenue Sharing program would:

—provide $2.5 billion of budget authority in fiscal year 1972 and $5.3 billion in fiscal year 1973 to help relieve the fiscal plight of State and local governments;

—enable those units of government closest to the people to determine how the funds would be spent to meet local needs and priorities; and

—reduce pressures to raise State and local taxes.

The special revenue sharing programs would provide assistance to State and local governments for six broad purposes, with discretion in the use of these funds to be left primarily to State and local governments. The following table shows the categories proposed and the first full year budget authority that would be provided for each one:

REVENUE SHARING PROPOSAL FOR FIRST FULL YEAR

Description	Billions
General revenue sharing	$5.3
Special revenue sharing:	
Urban community development	2.3
Rural community development	1.1
Education	3.2
Manpower training	2.0
Law enforcement	0.9
Transportation	2.8
Total	17.6

In total, these revenue sharing proposals would provide $17½ billion to State and local government in their first full year of operation. The magnitude of the fiscal crisis and the inefficiency and unresponsiveness of the present grant system make favorable action during this session of Congress an urgent need. We can ill-afford further delay.

Reorganization of the executive branch.—In my 1971 State of the Union message, I proposed reform of the executive branch by regrouping functions now scattered among seven cabinet departments and several independent agencies into four new departments organized around the major domestic purposes of government: Community development, natural resources, human resources, and economic affairs.

In my message on departmental reorganization, which I transmitted to the Congress on March 25, 1971, I described in detail the need for a comprehensive restructuring of the domestic executive departments to equip them to serve our Nation in the last third of this century. I cited the fragmentation of Federal responsibility for education matters, for manpower programs, for the development and conservation of water resources, for the management of public lands, and for assisting communities in meeting their needs for water and sewer services.

Typically, three or four separate departments or agencies are now engaged in administering overlapping or conflicting programs concerned with a single government objective. This dispersion and duplication of related functions has increased the costs of administration, generated interagency conflict and rivalry, weakened the departmental secretary as a leader in program development and execution, and imposed inexcusable inconvenience on the public being served. The excessive number of departments and agencies independently pursuing related goals has also frustrated able officials at all levels, impeded the decentralization of Federal operations, and made the coordination of administration in the field inordinately difficult.

By pulling together under each secretary the bulk of the programs which contribute to the achievement of a stated departmental mission, we can assure the prompt decisionmaking, the improvement of procedures, and the integration of Federal activities which we need for effective government.

Legislation and detailed plans for the reorganization have been transmitted to the Congress. I urge the early enactment of these basic proposals. They are vital elements of my strategy to narrow the gap between what the Federal Government promises and what it delivers.

Federal Assistance Review (FAR).—In 1969, I initiated the Federal Assistance Review program to streamline the Federal grant system. Primary emphasis was placed on improving the operation of Federal programs to strengthen the capacity of State and local governments. Achievements include:

—standardization of regional boundaries;

—simplification of Federal review procedures for grant applications;

—substantial delegation of authority to Federal field offices;

—a system for informing Governors and State legislatures of approval action on all Federal grants;

—a Project Notification and Review System, utilizing State and regional clearinghouses to facilitate State and local review of Federal grant applications at the formative stage;

—a pilot integrated grant administration program, enabling State and local governments to apply for several Federal assistance grants through a single application; further consolidation and joint funding authority is being sought under proposed legislation; and

—more participation by State and local officials in determining how Federal funds are used to respond to local needs.

Federal regional councils.—As part of the FAR effort, Federal Regional Councils, consisting of the regional directors of the major human resources agencies, were established in each of the 10 regions. The Councils have now demonstrated considerable potential for increasing Federal responsiveness and coordination at the State and local level.

I shall shortly constitute the Councils formally as bodies within which regional directors of the major grant agencies develop common strategies and mechanisms for program delivery, review program plans jointly with Governors and mayors, and resolve regional interagency issues expeditiously.

Technical assistance.—Since 1969, the Federal Government has offered broad-based organization and management assistance to State and local governments who have requested it. The assistance has taken the form of a review of the organizational structures and the major management processes of each requesting government. Improvements are then suggested. Subsequently, technical and other assistance is available to help the governments implement improvements they think are important. Even though resources are limited, I intend to encourage this form of technical assistance.

Reforming the budget process.—The American people deserve, and our Government requires, a more orderly and more rational budget process.

The preparation of this budget, like those of other recent years, has been handicapped by the delays in enactment of appropriations for the fiscal year which began last July 1. *There is still one 1972 appropriation bill which has not been enacted* even as I write this, 12 months after I submitted the 1972 budget. Moreover, the uncertainties and hesitation caused by these delays in congressional action have hindered the orderly management of the Government.

There has been excessive attention to details and virtually no attention paid to overall totals or the effect of individual irresponsible acts of spending on the budget totals. Any procedural reform that encouraged the Congress to be aware of the overall effect of their individual actions would have substantial benefits for us all.

There have been delays of many months in the enactment of regular appropriation bills, and there have also been periods in which temporary appropriations have been permitted to expire, leaving some agencies with no authority to continue operations.

Changes in the way the Congress conducts its business are its business. But, in the matter of the budget process, the results of the present methods have seriously affected how well I can administer and manage the executive branch.

THE LONGER VIEW

In 1976, our Nation will celebrate its 200th birthday. Three basic questions must be answered as we look toward a proper celebration of our bicentennial.

- How can we best achieve our great national goals?
- What role should the Federal Government have in this effort?
- How can we best rededicate ourselves to the ideal of personal freedom?

In considering these questions, we cannot ignore the hard fact that the increase in uncommitted resources between now and 1976 will be small in comparison with the magnitude of the tasks, forcing us to make difficult decisions about priorities.

My basic preferences in allocating our national resources are clear.

First, I believe that to avoid permanent inflation and waste we should assure that we count the costs before we make spending decisions. We can do that by adhering to the principle that spending must not exceed the level at which the budget would be balanced if the economy were at full employment.

Second, I believe that an increasing share of our national resources must be returned to private citizens and State and local governments to enable them—rather than the Federal Government—to meet individual and community needs.

Responsible budgeting.—The first principle—the full employment budget principle—imposes a necessary discipline on Federal spending.

Last year, the budget margin projected for 1976—the potential Federal budget surplus, *assuming full employment and only the programs and tax structure in existence or proposed then (1971)*—was $30 billion. Actions taken in the last 12 months and those proposed in this budget will reduce that margin to only $5 billion. This margin is less than $25 for each man, woman, and child in the expected 1976 population, and is less than 1.6% of projected 1976 budget receipts. And yet, it must be sufficient to cover the 1976 costs of all new proposals not included in this budget.

The moral is clear. A strong fiscal discipline will be necessary in the years ahead if we are to preserve the buying power of the dollar. New spending programs must be evaluated against the most stringent of standards: *do they have enough merit to warrant increases in taxes or elimination of existing programs?*

This Administration has measured its proposals against this standard. I have made the hard choices necessary to assure that they can be financed within a full-employment budget policy.

I urge the Congress to engage in a similar self-discipline in making the hard choices that will be required during the next few years. This Administration will vigorously oppose irresponsible and shortsighted spending proposals that would commit large sums of Federal money to schemes that are politically attractive but would endanger an inflation-free prosperity.

CONCLUSION

There will be those who contend that in this budget their favorite programs are not financed, or are not financed as much as they want them to be.

They will be absolutely right.

Government expenses increase each year because special interest groups, representing only those who stand to benefit from their program, persuade decisionmakers that more resources are needed for those programs without regard to the effect on the total budget. The cost is multiplied by geometric progression when this tactic is repeated for literally hundreds of programs. Seldom do any of these groups recommend additional taxes to finance their proposed spending.

Then inflationary factors, frequently induced by the large total volume of spending resulting from individual decisions made without consideration of the larger picture, force the cost of these programs upward. At the same time the special constituency benefiting from the program is enlarged and strengthened, its demands are correspondingly increased, and the cycle continues to feed upon itself.

Taken together, what is good for all the special interests is bad for the public interest. Our strength is in our ability to act as one nation, not as a conglomerate of warring and greedy factions.

For this reason my 1973 budget, large as it is, will not be large enough to satisfy many. However, I hope the American people will make their desire for less pervasive government known in unmistakable terms to their elected representatives. It is essential to preserve the private enterprise system, with its competitive spirit and its work ethic, which has done so much to inspire the independent and help the dependent and which has made this Nation the economic example to the rest of the world.

That system has enabled us to secure, for our people, a far higher standard of living than any experienced, or even envisioned, by the rest of the civilized world.

I do not wish it said of my Administration that we furthered or encouraged the process of discarding that heritage. So, I have emphasized fiscal responsibility and downward pressure on Federal expenditures, rather than simply accept all requests of all special groups and hope that the inevitable need for new taxes could be delayed as long as possible.

I am not averse to a day of reckoning, but when it comes, I want it to be said that this Administration foresaw the danger, held spending to amounts that could be paid from full-employment revenues, and took all steps possible to reduce the need for raising taxes so that the Federal Government plays a smaller, not a larger, role in the life of each of us. In this way, every citizen will have a larger share of the fruits of his labor to spend the way he or she freely chooses.

RICHARD NIXON.

MANPOWER REVENUE SHARING

Following is the text, as made available by the White House, of President Nixon's Feb. 7 message to Congress:

TO THE CONGRESS OF THE UNITED STATES:

There are few issues of greater concern today, to the Congress and to the President, than the state of the American economy. We are passing from a period when the economy was inflated by the strains of war to a time when it will be challenged by the needs of peace.

Adding to the inevitable problems of transition has been the increasingly vigorous economic competition of other countries. We welcome this competition, but we must also realize that it requires us to give renewed attention to increasing American productivity—not only to ensure the continued improvement in our own standard of living, but also to keep our Nation's goods competitive in the world's markets, thereby providing jobs for American workers.

During the late fifties and early sixties our annual rate of increase in labor productivity averaged 3.4 percent. But by the mid-sixties it had begun its drop to an average of only 1.8 percent.

We are taking important steps to revive the productivity of American labor. Our New Economic Policy is shrinking the bulge of inflation. We are proposing a new program to promote technological progress—for advances in research and development are essential ingredients of rising productivity. But technological advance is not the whole story: increase in the skills of our labor force also play a large part.

We are not interested in the competitiveness of our labor force for its own sake. We are concerned about the individual American—concerned that he learn the skills to gain employment or learn more skills to gain better employment. We are concerned about the health of our economy, knowing that a strong, highly productive economy is the individual American's best insurance against unemployment. This is why the Federal Government provides manpower training—to increase the opportunities of jobless Americans to share in the abundance of America.

Today, I again urge that the Congress enable us to improve our manpower programs by enacting the Manpower Revenue Sharing Act.

Ten years ago, the Congress recognized Federal responsibility for comprehensive manpower training by passing the Manpower Development and Training Act of 1962. The MDTA and the Economic Opportunity Act of 1964 have grown to include over a dozen separate, narrow grant programs, each with its own purposes. Yet, even though manpower programs have grown in number, the need for manpower training has outpaced the capability of these older programs to provide services. Our commitment is strong, but we have not bridged the gap between the promises and the performance of Federal manpower programs. Something better is needed—on this we can all agree.

The Old Way: A Need for Reform

Like the field of manpower training, many other areas of Federal assistance are suffering from a hardening of governmental arteries. Federal programs are meant to meet the needs of individual citizens living in 50 States and in thousands of communities, but those diverse needs are not being met by rigid, standardized Federal programs. Instead, the pressure on State and local resources is building to the breaking point. The traditional answer would be the establishment of even more separate categories of Federal aid.

Federal aid is needed, but the proliferation of Federal plans, programs, categories, and requirements has compounded the individual problems faced by American communities today. Frequently, Federal involvement has merely generated a false sense of security—a security which has been betrayed by the continuing multiplication of communities' social needs and the failure of government to meet those needs.

Federal aid outlays account for 21 percent of State and local revenues today, but many Federal grants require State and local officials to match some percentage of Federal aid with local money which could be better spent in other ways to solve local problems. In many cases, State and local officials must decide either to accept Federal aid with its accompanying allocation of State and local funds or to receive no Federal aid at all.

Federal maintenance of effort provisions further distort local priorities by requiring State and local governments to continue projects irrespective of their effectiveness in meeting their own needs. Once again, our communities lose more of the flexibility which would enable them to meet what they consider their most pressing needs.

Frustrating and time-consuming project approval requirements, a jungle of red tape, often make it impossible for State and local governments to count on having Federal money when it is needed. No matter how pressing some needs may be, communities must wait, sometimes months or even years, for the slowly grinding wheels of bureaucracy to consider each grant in minute detail.

The real problem lies not with the Federal Government's intentions, but with how it tries to meet communities' needs—by undertaking one narrow, inflexible program after another. The number of separate categories has grown until no one is sure of their boundaries. In 1963, there were only 160 individual grant programs amounting to about $8.6 billion, but now there are over 1,000 such programs amounting to almost $40 billion. Each rigid category of additional aid reflects the worst kind of arrogance: the presumption that only the Federal Government knows local needs and how to meet them.

If we have faith in the American people—and I for one do—then we must recognize that in thousands of communities, each with its own problems and priorities, there live people quite capable of determining and meeting their own needs and in all probability doing a better job of it than the Washington bureaucracy. Quite simply, today's local needs are likely to be met best by local solutions.

The time has clearly come to reform the way in which the Federal Government aids local and State authorities. The time has clearly come when those who serve at the State and local level and are charged with the responsibility for finding workable solutions to State and local problems should be given a chance. Clearly, it is time that Federal aid became truly that, aid, not rigid and often confusing control.

Waste, confusion, and inefficiency are too often the price paid by local and State governments for Federal aid under the present system. Last year the Federal Government discovered the following cases, to cite just a few examples:

• One Northcentral State had 93 people on its government payroll to do nothing but apply for Federal education grants.

• A study of grant programs in one Western city revealed that only 15 percent of the Federal funds to that city went through its mayor or elected government.

• Federal demands on the time and attention of local officials is particularly serious. In one small Midwestern city, a part-time mayor had to attend sixteen separate evening meetings per month, one with Federal officials from each of the sixteen separate grant programs in which his small city participates.

The New Way: Special Revenue Sharing

In a series of special messages to the Congress last year, I proposed Special Revenue Sharing, a new system of Federal aid which would serve the purposes of our State and local governments better than the system of narrow Federal grant programs now operating. I proposed that funds be made available to States and localities for six broad purposes—manpower, law enforcement, education, transportation, urban community development, and rural community development—to be used, for each of these purposes, as they see fit to meet their particular needs. Those proposals, if enacted, would consolidate over 130 separate programs into six general purpose areas. Under our Special Revenue Sharing proposals, in the first full year of operation, $12.3 billion in Federal funds would be provided to States and localities for those six broad purposes. These funds would be free from matching requirements, maintenance of effort restrictions, presently rigid prior Federal project approval requirements, and, best of all, inflexible Federal plans. But there are two major stipulations: (1) the money is subject to all the civil rights requirements of Title VI of the Civil Rights Acts of 1964, and (2) no government unit would receive less money under these proposals than it did under the old system of narrow Federal grants.

Special Revenue Sharing is not a wholesale dismantling of the Federal grants system, as some critics have charged. It is a careful effort to decide which level of government can best deal with a particular problem and then to move the necessary funds and decision-making power to that level of government. When a Federal approach is needed we should take that road, but when a local approach is better we should move the resources and power to that level.

I realize that these are challenging concepts, which have major implications for the structure of American government—Federal, State and local—and for the effectiveness with which government serves the people. They require us in Washington to give up some of our power, so that more power can be returned to the States, to the localities, and to the people, where it will be better used. It is appropriate, therefore, that the Congress give full consideration to all of these proposals for fundamental reform and move rapidly to create effective programs to meet today's needs.

Manpower Services for the Seventies

I recognize that it is incumbent upon those who propose change to justify the changes. I believe our experience with Federal manpower programs over the last 10 years justifies the changes we are proposing.

All those represented in the current array of patchwork manpower programs—the schools, private employers, public agencies, nonprofit groups, not to mention the unemployed workers—know that the present system is not delivering the jobs, the training, and the other manpower services that this Nation needs and has a right to expect.

As we begin the second decade of comprehensive manpower assistance for our unemployed and underemployed citizens we know we must do better, and we can do better. It is time for a change.

Manpower experts throughout the Nation agree that the necessary reform of the Nation's system of manpower training should have as its three basic goals the decategorization, the decentralization, and the consolidation of existing manpower development efforts.

The Manpower Revenue Sharing Act that I have proposed would allow us to achieve those goals. It would benefit citizens in every corner of the Nation and offer renewed hope to members of our society who have lacked opportunity—hope for jobs, for advancement, and for a better standard of living. It would establish a new framework of constructive partnership for manpower training among Federal, State, and local governments. Its principles are simple and fundamental, yet far-reaching.

The Principles of Manpower Special Revenue Sharing

First, the Manpower Revenue Sharing Act does not mandate any existing categorical program or guarantee its perpetuation—irrespective of its performance—in any community. However, it would not prohibit the continuation of any project which a particular locality feels effectively serves its own and its workers' needs. It is time to end the restrictiveness of the old, narrow programs which have frustrated communities' efforts to develop manpower programs geared to their own needs and circumstances.

In its first full year of operation, the Manpower Revenue Sharing Act would provide $2 billion for manpower purposes, of which $1.7 billion would be divided among State and local units of government—without unnecessary red tape—using a formula based on the size of their labor force and the numbers of unemployed and disadvantaged. The remainder would be used by the Secretary of Labor to meet the generalized national needs of this new system.

It would authorize a broad range of services, including:

• classroom instruction in both remedial education and occupational skills;

• training on the job with both public and private employers, aided by manpower subsidies;

• job opportunities, including work experience and short-term employment for special age groups and the temporarily unemployed, and transitional public service employment at all levels of government.

These services, all designed to help move people toward self-supporting employment, augmented by temporary income support, relocation assistance, child care and other supportive services authorized by the Act, would make it possible for our communities to mount integrated manpower development programs truly responsive to their own priority needs.

The second major goal of Manpower Special Revenue Sharing is to increase substantially reliance upon State and local governments to manage major manpower activities. Local governments are often powerless when jobs are not to be had. It is time we equipped our local governments with the resources and decision-making power to meet their responsibilities.

The Manpower Revenue Sharing Act meets this objective. It would provide communities with the resources they need to help get people into jobs and job-training. Decisions on what needs to be done to improve specific local manpower conditions cannot and should not be made in Washington. They should be delegated to the area where the unemployed person lives and wants to work.

The third way to move toward a new era in manpower development is through consolidation of the multiple, frequently inconsistent, funding authorizations for manpower activities. Even members of the congressional Appropriations Committees frequently chafe under the unmanageable task of sorting out the confusing array of alphabetical "programs" created by existing manpower enactments. While a good deal of untangling has been done by administrative action, the only durable solution is an overall reform.

The Manpower Revenue Sharing Act would replace the two major pieces of legislation which have spawned most of the acronym programs—the Manpower Development and Training Act and Title I of the Economic Opportunity Act—with a single statute which incorporates the flexibility needed by State and local government.

The Manpower Revenue Sharing Act submitted to the Congress in March of 1971 incorporates all three of these vital concepts. I believe that the application of these principles in the Manpower Revenue Sharing Act is sound, but the principles are more important than the details. Reasonable men may disagree on the specifics of any important legislation, but there comes a time when its principles must be earnestly debated and decisions made. For the principles of Manpower Special Revenue Sharing, that time has come. The fine points of this legislation, which were discussed in my message of March 4, 1971, are open to refinement, but I believe the principles of Special Revenue Sharing are too important to be eviscerated.

Our country needs new manpower legislation. Let us now write a new charter for the second decade of manpower development that will produce solid performance—for the economy, for the unemployed and underemployed, and for government itself.

Restoring the American Spirit

The Special Revenue Sharing approach to providing Federal help would enable us to deal more effectively with many of this Nation's most pressing problems. But it would do much more. It would help to restore the American spirit.

In recent years many Americans have come to doubt the capacity of government—at all levels—to meet the needs of an increasingly complex Nation. They have watched as the power to effect change in their communities has moved gradually from the local level, with the reality of friends and community, to the national center, to Washington. There was a time when the increasing centralization of government fostered a greater sense of national purpose. But more recently, the weight of unfulfilled promises reinforced by the growing complexity of social problems has caused many Americans to doubt the capability of our system of government.

By providing new resources to the levels of government closest to the problems and closest to the people involved—people who may see their problems in a different light than the Federal Government—both General and Special Revenue Sharing will do much to revive the confidence and spirit of our people. A free and diverse Nation needs a diversity of approaches; a free Nation should invest its faith in the right and ability of its people to meet the needs of their own communities. No greater sense of confidence can be found than that of a community which has solved its own problems and met its own needs.

Confidence in government is nowhere under greater challenge than among the young, yet the future of America depends upon the involvement of our young in the day-to-day business of governing this land. By making resources available to the more localized units of government, where more people can play a more direct role—and by placing the power of decision where the people are—I hope that many of the young will come to realize that their participation can truly make a difference.

This purpose—this philosophy—is at the heart of Special Revenue Sharing.

The people's right to change what does not work is one of the greatest principles of our system of government—and that principle will be strengthened as the governments closest to the people are strengthened. Though the Federal Government has tried with intelligence and vigor to meet the people's needs, many of its purposes have gone unfulfilled for far too long. Now, let us help those most directly affected to try their hand. American society and American government can only benefit from ensuring to our citizens the fullest possible opportunity to make their communities better places, for themselves, for their families, and for their neighbors.

RICHARD NIXON

RURAL DEVELOPMENT

Following is the text, as made available by the White House, of President Nixon's Feb. 1 message to Congress on rural development.

TO THE CONGRESS OF THE UNITED STATES:

From the very beginnings of our history, the vitality of rural America has been at the heart of our Nation's strength. It is essential that we preserve and expand that vitality in the years ahead. For America will not be able to look eagerly to the future with a sense of promise and hope unless those who live in its rural areas are able to share in this vision. To help improve the quality of life in the American countryside, I am today presenting a series of proposals designed to marshal more effectively the energies of the private sector and of government at all levels in a cooperative program of rural development.

The Problems of Rural America

All Americans have a high stake in rural development. For the problems which many rural areas are now experiencing are directly linked to those of our cities and suburbs. Changing patterns of life in rural America have changed the pattern of life in all of America.

A central cause of these changing patterns has been the increasing mechanization of agriculture and of other natural resource industries such as mining and lumber—a process which has resulted in a substantial reduction in jobs in these occupations in recent years. While employment opportunities in other occupations have more than offset these declines, the overall growth of economic opportunity in rural America has lagged far behind that of our urban areas. Today, dramatic disparities exist between metropolitan and rural areas in such indices as per capita income, housing standards, educational attainment and access to medical care.

At the same time, political institutions designed to deal with simpler problems in simpler times have frequently been unable to cope with these new challenges. The Federal Government often finds that it is too remote and too unwieldy to respond with precision to State and local needs. State and local governments are frequently too impoverished or too fragmented to undertake the necessary planning and development activities. Their problems are accentuated by the fact that widely dispersed rural population inevitably means a higher expenditure per person for most government programs.

One result of all these factors is that semi-deserted country towns—once centers of life for the surrounding countryside—stand today as stark reminders of unused and abandoned rural resources. In each of the three decades since 1940, half of our counties (not always the same ones) have lost population. Two out of every five of our counties lost population in all three decades. As I said in my State of the Union Message two years ago, many of our rural areas are being emptied of their people and their promise.

In many cases, those who have left the countryside have simply taken their problems with them. Indeed, many have seen their problems intensify as they have settled in overcrowded urban areas.

It is striking to realize, as I noted in this year's Message on the State of the Union, that even if we had a population of one billion—nearly five times the current level—our area is so great that we would still not be as densely populated as many European nations are at present. Our problems are not so much those of numbers as of distribution. And their solution requires the revitalization of the American countryside.

Changing our Approach

In seeking to solve the problems of rural areas, we must not simply seek more money from the Congress and the taxpayers. In the past decade we have seen the folly of pouring money into projects which were ill-considered and lacking in local support. What we must now seek instead is a fundamental change in the way government approaches the entire developmental challenge.

The Federal Government has spent considerable sums on rural development. Programs which we have recommended for inclusion in our rural development Revenue Sharing plan alone are spending almost $1 billion this year and this is only a small part of our overall rural development spending. And yet, despite this substantial funding, the problems have continued to grow. What is it that has been missing from our rural development programs?

MORE CONTROL AT THE STATE AND LOCAL LEVEL

I believe that a major missing ingredient has been effective control of development programs at lower levels of government. Because we have relied so exclusively on Federal funds—handed out through bureaucratic processes and through narrow categorical grants—too many decisions have been made in Washington and too few have been made in rural America. I believe this is wrong. I believe we should return power to officials who are selected at the State and local levels.

As long as the Federal Government sets rigid rules, both through legislative and administrative guidelines, there is little room for local initiative. Under our present system, a project that does not meet Federal standards does not get funded. This means that the talents of local government officials, of leaders in the private sector, and of public-spirited citizens cannot be fully utilized. Almost all of the success stories that can be found in rural economic development have occurred because local officials and private leaders have entered into a public-spirited partnership and have taken the initiative. We must do all we can to encourage such partnerships.

IMPROVED PLANNING

Even as we seek to decentralize, we must also work to improve planning. In many respects these goals represent two sides of the same coin. For plans which are developed at levels close to the people are likely to be more realistic, more imaginative and more useful than abstract blueprints which are drawn up far away from the scene of the action or which are altered to meet rigid Federal rules. Effective development does not require plans that can survive the scrutiny of Washington. Effective development requires plans that people believe in and will work to accomplish.

MORE ADEQUATE PUBLIC AND PRIVATE RESOURCES

More adequate development also requires more adequate resources. This does not simply mean more Federal money; it also means that Federal funds now available must be freed from the inhibiting restrictions within which they are now entangled. Funds which are free of these restrictions can be used in each locality where the needs are greatest, eliminating a great deal of inefficiency and waste.

But Federal grant money provides only a part of the Federal contribution to rural America. Adequate credit resources can also be extremely important in developing community facilities and in attracting private investment. In the end it is not Federal money, nor even the vast sums spent by State and local governments, which hold the key to rural development. The private sector has an enormous role to play and public efforts must keep this fact centrally in mind.

HELPING THE FARMER AND PROTECTING THE ENVIRONMENT

Rural America cannot move forward effectively into the future unless it respects those elements which have been the base of its strength in the past. We cannot build a stronger rural economy, for example, unless we also build a stronger agricultural economy. While we must work to change the American countryside, we must never do so at the expense of those who produce our food and fiber. We must work to create a better life for American farmers even as we provide an expanded range of opportunities for those who are no longer needed on the farm.

Even as we do more to promote agricultural prosperity, so we must do more to protect the rural environment. Just as development must not come at the expense of the farmer, so it must not come at the expense of environmental concerns. We cannot fully develop the American countryside if we destroy the beauty and the natural resources which are so much a part of its essential value.

BASIC PRINCIPLES

These then are the basic principles which should guide our new approach to rural community development:

We must treat the problems of rural America as a part of a general strategy for balanced growth.

We must reverse the flow of power to the Federal Government and return more power to State and local officials.

We must fight the rigidities of narrowly focused categorical grants.

We must facilitate more adequate advance planning.

We must reorganize the Federal Government so that it can more effectively support planning and execution at the State and local level.

We must provide adequate resources and credit, in ways which attract greater private resources for development.

We must develop rural America in ways which protect agriculture and the environment.

On the basis of these principles, we have prepared the following recommendations for action—including proposals which have been submitted earlier and a number of new initiatives.

Proposals Already Submitted to the Congress

DEPARTMENT OF COMMUNITY DEVELOPMENT

One of the most significant barriers to effective planning and coordination in rural areas has been the fragmentation of Federal efforts. Too many programs which should be closely related are operating as very separate entities. As a result, State and community leaders must often run a complex obstacle course in order to obtain development assistance. Frequently there is poor coordination and wasteful duplication and in some cases the action of one Federal agency actually conflicts with that of another.

The principal reason for this fragmentation has been the failure of the Government to recognize the inter-relationship among rural, suburban and urban problems and the need to strengthen the essential social and economic partnership between rural America and our great metropolitan centers.

I believe the proper solution to this problem is to gather the principal Federal programs which support community development within a single new Department of Community Development.

This new department would both simplify and expedite the tasks of State and local governments through a broad range of program and technical support efforts. Because fewer questions would have to be resolved in Washington at the interagency level, the new department would also expedite the decentralization of Federal decision-making which this administration has already begun. The new Department of Community Development would take over most of the functions now performed by the Department of Housing and Urban Development; some of the functions of the Department of Transportation, the Office of Economic Opportunity and the Small Business Administration; and the responsibilities of the Department of Commerce with respect to the Title V regional commissions.

Under our revised plan for executive reorganization, the Department of Agriculture would remain as a separate department focusing on the needs of farmers. But a number of present Department of Agriculture development functions would be moved to the new Department of Community Development, including the Farmers Home Administration loan and grant programs for rural community water and sewer systems and for rural housing; the Rural Electrification Administration loan programs for electric and telephone systems; the recently established Rural Telephone Bank; research programs related to rural community development conducted by the Economic Development Division of the Economic Research Service; and the programs of the recently established Rural Development Service.

Comprehensive reorganization would mean that every Federal dollar spent on rural development could have a far greater impact. I again call on the Congress to establish this new department, which would be uniquely capable of launching a well-developed, well-coordinated campaign to achieve the nation's community development goals.

A REVENUE SHARING PLAN FOR RURAL AMERICA

Our revenue sharing plan for rural America proposes to unite the funding for a number of existing programs into a single more flexible resource for rural community development. Our proposed program would add $179 million to the various programs to be consolidated, bringing the total annual program to a level of $1.1 billion. Each State would receive at least as much under revenue sharing as it receives under the current system of categorical grants. The program would take effect at the beginning of Fiscal Year 1974.

Rural community development revenue sharing funds would be paid out to the States and to Puerto Rico, the Virgin Islands and Guam according to a formula which takes three factors into account: the State's rural population, the State's rural per capita income in comparison to the national average, and the State's change in rural population compared to the change in population in all States. In addition, every State would receive a minimum amount to assure that all States participate in the program.

The revenue sharing proposal incorporates a requirement for statewide development plans to ensure that activities carried on under the rural community development revenue sharing program could be coordinated with activities under the other general and special revenue sharing proposals, including those for urban community development and for transportation. Each year the States would prepare a comprehensive statewide development plan which would outline spending intentions for programs in rural areas and smaller cities, as well as in metropolitan and suburban areas. It would be the responsibility of the Governor of each State to draw up this statewide plan. This process would be supported by another major administration initiative, our proposed $100 million planning and management grant program.

The development plan would be formulated through a consultative process which would consider plans submitted by multi-jurisdictional planning districts, which the Governors could establish with rural revenue sharing funds. These local planning organizations would be composed of local elected officials and would be established in all areas of the State. One member from each of these district planning bodies would sit on a panel to assist the Governor in the comprehensive planning process.

This process for developing a statewide plan would ensure that public officials and the general public itself would focus attention on the inter-relationships between rural and urban development within each State. The plan would identify potential growth areas and development sites as well as areas which are of special environmental concern. The plan could also take into account interstate projects and programs developed through the regional commission mechanism.

The rural community development revenue sharing program represents a reaffirmation of faith in State and local governments. It is based on the concept that local people have the best understanding of local problems and on the belief that they have the will and the ability to move vigorously and intelligently to solve them. The revenue sharing approach removes the often stifling and always frustrating strictures which require that Federal grants be used for narrow purposes. It provides the flexibility which State and local governments need in order to fund those projects which they themselves believe would best ensure rational development in their areas and most effectively enhance the quality of life.

The development plans drawn up under this program would cover an entire State. Rural revenue sharing funds would be spent largely outside metropolitan areas while urban revenue sharing funds would be used within those areas. It is important to note, however, that rural areas include almost 2800 of the more than 3100 counties in the United States.

New Proposals

Revenue sharing and reorganization can have a great long-range significance for rural America. But we must also take a number of other steps which I am outlining today, including two major new proposals. The first involves a new approach to rural financial assistance. The second concerns added authorities for improving the environment and attaining conservation objectives in rural America.

EXPANDED CREDIT FOR RURAL AMERICA

I am recommending today a new rural community development credit sharing authority which would give the Secretary of Agriculture and the State Governors new tools to help revitalize rural areas. Under this proposal, a new Rural Development Credit Fund would be established to provide loans, loan insurance and loan guarantees to the States for their use in assisting development. This credit would be made available through the Farmers Home Administration for up to 80 percent of the cost of establishing or improving businesses which help create economic growth in rural areas. This fund would also make loans and guarantees for sewer and water facilities and other public works and community facilities, such as industrial parks and community centers, which work directly or indirectly to improve employment opportunities.

Loans and guarantees would be made in accordance with the State development plan required under rural revenue sharing. The States would select specific projects which are consistent with this development plan.

A significant new feature of this credit-sharing proposal is the requirement that most of the authorizations be divided among the States according to the same formula established for rural community development revenue sharing. Specifically, 80 percent of the loan funds for commercial and industrial development and for community facilities would be allocated to the States on a formula basis. The remaining 20 percent of loan authorities would be administered by the Secretary of Agriculture. A large portion of the authorization—65 percent in each fiscal year—would be reserved for commercial and industrial development uses and the remainder would be available for community development purposes. Each State would know in advance the amount of grants and credit it could commit according to its plan each year.

This proposal would involve private lending institutions as fully as possible in the rural revitalization effort. Financial assistance would not be provided under the program unless it was clear that firms and communities could not obtain credit elsewhere. Fully three-quarters of each year's authorization would have to be in the form of a guarantee of loans made by private financial institutions. Hopefully, almost all loans could be made by this sector of our economy.

In addition to the direct involvement of private banks, this program would also emphasize loans to private entrepreneurs for job creation through commercial and industrial development. Since some equity would be required, these business decision-makers would be far more likely to make realistic, workable development decisions than far-removed Federal bureaucrats can now do. It is also likely that these market-oriented decisions would provide sounder, long-term employment opportunities. This combination of Federal funding, local intiative and statewide planning utilizing the private market economy should produce a far more productive use of our resources.

I am proposing an authorization level for this credit-sharing program, which includes the existing Farmers Home Administration water and sewer program, of $1.3 billion in fiscal year 1974.

My new proposals also involve additional features and technical improvements which would streamline and improve the effectiveness of farm and rural loan programs now administered by the Department of Agriculture. Among these are proposals to increase the farm operating loan limit to $50,000 and to increase the limit on new loans to be held in the agricultural credit insurance fund from $100 million to $500 million. This latter provision would provide adequate levels to ensure that the expanded loan and guarantee program would have a substantial impact on rural areas.

In summary, this new approach to credit assistance contains several advantageous features:

(1) It would establish a direct link between credit assistance and revenue sharing since both programs would be administered according to the same statewide plan.

(2) It would expand the role of private lending institutions. Firms otherwise unable to obtain credit would have a chance to mature under this plan so that they could borrow from private lending institutions at a later time without Federal guarantees.

(3) The plan could work through a delivery system for servicing loans which are already in operation—the Farmers Home Administration, which has offices in more than 1,700 counties. There is an office within a relatively short distance of practically every rural community in the United States. This whole system, moreover, could be readily transferred to a new Department of Community Development.

(4) Projects could be jointly financed by a number of Federal agencies, such as Small Business Administration, the Department of Housing and Urban Development, and the Environmental Protection Agency, as well as by other private and public State and local agencies.

(5) Improved planning and program coordination would be possible under statewide plans which grow out of the needs and suggestions of multi-jurisdictional planning districts already established in more than half of the States. These planning bodies would also provide expertise for communities that are too small to employ their own development experts.

IMPROVING THE RURAL ENVIRONMENT

To help carry out our environmental concerns, I propose that the Secretary of Agriculture be authorized to share the costs of long-term conservation in watershed areas. Such an authorization has worked most successfully under the Great Plains program. This measure would foster the orderly establishment of needed land treatment measures within the small watershed areas of the country.

In addition, technical and cost-sharing assistance should be authorized within watershed areas for the improvement of water quality. This would mean that, for the first time, Federal cost-sharing would be made available to improve water quality on a year-round basis. Such technical and cost-sharing assistance should also be provided in Resource Conservation and Development Project areas.

Finally, the Secretary of Agriculture should be authorized to inventory and to monitor soil, water, and related resources and to issue a national land inventory report at five-year intervals. Such data could be used at all levels of government in land use policy planning.

All these proposals would broaden the dimensions of Federal service and would give new impetus to the entire rural development task. But I would emphasize again that this task must be one in which the people themselves are directly involved—and it must begin in rural America. Our proposals would provide rural people and communities with the tools they need to achieve their goals and I hope these recommendations will receive early and favorable consideration.

Results of our Increased Emphasis on Rural Development

These essential steps now depend on action by the Congress. But while action on past proposals has been pending, we have also been taking a number of administrative steps to improve our rural development programs and have substantially increased program funding. For example:

• The funding of principal rural development programs in the Department of Agriculture this year ($2.8 billion) is more than four times that of fiscal year 1961 and twice that of fiscal year 1969. Twenty-nine of the thirty-four rural development programs in that department have been expanded since 1969.

• Since 1969, the Department of Housing and Urban Development has nearly tripled its grants for non-metropolitan planning districts. It funded 155 districts which received $3.4 million in grants in the last complete fiscal year.

• Rural housing assistance, with an emphasis on low and moderate income families, has reached a record level of $1.6 billion under the Farmers Home Administration program—more than triple the 1969 level.

• Research on rural development and housing is estimated at $9 million this year, more than double that of 1969.

• Funding for community sewer and water facilities has reached a record high level of $300 million in loans, plus $42 million in direct grants. This represents an increase of almost 80 percent over the level provided two years ago.

• Soil Conservation Service resource conservation and development, flood prevention, and watershed programs have expanded

from $103 million in fiscal 1969 to an estimated $156 million this year.

• With the recent release of an additional $109 million in funds for rural electrification, total available funds for the Rural Electrification Administration have been increased to $438 million for the current fiscal year. REA loans from 1969 to 1971 totaled more than $1.4 billion. Since 1969, REA-financed systems connected 700,000 new electric services and 420,000 telephone users—the largest three-year growth since the 1950's.

• The Rural Telephone Bank, with an initial Federal subscription of $60 million in the first two years, has been established to provide new credit resources for telephone cooperatives seeking to improve rural communications.

• Extension Service community development activities this year attained a funding level estimated at $12.7 million, an increase of $3.7 million over 1969 levels.

• To broaden the role of the employment service in serving our rural population, a Rural Manpower Service has been established in the Department of Labor.

• A cooperative program called Concerted Services in Training and Education has involved several Federal agencies as well as local organizations in helping individuals better utilize Federal programs.

• A special office has been created within the Department of Health, Education, and Welfare to focus on special problems of human resource development in rural areas.

This expansion of Federal efforts to stimulate the development of rural communities has been paralleled by the increased efforts of individual citizens, civic organizations, private enterprise and government at the State, county and municipal level. There are many evidences of the resulting overall progress.

• Outmigration from rural communities slowed from 4.6 million during the 1950's to 2.4 million during the 1960's. Most of the population losses during the 1960's occurred in the Great Plains and inter-mountain areas of the West, but gains were realized in parts of the Southern Piedmont, the middle Tennessee Valley, eastern Oklahoma, and northern and western Arkansas. This is evidence that the migratory tide can be slowed—and in some instances even reversed.

• Income per capita in rural America is growing faster than in metropolitan America, though it still remains below the urban level.

• While the incidence of poverty is greater in rural than in urban America, its reduction rate is nearly twice as fast.

• Non-farm employment outside the metropolitan centers has generally grown at a slightly faster rate than employment in metropolitan areas. Manufacturing employment is expanding more rapidly in rural areas than in the large cities.

• Although rural America still contains about two-thirds of our inadequate housing, the ratio of inadequate to adequate rural housing units has been reduced from one-third to one-seventh in recent years. Rural electric and telephone services have improved; more than 98 percent of America's farms are now electrified.

• During the past three years, per capita farm income has averaged about 75 percent that of non-farm workers. This is still too low, but it represents a significant improvement over the past decade.

• The median years of schools completed by persons 25 to 29 years of age is now about the same—12 years plus—in metropolitan and non-metropolitan areas.

All of these signs of progress are most encouraging. But this record is not something to stand on—it is something to build on. Much significant work has already been done—but the most important tasks are still before us.

The longer we put off these tasks the more difficult they will be. With the cooperation of the Congress we can promptly take up this work, opening new doors of opportunity for all who seek a better life in rural America.

RICHARD NIXON

HEALTH CARE: REQUESTS FOR ACTION ON THREE PROGRAMS

Following is the text, as made available by the White House, of President Nixon's March 2 message to Congress on health care.

TO THE CONGRESS OF THE UNITED STATES:

An all-directions reform of our health care system—so that every citizen will be able to get quality health care at reasonable cost regardless of income and regardless of area of residence—remains an item of highest priority on my unfinished agenda for America in the 1970s.

In the ultimate sense, the general good health of our people is the foundation of our national strength, as well as being the truest wealth that individuals can possess.

Nothing should impede us from doing whatever is necessary to bring the best possible health care to those who do not now have it—while improving health care quality for everyone—at the earliest possible time.

In 1971, I submitted to the Congress my new National Health Strategy which would produce the kind of health care Americans desire and deserve, at costs we all can afford.

Since that time, a great national debate over health care has taken place. And both branches of the Congress have conducted searching examinations of our health needs, receiving and studying testimony from all segments of our society.

The Congress has acted on measures advancing certain parts of my National Health Strategy:

• The Comprehensive Health Manpower Training Act of 1971 and the Nurse Training Act of 1971, which I signed last November, will spur the greatest effort in our history to expand the supply of health personnel. Additionally and importantly, it will attract them to the areas of health care shortages, helping to close one of the most glaring gaps in our present system.

• The Congress also passed the National Cancer Act which I proposed last year. This action opens the way for a high-intensity effort to defeat the No. 2 killer and disabler of our time, an effort fueled by an additional $100 million in the last year. A total of $430 million is budgeted for cancer programs in fiscal year 1973, compared to $185 million in fiscal year 1969.

• The Congress responded to my statement of early 1970 on needed improvements in veterans medical care by authorizing increased funds in 1971 and 1972, increases which have brought the VA hospital-to-patient ratios to an all-time high and have provided many additional specialty and medical services, including increased medical manpower training.

• The Congress also created a National Health Service Corps of young professionals to serve the many rural areas and inner city neighborhoods which are critically short on health care. By mid-summer, more than 100 communities around the Nation will be benefiting from these teams.

These are important steps, without doubt, but we still must lay the bedrock foundations for a new national health care system for all our people.

The need for action is critical for far too many of our citizens.

The time for action is now.

I therefore again urge the Congress to act on the many parts of my health care program which are still pending so that we can end—at the earliest possible time—the individual anguishes, the needless neglects and the family financial fears caused by the gaps, inequities and maldistributions of the present system.

The United States now spends more than $75 billion annually on health care—and for most people, relatively good service results.

Yet, despite this huge annual national outlay, millions of citizens do not have adequate access to health care. Our record in this field does not live up to our national potential.

That sobering fact should summon us to prompt but effective action to reform and reorganize health care practices, while simultaneously resisting the relentless inflation of health care costs.

More Than Money Is Needed

When the subject of health care improvements is mentioned, as is the case with so many other problems, too many people and too many institutions think first and solely of money—bills, payments, premiums, coverages, grants, subsidies and appropriations.

But far more than money is involved in our current health care crisis.

More money is important—but any attempted health care solution based primarily on money is simply not going to do the job.

In health care as in so many other areas, the most expensive remedy is not necessarily the most effective one.

One basic shortcoming of a solution to health care problems which depends entirely on spending more money, can be seen in the Medicare and Medicaid programs. Medicare and Medicaid did deliver needed dollars to the health care problems of the elderly and the poor. But at the same time, little was done to alter the existing supply and distribution of doctors, nurses, hospitals and other health resources. Our health care supply, in short, remained largely the same while massive new demands were loaded onto it.

The predictable result was an acute price inflation, one basic cause of our health economic quandary of the past 11 years.

In this period, national health expenditures rose by 188 percent, from $26 billion in fiscal 1960 to $75 billion in fiscal 1971. But a large part of this enormous increase in the Nation's health expenditure went, not for more and better health care, but merely to meet price inflation.

If we do not lessen this trend, all other reform efforts may be in vain.

That is why my National Health Strategy was designed with built-in incentives to encourage sensible economies—in the use of health facilities, in direct cost-control procedures, and through more efficient ways to bring health care to people at the community level. That is also why we have given careful attention to medical prices in Phase II of the Economic Stabilization Program.

Several months ago, the Price Commission ruled that increases in physician fees must be kept to within 2-½ percent. Rules also were issued to hold down runaway price increases among hospitals, nursing homes and other health care institutions. All of these efforts were directed toward our goal of reducing the previous 7.7 percent annual price increase in total health care costs to half of that level, 3.85 percent this year.

These actions should buy us some time. But they are, at best, a temporary tourniquet on health care price inflation.

We must now direct our energies, attentions and action to the long-range factors affecting the cost, the quality and the availability of medical care.

My overall program, of course, is one that would improve health care for everyone. But it is worthy of special note that these recommendations have a particular importance and a high value for older Americans, whose health care needs usually rise just as their incomes are declining.

We Should Build On Present Strengths

When we examine the status of health care in America, we always must be careful to recognize its strengths. For most Americans, more care of higher quality has been the result of our rising national investment in health, both governmental and private.

We lead the world in medical science, research and development. We have obliterated some major diseases and drastically reduced the incidence of others. New institutions, new treatments and new drugs abound. There has been a marked and steady gain in the number of people covered by some form of health insurance to 84 percent of those under 65, and coverages have been expanding. Life expectancy has risen by 3.4 percent since 1950 and the maternal death rate has declined 66 percent. Days lost from work in the same period are down 3.5 percent and days lost from school have declined 7.5 percent—both excellent measures of the general good state of our health.

All of this is progress—real progress.

It would be folly to raze the structure that produced this progress—and start from scratch on some entirely new basis—in order to repair shortcomings and redirect and revitalize the thrust of our health system.

To nationalize health care as some have proposed, and thus federalize medical personnel, institutions and procedures—eventually if not at the start—also would amount to a stunning new financial burden for every American taxpayer.

The average household would pay more than $1,000 a year as its share of the required new Federal expenditure of more than $80 billion each and every year. Such a massive new Federal budget item would run counter to the temper of the American taxpayer.

Also, such a massive new Federal budget item would run counter to the efforts of this Administration to decentralize programs and revenues, rather than bring new responsibilities to Washington.

And, finally, such a massive new Federal budget requirement would dim our efforts to bring needed Federal actions in many new areas—some of which bear directly on health, such as environmental protection.

Clearly we must find a better answer to the deficiencies in our health care system. Unfortunately, such deficiencies are not difficult to identify:

- In inner cities and in many rural areas, there is an acute shortage of physicians. Health screening under various government programs has found that appalling percentages of young people, mostly from deprived areas, have not seen a doctor since early childhood, have never seen a dentist and have never received any preventive care.

- General practitioners are scarce in many areas and many people, regardless of income or location, have difficulty obtaining needed medical attention on short notice.

- Our medical schools must turn away qualified applicants.

- While we emphasize preventive maintenance for our automobiles and appliances, we do not do the same for our bodies. The private health insurance system, good as it is, operates largely as standby emergency equipment, not coming into use until we are stricken and admitted to the most expensive facility, a hospital.

- Relative affluence is no ultimate protection against health care costs. A single catastrophic illness can wipe out the financial security of almost any family under most present health insurance policies.

To remedy these problems, however, will require far more than the efforts of the Federal Government—although the Federal role is vital and will be met by this Administration.

It is going to take the complementing efforts of many other units, of government at the State and local levels; of educational and health organizations and institutions of all kinds; of physicians and other medical personnel of all varieties; of private enterprise and of individual citizens.

My National Health Strategy is designed to enlist all those creative talents into a truly national effort, coordinated but not regimented by four guiding principles:

Capitalizing on Existing Strengths. We resolve to preserve the best in our existing health care system, building upon those strong elements the new programs needed to correct existing deficiencies.

Equal Access for all to Health Care. We must do all we can to end any racial, economic, social or geographical barriers which may prevent any citizen from obtaining adequate health protection.

Balanced Supply and Demand. It makes little sense to expand the demand for health care without also making certain that proper increases take place in the number of available physicians and other medical personnel, in hospitals and in other kinds of medical facilities.

Efficient Organization. We must bring basic reorganizations to our health care system so that we can cease reinforcing inequities and relying on inefficiencies. The exact same system which has failed us in many cases in the past certainly will not be able to serve properly the increased demands of the future.

Major Actions Awaited

Three major programs now awaiting action in the Congress after substantial hearings and study, would give life to these principles.

- The National Health Insurance Partnership Act,
- The Health Maintenance Organization Assistance Act,
- and H.R. 1, my welfare reform bill which also would amend Medicare and Medicaid in several significant ways.

THE NATIONAL HEALTH INSURANCE PARTNERSHIP ACT

This proposal for a comprehensive national health insurance program, in which the public and private sector would join, would guarantee that no American family would have to forego needed medical attention because of inability to pay.

My plan would fill gaps in our present health insurance coverage. But, beyond that, it would redirect our entire system to better and more efficient ways of bringing health care to our people.

There are two critical parts of this Act:

1. The National Health Insurance Standards Act would require employers to provide adequate health insurance for their employees, who would share in underwriting its costs. This approach follows precedents of long-standing under which personal security—and thus national economic progress—has been enhanced by requiring employers to provide minimum wages and disability and retirement benefits and to observe occupational health and safety standards.

Required coverages would include not less than $50,000 protection against catastrophic costs for each family member; hospital services; physician services both in and out of a hospital; maternity care; well-baby care (including immunizations); laboratory expenses and certain other costs.

The proposed package would include certain deductibles and coinsurance features, which would help keep costs down by encouraging the use of more efficient health care procedures.

It would permit many workers, as an alternative to paying separate fees for services, to purchase instead memberships in a Health Maintenance Organization. The fact that workers and unions would have a direct economic stake in the program would serve as an additional built-in incentive for avoiding unnecessary costs and yet maintaining high quality.

The national standards prescribes, moreover, would necessarily limit the range within which benefits could vary. This provision would serve to sharpen competition and cost-consciousness among insurance companies seeking to provide coverage at the lowest overall cost.

Any time the Federal Government, in effect, prescribes and guarantees certain things it must take the necessary follow-through steps to assure that the interests of consumers and taxpayers are fully protected.

Accordingly, legislative proposals have been submitted to the Congress within recent weeks for regulating private health insurance companies, in order to assure that they can and will do the job, and that insurance will be offered at reasonable rates. In addition, States would be required to provide group-rate coverage for people such as the self-employed and special groups who do not qualify for other plans.

2. Another vital step in my proposed program is the Family Health Insurance Plan (FHIP) which would meet the needs of poor families not covered by the National Health Insurance Standards Act because they are headed by unemployed or self-employed persons whose income is below certain levels. For a family of four, the ceiling for eligibility would be an annual income of $5,000. FHIP would replace that portion of Medicaid designed to help such families. Medicaid would remain for the aged poor, the blind, the disabled and some children.

HEALTH MAINTENANCE ORGANIZATIONS

Beyond filling gaps in insurance coverage, we must also turn our attention to how the money thus provided will be spent—on what kind of services and in what kind of institutions. This is why the Health Maintenance Organization concept is such a central feature of my National Health Strategy.

The HMO is a method for financing and providing health care that has won growing respect. It brings together into a single organization the physician, the hospital, the laboratory and the clinic, so that patients can get the right care at the right moment.

HMO's utilize a method of payment that encourages the prevention of illness and promotes the efficient use of doctors and hospitals. Unlike traditional fee-for-service billing, the HMO contracts to provide its comprehensive care for a fixed annual sum that is determined in advance.

Under this financial arrangement, the doctors' and hospitals' incomes are determined not by how much the patient is sick, but by how much he is well. HMO's thus have the strongest possible incentive for keeping well members from becoming ill and for curing sick members as quickly as possible.

I do not believe that HMO's should or will entirely replace fee-for-service financing. But I do believe that they ought to be everywhere available so that families will have a choice between these methods. The HMO is no mere drawing-board concept—more than 7 million Americans are now HMO subscribers and that number is growing.

Several pieces of major legislation now before the Congress would give powerful stimulus to the development of HMO's:

1. The Health Maintenance Organization Assistance Act would provide technical and financial aid to help new HMO's get started, and would spell out standards of operation;

2. The National Health Insurance Partnership Act described above requires that individuals be given a choice between fee-for-service or HMO payment plans;

3. H.R. 1 contains one provision allowing HMO-type reimbursement for Medicare patients and another that would increase the Federal share of payments made to HMO's under State Medicaid programs.

I urge that the Congress give early consideration to these three measures, in order to hasten the development of this efficient method for low-cost, one-stop health service. Meantime, the Administration has moved forward in this area on its own under existing legislative authorities.

Last year, while HMO legislation was being prepared, I directed the Department of Health, Education, and Welfare to focus existing funds and staff on an early HMO development effort. This effort has already achieved payoffs:

To date, 110 planning and development grants and contracts have been let to potential HMO sponsors and some 200,-000 Medicaid patients are now enrolled in HMO-type plans. Also, in a few months, 10 Family Health Centers will be operating with federally-supported funds to provide prepaid health care to persons living in underserved areas. Each of these Centers can develop into a full-service HMO. I have requested funds in 1973 to expand this support.

To keep this momentum going I have included in the fiscal year 1972 supplemental budget $27 million for HMO development, and requested $60 million for this purpose in fiscal year 1973.

I will also propose amendments to the pending HMO Assistance Act that would authorize the establishment of an HMO loan fund.

THE NATIONAL NEED FOR H.R. 1

One of the greatest hazards to life and health is poverty. Death and illness rates among the poor are many times those for the rest of the Nation. The steady elimination of poverty would in itself improve the health of millions of Americans.

H.R. 1's main purpose is to help people lift themselves free of poverty's grip by providing them with jobs, job training, income supplements for the working poor and child care centers for mothers seeking work.

For this reason alone, enactment of H. R. 1 must be considered centerpiece legislation in the building of a National Health Strategy.

But H.R. 1 also includes the following measures to extend health care to more Americans—especially older Americans—and to control costs:

Additional Persons Covered

• Persons eligible for Part A of Medicare (hospital care) would be automatically enrolled in Part B (physician's care).

• Medicare (both Parts A and B) would be extended to many disabled persons not now covered.

H. R. 1 as it now stands, however, would still require monthly premium payments to cover the costs of Part B. I have recommended that the Congress eliminate this $5.80 monthly premium payment and finance Medicare coverage of physician services through the social security payroll tax. This can be done within the Medicare tax rate now included in H. R. 1. If enacted, this change would save $1.5 billion annually for older Americans and would be equivalent to a 5 percent increase in social security cash benefits.

Cost Control Features

• Medicare and Medicaid reimbursement would be denied any hospital or other institution for interest, depreciation and service charges on any construction disapproved by local or regional health planning agencies. Moreover, to strengthen local and regional health planning agencies, my fiscal year 1973 budget would increase the Federal matching share. In addition, grants to establish 100 new local and 20 new State planning agencies would bring health planning to more than 80 percent of the Nation's population.

• Reviews of claim samples and utilization patterns, which have saved much money in the Medicare program, would be applied to Medicaid.

• The efficiency of Medicaid hospitals and health facilities would be improved by testing various alternative methods of reimbursing them.

• Cost sharing would be introduced after 30 days of hospitalization under Medicare.

• Federal Medicaid matching rates would decline one-third after the first 60 days of care.

• Federal Medicaid matching rates would be increased 25 percent for services for which the States contract with HMO's or other comprehensive health care facilities.

These latter three revisions are aimed at minimizing inefficient institutional care and encouraging more effective modes of treatment.

Research And Prevention Programs

My overall health program encompasses actions on three levels: 1) improving protection against health care costs, 2) improving the health care system itself, and 3) working creatively on research and prevention efforts, to eradicate health menaces and to hold down the incidence of illnesses.

A truly effective national health strategy requires that a significant share of Federal research funds be concentrated on major health threats, particularly when research advances indicate the possibility of breakthrough progress.

Potentially high payoff health research and prevention programs include:

Heart Disease. If current rates of incidence continue, some 12 million Americans will suffer heart attacks in the next 10 years.

I shortly will assign a panel of distinguished professional experts to guide us in determining why heart disease is so prevalent and what we should be doing to combat it. In the meantime, the fiscal year 1973 budget provides funds for exploring:

• The development of new medical devices to assist blood circulation and improved instruments for the early detection of heart disease; and

• Tests to explore the relationship of such high-risk factors as smoking, high blood pressure and high blood fats to the onset and progression of heart disease.

Cancer. The National Cancer Act I signed into law December 23, 1971, creates the authority for organizing an all-out attack on this dread disease. The new cancer program it creates will be directly responsive to the President's direction.

This new program's work will be given further momentum by my decision last October to convert the former biological warfare facility at Fort Detrick, Maryland into a cancer research center.

To finance this all-out research effort, I have requested that an additional $93 million be allocated for cancer research in fiscal year 1973, bringing the total funding available that year to $430 million.

In the past two and one-half years, we have more than doubled the funding for cancer research, reflecting this Administration's strong commitment to defeat this dread killer as soon as humanly possible.

Alcoholism. One tragic and costly illness which touches every community in our land is alcoholism. There are more than 9 million alcoholics and alcohol abusers in our Nation.

The human cost of this condition is incalculable—broken homes, broken lives and the tragedy of 28,000 victims of alcohol-related highway deaths every year.

The recently established National Institute of Alcohol Abuse and Alcoholism will soon launch an intensive public education program through television and radio and will continue to support model treatment projects from which States and communities will be able to pattern programs to fight this enemy.

Meanwhile, the Department of Health, Education, and Welfare and the Department of Transportation are funding projects in 35 States to demonstrate the value of highway safety, enforcement and education efforts among drinking drivers. The Veterans Administration will increase the number of its Alcohol Dependence Treatment Units by more than one-third, to 56 units in fiscal year 1973.

Drug Abuse. Drug abuse now constitutes a national emergency.

In response to this threat and to the need for coordination of Federal programs aimed at drug abuse, I established the Special Action Office for Drug Abuse Prevention within the Executive Office of the President. Its special areas of action are programs for treating and rehabilitating the drug abuser and for alerting our young people to the dangers of drug abuse.

I have proposed legislation to the Congress which would extend and clarify the authority of this Office. I am hopeful that Senate and House conferees will soon be able to resolve differences in the versions passed by the two branches and emerge with a single bill responsive to the Nation's needs.

The new Special Action Office, however, has not been idly awaiting this legislation. It has been vigorously setting about the task of identifying the areas of greatest need and channelling Federal resources into these areas.

The Department of Defense, for example, working in close coordination with the Special Action Office, has instituted drug abuse identification, education, and treatment programs which effectively combatted last year's heroin problem among our troops in South Vietnam. Indications are that the corner has been turned on this threat and that the incidence of drug dependence among our troops is declining.

The Veterans Administration, again in coordination with the Special Action Office, has accomplished more than a six-fold increase in the number of drug dependency treatment centers in fiscal year 1972, with an increase to 44 centers proposed in fiscal year 1973.

In fiscal year 1972, I have increased funds available for the prevention of drug abuse by more than 130 percent. For fiscal year 1973, I have requested over $365 million to treat the drug abuser and prevent the spread of the affliction of drug abuse.

This is more than eight times as much as was being spent for this purpose when this Administration took office.

Sickle Cell Disease. About one out of every 500 black infants falls victim to the painful, life-shortening disease called sickle cell anemia. This inherited disease trait is carried by about two million black Americans.

In fiscal year 1972, $10 million was allocated to attack this problem and an advisory committee of prominent black leaders was organized to help direct the effort. This committee's recommendations are in hand and an aggressive action program is ready to start.

To underwrite this effort, I am proposing to increase the new budget for sickle cell disease from $10 million in fiscal 1972 to $15 million in fiscal 1973.

The Veterans Administration's medical care system also can be counted on to make an important contribution to the fight against sickle cell anemia.

Eight separate research projects concerning sickle cell anemia are underway in VA hospitals and more will be started this year. All 166 VA hospitals will launch a broad screening, treatment and educational effort to combat this disease.

On any given day, about 17,000 black veterans are in VA hospitals and some 116,000 are treated annually.

All these expanded efforts will lead to a better and longer life for thousands of black Americans.

Family Planning Services. Nearly threee years ago, I called for a program that would provide family planning services to all who wanted them but could not afford their cost. The timetable for achieving this goal was five years.

To meet that schedule, funding for services administered by the National Center for Family Planning for this program has been steadily increased from $39 million in fiscal year 1971 to $91 million in fiscal year 1972. I am requesting $139 million for this Center in fiscal year 1973.

Total Federal support for family planning services and research in fiscal 1973 will rise to $240 million, a threefold increase since fiscal year 1969.

Venereal Disease. Last year, more than 2.5 million venereal disease cases were detected in the United States. Two-thirds of the victims were under 25.

A concentrated program to find persons with infectious cases and treat them is needed to bring this disease under control. I am, therefore, recommending that $31 million be allocated for this purpose in fiscal year 1973, more than two and one-half times the level of support for VD programs in 1971.

Health Education. Aside from formal treatment programs, public and private, the general health of individuals depends very much on their own informed actions and practices.

Last year, I proposed that a National Health Education Foundation be established to coordinate a nationwide program to alert people on ways in which they could protect their own health. Since that time, a number of public meetings have been held by a committee I established then to gather views on all aspects of health education. The report of this committee will be sent to me this year.

The committee hopes to define more explicitly the Nation's need for health education programs and to determine ways of rallying all the resources of our society to meet this need.

Consumer Safety. More than a half century has passed since basic legislation was enacted to ensure the safety of the foods and drugs which Americans consume. Since then, industrial and agricultural revolutions have generated an endless variety of new products, food additives, industrial compounds, cosmetics, synthetic fabrics and other materials which are employed to feed, clothe, medicate and adorn the American consumer.

These revolutions created an entirely new man-made environment—and we must make absolutely certain that this new environment does not bring harmful side-effects which outweigh its evident benefits.

The only way to ensure that goal is met is to give the agency charged with that responsibility the resources it needs to meet the challenge.

My budget request for the Food and Drug Administration for fiscal year 1973 represents the largest single-year expansion in the history of this agency—70 percent. I believe this expansion is amply justified by the magnitude of the task this agency faces.

In the past year, the foundations for a modern program of consumer protection have been laid. The FDA has begun a detailed review of the thousands of non-prescription drug products now marketed. The pharmaceutical industry has been asked to cooperate in compiling a complete inventory of every drug available to the consumer.

Meanwhile, I have proposed the following legislation to ensure more effective protection for consumers.

• A wholesome fish and fish products bill which provides for the expansion of inspections of fish handlers and greater authority to assure the safety of fish products.

• A Consumer Product Safety bill which would authorize the Federal Government to establish and enforce new standards for product safety.

• Medical device legislation which would not only authorize the establishment of safety standards for these products, but would also provide for premarketing scientific review when warranted.

• A drug identification bill now before the Congress would provide a method for quickly and accurately identifying any pill or tablet. This provision would reduce the risk of error in taking medicines and allow prompt treatment following accidental ingestion.

• The Toxic Substances Control Act that I proposed last year also awaits action by the Congress. This legislation would require any company developing a new chemical that may see widespread use to test it thoroughly beforehand for possible toxic effects.

Nursing Homes. If there is one place to begin upgrading the quality of health care, it is in the nursing homes that care for older Americans. Many homes provide excellent care and concern, but far too many others are callous, understaffed, unsanitary and downright dangerous.

Last August I announced an eight-point program to upgrade the quality of life and the standards of care in American nursing homes. The Federal interest and responsibility in this field is clear, since Federal programs including Medicare and Medicaid provide some 40 percent of total nursing home income nationally.

That HEW effort is well underway now:

Federal field teams have surveyed every State nursing home inspection program, and as a result 38 of 39 States found to have deficiencies have corrected them. The 39th is acting to meet Federal standards. To help States upgrade nursing homes, I have proposed legislation to pay 100 percent of the costs of inspecting these facilities.

Meanwhile, at my direction, a Federally-funded program to train 2,000 State nursing home inspectors and to train 41,000 nursing home employees is also underway. The Federal field force for assisting nursing homes is being augmented and fire, safety and health codes have been strengthened.

One way to measure the results of these efforts is to learn how patients in nursing homes feel about the care they are given. We have therefore also begun a program to monitor the complaints and suggestions of nursing home residents.

Applying Science and Technology. In my State of the Union message, I proposed a new Federal partnership with the private sector to stimulate civilian technological research and development. One of the most vital areas where we can focus this partnership—perhaps utilizing engineers and scientists displaced from other jobs—is in improving human health. Opportunities in this field include:

1. Emergency Medical Services: By using new technologies to improve emergency care systems and by using more and better trained people to run those systems, we can save the lives of many heart attack victims and many victims of auto accidents every year. The loss to the Nation represented by these unnecessary deaths cannot be calculated. I have already allocated $8 million in fiscal year 1972 to develop model systems and training programs and my budget proposes that $15 million be invested for additional demonstrations in fiscal year 1973.

2. Blood: Blood is a unique national resource. An adequate system for collecting and delivering blood at its time and place of need can save many lives. Yet we do not have a nationwide system to meet this need and we need to draw upon the skills of modern management and technology to develop one. I have therefore directed the Department of Health, Education, and Welfare to make an intensive study and to recommend to me as soon as possible a plan for developing a safe, fast and efficient nationwide blood collection and distribution system.

3. Health Information Systems: Each physician, hospital and clinic today is virtually an information island unto itself. Records and billings are not kept on the same basis everywhere, laboratory tests are often needlessly repeated and vital patient data can get lost. All of these problems have been accentuated because our population is so constantly on the move. The technology exists to end this chaos and improve the quality of care. I have therefore asked the Secretary of Health, Education, and Welfare to plan a series of projects to demonstrate the feasibility of developing integrated and uniform systems of health information.

4. Handicapping Conditions: In America today there are half a million blind, 850,000 deaf and 15 million suffering paralysis and loss of limbs. So far, the major responses to their need to gain self-sufficiency, have been vocational rehabilitation and welfare programs. Now the skills that took us to the moon and back need to be put to work developing devices to help the blind see, the deaf hear and the crippled move.

Toward A Better Health Care System

Working together, this Administration and the Congress already have taken some significant strides in our mutual determination to provide the best, and the most widely available, health care system the world has ever known.

The time now has come to take the final steps to reorganize, to revitalize and to redirect American health care—to build on its historic accomplishments, to close its gaps and to provide it with the incentives and sustenance to move toward a more perfect mission of human compassion.

I believe that the health care resources of America in 1972, if strengthened and expanded as I have proposed in this Message, will be more than sufficient to move us significantly toward that great goal.

If the Administration and the Congress continue to act together—and act on the major proposals this year, as I strongly again urge—then the 1970s will be remembered as an era in which the United States took the historic step of making the health of the entire population not only a great goal but a practical objective.

RICHARD NIXON

MINORITY ENTERPRISES

Following is the text, as made available by the White House, of President Nixon's March 20 message to Congress on minority enterprise.

TO THE CONGRESS OF THE UNITED STATES:

From its start, America has prided itself on being a land of opportunity.

In recent years, we have done much to press open new doors of opportunity for millions of Americans to whom those doors had previously been barred, or only half-open. In jobs, housing, education, old obstacles are being removed. But for Blacks, Mexican-Americans, Puerto Ricans, Indians and other minorities who have known discrimination, economic opportunity must also increasingly be made to mean a greater chance to know the satisfactions, the rewards and the responsibilities of business ownership. Such opportunities are not only important in themselves; they also help make possible the economic and social advances that are critical to the development of stable and thriving communities on which the social and economic vitality of the nation as a whole depend.

Despite a long history of frustration and lost potential, minority Americans want business ownership—and they should. Potential minority entrepreneurs are eager to join the mainstream of the nation's commerce. Many need help in getting started—and increasing numbers are getting that help. A working coalition of the government, the private sector and minority communities is moving rapidly to provide disadvantaged Americans with opportunities to own and control their own successful businesses.

The principal need of minority business today is for a greater supply of investment capital. Technical assistance, training, promotion and business opportunities are all fundamentally related to investment capital, that centripetal force which draws together the people, skills, equipment and resources necessary to operate a profitable business.

The coalition of public and private sectors and minority interests supporting disadvantaged business enterprise must be strengthened now, if we are to achieve the goal of generating the additional investment capital needed.

Today, therefore, I am turning to the Congress for its cooperation and help. I urge the approval by the Congress of the following:

• first, the Minority Enterprise Small Business Investment Act of 1972;

• second, a budget request for the Office of Minority Business Enterprise of $63.6-million for fiscal 1973;

• third, a variety of other small business legislation currently pending in Congress which will directly and collaterally aid minority enterprise.

The Pressing Need

The nation's Black, Spanish-speaking and Indian and other minorities constitute about one-sixth of the American population. Yet in 1967—the last year for which final figures are available—these American minorities accounted for well below one percent of the total business income of the nation. Gross receipts of almost $1.5-trillion were reported in that year by all American businesses. Of this amount, minority-owned firms received only $10.6-billion, or less than one percent. In the United States today, there are more than 8 million businesses; minority Americans presently own only about 4 percent of these businesses, despite the fact that they constitute almost 17 percent of our population.

These statistics starkly summarize the gross disparity of the minority enterprise imbalance, but they do not adequately outline the broader effects on our society at large. The human cost, in terms of lost potential and lowered horizons, is immeasurable.

Responding to Minority Needs

Recognizing the need for government incentives and leadership, I took steps in my first months in office to awaken the federal establishment and the private sector to the potential for development of minority business. First, I established the Office of Minority Business Enterprise (OMBE) within the Department of Commerce to plan and coordinate comprehensive minority business development. Secondly, the Small Business Administration (SBA) undertook to increase minority participation in its many business programs. Thirdly, I directed all federal departments and agencies to respond to the aspirations and needs of minority entrepreneurs, particularly by use of their procurement powers.

Progress Report

I am pleased to report to the Congress that our efforts to stimulate the federal government and private sector have been highly productive. A comprehensive statement of accomplishments was published in January of this year entitled, "Progress of the Minority Business Enterprise Program." Let me summarize the highlights of that report for you and outline our current status.

Office of Minority Business Enterprise. Only the private sector working with the government can reverse a century's discouragement of minority enterprise; the government cannot do it alone. The nation's established corporations, financial institutions, professional associations, foundations, and religious organizations are indispensable to meet the demand of minority businessmen for seed capital, operating funds, suppliers, markets, expert technical and management assistance and related business essentials.

Three years ago, there were no precedents, no rule books, no methods, no blueprints on how to focus the resources of these groups on a common objective. OMBE's greatest achievement during these past three years has been to forge an alliance of government, private sector and minority business interests. The office has succeeded in launching a carefully contoured, integrated set of programs that will work to engage minority entrepreneurs fully in our nation's economic life.

Gains. Since the establishment of OMBE, American minorities have gained greater access to both government and private sector contracts and concessions, business loans and loan guarantees, technical and management assistance, and other business aid. This access has been developed without reducing programs available to non-minority small businessmen. Federal assistance, channeled through these vehicles, has been enlarged from less than $200-million in 1969 to some $700-million currently, and the $1-billion threshold for fiscal 1973—five times the 1969 level—is within reach. New markets have been opened as minority suppliers and businessmen have expanded their operations and sales in unprecedented volume.

Funding OMBE and SBA. Our efforts on behalf of minority business secured substantial congressional approval, and OMBE was appropriated a supplemental budget increase of $40-million for the last six months of fiscal 1972, as I requested. I am hopeful that both the House and Senate will give favorable consideration to our present request for a fiscal 1973 OMBE budget of $63.6-million to provide urgently needed technical and management assistance to minority business. Together, these budgets will total more than $100-million. This figure offers a dramatic index of the commitment of this administration to the purposes of an office which was originally funded for fiscal year 1972 with less than four million dollars.

OMBE is a coordinating agency of the federal government, and as such does not itself engage directly in business financing. Direct loans, loan guarantees, surety bonding, lines of credit, and contract set-asides are supplied by the Small Business Administration (SBA) to small businessmen, including minority businessmen.

The Immediate Need: MESBIC Legislation

Enactment of the administration's proposed Minority Enterprise Small Business Investment Act of 1972 would give major impetus to the minority enterprise program, and would create a more productive mechanism to achieve its objectives.

Background. When the Congress passed the Small Business Investment Act of 1958, it recognized that small business generally lacks seed money and working capital. To give incentives for small business investment, the act empowered SBA to license "Small Business Investment Companies" (SBICs). Such companies are private investment institutions capitalized at a minimum of $150,000 from private sources. SBICs are eligible to borrow from SBA at an incentive ratio of $2 from SBA for every $1 of its private capital. Thus, a $150,000 SBIC can borrow $300,000 from SBA for investment in its own account. Also, after it raises $1-million in private capital, a SBIC is eligible to borrow $3 from SBA for every $1 of private capital.

Because of these incentives, substantial amounts of private capital have been invested in small business through SBICs. More than 40,000 small business financings have been completed by SBICs from the program's inception, totaling $1.9-billion in risk capital. *But only a small fraction of that amount has gone into minority businesses*, because usually risks and costs are even higher for minority small businesses than for small businesses generally.

MESBICS

To fill the need for minority enterprise high risk capital, the SBA evolved the *Minority Enterprise* Small Business Investment Company (MESBIC). A MESBIC is a specialized SBIC: 1) it limits its investment to minority enterprises; 2) it is supported by financially sturdy institutional sponsors; 3) it is underwritten in large part by its sponsors.

In 1969 OMBE joined with SBA in launching a national network of MESBICs with SBA licensing and regulating MESBICs and OMBE promoting them. Today, 47 MESBICs operate throughout the nation with private funds totaling in excess of $14-million. Since MESBIC seed capital has the potential of freeing $15 for investment in minority enterprises for every one privately invested dollar, more than $210-million is currently available through this program. All this is achieved at relatively low cost to the government.

MESBICs have the potential of becoming sophisticated investment companies, knowledgeable in the peculiar problems of minority business investment, and able to bring sound business principles and practices to their tasks. Seeking a fair return on investment, MESBICs can act effectively to raise the success prospects of portfolio companies.

MESBIC Limitations. Despite the proven values of the MESBIC mechanism, it labors under burdens which endanger further development. The cost of administering minority business investments and the risk of early loss are both very high. Moreover, the short term success pattern of minority businesses has not been sufficiently encouraging to enable them to attract equity investment in normal competitive markets. But the recent successes of minority enterprises have shown that they can compete if they are given enough equity assistance to carry them through this early period.

The Minority Enterprise Small Business Investment Act of 1972

The primary object of my message today is to urge that the proposed Minority Enterprise Small Business Investment Act be acted on favorably and with dispatch by the House in its upcoming small business hearings. This act will restructure SBA financing of MESBICs so that they can operate on a fiscally sound basis.

Provisions of the Act. The legislation proposes a statutory definition of a MESBIC and authority to organize it as a non-profit corporation. This status would facilitate foundation investments and tax-deductible gifts to MESBICs.

Building on our experience with SBICs and MESBICs, the act would reduce the level of private capital required to qualify for $3 to $1 assistance from SBA, from $1-million to $500,000; provide increased equity to MESBICs in the form of preferred stock to be purchased by SBA in place of part of the debt instruments purchased by SBA from MESBICs under current law; and lower the interest rate on SBA loans to MESBICs to three points below the normal rate set by the Treasury during the first five years of the loan.

Restructuring Effects of the Act. The immediate impact of this legislation would be to materially restructure the MESBIC program and stimulate increased private investment and gifts to MESBICs, resulting in greatly increased capital for minority business enterprises, at startlingly small federal cost.

The legislation would: Lower the high cost of starting the investment program of a MESBIC; allow MESBICs to take advantage of full SBA financing; enable MESBICs to invest more in equity securities and to reduce interest rates to portfolio companies; provide special incentives to existing smaller MESBICs which have pioneered the program.

In the act, I am proposing a fairer partnership between the private and public sectors—a partnership that would yield enabling capital for minority enterprise. The MESBIC program is sound, practical and necessary. It equitably extends our free enterprise system by making it work for all Americans.

Conclusion

Opening wider the doors of opportunity for one-sixth of our people is a social necessity, which responds to an imperative claim on our conscience. It also is an economic necessity. By stimulating minority enterprise—by permitting more of our people to be more productive, by creating new businesses and new jobs, by raising the sights and lifting the ambitions of millions who are enabled to see that others who started under handicaps like theirs are writing records of economic success— we help to stimulate the whole economy.

I therefore urge the Congress to give its swift approval to the Minority Enterprise Small Business Investment Act of 1972, to my fiscal year 1973 budget request for $63.6-million for OMBE, and to our other small business proposals currently pending in the Congress.

Hard work, private risk, initiative, and equal chance at success—these are the American way. Helping ensure for all of our people an opportunity to participate fully in the economic system that has made America the world's strongest and richest nation—this too is the American way. And this lies at the heart of our program for minority enterprise.

RICHARD NIXON

FOREIGN AID MESSAGE

Following is the text, as made available by the White House, of President Nixon's March 14 message to Congress on foreign aid.

TO THE CONGRESS OF THE UNITED STATES:

Today I am transmitting to the Congress legislation which would authorize funding for my foreign aid proposals for the coming fiscal year. This draft bill, which is entitled the Foreign Assistance Act of 1972, also contains provisions to make our military assistance more effective.

As I have often indicated, our foreign assistance programs are a central element in our foreign policy for the 1970s. For it is as dangerous for this nation to ignore the problems of poverty and hunger and the need for security in other nations as it is to ignore our own domestic needs.

The Congress, acting after two-thirds of the current fiscal year had already passed, drastically reduced my foreign assistance requests for fiscal year 1972. In my judgment, the amounts appropriated for both security and development assistance in fiscal year 1972 are below the minimum level required to attain our foreign policy and national security goals. These reductions have created difficult problems in essential programs and in our relations with several countries. A repetition of these reductions and delays in 1973 would call into serious question the firmness of our commitments abroad and could have a destabilizing effect at a time when calm confidence in our support and perseverance will be critically needed. I therefore urge the Congress to act promptly to authorize and appropriate the full amounts requested for foreign assistance in fiscal year 1973.

In forwarding the Foreign Assistance Act of 1972, I would also underscore the points I made in my message to the Congress on April 21, 1971. In that message I addressed the need for fundamental reform of foreign assistance and recommended a major reorganization of these programs. I hope that the Congress will give closer consideration to these proposals in this session, and that together we can develop the most effective program possible, one that truly merits the broad bipartisan support that foreign aid has enjoyed in the past.

SECURITY ASSISTANCE

As I pointed out in my annual Report to the Congress on Foreign Policy last month: "Security assistance is a cornerstone of our foreign policy and of Free World security..." We live today in a period of transition in world affairs, in a time in which the United States is taking bold initiatives to build a new structure of peace, while asking our friends and allies to assume a greater responsibility for their own defense.

As we begin to make adjustments in our international role, it is especially critical that we maintain a firm United States commitment to an adequate level of security assistance. For without such adequate levels, our friends and allies will lack the confidence required for successful international cooperation in an era of negotiations. And without adequate security assistance, we cannot safely reduce our military presence abroad.

I am therefore requesting authorizations for security assistance programs totaling $2,151-million in fiscal year 1973: $780-million for grant military assistance, $527-million for military credit sales, and $844-million for security supporting assistance, of which an estimated $50-million is intended for Israel.

NARCOTICS CONTROL

I am requesting that a separate appropriation of $42.5-million be authorized for the support of international narcotics control activities. Control of illicit drug production and trafficking is one of the highest priorities of my administration. I believe the authorization and appropriation of funds specifically for this purpose is essential to clearly demonstrate the determination of the administration, the Congress, and the American people to overcome this serious menace.

SOUTH ASIA RELIEF AND RECONSTRUCTION ASSISTANCE

I am also proposing the authorization of $100-million in fiscal year 1973 for refugee relief and humanitarian assistance in South Asia. This sum would be in addition to the $200-million appropriated for this purpose for the current fiscal year.

The damage and destruction growing out of the war between India and Pakistan has truly been immense. We have indicated our willingness to work with other donors under the auspices of the United Nations to provide relief and rehabilitation to those in need.

The secretary general of the United Nations has issued an assessment of these needs and a special appeal for support. We have already made an initial contribution to this effort and will continue to contribute in the light of the efforts of others and further assessments of need. The $100-million which I am requesting would enable us to continue to participate generously, along with other nations, in this important work.

RICHARD NIXON

WELFARE REFORM

Following is the text, as made available by the White House, of President Nixon's March 27 message to Congress on welfare reform.

TO THE CONGRESS OF THE UNITED STATES:

The American welfare system is a national disgrace.

Thirty-one months ago, I first proposed to the Congress my plan for total reform of that system.

Since that time, the welfare situation has continued to worsen, and sweeping changes have become even more imperative.

There can be absolutely no excuse for delaying those changes any further. The present system must be reformed.

Its shocking inequities continue to drain incentive from the many poor who work but who see some families making as much or more on welfare.

Its widely varying, discriminatory benefits continue to force needy families, millions of children, and the needy aged, blind and disabled into a web of inefficient rules and economic contradictions.

Its vast costs have continued to escalate, undermining state and local governments and threatening to erode taxpayer support for a welfare system of any kind.

The present system continues to contribute to the breakup of poor families, rather than reenforcing the role of the family in our national life. The welfare life-style continues to dehumanize those who are caught in it, and threatens now to create yet another "welfare generation."

Now is the Time for Action

This year must be the year in which we raze the ramshackle welfare system, patched up so many times in the past but still basically unchanged since it was first enacted as emergency legislation in the mid-1930s. In its place, we must build a new system, taking a new direction. We must create an environment that will draw forth and support—rather than smother—the innate ambitions and personal obligations of all needy Americans.

Last December, the Congress did pass transitional legislation which took parts of my welfare reform package—certain of the work fare provisions for job training and work requirements for all employable welfare recipients—and applied them to the present system of welfare. These actions will become effective later this year.

Acceptance of those workfare provisions by the Congress was a step in the right direction, as I said when I signed the measure. But it is still part of the patchwork approach. Now something far better than a patchwork approach is required if the needy are to receive rational assistance, if waste and inefficiency are to be abolished, and if America's work incentive-job reward system is to be placed within reach of every citizen.

We should never forget that it is precisely this system that has enabled us to develop the highest standard of living—with the most widely shared advantages—in the history of the world. We should continue to rely on it as we drive to close the final gaps between economic promise and economic reality.

On June 22 of last year the House of Representatives, for the second time, passed by a wide majority omnibus legislation which would implement my overall welfare reform. This legislation is now being closely scrutinized by the Senate Finance Committee, whose able chairman, Senator Long, has assured me that the committee will report HR 1 to the Senate floor as soon as possible. HR 1 continues to have my full support, and I hope that it will be enacted into law this year in the basic form approved by the House of Representatives.

We need reform this year so that, instead of pouring billions more into a system universally recognized as a failure, we can make a new start.

We must not forget that HR 1 contains basic reforms in social security and medical benefits, as well as welfare reform.

These benefits, by themselves, are pathbreaking in scope and impact—including a further 5-percent benefit increase in social security, the automatic adjustment of social security benefits in the future to make them inflation proof, and a host of additional reforms discussed in my recent message to the Congress on older Americans. As I said in that message, even one more year of delay in the passage of HR 1 would cost older Americans some $5-½-billion in annual benefits.

HR 1 clearly lies at the heart of economic progress of millions of Americans in 1972—and into the future. It is the most important single piece of social legislation to come before the Congress in several decades. I strongly urge the Congress to pass it as soon as possible this year. No legislation should have a higher priority.

The Welfare Mess Worsens

When I first presented my welfare reform proposal to the Congress on August 11, 1969, I declared that "America's welfare system is a failure that grows worse every day."

Nine hundred and fifty eight days have passed since that message and that comment. The welfare landscape today is a greater fiscal and ethical wasteland than ever:

• Injustice and inequities are widespread: There are glaring differences between welfare benefits paid in various parts of the country—they can range from $60 a month to $326 a month for a woman with three children, depending on in which state she happens to live. Moreover, too many Americans can get more money by going on welfare than by going to work. There is no real requirement that a recipient seek, much less accept, a job.

• The basic immorality of the system still prevails: In most states welfare still offers a man a bounty to desert his family.

• Incentive continues to be penalized: A man working hard for low wages can see neighboring families on welfare that are better off than his own family.

• Millions of children suffer: They are forced to live in degrading and deplorable conditions because the present system precludes their families from any benefits.

• Waste continues unabated: State quality control surveys indicate that as many as one in 20 welfare recipients may actually be ineligible for benefits, and that inaccurate payments are being given to as many as one case in every four—a potential total annual waste of more than $500-million.

• Administration remains a quagmire of red tape: There are 1,152 separate state and local welfare jurisdictions, with separate eligibility determinations and administrative procedures—making program integrity a virtual impossibility.

What we have in short, is a crazy quilt of injustice and contradiction that has developed in bits and pieces over the years with little serious thought of basic reform. I believe that HR 1 is the best and most comprehensive answer yet devised to meet this challenge.

Fiscal Crisis: Washington and the States

The present welfare system is not only morally bankrupt—but is a significant factor in driving the states toward fiscal bankruptcy.

Since I first proposed reform in 1969, the costs of maintaining the present system have mounted at an alarming rate. Each day of delay means further costs—without any offsetting benefits. For example:

• Welfare costs have skyrocketed from $6.2-billion in 1969 to an estimated $9.4 billion in 1971, a 51-percent increase in just two years.

• The overall welfare caseload has risen from 9.6 million people in 1969 to 13.5 million today. It has been estimated that, if no changes are made, 17.3 million people will be on welfare in 1974, an 80-percent rise in just five years.

What we have on our hands is nothing less than a social and political time bomb. And, in a development of concern to all of us, the patience and support of the American public for welfare programs has been slipping dangerously. Those who are truly needy are becoming scapegoats in the eyes of taxpayers understandably angered about waste and inconsistency.

What we are seeking is an end to the need for public support for people who are essentially employable, but have not been able to work for reasons beyond their control, just will not work, or will not even make themselves available for work-related training—and this is what HR 1 would cure.

We also need to establish a nationally uniform system of efficient aid for totally needy families and the old and infirm—and HR 1 would achieve that goal, too.

Outline of Reform

My program, as embodied in HR 1, would place a floor beneath the income of all American families not able to adequately support themselves. Its payments would vary, according to family size and resources, from a minimum of $1,600 to a maximum of $3,600. The basic benefit for a family of four with no other income would be $2,400.

Employable adult members of such families would have to register with the Department of Labor in its Opportunities for Families Program for manpower services, work training and employment availability before any benefits were paid to such persons. Exceptions would include mothers of children younger than 6, and mothers whose husbands were either working or registered for work.

Families without employable adult members would not be subject to registration requirements but would receive the same basic benefits under the Department of Health, Education, and Welfare's Family Assistance Program.

For the first time in our history, national wage supplements would be paid to the working poor on a proportionate sliding scale designed to spur, rather than kill, the incentive to start working and keep on earning.

Eligible persons would be able to keep the first $720 earned during the year without reduction in their supplements. As job income rose beyond that, supplements would be reduced by two-thirds of job income until a cut-off point were reached and the recipient had attained a degree of self-sufficiency.

A family of four thus could earn $720 and receive a benefit of $2,400—for a total income of $3,120. When such a family's earnings reached $3,600, it still would be eligible for a supplement of $480 for a total income of $4,080.

When such a family reached earnings of $4,320 it would move completely out of the federal assistance program.

Under the terms of HR 1, the Opportunities for Families program, the Family Assistance Plan and programs for the needy, aged, blind and disabled would be totally financed by the federal government—thereby providing much-needed financial relief for the states, which now share welfare costs.

In several respects, the proposed payments to the working poor constitute the basic conceptual foundation of my new approach.

These payments would encourage those who are working to keep on working, rather than sliding into welfare dependency. And they would motivate welfare recipients to start work.

We must hit head-on the cruel fallacy that any income, no matter how low, is sufficient for an American family merely because that money comes from full-time work.

We must establish the more humane and relevant principle that the total income of each American family must reach a certain minimum standard.

Another foundation of my approach is the strong work requirement and the provisions which would help implement that requirement, including child care benefits, manpower services, job training and job locating, and a program of 200,000 transitional public service jobs.

Recipients, with very few exceptions, would have to register for training and accept jobs which were offered, or benefits would be terminated for that recipient.

An entirely separate, new federal program would be established for needy aged, blind and disabled individuals and couples. While no work requirements would be included, of course, those who could work would be provided with strong incentives for doing so.

The current state payments to such individuals and couples, varying widely across the nation, would be replaced by a federal benefit of $130 a month for the aged, blind, or disabled individual, rising to $150 in two steps. For a couple in these categories, $195 a month would be provided, rising to $200. Such benefits now can be as low as $70 a month for an individual and $97 a month for a couple.

In all, some $2-billion in new money would go directly into the hands of the aged, blind and disabled in the first full year.

Tight Administration and Program Integrity

Those who receive welfare, while they are the most visible victims, are not the only ones who suffer because of the myriad confusions and contradictions of the present welfare mess. The taxpayers are victims as well, for they are paying for a program that not only fails to accomplish its objectives, but is virtually impossible to administer.

Welfare administration is woefully outmoded in this country, with its 1,152 separate state and local welfare jurisdictions. Although virtually all have the same basic programs—Aid to the Blind, Aid to the Disabled, Aid to the Aged, and Aid to Families with Dependent Children—each operates with its own eligibility determination and administrative methods.

In the administrative area, especially, there is nearly an incomprehensible variety of management philosophies, operating policies and methods, and personnel arrangements. Only 20 percent of these jurisdictions have automated management techniques.

Under such conditions, it is not surprising that there are major management problems which exacerbate the skyrocketing costs and add to the growing public concern about welfare. Moreover, because of current open end financing arrangements, states and localities have what amounts to a blank check on the federal treasury for this activity.

Thousands of dedicated people are doing their best to operate this ponderous machinery. But this system has been patched and repaired too many times. The frustration of current state program managers has resulted in very substantial support among Governors and state welfare administrators for federal administration of the benefit payments function.

In recent months we have documented the failings of the current system, including the absence of cross-checks of records in adjacent areas, inadequate verification of income and benefits from a variety of benefit programs, and rapid turnover of personnel.

While decentralized management is highly desirable in many fields and is indeed central to my philosophy of government, I believe that many of these problems in welfare administration can best be solved by using a national automated payments system, which would produce economies and considerably increase both equity of treatment and tightened administration.

Such a unified system—partially modeled on the Social Security system—would reduce errors and provide greater controls for fraud and duplicate payments.

HR 1 would require each recipient to have a social security number for identification to prevent duplicate benefits and to facilitate the receiving of recipient income information from such sources as the Social Security Administration, the Internal Revenue Service, the Veterans Administration, and other units.

National administration and standards would also ensure equitable treatment for individuals: they would no longer be subject to conflicting rules in different areas, to delays caused by back-ups, and to the confusing tangle of red tape.

Under such a system, states and counties would be freed to concentrate on social services to recipients, making use of their closer understanding of the needs of local residents.

An Investment in the Future

Because we want a better system—not just a new one—welfare reform will cost more in the early years and cover more needy people.

Against the increased initial costs of my proposals in HR 1, however, we must weigh the unknown future costs—both human and fiscal—if the present chaotic system, with its present soaring growth rates, is continued. The new system contained in HR 1 would be far less costly in the long run—both in terms of dollars and in terms of people.

Historians of the future no doubt will focus on America's 200th birthday—and the years leading up to that significant anniversary—as one important point for measuring the progress of our republic.

They will find, of course, that over 200 years America's mastery of the industrial revolution, its bountiful economic system, its military might and its technological triumphs helped to make it preeminent in the family of nations.

They will rightfully highlight our moon landings, our deep space probes, our satellite communications, our electronic innovations, and our extraordinary gross national product.

Penetrating observers, however, will also ask other questions:

What did all of this mean to the average American?

What was the quality of the daily life and the basic spirit of all the American people in the 1970s?

How, in particular, did our great nation provide for those citizens who—through no fault of their own—were unable from time to time to provide for themselves and their families?

I believe that the program contained in HR 1 will stand us in good stead when such historical evaluations are considered, for this is a program which has grown out of a fundamental concern for our least fortunate citizens.

The enactment of HR 1 would demonstrate both our concern for what is responsible and our concern for what is compassionate.

RICHARD NIXON

SCHOOL BUSING

Following is the text, as made available by the White House, of President Nixon's March 17 message to Congress on school busing.

TO THE CONGRESS OF THE UNITED STATES:

In this message, I wish to discuss a question which divides many Americans. That is the question of busing.

I want to do so in a way that will enable us to focus our attention on a question which unites all Americans. That is the question of how to ensure a better education for all of our children.

In the furor over busing, it has become all too easy to forget what busing is supposed to be designed to achieve: equality of educational opportunity for all Americans.

Conscience and the Constitution both require that no child should be denied equal educational opportunity. That Constitutional mandate was laid down by the Supreme Court in *Brown* v. *Board of Education* in 1954. The years since have been ones of dismantling the old dual school system in those areas where it existed—a process that has now been substantially completed.

As we look to the future, it is clear that the efforts to provide equal educational opportunity must now focus much more specifically on education: on assuring that the opportunity is not only equal, but adequate, and that in those remaining cases in which desegregation has not yet been completed it be achieved with a greater sensitivity to educational needs.

Acting within the present framework of Constitutional and case law, the lower Federal courts have ordered a wide variety of remedies for the equal protection violations they have found. These remedies have included such plans as redrawing attendance zones, pairing, clustering and consolidation of school districts. Some of these plans have not required extensive additional transportation of pupils. But some have required that pupils be bused long distances, at great inconvenience. In some cases plans have required that children be bused away from their neighborhoods to schools that are inferior or even unsafe.

The maze of differing and sometimes inconsistent orders by the various lower courts has led to contradiction and uncertainty, and often to vastly unequal treatment among regions, States and local school districts. In the absence of statutory guidelines, many lower court decisions have gone far beyond what most people would consider reasonable, and beyond what the Supreme Court has said is necessary in the requirements they have imposed for the reorganization of school districts and the transportation of school pupils.

All too often, the result has been a classic case of the remedy for one evil creating another evil. In this case, a remedy for the historic evil of racial discrimination has often created a new evil of disrupting communities and imposing hardship on children—both black and white—who are themselves wholly innocent of the wrongs that the plan seeks to set right.

The 14th Amendment to the Constitution—under which the school desegregation cases have arisen—provides that "The Congress shall have power to enforce, by appropriate legislation, the provisions of this article."

Until now, enforcement has been left largely to the courts—which have operated within a limited range of available remedies, and in the limited context of case law rather than of statutory law. I propose that the Congress now accept the responsibility and use the authority given to it under the 14th Amendment to clear up the confusion which contradictory court orders have created, and to establish reasonable national standards.

The legislation I propose today would accomplish this.

It would put an immediate stop to further new busing orders by the Federal courts.

It would enlist the wisdom, the resources and the experience of the Congress in the solution of the vexing problems involved in fashioning school desegregation policies that are true to the Constitutional requirements and fair to the people and communities concerned.

It would establish uniform national criteria, to ensure that the Federal courts in all sections and all States would have a common set of standards to guide them.

These measures would protect the right of a community to maintain neighborhood schools—while also establishing a shared local and Federal responsibility to raise the level of education in the neediest neighborhoods, with special programs for those disadvantaged children who need special attention.

At the same time, these measures would not roll back the Constitution, or undo the great advances that have been made in ending school segregation, or undermine the continuing drive for equal rights.

Specifically, I propose that the Congress enact two measures which together would shift the focus from more transportation to better education, and would curb busing while expanding educational opportunity. They are:

1. The Equal Educational Opportunities Act of 1972. This would:

• Require that no State or locality could deny equal educational opportunity to any person on account of race, color or national origin.

• Establish criteria for determining what constitutes a denial of equal opportunity.

• Establish priorities of remedies for schools that are required to desegregate, with busing to be required only as a last resort, and then only under strict limitations.

• Provide for the concentration of Federal school-aid funds specifically on the areas of greatest educational need, in a way and in sufficient quantities so they can have a real and substantial impact in terms of improving the education of children from poor families.

2. The Student Transportation Moratorium Act of 1972. This would provide a period of time during which any future, new busing orders by the courts would not go into effect, while the Congress considered legislative approaches—such as the Equal Educational Opportunities Act—to the questions raised by school desegregation cases. This moratorium on new busing would be effective until July 1, 1973, or until the Congress passed the appropriate legislation, whichever was sooner. Its purpose would not be to contravene rights under the 14th Amendment, but simply to hold in abeyance further busing orders while the Congress investigated and considered alternative methods of securing those rights—methods that could establish a new and broader context in which the courts could decide desegregation cases, and that could render busing orders unnecessary.

Together, these two measures would provide an immediate stop to new busing in the short run, and constructive alternatives to busing in the long run—and they would give the Congress the time it needs to consider fully and fairly one of the most complex and difficult issues to confront the Nation in modern times.

Busing: The Fears and Concerns

Before discussing the specifics of these proposals, let me deal candidly with the controversy surrounding busing itself.

There are some people who fear any curbs on busing because they fear that it would break the momentum of the drive for equal rights for blacks and other minorities. Some fear it would go further, and that it would set in motion a chain of reversals that would undo all the advances so painfully achieved in the past generation.

It is essential that whatever we do to curb busing be done in a way that plainly will not have these other consequences. It is vitally important that the Nation's continued commitment to equal rights and equal opportunities be clear and concrete.

On the other hand, it is equally important that we not allow emotionalism to crowd out reason, or get so lost in symbols that words lose their meaning.

One emotional undercurrent that has done much to make this so difficult an issue is the feeling some people have that to oppose busing is to be anti-black. This is closely related to the arguments often put forward that resistance to any move, no matter what, that may be advanced in the name of desegregation is "racist." This is dangerous nonsense.

There is no escaping the fact that some people oppose busing because of racial prejudice. But to go on from this to conclude that "anti-busing" is simply a code word for prejudice is an exercise in arrant unreason. There are right reasons for opposing busing, and there are wrong reasons—and most people, including large and increasing numbers of blacks and other minorities, oppose it for reasons that have little or nothing to do with race. It would compound an injustice to persist in massive busing simply because some people oppose it for the wrong reasons.

For most Americans, the school bus used to be a symbol of hope—of better education. In too many communities today, it has become a symbol of helplessness, frustration and outrage—of a wrenching of children away from their families, and from the schools their families may have moved to be near, and sending them arbitrarily to others far distant.

It has become a symbol of social engineering on the basis of abstractions, with too little regard for the desires and the feelings of those most directly concerned: the children, and their families.

Schools exist to serve the children, not to bear the burden of social change. As I put it in my policy statement on school desegregation 2 years ago (on March 24, 1970):

"One of the mistakes of past policy has been to demand too much of our schools: They have been expected not only to educate, but also to accomplish a social transformation. Children in many instances have not been served, but used—in what all too often has proved a tragically futile effort to achieve in the schools the kind of multiracial society which the adult community has failed to achieve for itself.

"If we are to be realists, we must recognize that in a free society there are limits to the amount of Government coercion that can reasonably be used; that in achieving desegregation we must proceed with the least possible disruption of the education of the Nation's children; and that our children are highly sensitive to conflict, and highly vulnerable to lasting psychic injury.

"Failing to recognize these factors, past policies have placed on the schools and the children too great a share of the burden of eliminating racial disparities throughout our society. A major part of this task falls to the schools. But they cannot do it all or even most of it by themselves. Other institutions can share the burden of breaking down racial barriers, but only the schools can perform the task of education itself. If our schools fail to educate, then whatever they may achieve in integrating the races will turn out to be only a Pyrrhic victory."

The Supreme Court has also recognized this problem. Writing for a unanimous Court in the *Swann* case last April, Chief Justice Burger said:

"The constant theme and thrust of every holding from *Brown I* to date is that state-enforced separation of races in public schools is discrimination that violates the Equal Protection Clause. The remedy commanded was to dismantle dual school systems.

"We are concerned in these cases with the elimination of the discrimination inherent in the dual school systems, not with myriad factors of human existence which can cause discrimination in a multitude of ways on racial, religious, or ethnic grounds. The target of the cases from *Brown I* to the present was the dual school system. The elimination of racial discrimination in public schools is a large task and one that should not be retarded by efforts to achieve broader purposes lying beyond the jurisdiction of school authorities. One vehicle can carry only a limited amount of baggage....

"Our objective in dealing with the issues presented by these cases is to see that school authorities exclude no pupil of a racial minority from any school, directly or indirectly, on account of race; it does not and cannot embrace all the problems of racial prejudice, even when those problems contribute to disproportionate racial concentrations in some schools."

In addressing the busing question, it is important that we do so in historical perspective.

Busing for the purpose of desegregation was begun—mostly on a modest scale—as one of a mix of remedies to meet the requirements laid down by various lower Federal courts for achieving the difficult transition from the old dual school system to a new, unitary system.

At the time, the problems of transition that loomed ahead were massive, the old habits deeply entrenched, community resistance often extremely strong. As the years wore on, the courts grew increasingly impatient with what they sometimes saw as delay or evasion, and increasingly insistent that, as the Supreme Court put it in the *Green* decision in 1968, desegregation plans must promise "realistically to work, and...to work, *now.*"

But in the past 3 years, progress toward eliminating the vestiges of the dual system has been phenomenal—and so too has the shift in public attitudes in those areas where dual systems were formerly operated. In State after State and community after community, local civic, business and educa-

tional leaders of all races have come forward to help make the transition peacefully and successfully. Few voices are now raised urging a return to the old patterns of enforced segregation.

This new climate of acceptance of the basic Constitutional doctrine is a new element of great importance: for the greater the elements of basic good faith, of desire to make the system work, the less need or justification there is for extreme remedies rooted in coercion.

At the same time, there has been a marked shift in the focus of concerns by blacks and members of other minorities. Minority parents have long had a deep and special concern with improving the quality of their children's education. For a number of years, the principal emphasis of the concern—and of the Nation's attention—was on desegregating the schools. Now that the dismantling of the old dual system has been substantially completed there is once again a far greater balance of emphasis on improving schools, on convenience, on the chance for parental involvement—in short, on the same concerns that motivate white parents—and, in many communities, on securing a greater measure of control over schools that serve primarily minority-group communities. Moving forward on desegregation is still important—but the principal concern is with preserving the principle, and with ensuring that the great gains made since *Brown*, and particularly in recent years, are not rolled back in a reaction against excessive busing. Many black leaders now express private concern, moreover, that a reckless extension of busing requirements could bring about precisely the results they fear most: a reaction that would undo those gains, and that would begin the unraveling of advances in other areas that also are based on newly expanded interpretations of basic Constitutional rights.

Also, it has not escaped their notice that those who insist on system-wide racial balance insist on a condition in which, in most communities, every school would be run by whites and dominated by whites, with blacks in a permanent minority—and without escape from that minority status. The result would be to deny blacks the right to have schools in which they are the majority.

In short, this is not the simple black-white issue that some simplistically present it as being. There are deep divisions of opinion among people of all races—with recent surveys showing strong opposition to busing among black parents as well as among white parents—not because they are against desegregation but because they are for better education.

In the process of school desegregation, we all have been learning; perceptions have been changing. Those who once said "no" to racial integration have accepted the concept, and believe in equality before the law. Those who once thought massive busing was the answer have also been changing their minds in the light of experience.

As we cut through the clouds of emotionalism that surround the busing question, we can begin to identify the legitimate issues.

Concern for the quality of education a child gets is legitimate.

Concern that there be no retreat from the principle of ending racial discrimination is legitimate.

Concern for the distance a child has to travel to get to school is legitimate.

Concern over requiring that a child attend a more distant school when one is available near his home is legitimate.

Concern for the obligation of government to assure, as nearly as possible, that all the children of a given district have equal educational opportunity is legitimate.

Concern for the way educational resources are allocated among the schools of a district is legitimate.

Concern for the degree of control parents and local school boards should have over their schools is legitimate.

In the long, difficult effort to give life to what is in the law, to desegregate the Nation's schools and enforce the principle of equal opportunity, many experiments have been tried. Some have worked and some have not. We now have the benefit of a fuller fund of experience than we had 18 years ago, or even 2 years ago. It has also become apparent that community resistance—black as well as white—to plans that massively disrupt education and separate parents from their children's schools, makes those plans unacceptable to communities on which they are imposed.

Against this background, the objectives of the reforms I propose are:

- To give practical meaning to the concept of equal educational opportunity.
- To apply the experience gained in the process of desegregation, and also in efforts to give special help to the educationally disadvantaged.
- To ensure the continuing vitality of the principles laid down in *Brown* v. *Board of Education.*
- To downgrade busing as a tool for achieving equal educational opportunity.
- To sustain the rights and responsibilities vested by the States in local school boards.

The Equal Educational Opportunities Act

In the historic effort since 1954 to end the system of State-enforced segregation in the public schools, all three branches of Government have had important functions and responsibilities. Their roles, however, have been unequal.

If some of the Federal courts have lately tended toward extreme remedies in school desegregation cases—and some have—this has been in considerable part because the work has largely gone forward in the courts, case-by-case, and because the courts have carried a heavy share of the burden while having to operate within a limited framework of reference and remedies. The efforts have therefore frequently been disconnected, and the result has been not only great progress but also the creation of problems severe enough to threaten the immense achievement of these 18 difficult years.

If we are to consolidate our gains and move ahead on our problems—both the old and the new—we must undertake now to bring the leaven of experience to the logic of the law.

Drawing on the lessons of experience, we must provide the courts with a new framework of reference and remedies.

The angry debate over busing has at one and the same time both illuminated and obscured a number of broad areas in which realism and shared concern in fact unite most American parents, whatever their race. Knowledge of such shared concerns is the most precious product of experience; it also is the soundest foundation of law. The time is at hand for the legislative, executive and judicial branches of Government to act on this knowledge, and by so doing to lift the sense of crisis that threatens the education of our children and the peace of our people.

The Equal Educational Opportunities Act that I propose today draws on that experience, and is designed to give the courts a new and broader base on which to decide future cases, and to place the emphasis where it belongs: on better education for all of our children.

Equal Opportunity: The Criteria. The act I propose undertakes, in the light of experience, both to prohibit and to define the denial of equal educational opportunity. In essence, it provides that:

- No State shall deny equal educational opportunity to any person on account of race, color or national origin.
- Students shall not be deliberately segregated either among or within the public schools.
- Where deliberate segregation was formerly practiced, educational agencies have an affirmative duty to remove the vestiges of the dual system.
- A student may not be assigned to a school other than the one nearest his home, if doing so would result in a greater degree of racial segregation.

- Subject to the other provisions of the act, the assignment of students to their neighborhood schools would not be considered a denial of equal educational opportunity unless the schools were located or the assignment made for the purpose of racial segregation.
- Racial balance is not required.
- There can be no discrimination in the employment and assignment of faculty and staff.
- School authorities may not authorize student transfers that would have the effect of increasing segregation.
- School authorities must take appropriate action to overcome whatever language barriers might exist, in order to enable all students to participate equally in educational programs. This would establish, in effect, an educational bill of rights for Mexican-Americans, Puerto Ricans, Indians and others who start under language handicaps, and ensure at last that they too would have equal opportunity.
- Through Federal financial assistance and incentives, school districts would be strongly encouraged not only to avoid shortchanging the schools that serve their neediest children, but beyond this to establish and maintain special learning programs in those schools that would help children who were behind to catch up. These incentives would also encourage school authorities to provide for voluntary transfers of students that would reduce racial concentrations.

Thus, the act would set standards for all school districts throughout the Nation, as the basic requirements for carrying out, in the field of public education, the Constitutional guarantee that each person shall have equal protection of the laws. It would establish broad-based and specific criteria to ensure against racial discrimination in school assignments, to establish the equal educational rights of Mexican-Americans, Puerto Ricans and others starting with language handicaps, to protect the principle of the neighborhood school. It would also provide money and incentives to help ensure for schools in poor neighborhoods the fair treatment they have too often been denied in the past, and to provide the special learning and extra attention that children in those neighborhoods so often need.

Denial of Equal Opportunity: The Remedies. In the past, the courts have largely been left to their own devices in determining appropriate remedies in school desegregation cases. The results have been sometimes sound, sometimes bizarre—but certainly uneven. The time has come for the Congress, on the basis of experience, to provide guidance. Where a violation exists, the act I propose would provide that:

- The remedies imposed must be limited to those needed to correct the particular violations that have been found.
- School district lines must not be ignored or altered unless they are clearly shown to have been drawn for purposes of segregation.
- Additional busing must not be required unless no other remedy can be found to correct the particular violation that exists.
- A priority of remedies would be established, with the court required to use the first remedy on the list, or the first combination of remedies, that would correct the unlawful condition. The list of authorized remedies—in order—is:

(1) Assigning students to the schools closest to their homes that provide the appropriate level and type of education, taking into account school capacities and natural physical barriers;

(2) Assigning students to the schools closest to their homes that provide the appropriate level and type of education, considering only school capacities;

(3) Permitting students to transfer from a school in which their race is a majority to one in which it is a minority;

(4) Creation or revision of attendance zones or grade structures without necessitating increased student transportation;

(5) Construction of new schools or the closing of inferior schools;

(6) The use of magnet schools or educational parks to promote integration;

(7) Any other plan which is educationally sound and administratively feasible. However, such a plan could not require increased busing of students in the sixth grade or below. If a plan involved additional busing of older children, then: (a) It could not be ordered unless there was clear and convincing evidence that no other method would work; (b) in no case could it be ordered on other than a temporary basis; (c) it could not pose a risk to health, or significantly impinge on the educational process; (d) the school district could be granted a stay until the order had been passed on by the court of appeals.

• Beginning with the effective date of the act, time limits would be placed on desegregation orders. They would be limited to 10 years' duration—or 5 years if they called for student transportation—provided that during that period the school authorities had been in good-faith compliance. New orders could then be entered only if there had been new violations.

These rules would thus clearly define what the Federal courts could and could not require; however, the States and localities would remain free to carry out voluntary school integration plans that might go substantially beyond the Federal requirements.

This is an important distinction. Where busing would provide educational advantages for the community's children, and where the community wants to undertake it, the community should—and will—have that choice. What is objectionable is an arbitrary Federal requirement—whether administrative or judicial—that the community must undertake massive additional busing as a matter of Federal law. The essence of a free society is to restrict the range of what must be done, and broaden the range of what may be done.

Equal Opportunity: Broadening the Scope. If we were simply to place curbs on busing and do nothing more, then we would not have kept faith with the hopes, the needs—or the rights—of the neediest of our children.

Even adding the many protections built into the rights and remedies sections of the Equal Educational Opportunities Act, we would not by this alone provide what their special needs require.

Busing helps some poor children; it poses a hardship for others; but there are many more, and in many areas the great majority—in the heart of New York, and in South Chicago, for example—whom it could never reach.

If we were to treat busing as some sort of magic panacea, and to concentrate our efforts and resources on that as the principal means of achieving quality education for blacks and other minorities, then in these areas of dense minority concentration a whole generation could be lost.

If we hold massive busing to be, in any event, an unacceptable remedy for the inequalities of educational opportunity that exist, then we must do more to improve the schools where poor families live.

Rather than require the spending of scarce resources on ever-longer bus rides for those who happen to live where busing is possible, we should encourage the putting of those resources directly into education—serving all the disadvantaged children, not merely those on the bus routes.

In order to reach the great majority of the children who most need extra help, I propose a new approach to financing the extra efforts required: one that puts the money where the needs are, drawing on the funds I have requested for this and the next fiscal year under Title I of the Elementary and Secondary Education Act of 1965 and under the Emergency School Aid Act now pending before the Congress.

As part of the Equal Educational Opportunities Act, I propose to broaden the uses of the funds under the Emergency School Aid Act, and to provide the Secretary of Health, Education and Welfare with additional authority to encourage effective special learning programs in those schools where the needs are greatest.

Detailed program criteria would be spelled out in administrative guidelines—but the intent of this program is to use a major portion of the $1.5 billion Emergency School Aid money as, in effect, incentive grants to encourage eligible districts to design educational programs that would do three things:

• Assure (as a condition of getting the grant) that the district's expenditures on its poorest schools were at least comparable to those on its other schools.

• Provide, above this, a compensatory education grant of approximately $300 per low-income pupil for schools in which substantial numbers of the students are from poor families, if the concentration of poor students exceeds specified limits.

• Require that this compensatory grant be spent entirely on basic instructional programs for language skills and mathematics, and on basic supportive services such as health and nutrition.

• Provide a "bonus" to the receiving school for each pupil transferring from a poor school to a non-poor school where his race is in the minority, without reducing the grant to the transferring school.

Priority would be given to those districts that are desegregating either voluntarily or under court order, and to those that are addressing problems of both racial and economic impaction.

Under this plan, the remaining portion of the $1.5 billion available under the Emergency School Aid Act for this and the next fiscal year would go toward the other kinds of aid originally envisaged under it.

This partial shift of funds is now possible for two reasons: First, in the nearly 2 years since I first proposed the Emergency School Aid Act, much of what it was designed to help with has already been done. Second, to the extent that the standards set forth in the Equal Educational Opportunities Act would relieve desegregating districts of some of the more expensive requirements that might otherwise be laid upon them, a part of the money originally intended to help meet those expenses can logically be diverted to these other, closely related needs. I would stress once again, in this connection, the importance I attach to final passage of the Emergency School Aid Act: those districts that are now desegregating still need its help, and the funds to be made available for these new purposes are an essential element of a balanced equal opportunity package.

I also propose that instead of being terminated at the end of fiscal 1973, as presently scheduled, the Emergency School Aid Act continue to be authorized at a $1 billion annual level—of which I would expect the greatest part to be used for the purposes I have outlined here. At the current level of funding of Title I of the Elementary and Secondary Education Act of 1965, this would provide a total approaching $2.5 billion annually for compensatory education purposes.

For some years now, there has been a running debate about the effectiveness of added spending for programs of compensatory or remedial education. Some have maintained there is virtually no correlation between dollar input and learning output; others have maintained there is a direct correlation; experience has been mixed.

What does now seem clear is that while many Title I experiments have failed, many others have succeeded substantially and even dramatically; and what also is clear is that without the extra efforts such extra funding would make possible, there is little chance of breaking the cycle of deprivation.

A case can be made that Title I has fallen short of expectations, and that in some respects it has failed. In many cases, pupils in the programs funded by it have shown no improvement whatever, and funds have frequently been misused or squandered foolishly. Federal audits of State Title I efforts have found instances where naivete, inexperience, confusion, despair, and even clear violations of the law have thwarted the act's effectiveness. In some instances, Title I funds have been illegally spent on unauthorized materials and facilities, or used to fund local services other than those intended by the act, such as paying salaries not directly related to the act's purposes.

The most prevalent failing has been the spending of Title I funds as general revenue. Out of 40 States audited between 1966 and 1970, 14 were found to have spent Title I funds as general revenue.

Too often, one result has been that instead of actually being concentrated in the areas of critical need, Title I moneys have been diffused throughout the system; and they have not reached the targeted schools—and targeted children—in sufficient amounts to have a real impact.

On the positive side, Title I has effected some important changes of benefit to disadvantaged children.

First, Title I has encouraged some States to expand considerably the contributions from State and local funds for compensatory education. In the 1965-66 school year, the States spent only $2.7 million of their own revenues, but by the 1968-69 school year—largely due to major efforts by California and New York—they were contributing $198 million.

Second, Title I has better focused attention on pupils who previously were too often ignored. About 8 million children are in schools receiving some compensatory funds. In 46 States programs have been established to aid almost a quarter of a million children of migratory workers. As an added dividend, many States have begun to focus educational attention on the early childhood years which are so important to the learning process.

Finally, local schools have been encouraged by Title I to experiment and innovate. Given our highly decentralized national educational system and the relatively minor role one Federal program usually plays, there have been encouraging examples of programs fostered by Title I which have worked.

In designing compensatory programs, it is difficult to know exactly what will work. The circumstances of one locality may differ dramatically from those of other localities. What helps one group of children may not be of particular benefit to others. In these experimental years, local educational agencies and the schools have had to start from scratch, and to learn for themselves how to educate those who in the past had too often simply been left to fall further behind.

In the process, some schools did well and others did not. Some districts benefited by active leadership and community involvement, while others were slow to innovate and to break new ground.

While there is a great deal yet to be learned about the design of successful compensatory programs, the experience so far does point in one crucial direction: to the importance of providing sufficiently concentrated funding to establish the educational equivalent of a "critical mass," or threshold level. Where funds have been spread too thinly, they have been wasted or dissipated with little to show for their expenditure. Where they have been concentrated, the results have been frequently encouraging and sometimes dramatic.

In a sample of some 10,000 disadvantaged pupils in California, 82 percent of those in projects spending less than $150 extra per pupil showed little or no achievement gain. Of those students in projects spending over $250 extra per pupil, 94 percent gained more than one year per year of exposure; 58 percent gained between 1.4 and 1.9 years per year of exposure. Throughout the country States as widely separated as Connecticut and Florida have recognized a correlation between a "critical mass" expenditure and marked effectiveness.

Of late, several important studies have supported the idea of a "critical mass" compensatory expenditure to afford disadvantaged pupils equal educational opportunity. The New York State Commission on the Quality, Cost and Financing of Elementary and Secondary Education, the National Educational Finance Project, and the President's Commission on School Finance have all cited the importance of such a sub-

stantial additional per pupil expenditure for disadvantaged pupils.

The program which I propose aims to assure schools with substantial concentrations of poor children of receiving an average $300 compensatory education grant for each child.

In order to encourage voluntary transfers, under circumstances where they would reduce both racial isolation and low-income concentration, any school accepting such transfers would receive the extra $300 allotted for the transferring student plus a bonus payment depending on the proportion of poor children in that school.

One key to the success of this new approach would be the "critical mass" achieved by both increasing and concentrating the funds made available; another would be vigorous administrative follow-through to ensure that the funds are used in the intended schools and for the intended purposes.

The Student Transportation Moratorium Act

In times of rapid and even headlong change, there occasionally is an urgent need for reflection and reassessment. This is especially true when powerful, historic forces are moving the Nation toward a conflict of fundamental principles—a conflict that can be avoided if each of us does his share, and if all branches of Government will join in helping to redefine the questions before us.

Like any comprehensive legislative recommendation, the Equal Educational Opportunities Act that I have proposed today is offered as a framework for Congressional debate and action.

The Congress has both the Constitutional authority and a special capability to debate and define new methods for implementing Constitutional principles. And the educational, financial and social complexities of this issue are not, and are not properly, susceptible of solution by individual courts alone or even by the Supreme Court alone.

This is a moment of considerable conflict and uncertainty; but it is also a moment of great opportunity.

This is not a time for the courts to plunge ahead at full speed.

If we are to set a course that enables us to act together, and not simply to do more but to do better, then we must do all in our power to create an atmosphere that permits a calm and thoughtful assessment of the issues, choices and consequences.

I propose, therefore, that the Congress act to impose a temporary freeze on new busing orders by the Federal courts—to establish a waiting period while the Congress considers alternative means of enforcing 14th Amendment rights. I propose that this freeze be effective immediately on enactment, and that it remain in effect until July 1, 1973, or until passage of the appropriate legislation, whichever is sooner.

This freeze would not put a stop to desegregation cases; it would only bar new orders during its effective period, to the extent that they ordered new busing.

This, I recognize, is an unusual procedure. But I am persuaded that the Congress has the Constitutional power to enact such a stay, and I believe the unusual nature of the conflicts and pressures that confront both the courts and the country at this particular time requires it.

It has become abundantly clear, from the debates in the Congress and from the upwelling of sentiment throughout the country, that some action will be taken to limit the scope of busing orders. It is in the interest of everyone—black and white, children and parents, school administrators and local officials, the courts, the Congress and the executive branch, and not least in the interest of consistency in Federal policy, that while this matter is being considered by the Congress we not speed further along a course that is likely to be changed.

The legislation I have proposed would provide the courts with a new set of standards and criteria that would enable them to enforce the basic Constitutional guarantees in different ways.

A stay would relieve the pressure on the Congress to act on the long-range legislation without full and adequate consideration. By providing immediate relief from a course that increasing millions of Americans are finding intolerable, it would allow the debate on permanent solutions to proceed with less emotion and more reason.

For these reasons—and also for the sake of the additional children faced with busing now—I urge that the Congress quickly give its approval to the Student Transportation Moratorium Act.

No message to the Congress on school desegregation would be complete unless it addressed the question of a Constitutional amendment.

There are now a number of proposals before the Congress, with strong support, to amend the Constitution in ways designed to abolish busing or to bar the courts from ordering it.

These proposals should continue to receive the particularly thoughtful and careful consideration by the Congress that any proposal to amend the Constitution merits.

It is important to recognize, however, that a Constitutional amendment—even if it could secure the necessary two-thirds support in both Houses of the Congress—has a serious flaw: it would have no impact this year; it would not come into effect until after the long process of ratification by three-fourths of the State legislatures. What is needed is action now; a Constitutional amendment fails to meet this immediate need.

Legislation meets the problem now. Therefore, I recommend that as its first priority the Congress go forward immediately on the legislative route. Legislation can also treat the question with far greater precision and detail than could the necessarily generalized language of a Constitutional amendment, while making possible a balanced, comprehensive approach to equal educational opportunity.

Conclusion

These measures I have proposed would place firm and effective curbs on busing—and they would do so in a Constitutional way, aiding rather than challenging the courts, respecting the mandate of the 14th Amendment, and exercising the responsibility of the Congress to enforce that Amendment.

Beyond making these proposals, I am directing the Executive departments to follow policies consistent with the principles on which they are based—which will include intervention by the Justice Department in selected cases before the courts, both to implement the stay and to resolve some of those questions on which the lower courts have gone beyond the Supreme Court.

The Equal Educational Opportunities Act I have proposed reflects a serious and wide-ranging process of consultation—drawing upon the knowledge and experience of legislators, Constitutional scholars, educators and government administrators, and of men and women from all races and regions of the country who shared with us the views and feelings of their communities.

Its design is in large measure the product of that collaboration. When enacted it would, for the first time, furnish a framework for collaborative action by the various branches of Federal and local government, enabling courts and communities to shape effective educational solutions which are responsive not only to Constitutional standards but also to the physical and human reality of diverse educational situations.

It will create more local choice and more options to choose from; and it will marshal and target Federal resources more effectively in support of each particular community's effort.

Most importantly, however, these proposals undertake to address the problem that really lies at the heart of the issue at this time: the inherent inability of the courts, acting alone, to deal effectively and acceptably with the new magnitude of educational and social problems generated by the desegregation process.

If these proposals are adopted, those few who want an arbitrary racial balance to be imposed on the schools by Federal fiat will not get their way.

Those few who want a return to segregated schools will not get their way.

Those few who want a rollingback of the basic protections black and other minority Americans have won in recent years will not get their way.

This Administration means what it says about dismantling racial barriers, about opening up jobs and housing and schools and opportunity to all Americans.

It is not merely rhetoric, but our record, that demonstrates our determination.

We have achieved more school desegregation in the last 3 years than was achieved in the previous 15.

We have taken the lead in opening up high-paying jobs to minority workers.

We have taken unprecedented measures to spur business ownership by members of minorities.

We have brought more members of minorities into the middle and upper levels of the Federal service than ever before.

We have provided more support to black colleges than ever before.

We have put more money and muscle into enforcement of the equal opportunity laws than ever before.

These efforts will all go foward—with vigor and with conviction. Making up for the years of past discrimination is not simply something that white Americans owe to black Americans—it is something the entire Nation owes to itself.

I submit these proposals to the Congress mindful of the profound importance and special complexity of the issues they address. It is in that spirit that I have undertaken to weigh and respect the conflicting interests; to strike a balance which is thoughtful and just; and to search for answers that will best serve all of the Nation's children. I urge the Congress to consider them in the same spirit.

The great majority of Americans, of all races, want their Government—the Congress, the Judiciary and the Executive—to follow the course of deliberation, not confrontation. To do this we must act calmly and creatively, and we must act together.

The great majority of Americans, of all races, want schools that educate and rules that are fair. That is what these proposals attempt to provide.

RICHARD NIXON

EXECUTIVE REORGANIZATION

Following is the text, as made available by the White House, of President Nixon's March 29 message to Congress on executive reorganization.

TO THE CONGRESS OF THE UNITED STATES:

The sand is running in the glass, and the hour is growing late, for enactment of a critically needed reform, one that merits the very best support which you as legislators for 208 million Americans, and I as their Chief Executive, are able to give it.

That reform is reorganization of the executive branch of the federal government—the most comprehensive and carefully planned such reorganization since the executive was first constituted in George Washington's administration 183 years ago. Its purpose is to make American government a more effective servant to, and a more responsive instrument of, the American people. Its method is to organize departments around the ends which public policy seeks, rather than (as too often in the past) around the means employed in seeking them.

The broad outlines of the reorganization proposals which I presented to the Congress just over a year ago are now well known. The seven domestic departments which sprang into being under pressure of necessity one at a time since 1849 would be viewed as a single system for the first time, and their functions regrouped accordingly. The product would be four entirely new, goal-oriented departments concerned with our communities, our earth, our economy, and our potential as individuals—plus a revitalized fifth department concerned with keeping America in food and fiber.

A Department of Community Development, a Department of Natural Resources, a Department of Economic Affairs, and a Department of Human Resources would be created to replace the present Departments of Interior, Commerce, Labor, Health, Education, and Welfare and Housing and Urban Development, and Transportation. And the Department of Agriculture—under our plans as I ordered them revised last fall—would be streamlined to increase its ability to serve the farmer and so to serve us all. Several independent federal agencies would be drawn into the consolidation process as appropriate. Further management reforms would be instituted within the new departments, to provide authority commensurate with responsibility at every level and to make form follow function intelligently.

Electing Better Government Machinery

I do not speak lightly or loosely in characterizing this measure as critically needed. To say that we must prepare government to perform satisfactorily in the years ahead is only another way of saying that we must provide for its very survival. This republic, soon to begin its third century, will surely grow old unless we take wise and decisive action to keep it young. "Adapt or die"—the Darwinian choice is ours to make.

Hard evidence of this danger abounds—dismal statistics about the low effectiveness of federal spending, case upon case of national problems stubbornly resisting national programs. "Most Americans today," as I put it in announcing these executive reorganization proposals in my 1971 state of the union message, and again in transmitting the detailed legislation for them, "are simply fed up with government at all levels."

For us here and now to make a strong beginning at making government work better for the ordinary citizen would hearten the nation immensely and it would do so honestly by getting at the real roots of the fed-up feeling. Yet some may question whether this political year is a time when public men can afford to meet public frustrations head on. "Mollifying gestures, yes," they may say in effect, "but fundamental reform, no—at least not in 1972." Our reply should be that this is a most appropriate year to move ahead with reorganization.

For what is it, after all, that the people want and deserve from the public processes of any year, an election year especially? More effective government. One way they seek to get it is by calling the officials who run the government to account at the polls, as is being done in 1972. Another way is by regulating the federal purse strings through their elected representatives in the Congress, as is also being done in 1972. Yet this necessary periodic scrutiny of men and money alone will not reach the heart of the problem. For it is axiomatic among those who know Washington best that, as I pointed out in my earlier message on this subject, "the major cause of the ineffectiveness of government is not a matter of men or of money (but) principally a matter of machinery." We cannot, therefore, in good conscience hold out to the people the hope that this will be a year of change for the better, if we fail to come to grips with reform of government's jerry-built mechanisms.

Institutional structure here in Washington tends to coast along all too comfortably under the protection of an inertia which does not shield elected officials and public expenditures. These last come up for renewal every one, two, four, or six years; not so the structure, which endures with little or no burden of proof for its own worthiness to continue. Now, though, the structure has been weighed in the balances and found wanting.

In less sweeping reorganizations than the one I am urging, of course, a President can institute changes through plans submitted under the Reorganization Act, whereby the burden of proof rests with defenders of the status quo. However such authority no longer extends to the creation, consolidation, or abolition of executive departments. In any event we would have felt it wise to submit so massive a reform as this one for regular statutory enactment, so as to permit consideration of amendments and to provide time for full hearings and review. My hope now is that the Congress will honor the best spirit of democratic change by electing now, in this election year, to modernize the executive structure and redeem the flagging public faith in our ability to order our national affairs effectively.

An Opportunity We Must Not Lose

Considerations of practicality, equally with those of principle, make the present time the best time to move ahead on this reform. The efforts of the past several years have amassed significant momentum toward overcoming the inertia which protects obsolete institutions. My proposals of last March 25 have behind them the weight of two years' exhaustive study and analysis by my Advisory Council on Executive Organization, and behind that the substantially similar recommendations of President Johnson's task forces of 1964 and 1967 on government organization. Since I laid those proposals before the Congress, the Administration and the Government Operations Committees in both Houses have made further headway on perfecting the reform legislation. A spirit of cooperation has been established; good faith and constructive attitudes have been demonstrated on all sides. We must not let these gains go to waste.

The pace of progress so far has not been disappointing, for no measure this broad and this complex can or should be pushed through the Congress overnight. What would be deeply disappointing, though—to me, and far more importantly to millions of Americans who deserve better than their government is now organized to give them—is to lose, in this rapidly passing second session of the 92nd Congress, our opportunity to record some solid achievement by creating at the very least one, and hopefully two or more, of the four proposed new departments.

The men and women who begin a new presidential term and a new Congress next January should not have to start over again on reorganization. They will not have to, if we push ahead now with the realism to see what is wrong with the old structures, the vision to see what benefits new forms can bring, and the courage to take the long step from old to new.

Obsolete Structure: How It Hurts

What is wrong, and what reorganization could do to set it right, is best illustrated with two actual examples. We cannot remind ourselves often enough that this matter of government organization is no mere shuffling of abstract blocks and lines on a wall chart—that it has to do with helping real people, building real communities, husbanding real resources.

The plethora of diverse and fragmented federal activities aimed at assisting our communities is a glaring case in point. If there is any one social concept which has clearly come of age in recent years, that concept would certainly be the idea of balanced, comprehensively planned community development. Yet where do we find this reflected in government organization? We grope toward it, as with the well-intentioned and (at the time) fairly progressive formation of a Department of Housing and Urban Development; but even that step was premised on an unrealistic, artificial, and harmful distinction between urban and rural communities. In altogether too many instances the dollars and efforts earmarked for communities end up producing more derangement than development.

This is hardly surprising when we consider that:

• A city or town may now seek federal grants or loans for sewer or sewage treatment facilities from three departments and one independent agency, each with different criteria, different procedures, and a separate bureaucracy.

• Responsibilities for housing assistance are also entrusted to different offices in some of the same departments, and to several other entities as well.

• Highway and mass transit programs have been isolated in a separate department with only partial consideration for what such programs do to our communities, large and small, forcing us to learn the hard way that highways and mass transit must be developed integrally with land use decisions, housing plans, and provisions for other essential community facilities.

Efforts have been made to clarify agency roles on the basis of urban/rural, type of facility, type of applicant, etcetera—but the real need is for unified authority, not artificial jurisdictional clarifications. In sum, it has become painfully clear that effective integration of all federal activities relating to community development can be achieved only under a vigorous new Department of Community Development created expressly for that purpose.

The conservation and development of our rivers offers another pointed example. This important trust, where stakes are high and mistakes irretrievable, has at present so many guardians in Washington that in the crunch it sometimes seems to have none at all. The Department of the Interior, the Department of Agriculture, and the U.S. Army Corps of Engineers, together with several independent agencies, are all empowered to plan river basin development to build dams and impound water, and to control water use. Elaborate interagency coordination efforts and all good intentions have not prevented waste and error from thriving under this crippling fragmentation of responsibility. Such costly fiascos as the reservoir built by the Bureau of Reclamation for drinking water supply but severely polluted and depleted by conflicting Soil Conservation Service projects upstream have been repeated too frequently. The answer? A unified Department of Natural Resources, where comprehensive authority to develop and manage water resources would be concentrated under a single departmental secretary.

Additional examples of dispersed responsibility could be cited in such areas as consumer protection, manpower and job training programs, and economic development activities. In each case, obsolete departmental structures have made it difficult to move forward effectively.

Even the newest of our domestic departments, like Housing and Urban Development and Transportation, now see the challenges of the seventies and beyond outrunning their own relatively narrow mandates. Departmental missions long circumscribed by law or historical development are suddenly outgrown; departmental preoccupations with limited constituencies no longer serve the public interest as reliably as before. Too often the ability of one department to achieve an important goal proves dependent upon the authority and resources of other departments, departments which inevitably attach only secondary importance to that goal. The new federal commitments undertaken year by year are increasingly difficult to locate in any one department—usually several can claim partial jurisdiction, but none can show full ability to follow through and get the job done.

Decentralization and Accountability

The solution to this rapidly worsening snarl of problems is regrouping of related programs by major purpose in a smaller number of executive departments. Besides opening the way for sharp improvements in government performance, such a consolidation would make the executive branch more sensitive to national needs and more responsive to the will of the people, in two ways.

First, it would decentralize decision-making. Far too many matters must now be handled above the department level by the Executive Office of the President or within the White House itself—not because of the inherent importance of those matters, but because no single department or agency head has broad

enough authority to make and enforce decisions on them. But the four new secretaries created by my reorganization proposal would have such breadth of authority. Their resultant ability to conduct domestic policy on the President's behalf should speed, streamline, and strengthen the whole process significantly.

Comparable decentralization could also be achieved within each department. At present, too many questions can be decided only in Washington, because of the multiplicity of field organizations and the limited authority of their regional directors. By enlarging the scope of responsibility of the departmental secretaries and by giving them the tools they need, we could facilitate broad delegation of authority to appropriate field officials. And this in turn means that citizens across the country would receive faster and better service from their federal government.

Secondly, the new alignment of domestic departments would enhance the accountability of federal officials to the people. It is easy to see how the new secretaries, each with his or her own broad area of responsibility to discharge, would be useful to the President and the Congress in monitoring compliance with direction and accomplishment of objectives. Once scattered responsibility was concentrated, today's frequently used and often quite accurate excuse, "It was the other fellow's fault," would no longer apply.

More importantly, though, whatever slack and tangle can be taken out of the lines of control within the federal establishment will then result in a tightening of those same lines between elected federal officials and a democratic electorate. Notwithstanding the famous sign on President Truman's desk—"The buck stops here"—there will be no stopping of the buck, no ultimate clarification of blame and credit, and no assurance that voters will get what they contracted for in electing Presidents, senators, and congressmen, until the present convoluted and compartmentalized Washington bureaucracy can be formed anew and harnessed more directly to the people's purposes.

Cooperating for Reform

Where, then, does the reform effort stand today? I am pleased to note that the Congress, acting through its Committees on Government Operations, has held extensive hearings on my proposals; that testimony, most of it favorable, has been taken from a broad, bipartisan array of expert witnesses; and that committee work on the House side is nearly complete on the bill to establish a Department of Community Development.

For our part, we in the administration have continued working to perfect the legislation and the management concepts set forth in my message of March 25, 1971. The Office of Management and Budget has taken the lead in working with members of the Congress, adopting a flexible and forthcoming approach which has led to refinements in our legislation: one to clarify responsibility for highway safety, another to remove doubts concerning the reform's impact on the Appalachian Regional Commission and the Title V regional planning and development commissions, another to guarantee Community Development participation in airport access and siting decisions, and several more. They have also clarified that the reorganization need not entail any shift in congressional committee jurisdiction.

I am confident that this refinement and clarification process has improved our bills. I pledge the fullest continuing cooperation of my Administration in seeing that the Congress has what it needs to move forward.

Community Development and Natural Resources: Achievable Goals for 1972

There is still much work to do. For all the excellent hearings conducted to date, action has yet to be completed on any of the departmental bills which were sent to the Congress 370 days ago. Yet their passage by this Congress is still possible—

especially for the Departments of Community Development and Natural Resources.

I would call special attention to HR 6962, the legislation for a Department of Community Development, which has now undergone 15 days of hearings in the House Government Operations Committee. Prompt, favorable action on this bill would represent a much-needed victory for common sense and the public good. Its defeat or emasculation would serve no interest except entrenched privilege and private advantage, and would cruelly disserve the interest of literally thousands of urban and rural communities with millions of people who are tired of waiting for Washington to get itself together and help them.

I urge all those concerned with the cause of executive reorganization to redouble their efforts to bring HR 6962 to my desk for signature during 1972—and, further, to press ahead on enactment of HR 6959, the Department of Natural Resources bill, and of legislation for the other two new departments which we need to govern effectively in the seventies.

Organizing to Meet the Challenges of Peace

Twenty-five years ago, when the United States was realizing that World War II had marked not the end, but only the beginning, of its leadership responsibilities in the world, a reorganization of the executive machinery in the defense area was undertaken. That reform, which created the Department of Defense, marks the only major streamlining of the cabinet and the only departmental consolidation in our history. The new structure thus established has served America and the free world well in the challenging period since.

Now the time has come to take a similar bold and visionary step on the domestic side of national affairs. The 1960s, troubled, eventful, and full of progress as they were, were only the prelude to a period of still faster change in American life. The peace which we find increasing reason to hope will prevail during the coming generation is already permitting us to turn somewhat from the formerly absorbing necessity to "provide for the common defense," the necessity which motivated the last major executive branch reorganization.

Other great purposes now move to the foreground: "to form a more perfect union, establish justice, insure domestic tranquility,...promote the general welfare, and secure the blessings of liberty to ourselves and our posterity." To serve these purposes, let us act decisively once again, and forge new institutions to serve a new America.

RICHARD NIXON

DOCK STRIKE MESSAGE

Following is the text, as made available by the White House, of President Nixon's Feb. 2 message to Congress on the West Coast longshoremen's strike.

TO THE CONGRESS OF THE UNITED STATES:

As the dock strike on the West Coast continues to impose a cruel and intolerable burden upon the American people, I appeal once again to the Congress for emergency action to end these transportation disputes.

There are now two bills before the Congress dealing with transportation stoppages, and immediate action is urgently required on both:

• S. J. Resolution 187, which would quickly halt the West Coast strike and lead to a fair and early settlement under binding arbitration.

• And the Crippling Strikes Prevention Act, S. 560, which would grant the executive branch sufficient authority so that future disruptions in the transportation industry could be averted.

The American public is rightly frustrated today by the inaction of Congress in ending the West Coast strike. Some crops are rotting while others are stalled in their bins, export customers are looking for more dependable trading partners, and jobs and businesses are threatened with extinction. Tens of thousands of people, who share no part of this dispute, are suffering needlessly.

Yet our Government stands idly by, paralyzed because the executive branch has exhausted all available remedies and the Congress has been unwilling to enact necessary legislation. This failure to act in time of need speaks directly to the question of why some Americans have lost confidence in their government.

We must act now, swiftly and decisively. Twelve days ago I proposed special legislation to end this strike and asked for enactment within a week. For inexplicable reasons, that deadline has passed without a response, and I must report to the American people today that I cannot predict when relief will come. To say that I am disappointed is to state the case in its mildest terms.

For those who argue that the Government should not interfere with collective bargaining, the short answer is that the bargaining in this case has thus far failed—and failed badly for 15 months. I share the belief that Government ordinarily should not tamper with the freedom of bargaining, but when the processes have broken down and the Nation's health and safety are at stake we in public office have no right to turn our heads.

I am also aware that some members of Congress believe this strike will soon be settled at the bargaining table. I sincerely hope they are right, and I urge the parties to continue their bargaining, but the 15 months of fruitless bargaining which have already passed convince me that we cannot depend on this solution.

Issues of Great Urgency

In the absence of an agreement, the critical question is whether all of us in Washington sense the urgency of these issues. I can assure you that the farmer whose grain is wasting away and the exporter who has lost his contract regard this strike as a matter of utmost urgency, and I plead with the Congress to recognize their plight.

For two years I have been trying to impress upon the Congress the need for new legislation in this field. In 1970, during the 91st Congress, and again in 1972 during the 92nd Congress, I proposed the comprehensive crippling strikes prevention program so that future transportation stoppages could be resolved. There has been precious little response. Yet I am confident that if the Congress had enacted those measures, there might have been no strike on the West Coast and the issue in dispute would have been fairly settled.

Let us resolve that this stoppage on the West Coast will be the last of its kind. The Congress should act immediately to end the West Coast strike and, with utmost dispatch, pass the Crippling Strikes Prevention Act.

The Crippling Strikes Prevention Act

Certainly the more far-reaching of the two proposals on which I am seeking action is the Crippling Strikes Prevention Act. It would give the President additional—and, in my opinion, essential—new authority to deal with emergency disputes in the railroad, airlines, maritime, longshore, and trucking industries.

First, it would discontinue the emergency strike provisions of the Railway Labor Act of 1926 and provide that all transportation disputes be settled under the Taft-Hartley Act. Currently, disputes in the railroad and airline industries are subject to the Railway Labor Act while all other emergency transportation disputes are governed by the Taft-Hartley Act. Of the two acts, the railway labor law is clearly the inferior. Under it, the President can delay a strike or lockout for 60 days by appointing an Emergency Board to study the issues and recommend a settlement. Unfortunately, these provisions only seem to discourage hard bargaining because the parties are hesitant to compromise their position before the Board is appointed, and then, recognizing that the Board will probably seek a middle position, the parties tend to adopt a more extreme stance in order to pull the Board in their direction. Thus the gap widens between the disputants and because neither the Board nor the President has any additional authority, strikes often resume at the end of the 60-day period. These resumptions have occurred at the rate of more than one per year since 1947, and four times during this administration alone I have been forced to ask Congress for special legislation. This a sorry record, best consigned to our history books.

Three New Options

Secondly, I propose a major revision of the Taft-Hartley Act to give the President three new options in the case of all emergency disputes in the transportation industry. Under current provisons of this Act, the President may appoint a Board of Inquiry when he believes that a work stoppage imperils the Nation's health or safety. Upon receiving a report from the Board on the status of the strike, the President may direct the Attorney General to petition a Federal District Court to enjoin the strike for an 80-day "cooling-off" period. But there the formal authority of the Federal Government ends: the Board of Inquiry may issue no recommendation on a settlement and the President has no additional options when the 80-day period elapses except to ask for emergency legislation. On nine of 30 occasions when this machinery has been invoked since 1947, a strike or lockout has resumed after the 80-day period, as it has now on the West Coast.

To permit a more flexible Federal response, I propose that the President be granted three options when the "cooling-off" period fails to produce a settlement:

• First, he could extend the period for 30 days, a most useful device if the dispute seems to be near an end.

• Secondly, he could require partial operation of the troubled industry, so that those segments essential to the national health or safety could be kept in operation for an additional 180 days.

• Or thirdly, he could invoke a "final offer selection" procedure whereby the final offers of each party would be submitted to a neutral panel. This panel would select, without amendment, the most reasonable of the offers as the final and binding contract between the parties. Unlike bargaining which now occurs under the Railway Labor Act or under arbitration, this approach would encourage the parties to narrow their positions so that they could persuade the panel of their reasonableness. Thus genuine negotiations and settlement would be encouraged automatically.

Among the additional features of this proposal is the establishment of a National Special Industries Commission to conduct a two-year study of labor relations in industries which are especially subject to national emergency disputes.

As I informed the Congress two years ago, the Crippling Strikes Prevention Act creates a balance between two cherished but sometimes inconsistent principles: the protection of the national health and safety against damaging work stoppages, and the protection of collective bargaining from interference by the Government. "Ideally," I said then, "we would provide maximum public protection with minimum Federal interference."

Without doubt, my proposal would tip the present scales back in the direction of greater protection for the public, but we must face up to the hard realities that the old way simply has not worked. The scales, in fact, have been heavily weighted against the public. The actions I propose would not only correct the balance but would also preserve and enhance the processes of collective bargaining.

The West Coast Dispute

The present tie-up on the West Coast vividly illustrates why we need the Crippling Strikes Prevention Act. Both the failure of negotiations and the resulting economic losses have been a painful lesson for us all.

Talks and negotiations between the parties have dragged on for 15 months, and I have used every remedy at my command, but to no avail. The Taft-Hartley machinery has been tried, and it has failed. Two extensions in time have been arranged by Government mediators, and twice the mediators' efforts have fallen short. And I have met personally with the parties. Yet this strike has resumed. In my view, it is abundantly clear that present legislation is inadequate and that we need comprehensive solutions.

Only now are we beginning to realize the full damages of the first 100-day strike which closed down the West Coast ports between July 1 and October 9, 1971. I recounted some of these losses to the Congress in my message 12 days ago, but the facts bear emphasis:

• It is estimated that American exports would have been $600 million higher during this 100-day period except for the work stoppage.

• The strike was particularly hard on our farmers, who have been exporting the product of one cropland acre out of four. During the June-September period, farm exports, from the West Coast dropped from $288 million in the same period in 1970 to $73 million in 1971.

• Wheat farmers suffered the worst calamities of all, as their sales to major Far Eastern markets fell off drastically. Japan, for instance, purchases over 50 percent of her wheat from the United States. Since April, we have lost sales to Japan of at least 25 million bushels of wheat values at $40 million. Ominously, the day after the strike resumed last month, the Japanese purchased 8.7 million bushels of wheat for a spring delivery, but only 1.6 million bushels were bought from the United States.

• Our merchant fleet also sustained heavy losses, as did exporters of vegetables, rice, cotton, and livestock, and wood products, and numerous related industries.

Appalling Human Costs

Overall, the 100-day strike thrust a spike into our progress toward economic recovery, threatened our balance of payments, and undermined the confidence of foreign buyers who need to rely upon dependable deliveries. But the most appalling costs were in human terms—those tens of thousands who were not parties to the dispute but suffered because of it.

Those same people are suffering needlessly again, as the costs of resuming the strike begin to mount. I met yesterday with the Governors of California and Washington, whose States along with Oregon lost an estimated total of $23.5 million a day during the 100-day strike, and they have reported to me that the cost of this resumption is intolerable to their economies. The State of Hawaii is also beginning to feel the punishment. If the strike persists for several weeks, we can anticipate a significant increase in unemployment on the West Coast and huge financial losses for many people across the country.

We can and must end this dispute. Because the parties have already been bargaining under different ground rules for many months, I do not think it would be fair or wise in this case to impose the "final offer selection" solution which I am proposing in the more comprehensive Crippling Strikes Prevention Act. I also see no merit in another "cooling-off" extension, because it offers little hope of resolution and it only increases the uncertainty in foreign markets. Instead, I urge the adoption of a plan for settlement by arbitration. As I explained to the Congress 12 days ago, I am asking that a three-member arbitration board be appointed by the Secretary of Labor to hear all the issues and then issue a settlement that would be binding for at least 18 months. No strike or lockout would be permitted from the day this legislation is enacted until the expiration of the binding settlement established by the board.

I strongly favor free collective bargaining, but the time has come for decisive action. I call upon the Congress to take such action on both this emergency bill and the Crippling Strikes Prevention Act.

RICHARD NIXON

BICENTENNIAL MESSAGE

Following is the text, as made available by the White House, of President Nixon's Feb. 4 message to Congress on the American Bicentennial and the District of Columbia.

TO THE CONGRESS OF THE UNITED STATES:

"Seafaring is necessary" says the Latin inscription on an old building in one of the great European port cities; "mere living is not." This same spirit of movement, venture, and quest animates the whole sweep of America's story—from its discovery by men who lived for sailing, to its founding as a nation by men who lived for liberty, to its modern maturity as the world's preeminent power—and it will do so still, 4 years hence, when we observe the Bicentennial of American independence. The Nation could not if it wanted to, and should not if it could, drop anchor somewhere in 1976 and savor the occasion at leisure. By its very nature it can only speed through the year as through any other, under full sail, on into a new century.

The central challenge of our Bicentennial preparations, therefore, is to plan for an observance "on the move." Many groups—public and private, national and local—have already devoted several years of creative thought and effort to meeting this challenge. The common goal to which ·all subscribe has nowhere been stated better than in the 1970 report of the celebration's official planning and coordinating body, the American Revolution Bicentennial Commission (ARBC): "to forge a new national commitment—a new Spirit for '76—a commitment which will unite the nation in purpose and dedication to the advancement of human welfare as we move into Century III of American National Life."

We can best forge such a spirit, the Commission went on to recommend, by approaching the Bicentennial as an occasion both for understanding our heritage better and for quickening the progress toward our horizons—not just in one chosen location or a few, but in every State, city, and community. The Commission's goal and the principles deriving from it have my strongest support, and I have followed with interest the ARBC's further work as well as that of the individual Bicentennial Commissions already set up or now being formed by each State and territory, Puerto Rico, and the District of Columbia.

The Bicentennial in Washington

Since the Federal Government has special responsibility for District of Columbia affairs, my closest contact has been with the planning effort now underway here in the District—and I have found its progress thus far most impressive. And so it should be. For while no one city will dominate this truly national anniversary, Washington—which was built to be the Capital of the Republic born in 1776 and seat of the Government constituted in 1787, and which has been in many ways a center of the hopes of all Americans in all generations since—has a unique role to play. As its plans are made known, they may well serve as a stimulus and an example for the equally important plans being made in thousands of other communities. Both to ensure that Washington itself is ready for 1976 and to spur Bicentennial activity all across the country, I shall outline to the Congress today an action plan for Federal partnership in the District of Columbia's Bicentennial observance.

My proposals follow two basic themes. One is the quest for quality of life—today's name for the age-old aspiration which Jefferson at the Nation's birth called "the pursuit of happiness." Here is the very essence of a Bicentennial celebrated "on the move." The past success of this quest, its present vigor, and its future prospects will provide a telling measure for our self-assessment as the great milestone nears. Such a theme's immediacy will call up exertion as well as congratulation—not only a birthday party but an actual rebirth.

The second theme which I would stress is dual excellence for Washington. In choosing which Bicentennial projects to pursue among myriad worthy possibilities, an old question arises again and again: Washington for Washingtonians, or Washington for all Americans? A kind of civic schizophrenia has troubled this city from the earliest days of its double existence as both a national capital and a community in its own right. Solutions going to both extremes have had their advocates—yet there is a better answer than either making thousands of people reside neglected in a strictly Federal city that is "a nice place to visit," or making millions of other people receive their governance from a narrowly provincial and self-centered capital where officials and visitors are classed as outsiders.

The Bicentennial Era, I am convinced, is the right time for Washington to gain a new and more expansive sense of itself, and to find in its dual identity an opportunity for dual excellence unparalleled among American cities. The seat of government can excel as an exemplary living city, at the same time the home of 750,000 local residents excels as a gracious host to fellow-citizens and foreign visitors who may number 40 million during 1976 alone.

The projects proposed in this message, then, treat quality of life in the Nation's Capital as indivisible. They aim for dual excellence, in the conviction that a more liveable city is a more visitable one, and vice versa. For the most part, they emphasize physical construction—not by any means because public works are the sum total of our Bicentennial intentions for the District, but only because building time is already becoming critically short. Activities of many other types, such as commemorative events, pageantry, and social and cultural programs, which will of course be essential to the human dimension of the Bicentennial but which require somewhat shorter lead-times, are also being planned. Reports on these activities and, in many cases, requests for approval and funding will be submitted to the Congress as we move toward 1976.

One further note on Bicentennial concerns not mentioned here but certainly not forgotten: It is my feeling that nothing we could do for the District of Columbia during the next 4 years would be more meaningful or more appropriate to the Spirit of '76 than granting this city and its people first-class status: voting representation in the Congress. I am encouraged by the apparently warmer climate for this reform on Capitol Hill in 1972, and it will continue to have my support.

Fort Lincoln New Town

Speaking at the National Archives last summer in a ceremony inaugurating the Bicentennial Era, I described an unusual painting which hangs in the Roosevelt Room across from the Oval Office in the White House. The scene portrayed is the signing of the Declaration of Independence—but for some reason the canvas was never finished, and many of the figures in the crowded hall are just sketched in, or left blank. The symbolism of this, I said, is that "the American Revolution is unfinished business, with important roles still open for each of us to play." A broad cross-section of District of Columbia citizens have now begun playing their roles in the continuing drama by serving on Mayor Washington's recently formed Bicentennial Assembly and Bicentennial Commission. We in the administration found the work of the old local Commission quite valuable in formulating our own plans for 1976, and we look forward to working closely with the reorganized two-level planning group in the future.

One of the strongest strains of community opinion identified by local representatives like these is a commitment to revitalizing the urban heart of this Washington area. This, not flight to the suburbs or complacent satisfaction with the status quo, seems to arouse hope and determination at the neighborhood level. At the same time it seems a most appropriate cornerstone for a Bicentennial program designed to lift the quality of Washington life.

Accordingly, I shall initiate immediate Federal action to move ahead on plans for building a new town at Fort Lincoln in Northeast Washington. Fort Lincoln, over 300 acres of open land which received its name as a military post a century ago and which was long the site of the National Training School for Boys, offers an ideal chance to create not just another urban project where homes are razed and the human factor is designed out, but a totally new community planned around people. More than 4,000 dwellings for families of varied incomes are envisioned—three-quarters of them owner-occupied, to provide an anchor of stability in the development.

Innovative public transportation and communications systems and experimental educational programs would help knit the community together. Both the installation of these features and the construction work itself would be used as demonstration settings for some of the social-benefit technology applications which I proposed in my State of the Union message. Also integral to the new town would be a Federal employment center for 5,000 to 10,000 employees, and a possible satellite campus for the Federal City College. The development would be financed through public-private partnership, with the initial Federal investment (supplemented by District contributions which will need approval by the Congress) likely to be matched several times over in related private investment.

"The city lives!"—a rallying cry which meets with considerable skepticism in some quarters today—would be the assurance forcefully offered to Washingtonians and the world by a Fort Lincoln town occupied and operating in 1976. We are determined to make it happen.

Neighborhood Social Development

The Fort Lincoln idea is not new, but the impetus behind it is—a neighborhood, community-based impetus, with which I am delighted to associate this administration. In order to demonstrate our support for this kind of bootstrap Bicentennial initiative, we shall ask the Congress to make available several million dollars in Federal funds to supplement the local funds set aside to carry out the social development project proposals which will be gathered by the local Bicentennial Commission and Assembly in neighborhoods all over Washington beginning this spring. None of these latter projects will approach the scale of Fort Lincoln, but most will be no less soundly rooted in ordinary people's knowledge of their own needs. The process of listening and response, as well as the project implementation itself, will make for a healthier and more progressive city.

We are also increasing our efforts to assist in redevelopment of the inner-city areas devastated by the riots of April 1968. Two recent ground-breakings give evidence that the work is moving ahead, but also remind us of how much is left to do. The job, of course, is not the Federal Government's alone, but we must and shall contribute our full share and see the obligation through at an accelerated pace.

More Community Parks

One frequently voiced need is for more parkland—not just in the ceremonial center of the city, but out in the residential sections as well. Planning is now underway for a joint Federal-District park development program focusing on underused,

publicly owned land near the Anacostia River, close to some of the District's most crowded neighborhoods. New recreational facilities will be constructed, to permit intensive use of the sorely needed new parks by Anacostia residents. Also within the Anacostia Basin, improvements will be carried out at the National Arboretum. Another major green-space project planned for completion by 1976 is the Fort Circle Parks, 17 outposts of the Army's old defensive system around the periphery of the District of Columbia, some dating back as far as the War of 1812. Strips of parkland are to link all the forts into a continuous belt containing bike trails, hiking paths, community recreation facilities, and campsites. Further, the District and the Interior Department will cooperate in rehabilitating and upgrading smaller parks in many areas of the city. I ask the Congress to approve the funds requested in my 1973 budget to move all of these projects forward on schedule.

A New Downtown Center

I also support, as vital to the kind of development momentum Washington must have to hold its head up among American cities in the Bicentennial Era, the District government's intention to construct a major convention center-sports arena complex near Mount Vernon Square.

This project would help to counter the centrifugal forces which are pushing both the leisure activities of local people and the major gatherings of out-of-town visitors away from the centers of many major cities. It would mean new business and investment and jobs for blocks around. And it would inject new life into nearby neighborhoods—provided, of course, that the legitimate concerns of merchants, working people, and residents in those neighborhoods receive fair consideration in the planning and location process. The scope of Federal assistance, however, should be appropriately limited, since I believe that a development largely local in function and benefits should have substantial local financing as well.

Following Through: Education and Transportation

New communities, new parks, new focal points for downtown business—all will help Washington carry through the ARBC's "Horizons '76" theme of honoring our founding principles by forging a better future with them. So too will two other ongoing District efforts, for which Congressional assistance requested during the last session is still much needed: our public colleges and our METRO subway system.

Washington Technical Institute is proceeding with plans for buildings at its new permanent location on the north side of the former Bureau of Standards site in Northwest Washington. Federal City College remains in scattered lease space throughout the city despite explosive enrollment growth in the past 4 years; it hopes to occupy a campus of its own in and around the old District Library building north of Mount Vernon Square, as well as satellite locations elsewhere. The Congress can help to expedite these campus development efforts by enacting the D.C. Capital Financing Act, which makes special provision for funding college construction through direct Federal grants rather than through Treasury loans as at present.

In my D.C. message urging this action last April, I noted that WTI and the new International Center which is to share the Bureau of Standards site will in the future symbolize "side by side the Capital City's dedication to human development and to international understanding." Action by the Congress late in 1971 cleared the way for actual sale to foreign governments of lots at the International Center to begin last week. By 1976 the cluster of new chanceries there will be a pride to Americans and foreign guests alike. Let us now make sure that the District's public colleges will also be a showplace in the Bicentennial year. Ample and balanced opportunities in higher education are essential, if we are to convince millions of 1976 student visitors that the District takes care of its own.

METRO, and all of the other elements which with it will comprise a balanced modern transportation system for greater Washington, are central to Bicentennial plans for the District. We need the pride of achievement in areawide cooperation which the system will give all communities taking part. We need its people-moving capacity to cope with visitor traffic which may average up to 100,000 people daily throughout the anniversary year. I am today renewing the commitment of all the agencies and resources of the Federal Government toward maximum progress on the entire transportation system—subway, freeways, bridges, parking, and support facilities—before 1976. The action of the Congress in December to support continued METRO funding was enormously heartening to the people of the Capital region; it gave, in fact, a glimmer of hope to beleaguered commuters everywhere. The grim Thanksgiving prospect of a great many excavated streets to fill back in has now become the far brighter prospect of at least 24 miles of operating subway—the most modern anywhere—by 1976. Urgently needed now is prompt approval by the Congress of Federal guarantees for METRO revenue bonds—the next essential step to getting the trains running.

To Welcome 40 Million Guests

Both the sheer visitor volume anticipated at the height of the bicentennial observance, and the important goal of eliminating a "them and us" polarity between city residents and their guests from around the world, dictate that past patterns which have made the Mall and its immediate environs a sort of "tourist ghetto" must now go. All of Washington must be made not only hospitable and attractive to the visitor—which the proposals just outlined should go far toward achieving—but easily accessible as well. I have directed the Secretary of Transportation to coordinate interagency action plans for supplementing those subway lines in service by 1976 with a coordinated network of other public transportation on which visitors can move from fringe parking areas (to be developed under these plans) to points of interest nearer the city center.

At the hub of this network should be new National Visitors Center in and around Union Station. Such a facility, desirable for all years, becomes indispensable as we look to the Bicentennial. I have therefore charged the Secretary of the Interior, in consultation with the Secretary of Transportation, to take immediate action to move the National Visitors Center out of the talk stage, and to prepare new proposals for bringing it to completion by 1976. When Union Station was built early in this century at the height of the railroad era, one of its express purposes was to permit removal of an unsightly terminal and tracks from the east end of the Mall. Its rehabilitation in the seventies as the Capital's principal reception and orientation point for travelers on all modes of ground transportation would be most appropriate, and would once again relieve the Mall and downtown areas of much traffic congestion. An "air rights" parking garage for buses and visitors' cars, convenient public transit connections, and a central information facility tied in with a citywide tourist guidance and information system would be the major features of the project.

Here is an opportunity for public and private resources to combine to fill a Bicentennial need. Notwithstanding the collapse of previous railroad financing plans for the Center at the time of the Penn Central bankruptcy, I have asked Secretaries Morton and Volpe to seek substantial railroad participation as they formulate the new proposals. I shall submit these to the Congress as soon as possible, with hopes of rapid approval.

Another step which should promote smoother tourist flow to major attractions is construction of a METRO station at Arlington National Cemetery. This station, for which planning funds are requested in my new budget, would speed movement from Washington over to the Arlington shrine, which by 1976 will be enhanced with numerous improvements including a new Memorial Chapel and columbarium. At the same time it would offer the arriving visitor one more convenient transfer point from private to public transportation on the way into the Capital itself.

Bicentennial Gardens

Moving in toward the center of the city, what will the 1976 visitor find along the Mall? Most strikingly new and charming, perhaps, would be a park and recreation center called Bicentennial Gardens, which I propose be developed in the open land along Constitution Avenue between the Washington Monument and Lincoln Memorial. Since the last of the old World War I "tempos" were removed from the West Mall in 1970, we have explored many alternative plans for developing in their place facilities for people of all ages, incomes, and interests, residents and tourists alike, to enjoy.

The Bicentennial Gardens plan, which will soon be ready to present in detail but which of course remains open to the ideas and desires of those for whom it is intended, might be called an American cousin of Copenhagen's beloved Tivoli. It follows the present contours of the land on a low profile in keeping with other Mall developments. A restaurant, smaller eating areas, an open-air theater, a bandshell, an area for ice skating, a children's play area, fountains, gardens, a boating lake, and walking paths are examples of the kind of features that might be included. There could be underground parking to accommodate tour buses, a terminal for the tourist trams, and a visitors center in the middle of the Gardens. With such a development, the Mall's attractions would be better balanced and dispersed, evening activities now concentrated in the Smithsonian Quadrangle would have a second focal point, and mingling of Washingtonians and visitors in a pleasant year-round setting would be encouraged. Quality of life for everyone in the Capital would be enhanced.

The Mall in 1976

The three major monuments and memorials in easy reach of Bicentennial Gardens are to be renovated and improved in a 4-year Park Service program beginning with this year's budget now before the Congress. Another facelifting project along the whole length of the Mall, and on the Ellipse as well, will reconstruct roadways, add walks, bikeways, plantings, and fountains, and provide for a new Ceremonial Drive. This work too is budgeted for fiscal year 1973 and beyond, to be completed by 1976.

The Mall east of the Washington Monument should also have a new look for the Bicentennial. Besides the Hirshhorn Museum and National Gallery of Art addition which are now being constructed, there will be a handsome new building for one of the Mall's oldest tenants, the Smithsonian Institution. This structure, which will house the National Air and Space Museum with exhibits ranging from Kitty Hawk to Hadley Rille and with a former astronaut in charge, can be ready in 1976 if the Congress will move now to approve FY 1973 construction funds for it; the plans are nearly complete. The Smithsonian also plans restoration of the historic Arts and Industries Building to its original 1880s appearance, as a fit setting for the Nation's Centennial exhibits which it displayed following the Philadelphia Exposition nearly a century ago and will display again for the Bicentennial, and construction of a major new "Nation of Nations" exhibit in the Museum of History and Technology to illustrate America's multicultural tradition. Both projects are the subject of FY 1973 budget requests.

A fourth important undertaking by the Smithsonian—not on the Mall but rather a part of the effort to give the bicentennial activities metropolitan scope—is the Bicentennial Outdoor Museum planned for old Fort Foote, Maryland, on the Potomac in Prince Georges Country. The restored fort is to serve as the scene for re-creation of Revolutionary events such as encampments, war-time life, and parades for 1976. I ask prompt congressional action on legislation to approve the Bicentennial Outdoor Museum and to authorize appropriations for planning it.

Realizing a Vision: Pennsylvania Avenue

As L'Enfant's majestic expanse of Mall provides an axis along which Washington visitors can honor and relive the American past, so Pennsylvania Avenue, leaving the Mall by the new reflecting pool in front of the Capitol and angling away from it a long mile up to the White House, forms the main axis of government activity shaping the American present and future. This avenue, then, also demands attention as we move to dress up the heart of the city for our two hundredth birthday. By 1976, let us complete the great Federal Triangle office complex in the spirit of the McMillan Commission's original vision 70 years ago. Let us build at its center a Grand Plaza worthy of the name, by transforming what is now a parking lot into a people-oriented park for government workers and visitors to enjoy. (Visitors will also benefit from the new information and orientation center to be opened in the Great Hall of the Commerce Building by 1976, intended to introduce citizens to the activities of all the executive departments and agencies.) I have requested funds in my budget for fiscal year 1973 to move forward on the Federal Triangle and Grand Plaza projects; with the cooperation of the Congress the work will begin in the near future.

The north side of Pennsylvania Avenue, and with it many blocks of the downtown area, can also be revitalized or well on the way by the time we celebrate the Bicentennial. The FBI building now rising north of the Avenue symbolizes half of the answer—Federal construction—and can stand completed and in use by 1976 with continued congressional support. A further appropriation for this project is included in my new budget requests.

The other half of the answer for Pennsylvania Avenue is coordinated development planning which will mobilize the private sector and help bring commercial and residential activity back to this part of the city. The heart of Washington must not become so dominated by Federal buildings that it sits abandoned and lifeless on evenings and weekends. The two Presidents before me initiated steps to prevent this, and to make the Avenue instead a corridor of lively and varied activity, public and private—and my administration has continued to press this effort. In September 1970 I announced my strong support for a legislative proposal to establish a development corporation to accomplish the needed revitalization. Since then the proposal has been substantially modified in a good faith effort to accommodate all interests and segments of opinion. Once again, I urge the Congress to act quickly and favorably on the Pennsylvania Avenue Bicentennial Development Corporation bill.

When I first expressed support for the corporation plan nearly 17 months ago, I called it "an opportunity to fulfill, in this city, at this time, a magnificent vision of the men who founded our Nation, and at the same time to create a standard for the rest of the Nation by which to measure their own urban achievement, and on which to build visions of their own." It is not an opportunity that waits forever, though; of the time available between that 1970 statement and the beginning of the Bicentennial year, more than a fourth is already gone. Every month that passes without this legislation further dims our chances of giving all Americans one birthday present they ought to have—a Capital "main street" to be proud of.

The Next Four Years

Both local and Federal plans for the Bicentennial celebration here in the Nation's Capital are far from complete at present. It is right that they should continue to evolve and expand as we move toward 1976. This message, however, attempts to set the tone and theme for Federal participation over the course of the next 4 years, and also to convey some of the aspirations of Washingtonians themselves without presuming to dictate what those aspirations should be.

The various levels and jurisdictions of government in the Washington area are well organized to follow through on the proposals I make today and to supervise further planning. The American Revolution Bicentennial Commission, with its distinguished bipartisan membership headed by David J. Mahoney, continues to provide excellent national leadership. The District government is well served by the responsive local Assembly and Commission structure to which I referred above; Mayor Washington is also establishing liaison with suburban planning bodies and with State officials of both Virginia and Maryland. The massive and diverse physical construction effort outlined in this message has been coordinated through a full-time District of Columbia bicentennial task force within the General Services Administration, until recently headed with great skill by Administrator Robert Kunzig. Now that Mr. Kunzig has become a Federal judge, I shall ensure that this coordination work is carried forward at the same high standard.

Under such direction and with the support of the Congress, we can achieve our Bicentennial goal of dual excellence in the District of Columbia, and we can realize by 1976 a dramatic improvement in the quality of Washington life for all whose physical or spiritual home this great Capital is. And by so doing we can help to inspire and encourage the preparations of other communities all across the country for a truly magnificent Bicentennial.

RICHARD NIXON

OLDER AMERICANS

Following is a partial text, as made available by the White House, of President Nixon's March 23 message to Congress on older Americans.

TO THE CONGRESS OF THE UNITED STATES:

When I addressed the White House Conference on Aging last December, I pledged that I would do all I could to make 1972 a year of action on behalf of older Americans. This message to the Congress represents an important step in fulfilling that promise.

Many of the actions which are outlined in this message have grown out of concerns expressed at the White House conference and at related meetings across the country. The message also discusses a number of steps that have already been taken or that were announced at an earlier date. All of these actions are part of our comprehensive strategy for helping older Americans.

The momentum which has been generated by all these steps—old and new—will move us toward the great national objectives which the White House conference set forth. I pledge that this momentum will be sustained as we follow through on these initiatives and as we keep other recommendations of the White House conference at the top of our agenda, under continuing review.

This message, then, does not represent the last word I will have to say on this important subject. It does, however, identify those administrative steps which we are taking immediately to help older Americans, along with a number of legislative initiatives which should be of highest priority on this year's congressional agenda.

We often hear these days about the "impatience of youth." But if we stop to think about the matter, it is the elderly who have the best reason to be impatient. As so many older Americans have candidly told me, "We simply do not have time to wait while the government procrastinates. For us, the future is now." I believe this same sense of urgency should characterize the government's response to the concerns of the elderly. I hope and trust that the Congress will join me in moving forward in that spirit.

A COMPREHENSIVE STRATEGY FOR MEETING COMPLEX PROBLEMS

The role of older people in American life has changed dramatically in recent decades. For one thing, the number of Americans 65 and over is more than six times as great today as it was in 1900—compared to less than a 3-fold increase in the population under 65. In 1900, one out of every 25 Americans was 65 or over; today one in ten has reached his 65th birthday.

While the number of older Americans has been growing so rapidly, their traditional pattern of living has been severely disrupted. In an earlier era, the typical American family was multi-generational—grandparents and even greatgrandparents lived in the same household with their children and grandchildren, or at least lived nearby. In recent years, however, the ties of family and of place have been loosened—with the result that more and more of our older citizens must live apart or alone. The rapid increase in mandatory retirement provisions has compounded this trend toward isolation. Under such conditions, other problems of older persons such as ill health and low income have become even more burdensome. And all of these difficulties are intensified, of course, for members of minority groups and for those who are blind or deaf or otherwise handicapped.

The sense of separation which has characterized the lives of many older Americans represents a great tragedy for our country. In the first place, it denies many older citizens the sense of fulfillment and satisfaction they deserve for the contributions they have made throughout their lifetimes. Secondly, it denies the country the full value of the skills and insights and moral force which the older generation is uniquely capable of offering.

The major challenge which confronts us, then, as we address the problems of older Americans is the new generation gap which has emerged in recent decades between those who are over 65 and those who are younger. The way to bridge this gap, in my judgment, is to stop treating older Americans as a burden and to start treating them as a resource. We must fight the many forces which can cause older persons to feel dependent or isolated and provide instead continuing opportunities for them to be self-reliant and involved.

If we can accomplish this goal, our entire Nation will reap immense benefits. As I put it in my speech to the White House Conference on Aging, "...any action which enhances the dignity of older Americans enhances the dignity of all Americans, for unless the American dream comes true for our older generation, it cannot be complete for any generation."

From its very beginnings, this administration has worked diligently to achieve this central objective. To assist me in this effort, I established a special task force on aging in 1969. In that same year, I elevated the commissioner on aging, John Martin, to the position of special assistant to the President on aging, the first such position in history. Later, I created a new cabinet-level committee on aging, under the leadership of the secretary of health, education and welfare, to ensure that the concerns of the aging were regularly and thoroughly considered by this administration and that our policies to help older persons were effectively carried out. To provide greater opportunity for older Americans to express their own concerns and to recommend new policies, I convened the White House Conference on Aging—which met last December and which was preceded and followed by many other meetings at the grassroots level. I asked the cabinet-level committee on aging to place the recommendations of the conference at the top of its agenda. And I also asked the chairman of the conference, Arthur Flemming, to stay on as the first special consultant to the President on aging, so that the voice of older Americans would continue to be heard at the very highest levels of the government.

One dimension of our efforts over the last three years is evident when we look at the federal budget. If our budget proposals are accepted, overall federal spending for the elderly in fiscal year 1973 will be $50-billion, nearly 150 percent of what it was when this administration took office. One particularly important example of increased concern for the elderly is the fact that over-all federal spending under the Older Americans Act alone has grown from $32-million in fiscal year 1969 to a proposed $257-million in fiscal year 1973—an eight-fold increase. This figure includes the $157-million I originally requested in my 1973 budget, plus an additional $100-million which I am requesting in this message for nutrition and related services.

How much money we spend on aging programs is only one part of the story, however. How we spend it is an equally important question. It is my conviction that the complex, interwoven problems of older Americans demand, above all else, a comprehensive response, one which attacks on a variety of fronts and meets a variety of problems.

This message outlines the comprehensive strategy which this administration had developed for bridging the new generation gap and enhancing the dignity and independence of older Americans. That strategy has five major elements:

1. Protecting the income position of the elderly;
2. Upgrading the quality of nursing home care;
3. Helping older persons live dignified, independent lives in their own homes or residences—by expanding and reforming service programs;
4. Expanding opportunities for older people to continue their involvement in the life of the country; and
5. Reorganizing the federal government to better meet the changing needs of older Americans.

A SUMMARY OF MAJOR INITIATIVES

In addition to discussing important actions which have been taken in the past or are now underway, this message focuses attention on the following major items of new and pending business.

1. To protect the income position of older Americans, the Congress should:
   • Enact HR 1 as soon as possible, thus providing older Americans with $5½-billion of additional annual income. HR 1 would increase social security benefits by 5 percent, make social security inflation-proof, increase widow, widower and delayed retirement benefits, liberalize earnings tests, and establish a floor under the income of older Americans for the first time;
   • Repeal the requirement that participants in part B of Medicare must pay a monthly premium which is scheduled to reach $5.80 this July. This step would make available to older persons an additional $1.5-billion—the equivalent of roughly another 4 percent increase in social security benefits for persons 65 and over;
   • Strengthen the role played by private pension plans by providing tax deductions to encourage their expansion, requiring the vesting of pensions, and protecting the investments which have been made in these funds;
   • Enact revenue sharing proposals designed to provide the opportunity for significant property tax relief; and
   • Enact my proposed consumer protection legislation which deals with problems which are especially acute for older citizens.

   The administration will:
   • Continue its investigation of alternative methods for financing public education in such a manner as to relieve the present heavy reliance on property taxes;
   • Propose major improvements in the military retirement system, including a one-time recomputation of retired pay;
   • Continue the battle against price inflation, with special emphasis in the health care field;
   • Develop a program to foster greater awareness among older citizens of their legal rights under the Interstate Land Sales Full Disclosure Act; and
   • Develop a program designed to help each state create consumer education programs for older citizens.

2. To upgrade the quality of nursing home care, the Congress should:

• Make it possible for the federal government to assume the entire cost of state inspection of homes receiving payments under the Medicaid program; and

• Approve my request for additional funds for training nursing home personnel.

The administration will:

• Continue to strengthen and expedite other portions of my 8-point program for upgrading nursing homes, including my commitment to withdraw federal funds from those homes that refuse to meet standards and to make adequate alternative arrangements for those who are displaced from substandard homes; and

• Develop proposals for protecting older persons in the purchase of nursing home services.

3. To help older persons live dignified, independent lives in their own homes or residences, the Congress should:

• Appropriate the $100-million I requested for the Administration on Aging in my 1973 budget;

• Appropriate an additional $100-million for nutritional and related purposes;

• Appropriate $57-million for other programs under the Older Americans Act, bringing total spending under this act to $257-million—an eight-fold increase over fiscal year 1969;

• Renew and strengthen the Older Americans Act, which so many older persons rightly regard as landmark legislation in the field of aging—extending it for an indefinite period rather than for a specified period of years;

• Create a new, coordinated system for service delivery under this act, so that the Administration on Aging can help develop goals for such services, while state and area agencies create specific plans for achieving these goals; and

• Allow states and localities to use some of the funds now in the highway trust fund to finance their mass transit programs, including special programs to help the elderly.

The administration will:

• Ensure that departments and agencies involved in the field of aging identify the portion of their total resources that are available for older persons and ensure that use of these resources is effectively coordinated all across the government;

• Strengthen the role already played by local officials of the Social Security Administration and other agencies in providing information about federal services to older persons and in receiving their complaints;

• Launch this summer a new project FIND—a program which will enlist the services of government workers at the grassroots level in an outreach effort to locate older persons who are not involved in federal nutrition programs and who should be;

• Step up efforts to meet the special transportation needs of older Americans, giving priority to community requests for capital grants that aid the elderly from the urban mass transportation fund;

• Provide more and better housing for older Americans by issuing new guidelines for two HUD programs to make the more readily applicable to the elderly, by extending the mortgage maturity for the FHA-insured nursing home program, by drawing upon research of the Law Enforcement Assistance Administration to reduce crime, by encouraging the provisions of more space for senior centers within housing projects for the elderly, and by developing training programs in the management of housing for older persons.

4. To expand opportunities for older persons to continue their involvement in the life of our country, the Congress should:

• Appropriate the funds I have requested for such action programs as Retired Senior Volunteers and Foster Grandparents;

• Authorize the ACTION agency to expand person-to-person volunteer service programs, helping more older Americans to work both with children and with older persons who need their help; and

• Broaden the Age Discrimination in Employment Act of 1967 to include state and local governments.

The administration will:

• Work with 130 national voluntary groups across the country in a special program to stimulate volunteer action; and

• Develop a national program to expand employment opportunities for persons over 65, through programs such as Senior Aides and Green Thumb, by urging state and local governments to make job opportunities available under the Emergency Employment Act of 1971, by working through the public employment offices to open part-time job opportunities in both the public and private sector, and by reaffirming federal policy against age discrimination in appointment to federal jobs.

5. To improve federal organization for future efforts, the administration will:

• Strengthen the secretary of health, education and welfare's advisory committee on older Americans—providing it with permanent staff capability to support its increased responsibilities;

• Arrange for the commissioner of aging, in his capacity as chairman of the advisory committee on aging, to report directly to the secretary of health, education and welfare;

• Create a technical advisory committee on aging research in the office of the secretary of health, education and welfare to develop a comprehensive plan for economic, social, psychological, health and education research on aging.

RICHARD NIXON

ECONOMIC MESSAGE

Following is the text of President Nixon's Jan. 27 economic message to Congress.

TO THE CONGRESS OF THE UNITED STATES:

The American economy is beginning to feel the effects of the new policies launched last August.

I undertook the New Economic Policy because it was becoming clear that not enough was being done to meet our ambitious goals for the American economy. The new measures are designed to bring the Nation to higher employment, greater price stability, and a stronger international position.

The essence of the New Economic Policy is not the specific list of measures we announced on August 15; it is the determination to do all that is necessary to achieve the Nation's goals.

Nineteen hundred and seventy-one was in many ways a good economic year. Total employment, total output, output per person, real hourly earnings, and real income after tax per person all reached new highs. The inflation which had plagued the country since 1965 began to subside. In the first 8 months of the year the rate of inflation was 30 percent less than in the same months of 1970.

But I did not believe this was enough to meet the Nation's needs. Although the rate of inflation had declined before August it was still too high. Although unemployment stopped rising, it remained near 6 percent. In the first part of the year our international balance-of-payments deficit—the excess of our payments to the rest of the world over their payments to us—had risen far too high.

The conditions called for decisive actions. On August 15, I announced these actions.

First, I imposed a 90-day freeze on prices, wages and rents.

Second, I suspended conversion of dollars into gold and other reserve assets.

Third, I imposed a temporary surcharge on imports generally at the rate of 10 percent.

Fourth, I proposed a number of tax changes intended to stimulate the economy, including repeal of the excise tax on automobiles, a tax credit for investment, and reduction of income taxes on individuals. At the same time I took steps to keep the budget under control.

The package of measures was unprecedented in scope and degree. My Administration had struggled for 2½ years in an effort to check the inflation we inherited by means more consistent with economic freedom than price-wage controls. But the inflationary momentum generated by the policy actions and inactions of 1965-68 was too stubborn to be eradicated by these means alone. Or at least it seemed that it could only be eradicated at the price of persistent high unemployment—and this was a price we would not ask the American people to pay.

Similarly, more than a decade of balance-of-payments deficits had built up an overhang of obligations and distrust which no longer left time for the gradual methods of correction which had been tried earlier.

The measures begun on August 15 will have effects continuing long into the future. They cannot be fully evaluated by what has happened in the little over 5 months since that date. Still the results up to this point have been extremely encouraging.

The freeze slowed down the rate of inflation dramatically. In the 3 months of its duration the index of consumer prices rose only 0.4 percent, compared to 1.0 percent in the previous 3 months. The freeze was a great testimonial to the public spirit of the American people, because that result could have been achieved with the small enforcement staff we had only if the people had been cooperating voluntarily.

The freeze was followed by a comprehensive, mandatory system of controls, with more flexible and equitable standards than were possible during the first 90 days. General principles and specific regulations have been formulated, staffs have been assembled and cases are being decided. This effort is under the direction of citizens on the Price Commission and Pay Board, with advice from other citizens on special panels concerned with health services, State and local government, and rent. These citizens are doing a difficult job, doing it well and the Nation is in their debt.

While this inflation-control system was being put in place, vigorous action was going forward on the international front. The suspension of the convertibility of the dollar was a shock felt around the world. The surcharge emphasized the need to act swiftly and decisively to improve our position. Happily, the process of adjustment began promptly, without disrupting the flow of international business. Other currencies rose in cost relative to the U.S. dollar. As a result, the cost of foreign goods increased relative to the cost of U.S. goods, improving the competitive position of American workers and industries. International negotiations were begun to stabilize exchange rates at levels that would help in correcting the worldwide disequilibrium, of which the U.S. balance-of-payments deficit was the most obvious symptom. These negotiations led to significant agreements on a number of points:

1. Realignment of exchange rates, with other currencies rising in cost relative to the dollar, as part of which we agreed to recommend to Congress that the price of gold in dollars be raised when progress had been made in trade liberalization.

2. Commitment to discussion of more general reform of the international monetary system.

3. Widening of the permitted range of variation of exchange rates, pending other measures of reform.

4. Commitment to begin discussions to reduce trade barriers, including some most harmful to the United States.

5. Assumption of a larger share of the costs of common defense by some of our allies.

6. Elimination of the temporary U.S. surcharge on imports.

The third part of the August 15 action was the stimulative tax program. Enactment of this package by Congress, although not entirely in the form I had proposed, put in place the final part of my New Economic Policy.

In part as a result of this program, economic activity rose more rapidly in the latter part of the year. In the fourth quarter real output increased at the annual rate of 6 percent, compared with about 3 percent in the 2 previous quarters. Employment rose by about 1.1 million from July to December, and only an extraordinarily large rise of the civilian labor force—1.3 million —kept unemployment from falling.

Nineteen hundred and seventy-two begins on a note of much greater confidence than prevailed 6 or 12 months ago. Output is rising at a rate which will boost employment rapidly and eat into unemployment. There is every reason to expect this rate of increase to continue. The Federal Government has contributed impetus to this advance by tax reductions and expenditure increases. The Federal Reserve has taken steps to create the monetary conditions necessary for rapid economic expansion.

The operation of the new control system in an economy without inflationary pressure of demand holds out great promise of sharply reducing the inflation rate. We are converting the fear of perpetual inflation into a growing hope for price stability. We are lifting from the people the frustrating anxiety about what their savings and their income will be worth a year from now or 5 years from now.

For the first time in over a decade the United States is moving decisively to restore strength to its international economic position.

The outlook is bright, but much remains to be done. The great problem is to get the unemployment rate down from the 6-percent level where it was in 1971. It was reduced from that level in the sixties by a war buildup; it must be reduced from that level in the seventies by the creation of peacetime jobs.

It is obvious that the unemployment problem has been intensified by the reduction of over 2 million defense-related jobs and by the need to squeeze down inflation. But 6 percent unemployment is too much, and I am determined to reduce that number significantly in 1972.

To that end I proposed the tax reduction package in 1971. Federal expenditures will rise by $25.2 billion between last fiscal year and fiscal 1972. Together these tax reductions and expenditure increases will leave a budget deficit of $38.8 billion this year. If we were at full employment in the present fiscal year, expenditures would exceed receipts by $8.1 billion. This is strong medicine, and I do not propose to continue its use, but we have taken it in order to give a powerful stimulus to employment.

We have imposed price and wage controls to assure that the expansion of demand does not run to waste in more inflation but generates real output and real employment.

We have suspended dollar convertibility and reduced the international cost of the dollar which will help restore the competitive position of U.S. workers and thereby generate jobs for them.

We have instituted a public service employment program to provide jobs directly for people who find it especially hard to get work.

We have expanded the number of people on federally assisted manpower programs to record levels.

We have established computerized Job Banks to help match up jobseekers and job vacancies.

We have proposed welfare reform to increase incentives to employment.

We have proposed special revenue sharing for manpower programs, to make them more effective.

We have proposed revision of the minimum wage system to remove obstacles to the employment of young and inexperienced workers.

We expect that these measures, and others, will contribute to a substantial reduction of unemployment.

In addition to getting unemployment down, a second major economic task before us is to develop and apply the price-wage control system, which is still in its formative stage, to the point where its objective is achieved. The objective of the controls is a state of affairs in which reasonable price stability can be maintained without controls. That state of affairs can and will be reached. How long it will take, no one can say. We will persevere until the goal is reached, but we will not keep the controls one day longer than necessary.

The success of the stabilization program depends fundamentally upon the cooperation of the American people. This means not only compliance with the regulations. It means also mutual understanding of the difficulties that all of us—working people, businessmen, consumers, farmers, Government officials —encounter in this new and complicated program. Our experience in the past few months convinces me that we shall have this necessary ingredient for success.

We embarked last year on another great task—to create an international economic system in which we and others can reap the benefits of the exchange of goods and services without danger to our domestic economies. Despite all the troubles in this field in recent years both the American people and our trading partners are enjoying on a larger scale than ever before what is the object of the whole international economic exercise— consumption of foreign goods that are better or cheaper or more interesting than domestic goods, as well as foreign travel and profitable investment abroad.

We don't want to reduce these benefits. We want to expand them. To do that, we in the United States must be able to pay in the way that is best—chiefly by selling abroad those things that we produce best or more cheaply, including the products of our agriculture and our other high-technology industries. This is our objective in the international discussions launched by our acts of last year and continuing this year.

These tasks, in which Government takes the lead, are superimposed on the fundamental task of the American economy, upon which the welfare of the people most depends and which is basically performed by the people and not by the Government. That fundamental task is the efficient and innovative production of the goods and services that the American people want. That is why I have emphasized the need for greater productivity and a resurgence of the competitive spirit.

The outstanding performance of the American economy in this respect provides a background of strength which permits the Government to face its economic problems with confidence and to bring about a new prosperity without inflation and without war.

RICHARD NIXON

SUMMARY TEXT OF NIXON'S FOREIGN POLICY MESSAGE

Following is the text, as made available by the White House, of the summary chapter of President Nixon's Feb. 9 report to Congress on U.S. foreign policy.

1971—The Watershed Year: An Overview

This is the third Report of this kind which I have made to the Congress. It comes after a year of dramatic developments. The earlier Reports set forth fully this Administration's analysis of the world situation. They expressed the conviction that new conditions required fundamental changes in America's world role. They expounded our conception of what that role should be.

In short, they foreshadowed a transformation of American foreign relations with both our friends and our adversaries.

For three years, our policies have been designed to move steadily, and with increasing momentum, toward that transformation.

1971 was the watershed year. The foundation laid and the cumulative effect of the actions taken earlier enabled us to achieve, during the past year, changes in our foreign policy of historic scope and significance:

- An opening to the Peoples Republic of China.
- The beginning of a new relationship with the Soviet Union.
- The laying of a foundation for a healthier and more sustainable relationship with our European allies and Japan.
- The creation of a new environment for the world's monetary and trade activities.

This Report is addressed to those and other developments. It is, however, a companion piece to the two earlier Reports, for without an understanding of the philosophical conception upon which specific actions were based, the actions themselves can neither be adequately understood nor fairly judged. This account of a year of intense action, therefore, properly begins with a brief review of the intellectual foundation on which those actions rest.

A Changed World

In the first two Reports, I stressed the fact that the postwar period of international relations had ended, and that it was the task of this Administration to shape a new foreign policy to meet the requirements of a new era. I set forth at some length the changes in the world which made a new policy not only desirable, but necessary.

1. The recovery of economic strength and political vitality by Western Europe and Japan, with the inexorable result that both their role and ours in the world must be adjusted to reflect their regained vigor and self-assurance.

2. The increasing self-reliance of the states created by the dissolution of the colonial empires, and the growth of both their ability and determination to see to their own security and well-being.

3. The breakdown in the unity of the Communist Bloc, with all that implies for the shift of energies and resources to purposes other than a single-minded challenge to the United States and its friends, and for a higher priority in at least some Communist countries to the pursuit of national interests rather than their subordination to the requirements of world revolution.

4. The end of an indisputable U.S. superiority in strategic strength, and its replacement by a strategic balance in which the U.S. and Soviet nuclear forces are comparable.

5. The growth among the American people of the conviction that the time had come for other nations to share a greater portion of the burden of world leadership; and its corollary that the assured continuity of our longterm involvement required a responsible, but more restrained American role.

The Philosophy of a New American Foreign Policy

The earlier reports also set forth the philosophical convictions upon which this Administration was proceeding to reshape American policies to the requirements of the new realities. The core principles of this philosophy are:

- A leading American role in world affairs continues to be indispensable to the kind of world our own well-being requires.
- The end of the bipolar postwar world opens to this generation a unique opportunity to create a new and lasting structure of peace.
- The end of bi-polarity requires that the structure must be built with the resources and concepts of many nations—for only when nations participate in creating an international system do they contribute to its vitality and accept its validity.
- Our friendships are constant, but the means by which they are mutually expressed must be adjusted as world conditions change. The continuity and vigor of our alliances require that our friends assume greater responsibilities for our common endeavors.
- Our enmities are not immutable, and we must be prepared realistically to recognize and deal with their cause.

• This requires mutual self-restraint and a willingness to accommodate conflicting national interests through negotiation rather than confrontation.

• Agreements are not, however, an end in themselves. They have permanent significance only when they contribute to a stable structure of peace which all countries wish to preserve because all countries share its benefits.

• The unprecedented advances in science and technology have created a new dimension of international life. The global community faces a series of urgent problems and opportunities which transcend all geographic and ideological borders. It is the distinguishing characteristic of these issues that their solution requires international cooperation on the broadest scale.

• We must, therefore, be willing to work with all countries—adversaries as well as friends—toward a structure of peace to which all nations contribute and in which all nations have a stake.

The Breakthrough—Actions We Have Taken

This Report is an accounting of the application of that philosophy to American foreign policy. It is beyond dispute that we have made signal progress. Taken together, the initiatives of 1971 constitute a profound change in America's world role.

The heart of our new conception of that role is a more balanced alliance with our friends—and a more creative connection with our adversaries.

Breakthroughs with Our Adversaries. Toward our two principal adversaries, the Peoples Republic of China and the Soviet Union, we faced dissimilar problems. With China, the task was to establish a civilized discourse on how to replace estrangement with a dialogue serving to benefit both countries. With the Soviet Union, we already had the discourse. We had examined at great length the general principles upon which the policies of both countries must be based, if we were to move from the mere assertion to the harmonization of conflicting national interests. The task was to make this discourse fruitful by moving to the achievement of concrete arrangements of benefit both to the Soviet Union and ourselves.

We have, in 1971, made striking progress toward both goals:

1. The Peoples Republic of China. We have ended a 25 year period of implacable hostility, mutually embraced as a central feature of national policy. Fragile as it is, the rapprochement between the most populous nation and the most powerful nation of the world could have greater significance for future generations than any other measure we have taken this year.

This initiative was the fruit of almost three years of the most painstaking, meticulous, and necessarily discreet preparation. It is an essential step in tempering animosities which have their roots in the past and which stand in the way of our hopes for the future.

My visit to Peking in February will certainly not bring a quick resolution of the deep differences which divide us from the Peoples Republic of China. But it will be a beginning, and it will signal the end of a sterile and barren interlude in the relationship between two great peoples. Finally, it will represent a necessary and giant step toward the creation of a stable structure of world peace.

2. The Soviet Union. We have succeeded in giving a new momentum to the prospects for more constructive relations through a series of concrete agreements which get at the cause of the tension between our two countries. The agreements vary in importance, but together provide serious grounds for believing that a fundamental improvement in the U.S.-Soviet relationship may be possible.

• In February, we agreed on a treaty barring weapons of mass destruction from the ocean floor.

• In May, we broke the deadlock which had developed in the talks on limiting strategic arms, and agreed on a framework which made it possible to resume progress.

• In September, we agreed on a draft treaty prohibiting the production or possession of biological and toxin weapons.

• In September, we and our British and French allies reached an agreement with the Soviet Union on Berlin to end the use of the citizens of West Berlin as Cold War hostages, and to reduce the danger of Berlin once again becoming the focus of a sharp and dangerous international confrontation.

• In September, we agreed on a more reliable "Hot Line" communication between Washington and Moscow, and on measures for notification and consultation designed to reduce the risk of an accidental nuclear war.

• In November, the visit of the American Secretary of Commerce to Moscow and the beginning of conversations looking toward a general normalization of economic relations.

These steps can represent the start of a new relationship with the Soviet Union. There were, however, other developments in 1971 which make it unclear whether we are now witnessing a permanent change in Soviet policy or only a passing phase concerned more with tactics than with a fundamental commitment to a stable international system. Soviet weapons development and deployment activity, Soviet arms policy in the Middle East, Soviet behavior during the India-Pakistan crisis and the expanionist implications of Soviet naval activities, all raise serious questions.

Nonetheless, the number and scope of the positive developments led us to conclude that a meeting at the highest level was appropriate and might provide the stimulus for additional progress, particularly in the fields of arms limitation and economic cooperation. Thus, in May, for the first time in our history, the President of the United States will visit Moscow. We go to that meeting with hope and determination to succeed.

Breakthrough with Our Allies. With our principal allies in Western Europe and Japan, the need was to shape our relationship into a more mature political partnership. Our alliances must now be flexible enough to permit members to pursue autonomous policies within a common framework of strategic goals. Our allies are no longer willing to have the alliance rest only on American prescriptions—and we are no longer willing to have our alliances depend for their potency and sustenance primarily on American contributions.

European unity, and Japan's status as the third greatest industrial power, lead inevitably to economic competition between us. We recognize also the necessity and right of a reinvigorated Europe and Japan to pursue their own political initiatives, just as we wish to pursue ours.

Our alliances, therefore, can no longer draw their cohesion only from our agreement on what we are against. We need instead a clearer focus on what we are for.

Our alliances are no longer addressed primarily to the containment of the Soviet Union and China behind an American shield. They are, instead, addressed to the creation with those powers of a stable world peace. That task absolutely requires the maintenance of the allied strength of the noncommunist world.

Within that framework, we expect and welcome a greater diversity of policy. Alliance does not require that those tendencies be stifled, but only that they be accommodated and coordinated within an overall framework of unity and common purpose.

In 1971, important actions were taken to put that theory into fruitful practice.

1. The Removal of the Economic Threat to Allied Unity. The old international monetary and trading system had begun to undermine our alliance system. It had become unfair, in one aspect or another, both for us and our major trading partners and allies.

• It led inevitably to recurrent international monetary crises.

• Its dependence on the dollar as a reserve currency was seen by others as enabling us to escape monetary and fiscal discipline in domestic policy.

• Its rigidity limited our ability to redress our imbalance of payments while enabling others to alter their currencies to improve their own trading position.

• We have helped in persuading the world community to recognize the dangers of, and take effective measures to control, excessive population growth.

• We are participating in a major effort to focus the world's attention and resources constructively on the threat to the global environment.

• We have consistently asserted and worked to stimulate the general world interest in space exploration and global communications.

• We have provided leadership in the efforts of the world community to meet the challenge of air piracy.

Our Basic National Purpose—and Vietnam

Each of the initiatives described is significant in itself. But, their true significance lies in the fact that they are all part of a whole, each contributing to our basic purpose of building a stable peace.

During much of the previous decade, our national effort to reach that goal had been disrupted by our concentration on the war in Southeast Asia. We therefore faced the exigent need to reshape the American role in Vietnam so that it contributed to, rather than inhibited, progress toward the national goal of secure world peace.

We promised to end the conflict, but in a way that did not mock our effort to bring about a stable peace. On January 25, 1972 I described our thirty-month effort to reach peace through secret negotiations. I also presented our new proposals which clearly make possible a peaceful settlement which entrusts the political future of South Vietnam to the South Vietnamese. Alternatively, as we offered to do over nine months ago, we are ready to conclude a settlement of military issues only. To date, however, our earnest efforts to end the war for all participants through negotiations have foundered on Communist obstinacy. That has left us no choice but to move toward ending the war for America through Vietnamization of the conflict.

We have come a long way. In Vietnam, we have changed the very nature of the U.S. involvement. Our ground combat role has effectively ended. When I came into office, the American troop ceiling in Vietnam was 549,500, and we were suffering an average of more than 1,000 casualties a month. As I write this Report, our troop level has dropped below 139,000—and will be no higher than 69,000 by the first day of May. In December 1971 our combat deaths were down to 17. Air sorties, budget costs, draft calls—all have sharply declined.

Those facts represent the transformation of the American role in Vietnam. We have done this, as we promised to do, without abandoning our commitments to our allies. As our role has diminished, South Vietnam has been able increasingly to meet its own defense needs and provide growing security to its people.

Progress Was Tempered by Disappointments

During the year there were several sharp disappointments:

• The greatest was the failure of our intense public and private efforts to end the Vietnam War through a negotiated settlement. Such a settlement continues to be available to our enemy whenever he is prepared to negotiate in earnest. The only serious barrier to a settlement which remains is the enemy's insistence that we cooperate with him to force on our ally at the negotiating table a solution which the enemy cannot force upon him in the field, and is unwilling to entrust to a political process. That we are not willing to do.

We are ready to reach an agreement which allows the South Vietnamese to determine their own future without outside interference. This goal can be reached whenever Hanoi distinguishes between a settlement and a surrender.

• In South Asia, we made a determined year-long effort to prevent a war. We did not succeed. Our deep interest in the well-being of both India and Pakistan compounded our disap-

pointment. We attempted to moderate the crisis with a massive relief effort and with an intense diplomatic campaign to promote a political solution. But war had its own momentum. The violation of peace in South Asia had ominous implications for the stability of other areas of tension in the world and for our efforts to establish a more hopeful relationship with our adversaries.

• In the Middle East, we were unable to make a breakthrough toward peace. Although the ceasefire resulting from our initiative in 1970 was maintained, it did not prove possible to engage the parties in negotiations, and consequently no progress was made toward the essential requirement of Middle-Eastern peace: an arrangement which rests the security of all on something more reliable than the good will of a nation's adversaries.

• In Latin America, we have yet to work out with our friends a solution of the conflict between their desire for our help and their determination to be free of dependence upon us. The thrust for change in Latin America, and our response to it, have yet to shape themselves into a pattern permitting us to make as full a contribution as we wish and our Hemisphere friends expect.

• In Africa, we have witnessed the growing maturity of the newly independent states, and the increasing concentration of their governments on the hard tasks of internal development. This is a heartening process, and it is one which deserves our encouragement. It is, therefore, a sharp disappointment, both to us and to our African friends, that our shrinking aid appropriations may prevent us from matching our expressions of good will with the material assistance which African countries wart and need.

• In the United Nations we were unable to preserve a place for the Republic of China.

Unfinished Business

In 1971, we passed a critical point in creating a new world role for the United States. But we are far from having completed the task. In almost every case, a listing of what we have done serves as an illustration of how far we still have to go. Our accomplishments as well as our disappointments define the agenda for the future. In all candor, I must say that the salient feature of the current state of U.S. foreign policy is the need for more progress on a whole series of pressing problems:

• We need to prove, through additional concrete accomplishments, the benefit to both the Soviet Union and ourselves of mutual self-restraint and willingness to accommodate rather than merely assert our respective national interests.

• We need to continue the hopeful but delicate process of creating a better relationship between ourselves and the Peoples Republic of China.

• We need to bring the arms race under control. Nothing would do more for our material and psychological well-being than to lighten this burden. It is axiomatic that it cannot be done at the sacrifice of our national security; but if it can be done without such a sacrifice, nothing would contribute more to our national security.

• We need to find the most effective way to help the poorer nations. Yet we now find ourselves in national disarray regarding our approach to economic assistance. Our wealth, our humanitarian traditions, and our interests dictate that we have an active foreign assistance program. The world looks to us for help in this area, and it is right that we should respond. I am prepared to work with the Congress to that end.

• We need to finish the construction with our partners of a reformed trade and monetary system which sustains our unity by encouraging the economic well-being of all.

• We need to continue, with both our friends and our adversaries, to build an international system which all will work to preserve because all recognize their stake in its preservation.

• We need to deal realistically with the fact that the United Nations is facing what I can only call a crisis of confidence. Whatever its current weaknesses, the UN makes an essential

- It contributed to a chronic U.S. imbalance of payments.
- It placed severe strains on our political relations with some of our closest friends and allies.

Both political and economic common sense dictated vigorous action—in our own national interest, in that of our allies, and in our shared interest in allied unity. What we needed was not a patch work adjustment, but a more fundamental change in the manner in which the non-Communist world's economy is managed.

Despite the general dissatisfaction, the inertia of the existing system and the conventional opposition to drastic change was tremendous. Hard steps were necessary to bring home to other countries that we were serious, and that reform of the international trade environment and a general realignment of currency values could no longer be delayed.

We, therefore, took drastic unilateral measures on August 15. Paradoxically, these were taken in order to stimulate a multilateral settlement of the problem. We did not in the period that followed resort to bilateral agreements. We sought instead a new international agreement which all would participate in creating.

In December of 1971, the general realignment of currencies took place. That was the necessary first step. With our partners we will, over the next year or two, pursue a more balanced monetary system and a more equitable trading environment. Most important of all, we have acted together to meet our economic problems in a way which strengthens our unity and guarantees our continued cooperation. We have, therefore, put behind us the imminent danger that conflicting economic interests would lead to the unravelling of free world cohesion.

2. The Evolution of Our Political and Defense Relationships. Our partnerships today comprise a varied and dynamic coalition of self-assured and independent states. In this Administration, the United States has shifted from the predominant role it played in the postwar period to a new role of accepting and encouraging initiative and leadership from our allies. Our basic common interests establish the requirement, and maturity and statesmanship furnish the tools for the preservation of the basic harmony of our policies.

In consonance with our new approaches to China and the Soviet Union, we supported a series of measures by our allies looking toward more autonomous policies. Both our initiatives and theirs were confirmed and coordinated at the end of the year in a series of meetings with the leaders of our principal allies.

- We welcomed the British decision to join the movement of European integration. A stronger Europe and more dynamic Britain are in the common interest of the West. I discussed with Prime Minister Heath at Bermuda the implications of that decision for the traditional special U.S.-U.K. relationship, and we reached agreement on how to harmonize our continuing friendship with Britain's new policies.
- We recognized France's special concerns as to the nature of the exchange rate adjustment. We met with President Pompidou in the Azores and agreed to a mutual adjustment that made possible the association of all major allies in the ensuing solution.
- We reaffirmed our acceptance of West Germany's desire for a more normal relationship with her Eastern neighbors. At Key Biscayne, we met with Chancellor Brandt and agreed upon the crucial and central role that Germany's participation in the Atlantic Alliance plays in Germany's future, including her future hopes for further improvement in her relations with Eastern Europe.
- With all our European allies we have stressed that the justification for the continued American military presence in Europe can only come from a clear and well-thought-out common strategy, and a consensus on how to share its responsibilities more equitably.
- We met with Prime Minister Sato at San Clemente, and agreed to the expedited return of Okinawa to Japan. This removes from our agenda an issue of vast potential for the dis-

ruption of the U.S.-Japanese friendship. We also indicated that we would regard a larger Japanese role in the economic and political affairs of Asia not as a substitute for or interference with our role, but as natural, necessary and proper. We clarified the fact that our initiative toward China is consistent with the continuity of the close U.S.-Japanese relationship.

The Problem of Timing

These were the most dramatic manifestations of our new policy towards both friends and adversaries. In the nature of things, progress in all areas could not be achieved simultaneously—and this led for a time to understandable concern that our interests in some areas were being sacrificed to the need for progress in others. Our approach to China had an impact on Japan, as did our negotiations with the Soviet Union on our friends in Western Europe. Our unilateral economic measures affected both. As a result, our relations with our allies appeared for a period of several months to be somewhat out of phase with the innovations taken in our relations with our adversaries.

By the end of the year, however, it was clear that our initiatives toward both our friends and our adversaries were in basic harmony. Progress in each contributed to progress in the other. In phase, each reinforced and gave added momentum to the other.

The total effect was an integrated and consistent adjustment of U.S. foreign policy to the requirements of a changed world.

Other Areas of Progress

There were other areas in which important, if quieter, progress was made in 1971 toward shaping the new American role in the world.

In our relations with all countries we proceeded to give effect to our new policy of insisting that the United States has neither the prescriptions nor the resources for the solution of problems in which ours is not the prime national interest. It is coming to be widely understood that we are in earnest when we say that it is for others to formulate solutions to these problems, and that our contribution should be viewed as a supplement to the application of major resources from those primarily at interest.

Latin America. We have looked to our Latin American neighbors for their initiatives and leadership. We are encouraging them to shape the political and economic framework in which our own contribution to common aims can be most effective.

Asia. We have helped our Asian allies create a greater capability to meet their own defense needs. This has enabled us to reduce substantially our military presence there, without abandoning our commitments to those steadfast friends. Indeed, by adhering to this pattern of building greater local capability, we have in three years reduced the American military presence in Asia from almost 800 thousand to less than 300 thousand without endangering the stability of the area or abandoning our commitments to our friends.

Africa. We have followed a deliberate policy of restraint in involvement in the political problems of Africa, while increasing our contribution to worthy African-initiated development activities.

New Dimension of Diplomacy. We have taken the initiative in stimulating international action on many of the issues which constitute the new dimension of diplomacy:
- We are making a major effort to reach world wide agreement in 1973 on a new Law of the Sea. Such an agreement is needed to ensure that the vast potential of the ocean and its resources serves to benefit mankind rather than becoming a new source of conflict between nations.
- We have taken the lead in organizing a concerted international effort to control narcotics.

contribution to the structure of world peace and thus to mankind's future.

This Report is, therefore, presented with a very sober awareness of how great a task still lies before the nation. We are still engaged in the essential job of redefining our role in the world. It must do justice to our capacity and obligation for leadership. It must also recognize our limitations. Above all, it must be based on a solid consensus of American public understanding and support. It is my hope that this report will help engender that support among the people of the nation and the Congress which represents them.

We believe the direction we have established and the actions we have taken commend themselves to such support.

SOCIAL SERVICES

Following is the text, as made available by the White House, of President Nixon's May 18 message to Congress on consolidation of federal social services programs.

TO THE CONGRESS OF THE UNITED STATES:

In responding to steady public demand over recent decades for more and more human services, the federal government created a host of assistance programs designed to meet a wide variety of human needs.

These many programs were established one-by-one over a considerable number of years. Each of the target problems was examined in isolation, and a program to alleviate each problem was devised separately—without regard to programs which had been, or would be, developed for allied problems.

The result is that a compassionate government unwittingly created a bureaucratic jungle that baffles and shortchanges many citizens in need. The unintended administrative snarl wastes taxpayers' money. And it frustrates needed efforts to treat "the whole person."

The Allied Services Act of 1972, which I am proposing today, would give state and local officials authority to consolidate the planning and implementation of the many separate social service programs into streamlined, comprehensive plans—each custom-designed for a particular area.

Such plans could eventually make it possible to assess the total human service needs of an entire family at a single location with a single application. Most applicants need more than one service, and now must trudge to office after office applying for assistance from one program at a time—with the result that they may not obtain all the services they need, or may be discouraged altogether from seeking help.

The Department of Health, Education and Welfare administers some 200 different human assistance programs in about a dozen major fields—to help needy citizens with such services as mental health, vocational rehabilitation, manpower training, food and nutrition, special programs for the aged, education, juvenile counseling, alcoholism and drug abuse, housing and public health.

Each of these programs has its own eligibility rules, application forms, management, and administrative policies. Each program usually has its own office location and its own geographical coverage area.

Federal rules and regulations, in short, now keep each social service program locked up in a little world of its own. This is not only wasteful and inefficient—it also prevents state and local efforts to close the gaps in social service delivery systems.

As I stated in my State of the Union Message this year, "We need a new approach to the delivery of social services—one which is built around people and not around programs. We need an approach which treats a person as a whole and which treats the family as a unit."

For the uninformed citizen in need, the present fragmented system can become a nightmare of confusion, inconvenience, and red tape.

The father of a family is helped by one program, his daughter by another, and his elderly parents by a third. An individual goes to one place for nutritional help, to another for health services, and to still another for educational counseling.

They are not the only victims of fragmented services—others include the taxpayers, and the public officials and government employees seeking to operate these diverse programs. Vast amounts of time, money and energy are expended in administrative procedures which overlap and duplicate—rather than being efficiently organized to help people.

The Allied Services Act of 1972 would give state and local governments greater legal freedom and planning tools needed for the long-overdue job of modernizing the delivery of social services, and to consolidated programs. This process would begin at the option of elected state and local officials, and would be highly responsive to their needs.

It would permit knowledgeable state and local people to break through rigid categorical walls, to open up narrow bureaucratic compartments, to consolidate and coordinate related programs in a comprehensive approach to related social aid problems—designed to match widely-varying state and local needs.

Under the act, the federal government would make dollars available for the costs of developing consolidated plans, and it would also be prepared to underwrite the administrative start-up costs when the comprehensive services program went into effect.

To encourage and facilitate such unified services, the Secretary of Health, Education and Welfare would be empowered by the Act to approve the transfer of up to 25 percent of any existing program's funds into any other purpose or programs involved in an approved local allied service plan—a logical flexibility now hindered by federal program regulations.

The Secretary also could provide a waiver of any existing program regulation which barred or hampered an existing program from participating in such activity.

The Allied Services Act charts a new course for the delivery of social services. It is a complex reform proposal with many major ramifications for many established groups—government and private—on the federal, state and local levels.

The consideration and eventual passage of this legislation by the Congress would only be a start. At the same time, human service delivery reform would have to be debated all across the country by affected governments and groups, in order to decide how they would make best use of the proposed freedoms and incentives in their particular areas.

This is one more effort by my administration to make government more sensible, more responsive and more effective at the local level—where most citizens actually meet the practical impact of government.

In this important proposal, as in my recommendations for revenue sharing, we would summon forth the creative energies and the local expertise of state and local officials, rather than keeping them strapped in a straitjacket of inflexible federal regulations.

They would be freed—and thus would be challenged—to direct the development of customized, comprehensive social services plans to treat the special needs, resources and desires of their particular areas.

Such efforts should result in government built for people, geared for across-the-board performance, and designed for results rather than bureaucratic ritual.

If we bring this about, we shall not only be providing better social services—we also shall be taking a giant step toward the restoration of the people's confidence in the common sense performance of their government.   RICHARD NIXON

ADDRESS TO CONGRESS

Following is the text, as made available by the White House, of President Nixon's address to a joint session of Congress June 1 immediately on his return from Russia, Iran and Poland.

Your welcome in this great chamber tonight has special meaning for Mrs. Nixon and me. We feel very fortunate to have traveled abroad so often representing the United States. But we both agree after each trip that the best part of any trip abroad is coming home to America again.

During the past 13 days we have flown more than 16,000 miles and visited four countries. Everywhere we went—to Austria, to the Soviet Union, to Iran, to Poland—we could feel the quickening pace of change in old international relationships, and the people's genuine desire for friendship with the American people. Everywhere new hopes are rising for a world no longer shadowed by fear and want and war. As Americans we can be proud that we now have an historic opportunity to play a great role in helping to achieve man's oldest dream—a world in which all nations can enjoy the blessings of peace.

On this journey we saw many memorable sights; but one picture will always remain indelible in our memory—the flag of the United States of America flying high in the spring breeze above Moscow's ancient Kremlin fortress.

To millions of Americans for the past quarter century, the Kremlin has stood for implacable hostility toward all that we cherish. To millions of Russians, the American flag has long been held up as a symbol of evil. No one would have believed, even a short time ago, that those two apparently irreconcilable symbols would be seen together as we saw them for these few days.

This does not mean that we bring back from Moscow the promise of instant peace, but we do bring the beginning of a process that can lead to a lasting peace. That is why I have taken the extraordinary action of requesting this special Joint Session of the Congress—because we have before us an extraordinary opportunity.

I have not come here this evening to make new announcements in a dramatic setting. This summit has already made its news. It has barely begun, however, to make its mark on our world. I ask you to join me tonight—while events are fresh, while the iron is hot—in starting to consider how we can help make that mark what we want it to be.

The foundation has been laid for a new relationship between the two most powerful nations on earth. Now it is up to us—to all of us here in this chamber and to all of us across America—to join with other nations in building a new house upon that foundation—one that can be a home for the hopes of mankind and a shelter against the storms of conflict.

As a preliminary, therefore, to requesting your concurrence in some of the agreements we reached and your approval of funds to carry out others, and also as a keynote for the unity in which the government and this nation must go forward from here, I am rendering this immediate report to the Congress on the results of the Moscow summit.

The pattern of U.S.-Soviet summit diplomacy in the cold war trend is well known. One meeting after another produced a short-lived euphoric mood—the spirit of Geneva, the spirit of Camp David, the spirit of Vienna, the spirit of Glassboro—without producing significant progress on the really difficult issues.

Early in this Administration, therefore, I stated that the prospect of concrete results, not atmospherics, would be our criterion for meeting at the highest level. I also announced our intention to pursue negotiations with the Soviet Union across a broad front of related issues, with the purpose of creating a momentum of achievement in which progress in one area could contribute to progress in others.

This is the basis on which we prepared for and conducted last week's talks. This was a working summit. We sought to establish not a superficial spirit of Moscow, but a solid record of progress on solving the difficult issues which for so long have divided our two nations and the world. Reviewing the number and scope of the agreements that emerged, I think we have accomplished that goal.

Recognizing the responsibility of the advanced industrial nations to set an example in combatting mankind's common enemies, we and the Soviets have agreed to cooperate in efforts to reduce pollution and enhance environmental quality. We have agreed to work together in the field of medical science and public health, particularly in the conquest of cancer and heart disease.

Recognizing that the quest for useful knowledge transcends the differences between ideologies and social systems, we have agreed to expand U.S.-Soviet cooperation in many areas of science and technology.

We have joined in plans for an exciting new adventure in the cooperative exploration of space, which will begin—subject to Congressional approval of funding—with a joint orbital mission of an Apollo vehicle and a Soyuz spacecraft in 1975.

By forming habits of cooperation and strengthening institutional ties in areas of peaceful enterprise, these four agreements will create on both sides a steadily growing vested interest in the maintenance of good relations between our two countries.

Expanded U.S.-Soviet trade will also yield advantages to both of our nations. When the two largest economies in the world start trading with each other on a much larger scale, living standards in both nations will rise, and the stake which both have in peace will be increased.

Progress in this area is proceeding on schedule. At the summit, we established a Joint Commercial Commission which will complete the negotiations for a comprehensive trade agreement between the U.S. and the USSR.

We expect the final terms of such an agreement to be settled, later this year. Two further accords which were reached last week have a much more direct bearing on the search for peace and security.

One is the agreement between the American and Soviet navies aimed at significantly reducing the chances of dangerous incidents between our ships and aircraft at sea.

Second, and most important, there is the treaty and related executive agreement which will limit, for the first time, both offensive and defensive strategic nuclear weapons in the arsenals of the United States and the USSR.

Three-fifths of all the people alive in the world today have spent their whole lifetimes under the shadow of a nuclear war which could be touched off by the arms race among the great powers. Last Friday in Moscow we witnessed the beginning of the end of that era which began in 1945. We took the first step toward a new era of mutually agreed restraint and arms limitations between the two principal nuclear powers.

With this step we have enhanced the security of both nations. We have begun to check the wasteful and dangerous spiral of nuclear arms which has dominated relations between our two countries for a generation. We have begun to reduce the level of fear by reducing the causes of fear, for our two peoples and for all peoples.

The ABM Treaty will be submitted promptly for the Senate's advice and consent to ratification, and the interim agreement on offensive weapons will be submitted to both houses for concurrence. We can undertake agreements as important as these only on a basis of full partnership between the Executive and Legislative branches.

I encourage the fullest national scrutiny of these accords, and I am confident such examination will underscore the truth of what I told the Soviet people on television several nights ago: that this is an agreement in the interest of both nations. From the standpoint of the United States, when we consider what the strategic balance would have looked like later in the Seventies if there had been no arms limitation, it is clear that the agreements forestall a major spiralling of the arms race—one which would have worked to our disadvantage, since we have no current building programs for the categories of weapons frozen, and since no new building program could have produced any new weapons in those categories during the period of the freeze.

I have studied the strategic balance in great detail with my senior advisers for more than three years. I can assure the

Congress and the American people tonight that the present and planned strategic forces of the United States are without question sufficient for the maintenance of our security and the protection of our vital interests.

No power on earth is stronger than the United States of America today. None will be stronger than the United States of America in the future.

This is the only national defense posture which can ever be acceptable to the United States. This is the posture I ask the Senate to protect by approving the arms limitation treaty. And this is the posture which, with the responsible cooperation of the Congress, I will take all necessary steps to maintain in our future defense programs.

In addition to the talks which led to the specific agreements I have listed, I also had full, frank and extensive discussions with General Secretary Brezhnev and his colleagues about several parts of the world where American and Soviet interests have come in conflict.

With regard to the reduction of tensions in Europe, we recorded our intention of proceeding later this year with multilateral consultations looking toward a conference on security and cooperation in Europe. We have also jointly agreed to move forward with negotiations on mutual and balanced force reductions in central Europe.

The problem of ending the Vietnam war, which engages the hopes of all Americans, was one of the most extensively discussed subjects of our agenda. It would only jeopardize the search for peace if I were to review here all that was said on that subject. I will simply say this: each side obviously has its own point of view and its own approach to this very difficult issue. But at the same time, both the United States and the Soviet Union share an overriding desire to achieve a more stable peace in the world. I emphasize to you once again that this Administration has no higher goal than bringing the Vietnam war to an early and honorable end. We are ending the war in Vietnam, but we shall end it in a way which will not betray our friends, risk the lives of the courageous Americans still serving in Vietnam, break faith with those held prisoners, or stain the honor of the United States.

Our summit conversations about the Middle East situation were also full, frank, and extensive. I reiterated the American people's commitment to the survival of Israel and to a settlement just to all the countries in the area. Both sides stated in the communique their intention to support the Jarring peace mission and other appropriate efforts to achieve this objective.

The final achievement of the Moscow conference was the signing of a landmark declaration entitled "basic principles of mutual relations between the United States and the USSR". As these twelve basic principles are put into practice, they can provide a solid framework for the future development of American-Soviet relations.

They begin with the recognition that two nuclear nations, each of which has the power to destroy humanity, have no alternative but to coexist peacefully—because in a nuclear war there would be no winners, only losers.

The basic principles commit both sides to avoid direct military confrontation and to exercise constructive leadership and restraint with respect to small conflicts which could drag the major powers into war.

They disavow any intention to create spheres of influence or to conspire against the interests of any other nation—a point I would underscore by saying once again tonight that America values its ties with all nations—from our oldest allies in Europe and Asia, as I emphasized by my visit to Iran, to our good friends in the third world, to our new relationship with the People's Republic of China.

The improvement of relations depends not only on words but on actions. The principles to which we agreed in Moscow are like a road map. Now that the map has been laid out, it is up to each country to follow it. The United States intends to adhere to these principles. The leaders of the USSR have indicated a similar intention.

However, we must remember that Soviet ideology still proclaim hostility to some of America' most basic values. The Soviet leaders remain committed to that ideology. Like the nation they lead, they are and will continue to be totally dedicated competitors of the United States.

As we shape our policies for the period ahead, therefore, we must maintain our defenses at an adequate level until there is mutual agreement to limit forces. The time-tested policies of vigilance and firmness which brought us to the Summit are the only ones that can safely carry us forward to further progress in reaching agreements to reduce the danger of war.

Our successes in the strategic arms talks and in the Berlin negotiations, which opened the road to Moscow, came about because over the past three years we have consistently refused proposals for unilaterally abandoning the ABM, unilaterally pulling back our forces from Europe, and drastically cutting the defense budget. The Congress deserves the appreciation of the American people for having the courage to vote such proposals down and to maintain the strength America needs to protect its interests.

As we continue the strategic arms talks, seeking a permanent offensive weapons treaty we must bear the lessons of the earlier talks well in mind.

By the same token, we must stand steadfastly with our NATO partners if negotiations leading to a new detente and mutual reduction of forces in Europe are to be productive. Maintaining the strength, integrity and steadfastness of our free world alliances is the foundation on which all of our other initiatives for peace and security in the world must rest. As we seek better relations with those who have been our adversaries, we will not let our friends and allies down.

We must keep our own economy vigorous and competitive if the opening for greater East-West trade is to mean anything, and if we do not wish to be shouldered aside in world markets by the growing potential of the economies of Japan, Western Europe, the USSR, and the People's Republic of China. For America to continue its role of helping to build a more peaceful world, we must keep America number one economically in the world.

We must maintain our own momentum of domestic innovation, growth, and reform if the opportunities for joint action with the Soviets are to fulfill their promise. As we seek agreements to build peace abroad, we must keep America moving forward at home.

Most importantly, if the new age we seek is ever to become a reality, we must keep America strong in spirit—a nation proud of its greatness as a free society and confident of its mission in the world. Let us be committed to our way of life as wholeheartedly as the Communist leaders with whom we seek a new relationship are committed to their system. Let us always be proud to show in our words and actions what we know in our hearts—that we believe in America.

These are the challenges of peace. They are in some ways more difficult than those of war. But we are equal to them. As we meet them, we will be able to go forward and explore the sweeping possibilities for peace which this season of summits has now opened up for the world.

For decades America has been locked in hostile confrontation with the two great Communist powers, the Soviet Union and the People's Republic of China. We were engaged with the one at many points and almost totally isolated from the other, but our relationships with both had reached a deadly impasse. All three countries were victims of the kind of bondage about which George Washington long ago warned: "The nation which indulges toward another in habitual hatred is a slave to its own animosity."

But now in the brief space of four months, these journeys to Peking and to Moscow have begun to free us from perpetual confrontation. We have moved toward better understanding, mutual respect, and point-by-point settlement of differences with both of the major Communist powers.

This one series of meetings has not rendered an imperfect world suddenly perfect. There still are deep philosophical differences, and there still are parts of the world in which age-old hatreds persist. The threat of war has not been eliminated—but it has been reduced. Now we are making progress toward a world in which leaders of nations will settle their differences by negotiation, not by force; and in which they learn to live with their differences so that their sons will not have to die for them.

It was particularly fitting that this trip, aimed at building such a world, should have concluded in Poland.

No country in the world has suffered more from war than Poland has—no country has more to gain from peace. The faces of the people who gave us such a heartwarming welcome in Warsaw yesterday told an eloquent story of suffering in the past and of hope for peace in the future. It made me more determined than ever that America must do all in its power to help that hope come true for all people.

As we continue that effort, our unity of purpose and action will be all-important.

For the summits of 1972 have not belonged just to one person or to one party or to one branch of our government alone. Rather they are part of a great national journey for peace. Every American can claim a share in the credit for the success of that journey so far; every American has a major stake in its success for the future.

An unparalleled opportunity has been placed in America's hands. Never has there been a time when hope was more justified or when complacency was more dangerous. We have made a good beginning. And because we have begun, history now lays upon us a special obligation to see it through. We can seize this moment or lose it; we can make good this opportunity to build a new structure of peace in the world, or let it slip away. Together, therefore, let us seize the moment so that our children and the world's children, live free of the fears and free of the hatreds that have been the lot of mankind through the centuries.

Then the historians of a future age will write of 1972, not that this was the year America went up to the summit and then down to the valley again—but that this was the year when America helped to lead the world up out of the lowlands of constant war, and onto the high plateau of lasting peace.

DISASTER RELIEF

Following is the text, as made available by the White House, of President Nixon's July 17 message to Congress seeking relief for victims of tropical storm Agnes.

TO THE CONGRESS OF THE UNITED STATES:

Tropical storm Agnes has caused unparalleled destruction in many areas of the eastern United States. More than 128,000 homes and businesses have been damaged or destroyed, and whole communities have been dealt a heavy blow. The losses to so many individuals cannot be measured only in terms of destruction of property and belongings; they must also be counted in terms of loss of jobs, disruption of families, personal privation, and anxiety about the future. In the whole history of our Nation, we have not before encountered such massive destruction over so wide-spread an area as a result of natural disaster.

Individuals, private groups and governments have responded magnificently to this calamity in the finest tradition of neighbor helping neighbors. The stamina, the courage and the spirit to fight back and recover are already evident throughout the devastated areas. My statement of July 12, 1972, summarized these impressive efforts. I also pointed out at that time, however, that an unparalleled disaster requires extraordinary measures to help in recovery. I announced my intention to recommend to the Congress supplementary and massive measures aimed at short and long-term recovery. I herewith transmit those recommendations, and the proposed legislation to carry them out.

My proposals are in three parts.

First, I propose the Agnes Recovery Act of 1972. This measure deals with disaster loans for homeowners, farmers and businessmen. Because of the unprecedented scope of the destruction, unprecedented measures to deal with it are required. Under the provisions of this proposal, disaster loans for Agnes victims would be changed from present law in the following ways:

• The maximum amount of principal which can be cancelled or forgiven would be increased from $2,500 to $5,000 on loans made by the Small Business Administration or the Farmers Home Administration.

• The forgiveness feature would be applicable to the first dollar of a loan rather than after the repayment of the first $500 of principal as is now the case.

• The interest rate on the loans would be dropped to 1 percent instead of its current rate of 5-1/8 percent.

This liberalized assistance to individual homeowners and small businessmen can mean the difference between recovery and bankruptcy or ruin. The situation is urgent. Individual people are now making decisions on whether to rebuild or not. While my proposal would apply retroactively to all victims of Agnes, it is important to them to know now the terms of assistance which will be available to them.

Therefore, I call on the Congress to respond to this emergency by acting on the Agnes Recovery Act so that it can become law within one week.

Second, I recommend supplemental appropriations totaling $1,569,800,000 for this emergency, the largest single request of its kind in our history. The vast majority of these funds would be used for disaster loans, with $1.3-billion for the Small Business Administration and $1.8-million for the Farmers Home Administration. The SBA funds would be used to provide loans for homeowners and small businessmen in disaster areas whose property has been damaged or destroyed. The FHA funds would provide sufficient personnel to process expeditiously loan requests in rural areas, for which adequate loan funds now exist. Also included in my supplemental request are:

• An additional $200-million for the President's Disaster Relief Fund, to speed repair and reconstruction of public facilities and to provide temporary housing, food and unemployment compensation.

• $40-million for the Economic Development Administration, $16-million for the Appalachian Regional Commission and $12-million for the Corps of Engineers, all to assist in the recovery of damaged communities. The funds for the Corps of Engineers would go toward flood control projects in the Susquehanna River Basin.

Third, I recommend that the existing authorization for appropriations for highway emergency relief be increased by $200-million. Current authority limits amounts to $50-million per year, which is clearly not adequate to cope with a disaster of this magnitude.

I urge that the Congress also act promptly on these second and third proposals.

The Federal Government must act quickly and decisively to do its part in providing relief and aiding recovery in a cooperative effort with the States and communities struck by Agnes. We can do no less. I am confident that the Congress will share this view.

RICHARD NIXON

PRESIDENT'S MESSAGE ON SPENDING

Following is the text, as made available by the White House, of President Nixon's July 26 special message to Congress.

TO THE CONGRESS OF THE UNITED STATES:

This is an urgent appeal for the Congress to join with me to avoid higher taxes, higher prices and a cut in purchasing power for everyone in the Nation.

Just when we have succeeded in cutting the rate of inflation in half, and just when we have succeeded in making it possible for America's workers to score their largest real spendable income gains in eight years, this tangible, pocketbook progress may be wiped out by proposed excessive spending.

Specifically, Federal spending for the fiscal year 1973 (which began on July 1, 1972) already is estimated to be almost $7 billion higher than was planned in my budget.

That figure by itself is bad enough. But even more spending beyond the budget—and beyond emergency flood relief funds —appears to be on the way.

The inevitable result would be higher taxes and more income-eating inflation in the form of higher prices.

I am convinced the American people do not want their family budgets wrecked by higher taxes and higher prices, and I will not stand by and permit such irresponsible action to undermine the clear progress we have made in getting America's workers off the inflation treadmill of the 1960's.

While specific Federal programs are important to many people and constituent groups, none is more important to all the American tax-payers than a concerted program to hold down the rate of taxes and the cost of living.

In view of this serious threat I again urge the Congress—in the economic interest of all American citizens—to enact a spending ceiling of $250 billion. I urgently recommended a spending ceiling when I submitted the fiscal 1973 budget earlier this year.

Our concern with sustaining the increasing purchasing power of all the people requires and demands such responsible action. Our concern with the cost of living requires and demands such responsible action. Our determination to avoid higher taxes requires and demands such action. The basic fiscal integrity of the Nation requires and demands such action.

At fault is the hoary and traditional procedure of the Congress, which now permits action on the various spending programs as if they were unrelated and independent actions. What we should have—and what I again seek today—is that an annual spending ceiling be set first, and that individual program allocations then be tailored to that ceiling. This is the anti-inflationary method I use in designing the Federal budget.

The present Congressional system of independent, unrelated actions on various spending programs means that the Congress arrives at total Federal spending in an accidental, haphazard manner. That is no longer good enough procedure for the American people, who now realize that their hard-won economic gains against inflation are threatened by every deficit spending bill— no matter how attractive the subject matter of that bill might be. And there are impressive gains which I am committed to help guard:

• We have achieved a substantial success in our battle against the inflation we inherited in 1969. Instead of the more than 6 percent of 1969, we are now down to a rate of 2.9 percent per year. Inflation has been cut in half.

• We have cut the personal income tax so that a family of four with an income of $5,000 has had its individual income taxes reduced by 66 percent since 1969, and a family of four with an income of $10,000 has had its income tax reduced by 26 percent since that date.

• We have thus brought about conditions in which real, spendable weekly earnings have risen four percent in the last year, the largest such gain since 1964.

If we permit unbridled increases in Federal spending to go on month after month, however, we are in real danger of losing the advantages of the tax cuts and our victories in the battle against inflation.

These are the compelling reasons which require me to ask again in the most urgent and explicit language I can frame that the Congress enact at the earliest possible opportunity a spending ceiling—without loopholes or exceptions—to force Government spending back to the $250 billion level in fiscal year 1973.

I again remind the Congress of the situation I cited last January, when I submitted the fiscal year 1973 budget:

"It will be a job-creating budget and a non-inflationary budget only if spending is limited to the amount the tax system would produce if the economy were operating at full employment."

"Those who increase spending beyond that amount will be responsible for causing more inflation."

Since that time, various Congressional actions and inactions have heavily underscored all of the reasons I then made for speedy passage of a spending ceiling.

Such a ceiling cannot be completely effective unless the Congress enacts it as I have requested—without exceptions and without loopholes. But if the Congress fails to do this, I do not propose to sit by and silently watch individual family budgets destroyed by rising prices and rising taxes—the inevitable end to spending of this magnitude.

With or without the cooperation of the Congress, I am going to do everything within my power to prevent such a fiscal crisis for millions of our people.

Let there be no misunderstanding: If bills come to my desk calling for excessive spending which threatens the Federal budget, I will veto them.

It is now generally recognized that the national economy is in a period of vigorous expansion. The Gross National Product soared at an annual growth rate of 8.9 percent in the second quarter of the year—the best such increase since 1965. About 2-1/2 million additional civilian jobs have been added in the last year.

We do not plan to reduce or restrict the very substantial fiscal stimulation we have already provided. But further massive Federal stimulation of the economy at this time—whatever its superficial political attractiveness—is certain to lead to the kind of inflation that even wage-price control machinery would find impossible to restrain.

In other words, the American people will have to pay, and pay quickly, for excessive Federal spending—either by higher taxes or by higher consumer prices, or both. Such an intolerable burden would shortly cause an end to the period of economic growth on which we are embarked.

There are desirable features in some of the individual bills now pending in the Congress, but to them have been attached some very excessive spending proposals.

The Federal Government cannot do everything that might be desirable. Hard choices must be made by the Congress in the national interest, just as a family must decide what it will buy with the money it has. Moreover, the experience of the past decade proved that merely throwing money at problems does not automatically or necessarily solve the problems.

I have every confidence that the American people, in this era of wide public awareness of inflation and wide public opposition to its clear causes, understand these realities about Federal spending.

I believe that all of us, the President and the Congress, have a clear duty to protect the national interest in general prosperity—and therefore to resist temptations to over-spend for desirable special programs, or to spend for partisan political advantage.

I favor and have submitted to the Congress responsible and effective programs designed to cleanse the air, to purify the water, to develop and preserve rural America, to improve education, and for many other worthy purposes. No individual and no political party has a monopoly on its concern for the people, individually and in groups. But I am required always to ask:

What is best for all the people? What are the hard choices that must be made so that the general welfare is secured? Of what use is it for us to pass these measures, and more, if they are going to destroy the family budget by higher prices and more taxes?

No matter what the political pressures, no matter how frequently I may be told that in an election year a President cannot veto a spending measure, I will simply not let reckless spending of this kind destroy the tax reductions we have secured and the hard-won successes we have earned in the battle against inflation. I intend to continue to do my utmost to preserve the American family budget and to protect it from the ravages of higher taxes and inflation.

The time for fiscal discipline has long since come. The threat demands bold and difficult decisions. Let the Congress make them now.

RICHARD NIXON

LABOR-HEW VETO

Following is the text, as made available by the White House, of President Nixon's Aug. 16 message to the House vetoing HR 15417, the Labor-HEW appropriations bill for fiscal 1973.

TO THE HOUSE OF REPRESENTATIVES:

Today, I must return without my approval HR 15417, the appropriations bill for the Department of Labor, the Department of Health, Education and Welfare and certain related agencies. Exceeding my budget recommendations by $1.8-billion, this bill is a perfect example of that kind of reckless Federal spending that just cannot be done without more taxes or more inflation, both of which I am determined to avoid.

Moreover, the bill fails to include a limitation on Federal matching payments for social services for public assistance recipients, although such a limitation was passed by the Senate. Because this is currently an open-ended program, this Congressional inaction could require a later supplemental reaching as high as $3.5-billion. By increasing the face amount of the bill on the one hand and failing to place a limitation on payments for social services on the other, the Congress has produced a budget overrun that could exceed $5-billion.

Purchasing Power

Inherent in this kind of spending, but not publicly specified by its sponsors, is a cut in purchasing power for every American family. No program has a higher priority than continued expansion of the purchasing power of all the people.

As I said in my special message of July 26: "I do not propose to sit by and silently watch individual family budgets destroyed by rising prices and rising taxes—the inevitable end to spending of this magnitude." Our mounting economic resurgence is at stake and I mean to protect it.

We have cut inflation in half, but spending such as this bill would clearly undermine that progress.

We have reduced Federal income taxes by 26 percent for a family of four making $10,000 a year but spending such as this would undermine that progress.

We have achieved conditions in which the purchasing power of the average production worker with three dependents has gained four percent in one year, the best increase since 1964, but spending such as this would undermine that progress.

What the Congress has done is to take my ample and carefully considered 1973 budget proposals and balloon them to fiscally dangerous dimensions.

This Administration is second to none in its concern for America's health, education and manpower program needs. From the very beginning we have consistently proposed and supported desirable programs in both the health research and health services areas, and we will continue to do so. For example, we proposed—and in November of 1971 I signed into law— the most comprehensive health manpower legislation in the Nation's history. This Administration launched the first separate Federal effort to combat sickle cell anemia. We have nearly doubled the Federal commitment to finding a cure for cancer. We have also proposed fundamental reform of education and manpower training programs coupled with recommendations for

major fund allocations for education revenue sharing, emergency school assistance and public service jobs.

The failure of the Congress to use balance and restraint in the framing of HR 15417 has turned it into a big-spending measure that impairs the Nation's economic health.

The budget request that I submitted to the Congress proposed an increase of $2.1-billion for the HEW programs contained in this bill. That addition permits substantial expansion over the fiscal year 1972 level while recognizing competing priorities in other areas and the necessary discipline of keeping total Federal spending within the limit of full employment revenues.

The Congress would add to my proposals $1.8-billion in new spending authority. Increases of this magnitude are clearly excessive and must be revised.

Aside from increasing the face amount of this bill to unacceptable levels, the Congress, as I have previously noted, threatens to bring on a separate fiscal crisis of a dimention involving billions of dollars by its continuing inaction with regard to the social services program of HEW. Under this program the Federal Government provides matching funds, on a three-to-one basis, for social services provided by the States for past, current and potential public assistance recipients.

Spending Limit

As I have previously proposed on several occasions, the Congress should place a ceiling on spending for this program which is now openended and not subject to any effective control by the Federal Government. But HR 15417 does not contain such a cutoff.

We now provide matching money for whatever amounts of services the States choose to provide. Since the authorizing legislation for the social services programs is vaguely written, the States have been able to include services far beyond what the Congress must have originally intended.

The result amounts to opening up a trap-door in the Federal Treasury through which billions are now flowing and through which more billions will pour unless the Congress enacts a specific limitation.

The rate of increase has been quickening. From 1970 to 1971, expenditures rose 37 percent. In 1972, they more than doubled—shooting up to more than $1.9-billion. In 1973, they threaten to more than double again as State claims approach $5-billion.

Elementary fiscal responsibility demands that this loophole for unlimited Federal funds for undefined services must be closed now. The Congress must harness this multi-billion-dollar runaway program by enacting a social services spending ceiling.

I also urge that the Congress, in drawing up a new measure, provide that the line items in the bill should not, in the aggregate, exceed my budget request. This could be accomplished either by revising the recommendations for each of the items, or by including a general provision in the bill which would limit spending to this overall aggregate amount.

I know the usual practice is to repass such a bill with a slight reduction and assume that the second bill will have to be signed.

Such action would obviously not satisfy the objections to this measure I have set forth here.

In returning this measure without my approval, I again urge the Congress to join with me to avoid higher taxes, higher prices and a resulting cut in purchasing power for the American people by enacting a general spending ceiling of $250-billion. That action would get us away from this Congressional creditcard approach to Government finances—an approach that will add up to bad news for everybody when the eventual and inevitable bills must be paid.

RICHARD NIXON

WILDERNESS AREAS MESSAGE

Following is the text, as made available by the White House, of President Nixon's Sept. 21 message to Congress proposing the inclusion of 16 areas in the National Wilderness Preservation System.

TO THE CONGRESS OF THE UNITED STATES:

Everywhere in America, we seek the horizons where escape is free and where despair can never catch up. We sense that our wilderness, more than a concept, is an experience, where we may find something of ourselves and of our world that we might never have known to exist.

Wide-winged birds soaring over remote treetops can set our dreams in new directions. Serrated cliffs can tell us about our geological past. Mountain flowers beside woodland trails can teach us vital lessons about our ecological relationships. Sea winds blowing across lonely beaches can refresh us for new accomplishments.

It is a prime objective of government to balance the use of land sensibly to ensure that the world of nature is preserved along with the world of man.

"A wilderness..." according to the epochal Wilderness Act of 1964, "is hereby recognized as an area where the earth and its community of life are untrammeled by man, where man himself is a visitor who does not remain." Within the National Wilderness Preservation System established by this act, the first 9.1 million acres of our country were set aside, to be conserved, unimpaired, in their natural state.

Today, I am proposing to the Congress 16 new wilderness areas which, if approved, would add 3.5 million acres to our wilderness system. This is the largest single incremental increase in the system since passage of the act.

Five would be located in our National Wildlife Refuge Areas. They are the Brigantine National Wildlife Refuge in New Jersey, the Blackbeard Island National Wildlife Refuge in Georgia, the Chassahowitzka National Wildlife Refuge in Florida, and the Lostwood National Wildlife Refuge and the Chase Lake National Wildlife Refuge in North Dakota. A sixth area, administered by the National Park Service, would be within the Cumberland Gap National Historical Park on the borders of Tennessee, Virginia, and Kentucky. These six additions would add 40,257 acres to the Wilderness Preservation System.

In the Western States, in units administered by the National Park Service, my proposals today would designate as wilderness 2,016,181 acres in Yellowstone National Park, 512,870 in the Grand Canyon complex, 646,700 acres in Yosemite National Park, and 115,807 acres in Grand Teton National Park.

I further propose for inclusion in our National Wilderness Preservation System an additional 216,519 acres in some of the most beautiful regions of our country. These would include designated areas in the Great Sand Dunes National Monument in Colorado, the Theodore Roosevelt National Memorial Park in North Dakota, the Badlands National Monument in South Dakota, the Guadalupe Mountains National Park in Texas, the Carlsbad Caverns National Park in New Mexico and the Haleakala National Park in Hawaii.

The 1964 Wilderness Act further directed the Secretaries of Agriculture and of the Interior to review federally owned lands which they administer and to report to the President, who transmits to the Congress their and his recommendations for those areas which qualify as wilderness as defined by the act. This wilderness review process, to be conducted in three phases, was to be completed by 1974.

Beginning in 1969, I accelerated this program, and on April 28, 1971, I forwarded to the Congress 14 new wilderness proposals which, when enacted, would substantially increase the acreage added since passage of the Wilderness Act. I warned that we would need redoubled effort by the Departments of Agriculture and the Interior in completing the review process and prompt action on these proposals by the Congress.

On February 8, 1972, I transmitted a second package of 18 new wilderness proposals to the Congress, which, if enacted, would designate 1.3 million additional acres as wilderness. At that time I reported that the September, 1974 statutory deadline for reviews could and would be met. I also pointed out that the majority of the wilderness areas recommended to date had involved western lands. Therefore, I directed the Secretaries of Agriculture and Interior to accelerate the identification of areas in the Eastern United States having wilderness potential.

The Congress has now received 78 wilderness proposals which would add 5.8 million acres to the original 9.1 million acres designated by the Congress.

To date, however, the Congress has acted on only 35 proposals, approving 1.7 million acres for inclusion in the system. This leaves pending 43 wilderness proposals encompassing 4.1 million acres.

I now urge the Congress—in this centennial year of our National Park System—to act quickly in favor of these new proposals as well as the ones already pending.

I am aware of the commercial opportunities in potential wilderness areas such as mining, lumbering, and recreational development. I believe we must achieve a sensible land use balance—America can have economic growth *and* the unspoiled nature of the wilderness.

Increasingly, in fact, the preservation of these areas has become a major goal of all Americans. The process of developing wilderness proposals is now exemplifying public participation and cooperation with the governmental process. Commercial and conservation groups—and individuals from all over the country—have, through public hearings and direct contact with government agencies, done much more than is generally realized to contribute to the wilderness program.

I believe the value of this cooperative effort between the public and their government officials is reflected in the wilderness proposals I am proud to submit today. This is an excellent example of the responsive way in which our government is meant to work.

The first man on earth, according to the scriptures was placed in a natural garden, and he was charged "to dress it and keep it." Our own great naturalist John Muir said that our "whole continent was a garden and...seemed to be favored above all the other wild parks and gardens of the globe."

The addition of these new areas to our national wilderness system will help to keep it that way.

RICHARD NIXON

WATER POLLUTION VETO

Following is the text, as made available by the White House, of President Nixon's Oct. 16 message to the Senate vetoing S 2770, the Federal Water Pollution Control Act Amendments of 1972.

TO THE SENATE OF THE UNITED STATES:

The pollution of our rivers, lakes and streams degrades the quality of American life. Cleaning up the Nation's waterways is a matter of urgent concern to me, as evidenced by the nearly tenfold increase in my budget for this purpose during the past four years.

I am also concerned, however, that we attack pollution in a way that does not ignore other very real threats to the quality of life, such as spiraling prices and increasingly onerous taxes. Legislation which would continue our efforts to raise water quality, but which would do so through extreme and needless overspending, does not serve the public interest. There is a much better way to get this job done.

For this reason, I am compelled to withhold my approval from S 2770, the Federal Water Pollution Control Act Amendments of 1972—a bill whose laudable intent is outweighed by its unconscionable $24 billion price tag. My proposed legislation, as reflected in my budget, provided sufficient funds to fulfill that same intent in a fiscally responsible manner. Unfortunately the Congress ignored our other vital national concerns and broke the budget with this legislation.

Environmental protection has been one of my highest priorities as President. The record speaks for itself. With the Council on Environmental Quality and the Environmental Protection Agency, we have established a strong new framework for developing and administering forceful programs in this problem area. I have proposed more than 25 far-reaching laws to deal with threats to the environment; most still await final action in the Congress. Pending enactment of new legislation, our enforcement agencies have cracked down on polluters under old laws seldom enforced by previous administrations.

The budget authority which I have requested for pollution control and abatement in fiscal year 1973 is more than four times the amount requested in 1969. Federal grants for local sewage treatment plant construction have increased almost tenfold, from an annual rate of $214 million appropriated up to the time I took office, to $2 billion in my budget for 1973. This dramatic growth in the share of Federal Government resources being devoted to the environment exceeds, many times over, the rate of increase for funds in most other major government programs.

Every environmental spending increase that I have proposed, however, has been within the strict discipline of a responsible fiscal policy—*a policy which recognizes as the highest national priority the need to protect the working men and women of America against tax increases and renewed inflation.* Specifically, the water pollution control bill which I originally sent to the Congress last year was fully consistent with the concept of a balanced, full-employment budget. It would have committed $6-billion in Federal funds over a three-year period, enough to continue and accelerate the momentum toward that high standard of cleanliness which all of us want in America's waters.

By contrast, the bill which has now come to my desk would provide for the commitment of a staggering, budget-wrecking $24 billion. Every extra dollar which S 2770 contemplates spending beyond the level of my budget proposals would exact a price from the consumer in the form of inflated living costs, or from the taxpayer in the form of a new Federal tax bite, or both.

Ironically, however, only a portion of the $18 billion by which my bill was fattened on Capitol Hill would actually go to buy more pollution control than the Administration bill would have done. One backward-looking provision, for example, would provide $750 million to reimburse State and local governments for work already completed on sewage treatment pants *between 1956 and 1966.* The precedent this would set for retroactive reimbursement in other matching grant programs is an invitation to fiscal chaos. Another provision would raise the Federal share of the cost of future facilities from 55 percent to 75 percent. Neither of these costly actions would, in any real sense, make our waters any cleaner: they would simply increase the burden on the Federal taxpayer.

There is a well-worn political axiom which says that any election year spending bill, no matter how ill-advised, defies veto by the President. But I say that any spending bill this year which would lead to higher prices and higher taxes defies signature by this President. I have nailed my colors to the mast on this issue; the political winds can blow where they may.

I am prepared for the possibility that my action on this bill will be overridden. The defeat of my proposal for a spending ceiling showed that many Senators and Congressmen are simply AWOL in our fight against higher taxes. And some have been lured to the wrong side of the fight by the false glitter of public works money for their districts or states. They seem to forget that it is their constituents' pockets from which the higher taxes must come as a result of their votes this week. Others, to their great credit, voted for the spending limit to try to hold taxes down. Taxpayers must be sad to learn that a majority are charge account Congressmen.

If this veto is not sustained, however, let the issue be clearly drawn. As with the spending ceiling, so with this bill, a vote to sustain the veto is a vote against a tax increase. A vote to override the veto is a vote to increase the likelihood of higher taxes.

Even if this bill is rammed into law over the better judgment of the Executive—even if the Congress defaults its obligation to the taxpayers—I shall not default mine. Certain provisions of S 2770 confer a measure of spending discretion and flexibility upon the President, and if forced to administer this legislation I mean to use those provisions to put the brakes on budget-wrecking expenditures as much as possible.

But the law would still exact an unfair and unnecessary price from the public. For I am convinced, on the basis of 26 years' experience with the political realities here in Washington, that the pressure for full funding under this bill would be so intense that funds approaching the maximum authorized amount could ultimately be claimed and paid out, no matter what technical controls the bill appears to grant the Executive.

I still hope, with millions of taxpayers, that at least one-third plus one of the members in one House will be responsible enough to vote for the public interest and sustain this veto. It should be noted that doing so would by no means terminate the existing Federal water quality programs, because the Environmental Protection Agency will continue to operate those programs until the merits of a new water bill can be dealt with as a first order of business in the new Congress.

I look forward to cooperating with the next Congress on a prudent bill, to achieve ends on which we are mutually agreed, and by means which I trust will take better account than S 2770 did of the working men and women who must ultimately pay the bill for environmental quality.

RICHARD NIXON

OCT. 21 VETO MESSAGE

I am withholding my approval from H.R. 56.

My objections to this bill are centered upon two of its titles which would establish a National Environmental Data System and create environmental centers in each State. While both of these titles sound desirable in theory, they would in reality lead to the duplication of information or would produce results unrelated to real needs and wasteful of talent, resources, and the taxpayers' money.

A third portion of H.R. 56 would direct the Federal Government to purchase the Klamath Indian Forest lands in Oregon. After studying this proposal carefully, I believe this purchase would be sound public policy, and if the next Congress provides the necessary funds, I shall happily approve the acquisition of these unique lands.

In the form now before me, Title I of this legislation calls for the establishment of an independent, centralized environmental data system for the acquisition, storage and dissemination of information relating to the environment. Data for the system would come from governmental, international and private sources. A Director, who would be under the guidance of the Council on Environmental Quality, would determine what data would actually be placed in the system and who would have access to the data.

I believe there are serious drawbacks to such a data system which would outweigh potential benefits. The collection of data and statistics on the supposition that some day they may be useful is in itself a highly dubious exercise. Data, taken out of the context of the questions they were specifically designed to answer, can even contribute to confusion or be misleading.

With this in mind, I believe the centralized collection of environmental data should be related to specific policies and programs. H.R. 56 fails to provide such a relationship and the question of whether this basic deficiency can be overcome, and a useful centralized system designed, is now under study by the Administration. In the meantime, the Environmental Protection Agency and other agencies have consistently worked to strengthen the acquisition and exchange of such data and this effort will continue.

Title II of this legislation authorizes the establishment of environmental centers in every State to conduct research in pollution, natural resource management, and other local, State or regional problems. The centers would also train environmental professionals and carry out a comprehensive education program.

Research is a vital part of our effort to come to grips with the environmental problems we face. This Administration is currently spending literally hundreds of millions of dollars through directed research efforts sponsored by the Environmental Protection Agency, the Department of the Interior, the National Oceanic and Atmospheric Administration, the Department of Agriculture, and the Department of Health, Education and Welfare—to name but a few. We will continue these programs and institute others where they are needed.

Academic talent and resources have a vital role to play in the success of our environmental research programs. As members of the academic community know, grants for research are awarded on the basis of not only the merits of the project, but also the capabilities of the institution to carry out its responsibilities. By creating research centers on a rigid State-by-State basis, and requiring that each be funded, the Congress is asking us to throw away our priorities and to fund programs regardless of their merits and in spite of the limited capabilities of some institutions. Equally important, this approach also ignores the competence and available capacity of already existing institutions and laboratories to carry out this vital research.

Further, I share the view of the Administrator of the Environmental Protection Agency that environmental problems are essentially national in scope, and that most problems, even though they may appear to be local in nature, really affect many other States and localities as well. To the extent there may be local problems, our present project-by-project approach in research can be used to marshal the best scientific talents, wherever they are located, to deal with such problems. Thus, there is clearly no justification for establishing up to 51 new environmental centers specifically charged with investigation of State and local environmental problems.

Titles III and IV of the bill direct the Secretary of Agriculture to purchase a tract of 113,000 acres in the Klamath Indian Forest in Oregon. I believe that acquisition of this forest area would mark a significant and worthwhile addition to our National Forest System while, at the same time, assuring full environmental protection to this scenic part of Oregon.

RICHARD NIXON

OCT. 27 VETO MESSAGE

I have promised the American people that I will do everything in my power to avoid the need for a tax increase next year. Today, I take another important step in the fulfillment of that sincere pledge.

This effort really began last January, when I submitted the Federal Budget for fiscal year 1973 to the Congress. As I explained at the time, that budget was carefully prepared so that all justified Federal programs could be provided without any need for higher taxes and without causing higher prices.

When it became clear that the Congress was exceeding the budget in many bills, I proposed that a spending ceiling of $250 billion be adopted as insurance against a 1973 tax increase.

The Congress rejected that spending ceiling. Instead, it approved spending far in excess of my no-new-taxes budget.

Some of these bills have presented very difficult decisions about whether to sign or to veto. A number of them have attractive features, or would serve very worthwhile purposes—and of course I have received strong advice that to veto them just a few days before the Presidential election would be politically very damaging.

However, in this memorandum are nine measures which I cannot sign without breaking my promise to the American people that I will do all in my power to avoid the necessity of a tax increase next year.

I made that promise in good faith, and I believe in keeping the promises I make—and in making only those promises that I am confident I can keep.

If I were to sign these measures into law, I would, in effect, be making promises that could not be kept—since the funds required to finance the promised services are not available, and would not be available without the higher taxes I have promised to resist.

I believe that political leaders must lay the facts on the line, to talk straight to the people and to deliver on the promises they make to the people.

Although the choices are not easy, I am withholding my approval from 9 Congressional spending programs that would breach the budget by $750 million in fiscal year 1973 and by nearly $2 billion in fiscal year 1974.

Each of these measures by itself might seem justifiable, or even highly desirable. But the hard fact is that they cannot be considered by themselves; each has to be considered in the broader context of the total budget—in terms of how that total weighs on the taxpayers, and how it affects the struggle to curb rising prices.

I am withholding my approval from the following bills:

Labor-HEW and Related Agencies Appropriation Act (H.R. 16654).

This is the second time I have vetoed inflated appropriations this year for the Department of Health, Education and Welfare. This amounts to a textbook example of the seeming inability or unwillingness of the Congress to follow a prudent and responsible spending policy. In my budget for fiscal year 1973, I requested that the Congress provide an increase of $2.1 billion over fiscal 1972 funds for the HEW programs contained in this bill. On top of that generous increase—which would have provided substantial expansion while recognizing competing priorities in other program areas—the Congress amassed a budget-breaking additional increase of $1.8 billion. I vetoed this in August because it was clearly excessive and unwarranted.

The bill now before me contains the same face amount as the measure I previously vetoed. In a partial concession to that veto, however, H.R. 16654 contains authority for the overspending to be held to $535 million—a result that would still amount to pressure for higher taxes.

This Administration is second to none in its demonstrated concern and clear accomplishments in health, education and manpower matters. My budget represented a balanced and rational approach to the funding of many high priority domestic programs in a time of tight budget resources, while continuing this Administration's shift of priorities and funds toward the human resources activities of the Government.

H.R. 16654 is as unwarranted as the version I vetoed last August.

Public Works and Economic Development Act Amendments of 1972 (H.R. 16071).

This bill would unnecessarily add vast new authorizations for Federal programs which have been shown to be ineffective in creating jobs or stimulating timely economic development. Public works projects have notoriously long lead times—so by the time this spending became fully effective, the need for such stimulation would be passed and the stimulation would be inflationary.

The bill would stimulate increased bureaucracy in the regional commissions by using them as a funding rather than a planning and coordinating level of Government.

It would also provide assistance to workers and firms affected by Federal environmental actions. These provisions would be highly inequitable and almost impossible to administer. The unemployment benefits provision would fragment and undermine our basic Federal-State unemployment insurance system and its costs would be essentially uncontrollable. The proposed pollution control facilities loan program has only vague and unspecified objectives.

Amendments to the Mining and Mineral Policy Act (S. 635).

This bill would authorize the Secretary of the Interior to provide matching categorical grants to establish and support a mineral research and training institute in each of the 50 States and Puerto Rico, as well as grants for related research and demonstration projects. It would fragment our research effort and destroy its priorities. Such an inflexible program would preclude us from taking advantage of the best research talents of the Nation—wherever they may be. The Federal Government's ongoing programs of similar and related kinds of research, currently funded at about $40 million annually, have provided a flexible and efficient means of meeting minerals problems of the highest national priority and can readily be adapted to continue to do so.

Airport Development Acceleration Act (S. 3755).

This bill would increase Federal expenditures and raise percentage participation in categorical grant programs with specific and limited purposes. I believe this would be inconsistent with sound fiscal policy. Airport development funds have been almost quadrupled since 1970 under this Administration.

Flood Control Act of 1972 (S. 4018).

This measure would authorize federal projects which would ultimately cost hundreds of millions of dollars. It contains projects never approved or recommended by the executive branch. In addition, it contains a number of objectionable features such as authorizing ill-defined and potentially costly new programs, and limiting my authority to establish criteria and standards to measure the feasibility of water resources projects in determining which ones to recommend for Congressional authorization. However, a number of projects in this bill are in my judgment justified and I will recommend legislation to authorize their construction early in the next Congress.

Upgrading of Deputy U.S. Marshals (H.R. 13895).

This would raise the pay of some 1,500 deputy marshals by as much as 38 percent, through wholesale across-the-board upgrading. There is no justification for this highly preferential treatment, which discriminates against all other Government employees who perform work of comparable difficulty and responsibility and whose pay is now the same as that of deputy marshals.

National Cemeteries Act of 1972 (H.R. 12674).

This bill would block the orderly system of surplus land disposal established by general law and Executive order, by requiring an unusual Congressional approval procedure before any VA land holdings larger than 100 acres could be sold.

These property transfer restrictions would undermine the executive branch's Government-wide system of property management and surplus property disposal which is designed to assure the best and fullest use of Federal property. It would impede the Legacy of Parks programs and the procedures for disposing of surplus Federal property under the Federal Property and Administrative Services Act and Executive Order 11508.

Also, the bill deals inconsistently with the serious problem of burial benefits for the Nation's veterans and war dead. It commissions a study of this problem at the same time it preempts the results of such a study by authorizing new burial benefits which would annually add $55 million to the Federal budget beginning next year. The Administrator of Veterans Affairs already is at work on such a study, which will identify the alternatives for improving burial and cemetery benefits. In the interim, it would be unwise to commit additional Federal resources as proposed by this bill.

Veterans Health Care Expansion Act of 1972 (H.R. 10880).

The liberalizing features of this bill would unnecessarily add hundreds of millions of dollars to the Federal budget. It would open the VA hospital system to nonveterans and would expand the type of direct medical services available from VA. By providing direct medical services to veterans' dependents, the bill runs counter to this Administration's national health strategy which would provide national financing mechanisms for health care and sharply reduce the Federal Government's role in the direct provision of services.

The bill also purports to set mandatory minimums on the number of patients treated in VA hospitals. In testimony on this bill, the Veterans Administration strongly objected to this provision on the grounds that it was totally unnecessary and could result in inefficient medical treatment and wasteful administrative practices. The tragic result would be a lower quality of medical care to all patients.

While I strongly support the VA health care system and will continue to encourage its improvement in the future, I cannot approve a bad bill.

Rehabilitation Act of 1972 (H.R. 8395).

This measure would seriously jeopardize the goals of the vocational rehabilitation program and is another example of Congressional fiscal irresponsibility. Its provisions would divert this program from its basic vocational objectives into activities that have no vocational element whatsoever or are essentially medical in character. In addition, it would proliferate a host of narrow categorical programs which duplicate and overlap existing authorities and programs. Such provisions serve only to dilute the resources of the vocational rehabilitation program and impair its continued valuable achievements in restoring deserving American citizens to meaningful employment.

H.R. 8395 also would create organization rigidities in the vocational rehabilitation program which would undermine the ability of the Secretary of HEW to management the program effectively. The bill also would establish numerous committees and independent commissions which are unnecessary, would waste the taxpayers' dollars, and would complicate and confuse the direction of this program. Finally, the bill would authorize funding far in excess of the budget request and far beyond what can be made available and used effectively.

RICHARD NIXON

OCT. 30 VETO MESSAGE

I have announced today the signing of H.R. 1—a bill which represents a tremendous forward step in improving the income position and health services for older Americans. Two other bills concerning the elderly have also come to me for signature—the Older Americans Comprehensive Service Amendments of 1972 (H.R. 15657) and the Research on Aging Act of 1972 (H.R. 14424). Although I support some of the goals of these two bills, careful review has persuaded me that neither bill provides the best means of achieving these goals. Both authorize unbudgeted and excessive expenditures and would also require duplications or fragmentations of effort which would actually impair our efforts to serve older Americans more effectively. I have decided therefore to withhold my approval from these two pieces of legislation.

Older Americans Comprehensive Service Amendments of 1972 (H.R. 15657).

Last March, I submitted to the Congress a plan for strengthening and expanding service delivery programs under the Older Americans Act. This program would begin the development of more comprehensive and better coordinated systems for delivering services at the local level. In addition, I submitted a proposal to broaden the highly successful Foster Grandparents Program. The Administration will continue its vigorous pursuit of both these objectives.

However, the Congress added to the bill containing these provisions a range of narrow, categorical service programs which would seriously interfere with our effort to develop coordinated services for older persons. This is particularly the case with two categorical manpower programs which were added on the floor of the Senate and were considered without regard to manpower programs already serving older persons. Furthermore, this bill would authorize new funding of more than $2-billion between now and fiscal year 1975—far beyond what can be used effectively and responsibly.

I cannot responsibly approve H.R. 15657.

Research on Aging Act of 1972 (H.R. 14424).

In my Special Message to the Congress on Older Americans last March, I also emphasized the need to develop a comprehensive, coordinated program of aging research—one which includes disciplines ranging from biomedical research to transportation systems analysis, from psychology and sociology to management science and economics. The Secretary of Health, Education and Welfare has since appointed a new Technical Advisory Committee for Aging Research to develop a plan for bringing together all the resources available to the Federal Government in the aging research field.

H.R. 14424, however, would set up an entirely separate aging research institute that would duplicate these activities. This bill would create additional administrative costs without enhancing the conduct of biomedical research for the aging. In fact, it could even fragment existing research efforts. This bill also contains a new grant program for mental health facilities for the aging which duplicates the more general and flexible authorities contained in the Community Mental Health Centers Act.

In sum, I feel that both research and mental health programs for the aging should be carried out in the broader context of research on life-span processes and comprehensive mental health treatment programs now underway.

H.R. 14424 would not enhance and could inhibit Federal efforts to respond to the needs of the elderly, and I cannot give it my approval.

RICHARD NIXON

MAJOR PRESIDENTIAL
STATEMENTS

INDOCHINA PROPOSAL

Following is the text of a proposal by the U.S. and South Vietnamese governments for an Indochina settlement, as released Jan. 25 by the White House.

1. There will be a total withdrawal from South Vietnam of all U.S. forces and other foreign forces allied with the government of South Vietnam within six months of an agreement.

2. The release of all military men and innocent civilians captured throughout Indochina will be carried out in parallel with the troop withdrawals mentioned in point 1. Both sides will present a complete list of military men and innocent civilians held throughout Indochina on the day the agreement is signed. The release will begin on the same day as the troop withdrawals and will be completed when they are completed.

3. The following principles will govern the political future of South Vietnam: The political future of South Vietnam will be left for the South Vietnamese people to decide for themselves, free from outside interference.

There will be a free and democratic presidential election in South Vietnam within six months of an agreement. This election will be organized and run by an independent body representing all political forces in South Vietnam which will assume its responsibilities on the date of the agreement. This body will, among other responsibilities, determine the qualification of candidates. All political forces in South Vietnam can participate in the election and present candidates. There will be international supervision of this election.

One month before the presidential election takes place, the incumbent President and Vice President of South Vietnam will resign. The Chairman of the Senate, as caretaker head of the government, will assume administrative responsibilities except for those pertaining to the election, which will remain with the independent election body.

The United States, for its part, declares that it:

• will support no candidate and will remain completely neutral in the election;

• will abide by the outcome of this election and any other political processes shaped by the South Vietnamese people themselves;

• is prepared to define its military and economic assistance relationship with any government that exists in South Vietnam.

Both sides agree that:

• South Vietnam, together with the other countries of Indochina, should adopt a foreign policy consistent with the military provisions of the 1954 Geneva Accords.

• Reunification of Vietnam should be decided on the basis of discussions and agreements between North and South Vietnam without constraint and annexation from either party, and without foreign interference.

4. Both sides will respect the 1954 Geneva Agreements on Indochina and those of 1962 on Laos. There will be no foreign intervention in the Indochinese countries and the Indochinese peoples will be left to settle their own affairs by themselves.

5. The problems existing among the Indochinese countries will be settled by the Indochinese parties on the basis of mutual respect for independence, sovereignty, territorial integrity and noninterference in each other's affairs. Among the problems that will be settled is the implementation of the principle that all armed forces of the countries of Indochina must remain within their national frontiers.

6. There will be a general ceasefire throughout Indochina, to begin when the agreement is signed. As part of the ceasefire, there will be no further infiltration of outside forces into any of the countries of Indochina.

7. There will be international supervision of the military aspects of this agreement including the ceasefire and its provisions, the release of prisoners of war and innocent civilians, the withdrawal of outside forces from Indochina, and the implementation of the principle that all armed forces of the countries of Indochina must remain within their national frontiers.

8. There will be an international guarantee for the fundamental national rights of the Indochinese peoples, the status of all the countries in Indochina, and lasting peace in this region.

Both sides express their willingness to participate in an international conference for this and other appropriate purposes.

JAN. 25 VIETNAM SPEECH

Following is the text of President Nixon's Jan. 25 speech on Vietnam as prepared for delivery on national television.

Good evening. I have asked for this television time tonight to make public a plan for peace that can end the war in Vietnam.

The offer that I shall now present, on behalf of the Government of the United States and the Government of South Vietnam, with the full knowledge and approval of President Thieu, is both generous and far reaching.

It is a plan to end the war now; it includes an offer to withdraw all American forces within six months of an agreement; its acceptance would mean the speedy return of all the prisoners of war to their homes.

Three years ago when I took office, there were 550,000 Americans in Vietnam; the number killed in action was running as high as 300 a week; there were no plans to bring any Americans home, and the only thing that had been settled in Paris was the shape of the conference table.

I immediately moved to fulfill a pledge I had made to the American people: to bring about a peace that could last, not only for the United States, but for the long-suffering people of Southeast Asia.

There were two honorable paths open to us.

The path of negotiation was, and is, the path we prefer. But it takes two to negotiate; there had to be another way in case the other side refused to negotiate.

That path we called Vietnamization. What it meant was training and equipping the South Vietnamese to defend themselves, and steadily withdrawing Americans as they developed the capability to do so.

The path of Vietnamization has been successful. Two weeks ago, you will recall, I announced that by May 1st, American forces in Vietnam would be down to 69,000. That means almost one-half million Americans will have been brought home from Vietnam over the past three years. In terms of American lives, the losses of 300 a week have been reduced by over 95 percent—to less than 10 a week.

But the path of Vietnamization has been the long voyage home. It has strained the patience and tested the perseverance of the American people. What of the shortcut, the shortcut we prefer, the path of negotiation?

Progress there has been disappointing. The American people deserve an accounting of why it has been disappointing. Tonight I intend to give you that accounting, and in so doing, I am going to try to break the deadlock in the negotiations.

We have made a series of public proposals designed to bring an end to the conflict. But early in this Administration, after ten months of no progress in the public Paris talks, I became convinced that it was necessary to explore the possibility of negotiating in private channels, to see whether it would be possible to end the public deadlock.

After consultation with Secretary of State Rogers, our Ambassador in Saigon and our chief negotiator in Paris, and with the full knowledge and approval of President Thieu, I sent Dr. Kissinger to Paris as my personal representative on August 4, 1969, 30 months ago, to begin these secret peace negotiations.

Since that time, Dr. Kissinger has traveled to Paris twelve times on these secret missions. He has met seven times with Le Duc Tho, one of Hanoi's top political leaders, and Minister Xuan Thuy, head of the North Vietnamese delegation to the Paris talks and he has met with Minister Xuan Thuy five times alone. I would like, incidentally, to take this opportunity to thank President Pompidou of France for his personal assistance in helping to make arrangements for these talks.

This is why I initiated these private negotiations: Privately, both sides can be more flexible in offering new approaches and also private discussions allow both sides to talk frankly, to take positions free from the pressures of public debate.

In seeking peace in Vietnam, with so many lives at stake, I felt we could not afford to let any opportunity go by—private or public—to negotiate a settlement. As I have stated on a number of occasions, I was prepared and I remain prepared to explore any avenue, public or private, to speed negotiations to end the war.

For thirty months, whenever Secretary Rogers, Dr. Kissinger or I were asked about secret negotiations we would only say we were pursuing every possible channel in our search for peace. There was never a leak, because we were determined not to jeopardize the secret negotiations. Until recently, this course showed signs of yielding some progress.

Now, however, it is my judgment that the purposes of peace will best be served by bringing out publicly the proposals we have been making in private.

Nothing is served by silence when the other side exploits our good faith to divide America and to avoid the conference table. Nothing is served by silence when it misleads some Americans into accusing their own government of failing to do what it has already done. Nothing is served by silence when it enables the other side to imply possible solutions publicly that it has already flatly rejected privately.

The time has come to lay the record of our secret negotiations on the table. Just as secret negotiations can sometimes break a public deadlock, public disclosure may help to break a secret deadlock.

Some Americans, who believed what the North Vietnamese led them to believe, have charged that the United States has not pursued negotiations intensively. As the record that I now will disclose will show, just the opposite is true.

Questions have been raised as to why we have not proposed a deadline for the withdrawal of all American forces in exchange for a cease-fire and the return of our prisoners of war; why we have not discussed the 7-point proposal made by the Vietcong last July in Paris; why we have not submitted a new plan of our own to move the negotiations off dead center.

As the private record will show, we have taken all these steps and more—and have been flatly rejected or ignored by the other side.

On May 31, 1971, eight months ago, at one of the secret meetings in Paris, we offered specifically to agree to a deadline for the withdrawal of all American forces in exchange for the release of all prisoners of war and a cease-fire.

At the next private meeting, on June 26, the North Vietnamese rejected our offer. They privately proposed instead their own 9-point plan which insisted that we overthrow the Government of South Vietnam.

Five days later, on July 1, the enemy publicly presented a different package of proposals—the 7-point Vietcong plan.

That posed a dilemma: Which package should we respond to, the public plan or the secret plan?

On July 12, at another private meeting in Paris, Dr. Kissinger put that question to the North Vietnamese directly. They said we should deal with their 9-point secret plan, because it covered all of Indochina including Laos and Cambodia, while the Vietcong 7-point proposal was limited to Vietnam.

So that is what we did. But we even went beyond that, dealing with some of the points in the public plan that were not covered in the secret plan.

On August 16, at another private meeting, we went further. We offered the complete withdrawal of U.S. and allied forces within nine months after an agreement on an overall settlement. On September 13, the North Vietnamese rejected that proposal. They continued to insist that we overthrow the South Vietnamese Government.

Now, what has been the result of these private efforts? For months, the North Vietnamese have been berating us at the public sessions for not responding to their side's publicly presented 7-point plan.

The truth is that we did respond to the enemy's plan, in the manner they wanted us to respond—secretly. In full possession of our complete response, the North Vietnamese publicly denounced us for not having responded at all. They induced many Americans in the press and in the Congress into echoing their propaganda—Americans who could not know they were being used by the enemy to stir up divisiveness in this country.

I decided in October that we should make another attempt to break the deadlock. I consulted with President Thieu, who concurred fully in a new plan. On October 11, I sent a private communication to the North Vietnamese that contained new elements that could move negotiations forward. I urged a meeting on November 1 between Dr. Kissinger and Special Advisor Le Duc Tho, or some other appropriate official from Hanoi.

On October 25, the North Vietnamese agreed to meet and suggested November 20th as the time for a meeting. On November 17, just three days before the scheduled meeting, they said Le Duc Tho was ill. We offered to meet as soon as he recovered, either with him, or immediately with any other authorized leader who could come from Hanoi.

Two months have passed since they called off that meeting. The only reply to our plan has been an increase in troop infiltration from North Vietnam and Communist military offensives in Laos and Cambodia. Our proposal for peace was answered by a step-up in the war.

That is where matters stand today.

We are being asked publicly to respond to proposals that we answered, and in some respects accepted, months ago in private.

We are being asked to set a terminal date for our withdrawals when we already offered one in private.

And the most comprehensive peace plan of this conflict lies ignored in a secret channel, while the enemy tries again for military victory.

That is why I have instructed Ambassador Porter to present our plan publicly at this Thursday's session of the Paris Peace Talks, along with alternatives to make it even more flexible.

We are publishing the full details of our plan tonight. It will prove beyond doubt which side has made every effort to make these negotiations succeed. It will show unmistakably that Hanoi—not Washington or Saigon—has made the war go on.

Here is the essence of our peace plan; public disclosure may gain it the attention it deserves in Hanoi.

Within six months of an agreement:

• We shall withdraw all U.S. and allied forces from South Vietnam.

• We shall exchange all prisoners of war.

• There shall be a cease-fire throughout Indochina.

• There shall be a new Presidential election in South Vietnam.

President Thieu will announce the elements of this election. These include international supervision; and an independent body to organize and run the election, representing all political forces in South Vietnam, including the National Liberation Front.

Furthermore President Thieu has informed me that within the framework of the agreement outlined above, he makes the following offer: He and Vice President Huong would be ready to resign one month before the new election. The Chairman of the Senate, as caretaker head of the government, would assume administrative responsibilities in South Vietnam, but the election would be the sole responsibility of the independent election body I have just described.

There are several other proposals in our new peace plan; for example, as we offered privately on July 26 of last year, we remain prepared to undertake a major reconstruction program throughout Indochina, including North Vietnam, to help all these peoples recover from the ravages of a generation of war.

We will pursue any approach that will speed negotiations.

We are ready to negotiate the plan I have outlined tonight and conclude a comprehensive agreement on all military and political issues. Because some parts of this agreement could prove more difficult to negotiate than

others, we would be willing to begin implementing certain military aspects while negotiations continue on the implementation of other issues, just as we suggested in our private proposal in October.

Or, as we proposed last May, we remain willing to settle only the military issues and leave the political issues to the Vietnamese alone. Under this approach, we would withdraw all U.S. and allied forces within six months in exchange for an Indochina cease-fire and the release of all prisoners. The choice is up to the enemy.

This is a settlement offer which is fair to North Vietnam and fair to South Vietnam. It deserves the light of public scrutiny by these nations and by other nations throughout the world. And it deserves the united support of the American people.

We made the substance of this generous offer privately over three months ago. It has not been rejected, but it has been ignored. I reiterate that peace offer tonight. It can no longer be ignored.

The only thing this plan does not do is to join the enemy to overthrow our ally, which the United States of America will never do. If the enemy wants peace, it will have to recognize the important difference between settlement and surrender.

This has been a long and agonizing struggle. But it is difficult to see how anyone, regardless of his past position on the war, could now say that we have not gone the extra mile in offering a settlement that is fair, fair to everybody concerned.

By the steadiness of our withdrawal of troops, America has proven its resolution to end our involvement in the war; by our readiness to act in the spirit of conciliation, America has proven its desire to be involved in the building of a permanent peace throughout Indochina.

We are ready to negotiate peace immediately.

If the enemy rejects our offer to negotiate, we shall continue our program of ending American involvement in the war by withdrawing our remaining forces as the South Vietnamese develop the capability to defend themselves.

If the enemy's answer to our peace offer is to step up their military attacks, I shall fully meet my responsibility as Commander-in-Chief of our Armed Forces to protect our remaining troops.

We do not prefer this course of action.

We want to end the war not only for America but for all the people of Indochina. The plan I have proposed tonight can accomplish that goal.

Some of our citizens have become accustomed to thinking that whatever our government says must be false, and whatever our enemies say must be true, as far as this war is concerned. Well, the record I have revealed tonight proves the contrary. We can now demonstrate publicly what we have long been demonstrating privately—that America has taken the initiative not only to end our participation in this war, but to end the war itself for all concerned.

This has been the longest, the most difficult war in American history.

Honest and patriotic Americans have disagreed as to whether we should have become involved at all nine years ago, and there has been disagreement on the conduct of the war. The proposal I have made tonight is one on which we all can agree.

Let us unite now, unite in our search for peace—a peace that is fair to both sides—a peace that can last.

Excerpts from Joint Nixon-Chou En-Lai Communique

Following are excerpted major positions adopted in the communique issued Feb. 27 by President Nixon and Chinese Premier Chou En-lai at Shanghai after their series of meetings:

REDUCING TENSIONS. The United States believes that the effort to reduce tensions is served by improving communication between countries that have different ideologies so as to lessen the risks of confrontation through accident, miscalculation or misunderstanding. Countries should treat each other with mutual respect and be willing to compete peacefully, letting performance be the ultimate judge. No country should claim infallibility and each country should be prepared to re-examine its own attitudes for the common good.

REVOLUTION. The Chinese side stated: Wherever there is oppression, there is resistance. Countries want independence, nations want liberation and the people want revolution—this has become the irresistible trend of history. All nations, big or small, should be equal; big nations should not bully the small and strong nations should not bully the weak. China will never be a superpower and it opposes hegemony and power politics of any kind. The Chinese side stated that it firmly supports the struggles of all the oppressed people and nations for freedom and liberation and that the people of all countries have the right to choose their social systems according to their own wishes and the right to safeguard the independence, sovereignty and territorial integrity of their own countries and oppose foreign aggression, interference, control and subversion. All foreign troops should be withdrawn to their own countries.

INDOCHINA. The United States stressed that the peoples of Indochina should be allowed to determine their destiny without outside intervention; its constant primary objective has been a negotiated solution; the eight-point proposal put forward by the Republic of Vietnam and the United States on January 27, 1972 represents a basis for the attainment of that objective; in the absence of a negotiated settlement the United States envisages the ultimate withdrawal of all U.S. forces from the region consistent with the aim of self-determination for each country of Indochina.

The Chinese side expressed its firm support to the peoples of Vietnam, Laos and Cambodia in their efforts for the attainment of their goal and its firm support to the seven-point proposal of the Provisional Revolutionary Government of the Republic of South Vietnam and the elaboration of February this year on the two key problems in the proposal, and to the Joint Declaration of the Summit Conference of the Indochinese Peoples.

TAIWAN. The Chinese side reaffirmed its position: The Taiwan question is the crucial question obstructing the normalization of relations between China and the United States; the Government of the People's Republic of China is the sole legal government of China; Taiwan is a province of China which has long been returned to the motherland; the liberation of Taiwan is China's internal affair in which no other country has the right to interfere; and all U.S. forces and military installations must be withdrawn from Taiwan.

The U.S. side declared: The United States acknowledges that all Chinese on either side of the Taiwan Strait maintain there is but one China and that Taiwan is a part of China. The United States Government does not challenge that position. It reaffirms its interest in a peaceful settlement of the Taiwan question by the Chinese themselves. With this prospect in mind, it affirms the ultimate objective of the withdrawal of all U.S. forces and military installations from Taiwan. In the meantime, it will progressively reduce its forces and military installations on Taiwan as the tension in the area diminishes.

EXCHANGES. The two sides agreed that it is desirable to broaden the understanding between the two peoples. To this end, they discussed specific areas in such fields as science, technology, culture, sports and journalism, in which people-to-people contacts and exchanges would be mutually beneficial. Each side undertakes to facilitate the further development of such contacts and exchanges.

FUTURE RELATIONS. The two sides agreed that they will stay in contact through various channels, including the sending of a senior U.S. representative to Peking from time to time for concrete consultations to further the normalization of relations between the two countries and continue to exchange views on issues of common interest.

ASIAN RELATIONS. There are essential differences between China and the United States and their social systems and foreign policies. However, the two sides agreed that countries, regardless of their social systems, should conduct their relations on the principles of respect for the sovereignty and territorial integrity of all states, non-aggression against other states, non-interference in the internal affairs of other states, equality and mutual benefit, and peaceful coexistence. International disputes should be settled on this basis, without resorting to the use or threat of force....

With these principles of international relations in mind the two sides stated that:

• Neither should seek hegemony in the Asia-Pacific region and each is opposed to efforts by any other country or group of countries to establish such hegemony; and

• Neither is prepared to negotiate on behalf of any third party or to enter into agreements or understandings with the other directed at other states.

Both sides are of the view that it would be against the interests of the peoples of the world for any major country to collude with another against other countries, or for major countries to divide up the world into spheres of interest.

ARRIVAL FROM CHINA

Following is the text, as made available by the White House, of President Nixon's Feb. 28 remarks at Andrews Air Force Base, Washington, D.C., on his arrival in the Capitol from his trip to China:

I want to express my very deep appreciation, and the appreciation of all of us, for this wonderfully warm welcome that you have given us, and for the support that we have had on the trip that we have just completed from Americans of both political parties and all walks of life across this land.

Because of the superb efforts of the hardworking members of the press who accompanied us—they got even less sleep than I did—millions of Americans in this past week have seen more of China than I did. Consequently, tonight I would like to talk to you not about what we saw, but what we did, to sum up the results of the trip and to put it in perspective.

When I announced this trip last July, I described it as a journey for peace. In the last 30 years, Americans have in three different wars gone off by the hundreds of thousands to fight, and some to die, in Asia and in the Pacific. One of the central motives behind my journey to China was to prevent that from happening a fourth time to another generation of Americans.

As I have often said, peace means more than the mere absence of war. In a technical sense, we were at peace with the Peoples Republic of China before this trip, but a gulf of almost 12,000 miles and 22 years of noncommunication and hostility separated the United States of America from the 750 million people who live in the Peoples Republic of China, and that is one-fourth of all of the people in the world.

As a result of this trip, we have started the long process of building a bridge across that gulf, and even now we have something better than the mere absence of war. Not only have we completed a week of intensive talks at the highest levels; we have set up a procedure whereby we can continue to have discussions in the future. We have demonstrated that nations with very big and fundamental differences can learn to discuss those differences calmly, rationally, and frankly, without compromising their principles. This is the basis of a structure for peace, where we can talk about differences, rather than fight about them.

The primary goal of this trip was to reestablish communication with the Peoples Republic of China after a generation of hostility. We achieved that goal. Let me turn now to our joint communique.

We did not bring back any written or unwritten agreements that will guarantee peace in our time. We did not bring home any magic formula which will make unnecessary the efforts of the American people to continue to maintain the strength so that we can continue to be free.

We made some necessary and important beginnings, however, in several areas. We entered into agreements to expand cultural, educational and journalistic contacts between the Chinese and American people. We agreed to work to begin and broaden trade between our two countries. We have agreed that the communications that have now been established between our governments will be strengthened and expanded.

Most important, we have agreed on some rules of international conduct which will reduce the risk of confrontation and war, in Asia and in the Pacific.

We agreed that we are opposed to domination of the Pacific area by any one power. We agreed that international disputes should be settled without the use of the threat of force and we agreed that we are prepared to apply this principle to our mutual relations.

With respect to Taiwan, we stated our established policy that our forces overseas will be reduced gradually as tensions ease, and that our ultimate objective is to withdraw our forces as a peaceful settlement is achieved.

We have agreed that we will not negotiate the fate of other nations behind their backs, and we did not do so in Peking. There were no secret deals of any kind. We have done all this without giving up any United States commitment to any other country.

In our talks, talks that I had with the leaders of the Peoples Republic and the Secretary of State had with the office of the government of the Peoples Republic in the foreign affairs area, we both realized that a bridge of understanding that spans almost 12,000 miles and 22 years of hostility, can't be built in one week of discussions. But we have agreed to begin to build that bridge, recognizing that our work will require years of patient effort. We made no attempt to pretend that major differences did not exist between our two governments, because they do exist.

This communique was unique in honestly setting forth differences rather than trying to cover them up with diplomatic double talk.

One of the gifts that we left behind in Hangchow was a planted sapling of the American redwood tree. As all Californians know, and as most Americans know, redwoods grow from saplings into the giants of the forest. But the process is not one of days or even years; it is a process of centuries.

Just as we hope that those saplings, those tiny saplings that we left in China, will grow one day into mighty redwoods, so we hope, too, that the seeds planted on this journey for peace will grow and prosper into a more enduring structure for peace and security in the Western Pacific.

But peace is too urgent to wait for centuries. We must seize the moment to move toward that goal now, and this is what we have done on this journey.

I am sure you realize it was a great experience for us to see the timeless wonders of ancient China, the changes that are being made in modern China. And one fact stands out among many others, from my talks with the Chinese leaders. It is their total belief, their total dedication, to their system of government. That is their right, just as it is the right of any country to choose the kind of government it wants.

But as I return from this trip, just as has been the case on my return from other trips abroad which have taken me to over 80 countries, I come back to America with an even stronger faith in our system of government.

As I flew across America today, all the way from Alaska, over the Rockies, the plains, and then on to Washington, I thought of the greatness of our country, and most of all, I thought of freedom, the opportunity, the progress that 200 million Americans are privileged to enjoy. I realized again this is a beautiful country, and tonight our prayer and my hope is that as a result of this trip, our children will have a better chance to grow up in a peaceful world.

ECONOMIC STABILIZATION

Following is the text, as made available by the White House, of President Nixon's March 23 executive order reorganizing the Pay Board and conforming previous orders affecting the Pay Board and the Price Commission to the extension of the Economic Stabilization Act which Congress passed in 1971.

AMENDING EXECUTIVE ORDER NO. 11640, FURTHER PROVIDING FOR THE STABILIZATION OF THE ECONOMY

By virtue of the authority vested in me by the Constitution and statutes of the United States, particularly the Economic Stabilization Act of 1970, as amended, it is hereby ordered as follows:

Section 1. Subsection (a) of section 1 of Executive Order No. 11640 of January 26, 1972, is amended by inserting in lieu of the first sentence thereof the following:

"The Pay Board and Price Commission established by sections 7 and 8 of Executive Order No. 11627 of October 15, 1971, are hereby continued, except to the extent that the language prescribing the composition of the Pay Board and the Price Commission has been modified by sections 7(b) and 8(b) of this Order, as amended, and shall act as agencies of the United States. The Chairman of each of these bodies, acting in accordance with the majority vote of its members, shall, pursuant to the goals established by the Cost of Living Council, take such steps as may be necessary, and authorized by or pursuant to this Order, to stabilize prices, rents, wages, and salaries."

Sec. 2. Subsection (b) of section 7 of Executive Order No. 11640 is amended by inserting in lieu of the first four sentences thereof the following:

"The Board shall be composed of such members as the President has appointed or may, from time to time, appoint and who are serving pursuant to such appointment. Such members shall be appointed by and with the advice and consent of the Senate; except that the foregoing requirement with respect to Senate confirmation does not apply to any member of the Board who was serving, pursuant to appointment by the President, on December 22, 1971, and who continues to serve pursuant to such appointment, after such time. The members of the Board shall serve at the pleasure of the President and one of the members designated by the President shall serve as Chairman."

Sec. 3. (a) Subsection (b) of section 8 of Executive Order No. 11640 is amended by inserting in lieu of the first two sentences thereof the following:

"The Commission shall be composed of such members as the President has appointed or may, from time to time, appoint and who are serving pursuant to such appointment. Such members shall be appointed by and with the advice and consent of the Senate; except that the foregoing requirement with respect to Senate confirmation does not apply to any member of the Commission who was serving, pursuant to appointment by the President, on December 22, 1971, and who continues to serve pursuant to such appointment, after such time."

Sec. 3. (b) The penultimate sentence of section 8(b) of Executive Order No. 11640 is amended by deleting "Executive Director of the Board" and inserting in lieu thereof "Executive Director of the Commission."

Sec. 4. All orders, regulations, circulars, or other directives issued and all other actions taken pursuant to Executive Order No. 11615, as amended, Executive Order No. 11627, as amended, and Executive Order No. 11640, and in effect on the date of this Order, are hereby confirmed and ratified, and shall remain in full force and effect, unless and until altered, amended, or revoked by competent authority.

RICHARD NIXON

INDOCHINA WAR

Following is the text, as made available by the White House, of President Nixon's April 26 radio-TV address on the Indochina war.

Good evening.

During the past three weeks you have been reading and hearing about the massive invasion of South Vietnam by the Communist armies of North Vietnam.

Tonight, I want to give you a first-hand report on the military situation in Vietnam, the decisions I have made with regard to the role of the United States in the conflict, and the efforts we are making to bring peace at the negotiating table.

Let me begin briefly by reviewing what the situation was when I took office, and what we have done since then to end American involvement in the war and to bring peace to the long-suffering people of Southeast Asia.

On January 20, 1969, the American troop ceiling in Vietnam was 549,000. Our casualties were running as high as 300 a week. Thirty thousand young Americans were being drafted every month.

Today, 39 months later, through our program of Vietnamization—helping the South Vietnamese develop the capability of defending themselves—the number of Americans in Vietnam by Monday, May 1, will have been reduced to 69,000. Our casualties—even during the present, all-out enemy offensive—have been reduced to 95 percent. And draft calls now average fewer than 5,000 men a month, and we expect to bring them to zero next year.

As I reported in my television address to the Nation on January 25, we have offered the most generous peace terms in both public and private negotiating sessions. Our most recent proposal provided for an immediate ceasefire; the exchange of all prisoners of war; the withdrawal of all forces within six months; and new elections in Vietnam, which would be internationally supervised, with all political elements including the Communists participating in and helping to run the elections. One month before such elections, President Thieu and Vice President Huong would resign.

Hanoi's contemptuous answer to this offer was a refusal even to discuss our proposals and, at the same time, a huge escalation of their military activities on the battlefield. Last October, the same month when we made this peace offer to Hanoi, our intelligence reports began to indicate that the enemy was building up for a major attack. Yet we deliberately refrained from responding militarily. Instead we patiently continued with the Paris talks, because we wanted to give the enemy every chance to reach a negotiated settlement at the bargaining table rather than to seek a military victory on the battlefield—a victory they cannot be allowed to win.

Finally, three weeks ago, on Easter weekend, they mounted their massive invasion of South Vietnam. Three North Vietnamese divisions swept across the Demilitarized Zone into South Vietnam—in a violation of the treaties they had signed in 1954 and in violation of the understanding they had reached with President Johnson in 1968, when he stopped the bombing of North Vietnam in return for arrangements which included their pledge not to violate the DMZ. Shortly after the invasion across the DMZ, another three North Vietnamese divisions invaded South Vietnam further south. As the offensive progressed, the enemy indiscriminately shelled civilian population centers in clear violation of the 1968 bombing halt understanding.

So the facts are clear. More than 120,000 North Vietnamese are now fighting in South Vietnam. There are no South Vietnamese troops anywhere in North Vietnam. Twelve of North Vietnam's thirteen regular combat divisions have now left their own soil in order to carry aggressive war onto the territory of their neighbors. Whatever pretext there was of a civil war in South Vietnam has not been stripped away.

What we are witnessing here—what is being brutally inflicted upon the Republic of Vietnam—is a clear case of naked and unprovoked aggression across an international border. There is only one word for it—invasion.

This attack has been resisted on the ground entirely by South Vietnamese forces, and in one area by South Korean forces. There are no United States ground troops involved. None will be involved. To support this defensive effort by the South Vietnamese, I have ordered attacks on enemy military targets in both North and South Vietnam by the air and naval forces of the United States.

I have here on my desk a report. I received it this morning from General Abrams. He gives the following evaluation of the situation:

The South Vietnamese are fighting courageously and well in their self-defense. They are inflicting very heavy casualties on the invading force, which has not gained the easy victory some predicted for it three weeks ago.

Our air strikes have been essential in protecting our own remaining forces and in assisting South Vietnam in their efforts to protect their homes and their country from a Communist takeover.

General Abrams predicts in this report that there will be several more weeks of very hard fighting. Some battles will be lost, he said, and others will be won by the South Vietnamese. But his conclusion is that if we continue to provide air and sea support, the enemy will fail in its desperate gamble to impose a Communist regime on South Vietnam, and the South Vietnamese will then have demonstrated their ability to defend themselves on the ground against future enemy attacks.

Based on this realistic assessment from General Abrams, and after consultation with President Thieu, Ambassador Bunker, Ambassador Porter, and my senior advisers in Washington, I have three decisions to announce tonight.

First, I have decided that Vietnamization has proved itself sufficiently that we can continue our program of withdrawing American forces without detriment to our overall goal of ensuring South Vietnam's survival as an independent country. Consequently, I am announcing tonight that over the next two months 20,000 more Americans will be brought home from Vietnam. This decision has the full approval of President Thieu and of General Abrams. It will bring our troop ceiling down to 49,000 by July 1—a reduction of half a million men since this Administration came into office.

Second, I have directed Ambassador Porter to return to the negotiating table in Paris tomorrow, but with one very specific purpose in mind. We are not resuming the Paris talks simply in order to hear more empty propaganda and bombast from the North Vietnamese and Viet Cong delegates, but to get on with the constructive business of making peace. We are resuming the Paris talks with the firm expectation that productive talks leading to rapid progress will follow through all available channels. As far as we are concerned, the first order of business will be to get the enemy to halt his invasion of South Vietnam, and to return the American prisoners of war.

Finally, I have ordered that our air and naval attacks on military installations in North Vietnam be continued until the North Vietnamese stop their offensive in South Vietnam.

I have flatly rejected the proposal that we stop the bombing of North Vietnam as a condition for returning to the negotiating table. They sold that package to the United States once before, in 1968, and we are not going to buy it again in 1972.

Now, let's look at the record. By July 1 we will have withdrawn over 90 percent of our forces that were in Vietnam by 1969. Before the enemy's invasion began, we had cut our air sorties in half. We have offered exceedingly generous terms for peace. The only thing we have refused to do is to accede to the enemy's demand to overthrow the lawfully constituted government of South Vietnam and to impose a Communist dictatorship in its place.

As you will recall, I have warned on a number of occasions over the past three years that if the enemy responded to our efforts to bring peace by stepping up the war I would act to meet that attack, for three good reasons: First, to protect our remaining American forces; second, to permit continuation of our withdrawal program, and third, to prevent the imposition of a Communist regime on the people of South Vietnam against their will, with the inevitable bloodbath that would follow for hundreds of thousands who have dared to oppose Communist aggression.

The air and naval strikes of recent weeks have been carried out to achieve these objectives. They have been directed only against military targets supporting the invasion of South Vietnam, and they will not stop until the invasion stops.

The Communists have failed in their efforts to win over the people of South Vietnam politically. General Abrams believes that they will fail in their efforts to conquer South Vietnam militarily. Their one remaining hope is to win in the Congress of the United States, and among the people of the United States the victory they cannot win among the people of South Vietnam or on the battlefield in South Vietnam.

The great question then is how we, the American people, will respond to this final challenge.

Let us look at what the stakes are—not just for South Vietnam, but for the United States and for the cause of peace in the world. If one country, armed with the most modern weapons by major powers can invade another nation and succeed in conquering it, other countries will be encouraged to do exactly the same thing—in the Mideast, in Europe, and in other international danger spots. If the Communists win militarily in Vietnam, the risk of war in other parts of the world would be enormously increased. But if, on the other hand, Communist aggression fails in Vietnam, it will be discouraged elsewhere and the chance for peace will be increased.

We are not trying to conquer North Vietnam or any other country in this world. We want no territory. We seek no bases. We have offered the most generous peace terms—peace with honor for both sides—with South Vietnam and North Vietnam each respecting the other's independence.

But we will not be defeated; and we will never surrender our friends to Communist aggression.

We have come a long way in this conflict. The South Vietnamese have made great progress and they are now bearing the brunt of the battle. We can now see the day when no more Americans will be involved there at all.

But as we come to the end of this long and difficult struggle, we must be steadfast. And we must not falter. For all that we have risked and all that we have gained over the years now hangs in the balance during the coming weeks and months. If we now let down our friends we shall surely be letting down ourselves and our future as well. If we now persist, future generations will thank America for her courage and her vision in this time of testing.

That is why I say to you tonight, let us bring our men home from Vietnam. But let us end it in such a way that the younger brothers and the sons of the brave men who have fought in Vietnam will not have to fight again in some other Vietnam at some time in the future.

Any man who sits here in this office feels a profound sense of obligation to future generations. No man who sits here has the right to take any action which would abdicate America's great tradition of world leadership or weaken respect for the Office of the President of the United States.

Earlier this year I traveled to Peking on an historic journey for peace. Next month I shall travel to Moscow on what I hope will also be a journey for peace. In the 18 countries I have visited as President I have found great respect for the Office of the President of the United States. I have reason to expect, based on Dr. Kissinger's report, that I shall find that same respect for the office I hold when I visit Moscow.

I do not know who will be in this office in the years ahead. But I do know that future Presidents will travel to nations abroad as I have, on journeys for peace. If the United States betrays the millions of people who have relied on us in Vietnam, the President of the United States, whoever he is, will not deserve nor receive the respect which is essential if the United States is to continue to play the great role we are destined to play of helping to build a new structure of peace in the world. It would amount to a renunciation of our morality, an abdication of our leadership among nations, and an invitation for the mighty to prey upon the weak all around the world. It would be to deny peace the chance peace deserves to have. This we shall never do.

My fellow Americans, let us therefore unite as a nation in a firm and wise policy of real peace—not the peace of surrender, but peace with honor—not just peace in our time, but peace for generations to come.

Thank you, and good night.

MAY 8 VIETNAM ADDRESS

Following is the text, as made available by the White House, of President Nixon's May 8 television and radio address on the situation in Vietnam.

Good evening. Five weeks ago, on Easter weekend, the Communist armies of North Vietnam launched a massive invasion of South Vietnam, an invasion that was made possible by tanks, artillery, and other advanced offensive weapons supplied to Hanoi by the Soviet Union and other Communist nations.

The South Vietnamese have fought bravely to repel this brutal assault. Casualties on both sides have been very high. Most tragically, there have been over 20,000 civilian casualties, including women and children, in the cities which the North Vietnamese have shelled in wanton disregard of human life.

As I announced in my report to the Nation 12 days ago, the role of the United States in resisting this invasion has been limited to air and naval strikes on military targets in North and South Vietnam. As I also pointed out in that report, we have responded to North Vietnam's massive military offensive by undertaking wide-ranging new peace efforts aimed at ending the war through negotiation.

On April 20th, I sent Dr. Kissinger to Moscow for four days of meetings with General Secretary Brezhnev and other Soviet leaders. I instructed him to emphasize our desire for a rapid solution to the war and our willingness to look at all possible approaches. At that time, the Soviet leaders showed an interest in bringing the war to an end on a basis just to both sides. They urged resumption of negotiations in Paris, and they indicated they would use their constructive influence.

I authorized Dr. Kissinger to meet privately with the top North Vietnamese negotiator, Le Duc Tho, on Tuesday, May 2nd, in Paris. Ambassador Porter, as you know, resumed the public peace negotiations in Paris on April 27th and again on May 4th. At those meetings, both public and private, all we heard from the enemy was bombastic rhetoric and a replaying of their demand for surrender. For example, at the May 2nd secret meeting, I authorized Dr. Kissinger to talk about every conceivable avenue toward peace. The North Vietnamese flatly refused to consider any of these approaches. They refused to offer any new approach of their own. Instead, they simply read verbatim their previous public demands.

Here is what over three years of public and private negotiations with Hanoi has come down to: The United States, with the full concurrence of our South Vietnamese allies, has offered the maximum of what any President of the United States could offer.

We have offered a de-escalation of the fighting. We have offered a cease-fire with the deadline for withdrawal of all American forces. We have offered new elections which would be internationally supervised with the Communists participating both in the supervisory body and in the elections themselves.

President Thieu has offered to resign one month before the elections. We have offered an exchange of prisoners of war in a ratio of 10 North Vietnamese prisoners for every one American prisoner that they release. And North Vietnam has met each of these offers with insolence and insult. They have flatly and arrogantly refused to negotiate an end to the war and bring peace. Their answer to every peace offer we have made has been to escalate the war.

In the two weeks alone since I offered to resume negotiations Hanoi has launched three new military offensives in South Vietnam. In those two weeks the risk that a Communist government may be imposed on the 17 million people of South Vietnam has increased and the Communist offensive has now reached the point that it gravely threatens the lives of 60,000 American troops who are still in Vietnam.

There are only two issues left for us in this war. First, in the face of a massive invasion do we stand by, jeopardize the lives of 60,000 Americans, and leave the South Vietnamese to a long night of terror? This will not happen. We shall do whatever is required to safeguard American lives and American honor.

Second, in the face of complete intransigence at the conference table do we join with our enemy to install a Communist government in South Vietnam? This, too, will not happen. We will not cross the line from generosity to treachery.

We now have a clear, hard choice among three courses of action: Immediate withdrawal of all American forces, continued attempts at negotiation, or decisive military action to end the war.

I know that many Americans favor the first course of action, immediate withdrawal. They believe that the way to end the war is for the United States to get out and to remove the threat to our remaining forces by simply withdrawing them.

From a political standpoint, this would be a very easy choice for me to accept. After all, I did not send over one-half a million Americans to Vietnam. I have brought 500,000 men home from Vietnam since I took office. But, abandoning our commitment in Vietnam here and now would mean turning 17 million South Vietnamese over to Communist tyranny and terror. It would mean leaving hundreds of American prisoners in Communist hands with no bargaining leverage to get them released.

An American defeat in Vietnam would encourage this kind of aggression all over the world, aggression in which smaller nations armed by their major allies, could be tempted to attack neighboring nations at will in the Mid-East, in Europe, and other areas. World peace would be in grave jeopardy.

The second course of action is to keep on trying to negotiate a settlement. Now this is the course we have preferred from the beginning and we shall continue to pursue it. We want to negotiate, but we have made every reasonable offer and tried every possible path for ending this war at the conference table.

The problem is, as you all know, it takes two to negotiate and now, as throughout the past four years, the North Vietnamese arrogantly refuse to negotiate anything but an imposition, and ultimately that the United States impose a Communist regime on 17 million people in South Vietnam who do not want a Communist government.

It is plain then that what appears to be a choice among three courses of action for the United States is really no choice at all. The killing in this tragic war must stop. By simply getting out, we would only worsen the bloodshed. By relying solely on negotiations, we would give an intransigent enemy the time he needs to press his aggression on the battlefield.

There is only one way to stop the killing. That is to keep the weapons of war out of the hands of the international outlaws of North Vietnam.

Throughout the war in Vietnam, the United States has exercised a degree of restraint unprecedented in the annals of war. That was our responsibility as a great nation, a nation which is interested—and we can be proud of this as Americans— as America has always been, in peace not conquest.

However, when the enemy abandons all restraint, throws its whole army into battle in the territory of its neighbor, refuses to negotiate, we simply face a new situation.

In these circumstances, with 60,000 Americans threatened, any President who failed to act decisively would have betrayed the trust of his country and betrayed the cause of world peace.

I therefore concluded Hanoi must be denied the weapons and supplies it needs to continue the aggression. In full coordination with the Republic of Vietnam I have ordered the following measures which are being implemented as I am speaking to you.

All entrances to North Vietnamese ports will be mined to prevent access to these ports and North Vietnamese naval operations from these ports. United States forces have been directed to take appropriate measures within the internal and claimed territorial waters of North Vietnam to interdict the delivery of any supplies. Rail and all other communications will be cut off to the maximum extent possible. Air and naval strikes against military targets in North Vietnam will continue.

These actions are not directed against any other nation. Countries with ships presently in North Vietnamese ports have already been notified that their ships will have three daylight periods to leave in safety. After that time, the mines will become active and any ships attempting to leave or enter these ports will do so at their own risk.

These actions I have ordered will cease when the following conditions are met: First, all American prisoners of war must be returned.

Second, there must be an internationally supervised cease-fire throughout Indochina.

Once prisoners of war are released, once the internationally supervised cease-fire has begun, we will stop all acts of force throughout Indochina, and at that time we will proceed with a complete withdrawal of all American forces from Vietnam within four months.

Now, these terms are generous terms. They are terms which would not require surrender and humiliation on the part of anybody. They would permit the United States to withdraw with honor. They would end the killing. They would bring our POWs home. They would allow negotiations on a political settlement between the Vietnamese themselves. They would permit all the nations which have suffered in this long war—Cambodia, Laos, North Vietnam, South Vietnam—to turn at last to the urgent works of healing and of peace. They deserve immediate acceptance by North Vietnam.

It is appropriate to conclude my remarks tonight with some comments directed individually to each of the major parties involved in the continuing tragedy of the Vietnam War. First, to the leaders of Hanoi, your people have already suffered too much in your pursuit of conquest. Do not compound their agony with continued arrogance; choose instead the path of a peace that redeems your sacrifices, guarantees true independence for your country and ushers in an era of reconciliation.

To the people of South Vietnam, you shall continue to have our firm support in your resistance against aggression. It is your spirit that will determine the outcome of the battle. It is your will that will shape the future of your country.

To other nations, especially those which are allied with North Vietnam, the actions I have announced tonight are not directed against you. Their sole purpose is to protect the lives of 60,000 Americans who would be gravely endangered in the event the Communist offensive continues to roll forward and to prevent the imposition of a Communist government by brutal aggression upon 17 million people.

I particularly direct my comments tonight to the Soviet Union. We respect the Soviet Union as a great power. We recognize the right of the Soviet Union to defend its interests when they are threatened. The Soviet Union in turn must recognize our right to defend our interests.

No Soviet soldiers are threatened in Vietnam. Sixty thousand Americans are threatened. We expect you to help your allies, and you cannot expect us to do other than to continue to help our allies, but let us, and let all great powers help our allies only for the purpose of their defense, not for the purpose of launching invasions against their neighbors.

Otherwise the cause of peace, the cause in which we both have so great a stake, will be seriously jeopardized.

Our two nations have made significant progress in our negotiations in recent months. We are near major agreement on nuclear arms limitation, on trade, on a host of other issues.

Let us not slide back toward the dark shadows of a previous age. We do not ask you to sacrifice your principles, or your friends, but neither should you permit Hanoi's intransigence to blot out the prospects we together have so patiently prepared.

We, the United States, and the Soviet Union, are on the threshold of a new relationship that can serve not only the interests of our two countries, but the cause of world peace. We are prepared to continue to build this relationship. The responsibility is yours if we fail to do so.

And finally, may I say to the American people, I ask you for the same strong support you have always given your President in difficult moments. It is you most of all that the world will be watching.

I know how much you want to end this war. I know how much you want to bring our men home and I think you know from all that I have said and done these past three and one-half years how much I, too, want to end the war to bring our men home.

You want peace. I want peace. But, you also want honor and not defeat. You want a genuine peace, not a peace that is merely a prelude to another war.

At this moment, we must stand together in purpose and resolve. As so often in the past, we Americans did not choose to resort to war. It has been forced upon us by an enemy that has shown utter contempt toward every overture we have made for peace. And that is why, my fellow Americans, tonight I ask for your support of this decision, a decision which has only one purpose, not to expand the war, not to escalate the war, but to end this war and to win the kind of peace that will last.

With God's help, with your support, we will accomplish that great goal.

Thank you and good night.

ADDRESS TO SOVIET PEOPLE

Following is the text, as made available by the White House, of President Nixon's May 28 address to the people of the Soviet Union. The address was carried on Soviet radio and television.

Dobry Vecher.

I deeply appreciate this opportunity your government has given me to speak directly with the people of the Soviet Union, to bring you a message of friendship from all the people of the United States and to share with you some of my thoughts about the relations between our two countries and about the way to peace and progress in the world.

This is my fourth visit to the Soviet Union. On these visits I have gained a great respect for the peoples of the Soviet Union, for your strength, your generosity, your determination, for the diversity and richness of your cultural heritage, for your many achievements.

In the three years I have been in office, one of my principal aims has been to establish a better relationship between the United States and the Soviet Union. Our two countries have much in common. Most important of all, we have never fought one another in war. On the contrary, the memory of your soldiers and ours embracing at the Elbe, as allies, in 1945, remains strong in millions of hearts in both of our countries. It is my hope that that memory can serve as an inspiration for the renewal of Soviet-American cooperation in the 1970's.

As great powers, we shall sometimes be competitors, but we need never be enemies.

Thirteen years ago, when I visited your country as Vice President, I addressed the people of the Soviet Union on radio and television, as I am addressing you tonight. I said then, "Let us have peaceful competition, not only in producing the best factories, but in producing better lives for our people. Let us cooperate in our exploration of outer space. Let our aim be not victory over other peoples, but the victory of all mankind over hunger, want, misery and disease, wherever it exists in the world."

In our meetings this week, we have begun to bring some of those hopes to fruition. Shortly after we arrived here on Monday afternoon, a brief rain fell on Moscow, of a kind that I am told is called a mushroom rain, a warm rain, with sunshine breaking through that makes the mushrooms grow and is therefore considered a good omen. The month of May is early for mushrooms, but as our talks progressed this week, what did grow was even better. A far-reaching set of agreements that can lead to a better life for both of our peoples, to a better chance for peace in the world.

We have agreed on joint ventures in space. We have agreed on ways of working together to protect the environment, to advance health, to cooperate in science and technology. We have agreed on means of preventing incidents at sea. We have established the commission to expand trade between our two nations.

Most important, we have taken an historic first step in the limitation of nuclear strategic arms. This arms control agreement is not for the purpose of giving either side an advantage over the other. Both of our nations are strong, each respects the strength of the other, each will maintain the strength necessary to defend its independence.

But in an unchecked arms race between two great nations, there would be no winners, only losers. By setting this limitation together, the people of both of our nations, and of all nations, can be winners. If we continue in the spirit of serious purpose that has marked our discussions this week, these agreements can start us on a new road of cooperation for the benefit of our people, for the benefit of all people.

There is an old proverb that says, "Make peace with man and quarrel with your sins." The hardships and evils that beset all men and all nations, these and these alone are what we should make war upon.

As we look at the prospects for peace, we see that we have made significant progress at reducing the possible sources of direct conflict between us. But history tells us that great nations have often been dragged into war without intending it, but by conflicts between smaller nations. As great powers, we can and should use our influence to prevent this from happening. Our goal should be to discourage aggression in other parts of the world and particularly among those smaller nations that look to us for leadership and example.

With great power goes great responsibility. When a man walks with a great tread, he must be careful where he sets his feet. There can be true peace only when the weak are as safe as the strong. The wealthier and more powerful our own nations become, the more we have to lose from war and the threat of war, anywhere in the world.

Speaking for the United States, I can say this. We covet no one else's territory, we seek no dominion over any other people, we seek the right to live in peace, not only for ourselves, but for all the peoples of this earth. Our power will only be used to keep the peace, never to break it, only to defend freedom, never to destroy it. No nation that does not threaten its neighbors has anything to fear from the United States.

Soviet citizens have often asked me, "Does America truly want peace?"

I believe that our actions answer that question far better than any words could do. If we did not want peace, we would have not reduced the size of our armed forces by a million men, by almost one-third, during the past three years. If we did not want peace, we would not have worked so hard at reaching an agreement on the limitation of nuclear arms, at achieving a settlement of Berlin, at maintaining peace in the Middle East, at establishing better relations with the Soviet Union, with the People's Republic of China, with other nations of the world.

Mrs. Nixon and I feel very fortunate to have had the opportunity to visit the Soviet Union, to get to know the people of the Soviet Union, friendly and hospitable, courageous and strong. Most Americans will never have a chance to visit the Soviet Union and most Soviet citizens will never have a chance to visit America. Most of you know our country only through what you read in your newspapers and what you hear and see on radio and television and motion pictures. This is only a part of the real America.

I would like to take this opportunity to try to convey to you something of what America is really like, not in terms of its scenic beauties, its great cities, its factories, its farms, or its highways, but in terms of its people.

In many ways, the people of our two countries are very much alike. Like the Soviet Union, ours is a large and diverse nation. Our people, like yours, are hard working. Like you, we Americans have a strong spirit of competition, but we also have a great love of music and poetry, of sports, and of humor. Above all, we, like you, are an open, natural and friendly people. We love our country. We love our children. And we want for you and for your children the same peace and abundance that we want for ourselves and for our children.

We Americans are idealists. We believe deeply in our system of government. We cherish our personal liberty. We would fight to defend it, if necessary, as we have done before. But we also believe deeply in the right of each nation to choose its own system. Therefore, however much we like our own system for ourselves, we have no desire to impose it on anyone else.

As we conclude this week of talks, there are certain fundamental premises of the American point of view which I believe deserve emphasis. In conducting these talks, it has not been our aim to divide up the world into spheres of influence, to establish a condominium, or in any way to conspire together against the interests of any other nation. Rather we have sought to construct a better framework of understanding between our two nations, to make progress in our bilateral relationship, to find ways of insuring that future frictions between us would never embroil our two nations, and therefore, the world, in war.

While ours are both great and powerful nations, the world is no longer dominated by two super powers. The world is a better and safer place, because its power and resources are more widely distributed.

Beyond this, since World War II, more than 70 new nations have come into being. We cannot have true peace unless they, and all nations, can feel that they share it.

America seeks better relations, not only with the Soviet Union, but with all nations. The only sound basis for a peaceful and progressive international order is sovereign equality and mutual respect. We believe in the right of each nation to chart its own course, to choose its own system, to go its own way, without interference from other nations.

As we look to the longer term, peace depends also on continued progress in the developing nations. Together with other advanced industrial countries, the United States and the Soviet Union share a two-fold responsibility in this regard.

On the one hand, to practice restraint in those activities, such as the supply of arms, that might endanger the peace of developing nations. And second, to assist them in their orderly economic and social development, without political interference.

Some of you may have heard an old story told in Russia of a traveler who was walking to another village. He knew the way, but not the distance. Finally he came upon a woodsman chopping wood by the side of the road and he asked the woodsman, "How long will it take to reach the village?"

The woodsman replied, "I don't know."

The traveler was angry, because he was sure the woodsman was from the village and therefore knew how far it was. And so he started off down the road again. After he had gone a few steps, the woodsman called out, "Stop. It will take you about 15 minutes."

The traveler turned and demanded, "Why didn't you tell me that in the first place?"

The woodsman replied, "Because then I didn't know the length of your stride."

In our talks this week with the leaders of the Soviet Union, both sides have had a chance to measure the length of our strides toward peace and security. I believe that those strides have been substantial and that now we have well begun the long journey which will lead us to a new age in the relations between our two countries. It is important to both of our peoples that we continue those strides.

As our two countries learn to work together, our people will be able to get to know one another better. Greater cooperation can also mean a great deal in our daily lives. As we learn to cooperate in space, in health and the environment, in science and technology, our cooperation can help sick people get well. It can help industries produce more consumer goods. It can help all of us enjoy cleaner air and water. It can increase our knowledge of the world around us.

As we expand our trade, each of our countries can buy more of the other's goods and market more of our own. As we gain experience with arms control, we can bring closer the day when further agreements can lessen the arms burden of our two nations and lessen the threat of war in the world.

Through all the pages of history, through all the centuries, the world's people have struggled to be free from fear, whether fear of the elements or fear of hunger or fear of their own rulers or fear of their neighbors in other countries. And yet, time and again, people have vanquished the source of one fear only to fall prey to another.

Let our goal now be a world free of fear. A world in which nation will no longer prey upon nation, in which human energies will be turned away from production for war and toward more production for peace, away from conquest and toward invention, development, creation. A world in which together we can establish that peace which is more than the absence of war, which enables man to pursue those higher goals that the spirit yearns for.

Yesterday, I laid a wreath at the cemetery which commemorates the brave people who died during the Seige of Leningrad in World War II. At the cemetery, I saw the picture of a 12 year old girl. She was a beautiful child. Her name was Tanya. The pages of her diary tell the terrible story of war. In the simple words of a child, she wrote of the deaths of the members of her family. "Geine in December, Grannie in January. Lyosha then next. Then Uncle Vafya, then Uncle Lyosha, then Mama and then the Savizhevs." And then finally, these words, the last words in her diary, "All are dead. Only Tanya is left."

As we work toward a more peaceful world, let us think of Tanya and of the other Tanya's and their brothers and sisters everywhere. Let us do all that we can to insure that no other children will have to endure what Tanya did and that your children and ours, all the children of the world can live their full lives together in friendship and in peace.

Spasibo y Do Svidaniya.

SOVIET COMMUNIQUE

Following is the text of a joint communique issued by President Nixon and Soviet leaders at the end of Moscow summit talks on May 29:

By mutual agreement between the United States of America and the Union of Soviet Socialist Republics, the President of the United States and Mrs. Richard Nixon paid an official visit to the Soviet Union from May 22 to May 30, 1972. The President was accompanied by Secretary of State William P. Rogers, assistant to the President Dr. H. A. Kissinger, and other American officials. During his stay in the U.S.S.R. President Nixon visited, in addition to Moscow, the cities of Leningrad and Kiev.

President Nixon and L. I. Brezhnev, general secretary of the Central Committee of the Communist Party of the Soviet Union, N. Podgorny, chairman of the Supreme Soviet of the U.S.S.R., and A. N. Kosygin, chairman of the Council of Ministers of the U.S.S.R., conducted talks on fundamental problems of American-Soviet relations and the current international situation.

Also taking part in the conversations were:

On the American side: William P. Rogers, secretary of state, Jacob D. Beam, American ambassador to the U.S.S.R., Dr. Henry A. Kissinger, assistant to the President for national security affairs, Peter M. Flanigan, assistant to the President, and Martin J. Hillenbrand, assistant secretary of state for European affairs.

On the Soviet side: A. A. Gromyko, minister of foreign affairs of the U.S.S.R., N. S. Patolichev, minister of foreign trade, V. V. Kuznetsov, deputy minister of foreign affairs of the U.S.S.R., A. F. Dobrynin, Soviet ambassador to the U.S.A., A. M. Aleksandrov, assistant to the general secretary of the Central Committee, C.P.S.U., G. M. Korniyenko, member of the collegium of the Ministry of Foreign Affairs of the U.S.S.R.

The discussions covered a wide range of questions of mutual interest and were frank and thorough. They defined more precisely those areas where there are prospects for developing greater cooperation between the two countries, as well as those areas where the positions of the two sides are different.

I. BILATERAL RELATIONS

Guided by the desire to place U.S.-Soviet relations on a more stable and constructive foundation, and mindful of their responsibilities for maintaining world peace and for facilitating the relaxation of international tension, the two sides adopted a document entitled: "Basic Principles of Mutual Relations Between the United States of America and the Union of Soviet Socialist Republics," signed on behalf of the U.S. by President Nixon and on behalf of the U.S.S.R. by General Secretary Brezhnev.

Both sides are convinced that the provisions of that document open new possibilities for the development of peaceful relations and mutually beneficial cooperation between the U.S.A. and the U.S.S.R.

Having considered various areas of bilateral U.S.-Soviet relations, the two sides agreed that an improvement of relations is possible and desirable. They expressed their firm intention to act in accordance with the provisions set forth in the above-mentioned document.

As a result of progress made in negotiations which preceded the summit meeting, and in the course of the meeting itself, a number of significant agreements were reached. This will intensify bilateral cooperation in areas of common concern as well as in areas relevant to the cause of peace and international cooperation.

Limitation of Strategic Armaments

The two sides gave primary attention to the problem of reducing the danger of nuclear war. They believe that curbing the competition in strategic arms will make a significant and tangible contribution to this cause.

The two sides attach great importance to the treaty on the limitation of anti-ballistic missile systems and the interim agreement on certain measures with respect to the limitation of strategic offensive arms concluded between them.

These agreements, which were concluded as a result of the negotiations in Moscow, constitute a major step towards curbing and ultimately ending the arms race.

They are a concrete expression of the intention of the two sides to contribute to the relaxation of international tension and the strengthening of confidence between states as well as to carry out the obligations assumed by them in the Treaty on the Nonproliferation of Nuclear Weapons Article VI. Both sides are convinced that the achievement of the above agreements is a practical step toward saving mankind from the threat of the outbreak of nuclear war. Accordingly, it corresponds to the vital interests of the American and Soviet peoples as well as to the vital interests of all other peoples.

The two sides intend to continue active negotiations for the limitation of strategic offensive arms and to conduct them in a spirit of good will, respect for each other's legitimate interests and observance of the principle of equal security.

Both sides are also convinced that the agreement on measures to reduce the risk of outbreak of nuclear war between the U.S.A. and the U.S.S.R. signed in Washington Sept. 30, 1971, serves the interest not only of the Soviet and American peoples, but of all mankind.

Commercial and Economic Relations

Both sides agreed on measures designed to establish more favorable conditions for developing commercial and other economic ties between the U.S.A. and the U.S.S.R. They agree that realistic conditions exist for increasing economic ties. These ties should develop on the basis of mutual benefit and in accordance with generally accepted international practice.

Believing that these aims would be served by conclusion of a trade agreement between the U.S.A. and the U.S.S.R., the two sides decided to complete in the near future the work necessary to conclude such an agreement. They agreed on the desirability of credit arrangements to develop mutual trade and of early efforts to resolve other financial and economic issues. It was agreed that a lend-lease settlement will be negotiated concurrently with a trade agreement.

In the interests of broadening and facilitating commercial ties between the two countries, and to work out specific arrangements, the two sides decided to create a U.S.-Soviet joint commercial commission. Its first meeting will be held in Moscow in the summer of 1972.

Each side will promote the establishment of effective working arrangements between organizations and firms of both countries and encouraging the conclusion of long-term contracts.

Maritime Matters, Incidents at Sea

The two sides agreed to continue the negotiations aimed at reaching an agreement on maritime and related matters. They believe that such an agreement would mark a positive step in facilitating the expansion of commerce between the United States and the Soviet Union.

An agreement was concluded between the two sides on measures to prevent incidents at sea and in air space over it between vessels and aircraft of the U.S. and Soviet navies. By providing agreed procedures for ships and aircraft of the two navies operating in close proximity, this agreement will diminish the chances of dangerous accidents.

Cooperation in Science and Technology

It was recognized that the cooperation now under way in areas such as atomic energy research, space research, health and other fields benefits both nations and has contributed positively to their over-all relations. It was agreed that increased scientific and technical cooperation on the basis of mutual benefit and shared effort for common goals is in the interest of both nations and would contribute to a further improvement in their bilateral relations. For these purposes the two sides signed an agreement for cooperation in the fields of science and technology. A U.S.-Soviet joint commission on scientific and technical cooperation will be created for identifying and establishing cooperative programs.

Cooperation in Space

Having in mind the role played by the U.S. and the U.S.S.R. in the peaceful exploration of outer space, both sides emphasized the importance of further bilateral cooperation in this sphere. In order to increase the safety of man's flights in outer space and the future prospects of joint scientific experiments, the two sides agreed to make suitable arrangements to permit the docking of American and Soviet spacecraft and stations. The first joint docking experiment of the two countries' piloted spacecraft, with visits by astronauts and cosmonauts to each other's spacecraft, is contemplated for 1975. The planning and implementation of this flight will be carried out by the U.S. National Aeronautics and Space Administration and the U.S.S.R. Academy of Sciences, according to principles and procedures developed through mutual consultations.

Cooperation in the Field of Health

The two sides concluded an agreement on health cooperation which marks a fruitful beginning of sharing knowledge about, and collaborative attacks on, the common enemies, disease and disability. The initial research efforts of the program will concentrate on health problems important to the whole world—cancer, heart diseases, and the environmental health sciences.

This cooperation subsequently will be broadened to include other health problems of mutual interest. The two sides pledged their full support for the health cooperation program and agreed to continue the active participation of the two governments in the work of international organizations in the health field.

Environmental Cooperation

The two sides agreed to initiate a program of cooperation in the protection and enhancement of man's environment. Through joint research and joint measures, the United States and the U.S.S.R. hope to contribute to the preservation of a healthful environment in their countries and throughout the world. Under the new agreement on environmental cooperation there will be consultations in the near future in Moscow on specific cooperative projects.

Exchanges in the Fields of Science, Technology, Education and Culture

Both sides note the importance of the agreement on exchanges and cooperation in scientific, technical, educational, cultural, and other fields in 1972-1973, signed in Moscow on April 11, 1972. Continuation and expansion of bilateral exchanges in these fields will lead to better understanding and help improve the general state of relations between the two countries. Within the broad framework provided by this agreement the two sides have agreed to expand the areas of cooperation, as reflected in new agreements concerning space, health, the environment and science and technology.

The U.S. side, noting the existence of an extensive program of English-language instruction in the Soviet Union, indicated its intention to encourage Russian-language programs in the United States.

II. INTERNATIONAL ISSUES

Europe

In the course of the discussions on the international situation, both sides took note of favorable developments in the relaxation of tensions in Europe.

Recognizing the importance to world peace of developments in Europe, where both world wars originated, and mindful of the responsibilities and commitments which they share with other powers under appropriate agreements, the U.S.A. and the U.S.S.R. intend to make further efforts to ensure a peaceful future for Europe, free of tensions, crises and conflicts.

They agree that the territorial integrity of all states in Europe should be respected.

Both sides view the Sept. 3, 1971, quadripartite agreement relating to the western sectors of Berlin as a good example of fruitful cooperation between the states concerned, including the U.S.A. and the U.S.S.R. The two sides believe that the implementation of that agreement in the near future, along with other steps, will further improve the European situation and contribute to the necessary trust among states.

Both sides welcomed the treaty between the U.S.S.R. and the Federal Republic of Germany signed on Aug. 12, 1970. They noted the significance of the provisions of this treaty as well as of other recent agreements in contributing to confidence and cooperation among the European states.

The U.S.A. and the U.S.S.R. are prepared to make appropriate contributions to the positive trends on the European continent toward a genuine detente and the development of relations of peaceful cooperation among states in Europe on the basis of the principles of territorial integrity and inviolability of frontiers, non-interference in internal affairs, sovereign equality in independence and renunciation of the use or threat of force.

The U.S. and U.S.S.R. are in accord that multilateral consultations looking toward a conference on security and cooperation in Europe could begin after the signature of the final quadripartite protocol of the agreement of Sept. 3, 1971. The two governments agree that the conference should be carefully prepared in order that it may concretely consider specific problems of security and cooperation and thus contribute to the progressive reduction of the underlying causes of tension in Europe. This conference should be convened at a time to be agreed by the countries concerned, but without undue delay.

Both sides believe that the goal of ensuring stability and security in Europe would be served by a reciprocal reduction of armed forces and armaments, first of all in central Europe. Any agreement on this question should not diminish the security of any of the sides. Appropriate agreement should be reached as soon as practicable between the states concerned on the procedures for negotiations on this subject in a special forum.

The Middle East

The two sides set out their positions on this question. They reaffirm their support for a peaceful settlement in the Middle East in accordance with Security Council Resolution 242.

Noting the significance of constructive cooperation of the parties concerned with the special representative of the U.N. secretary general, Ambassador Jarring, the U.S. and the U.S.S.R. confirm their desire to contribute to his mission's success and also declare their readiness to play their part in bringing about a peaceful settlement in the Middle East. In the view of the U.S. and the U.S.S.R., the achievement of such a settlement would open prospects for the normalization of the Middle East situation and would permit, in particular, consideration of further steps to bring about a military relaxation in that area.

Indochina

Each side set forth its respective standpoint with regard to the continuing war in Vietnam and the situation in the area of Indochina as a whole.

The U.S. side emphasized the need to bring an end to the military conflict as soon as possible and reaffirmed its commitment to the principle that the political future of South Vietnam should be left for the South Vietnamese people to decide for themselves, free from outside interference.

The U.S. side explained its view that the quickest and most effective way to attain the above-mentioned objectives is through negotiations leading to the return of all Americans held captive in the region, the implementation of an internationally supervised, Indochina-wide cease-fire and the subsequent withdrawal of all American forces stationed in South Vietnam within four months, leaving the political questions to be resolved by the Indochinese peoples themselves.

The United States reiterated its willingness to enter into serious negotiations with the North Vietnamese side to settle the war in Indochina on a basis just to all.

The Soviet side stressed its solidarity with the just struggle of the peoples of Vietnam, Laos and Cambodia for their freedom, independence and social progress. Firmly supporting the proposals of the DRV (North Vietnam) and the Provisional Revolutionary Government of the Republic of South Vietnam, which provide a realistic and constructive basis for settling the Vietnam problem, the Soviet Union stands for a cessation of bombings of the DRV, for a complete and unequivocal withdrawal of the troops of the U.S.A. and its allies from South Vietnam, so that the people of Indochina would have the possibility to determine for themselves their fate without any outside interference.

Disarmament Issues

The two sides note that in recent years their joint and parallel actions have facilitated the working out and conclusion of treaties which curb the arms race or ban some of the most dangerous types of weapons. They note further that these treaties were welcomed by a large majority of the states in the world, which became parties to them.

Both sides regard the convention on the prohibition of the development, production and stockpiling of bacteriological, biological and toxic weapons and on their destruction, as an essential disarmament measure. Along with Great Britain, they are the depositories for the convention which was recently opened for signature by all states. The U.S.A. and U.S.S.R. will continue their efforts to reach an international agreement regarding chemical weapons.

The U.S.A. and the U.S.S.R., proceeding from the need to take into account the security interests of both countries on the basis of the principle of equality, and without prejudice to the security interests of third countries, will actively participate in negotiations aimed at working out new measures designed to curb and end the arms race. The ultimate purpose is general and complete disarmament, including nuclear disarmament, under strict international control. A world disarmament conference could play a role in this process at an appropriate time.

Strengthening the United Nations

Both sides will strive to strengthen the effectiveness of the United Nations on the basis of strict observance of the U.N. charter.

They regard the United Nations as an instrument for maintaining world peace and security, discouraging conflicts, and developing international cooperation. Accordingly, they will do their best to support United Nations efforts in the interests of international peace.

Both sides emphasized that agreements and understandings reached in the negotiations in Moscow, as well as the contents and nature of these negotiations, are not in any way directed against any other country. Both sides proceed from the recognition of the role, the responsibility and the prerogatives of other interested states, existing international obligations and agreements, and the principles and purposes of the U.N. charter.

Both sides believe that positive results were accomplished in the course of the talks at the highest level. These results indicate that despite the differences between the U.S.A. and the U.S.S.R. in social systems, ideologies, and policy principles, it is possible to develop mutually advantageous cooperation between the peoples of both countries, in the interests of strengthening peace and international security.

Both sides expressed the desire to continue close contact on a number of issues that were under discussion. They agreed that regular consultations on questions of mutual interest, including meetings at the highest level, would be useful.

In expressing his appreciation for the hospitality accorded him in the Soviet Union, President Nixon invited General Secretary L. I. Brezhnev, Chairman N. V. Podgorny and Chairman A. N. Kosygin to visit the United States at a mutually convenient time. This invitation was accepted.

DECLARATION OF PRINCIPLES

Following is the text, as made available by the White House, of the declaration of basic principles of relations between the United States and the Soviet Union. It was signed by President Nixon and Communist Party Chief Leonid Brezhnev on May 29.

The United States of America and the Union of Soviet Socialist Republics,

Guided by their obligations under the Charter of the United Nations and by a desire to strengthen peaceful relations with each other and to place these relations on the firmest possible basis,

Aware of the need to make every effort to remove the threat of war and to create conditions which promote the reduction of tensions in the world and the strengthening of universal security and international cooperation,

Believing that the improvement of US-Soviet relations and their mutually advantageous development in such areas as economics, science and culture, will meet these objectives and contribute to better mutual understanding and business-like cooperation, without in any way prejudicing the interests of third countries,

Conscious that these objectives reflect the interests of the peoples of both countries,

Have agreed as follows:

First. They will proceed from the common determination that in the nuclear age there is no alternative to conducting their mutual relations on the basis of peaceful coexistence. Differences in ideology and in the social systems of the USA and the USSR are not obstacles to the bilateral development of normal relations based on the principles of sovereignty, equality, non-interference in internal affairs and mutual advantage.

Second. The USA and the USSR attach major importance to preventing the development of situations capable of causing a dangerous exacerbation of their relations. Therefore, they will do their utmost to avoid military confrontations and to prevent the outbreak of nuclear war. They will always exercise restraint in their mutual relations, and will be prepared to negotiate and settle differences by peaceful means. Discussions and negotiations on outstanding issues will be conducted in a spirit of reciprocity, mutual accommodation and mutual benefit.

Both sides recognize that efforts to obtain unilateral advantage at the expense of the other, directly or indirectly, are inconsistent with these objectives. The prerequisites for maintaining and strengthening peaceful relations between the USA and the USSR are the recognition of the security interests of the Parties based on the principle of equality and the renunciation of the use or threat of force.

Third. The USA and the USSR have a special responsibility, as do other countries which are permanent members of the United Nations Security Council, to do everything in their power so that conflicts or situations will not arise which would serve to increase international tensions. Accordingly, they will seek to promote conditions in which all countries will live in peace and security and will not be subject to outside interference in their internal affairs.

Fourth. The USA and the USSR intend to widen the juridical basis of their mutual relations and to exert the necessary efforts so that bilateral agreements which they have concluded and multilateral treaties and agreements to which they are jointly parties are faithfully implemented.

Fifth. The USA and the USSR reaffirm their readiness to continue the practice of exchanging views on problems of mutual interest and, when necessary, to conduct such exchanges at the highest level, including meetings between leaders of the two countries.

The two governments welcome and will facilitate an increase in productive contacts between representatives of the legislative bodies of the two countries.

Sixth. The Parties will continue their efforts to limit armaments on a bilateral as well as on a multilateral basis. They will continue to make special efforts to limit strategic armaments. Whenever possible, they will conclude concrete agreements aimed at achieving these purposes.

The USA and the USSR regard as the ultimate objective of their efforts the achievement of general and complete disarmament and the establishment of an effective system of international security in accordance with the purposes and principles of the United Nations.

Seventh. The USA and the USSR regard commercial and economic ties as an important and necessary element in the strengthening of their bilateral relations and thus will actively promote the growth of such ties. They will facilitate cooperation between the relevant organizations and enterprises of the two countries and the conclusion of appropriate agreements and contracts, including long-term ones.

The two countries will contribute to the improvement of maritime and air communications between them.

Eighth. The two sides consider it timely and useful to develop mutual contacts and cooperation in the fields of science and technology. Where suitable, the USA and the USSR will conclude appropriate agreements dealing with concrete cooperation in these fields.

Ninth. The two sides reaffirm their intention to deepen cultural ties with one another and to encourage fuller familiarization with each other's cultural values. They will promote improved conditions for cultural exchanges and tourism.

Tenth. The USA and the USSR will seek to ensure that their ties and cooperation in all the above-mentioned fields and in any others in their mutual interest are built on a firm and long-term basis. To give a permanent character to these efforts, they will establish in all fields where this is feasible joint commissions or other joint bodies.

Eleventh. The USA and the USSR make no claim for themselves and would not recognize the claims of anyone else to any special rights or advantages in world affairs. They recognize the sovereign equality of all states.

The Development of US-Soviet relations is not directed against third countries and their interests.

Twelfth. The basic principles set forth in this document do not affect any obligations with respect to other countries earlier assumed by the USA and the USSR.

Moscow, May 29, 1972

For the United States of America

RICHARD NIXON
President of the United States
of America

For the Union of Soviet
Socialist Republics

LEONID I. BREZHNEV
General Secretary of the
Central Committee, CPSU

U.S.-SOVIET MISSILE PACTS
Nixon Message

Following is the text, as made available by the White House, of President Nixon's June 13, 1972, message to Congress requesting ratification of the defensive arms treaty and offensive arms agreement signed in Moscow May 26.

TO THE SENATE OF THE UNITED STATES:

I transmit herewith certified copies of the Treaty on the Limitation of Anti-Ballistic Missile Systems and the Interim Agreement on Certain Measures with respect to the Limitation of Strategic Offensive Arms signed in Moscow on May 26, 1972. Copies of these agreements are also being forwarded to the Speaker of the House of Representatives. I ask the Senate's advice and consent to ratification of the Treaty, and an expression of support from both Houses of the Congress for the Interim Agreement on Strategic Offensive Arms.

These agreements, the product of a major effort of this administration, are a significant step into a new era of mutually agreed restraint and arms limitation between the two principal nuclear powers.

The provisions of the agreements are explained in detail in the Report of the Secretary of State, which I attach. Their main effect is this: The ABM Treaty limits the deployment of anti-ballistic missile systems to two designated areas, and at a low level. The Interim Agreement limits the overall level of strategic offensive missile forces. Together the two agreements provide for a more stable strategic balance in the next several years than would be possible if strategic arms competition continued unchecked. This benefits not only the United States and the Soviet Union, but all the nations of the world.

The agreements are an important first step in checking the arms race, but only a first step; they do not close off all avenues of strategic competition. Just as the maintenance of a strong strategic posture was an essential element in the success of these negotiations, it is now equally essential that we carry forward a sound strategic modernization program to maintain our security and to ensure that more permanent and comprehensive arms limitation agreements can be reached.

The defense capabilities of the United States are second to none in the world today. I am determined that they shall remain so. The terms of the ABM Treaty and Interim Agreement will permit the United States to take the steps we deem necessary to maintain a strategic posture which protects our vital interests and guarantees our continued security.

Besides enhancing our national security, these agreements open the opportunity for a new and more constructive U.S.-Soviet relationship, characterized by negotiated settlement of differences, rather than by the hostility and confrontation of decades past.

These accords offer tangible evidence that mankind need not live forever in the dark shadow of nuclear war. They provide renewed hope that men and nations working together can succeed in building a lasting peace.

Because these agreements effectively serve one of this Nation's most cherished purposes—a more secure and peaceful world in which America's security is fully protected—I strongly recommend that the Senate support them, and that its deliberations be conducted without delay.

RICHARD NIXON

AGREED INTERPRETATIONS

Following is the text, as made available by the White House June 13, of the agreed interpretations by the United States and the Soviet Union on the defensive arms treaty and the offensive arms agreement signed in Moscow May 26.

1. Agreed Interpretations.

(a) *Initialed Statements.*

The texts of the statements set out below were agreed upon and initialed by the Heads of the Delegations on May 26, 1972.

ABM Treaty

(A)

The Parties understand that, in addition to the ABM radars which may be deployed in accordance with subparagraph (a) of Article III of the Treaty, those non-phased-array ABM radars operational on the date of signature of the Treaty within the ABM system deployment area for defense of the national capital may be retained.

(B)

The Parties understand that the potential (the product of mean emitted power in watts and antenna area in square meters) of the smaller of the two large phased-array ABM radars referred to in subparagraph (b) of Article III of the Treaty is considered for purposes of the Treaty to be three million.

(C)

The Parties understand that the center of the ABM system deployment area centered on the national capital and the center of the ABM system deployment area containing ICBM silo launchers for each Party shall be separated by no less than thirteen hundred kilometers.

(D)

The Parties agree not to deploy phased-array radars having a potential (the product of mean emitted power in watts and antenna area in square meters) exceeding three million, except as provided for in Articles III, IV and VI of the Treaty, or except for the purposes of tracking objects in outer space or for use as national technical means of verification.

(E)

In order to insure fulfillment of the obligation not to deploy ABM systems and their components except as provided in Article III of the Treaty, the Parties agree that in the event ABM systems based on other physical principles and including components capable of substituting for ABM interceptor missiles, ABM launchers, or ABM radars are created in the future, specific limitations on such systems and their components would be subject to discussion in accordance with Article XIII and agreement in accordance with Article XIV of the Treaty.

(F)

The Parties understand that Article V of the Treaty includes obligations not to develop, test or deploy ABM interceptor missiles for the delivery by each ABM interceptor missile of more than one independently guided warhead.

(G)

The Parties understand that Article IX of the Treaty includes the obligation of the US and the USSR not to provide to other States technical descriptions or blueprints specially worked out for the construction of ABM systems and their components limited by the Treaty.

Interim Agreement

(H)

The Parties understand that land-based ICBM launchers referred to in the Interim Agreement are understood to be launchers for strategic ballistic missiles capable of ranges in excess of the shortest distance between the northeastern border of the continental U.S. and the northwestern border of the continental USSR.

(I)

The Parties understand that fixed land-based ICBM launchers under active construction as of the date of signature of the Interim Agreement may be completed.

(J)

The Parties understand that in the process of modernization and replacement the dimensions of land-based ICBM silo launchers will not be significantly increased.

(K)

The Parties understand that dismantling or destruction of ICBM launchers of older types deployed prior to 1964 and ballistic missile launchers on older submarines being replaced by new SLBM launchers on modern submarines will be initiated at the time of the beginning of sea trials of a replacement submarine, and will be completed in the shortest possible agreed period of time. Such dismantling or destruction, and timely notification thereof, will be accomplished under procedures to be agreed in the Standing Consultative Commission.

(L)

The Parties understand that during the period of the Interim Agreement there shall be no significant increase in the number of ICBM or SLBM test and training launchers, or in the number of such launchers for modern land-based heavy ICBMs. The Parties further understand that construction or conversion of ICBM launchers at test ranges shall be undertaken only for purposes of testing and training.

(b) *Common Understandings.*

Common understanding of the Parties on the following matters was reached during the negotiations:

A. Increase in ICBM Silo Dimensions

Ambassador Smith made the following statement on May 26, 1972: "The Parties agree that the term 'significantly increased' means that an increase will not be greater than 10-15 percent of the present dimensions of land-based ICBM silo launchers."

Minister Semenov replied that this statement corresponded to the Soviet understanding.

B. Location of ICBM Defenses

The U.S. Delegation made the following statement on May 26, 1972: "Article III of the ABM Treaty provides for each side one ABM system deployment area centered on its national capital and one ABM system deployment area containing ICBM silo launchers. The two sides have registered agreement on the following statement: 'The Parties understand that the center of the ABM system deployment area centered on the national capital and the center of the ABM system deployment area containing ICBM silo launchers for each Party shall be separated by no less than thirteen hundred kilometers.' In this connection, the U.S. side notes that its ABM system deployment area for defense of ICBM silo launchers, located west of the Mississippi River, will be centered in the Grand Forks ICBM silo launcher deployment area." (See Initialed Statement (C).)

C. ABM Test Ranges

The U.S. Delegation made the following statement on April 26, 1972: "Article IV of the ABM Treaty provides that 'the limitations provided for in Article III shall not apply to ABM systems or their components used for development or testing, and located within current or additionally agreed test ranges.' We believe it would be useful to assure that there is no misunderstanding as to current ABM test ranges. It is our understanding that ABM test ranges encompass the area within which ABM components are located for test purposes. The current U.S. ABM test ranges are at White Sands, New Mexico, and at Kwajalein Atoll, and the current Soviet ABM test range is near Sary Shagan in Kazakhstan. We consider that non-phased array radars of types used for range safety or instrumentation purposes may be located outside of ABM test ranges. We interpret the reference in Article IV to 'additionally agreed test ranges' to mean that ABM components will not be located at any other test ranges without prior agreement between our Governments that there will be such additional ABM test ranges."

On May 5, 1972, the Soviet Delegation stated that there was a common understanding on what ABM test ranges were, that the use of the types of non-ABM radars for range safety or instrumentation was not limited under the Treaty, that the reference in Article IV to "additionally agreed" test ranges was sufficiently clear, and that national means permitted identifying current test ranges.

D. Mobile ABM Systems

On January 28, 1972, the U.S. Delegation made the following statement: "Article V(1) of the Joint Draft Text of the ABM Treaty includes an undertaking not to develop, test, or deploy mobile land-based ABM systems and their components. On May 5, 1971, the U.S. side indicated that, in its view, a prohibition on deployment of mobile ABM systems and components would rule out the deployment of ABM launchers and radars which were not permanent fixed types. At that time, we asked for the Soviet view of this interpretation. Does the Soviet side agree with the U.S. side's interpretation put forward on May 5, 1971?"

On April 13, 1972, the Soviet Delegation said there is a general common understanding on this matter.

E. Standing Consultative Commission

Ambassador Smith made the following statement on May 23, 1972: "The United States proposes that the sides agree that, with regard to initial implementation of the ABM Treaty's Article XIII on the Standing Consultative Commission (SCC) and of the consultation Articles to the Interim Agreement an offensive arms and the Accidents Agreement, agreement establishing the SCC will be worked out early in the follow-on SALT negotiations; until that is completed, the following arrangements will prevail: when SALT is in session, any consultation desired by either side under these articles can be carried out by the two SALT Delegations; when SALT is not in session, *ad hoc* arrangements for any desired consultations under these Articles may be made through diplomatic channels."

Minister Semenov replied that, on an *ad referendum* basis, he could agree that the U.S. statement corresponded to the Soviet understanding.

F. Standstill

On May 6, 1972, Minister Semenov made the following statement: "In an effort to accommodate the wishes of the U.S. side, the Soviet Delegation is prepared to proceed on the basis that the two sides will in fact observe the obligations of both the Interim Agreement and the ABM Treaty beginning from the date of signature of these two documents."

In reply, the U.S. Delegation made the following statement on May 20, 1972: "The U.S. agrees in principle with the Soviet statement made on May 6 concerning observance of obligations beginning from date of signature but we would like to make clear our understanding that this means that, pending ratification and acceptance, neither side would take any action prohibited by the agreements after they had entered into force. This understanding would continue to apply in the absence of notification by either signatory of its intention not to proceed with ratification or approval."

The Soviet Delegation indicated agreement with the U.S. statement.

2. Unilateral Statements.

(a) The following noteworthy unilateral statements were made during the negotiations by the United States Delegation:—

A. Withdrawal from the ABM Treaty

On May 9, 1972, Ambassador Smith made the following statement: "The U.S. Delegation has stressed the importance the U.S. Government attaches to achieving agreement on more complete limitations on strategic offensive arms, following agreement on an ABM-Treaty and on an Interim Agreement on certain measures with respect to the limitation of strategic offensive arms. The U.S. Delegation believes that an objective of the follow-

on negotiations should be to constrain and reduce on a long-term basis threats to the survivability of our respective strategic retaliatory forces. The USSR Delegation has also indicated that the objectives of SALT would remain unfulfilled without the achievement of an agreement providing for more complete limitations on strategic offensive arms. Both sides recognize that the initial agreements would be steps toward the achievement of more complete limitations on strategic arms. If an agreement providing for more complete strategic offensive arms limitations were not achieved within five years, U.S. supreme interests could be jeopardized. Should that occur, it would constitute a basis for withdrawal from the ABM Treaty. The U.S. does not wish to see such a situation occur, nor do we believe that the USSR does. It is because we wish to prevent such a situation that we emphasize the importance the U.S. Government attaches to achievement of more complete limitations on strategic offensive arms. The U.S. Executive will inform the Congress, in connection with Congressional consideration of the ABM Treaty and the Interim Agreement of this statement of the U.S. position."

B. Land-Mobile ICBM Launchers

The U.S. Delegation made the following statement on May 20, 1972: "In connection with the important subject of land-mobile ICBM launchers, in the interest of concluding the Interim Agreement the U.S. Delegation now withdraws its proposal that Article I or an agreed statement explicitly prohibit the deployment of mobile land-based ICBM launchers. I have been instructed to inform you that, while agreeing to defer the question of limitation of operational land-mobile ICBM launchers to the subsequent negotiations on more complete limitations on strategic offensive arms, the U.S. would consider the deployment of operational land-mobile ICBM launchers during the period of the Interim Agreement as inconsistent with the objectives of that Agreement."

C. Covered Facilities.

The U.S. Delegation made the following statement on May 20, 1972: "I wish to emphasize the importance that the United States attaches to the provisions of Article V, including in particular their application to fitting out or berthing submarines."

D. "Heavy" ICBMs

The U.S. Delegation made the following statement on May 26, 1972: "The U.S. Delegation regrets that the Soviet Delegation has not been willing to agree on a common definition of a heavy missile. Under these circumstances, the U.S. Delegation believes it necessary to state the following: The United States would consider any ICBM having a volume significantly greater than that of the largest light ICBM now operational on either side to be a heavy ICBM. The U.S. proceeds on the premise that the Soviet side will give due account to this consideration."

E. Tested in ABM Mode

On April 7, 1972, the U.S. Delegation made the following statement: "Article II of the Joint Draft Text uses the term 'tested in an ABM mode,' in defining ABM components, and Article VI includes certain obligations concerning such testing. We believe that the sides should have a common understanding of this phrase. First, we would note that the testing provisions of the ABM Treaty are intended to apply to testing which occurs after the date of signature of the Treaty, and not to any testing which may have occurred in the past. Next, we would amplify the remarks we have made on this subject during the previous Helsinki phase by setting forth the objectives which govern the U.S. view on the subject, namely, while prohibiting testing of non-ABM components for ABM purposes: not to prevent testing of ABM components, and not to prevent testing of non-ABM components for non-ABM purposes. To clarify our inter-

its decision to the other Party six months prior to withdrawal from the Treaty. Such notice shall include a statement of the extraordinary events the notifying Party regards as having jeopardized its supreme interests.

Article XVI

1. This Treaty shall be subject to ratification in accordance with the constitutional procedures of each Party. The Treaty shall enter into force on the day of the exchange of instruments of ratification.

2. This Treaty shall be registered pursuant to Article 102 of the Charter of the United Nations.

Done at Moscow on May 26, 1972, in two copies, each in the English and Russian languages, both texts being equally authentic.

FOR THE UNITED STATES
OF AMERICA

FOR THE UNION OF SOVIET
SOCIALIST REPUBLICS

RICHARD NIXON
President of the United
States of America

LEONID I. BREZHNEV
General Secretary of the Central
Committee of the CPSU

AGREEMENTS ON OFFENSIVE MISSILES

THE PROTOCOL

Following is the text, as made available by the White House, of the protocol to the interim agreement between the United States of America and the Union of Soviet Socialist Republics on certain measures with respect to the limitation of strategic offensive arms:

The United States of America and the Union of Soviet Socialist Republics, hereinafter referred to as the Parties,

Having agreed on certain limitations relating to submarine-launched ballistic missile launchers and modern ballistic missile submarines, and to replacement procedures, in the Interim Agreement,

Have agreed as follows:

The Parties understand that, under Article III of the Interim Agreement, for the period during which that Agreement remains in force:

The US may have no more than 710 ballistic missile launchers on submarines (SLBMs) and no more than 44 modern ballistic missile submarines. The Soviet Union may have no more than 950 ballistic missile launchers on submarines and no more than 62 modern ballistic missile submarines.

Additional ballistic missile launchers on submarines up to the above-mentioned levels, in the U.S. - over 656 ballistic missile launchers on nuclear-powered submarines, and in the U.S.S.R. - over 740 ballistic missile launchers on nuclear-powered submarines, operational and under construction, may become operational as replacements for equal numbers of ballistic missile launchers of older types deployed prior to 1964 or of ballistic missile launchers on older submarines.

The deployment of modern SLBMs on any submarine, regardless of type, will be counted against the total level of SLBMs permitted for the U.S. and the U.S.S.R.

This Protocol shall be considered an integral part of the Interim Agreement.

FOR THE UNITED STATES
OF AMERICA

FOR THE UNION OF SOVIET
SOCIALIST REPUBLICS

RICHARD NIXON
The President of the United
States of America

LEONID I. BREZHNEV
The General Secretary of the
Central Committee of the CPSU

INTERIM AGREEMENT

Following is the text, as made available by the White House, of the Interim Agreement between the Union of Soviet Socialist Republics and the United States of America on certain measures with respect to the limitation of strategic offensive arms:

The Union of Soviet Socialist Republics and the United States of America hereinafter referred to as the Parties,

Convinced that the Treaty on the Limitation of Anti-Ballistic Missile Systems and this Interim Agreement on Certain Measures with Respect to the Limitation of Strategic Offensive Arms will contribute to the creation of more favorable conditions for active negotiations on limiting strategic arms as well as to the relaxation of international tension and the strengthening of trust between States,

Taking into account the relationship between strategic offensive and defensive arms,

Mindful of their obligations under Article VI of the Treaty on the Non-Proliferation of Nuclear Weapons,

Have agreed as follows:

Article I

The Parties undertake not to start construction of additional fixed land-based intercontinental ballistic missile (ICBM) launchers after July 1, 1972.

Article II

The Parties undertake not to convert land-based launchers for light ICBMs, or for ICBMs of older types deployed prior to 1964, into land-based launchers for heavy ICBMs of types deployed after that time.

Article III

The Parties undertake to limit submarine-launched ballistic missile (SLBM) launchers and modern ballistic missile submarines to the numbers operational and under construction on the date of signature of this Interim Agreement, and in addition launchers and submarines constructed under procedures established by the Parties as replacements for an equal number of ICBM launchers of older types deployed prior to 1964 or for launchers on older submarines.

Article IV

Subject to the provisions of this Interim Agreement, modernization and replacement of strategic offensive ballistic missiles and launchers covered by this Interim Agreement may be undertaken.

Article V

1. For the purpose of providing assurance of compliance with the provisions of this Interim Agreement, each Party shall use national technical means of verification at its disposal in a manner consistent with generally recognized principles of international law.

2. Each Party undertakes not to interfere with the national technical means of verification of the other Party operating in accordance with paragraph 1 of this Article.

3. Each Party undertakes not to use deliberate concealment measures which impede verification by national technical means of compliance with the provisions of this Interim Agreement. This obligation shall not require changes in current construction, assembly, conversion, or overhaul practices.

national capital, a Party may deploy: (1) no more than one hundred ABM launchers and no more than one hundred ABM interceptor missiles at launch sites, and (2) ABM radars within no more than six ABM radar complexes, the area of each complex being circular and having a diameter of no more than three kilometers; and

(b) within one ABM system deployment area having a radius of one hundred and fifty kilometers and containing ICBM silo launchers, a Party may deploy: (1) no more than one hundred ABM launchers and no more than one hundred ABM interceptor missiles at launch sites; (2) two large phased-array ABM radars comparable in potential to corresponding ABM radars operational or under construction on the date of signature of the Treaty in an ABM system deployment area containing ICBM silo launchers, and (3) no more than eighteen ABM radars each having a potential less than the potential of the smaller of the above-mentioned two large phased-array ABM radars.

Article IV

The limitations provided for in Article III shall not apply to ABM systems or their components used for development or testing, and located within current or additionally agreed test ranges. Each Party may have no more than a total of fifteen ABM launchers at test ranges.

Article V

1. Each Party undertakes not to develop, test, or deploy ABM systems or components which are sea-based, air-based, space-based, or mobile land-based.

2. Each Party undertakes not to develop, test, or deploy ABM launchers for launching more than one ABM interceptor missile at a time from each launcher, nor to modify deployed launchers to provide them with such a capability, nor to develop, test, or deploy automatic or semi-automatic or other similar systems for rapid reload of ABM launchers.

Article VI

To enhance assurance of the effectiveness of the limitations on ABM systems and their components provided by this Treaty, each Party undertakes:

(a) not to give missiles, launchers, or radars, other than ABM interceptor missiles, ABM launchers, or ABM radars, capabilities to counter strategic ballistic missiles or their elements in flight trajectory, and not to test them in an ABM mode; and

(b) not to deploy in the future radars for early warning of strategic ballistic missile attack except at locations along the periphery of its national territory and oriented outward.

Article VII

Subject to the provisions of this Treaty, modernization and replacement of ABM systems or their components may be carried out.

Article VIII

ABM systems or their components in excess of the numbers or outside the areas specified in this Treaty, as well as ABM systems or their components prohibited by this Treaty, shall be destroyed or dismantled under agreed procedures within the shortest possible agreed period of time.

Article IX

To assure the viability and effectiveness of this Treaty, each Party undertakes not transfer to other States, and not to deploy outside its national territory, ABM systems or their components limited by this Treaty.

Article X

Each Party undertakes not to assume any international obligations which would conflict with this Treaty.

Article XI

The Parties undertake to continue active negotiations for limitations on strategic offensive arms.

Article XII

1. For the purpose of providing assurance of compliance with the provisions of this Treaty, each Party shall use national technical means of verification at its disposal in a manner consistent with generally recognized principles of international law.

2. Each Party undertakes not to interfere with the national technical means of verification of the other Party operating in accordance with paragraph 1 of this Article.

3. Each Party undertakes not to use deliberate concealment measures which impede verification by national technical means of compliance with the provisions of this Treaty. This obligation shall not require changes in current construction, assembly, conversion, or overhaul practices.

Article XIII

1. To promote the objectives and implementation of the provisions of this Treaty, the Parties shall establish promptly a Standing Consultative Commission, within the framework of which they will:

(a) consider questions concerning compliance with the obligations assumed and related situations which may be considered ambiguous;

(b) provide on a voluntary basis such information as either Party considers necessary to assure confidence in compliance with the obligations assumed;

(c) consider questions involving unintended interference with national technical means of verification;

(d) consider possible changes in the strategic situation which have a bearing on the provisions of this Treaty;

(e) agree upon procedures and dates for destruction or dismantling of ABM systems or their components in cases provided for by the provisions of this Treaty;

(f) consider, as appropriate, possible proposals for further increasing the viability of this Treaty, including proposals for amendments in accordance with the provisions of this Treaty;

(g) consider, as appropriate, proposals for further measures aimed at limiting strategic arms.

2. The Parties through consultation shall establish, and may amend as appropriate, Regulations for the Standing Consultative Commission governing procedures, composition and other relevant matters.

Article XIV

1. Each Party may propose amendments to this Treaty. Agreed amendments shall enter into force in accordance with the procedures governing the entry into force of this Treaty.

2. Five years after entry into force of this Treaty, and at five-year intervals thereafter, the Parties shall together conduct a review of this Treaty.

Article XV

1. This Treaty shall be of unlimited duration.

2. Each Party shall, in exercising its national sovereignty, have the right to withdraw from this Treaty if it decides that extraordinary events related to the subject matter of this Treaty have jeopardized its supreme interests. It shall give notice of

Article VI

To promote the objectives and implementation of the provisions of this Interim Agreement, the Parties shall use the Standing Consultative Commission established under Article XIII of the Treaty on the Limitation of Anti-Ballistic Missile Systems in accordance with the provisions of that Article.

Article VII

The Parties undertake to continue active negotiations for limitations on strategic offensive arms. The obligations provided for in this Interim Agreement shall not prejudice the scope or terms of the limitations on strategic offensive arms which may be worked out in the course of further negotiations.

Article VIII

1. This Interim Agreement shall enter into force upon exchange of written notices of acceptance by each Party, which exchange shall take place simultaneously with the exchange of instruments of ratification of the Treaty on the Limitation of Anti-Ballistic Missile Systems.

2. This Interim Agreement shall remain in force for a period of five years unless replaced earlier by an agreement on more complete measures limiting strategic offensive arms. It is the objective of the Parties to conduct active follow-on negotiations with the aim of concluding such an agreement as soon as possible.

3. Each Party shall, in exercising its national sovereignty, have the right to withdraw from this Interim Agreement if it decides that extraordinary events related to the subject matter of this Interim Agreement have jeopardized its supreme interests. It shall give notice of its decision to the other Party six months prior to withdrawal from this Interim Agreement. Such notice shall include a statement of the extraordinary events the notifying Party regards as having jeopardized its supreme interests.

Done at Moscow on May 26, 1972, in two copies, each in the Russian and English languages, both texts being equally authentic.

FOR THE UNION OF SOVIET   FOR THE UNITED STATES
     SOCIALIST REPUBLICS   OF AMERICA

LEONID I. BREZHNEV   RICHARD NIXON
General Secretary of the Central   The President of
Committee of the CPSU   the United States

ECONOMIC STATEMENT

Following is the text, as made available by the White House, of President Nixon's introduction to the Aug. 13 report of the Council of Economic Advisers.

It is now almost exactly a year since the New Economic Policy was launched on August 15, 1971. What has happened since then adds up to solid economic gains which are a tribute to the public spirit of the people, as well as tangible pocketbook progress for the people.

The actions of last August 15 were designed to intensify previous measures that had reduced the rate of inflation and had started economic resurgence. They included a freeze on wages and prices to help reduce the inflation further, tax reductions to speed up the expansion and get unemployment down, and steps in international finance and trade to lay the basis for increasing the competitiveness of the United States in the world economy.

The August 15 policy consisted of actions the Government would take. But, as I said in my speech that night, the key to success would be in the hands of the American people.

I asked for public cooperation on the ground of patriotism—for the sake of America's economic health. But I also asked for cooperation on the ground of intelligent self-interest. Only by acting together could we get off the inflationary treadmill which for years had been keeping all of us from enjoying the rising prosperity. the American economy was capable of producing.

This report by the Council of Economic Advisers describes what has happened since the New Economic Policy was adopted. The performance has been impressive:

• The rate of increase in the cost of living, which had been cut by one-third before the freeze, has now been cut in half.

• There are 2.5 million more civilian jobs than there were one year ago.

• The unemployment rate has declined from about 6 percent to 5 ½ percent.

• Our economy is growing at a rate of almost 9 percent a year, the highest since 1965.

• Workers' real weekly spendable earnings have risen 4 percent in the last year, three times the average rate from 1960 to 1968.

• We have led the world on the path to international financial and trade reform which will substantially help us to improve our international competitive position as well as help other countries strengthen their economies.

I want to emphasize that the success of the New Economic Policy has been due to the cooperation of the American people.

This cooperation has taken many forms:

• Voluntary compliance by workers, businesses, landlords, consumers and tenants with the price-wage freeze and then with Phase II has been remarkable.

• During the period when the Phase II program was being developed, leaders of business, labor, agriculture, and State and local governments were most helpful in consulting with the Federal officials involved. In the following months, many outstanding citizens have participated in running the program.

• Productivity—output per man-hour—rose 4.3 percent in the past year, the biggest year-to-year gain since early 1966. Such an increase of productivity is impossible without the positive mutual contributions of labor and management.

• The fraction of working time lost from strikes has been at an exceptionally low level.

The American people can congratulate themselves on their performance in the past year and are increasingly enjoying the tangible benefits of what they and their Government have done together.

We still have economic problems to solve, however, and again the key to success lies in the hands of the people. We must firmly establish a lower rate of inflation—both in fact and in the public expectations which help shape the economic future. While we have cut the rate of inflation in half the price of food remains a major concern. We have to get the unemployment rate down much further. We have to continue to improve U.S. competitiveness to strengthen our international economic position.

To accomplish all these things will require continued efforts by everyone—including the Government—to comply with the letter and the spirit of the price-wage control system and to raise productivity even higher.

The critical point at which the help and understanding of the American people is now needed is the Federal budget. If we allow Federal expenditures to soar again, to a point far exceeding the revenues even under conditions of full employment— as they did between 1965 and 1968—we will risk destroying the hard-won gains we have already made. The result would be big increases in the cost of living, or big new taxes—or the first followed by the second.

This Administration is determined to do its best to resist this course by keeping the budget under control, and I have urgently called upon the Congress for help.

But the outcome will depend most of all on the wishes of the American people: If the people insist on spending beyond the $250-billion ceiling I have urged, such spending will be done. But if the people join me in insisting that Federal spending be held down, to avoid reviving inflation now and paying higher taxes soon, the Government will act responsibly.

This critical situation poses a great test of our mature determination to manage our economic affairs soundly. I am confident that we will meet it, and that our national economy—which includes all of us—will continue to rise to new heights of prosperous greatness.

RICHARD NIXON

ACCEPTANCE SPEECH

Following is the text, after preliminary remarks, of President Nixon's Aug. 23 speech in Miami Beach, Fla., accepting the Republican nomination for President in 1972.

...And speaking in a very personal sense, I express my deep gratitude to this convention for the tribute that you have paid to the best campaigner in the Nixon family, my wife, Pat. In honoring her, you have honored millions of women in America who contributed in the past and will contribute in the future so very much to better government in this country.

And again, as I did last night when I was not at the convention, I express the appreciation of all of the delegates and of all America for letting us see young America at its best at our convention.

As I express my appreciation to you. I want to say that you have inspired us with your enthusiasm, with your intelligence, with your dedication at this convention. You have made us realize that this is a year when we can prove the experts' predictions wrong because we set as our goal winning a majority of the new voters for our ticket this November.

And I pledge to you, I pledge to you all of the new voters in America who are listening here in this convention hall that I will do everything that I can over these next four years to make your support be one that you can be proud of, because as I said to you last night—and I feel it very deeply in my heart—years from now I want you to look back and be able to say that your first vote was one of the best votes you ever cast in your life.

Mr. Chairman, I congratulate the delegates to this convention for renominating as my running mate the man who has so eloquently and graciously introduced me, Vice President Ted Agnew.

I thought he was the best man for the job four years ago. I think he is the best man for the job today, and I'm not going to change my mind tomorrow.

And finally, as the Vice President has indicated, you have demonstrated to the nation that we can have an open convention without dividing Americans into quotas. Let us commit ourselves to root out every vestige of discrimination in this country of ours.

But, my fellow Americans, the way to end discrimination against some is not to begin discrimination against others.

Dividing Americans into quotas is totally alien to the American tradition. Americans don't want to be part of a quota—they want to be part of America.

And this nation proudly calls itself the United States of America. Let's reject any philosophy that would make us the divided people of America.

In that spirit I address you tonight, my fellow Americans, not as a partisan of party which would divide us but as a partisan of principles which can unite us. Six weeks ago our opponents at their convention rejected many of the great principles of the Democratic party. To those millions who have been driven out of their home in the Democratic party, we say, come home. We say come home not to another party, but we say come home to the great principles we Americans believe in together.

And I ask you, my fellow Americans, tonight to join us, not in a coalition held together only by a desire to gain power. I ask you to join us as members of a new American majority bound together by our common ideals.

I ask everyone listening to me tonight—Democrats, Republicans, independents—to join our majority, not on the basis of the party label you wear in your lapel but on the basis of what you believe in your hearts.

And in asking for your support, I shall not dwell on the record of our Administration, which has been praised, perhaps too generously, by others at this convention.

We have made great progress in these past four years.

It can truly be said that we have changed America and that America has changed the world. As a result of what we have done, America today is a better place and the world is a safer place to live in than was the case four years ago.

We can be proud of that record but we shall never be satisfied. A record is not something to stand on, it's something to build on.

And tonight I do not ask you to join our new majority because of what we have done in the past. I ask your support of the principles I believe should determine America's future.

The choice, the choice in this election is not between radical change and no change, the choice in this election is between change that works and change that won't work.

I begin with an article of faith. It has become fashionable in recent years to point up what is wrong with what is called the American system. The critics contend it is so unfair, so corrupt, so unjust that we should tear it down and substitute something else in its place.

I totally disagree. I believe in the American system.

I have traveled to 80 countries in the past 25 years, and I have seen communist systems, I've seen socialist systems, I have seen systems that are half-socialist and half-free.

Every time I come home to America I realize how fortunate we are to live in this great and good country.

Every time I am reminded that we have more freedom, more opportunity, more prosperity than any people in the world, that we have the highest rate of growth of any industrial nation, that Americans have more jobs at higher wages than in any country in the world, that our rate of inflation is less than that of any industrial nation, that the incomparable productivity of America's farmers has made it possible for us to launch a winning war against hunger in the United States, and that the productivity of our farmers also makes us the best-fed people in the world with the lowest percentage of the family budget going to food of any country in the world.

We can be very grateful in this country that the people on welfare in America would be rich in most of the nations of the world today.

Now my fellow Americans, in pointing up those things we do not overlook the fact that our system has its problems. Our administration, as you know, has provided the biggest tax cut in history, but taxes are still too high. That is why one of the goals of our next administration is to reduce the property tax, which is such an unfair and heavy burden on the poor, the elderly, the wage earner, the farmer and those on fixed incomes.

As all of you know, we have cut inflation in half in this administration, but we've got to cut it further. We must cut it further so that we can continue to expand on the greatest accomplishment of our new economic policies—for the first time in five years wage increases in America are not being eaten up by price increases.

And as a result of the millions of new jobs created by our new economic policies, unemployment today in America is less than the peacetime average of the sixties, but we must continue the unparalleled increase in new jobs so that we can achieve the great goal of our new prosperity—a job for every American who wants to work, without war and without inflation.

The way to reach this goal is to stay on the new road we have charted to move America forward and not to take a sharp detour to the left which would lead to a dead end for the hopes of the American people.

And this points up one of the clearest choices in this campaign. Our opponents believe in a different philosophy. Theirs is the politics of paternalism, where master planners in Washington make decisions for people.

Ours is the politics of people—where people make decisions for themselves.

The proposal that they have made to pay $1,000 to every person in America insults the intelligence of the American voters. Because you know that every politician's promise has a price—the taxpayers pays the bill.

The American people are not going to be taken in by any scheme where Government gives money with one hand and then takes it away with the other.

And their platform promises everything to everybody but at a net increase in the budget of $144-billion, but listen to what it means to you, the taxpayers of the country.

That would mean an increase of 50 per cent in what the taxpayers of America pay. I oppose any new spending programs, which will increase the tax burden on the already burdened American taxpayers.

And they have proposed legislation which would add 82-million people to the welfare rolls. I say that instead of providing incentives for millions of more Americans to go on welfare, we need a program which will provide incentives for people to get off of welfare and to get to work.

We believe that it is wrong for anyone to receive more on welfare than for someone who works. Let us be generous to those who can't work, without increasing the tax burden of those who do work.

And while we're talking about welfare, let us quit treating our senior citizens in this country like welfare recipients. They have worked hard all their lives to build America, and as the builders of America they haven't asked for a handout. What they ask for is what they have earned, and that is retirement in dignity and self-respect. Let's give that to our senior citizens.

And now when you add up the cost of all of the programs our opponents have proposed, you reach only one conclusion: they would destroy the system which has made America No. 1 in the world economically.

Listen to these facts: Americans today pay one-third of all of their income in taxes. If their programs were adopted, Americans would pay over one-half of what they earn in taxes. This means that if their programs are adopted, American wage-earners would be working more for the Government than they would for themselves and once we cross this line, we cannot turn back, because the incentive which makes the American economic system the most productive in the world would be destroyed.

Theirs is not a new approach. It has been tried before in countries abroad and I can tell you that those who have tried it have lived to regret it.

We cannot and will not let them do this to America.

Let us always be true to the principle that has made American the world's most prosperous nation—that here in America a person should get what he works for and work for what he gets.

Let me illustrate the difference in our philosophies. Because of our free economic system, what we have done is to build a great building of economic wealth and might in America. It is by far the tallest building in the world, and we are still adding to it. Now, because some of the windows are broken, they say tear it down and start again. We say, replace the windows and keep building. That's the difference.

Let me turn now to a second area where my beliefs are totally different from those of our opponents. Four years ago crime was rising all over America at an unprecedented rate. Even our nation's capital was called the crime capital of the world. I pledged to stop the rise in crime.

In order to keep that pledge I promised in the election campaign that I would appoint judges to the Federal courts and particularly to the Supreme Court who would recognize that the first civil right of every American is to be free from domestic violence.

I have kept that promise. I am proud of the appointments I have made to the courts and particularly proud of those I have made to the Supreme Court of the United States.

And I pledge again tonight as I did four years ago that, whenever I have the opportunity to make more appointments to the courts, I shall continue to appoint judges who share my philosophy that we must strengthen the peace forces as against the criminal forces in the United States.

We have launched an allout offensive against crime, against narcotics, against permissiveness in our country.

And I want the peace officers across America to know that they have the total backing of their President in their fight against crime.

My fellow Americans, as we move toward peace abroad, I ask you to support our programs which will keep the peace at home.

And now, I turn to an issue of overriding importance, not only to this election but for generations to come—the progress we have made in building a new structure of peace in the world.

Peace is too important for partisanship.

There have been five Presidents in my political lifetime—Franklin D. Roosevelt, Harry Truman, Dwight Eisenhower, John F. Kennedy and Lyndon Johnson.

They had differences on some issues, but they were united in their beliefs that where the security of America or the peace of the world is involved, we are not Republicans, we are not Democrats, we are Americans first, last and always.

These five Presidents were united in their total opposition to isolation for America and in their belief that the interest of the United States and the interest of world peace required that America be strong enough and intelligent enough to assume the responsibilities of leadership in the world.

They were united in the conviction that the United States should have a defense second to none in the world. They were all men who hated war and were dedicated to peace.

But not one of these five men and no President in our history believed that America should ask an enemy for peace on terms that would betray our allies and destroy respect for the United States all over the world.

And as your President, I pledge that I shall always uphold that proud bipartisan tradition.

Standing in this convention hall four years ago, I pledged to seek an honorable end to the war in Vietnam. We have made great progress toward that end.

We have brought over half a million men home and more will be coming home. We have ended America's ground combat role. No draftees are being sent to Vietnam. We have reduced our casualties by 98 percent.

We've gone the extra mile—in fact, we've gone tens of war.

We have offered a cease-fire, a total withdrawal of all American forces, an exchange of all prisoners of war, internationally supervised free elections with the Communists participating in the elections and in the supervisions.

There are three things, however, that we have not and that we will not offer:

We will never abandon our prisoners of war.

And, second, we will not join our enemies in imposing a Communist government on our allies—the 17 million people of South Vietnam.

And we will never stain the honor of the United States of America.

Now, I realize that many—particularly in this political year—wonder why we insist on an honorable peace in Vietnam. From a political standpoint, they suggest that, since I was not in office when over a half a million American men were sent there, that I should end the war by agreeing to impose a Communist government on the people of South Vietnam and just blame the whole catastrophe on my predecessors.

This might be good politics. But it would be disastrous to the cause of peace in the world. If at this time we betray our allies, it will discourage our friends abroad and it will encourage our enemies to engage in aggression.

In areas like the Mideast, which are danger areas, small nations who rely on the friendship and support of the United States would be in deadly jeopardy.

To our friends and allies in Europe, Asia, the Mideast and Latin America, I say the United States will continue its great bipartisan tradition—to stand by our friends and never to desert them.

Now in discussing Vietnam, I have noticed that in this election year there's been a great deal of talk about providing amnesty for those few hundred Americans who chose to desert their country rather than to serve it in Vietnam.

I think it's time that we put the emphasis where it belongs. The real heroes are two and a half-million young Americans who chose to serve their country rather than desert it.

And I say to you tonight in these times when there is so much of a tendency to run down those who have served America in the past and who serve it today, let's give those who serve in our armed forces and those who have served in Vietnam the honor and the respect that they deserve and that they've earned.

Finally, in this connection, let one thing be clearly understood in this election campaign. The American people will not tolerate any attempt by our enemies to interfere in the cherished right of the American voter to make his own decision with regard to what is best for America without outside intervention.

Now, it is understandable that Vietnam has been a major concern in foreign policy, but we have not allowed the war in Vietnam to paralyze our capacity to initiate historic new policies to construct a lasting and just peace in the world.

And when the history of this period is written, I believe it will be recorded that our most significant contributions to peace resulted from our trips to Peking and to Moscow. The dialogue that we have begun with the People's Republic of China has reduced the danger of war and has increased the chance for peaceful cooperation between two great peoples.

And, within the space of four years in our relations with the Soviet Union, we have moved from confrontation to negotiation and then to cooperation in the interest of peace.

We have taken the first step in limiting the nuclear arms race.

We have laid the foundation for further limitations on nuclear weapons, and, eventually, of reducing the armaments in the nuclear area.

We can thereby not only reduce the enormous cost of the arms for both our countries, but we can increase the chances for peace.

More than on any other single issue, I ask you, my fellow Americans, to give us the chance to continue these great initiatives that can contribute so much to the future of peace in the world.

And it can truly be said that as a result of our initiatives the danger of war is less today than it was, the chances for peace are greater.

But a note of warning needs to be sounded. We cannot be complacent. Our opponents have proposed massive cuts in our defense budget which would have the inevitable effect of making the United States the second strongest nation in the world. For the United States unilaterally to reduce its strength with the naive hope that other nations would do likewise would increase the danger of war in the world. It would completely remove any incentive of other nations to agree to a mutual limitation to reduction of arms, the promising initiatives we have undertaken to limit arms would be destroyed, the security of the United States and all the nations in the world who depend upon our friendship and support would be threatened.

Let's look at the record on defense expenditures. We have cut spending in our Administration. It now takes the lowest percentage of our national product in 20 years. We should not spend more on defense than we need, but we must never spend less than we need.

What we must understand is spending what we need on defense will cost us money. Spending less than we need could cost us our lives or our freedom.

And so tonight, my fellow Americans, I say, let us take risks for peace, but let us never risk the security of the United States of America.

And it is for that reason that I pledge that we will continue to seek peace and the mutual reduction of arms. The United States during this period, however, will always have a defense second to none.

There are those who believe that we can entrust the security of America to the goodwill of our adversaries. And those who hold this view do not know the real world. We can negotiate limitation of arms, and we have done so. We can make agreements to reduce the danger of war, and we have done so. But one unchangeable rule of international diplomacy that I've learned over many, many years is that, in negotiations between great powers, you can only get something if you have something to give in return.

And that is why I say tonight, let us always be sure that when the President of the United States goes to the conference table he never has to negotiate from weakness.

There is no such thing as a retreat to peace.

My fellow Americans, we stand today on the threshold of one of the most exciting and challenging eras in the history of relations between nations. We have the opportunity in our time to be the peacemakers of the world.

Because the world trusts and respects us, and because the world knows that we shall only use our power to defend freedom, never to destroy it; to keep the peace, never to break it.

A strong America is not the enemy of peace, it is the guardian of peace.

The initiatives that we have begun can result in reducing the danger of arms as well as the danger of war which hangs over the world today.

Even more important, it means that the enormous creative energies of the Russian people and the Chinese people and the American people and all the great peoples of the world can be turned away from production of war and turned toward production for peace.

And in America it means that we can undertake programs for progress at home that will be just as exciting as the great initiative we have undertaken in building a new structure of peace abroad.

My fellow Americans. the peace dividend that we hear so much about has too often been described solely in monetary terms.

How much money we could take out of the arms budget and apply to our domestic needs. By far the biggest dividend, however, is that achieving our goal of a lasting peace in the world would reflect the deepest hopes and ideals of all the American people.

Speaking on behalf of the American people, I was proud to be able to say in my television address to the Russian people in May, we covet no one else's territory, we seek no dominion over any other nation, we seek peace, not only for ourselves, but for all the people of the world.

This dedication to idealism runs through America's history. During the tragic war between the states, Abraham Lincoln was asked whether God was on his side. He replied, "My concern is not whether God is on our side but whether we are on God's side."

May that always be our prayer for America.

We hold the future of peace in the world and our own future in our hands.

Let us reject, therefore, the policies of those who whine and whimper about our frustrations and call on us to turn inward. Let us not turn away from greatness.

The chance America now had to lead the way to a lasting peace in the world may never come again.

With faith in God and faith in ourselves and faith in our country, let us have the vision and the courage to seize the moment and meet the challenge before it slips away.

On your television screens last night, you saw the cemetery in Leningrad I visited on my trip to the Soviet Union where 300,-000 people died in the siege of that city during World War II. At

(Continued on p. 142-A)

PRESIDENTIAL NEWS CONFERENCES

FEBRUARY 10

Following is the text, as made available by the White House, of President Nixon's Feb. 10 impromptu news conference, his 23rd since taking office and his first since Nov. 11.

THE PRESIDENT: Ladies and gentlemen, before going to your other questions, I would like to make an announcement with regard to the details of the trip to Mainland China. This will not cover all the details, but it will at least cover those that have been announced at this time.

The official party will be announced from Florida, Key Biscayne, on Saturday the 12th. Of course, as you know, we have already announced that Dr. Kissinger, the Secretary of State, Mrs. Nixon and I will be going, and the other member of the official party at that time will be announced from Washington.

On Monday, I have an event that I think has already been announced, a meeting with Andre Malraux, and I am giving a dinner that night for him to which several Congressional leaders will be invited, as well as members of the official party, the Secretary of State and Dr. Kissinger.

In mentioning Andre Malraux, I do not want to reflect on many of the other experts—and there are many experts in this field of China—whose books have been brought to my attention. I do not want to indicate I have read them all, but I have been exposed to a great number. I asked him to come because there was an interesteing coincidence.

In 1969, when I met with President deGaulle in Paris, Mr. Malraux at that time was the Minister of Culture in the deGaulle Cabinet. We had a discussion prior to dinner on the subject of China generally, and I was particularly impressed with his analysis of the leaders. His book, at least one he has written, but his book—the one I particularly refer to was his Anti-Memoirs. I commend it to you not only for what it tells about China and its leaders, but also about France, its problems, and the whole World War II and post-World War II era.

I give you this only to indicate the breadth of the kind of briefings that all of us who are going to participate in the talks are trying to undertake. It is very different from the other meetings that we have had at the highest level with other governments. I have visited virtually all of the other countries, just as I have visited the Soviet Union.

But here it is essential to do an enormous amount of homework just to come up to the starting line. I don't want to say after having read as much as I have, and as much as I will be reading between now and the time we arrive, that I will be an expert, but at least I will be familiar with the men with whom we will be meeting and the problems that may be discussed.

Tuesday and Wednesday will be used primarily to finish up on many of the domestic matters that are, of course, the subject of matters that I will be discussing with Secretary Connally and Mr. Ehrlichman over this weekend, and also for further briefings from members of the NSC staff and the State Department on the China trip.

The time of departure has now been set. It will be 10:00 o'clock Thursday morning, the 17th, from Andrews. We will fly directly to Hawaii. We will spend Thursday night and all day Friday in Hawaii.

The following morning, Saturday morning, on the 19th, the press plane will go directly to Mainland China, stopping in Shanghai first, and arriving in Peking. The Chinese Government is arranging this so the members of the press can be on the ground prior to the time I will be arriving.

On that same day, Saturday, the 19th, the Presidential plane, the Spirit of '76, will fly to Guam, and we will stay overnight in Guam and then take off the next day, Monday, for Shanghai and Peking, arriving in Peking Monday morning at approximately 11:30 a.m.* The date, of course, is the 21st there and the 20th here. As you know, we cross the International Date Line on the way.

A couple of other points that I know have been raised in briefings and that I can only cover generally:

With regard to agenda, both governments have decided that we will not make any announcements on agenda items prior to the meetings. The agenda will be covered by a joint communique that will be issued at the conclusion of our talks and consequently, questions on agenda, what will be discussed and so forth, on the part of both sides, will not be answered either before we get there or during the course of the meetings, unless the two sides decide, while we are meeting, that an agenda item can properly be discussed or disclosed.

With regard to the itinerary itself, the itinerary, generally as you know, has been announced for three cities. With regard to what we do in each city, it is being kept flexible and no final decisions have been made and none will be announced at this time.

Mrs. Nixon's itinerary will be much more public than mine. And she will have an opportunity, which I hope many of you also will have, those of you who are going, to visit a number of institutions, places of interest in Peking and Hangchow and Shanghai. She, as you know, having traveled to perhaps more countries than any First Lady, is looking forward to this with a great deal of interest and I think as she demonstrated on her trip to Africa, her events, I think, will be worth covering.

One side note, and I am sure all of you who have been studying, as I have, will have noted this, is that one development in the 20th century China which is very significant, is the enormous elevation in the status of women. Total equality is now recognized and looking back over Chinese history, that is, of course, a very significant change.

Consequently, I think that Mrs. Nixon's activities will be significant for them. It will be, of course, very significant for us in the United States to see their schools and other institutions and how they compare with ours and the other countries that we visit.

As far as my agenda is concerned, there will not be a great deal of what I would call public—well, to put it perhaps rather plainly—sightseeing. There will be some. I mean actually I would hope to see some of the points of interest and the Chinese Government is arranging for some, but we have both agreed that this visit is one, taking place as it does at this time, in which first priority must be given to our talks and sightseeing and protocol must come second. And consequently, we have agreed that we will not get frozen into any extended travel within the cities which we will be visiting, in the event that that might interfere with an extended conversation that might be taking place.

I do not want to suggest here what the length of the talks will be, but, necessarily because we are in truth at a beginning, they will be much longer, both with Mr. Chou En-lai and Mr. Mao Tse-tung than with the leaders of other governments that we have visited, because there we are not starting at the beginning. We have the opportunity to come immediately to matters of substance.

Finally, in order to perhaps put the trip in context, you have heard me discuss it in various speeches that I have made. I really haven't much to add, because as I pointed out, the agenda items will be decided at the beginning of the meetings, but they will be published at the end of our meetings and by communique.

But I think we could say this, this trip should not be one which would create very great optimism or very great pessimism. It is one in which we must recognize that 20 years of hostility and virtually no communication will not be swept away by one week of discussion.

However, it will mark a watershed in the relations between the two governments; the post-war era with respect to the Peoples Republic of China and the United States, that chapter now comes to an end from the time that I set foot on the soil of Mainland China, and a new chapter begins.

Now, how the new chapter is written will be influenced, perhaps influenced substantially, by the talks that will take place. On our side and we believe also on their side we hope that

---

* The arrival in Peking is scheduled for 11:30 a.m. Monday, Peking Time, which is 10:30 p.m. Sunday, EST.

the new chapter will be one of more communication and that it will be a chapter that will be marked by negotiation, rather than confrontation and one that will be marked by the absence of armed conflict. These are our hopes.

We, of course, will now see to what extent those hopes can be realized in the first meetings.

I will go to any other questions.

U. S. Aid to China

Q: Mr. Malraux is quoted as having said that he is sure the first question Mao will ask you is will you provide aid to China and the rest of the trip, the success of the talks, will be determined by your answer. Can you give us any indication if that is true?

THE PRESIDENT: That gets into the area that I will decline to comment upon, because it involves the agenda items. I cannot really predict with much confidence as Mr. Malraux perhaps can, as to what Mr. Mao Tse-tung's questions will be.

So, consequently, I don't believe it would be proper to comment now on a question that has not yet been asked by him. If it is asked, I will have an answer.

Dialogue or Negotiation

Q: Mr. President, do you look upon your meeting with Chou En-lai and Mao Tse-tung as dialogue or negotiation?

THE PRESIDENT: They will be primarily dialogue. Here a very subtle but definite distinction is made between the talks that will take place in Peking and the talks that will take place in Moscow.

In the talks in Moscow there are certain subjects that we have been negotiating about and those subjects, therefore, will be negotiated, although, of course, there will be dialogue as well, dialogue is an essential part of negotiation.

In the case of Peking, there will necessarily have to be a substantial amount of dialogue before we can come to the point of negotiating on substantive matters. I should emphasize, too, that it has already been pointed out by Dr. Kissinger when he returned, that when we speak of these matters that they will be primarily bilateral matters. Beyond that, however, I will not go.

Peace Plan Critics

Q: Mr. Haldeman has had very strong words for critics of your peace proposal, saying that they are consciously aiding and abetting the enemy. Your statement was somewhat softer. The Democrats seem to still not think it is enough. Do you think that Mr. Haldeman's statement, since he is so close to you, and a lot of people interpret his thinking as very close to yours should be left to lie as it is or is there something further that you should say?

THE PRESIDENT: There is nothing further I should say. I think Mr. Ziegler covered the situation with regard to Mr. Haldeman and you ladies and gentlemen pressed him very hard on that on Monday.

I stated my position very clearly yesterday in my summary of the State of the World speech. We have here a situation where there is a difference of opinion among various candidates for the Presidency as to how they should conduct themselves at this time.

As I pointed out, I consider it a matter of judgment. I do not question the patriotism, I do not question the sincerity of people who disagree with me, because there are a lot of people who do disagree with me on this and other issues as well.

Perhaps to put it in a clearer context, I was a very vigorous critic of the policies that got us into Vietnam. I was a critic, for example, of the settlement which resulted in the partition of Laos, which opened the Ho Chi Minh Trail and paved the way for the invasion of the south by the North Vietnamese troops.

I was a critic of the policies and the actions which I think most observers would agree, contributed to the assassination of Diem and the succession of coups which then brought on further armed conflict. I was a strong critic of the conduct of the war before I was a candidate and after I was a candidate. But once I became a candidate and once when President Johnson announced he would no longer be a candidate and the peace talks began, I said then that as far as I was concerned, as a man seeking the Presidency, I would say nothing that would, in any way, jeopardize those peace talks.

So there is, in my view, and I do not ask others to hold it, I ask them to consider it, a very great difference between criticizing policies that got us into war and criticizing the conduct of war and criticisms by a Presidential candidate of a policy to end the war and to bring peace.

What we have here is a situation, as Secretary Rogers has pointed out, a situation where within one week after a very forthcoming peace proposal has been made, various Presidential candidates sought to propose another settlement which went beyond that.

My own candid judgment is that that kind of action has the effect, as I implied in my remarks yesterday, it has the effect of having the government in Hanoi consider at least that they might be well advised to wait until after the election rather than negotiate.

So my view is that as far as I was concerned that is why I did not criticize when I was a candidate for the President—after President Johnson started the negotiation. I thought it was good judgment then.

As far as others are concerned, they have to consult their own conscience. They apparently have determined that they wish to take another course of action. I disagree with the course of action. I would strongly urge at this point that all candidates for the Presidency, Republican and Democrat, review their public statements and really consider whether they believe that they are going to help the cause of peace or hurt it, whether they are going to encourage the enemy to negotiate or encourage him to continue the war.

I have stated my position very categorically. It is different from others. I respect the other opinions. You will have to let the people judge as to which is right.

South Vietnamese Government

Q: Mr. President, is there real flexibility in this country on the question of when President Thieu should resign and inflexibility in Saigon, is there a real difference and are you going to do anything about it?

THE PRESIDENT: Well, I notice the flap that has occurred from President Thieu's statement today, and based on his interpretation of what Secretary Rogers has said. I think the misunderstanding can be cleared up by what I now say.

Every proposal we have made in Paris has been a joint proposal by the Government of South Vietnam and the Government of the United States. Every proposal that we have made has been after consultation and after receiving suggestions from the Government of South Vietnam, as well as the Government of the United States.

The best example of that is the proposal that I announced on January 25th and which we presented on October 11th. The offer on the part of President Thieu to resign a month before the election was his idea. And we included it in the proposal. It was in my opinion a very statesmanlike thing for him to do and showed his devotion to the proposition of trying to find a way to break the political deadlock which has deadlocked these talks all along.

Now, at this point, I can say that any future proposals we make will be joint proposals of the Government of South Vietnam and the Government of the United States. As far as we are concerned, we have made an offer. It is forthcoming. Many have said it is as far as we should go. We are ready to negotiate on that offer, we and the Government of South Vietnam, but under no circumstances are we going to make any further proposals without the consultation with and the agreement of the Government of South Vietnam, particularly on political issues, because the political issues are primarily theirs to decide rather than ours.

And I would say also, that under no circumstances are we going to negotiate with our enemy, in a way that undercuts our ally.

We are not going to negotiate over the heads of our ally with our enemies to overthrow our ally. As I said in my speech on January 25th, we are ready to negotiate a settlement, but we are not going to negotiate a surrender either for the United States, nor are we going to negotiate the surrender of 15 million people of South Vietnam to the Communists.

As far as President Thieu and his government is concerned, and our government is concerned, the proposal we have made is a joint proposal. If there are to be any changes in that proposal—and we don't intend to make any unless and until there is some indication that the enemy intends to negotiate in good faith—it will be a joint proposal.

The next step is up to the enemy. Our proposal is on the table and it is going to stand there until we get a reply from them.

Vietnam as Issue

Q: You have said in the past that if the Democrats hope to make an issue of Vietnam, that the rug would be pulled out from under them. I think it is a fairly accurate quote. Do you feel that issue now remains a live issue, and are you disappointed that it does remain a part of the public dialogue in so intense a way?

THE PRESIDENT: I am very disappointed that the enemy has refused to negotiate, and I, as you know, have always pointed out that we have a two-track approach to ending the American involvement. Our favorite track is negotiation. That could have ended it in '69, '70, '71. We have made various proposals we think were the basis for negotiation.

The longest track is Vietnamization. That will end the American involvement in a predictable time, as I think most of us can see.

As far as pulling the rug out from under those who criticize—and it is not a partisan issue; there are Republicans as well as Democrats who have disagreements on this, I respect their disagreements.

As far as pulling the rug out is concerned, I would say I think America would be delighted to have the rug pulled out from under them on this issue if it brings peace and an end to the killing. That is what we are trying to do.

I would hope Presidential candidates, particularly, would consult their consciences before they make proposals which might be misread—might be; they would not intend it, I am sure—but might be misread by the enemy and thereby encourage them to wait until after the election before even discussing a very forthcoming proposal.

News Conferences

Q: Mr. President, why are you not, sir, holding news conferences with very much regularity or frequency? And what, in particular, do you have against televised news conferences? I believe it has been more than eight months since you held one of those.

THE PRESIDENT: Well, I will hold news conferences whenever I believe that they will serve the public interest.

As far as televised news conferences are concerned, I find that ladies and gentlemen in the Press Corps have a very vigorous difference of opinion as to which is the more valuable forum.

I remember the last time, or a few months ago, that I was in this office, the first time I had an in-office conference. Mr. Bailey, former head of the White House Correspondents, said, "This is the best kind of press conference." I am sure Mr. Rather thinks the best kind of press conference is one with him alone. (Laughter)

So I will have Q&A with one commentator. I have had questions and answers with some members of the press, as you know, alone. I will have in-office press conferences. Sometimes I have walked out in the room there, as I did when I announced the Soviet Summit, and have a press conference in the press room, so that whoever wants to may film it, and on other occasions we may have a televised press conference.

I would only say, finally, with regard to the televised press conference, it is no more work than one like this, and I would suggest that I do follow the columns of the commentators pretty well, and I noted that there was considerable—I wouldn't call it criticism—but eyebrow-raising as to "Why has the President been on television so much? He had A Day in the Life of the President. That took an hour of prime time. He had a half-hour the night before Christmas on CBS. Then he had an hour with Rather, another CBS. Then he had a State of the Union Message, and he took prime time for the purpose of making announcements on Vietnam in addition to all the rest."

Let me say, I think television has probably had as much of the President as it wants at this point, and that is why you are getting this kind of conference.

Advice for Haldeman

Q: Mr. President, you had some public advice today and yesterday about how critics of the war should conduct themselves. Do you have any public advice for Mr. Haldeman?

THE PRESIDENT: I have answered the question. Anything further?

Consultations With Thieu

Q: Mr. President, you have left open the question of your flexibility on President Thieu. He is upset. We had running stories from Saigon. In effect, you have said the policy is flexible. Do you plan to consult with him at some early point to soothe his feelings?

THE PRESIDENT: We already have. We are in constant consultation. I have discussed the matter with Ambassador Bunker. President Thieu knows first, as he said in his own statement, because if you will read it carefully, he pointed out he felt we had consulted him. He knows first that we have never made a proposal except when it was a joint proposal. He knows now that there will be no new proposals made unless it is a joint proposal and I trust that this press conference, I am having now with you ladies and gentlemen, will reassure not only him, but the people of South Vietnam as well on that point.

As far as flexibility is concerned, what Secretary Rogers was referring to was what we have always said that we have put a proposal on the table. We are ready to negotiate on it.

Now, that does not mean, however, that after having made such a proposal that two weeks later we are going to go a step further and say that we will go further than we have in that proposal. At this point, I emphasize here today we have made a proposal, we think it is reasonable.

The enemy has not responded to it. Until the enemy does respond to it, there will be no further proposals and no further concessions on our part.

Recognition of Bangladesh

Q: Mr. President, you spoke in your foreign policy report about sympathy for the aspiration of the East Bengali people. Could you give us some idea of the factors and the timing of the decision on the recognition of Bangladesh.

THE PRESIDENT: With regard to the problem of the Bengali people, first let me say that on the humanitarian side issue, as you know, both before the war, during the war, and after the war, the United States has been the most generous of all of the nations. We will continue to be. That is separate from the political side.

With regard to the political side, we have under study our whole relationship with the subcontinent and as part of that relationship, of course, the 70 million people in Bangladesh are involved. We have not yet made a decision with regard to recognition you should not expect a decision prior to the time that I return from China.

Anti-Busing Amendment

Q: Mr. President, what are your views on the constitutional amendments on busing now before the House and Senate?

THE PRESIDENT: Which one?

Q: Well, the amendments have to do—

THE PRESIDENT: There are several. Let me get at it this way. My views on busing are well known. I favor local control of local schools. I oppose busing for the purpose of racial balance. Those are my views which have been stated on many occasions.

The problem we have now is that some courts have handed down decisions which seem to differ from those views and so the question arises as to whether legislation on a constitutional amendment is necessary if we are to see that those views that I have just enunciated can properly be held and implemented.

Because if the courts, acting under the Constitution, decide that the views that I have held are unconstitutional, I, of course, will have to follow the courts.

Under these circumstances, therefore, I have ordered a study of the legislative route and of the constitutional amendments and, as part of that study, I have asked that Senator Brock, Senator Baker in the Senate and Congressman Steed, and Congressman Lent in the House, come to the White House on Monday for the purpose of discussing their amendment. The purpose of this discussion is to see whether the constitutional amendment approach is the best approach to this problem.

After I have met Monday, I will be glad to have Mr. Ziegler brief you on what the next step will be. I have not made a decision on it, but the matter is under consideration.

Neighborhood Legal Services

Q: Mr. President, what is your position on civil suits filed in the names of indigents by Neighborhood Legal Services lawyers against local and State governments? Is that a legitimate function of Neighborhood Legal Services Offices?

THE PRESIDENT: I am not going to get into that at this point.

Tax Reform

Q: Mr. President, on another Congressional matter, you have been receiving strong suggestions from especially Democrats on the proposed tax reforms. How do you intend to respond?

THE PRESIDENT: I didn't hear the first part of the question.

Q: The proposal for tax reforms, the suggestion that you submit a program for tax reform, has been broached by the Democrats. How do you respond?

THE PRESIDENT: First, there will be no increases in taxes this year. It is obvious that even if the Administration were to recommend tax reform this year, it would be impossible for the Congress, particularly the Ways and Means Committee, as much as it has on its plate, and the Finanace Committee, with welfare reform, revenue sharing and the rest, ever to get to it.

So there will be no tax increase this year.

Second, I pointed out in the State of the Union Message that we are studying the problem of the property tax. We are studying it first because it is the most regressive of all taxes and second, because in those States, and that is most of the States, where the property tax is the primary source for financing public education, recent court decisions indicate it may be unconstitutional.

Under these circumstances, that is why I have asked the MacElroy Commission and the Commission on Intergovern-mental Relations to study this problem as to how general tax reform might be undertaken which would meet the objections to the property tax and perhaps mitigate the inequities and find another source of revenue to replace it.

Now we come to the value added tax. The value added tax should be put in perspective. We have not recommended a value added tax and at the present time it is one of a number of proposals being considered by the Treasury Department, by the Domestic Council and the others with responsibility, as part of a general tax reform.

But one point that should be made is this: The property tax is regressive. In the event that we finally decide, after hearing from these two Commissions, that tax reform is necessary for the future, and it will have to be next year and not this, we are certainly not going to replace one regressive tax with another regressive tax.

That is why when you discuss value added—and Secretary Connally and I have had a long discussion about this just two days ago and we are going to discuss it again in Florida tomorrow, along with other problems of that type—when you discuss value added, it can't even be considered unless the formula can be found to remove its regressive features, if you had it across the board. I don't know whether such a formula can be found.

But to sum up, we have made no decision with regard to a value added tax. At the present time, we have not yet found a way, frankly, that we could recommend it to replace the property tax. But, with the obligation to face up to the need to reduce or reform property taxes, the Treasury Department necessarily is considering other methods of taxation.

And I emphasize again, there will be no new taxes this year and second, whenever any tax reform is recommended by this Administration, it will not be one which will replace one form of regression with another form of regression. It will not be one that increases the tax burden for America. It will be one that simply reforms it and makes it more equitable.

THE PRESS: Thank you, Mr. President.

Additional Questions

Q: Mr. President, we haven't had a press conference with you for three months. I wonder if we could have one or two more questions.

THE PRESIDENT: Oh, sure. Go ahead.

Policy on South Asia

Q: I would like to ask you, Mr. President, about statements made by the Administration officials during the India-Pakistani war. Mr. Kissinger told us, during that war, this Administration had no bias toward India. Subsequently, papers came to light quoting Mr. Kissinger saying he was getting hell from you every half hour because the government wasn't—

THE PRESIDENT: Every hour. (Laughter)

Q: —because the government wasn't tilting enough toward Pakistan.

THE PRESIDENT: Keep your good humor, otherwise you lose your colleagues.

Q: I am wondering from a credibility standpoint how do you reconcile these two things?

THE PRESIDENT: I remember being in this office on what I think was one of the saddest days of President Eisenhower's Presidency. At the time we had come out against the British, the French and the Israelis in the Suez crisis. We did so because we were against the war, not because we were anti-British, anti-French or anti-Israeli. As a matter of fact we are pro-British, pro-French, and pro-Israeli, but we are against the war more.

As far as India is concerned, for 25 years—and those of you who have followed me in the House well know this, as a Member of the House, as a Member of the Senate, as Vice President, when I was out of office, and now as President—I have supported every Indian aid program. I believed it very important for the world's largest non-Communist country to have a chance to make a success of its experiment in democracy, in comparison with its great neighbor to the north, which is the world's largest Communist country. That and, of course, other reasons were involved.

But as far as being anti-Indian is concerned, I can only say I was anti-war. We did everything that we could to avoid the war, as I pointed out. At this point, we are going to do everything we can to develop a new relationship with the countries on the subcontinent that will be pro-Indian, pro-Bangalese, pro-Pakistan, but mostly pro-peace.

That is what that part of the world needs. A million were killed in the war of partition. That is probably a modest figure. And then they went through the terrible agony again in 1965, and now they have gone through it again.

It was Prime Minister Nehru who told me more than anything else what the subcontinent needed was a generation of peace. That is where I got the phrase.

As far as we were concerned, I believed that our policies—certainly, we may have made mistakes—but our policies had the purpose of avoiding the war, of stopping it once it began, and now of doing everything we can to heal up the wounds.

Anderson Papers Leak

Q: Mr. President, has the Administration discovered sir, who was the source of the papers which were leaked to Mr. Anderson, and are you planning any action against that person if you know who it is?

THE PRESIDENT: Well, first, we have a lot of circumstantial evidence. Second, as a lawyer, I can say that we do not have evidence that I consider adequate or that the Attorney General considers adequate to take to court. You can be sure that the investigation is continuing. If the investigation gets a break which provides the kind of evidence which will stand up in court, we will present it; but we cannot go to court on circumstantial evidence.

Peace Negotiations

Q: Mr. President, a few moments ago you discussed your stand in 1968 with regard to the peace negotiations. We know now that there was really very little possibility—

THE PRESIDENT: As a matter of fact, you know it now, but I said it then, over and over again, to those who had to listen to my speech. I only had one in 1968, as you recall. (Laughter) That is what you wrote anyway.

But I pointed out that I thought there was very little chance, but I said as long,—and this was my phrase; I just read it this morning—as long as there was any chance whatever—and I could not be sure, because I wasn't being consulted—for a breakthrough at the peace table, I was going to say nothing that might destroy that chance. That was my view. It may have been wrong.

Q: Could I take sort of a different tact?

THE PRESIDENT: Sure, any way you want.

Candidates' Views

Q: As a consequence of your position in 1968, you were promising to end the war, but because of the negotiations that were going on, you felt yourself unable to tell the American people how you proposed to do it once elected President.

Now, it is almost four years since these negotiations, in a way, began with President Johnson's announcement of March 31, 1968. Do you think that under these circumstances it is fair to the American people and to your rival and to this Nation for those who seek the highest office and who have views on the war not to say how they would proceed if they were to become the next President?

THE PRESIDENT: All the candidates for the Presidency have a right to say what they want. They must determine whether they believe it is right to say it. I concluded in 1968 that, as one who was a potential President, and that was particularly true after I received the nomination, that while I had a right to criticize, it was not right to do so.

Now, each of these candidates may feel that the peace proposal that we have made is one that they don't think goes far enough. They may feel that we should make one that would overthrow the Government of South Vietnam, or some other proposal that would satisfy the enemy. They have a right to say that. The American people then will have to judge.

But I am suggesting now that we have made a proposal that is fair, it is forthcoming, it should be negotiated on, and the responsibility for the enemy's failing to negotiate may have to be borne by those who encourage the enemy to wait until after the election.

THE PRESS: Thank you again, Mr. President.

MARCH 24

Following is the text, as made available by the White House, of President Nixon's March 24 news conference.

THE PRESIDENT: We will take your questions first.

Q: In view of the suspension of the Paris peace talks, can you tell us if the hopes are dimming for a negotiated peace settlement and what you assess the situation is?

THE PRESIDENT: What we are trying to do there, Miss Lewine, and this is being done under my direction, is to break the filibuster. There has been a three and a half year filibuster on the peace talks on the part of the North Vietnamese. They refuse to negotiate seriously and they use the talks for the purpose of propaganda while we have been trying to seek peace. Whenever the enemy is ready to negotiate seriously, we are ready to negotiate and I would emphasize we are ready to negotiate in public channels or in private channels.

As far as the hopes for a negotiated peace are concerned; I would say that the way the talks were going, there was no hope whatever. I am not saying that this move is going to bring a negotiation. I do say, however, that it was necessary to do something to get the talks off dead center and to see whether the enemy continued to want to use the talks only for propaganda or whether they wanted to negotiate.

When they are ready, we are ready, but we are not going to continue to allow them to use this forum for the purpose of bullying the United States in a propaganda forum rather than in seriously negotiating peace, as we tried to do as exemplified by not only our private contacts in the 12 meetings that I discussed on January 25th, but also in my speech of January 25th, in which I made a very forthcoming offer.

Q: Was there any link between the ITT antitrust settlement and the contribution to San Diego as a convention city and do you think Mr. Kleindienst will be confirmed as the attorney general?

THE PRESIDENT: Well, I have noted that you ladies and gentlemen of the press have been pressing on this matter, as you should, because it is a matter of very great interest in the Senate and in the nation.

I will simply limit my remarks to these observations: First, Mr. Kleindienst is being considered for, as you have indicated, confirmation as attorney general of the United States. That is the purpose of the hearings. I had confidence when I appointed him that he was qualified for this position. I still have that confidence. I believe that he should be confirmed and I believe that he will be confirmed.

Now, as far as the hearings are concerned, there is nothing that has happened in the hearings to date that has in one way shaken my confidence in Mr. Kleindienst as an able, honest man, fully qualified to be attorney general of the United States.

However, I am not going to comment on any aspect of the hearing or any aspects of the case while the Senate is still conducting them and while the Senate is still trying to determine the authenticity of some of the evidence that is before it. That is a matter for the Senate committee under the chairmanship of Mr. Eastland to continue to consider, but I would point out that Mr. Kleindienst asked for these hearings.

We want the whole record brought out because as far as he is concerned, he wants to go in as attorney general with no cloud over him. He will not have any, in my opinion, once the hearings are concluded and what we are talking about will be proof, rather than simply charges which have not been substantiated.

Q: On another aspect which I think is not directly related to the ITT case, I wondered if you could give us your view on the proper role of the White House staff members in contact with the executive departments and regulatory agencies concerning matters that are before those departments or agencies.

My specific reference, of course, is to the involvement of Mr. Flanigan in some of these matters, but I wonder if you could give us, on a more general basis, what you consider the proper role and the limits of that role for the presidential aides in dealing with law enforcement matters.

THE PRESIDENT: A presidential aide must listen to all who come to the White House, as they do in great numbers on all sides of all cases with regard to conditions they have or causes that they may wish to work for, just as they go to members of the House and Senate and others in that connection.

What is improper is for a presidential aide to use influence for personal gain, and to use influence in any way that would not be in the public interest. As far as Mr. Flanigan is concerned, Mr. Ziegler has responded to that charge at considerable length with my total authority and his views represent mine and I have nothing further to say.

Q: Mr. President, how do you expect the war on inflation to succeed without the cooperation of George Meany and his friends?

THE PRESIDENT: The war on inflation will succeed with their cooperation, if possible, but without it, if necessary. I think the best indication of the fact that it is succeeding is that as far as that part of the consumer price index which is made up of those items that are under control, as Mr. Stein pointed out in his briefings yesterday, the wage-price controls have been effective.

The only part of the consumer price index or the major part of the consumer price index which resulted in what we thought was a disappointing increase in prices, at least a one-month increase, was the food index.

The food index, as we know, is not controlled. Now, so far as that food index is concerned, we discussed that at considerable length at the Cost of Living Council yesterday. What we found is that it is a mistake and totally unfair to make the farmer the scapegoat for the high meat prices and the high food prices.

Approximately one-third of what the prices are that the consumer pays in the grocery store or the supermarket for food, approximately only a third of that amount is a result of what the farmer receives as farm income. The other two-thirds goes to middlemen, to retailers and others, and our preliminary investigation of this situation shows that the spread between what the farmer receives and what the consumer pays in the grocery store and the supermarket has widened. It is too great.

That is the reason why the Price Commission is, on April 12th, as you know—I think it was announced this morning—is going to conduct a hearing on this matter to determine whether or not the profit margins in this period have gone beyond the guidelines that have been laid down.

I will simply say that as far as we are concerned, we can say that on the one hand we are glad to see that, looking at a

six-month period, the rate of inflation has decelerated. On the other hand, we are disappointed at even a one-month figure in which the rate of inflation is at the level it was this time.

We are particularly disappointed that the food component was as high as it was. That is why we welcome the reaction of the Price Commission looking into that component as it is, and then in the event those food prices do not start to move down, then another action will have to be taken. I am prepared to have such other action be taken.

I have directed those who have responsibility in this field to see what action can be taken. I would simply conclude by pointing out that to feel that the action that will be effective is to control or move on the one-third, that which the farmer receives as income for what he sells, is not the most effective way to do it.

One little example that I can use that I think is quite graphic, and Secretary Connally was discussing this matter in the Cost of Living Council yesterday. He said he had been in Texas and talked to a rancher who raised chickens. He said he got 30 cents a dozen. A couple of days later he got breakfast at the Hotel Pierre in New York and ordered a couple of eggs. It was $5 for two. That is at a rate of thirty dollars a dozen. Now, of course, the eggs also have to be transported, processed, cooked and served, but 30 cents a dozen to the farmer and thirty dollars a dozen to whoever buys those eggs in a restaurant, that is just too much, and we will have to get to that middleman one way or another.

Q: Will you give us your views on the general proposition of large political contributions either by corporations or individuals in terms of possibly getting something back for it?

THE PRESIDENT: Nobody gets anything back as far as the general contributions are concerned in this administration. As a matter of fact, I think some of our major complaints have been that many of our business people have not received the consideration that perhaps they thought that an administration that was supposed to be business-oriented would provide for it.

As far as such contributions are concerned, they should always, of course, comply with the law.

Second, as far as those who receive them are concerned, they must be accepted with no understandings, expressed or implied, that anything is to be done, or as a result of those contributions, that would not be done in the ordinary course of events.

Let me just say on that point that looking at ITT, which, as I understand, has been a contributor to a number of political causes over the years, it is significant to note—and I would hope that the members of the press would report this, because I have not seen this in many stories—it is significant to note that ITT became the great conglomerate that it was in the two previous administrations primarily, the Kennedy administration and the Johnson administration. It grew and grew and grew, and nothing was done to stop it.

In this administration we moved on ITT. We are proud of that record. We moved on it effectively. We required the greatest divestiture in the history of the antitrust law. We also, as a result of the consent decree, required that ITT not have additional acquisitions, so that it became larger.

Now, as Dean Griswold pointed out, that not only was a good settlement; it was a very good settlement. I think under the circumstances that gives the lie to the suggestion that this administration, in the handling of the ITT case, just using one example, was doing a favor for ITT. If we wanted to do a favor for ITT, we could just continue to do what the two previous administrations had done, and that is nothing; let ITT continue to grow. But we moved on it and moved effectively.

Mr. McLaren is justifiably proud of that record, and Dean Griswold is very proud of that record, and they should be.

Q: Mr. President, could we just ask about your speech the other night and your moves on the part of schools, particularly the blacks in our society? There are those who feel that in the combination of the constitutional issue that has been raised, in which you have asked that the courts have a moratorium, and at the same time by putting more money into black schools, what you are doing is, in effect, going back to the old doctrine of separate but equal facilities for blacks.

Could you comment on that?

THE PRESIDENT: Yes, I see that that charge has been made and I can see how that understanding or misunderstanding could develop.

Let me explain what we are trying to do and what I believe our proposals, if they are enacted by the Congress, will accomplish. In the first place, we have to analyze what the constitutional problem is. The Constitution under the Fourteenth Amendment provides for equal protection of the law. The Constitution does not provide, as a remedy, busing or any other device. The Constitution in the Fourteenth Amendment expressly grants power to the Congress to set up the remedies to accomplish the right of equal protection of the law.

Now, we turn now to busing. Let me relate this to *Brown versus the Board of Education. Brown versus the Board of Education,* as its name indicates, was about, primarily, education. *Brown versus the Board of Education* held, in effect, that legally segregated education was inherently inferior education. I agree with that.

On the other hand, how do we desegregate and thereby get better education? Here is where busing compounds the evil. Busing for the purpose of achieving racial balance not only does not produce superior education, it results in even more inferior education.

So what I was trying to do was to tackle the issue by saying we can and should have desegregation, but, we should not compound the evil of a dual school system, of legal segregation, by using a remedy which makes it even worse.

That is why I have concluded that first, a moratorium on busing for a year was the right move to make. I believe, incidentally, that the moratorium is constitutional. I believe it will be so held by the Supreme Court due to the fact that it deals with a remedy and not a right. That is the fundamental difference. Lawyers will disagree on that, but the court will decide and I believe the court will decide that the moratorium is constitutional.

That is why I also moved in another field. When we talk about education, we must remember that if we had busing at the maximum degree suggested by the most extreme proponents of busing, it would still leave the vast majority of black school children living in central cities, going to what are basically inferior schools; a lost generation, as I described it.

I decided that we could not allow that situation to continue without trying to move on it. How have we tried to move? We tried to move through a program which has not yet been fully tested. I am not sure that it will work, but we have to do something that is in the field of compensatory education; a program in which we, rather than doing it with a shotgun approach which has proved ineffective, that we use the critical mass approach, $300 as has been described per pupil, for the purpose of improving education in those schools where no plan for desegregation that anybody has suggested will ever affect. We cannot leave those people, those students there without having some action and some attention paid to them. One other thought with regard to this whole matter of compensatory education.

I have noted on one of the networks, not yours, but NBC's, a very thoughtful series to the effect that compensatory education is a failure. We looked into that. As a matter of fact, on the basis in which it has been used up to this point of a shotgun approach where you have $100, $150, $200 a student, it has not worked.

You have an example in the District of Columbia where over $300 has not helped. But on the other hand, in California and in four other states which came to our attention, we have found that there is substantial evidence to indicate that if we can get $300 a student or more into those schools, it will raise the level of education in those areas. That is why we are going down this road.

Another point I should cover, incidentally, since this subject has been raised, is the matter of new money. Let me say there is certainly a great deal of new money in this program. First, you must remember that the Congress has not yet passed and has not yet sent to my desk a request for $1-billion in emergency school aid funds that I have asked for. That $1-billion will go into this program.

Second, we have asked not only that that billion dollars come here, but that the program be four years, rather than simply one year, because our proposal, as you know, was simply a one shot proposal for $1.5-billion. So that means you have $2.5-billion in new money.

I would say in conclusion, I would like to be able to assure everybody here that this program of compensatory education concentrating money in some of these areas on students who will never be helped by any program of busing at all, no matter how extreme, I would like to say that it will succeed. I am not sure, but I do know that we cannot go on with the present situation where we leave them there growing up in inferior schools with no chance or hope.

I know Mr. Shultz believes and other experts that I have talked to that that critical mass approach will get at the problem. I want to say that as far as segregation and desegregation is concerned, this administration has made great progress in desegregation. There are more black students that go to majority white schools in the South than in the North at the present time. The dual school system has been virtually eliminated.

What we were trying to get at is the problem of busing, busing which was a bad means because it compounds the evil which *Brown versus the Department of Education* was trying to get at. Also it poisons relations between the races and creates racism and it was time for somebody to move on it in what I thought was a responsible way.

Q: To go back to the ITT case for a moment, since you have said that you see nothing improper in Mr. Flanigan's activities in the various cases you mentioned, will you permit him to testify before the Senate Judiciary Committee if he is invited to do so?

THE PRESIDENT: Mr. Ziegler responded to that question and I will not respond further.

Q: Would you care to comment on the primaries and do you expect Congressman Ashbrook to go right down the wire to the convention and go for the nomination?

THE PRESIDENT: I realize that a lot of you have political questions. You may remember, as, I think, the first president of the press club that I ever introduced at one of your meetings many, many years ago, that I stated several months ago that in presidential press conferences I would not answer questions on partisan political matters until after the Republican convention. That includes the Republicans. That includes the Democrats. That includes those who may leave the Republicans or leave the Democrats.

Q: And it is still your intention, Mr. President, not to campaign until after convention time?

THE PRESIDENT: It is. As a matter of fact, I will not be making any political speeches—well, you may call them political —but I will not be appearing, Mr. Warren, before any partisan political groups, making partisan political speeches, and I am not going to answer any partisan political questions one way or another in any presidential conference or in any other forum of this kind.

Between now and the Republican convention, I shall continue to meet the responsibilities as President of the United States and I will answer all questions in that area. I will not answer political questions. I will have plenty of time to answer them after the Republican convention.

Q: Mr. President, how do you assess the military situation in Vietnam, Laos and Cambodia, and will you be able to follow your schedule for withdrawal of troops and perhaps tell us something more of it?

THE PRESIDENT: I will not tell you more about the withdrawal at this time because as you know, we make these announcements at the time they are scheduled and on the basis of the situation as it exists then. Another announcement will be made before the first of May.

Secondly, with regard to our program for withdrawal, it has gone well, as you know. The casualties again are low this week, still not zero, which is our goal, but it is better than 200 or 300, which is what it was when we came in. As far as the military situation is concerned, an ominous enemy build-up continues. The press has very well reported the threats in the Laotian base on Long Cheng. There has been some sporadic mortar attacks in Cambodia and a considerable amount of action in South Vietnam. On the other hand, I received a report from General Abrams just a few days ago. He says that they still expect—he doesn't guarantee it—but he says they are still prepared for some attacks in this dry season. They have not come yet. He says if they do come he is confident that the South Vietnamese will be able to contain them. He is also confident that while the South Vietnamese lines, in the event the attacks are heavy, may bend, that they will not break. If this proves to be the case it will be the final proof that Vietnamization has succeeded.

Q: Mr. President, have you satisfied yourself, sir, that the Justice Department acted properly in quashing an investigation of campaign contributions in San Diego last year?

THE PRESIDENT: I covered that question.

Q: Mr. President, you spoke in terms of busing a moment ago and that the patterns of living are the root cause of it. Have you then thought of some new programs to try to break up the patterns that keep the blacks in the inner city, to try to get at integration in that way?

THE PRESIDENT: It is very difficult to try to find new programs because so many have been suggested and I imagine there are not any that could be classified as new. The breaking up of these patterns is something that probably is going to occur over a period of time as economic considerations and educational considerations come more into play. I am confident of this, that we cannot put, as I said, not in my statement on busing a few days ago, but in my original statement on the whole educational process last year, we cannot put the primary burden for breaking up these patterns on the educational system.

The purpose of education is to educate. Whenever a device is used to desegregate which results in inferior education, we are doing a grave disservice to the blacks who are supposed to be helped.

Q: Mr. President, is it a pragmatic observation to say that the world now is divided into three parts: The United States, China, and the Soviet Union?

THE PRESIDENT: Some would perhaps describe the world that way, but I think the world is much bigger and much more complicated. I don't think that you can rule out by such a simplistic observation the future of Latin America, the potential of Africa, the potential in South Asia and the rimland of Asia, the future of Japan which is an economic giant, even though it is a mini-military power.

At the present time, it could be said that the United States and the Soviet Union are the two major super powers from a military standpoint and that the Peoples Republic of China is the most populous nation in the world with the potential of becoming a super power, and therefore anyone who is interested in trying to build a structure of peace must deal with the relationships between these three great power centers now.

I think that is the key to the future. But we must also, at the same time, have politics that look to the future of Japan, the future of Western Europe, because it will play a major role, and of course the future of Latin America and Africa.

Q: Mr. President, you have sort of a pattern of making peace with enemies around the world. Are you next going to see Fidel Castro?

THE PRESIDENT: No. I have not been invited.

Q: Mr. President, do you have a comment, sir, on the recommendation of your commission on drugs that the use of marijuana in the home be no longer considered a crime?

THE PRESIDENT: I met with Mr. Shafer. I have read the report. It is a report which deserves consideration and it will receive it. However, as to one aspect of the report, I am in disagreement. I was before. I read it and reading it did not change my mind. I oppose the legalization of marijuana and that includes its sale, its possession, and its use. I do not believe you can have effective criminal justice based on the philosophy that something is half legal and half illegal. That is my position, despite what the commission has recommended.

Q: Mr. President, on your upcoming trip to Canada, do you intend to try to do something about getting us in a better trade position, and also, do you intend to take up the matter of the Great Lakes?

THE PRESIDENT: We are working out the agenda for our Canadian trip at the present time. I would have to say quite candidly that we have had very little success to date in our negotiations with our Canadian friends, which shows, incidentally, that sometimes you have more problems negotiating with your friends than you do with your adversaries. But that is as it should be. They have a right to their position and we have a right to ours. But we will discuss certainly trade and the Great Lakes and environment. I am sure we will also discuss the world situation in which Prime Minister Trudeau has some, based on my previous visits with him, some very constructive ideas to suggest.

In addition, on my trip to Canada, I will, of course, brief Prime Minister Trudeau personally on the results of my visit to China and also brief him prior to my going to the Soviet Union on my visit there.

I think it is very helpful that at this point we are meeting with our friends from Canada, although we will find that we have some very basic disagreements, probably, after the meeting as before.

Q: When you went to China there were a lot of people in this country who sincerely hoped that your trip would be helpful in terms of settling the Vietnam war in some fashion or another. Did you find that trip helpful in that respect and if so, can you tell us how?

THE PRESIDENT: At the time we went to China, I indicated that the purpose of that trip was to discuss relations between the two countries, and that its purpose was not to discuss the situation with regard to other nations.

Now, as far as the discussions that did take place, the agenda did include the whole range of problems in the world in which the People's Republic of China is interested, as we are interested.

As far as Vietnam is concerned, I don't think it would be helpful to indicate what was discussed or what was not discussed. Only time will tell what is going to happen there.

Q: Mr. President, there has been some question raised about Ambassador Watson's qualifications to negotiate with the Chinese in Paris. Do you still have confidence in his ability to negotiate exchange agreements with the Chinese?

THE PRESIDENT: Mr. Lisagor, the best test of that—and I should know—is how the negotiations are going. They are going very well. Mr. Watson is conducting them with great competence and, I understand, total sobriety.

I realize that there are those who raise questions about the personal conduct of an ambassador when he travels to his post. I see that some members of the House and Senate are raising such questions about that. I would say that people in glass houses should not throw stones.

Q: Do you plan to have any more breakfasts with George Meany, or do you consider that a political question?

THE PRESIDENT: Not at thirty dollars a dozen for eggs.

Seriously, Paul Healy, I do want to say that I respect Mr. Meany not only as a powerful labor union leader, but as a patriotic American who, at a time when many of his weak-spined business colleagues were ready to throw in the sponge with regard to the security of the United States and what was best for this country in dealing with its adversaries abroad, stood firm.

On the other hand, in this particular area, I think Mr. Meany, I respectfully say, has overstepped. In the latter part of the 19th Century this country determined that no business leader could take the attitude "The public be damned." In the latter part of the 20th Century that applies to both business leaders and labor leaders.

Mr. Meany, in this case, I am sure, thinks he is acting in the best interest of his members, but I would respectfully suggest that I believe that a great number of his members, possibly a majority, realize that wage increases that are eaten up by price increases are no wage increases at all. They will also remember, as they look at their income, that in the past six months since Phase 2 began, we have had an increase in real wages, something that we have not had for five years before that time in any significant degree, and while we have had this one month of bad figures—and believe me I am not satisfied with bad figures; I want these food prices down—nevertheless, our wage-price controls are working. We are going to reach our goal, in my opinion, or are going to come very close to it, cutting the rate of inflation in half.

Even though Mr. Meany is not with us, I think what we do is in the best interest of his members, and I hope in the end maybe he will invite me to breakfast.

Q: With respect to Mr. Agnew, do you still not feel like breaking up the winning combination?

THE PRESIDENT: I covered that question in a rather lengthy discussion with Mr. Rather, sitting in this room, a few months ago. My views are the same as they were then.

Q: Mr. President, I would like to ask one question on the forthcoming Moscow trip. Are you still hopeful of having a strategic arms limitation agreement not only to discuss, but hopefully to sign?

THE PRESIDENT: Mr. Semple, I realize that there are many of you here, I hope, who will be able to go on that trip who went to the PRC, and many who did not go to the PRC can also go.

The Moscow trip, at the present time, will be very different from the PRC trip in the sense that it will be primarily devoted to a number of substantive issues of very great importance. One of them may be SALT, if SALT is not completed before Moscow. It does not appear now likely that they can complete SALT before Moscow, because in my conversations with Ambassador Smith before he left, I found that while we are agreed in principle on the limitation of offensive and defensive weapons, that we are still very far apart on some fundamental issues—well, whether or not SLBM's should be included, matters of that sort.

Mr. Smith went back to the meetings, this time in Helsinki, with very full instructions from me, both written and oral, to do everything he could to attempt to narrow those differences. I believe that there is a good chance at this point, particularly in view of Mr. Brezhnev's quite constructive remarks in his speech the other day, that we may reach an agreement on SALT in Moscow on defense and offensive limitations, and also agreements in a number of other areas.

This is our goal, and I would say that at this time the prospects for the success of this summit trip are very good.

THE PRESS: Thank you, Mr. President.

APRIL 30 TEXAS REMARKS

Following is the text, as made available by the White House, of President Nixon's remarks and answers to questions of guests at the Floresville, Texas, ranch of Treasury Secretary John B. Connally on April 30.

THE PRESIDENT: Well, I want to say first of all that we are most grateful for the welcome that you have given us to Texas, and speaking in a very personal sense, I, of course, rather than saying Mr. Secretary, would like to say to John and Nellie Connally that we are particularly happy that we have had a chance to visit this ranch, to see a lot of old friends, and also to make some new friends, as well.

As I listened to John Connally, and as I listened to some of the things he had to say about me and my age, and as I thought back on some of those dope stories suggesting that he was no longer a potential candidate for anything, I began to wonder. (Laughter)

I would like to return the compliment, not simply because it is a case of when one man scratches your back, you scratch his in return—and, of course, it is much more pleasant when it is a lady—but nevertheless, whatever the case might be, I would like to say a word about the appointment that I made of John Connally as Secretary of the Treasury; how it was greeted with such surprise in many quarters, applause from some, a wonder among others, and criticism, of course, from many that you would expect.

Generally speaking, the line was, well, what does John Connally know about being Secretary of the Treasury? They recognized he was a fine lawyer, they recognized he was a very successful political leader in Texas, they recognized he had been a great Governor of this State, but what in the world did he know about being Secretary of the Treasury. And the country has found out.

All that I can say is this: When I named him to this position, I named him to the position because I had had the privilege of knowing him as a man through many years, and particularly well during the years I have been President. And based on the—and it is hard to realize it has been 18 months almost now that he has been in this position—based on those 18 months, I can say that John Connally, who has been a Governor and now a Cabinet Officer, and was a former Secretary of the Navy, is, in my view, a man who has demonstrated that he is capable of holding any job in the United States that he would like to pursue. (Applause)

I am just glad he is not seeking the Democratic nomination. (Laughter)

If I could just add to that by saying that we remember the new economic policy of August 15; we remember the United States at long last standing up for its position in international monetary affairs, in trade matters and the rest, and the leadership that the Secretary of the Treasury provided. We remember his leadership in the fight on inflation, in all of the other areas, but I also recall those times when clearly out of his special capacity as Secretary of the Treasury, his capacity as the head of the Cost of Living Council, as an advisor, as a friend, as a counsellor in all areas, I remember how much he has contributed to this Administration.

And to all those, I would add one final thing. Certainly his greatest contribution was bringing Nellie Connally to Washington, D.C. She has been a scintillating star on the Washington scene. Don't get the idea that that is bad, necessarily, but I can assure you that in our Cabinet Family and among those who have known her, be they Democrats or Republicans, they have all been as warmly affectionate towards her as the people of this State are, and we are so happy that here with their friends, we can share this special evening with you.

Because I know you have had a very splendid dinner tonight, and because I know this has probably never happened on this ranch before—well, at least if it has happened, it has never been done by one who held the office that I hold—I think that all of you would like to join me in raising our glasses to John and Nellie Connally.

Now, with that, let me just say a word with regard to what John has suggested. It did occur to him as we were sitting here that so many of our guests don't have the opportunity to talk with the one who happens to be the guest of honor as those who are at only the one table at which we are seated. It doesn't mean that there are many pearls of wisdom that are passed out here that you are missing, but I would say it does mean simply that perhaps on an occasion like this, since this is a party of close friends, and since this whole great State is covered, that I know that both Pat and I would have liked to have sat at every table and talked to each one of you.

So for the next few minutes, if you like, in a totally nonpartisan, not political way, if you would like to just rather imagine that we were sitting in your living room, and you were chatting and asking questions, I will try to answer them.

I can assure you, if I don't know the answers, John will.

So with that, in that very informal way, we will be glad to take any of your questions that you have for a few minutes, and we will not keep you too long, unless the questions take too long.

Q: Mr. President, do you anticipate any developments in Vietnam other than those courageous statements we heard on the television the other night, that you might tell us here?

THE PRESIDENT: I would respond by saying that the evaluation of the situation in Vietnam today is the same that I gave then.

As General Abrams reported then, and as he has updated his report as of today, the South Vietnamese on the ground are resisting very bravely a massive Communist North Vietnamese invasion of South Vietnam. That invasion will continue. The offensive will continue in its intensity, and we can expect over the next four to five weeks that there will be some battles lost for the South Vietnamese and some will be won, but it is his professional judgment—General Abrams' professional judgment—that the South Vietnamese will be able to hold and deny to the North Vietnamese their goal, which, of course, is to impose on the people of South Vietnam a Communist government.

Now to keep it all in perspective, let us understand that when we hear about this town or that one that is under attack, we must remember that as of this time, the North Vietnamese have utterly failed in their ability to rally the South Vietnamese people to their cause.

We also must remember that despite their moving in on certain territory and in certain towns, that over 90 percent of the people of South Vietnam are still under the government of South Vietnam, and not under control of the Communists.

So keeping it in perspective, while we can expect, and should expect, as is always the case in a war of any kind, and particularly a war of this type—we can expect some days when the news may be a South Vietnamese setback, and other days when it will be otherwise. It is the professional view of the man on the spot, best able to judge, that the South Vietnamese will be able to hold, provided—and this comes to what we do—provided the United States continues to furnish the air and naval support that we have been furnishing to stop this invasion.

Now, without repeating what I said last Wednesday night, but simply to underline it, I would like to make just two or three points quickly, frankly to this group of friends here in Texas.

Questions have been raised about the decision that I have made, which is to the effect that as long as the North Vietnamese were conducting an invasion, an offensive, in South Vietnam, and were killing South Vietnamese and Americans in South Vietnam, that I would, as Commander-in-Chief of our Armed Forces, order air and naval attacks on military targets in North Vietnam.

I realize that decision has caused considerable controversy in this country. I understand why that would be the case. There are many people who believe that the United States has done enough in South Vietnam; that what we should do is to find a way to get out as quickly as we can, and let whatever the consequences are flow from that, which would mean, of course, a Communist take-over.

Let me tell you the reasons why I feel that it is vitally important that the United States continue to use its air and naval power against targets in North Vietnam, as well as in South Vietnam, to prevent a Communist take-over and a Communist victory over the people of South Vietnam.

First because there are 69,000 Americans still in Vietnam—that will be reduced to 49,000 by the first of July—and I, as Commander-in-Chief have a responsibility to see to it that their lives are adequately protected, and I, of course, will meet that responsibility.

Second, because as we consider the situation in Vietnam, we must remember that if the North Vietnamese were to take over in South Vietnam, as a result of our stopping our support in the air and on the sea—we have no ground support whatever, there are no American ground forces in action in South Vietnam and none will be—but when we consider that situation, if there were such a take-over, we must consider the consequences.

There is first the consequence to the people of South Vietnam. We look back to what happened historically in 1954, when the North Vietnamese took over in North Vietnam, the Catholic Bishop of Danang estimated that at least 500,000 people in North Vietnam who had opposed the Communist take-over in the North were either murdered or starved to death in slave labor camps.

I saw something of that when Mrs. Nixon and I were in there in 1956, when we visited refugee camps where over a million North Vietnamese fled from the Communist tyranny to come to the South. If, at this particular point, the Communists were to take over in South Vietnam, you can imagine what would happen to the hundreds of thousands of South Vietnamese who sided with their own government and with the United States against the Communists. It would be a blood bath that would stain the hands of the United States for time immemorial.

That is bad enough. I know there are some who say we have done enough; they say what happens to the South Vietnamese at this particular time is something that should not be our concern. We have sacrificed enough for them. So let's put it in the terms of the United States alone, and then we really see why the only decision that any man in the position of President of the United States can make is to authorize the necessary aid and naval strikes that will prevent a Communist take-over.

In the event that one country like North Vietnam, massively assisted with the most modern technical weapons by two Communist superpowers—in the event that that country is able to invade another country and conquer it, you can see how that pattern would be repeated in other countries throughout the world—in the Mideast, in Europe, and in others as well.

If, on the other hand, that kind of aggression is stopped in Vietnam, and fails there, then it will be discouraged in other parts of the world. Putting it quite directly then, what is on the line in Vietnam is not just peace for Vietnam, but peace in the Mideast, peace in Europe, and peace not just for the five or six or seven years immediately ahead of us, but possibly for a long time in the future.

As I put it last Wednesday night, I want, and all America wants, to end the war in Vietnam. I want, and all Americans want, to bring our men home from Vietnam. But I want, and I believe all Americans want, to bring our men home and to end this war in a way that the younger brothers and the sons of the men who have fought and died in Vietnam won't be fighting in another Vietnam five or ten years from now. That is what this is all about.

Q: May we raise our glasses and pay tribute to the courage of the President of the United States.

THE PRESIDENT: I am most grateful for that toast. Incidentally, I hope the champagne holds out for the evening.

But I do want to say that in the final analysis, what is really on the line here, of course, is the position of the United States of America as the strongest free world power, as a constructive force for peace in the world.

Let us imagine for a moment what the world would be like if the United States were not respected in the world. What would the world be like if friends of the United States throughout the non-Communist world lost confidence in the United States? It would be a world that would be much less safe. It would be a world that would be much more dangerous, not only in terms of war, but in terms of the denial of freedom, because when we talk about the United States of America and all of our faults, let us remember that in this country we have never used our power to break the peace, only to restore it or keep it, and we have never used our power to destroy freedom, only to defend it.

Now, I think that is a precious asset for the world. I also feel one other thing, and I will close this rather long answer on this point: John Connally has referred to the office of the President of the United States. Earlier this evening I talked to President Johnson on the telephone. We are of different parties. We both served in this office. While I had my political differences with him, and he with me, I am sure he would agree that each of us in his way tries to leave that office with as much respect and with as much strength in the world as he possibly can—that is his responsibility—and to do it the best way he possibly can.

Let me say in this respect that I have noted that when we have traveled abroad to 18 countries, particularly even when we went to the People's Republic of China, the office of President—not the man, but the office of President—of the United States is respected in every country we visited. I think we will find that same respect in Moscow. But if the United States at this time leaves Vietnam and allows a Communist takeover, the office of President of the United States will lose respect and I am not going to let that happen.

Q: Mr. President, may I ask you about strategic targets in North Vietnam? I have been told for years by the pilots that there are dams up there that would be very much defeating to the North Vietnamese, who have defied what you have tried to prove in the way of peace. Is this true or false? Has this crossed your mind?

THE PRESIDENT: The question is with regard to the targets in North Vietnam, and particularly with regard to the dams and dikes, which many of the pilots believe would be very effective strategic targets.

I would say on that score that we have, as you know, authorized strikes, and we have made them over the past four weeks, since the Communist offensive began, in the Hanoi-Haiphong area.

I have also indicated, as this offensive continues, if it does continue, that we will continue to make strikes on military targets throughout North Vietnam.

Now, the problem that is raised with regard to dams or dikes is that, while it is a strategic target, and indirectly a military target, it would result in an enormous number of civilian casualties. That is something that we want to avoid. It is also something we believe is not needed.

Just let me say that as far as the targets in North Vietnam are concerned, that we are prepared to use our military and naval strength against military targets throughout North Vietnam, and we believe that the North Vietnamese are taking a very great risk if they continue their offensive in the South.

I will just leave it there, and they can make their own choice.

In other words, I believe that we can limit our strikes to military targets without going to targets that involve civilian casualties. That is what we have done, and we can do that in the future, and do the job.

Q: Mr. President, turn to domestic America. You know there are great misgivings in the press now about how America feels about itself, and where we are going to. I don't think there is anyone better equipped to tell us how you feel about where America is going; not today, but for its future and about its own confidence in itself, and I would like to hear your remarks.

THE PRESIDENT: The question relates to domestic America, the feeling that many Americans have that possibly we, in America, are losing confidence in ourselves. The question asks me to evaluate how I see the mood of America, and how I understand it, and what the future for America is in terms of confidence in itself.

That, of course, would allow a rather extended reply. Let me see if I can get at the heart of it. First, let me relate it to the last question.

I know there are those who say that the trouble with America's confidence, most of it, is due to the fact that we are involved in Vietnam, and that once the war in Vietnam is over that then the trouble on the campuses will go away, the division in the country, the polarization and all the rest. That is just nonsense.

Let me say the American people do not want war. We did not start this war. Let me say also that when I see people carrying signs saying "Stop the War," I am tempted to say "Tell it to Hanoi; they are the ones who have started the war, not the United States of America."

Nevertheless, while peace is our goal, and peace will be achieved—not just peace in our time, but we hope peace that will live for a generation or longer—that is why we went to Peking. That is why we are going to Moscow. That is why we are trying to end the war responsibly, in a way that would discourage those who would start war, rather than encourage them.

Let us well understand, if the United States, as a great nation, fails in Vietnam as we come to the end of this long road, and as we see the end, and as we know that it is not necessary to fail, I can think of nothing that would destroy the confidence of the American people more than that. So I would begin with that proposition by answering it on the negative side.

Now, turning to the domestic issue, what about the attitude of America toward itself? We often hear it said that we, in this country, are so divided about race issues, we are divided between labor and management, rich and poor, environmentalists, those who are against doing anything about the environment, and so forth and so on, that it is a rather hopeless future.

I would simply raise this one question in that respect. If you sit in Washington, if you limit yourself to the group that we in Washington generally talk to, and this is no reflection on them, because we all tend to be sort of victims of intellectual incest there, what happens is that you get the impression that everything is wrong with America; that the majority of the people of this country have lost faith in themselves, faith in their country; they no longer have the will to work, and the will to defend the country, the will to build a great nation.

That is a point of view. That point of view tends to be fed—and I say this, incidentally, not in anger, and perhaps more in sorrow—it tends to be fed by the tendency of some in the media—not all, but some in the media—constantly to emphasize a negative; I am speaking now more of the national media, rather than those who are out across the great, heartland of America—but the tendency to emphasize those negatives and to create in the minds of the American people the impression that this country, just before its 200th birthday, has reached the point where it has lost its sense of destiny; the American people no longer have the will to greatness which they once had.

I can only say that as I travel through America I find a different story. Let me point it out to you in a different way. I was talking to an Ambassador recently from a country in Europe who had just been accredited to this country. This was several months ago. This Ambassador told me that he had lived in Washington for a while, and then he had taken a trip out through the country. He said, "Mr. President, as I traveled through the country"—he had been to Illinois; he had been to California; he had also been to Texas; as a matter of fact, to Florida and Georgia and back to Washington, and he said, "I go out into the country and I see a different America than I see in Washington, D.C." I believe that the heart of America is still strong. I believe that the character of America is still strong. But I think now is the time when we must stand up against the trend toward permissiveness, the trend toward weakness, the trend toward something for nothing, and if we do that, this country is going to regain its self-confidence.

I believe that is what is going to happen.

Q: Mr. President, I would like to ask you this question: Mr.

Moncrief spoke my sentiments, and I think 99 percent of the people in Texas are in favor of what you are doing in Vietnam, but why is it in the East you get the newspapers and students and Members of the Congress and the Senate are complaining about what you are doing, but they never mention what the Communists, the North Vietnamese, are doing by invading South Vietnam, and they are killing thousands of people. They seem to think that is right, and what we are doing is wrong. Why don't they ever mention that?

THE PRESIDENT: I think that would be a very excellent editorial for somebody to write. (Applause)

Let me, in all fairness, say this: I do not question the patriotism of any critics of this war. Reasonable and honest and decent Americans can disagree about whether we should have gotten into Vietnam. They can disagree about how the war should be conducted, disagree about who is at fault now, and so forth, but let's look at the record as it is at the present time.

Since I have come into office we have withdrawn half a million men from Vietnam. We have offered everything that could be offered except impose a Communist government on the people of South Vietnam, and their answer has been massive invasion of South Vietnam by the North.

Now, under these circumstances, instead of the critics criticizing brave Americans flying dangerous air missions, hitting military targets in North Vietnam and military targets only, instead of criticizing them trying to prevent a Communist takeover, I think they should direct a little criticism to the Communists who are trying to keep this war going. That is what they ought to be doing.

Q: What are the possibilities of trade with China and Russia, as you now see it?

THE PRESIDENT: Looking at both of these countries, we must realise—and I know that there are many here who have traveled certainly to Russia, and to other Communist countries, although very few perhaps have been to China, at least in recent years—and looking at both of these countries realistically, as far as China is concerned, while we have now opened the door for a new relationship insofar as trade is involved, realistically, the amount of trade that the United States will have with the People's Republic of China will be considerably limited over a period of time.

The Japanese, for example, have found that out. They, of course, are much closer to Mainland China, and they have been trying to trade with them over a period of years, and yet they find that the amount of trade that they are able to have with the People's Republic of China is, frankly, much less than they expected when they began to open trade up.

We should not expect too much in the short range. We could expect a considerable amount further down the road.

Now, with the Soviet Union, this, of course, will be a major subject that will be discussed at the Summit meeting. There will be considerable opportunities for trade with the Soviet Union.

The Secretary of Agriculture, Mr. Butz, was there discussing the possibility of trade insofar as agricultural products are concerned—the selling of some of our grain to the Soviet Union.

We have also had discussions between the Secretary of Commerce, Mr. Stans, and Mr. Peterson, now the new Secretary of Commerce, is discussing this with the Russian delegation, and we expect more trade opportunities to develop with the Soviet Union.

Realistically, however, we must recognize that where you have a Communist country dealing with a capitalist country, or non-Communist country, the possibilities of trade are seriously limited because of an inability to have a method for financing it.

I know I have heard some American businessmen say wouldn't it be great if we could just sell just a few consumer items to 800 million Chinese. That is fine, but what are they going to sell us, and how are we going to finance it?

That is a problem, to a lesser extent, with the Soviet Union, but also a problem with them.

I would say then that these new relationships we have developed and are developing with the People's Republic of China and with the Soviet Union will certainly lead to more trade in the years ahead—trade in non-strategic items of course, so long as those countries are engaged in supporting activities such as those in Vietnam.

Q: Mr. President, leave it to John. He will work it out. (Laughter)

Q: Mr. President, one thing that is bothering me is what is the basis for the criticism of our bombing Haiphong and Hanoi? Were the United States in war, do you not think they would immediately bomb Washington and San Francisco and New York and isn't the quickest way to stop this war to stop the supplies that are going into South Vietnam from their friends?

THE PRESIDENT: The United States has shown restraint such as a great power has never shown in history in its handling of the war in Vietnam. At the present time, however, now that we have gone the extra mile in offering a peace settlement and peace terms, a cease fire, an exchange of prisoners of war—and Mr. Ross Perot can tell you about some of the things we have gone through there and the barbarism with which our prisoners of war are treated. We have offered a total withdrawal of all our forces within six months. President Thieu has offered to resign a month before new elections that would be internationally supervised in which the Communists would participate in the election and the supervisory body.

Having offered all of that, and then faced with this invasion, certainly the least the United States can do—and that is all I have ordered—is to use our air and sea power to hit military targets in North Vietnam. This is what we have done and that is what we are going to continue to do until they stop their invasion of South Vietnam.

Q: Mr. President, most of us who have observed the moves that you have made in raising the price of gold and expecting the rest of the world to let their currency float, are pleased. At least the ones who I know.

The greatness of the country is built on the willingness of its people to work. The success of this country is built on that. When Japan can settle a strike in two days, a shipping strike, and we take six months, why can't we do this a little more efficiently and quickly. When we take people away from their jobs and do not have them produce, we are losing the productive value of these people, and if we don't do this, will we not face a further devaluation in the ensuing months ahead?

THE PRESIDENT: I think most of you could hear the question. It relates to what I think is the totally correct policy of the Secretary of the Treasury in which we sought a new alignment of currency, we raised the price of gold, and as a result we improved the competitive position of American products in world markets.

But when we come to the fundamental point—and this is the one you are getting at—it is very simply this: Unless the United States is prepared to build a wall around itself, we have to compete with other nations in the world. Now in order to compete with other nations in the world, we who pay by far the highest wages in the world, have to be more productive than other people in the world, and that means that we can't afford work stoppages that are too long.

The strike that you refer to, the Longshoremen's strike, was one that certainly was not defendable and had enormously negative effects on the economy of this country.

We also, in that connection, if we are going to be competitive, have to have a tax structure which will encourage new investments in capital rather than discouraging it, and we also have to have, if I may boldly suggest it, a recognition of the need to respect what I call the work ethic in this country.

Now, briefly, on all three points. With regard to strikes of the Longshoremen, railroads, transportation generally, the Congress of the United States has had before it for the past two years a bill that would require, in effect compulsory arbitration of such disputes and bring them to a halt, and the Congress has not acted.

I think this, of course, is a major failure on the part of the Congress, and it is time that we had Congressmen and Senators—and incidentally, this is not partisan—Democrats or Republicans, that have the courage to go down to Washington and vote for legislation in the public interest that will stop these transportation tie-ups that we had on the docks and other places, and I think we should get them.

Second, with regard to the competitive position of American products in the world, there has been a lot of talk lately about the need for tax reform, and a great deal of criticism of so-called tax loopholes. I am not going to go into that in any detail, when I have the major expert on tax reform right here in front of me. And it is no accident he is on my right, incidentally, in this respect.

But I simply want to say this: One of the loopholes is supposed to be depreciation. Another loophole is supposed to be depletion. Now all of you here in this State know my own position on depletion and depreciation, and you also know that this Administration has been subjected to considerable criticism on the ground that we are for big business and we are for rich oil men and against people.

I will tell you what we are for. What we are for is for more jobs for America and for American industry to be able to compete abroad. Do you know where the most efficient steel plant in the world is? It is not in the United States. It is in Japan. Do you know where some of the most efficient new kinds of chemical plants in the world are? We have some very good ones in the United States, but the best new ones may be in Germany.

How did this happen? It didn't happen because our American businessmen are less imaginative, our scientists and engineers less capable. I believe we have the best in the world. But in both Japan and Germany, after they had gone through the devastation of World War II, they adopted a tax policy in terms of the depreciation that encouraged investment in new plants and equipment and research on a basis unheard of in any capitalist country in the world.

As far as I am concerned, that is why I strongly favor not only the present depreciation rate, but going even further than that, so we can get our plants and equipment more effective. This is why, in terms of depletion, rather than moving in the direction of reducing depletion allowance, let us look at the fact that all the evidence now shows that we are going to have a major energy crisis in this country in the 80's. To avoid that energy crisis we have to provide incentive rather than disincentive for people to go out and explore for oil. That is why you have depletion, and the people have got to understand it.

Now, if I can just spend a moment on the last point, the work ethic. First, let us well understand that there are millions of fine Americans who work hard, are proud of their work and they have made this country, they built this country and they are going to build it bigger in the future.

But let us also understand that there has developed—and this goes back to the earlier question which I could not answer too precisely because it is difficult to answer in an effective way a question so profound in its implication—but in recent years there has grown up the idea more and more and more of something for nothing; the idea that where a job is concerned that we will take those jobs only if they happen to be jobs that we consider as the term is used, not menial.

Let me ask any of you who have traveled to Los Angeles, to Miami, to New York and so forth, Denver, Dallas, anyplace, pick up your papers, look at the Help Wanted ads, and you will find thousands of Help Wanted ads in those particular papers, and yet you will find unemployment, and in the City of New York alone a million on the welfare rolls.

Now this is not always true. It may not even be true in a majority of cases. It is sometimes true, and very simply, it is that in case after case, an individual who is able to work refuses to work because the job is not one that he feels is up to his capability. He feels that it is too menial a job.

Well, I just have grown up in a different time. I say that no job is menial if it provides bread on the table and shelter for a family. Rather than for a man to have to go on public welfare, he ought to take the job.

It is that spirit that we need revived in this country, and we have to revive it not only down among those who might potentially be on welfare rolls, but up and down our whole society, because let us be quite honest in our own self-evaluation: The tendency, too often, in modern education, in some of our great colleges and great universities, is to downplay the necessity for excellence, for pride in work and all these other great values that have made this country what it is.

I just want to say on that point, I have great confidence in the future as far as America's competitive position is concerned, but let us make no mistake about it: Simply letting the dollar float, having realignments of currency, erecting temporary barriers, 10 or 15 percent surcharges or less, isn't going to do the trick. The United States will be able to compete in the world only when the United States and the people of this country are competitive in every sense of the word. We can do it, but we have to tighten our belts if we are going to meet that task.

SECRETARY CONNALLY: Ladies and gentlemen, the President has been going for about an hour. Let's see if we can take one more question, and we won't count this: Mr. President, the people here from Dallas, Corpus Christi, Houston, Austin, and in very recent months, I suppose, perhaps, the most emotional, most critical issue in those cities has been the question of busing. Do you have any comments on it?

THE PRESIDENT: My views on the merits of busing have been expressed on many occasions. I will repeat them only briefly, and then talk about the remedy briefly.

The reason that I am against busing for the purpose of achieving racial balance in our schools is that it leads to inferior education. Let's look at the situation with regard to what the whole busing controversy is about, and there are many lawyers here tonight, and all of you are, of course, familiar with the famous, landmark case of Brown versus the Board of Education in 1954.

The very title of that case tells us something. Brown versus the Board of Education, which provided that the dual school system had to be eliminated, was about education, and correctly, in the opinion of observers at that time, and I was one of them, and certainly most observers now, a system that legally sets up a dual school system and divides people according to race is one that could lead and would inevitably lead to inferior education. So Brown versus the Board of Education dealt with that problem.

That problem has been moved on very effectively, particularly during this Administration, to the great credit of those particularly in Southern States, where some of the dual school systems had to be removed. We now find that the South has gone really further than the North insofar as meeting the goal of getting rid of a dual school system.

Let's look at busing. Where busing comes in, in attempting to deal with the problem, a Board of Education or a court orders that school children be bused across town away from their neighborhood schools in order to create some artificial racial balance.

If you read the decisions, they never use the term "racial balance", but there are over 23 that we already have identified where that is exactly what the court was ordering.

Now, why do I believe this is wrong? Because in my view, when you bus children, particularly young children, away from their neighborhood school, into an unfamiliar neighborhood, whether they are black or white, it leads to inferior education. It also has some other disadvantages. It divides communities; it creates hostility among people that didn't exist before. I think that for that reason, we have got to find more effective ways to have equality of educational opportunity for all Americans than to use busing.

So that is why I have come up with these remedies: First, a moratorium on any new busing orders for a year. We have asked the Congress to act on that.

Second, I have ordered the Attorney General of the United States to intervene in those cases where the courts have gone beyond what the Supreme Court presently has laid down as the requirement insofar as eliminating the dual school system is concerned.

And then third, we have asked for the enactment of the Equal Educational Opportunity Act, under which we would upgrade education in inferior schools; but we would specifically provide that busing would not be required at all for children in the sixth grade and below, and then for any other cases above that, would be used not as the first resort, but only as a last resort, and then only temporarily.

It also provides, incidentally, when this Act is passed, that in those States that have had imposed upon them busing orders that went beyond what the new legislation would require, those cases could be reopened.

Now, where do you stand? At the present time, the Congress has had this request for legislation for over two months. It has not acted. The prospects for its acting do not appear hopeful at the present time. In my view, before the Congress goes home for its election recess, the Congress owes it to the American people to act, because unless it does act, it means that tens of thousands of students in scores of communities across this country are going to be subjected to busing orders that will provide inferior education for them, and that should be avoided. So I believe that the Congress should act to deal with the problem. If the Congress does not act, and refuses to face up to one problem, then the only resort that we have left is to proceed with the Constitutional amendment.

So under these circumstances, I realize that the position that I have taken is subject to honest criticism, honest debate by people who have considered the subject just as I tried to consider it, with the interest of better education as well as eliminating the dual school system, and providing equality of education for all concerned.

But I simply conclude my answer to this question by saying that in this country if you were to provide for—I am talking now about the most extreme advocates of busing—if you were to provide for busing students in the major metropolitan centers like New York, Chicago, Detroit and Los Angeles, in plans that go further than even the most liberal plans have ever provided, it would still leave the great majority of black children in inferior schools in central cities who would never get the benefit of a so-called better education.

So I say that the better answer is to upgrade the education for those children who would otherwise be a lost generation, but let's do not impair the education for all other children as a result of busing orders. That is the way I think we should approach it.

Q: Mr. President, your days and nights are very long, and we are very grateful for your services. As a newspaperman, I would like to exercise my prerogative and say thank you, Mr. President.

JUNE 22

Following is the text, as made available by the White House, of President Nixon's June 22 news conference.

THE PRESIDENT: Ladies and gentlemen:

Next week before the Congress recesses, I am planning to have a general news conference. Prior to that time, in talking to Mr. Ziegler, I found that a number of members of the press, looking back at previous news conferences, have indicated that there is a tendency for foreign policy and defense policy questions to dominate the conferences so much that questions on domestic policy do not get adequately covered.

As a matter of fact, I have noted several of you in your commentaries, after some news conferences, have indicated that we have not given enough attention to the domestic issues.

So, subsequently, after discussing the matter with Mr. Ziegler, I thought it would be useful this week, on this occasion, to have you here in the office for the purpose of covering domestic issues only. The session next week will be open to foreign policy, defense policy and domestic issues.

So, today we will take all questions on domestic issues and next week you can cover all three areas to the extent you wish to.

Q: Mr. O'Brien has said that the people who bugged his headquarters had a direct link to the White House. Have you had any sort of investigation made to determine whether this is true?

THE PRESIDENT: Mr. Ziegler and also Mr. Mitchell, speaking for the Campaign Committee, have responded to questions on this in great detail. They have stated my position and have also stated the facts accurately.

This kind of activity, as Mr. Ziegler has indicated, has no place whatever in our electoral process, or in our governmental process. And, as Mr. Ziegler has stated, the White House has had no involvement whatever in this particular incident.

As far as the matter now is concerned, it is under investigation, as it should be, by the proper legal authorities, by the District of Columbia police and by the FBI. I will not comment on those matters, particularly since possible criminal charges are involved.

Q: Mr. President, wholesale food prices have led an increase in the cost of living in the last few weeks. Are you considering any permanent controls over the price of food?

THE PRESIDENT: In the whole area of inflation we have had a period of pretty good news generally. As you know, in 1969 and early 1970 the rate of inflation, the CPI, peaked out at six percent. Since that time it has been moving down and particularly since the August 15 new policy with the control system was announced, it has now been cut approximately in half, running at around the rate of three percent. The most troublesome area however is the one you have referred to—food prices.

We cannot take too much comfort from the figures that came out yesterday because as you know they actually reflected a slight drop in food prices. I met yesterday, however, with the Quadriad and Mr. Stein reported that the weekly reports that we get which, of course, were not reflected in yesterday's numbers indicate that meat prices, particularly, are beginning to rise again and rising very fast.

For that reason, I have directed that the Cost of Living Council which will be meeting this afternoon look into this matter to see what further action can be taken to deal specifically with food prices, but particularly with meat prices.

Now with regard to meat prices, to give you an indication of the direction of my thinking, you can move on the control side. But as we all remember in that period immediately after World War II, when we had controls but too much demand and too little supply, and all the black markets, controls alone will not work unless you also move on the supply side.

At the present time, we have apparently a world shortage of meat, and particularly a shortage of meat in the United States where the demand is constantly going up, as the income of our people also goes up.

We have to get, therefore, at the problem of supply. Consequently, one of the areas that I am exploring is the quota system. I have directed our staff to check into the advisability of a temporary lifting of the quotas on imported meat which will move on the supply side. It will not affect the problem immediately, but at least it would affect it over the next few months.

That does not rule out, also, the possibility of moving on the control side and the control side is a matter where the Cost of Living Council is presently, or will be at four o'clock this afternoon, considering a number of options which I will consider as the matter develops.

Q: Mr. President, this may be a borderline question in the domestic field, but I believe it may fall there since the issues are before Congress. Could you tell us your view of the relationship between the development of offensive weapons, as proposed in your defense budget, and the SALT agreements?

THE PRESIDENT: I have noted the progress of the debate in the committee, and particularly the controversy, or alleged controversy and contradiction which seems in some quarters to have been developed between the views of the Secretary of Defense and the views that I have expressed, and the views that have been expressed by Dr. Kissinger and Secretary Rogers.

I think that I can put the thing in context best by first pointing out the Secretary of Defense's position, and then relating that position to the overall position of the United States in attempting to develop policy that will adequately protect the security of the United States and also move forward on the arms limitation front.

The Secretary of Defense has a responsibility, as I have a responsibility, to recommend to the Congress action that will adequately protect the security of the United States. Moving on that responsibility, he has indicated that if the SALT agreement is approved, and then if the Congress rejects the programs for offensive weapons not controlled by the SALT agreement, that this would seriously jeopardize the security of the United States. On that point he is correct.

What I would suggest to the Congress and would recommend to individual Congressmen and Senators, who will have the responsibility of voting on this matter, is the following course: First, the arms limitation agreements should be approved on their merits. I would not have signed those agreements unless I had believed that, standing alone, they were in the interest of the United States. As a matter of fact, the offensive limitation is one that is particularly in our interest because it covers arms where the Soviet Union has ongoing programs which will be limited in this five-year period, and in which we have no ongoing programs.

So, consequently, I would recommend and strongly urge that the Congress approve the ABM Treaty, and also the limited, temporary, offensive limitations curb. However, after the Congress moves in that field, all Congressmen and Senators—and this would, of course, concern them all—who are concerned about the security of the United States should then vote for those programs that will provide adequate offensive weapons in the areas that have been recommended by the Secretary of Defense and by the Administration.

Now the reason for that is two fold: First, because if we have a SALT agreement and then do not go forward with these programs, the Soviet Union will, within a matter of a very limited time, be substantially ahead of the United States overall; particularly in the latter part of the 70s.

If the United States falls into what is a definitely second position, an inferior position to the Soviet Union overall in its defense programs, this will be an open invitation for more instability in the world and an open invitation, in my opinion, for more potential aggression in the world, particularly in such potentially explosive areas as the Mideast.

Therefore, it is important from the standpoint of the United States being able to play its role of maintaining peace and security in the world, a role that the United States, of all the non-Communist nations is the only one capable of playing, it is essential that the United States not fall into an inferior position.

Therefore, the offensive weapons programs—which incidentally were not conceived after the SALT agreements, they were recommended prior to the SALT agreements and stand on their own because the Soviet Union has programs in which they are moving forward. As I pointed out the leaders, and you ladies and gentlemen were present there, or some of you were and the rest of you covered it through the broadcasting system, the Soviet Union is moving forward.

Mr. Brezhnev made it absolutely clear to me that in those areas that were not controlled by our offensive agreement that they were going ahead with their programs. For us not to would seriously jeopardize the security of the United States and jeopardize the cause of world peace, in my opinion.

Now, the second reason why those who vote for the Arms Limitation Agreement should vote for an on-going program in those areas not covered by it, is that this Arms Control Agreement, while very important, is only the first step and not the biggest step.

The biggest step remains. The biggest step is a permanent limitation on offensive weapons, covering other categories of weapons, and we trust eventually all categories of weapons. This would be as dramatic as the one step that we have already taken —this would be an even more dramatic step in limiting arms overall between the two super powers.

In the event that the United States does not have ongoing programs, however, there will be no chance that the Soviet Union will negotiate Phase 2 of an arms limitation agreement. I can say to the members of the press here that had we not had an ABM program in being there would be no SALT agreement today because there would be no incentive for the Soviet Union to stop us from doing something that we were doing; and, thereby, agree to stop something they were doing.

Now in the event that we do not therefore have any new offensive systems under way or planned, the Soviet Union has no incentive to limit theirs and so consequently and I have studied this very, very carefully, I can assure you that there is nothing I would like better than to be able to limit these expenses—I am convinced that to achieve our goal which is the goal, I think, of all Americans, to achieve our goal of an offensive limitations curb, covering all types of nuclear weapons, that it is essential for the United States to have an ongoing, offensive program. For that reason, I think that the position of the Secretary of Defense, speaking for the security of the United States, is a sound one.

I would hope that Members of the House and Senate, on reflection, would recognize that the SALT agreement, important as it is, by itself, does not deal with the total defense posture of the United States. By itself it is in the interest of the United States and it stands on its own, but by itself, without a continuing offensive program, we can be sure that the security interests of the United States would be very seriously jeopardized and the chances for a permanent offensive agreement would, in my opinion, be totally destroyed.

Q: Mr. President, is Mr. Ehrlichman correct when he says that you sometimes get irritated with us for our dumb and flabby questions so-called?

THE PRESIDENT: You are not dumb and flabby. No, I noted that comment and expected a question on it. I am afraid if I begin to characterize the questions you will begin to characterize my answers, but you probably will anyway. In any event, as far as questions are concerned, I think what Mr. Ehrlichman was referring to was the tendency in the big East Room conferences for questions to come in from all over the place and no follow-up, as there can be in a conference like this.

Sometimes the questions may appear somewhat less relevant. I have found, for example, although we do not rule out the big conference where everybody gets to come, I have found that these smaller sessions do provide an opportunity for members of the regular White House Press, who study these issues day by day and who know what is relevant and what is not relevant and who can follow up, I think that the possibility of dumb and flabby questions is much less and I don't, frankly, complain about it.

The other point that I should make is this: in looking over the transcripts of various press conferences, I have not seen many softballs and I don't want any because it is only the hardball that you can hit or strike out on.

Q: Mr. President, how badly do you want a welfare bill to pass Congress and how much are you willing to compromise either on the principle or the price tag of H.R. 1?

THE PRESIDENT: Well, as you know, I have been having a number of meetings on this matter over the past week and I will expect to have more during the next week and after the Congress returns from its vacation in Miami.

But, whatever the case may be, looking at the welfare program, I believe that the position that we have taken, a position that has been overwhelmingly approved by the House, is the right position.

It provides for welfare for those who need it. It provides also for those incentives that will move people from welfare rolls to jobs, and it does so at a cost we can afford. And all of those matters, I think, have to be taken into consideration in any program that we recommend.

Now, the tactical situation is that Mr. Ribicoff and several Republicans have indicated that unless the Administration moves toward their position, that we have no chance to get a bill.

First, I question their analysis on that point.

Secondly, I believe that on the merits, moving in that direction is the wrong step because it would substantially increase the cost of welfare and move in the direction that I think the country does not want and that I believe would not be in the interests of the welfare recipients themselves.

On the other side of the coin, when it was known that I had had, as I did have, long conversations with those who were advocating the movement toward the Ribicoff positions, the members of the Senate Finance Committee have requested equal time. I intend to give them equal time, of course, to hear their arguments, after the bill is written in its final form. As you know, it has not yet been finalized.

My own present intention, however, is to stay by our middle position. I think it is the right position and I believe that it is a position that can get through this Congress.

Now on that score, I would just point out that we can all go back and look at speeches that have been made and maybe a few columns that have been written, indicating that the Administration's failing to move from the position that we had taken on revenue sharing meant that we would never get revenue sharing.

Well, we got it today in the House because our position was sound and I think we are going to follow these same tactics and same position now. I will watch it, of course, day by day, because I want welfare reform and the country wants welfare reform, but we cannot have welfare reform that moves in the direction of increasing the cost and putting more people on, rather than getting them off.

Q: Sir, I have seen a letter from a high official in the Immigration Department of the State Department saying we had 4,-800,000 people in this country on temporary visas who were employed. I wonder in view of the large number who come in illegally if you don't think these two groups together have a great impact on our high rate of unemployment.

THE PRESIDENT: The President of Mexico spoke to me about the problem of illegal aliens and as you know, it is a problem in which many of our labor organizations are very vitally interested. It does certainly contribute to the unemployment problem. It is one which Administration after Administration has wrestled with without too much success.

It is one, however, after my consultation with the President of Mexico that I have asked the Department of Labor to examine to see what steps could be taken to see that illegal aliens and particularly those—the Mexican problem is the biggest one, as you know—those from our friends and neighbors to the south, if that could be brought into greater control.

Q: Two questions about recent Supreme Court decisions, if I may ask them as two questions, because I am asking in both cases if you have any plans for meeting the situation.

In the first case, the Supreme Court ruled your wiretapping program unconstitutional, saying that in cases of domestic security, wires could not be tapped without a court order. So my first question is whether you have any plans to ask Congress for legislation to restore that authority in the form of an amendment to the Safe Streets Act or other legislation.

In the second case, the Supreme Court left it up to Congress whether organized baseball came under antitrust laws. This being a matter of national interest, I wonder if you have any plans to ask for legislation to clarify the status of organized baseball.

THE PRESIDENT: On the first question, I think it is appropriate to point out that the wiretapping in cases of civilian activity, domestic civilian activity, is not, as you have described it, just this Administration's policy. As you know, this type of activity of surveillance has been undertaken, to my knowledge, going back to World War II. It reached its high point in 1963

when there were over 100 cases, as Mr. Hoover testified, in which there were taps used in cases involving domestic security.

Since that time the number of taps has gone down. It went down during the Johnson Administration, and it has sharply been decreased during the 3-1/2 years that this Administration has been in office.

Now, as far as the Supreme Court's decision is concerned, I see no need to ask for legislation to obtain that authority, because the Supreme Court's decision allows the Government, in a case that it believes necessary, to go to a court and get a court order for wiretapping. It simply prohibits wiretapping unless there is a court order. So we shall abide by that.

I should also point out that the Supreme Court's decision does not rule out wiretapping in the United States in domestic matters where there is a clear connection between the activity that is under surveillance and a foreign government. That, of course, allows us to move in the internal security matter where there is a clear connection between the two. So we will, of course, abide by the Supreme Court's decision in this instance, and I see no need to ask for additional authority from the Congress.

On the baseball matter, I must say I cannot even tell you who is in first place at the present time because I have not had a chance to check it lately.

Yes, I can. I called the Mayor of Houston and congratulated him on the fact that he had just been elected to be head of the Conference of Mayors, Mr. Louie Welch. He thought I was calling to congratulate him on the Astros being in first place.

In any event, as an old baseball fan, and the rest, I have no present thoughts on that. I would like, perhaps, to talk to Bowie Kuhn, who is a good lawyer and also interested in baseball.

Q: Mr. President, can you give us some of your reasons, sir, for deciding against debating your Democratic opponent this fall?

THE PRESIDENT: The question that he asked is requesting me to give reasons for deciding against debating my Democratic opponent this fall. As you ladies and gentlemen have often heard me say, and I will continue to hold this position, questions that deal with the campaign, questions that deal with matters that involve candidacy, are ones that I will respectfully not comment upon until after the Republican Convention. At that time I will be glad to take that question and answer it.

I have not made a decision on it yet. That is my point.

Q: Mr. President, can you tell us what your plans are for the Higher Education Bill? Do you intend to sign it?

THE PRESIDENT: I have to make the decision tomorrow. I will be very candid with you and tell you that it is one of the closest calls that I have had since being in this office. I have some of the members of my staff, and Members of the Congress who are enthusiastic for signing it, and others are just as enthusiastic for vetoing it.

I have mixed emotions about it. First, as far as many of the strictly educational provisions, they are recommendations of this Administration. I think they are very much in the public interest. If they could be separated from the rest of the bill, and stand on their own, there would not be any question about signing the bill. On the other hand, the Congress, as you know, did add a provision, Section 803, with regard to busing. It was certainly a well-intentioned position, but from a legal standpoint it is so vague and so ambiguous that it totally fails to deal with this highly volatile issue.

What brought that home to me was when I asked the Attorney General for an opinion as to whether or not it could deal with the problem of the busing order that has been handed down in Detroit. The answer is that it is highly doubtful that Section 803 of the Higher Education Act, in the event that it is signed into law, will deal with that problem, because of its vagueness and because of its ambiguity.

The Detroit case is perhaps the most flagrant example that we have of all the busing decisions, moving against all the principles that I, at least, believe should be applied in this area. It completely rejects the neighborhood school concept. It requires massive busing among 53 different school districts, including the busing of kindergarten children, up to an hour and a half a day, and it puts the objective of some kind of racial balance or attempting to achieve some kind of racial balance above that of superior education or quality education for all.

I believe that the fact that this Section 803 would not deal with the Detroit case means that we are going to have other cases of that type, possibly in other cities before school begins this fall and the responsibility, if we have them, and if we are unable to stop those orders from going into effect, falls squarely on the Congress because a very simple moratorium bill that I have sent to the Congress and asked for enactment of would stop this. And then the Congress moving forward and I am glad to see that there has been some movement in the Committee at least with the Equal Educational Opportunities Act, this action on the part of the Congress would deal with problems like the one in Detroit.

My own view is that in this whole area we face very serious problems this fall unless the Congress moves on the moratorium legislation, clear-cut and soon and before the school year begins.

I have digressed a little from the bill. It is a close call. I will make the decision tonight and will announce it tomorrow. But that gives you an idea of some of the things that have been going through my mind.

Q: But to follow that up, if you were to veto it, sir, what are the prospects do you think of getting a separate busing bill and higher education bill without busing?

THE PRESIDENT: As a matter of fact, that is one of the matters I have been discussing with the Congressional leaders —for example, Senator Griffin, who as you know is somewhat interested in this issue, because he comes from Michigan—and the prospects of getting the higher education bill here on the President's desk as it should be, in the proper form, and then getting an adequate, straight-out moratorium on new school busing orders, the prospects are, frankly, somewhat doubtful.

That is the reason why, in determining whether I sign this bill or veto it, it is a very close call, but I think my statement tomorrow will address that question.

I have an idea which way I am going to go but I promised to talk to one more Senator before I make the final decision and I will not tell you the direction.

Q: Is that the Senator from Tennessee?

THE PRESIDENT: As a matter of fact, Miss McClendon, you have touched upon a rather raw nerve there, because Nashville is a case that 803 might cover. I say might, because we are not even sure it would.

So consequently, the Senators from Tennessee strongly advocate signing this, even though it will not handle Detroit, because they say we are interested in Detroit, but more interested in Tennessee.

Miss Angelo.

Q: Mr. Mitchell has declined to make public the source of about $10 million of contributions to your re-election fund. I know that this is in the letter of the law, but I wonder in the spirit of the law of more openness what you think about that and might you make them public?

THE PRESIDENT: Mr. Ziegler has responded to that and Mr. Mitchell and Mr. Stans. I think it is Mr. Stans who has declined to do that. I support the position that Mr. Stans has taken.

When we talk about the spirit of the law and the letter of the law, my evaluation is that it is the responsibility of all, a high moral responsibility to obey the law and to obey it totally.

Now, if the Congress wanted this law to apply to contributions before the date in April that it said the law should take effect, it could have made it apply. The Congress did not apply it before that date and under the circumstances, Mr. Stans has said we will comply with the law as the Congress has written it and I support his decision.

Q: Mr. President, it has been decided that federal troops will be deployed to the Miami Beach area for both Presidential conventions. First, were you a part of that decision and secondly, what is your reaction to this?

THE PRESIDENT: Well, I was not a part of the decision, actually. I think that was probably done consistent with our policy of accepting, when requests are made, the advice of local officials as to the need for federal troops. I would hope that they would not be needed, but apparently the city of Miami Beach, the State officials in Florida, felt that they might not have adequate personnel to handle what might be conduct that would be quite explosive.

I will just make a guess at this point. I don't think that— well, at least speaking as to what goes on outside the convention halls is concerned—I don't think that we are going to have those great demonstrations and the violence and so forth that everybody has been predicting. I don't believe we are going to have another Chicago situation as we had in 1968.

I believe that many of the younger people who have engaged in such activities in the past are rather turned off by it now. I think they will try their best to, of course, affect the outcome of the conventions, both inside the hall and outside, but I think when it comes to violence, the kind of thing that we saw in Chicago, I think that fortunately while we are not through with it as we saw in the tragic incident involving Governor Wallace, I think that we are not going to have that great a problem. But the federal troops will be there if they are requested, but only if necessary.

Q: Mr. President, would you tell us what progress you are making toward keeping your promise about finding a way to relieve property taxes and provide fair and adequate financing for public schools and save the private schools?

THE PRESIDENT: First, with regard to the general problem of tax reform, I would like to commend Chairman Mills for the position that he has taken. I had breakfast with him and Congressman Byrnes and with Secretary Connally before I went to the Soviet Union.

We discussed the problem of tax reform. He is very interested in tax reform. I am interested in tax reform and, of course, I have noticed several candidates that have expressed themselves on this point.

The problem is that tax reform, or tax legislation, in an election year, as Mr. Mills who is one of the most experienced men in this field, and Mr. Byrnes, both agree, is simply not a wise course of action. It is hard enough to get a responsible tax law in a non-election year. In an election year it will be totally impossible.

Consequently, I think Chairman Mills' announcement that he will begin hearings on tax reform legislation early in the next session of the Congress shows high statesmanship. Now we will be ready for those hearings.

Secretary Connally instituted, at my request, an intensive study within the Treasury Department of how we could reform the tax system to make it more equitable and to make it more simple and also to deal with problems like property tax which fall on 65 million people and therefore are, in my view, unfair.

These studies have gone forward. Considerable progress has been made. Secretary Shultz is continuing these studies and I will make a decision on it prior to submitting the budget and will present recommendations to the next Congress dealing with these issues.

I will not at this time pre-judge the various proposals that have been presented before me. Certainly included in that decision will be relief for non-public schools. I am committed to that, and the approach of tax credits in this area will be included in that proposal.

Just so that somebody won't say I was trying to duck a hard one here, I know the question of value-added will come up. There has been a lot of speculation about that. Value-added— I have instructed or directed the Secretary of the Treasury, along with my Council of Economic Advisers—can be considered as a possible approach but only if we can find a non-retrogressive formula.

Tax reform should not be used as a cover for a tax increase. Value-added has to be evaluated under those circumstances.

One final point I will make is that as we move in this area we have to realize that we have had considerable tax reform over the past three years. Nine million poor people have been totally removed from the federal tax rolls. The lower income taxpayers have had reductions of 83 percent in their taxes since 1969 and middle-income taxpayers have had reductions of 13 percent.

But there are still inequities. One point I particularly want to emphasize: At a time when we have made some necessary reforms, some of which I have referred to, we have moved in the wrong direction in another way. The tax system, particularly the federal income tax system, is hopelessly complex. In law school I majored in tax law. As a lawyer I used to do quite a bit of tax work. I naturally don't take the time to make up my own income tax returns now. But when Manolo came in recently and asked me to help him figure out the forms, I had to send him to a lawyer and when that is the case with a man who is in basically not a high income bracket, then it is time to do something to make the system not only more equitable but make it more simple. It will put some lawyers and accountants out of business, but there are other things they can do.

Q: Are you saying these proposals won't come until after the first of the year?

THE PRESIDENT: We will make the proposal before the first of the year, but it will not be considered by the Congress until after the 1st of the year.

It would not be fair to the American people, it would not be fair to those, for example, interested in non-public school relief, to suggest that the Congress, in this sort of sputtering, start-and-stop period—I mean, they are stopping next week and they come back for six weeks and maybe come back after the Republican Convention and the rest—that they can enact tax reform. It is not going to happen, and I am aware of that.

Q: Mr. President, back on the subject of busing, are you moving at all toward the position of favoring an anti-busing constitutional amendment?

THE PRESIDENT: A constitutional amendment is a step that should be taken only if the legislative route proves to be inadequate or impossible—impossible due to the fact that the Congress will not enact it. As far as I am concerned, we do need action here. I prefer the legislative route. I think it is the most responsible route, but if the Congress does not act, then the only recourse left is for a constitutional amendment, and I will move in that direction. We must deal with the problem.

Q: Mr. President, do you think that there should be a court martial in the case of General Lavelle to bring out all the facts there, and what is your opinion about that?

THE PRESIDENT: First, that does deal with the foreign policy defense area, Vietnam and so forth. But since it does involve a current case, I will comment upon it.

The Secretary of Defense has stated his view on that, has made a decision on it. I think it was an appropriate decision. I will not go beyond that.

THE PRESS: Thank you, Mr. President.

JUNE 29

Following is the text, as made available by the White House, of President Nixon's June 29 news conference.

THE PRESIDENT: Mr. Cormier has the first question.

Q: Mr. President, I don't want to ask a soft or flabby question because, as you know, your associate John Ehrlichman has suggested that news conferences really are not all that important because we tend to ask that type of question too often.

So I want to submit one for the Ehrlichman Award this evening.

THE PRESIDENT: As long as it is not soft and flabby.

Q: Mindful that ending the war was one of your major campaign themes in 1968, mindful that our bombings in Indochina now are at a five year high, according to the Pentagon, mindful that the troops are still coming out, but even more are going into Thailand and the Seventh Fleet, I wonder if you can say with any confidence that you can end the war by January 20th of next year?

THE PRESIDENT: Mr. Cormier, we have made great progress in ending the war and particularly in ending American involvement in the war.

Since you have recounted the record to an extent, let me recount it also from the positive side.

When we came into office, there were 540,000 Americans in Vietnam. Our casualties were running as high as 300 a week and the cost was $22 billion a year. We have taken out 500,000 men since that time. Our casualties have been reduced 95 percent, down to two, that is too many, but from 300 to two. As far as the cost is concerned, instead of $22 billion a year, it is down to $7 billion a year.

As far as the situation on the negotiating front is concerned, instead of being in a position where we did not have a positive offer on the table, we have made what Mr. Brinkley at NBC characterized last night as being a very constructive offer, one in which in return for an all-of-Indochina ceasefire and in return for prisoners of war an accounting for all missing in action we would stop all military activities in Indochina and we would withdraw all Americans remaining within four months.

Now, having reached this position at this time, we believe that that is an excellent record. The only thing that we have not done is to do what the communists have asked and that is to impose a communist government on the people of South Vietnam against their will. This we will not do because that would reward aggression, it would encourage that kind of aggression and reduce the chances of peace all over the world in the years to come, and it would dishonor the United States of America.

On the negotiating front, we have informed the North Vietnamese, after consultation with the Government of Vietnam, that we will return to the negotiating table in Paris on April 13 (he meant July 13), Thursday; we have been informed by the North Vietnamese, the Viet Cong, that they, too, will return on that date. We will return to the negotiating table or will return to it on the assumption that the North Vietnamese are prepared to negotiate in a constructive and serious way. We will be prepared to negotiate in that way. If those negotiations go forward in a constructive and serious way, this war can be ended and it can be ended well before January 20. If they do not go forward on that basis, the United States will continue to meet its commitments, our bombing, as far as that is concerned, our mining is for the purpose only of preventing communist aggression from succeeding, to protect the remaining Americans, 40,000 or so, that are still in Vietnam, and to have some bargaining position in getting our POWs back.

One last point with regard to the POWs: I know that every American is concerned about these men. I have been somewhat concerned about them. I will only say that I have had some experience, and a great deal of experience as a matter of fact in this past year, in dealing with communist leaders. I find that making a bargain with them is not easy and you get something from them only when you have something they want to get from you. The only way we are going to get our POWs back is to be doing something to them, and that means hitting military targets in North Vietnam, retaining a residual force in South Vietnam, and continuing the mining of the harbors of Vietnam.

Only by having that kind of activity to go forward will they have any incentive to return our POWs rather than not to account for them as was the case when the French got out of Vietnam in 1954 and 15,000 French were never accounted for after that.

I shall never have that happen to the brave men who are POWs.

Q: Mr. President, before you ordered a resumption of the bombing of North Vietnam, General Lavelle authorized or initiated some unauthorized strikes there. In your view, did this affect any diplomatic negotiations going on at that time, and are you concerned that you apparently didn't know about that?

THE PRESIDENT: It did not affect the diplomatic negotiations. As a matter of fact, a meeting took place, a private meeting, between Dr. Kissinger and the negotiators in Paris on May 2nd, during the period that General Lavelle's activities were being undertaken, and you can be very sure if the North Vietnamese had wanted any pretext to complain about, they would have complained about that particular matter.

As far as this is concerned, as Admiral Moorer testified today, it wasn't authorized, it was directly against only those military targets which were the areas being used for firing on American planes, but since it did exceed authorization, it was proper for him to be relieved and retired, and I think it was the proper action to take, and I believe that will assure that kind of activity may not occur in the future.

Q: Mr. President, on May 8th, at the time of the mining of the harbors in North Vietnam, your assistant, Dr. Kissinger, predicted the mining would result in the drying up of supplies and the major offensive should be over around July 1st. Is that estimate still valid, and if so, do you have a timetable for the withdrawal of the support troops who have gone into the naval and air bases around Vietnam to support the South Vietnamese during the offensive?

THE PRESIDENT: Mr. Jarriel, the date of the effective mining and also the bombing of the military targets in North Vietnam, particularly the railroads and oil supplies, the situation in Vietnam has been completely turned around. I was looking at news magazines that came out the week before the mining was ordered, and I noted that each one of them has, as the heading, "The specter of defeat in Vietnam." That was the situation when we started.

It has been turned around. The South Vietnamese are now on the offensive. It is not over. We expect, perhaps, some more North Vietnamese offensive, but I believe now the ability of the South Vietnamese to defend themselves on the ground, with the support we give them in the air, has been demonstrated. The ability to defend themselves in An Loc and Kontum, and now in the area of Hue, is an indication that Vietnamization, as far as the ground activity is concerned, has proved to be a successful action. Now, as far as the future is concerned, I have already indicated that we will be returning to negotiations in July. That is the important area to watch at this time, as well as the battlefield. And as far as any future announcements are concerned, that will depend upon progress at the negotiating table and on the battlefront.

Q: Mr. President—

THE PRESIDENT: Mr. Rather. I remember your name. (Laughter)

MR. RATHER: Thank you. I remember your name, too.

The background of this question is your own statements made down in Texas, among other places, saying that you had not sanctioned and would not sanction the bombing of the dikes and dams in North Vietnam, because you considered it an inhumane act because of what it would do to civilians.

Within the past week there have been reports of eye-witnesses. One of these reports came from the French Press Agency, and another from the Swedish Ambassador in Hanoi, eyewitness reports claiming to have seen American planes hit dikes and dams.

The question is, has such bombing occurred, and if so, what steps are you taking to see it doesn't happen again?

THE PRESIDENT: Mr. Rather, we have checked those reports. They have proved to be inaccurate. The bombing of dikes is something, as you will recall from the gentleman who asked the question in Texas, was something that some people have advocated. The United States has used great restraints in its bombing policy and I think properly so. We have tried to hit only military targets and we have been hitting military targets. We have had orders out not to hit dikes because the results in terms of civil casualties would be extraordinary.

As far as any future activities are concerned, those orders still are in force. I do not intend to allow any orders to go out which would involve civilian casualties if it can be avoided. Military targets only will be allowed.

Q: Mr. President, last year, or at least early this year, General Abrams relayed to you the belief that the South Vietnamese could not hack it on the battlefield. The invasion from the north occurred and we responded with bombing.

When do you realistically think the South Vietnamese can do it alone without massive fire power from us?

THE PRESIDENT: Mr. Semple, I think that is being determined and also demonstrated at this time.

First, as far as the ground activities are concerned, they are being entirely undertaken by the South Vietnamese. American ground combat action has totally been finished in Vietnam. As far as Americans in Vietnam are concerned, this war is over in the future for many future draftees. No more draftees will be sent to Vietnam.

As far as that air action is concerned, as General Abrams or any military man will tell you, as they have told me, air action alone, without any fighting on the ground, cannot stop a determined enemy.

What happened in this case was that North Vietnam launched a massive offensive with huge tanks, bigger than those against which they were arrayed, with new and modern weapons. In order to provide an equalizer, and it was needed, we provided air support.

But I should also point this out, something that has been little noticed, 40 percent of all the tactical air sorties being flown over the battlefields of South Vietnam are not being flown by Americans, but by South Vietnamese.

So we see the South Vietnamese not only doing the ground fighting, but increasing their ability to fight in the air.

Finally, the success of our air strikes in the North and on the battlefield, the success in turning this battle around hastens the day when the South Vietnamese will be able to undertake the total activity themselves.

I am not going to put a date on it. I can only say the outcome of the present battle, how badly the North Vietnamese are hurt, will determine it, but I am very optimistic.

Q: To change the subject and not to be flabby, sir.

THE PRESIDENT: You would never be flabby.

Q: Thank you, sir.

Isn't it time you told us, will Agnew be on the ticket?

THE PRESIDENT: I know that that is a question that is very much on the minds of the delegates who will be coming to Miami in August. I will announce a decision on that, my views on it, well before the convention so that the delegates will know my views.

As far as the Vice President is concerned, my views with regard to his performance are the same that I reflected rather generously in my interview with Mr. Rather in January of this year. I think he had done a fine job as Vice President. I have very high confidence in him.

But the decision with regard to the Vice Presidency will not be announced until before the Republican Convention, in good time for them to make their own decision.

Mr. Horner.

Q: Mr. President, what role do you foresee in the future months after he returns from his present trip and after the election, for John Connally?

THE PRESIDENT: Mr. Horner, first the reports we have had on Mr. Connally's trip have been excellent. I think his trip to Latin America—and incidentally, also the trip that Dr. Arthur Burns made to Latin America—came at a good time and allowed the Latin American heads of State to express their views just as vigorously as did President Echeverria when he was here in this country. That is what we want, candid, vigorous talk between the heads of State in the American Hemisphere.

The discussions he is presently having in Australia, in New Zealand, Southeast Asia, India, Pakistan and so forth and later in Iran I know will be helpful. When he returns he will not undertake a permanent government assignment, but he has agreed to undertake special government assignments at that time. I have one in mind, a very important one, but I cannot announce it at this time. I will announce it when he returns and when he reports to me in San Clemente.

Ms. Cornell. (Laughter)

Q: Mr. President.

THE PRESIDENT: I said Ms.

Q: Thank you.

Can you tell us what took you back to the Paris peace table and would you support a coalition government, the formation of a coalition government or would you discuss it in Paris?

THE PRESIDENT: It would not be useful to indicate the discussions that took place in various places with regard to returning to the Paris peace table.

Let it suffice to say that both sides considered it in their interests to return to the Paris peace table. We would not have returned unless we thought there was a chance for more serious discussions and more constructive discussions than we have had in the past, although I must be quite candid and say that we have been disappointed in the past with regard to these discussions.

We have had 149 plenary sessions and no significant results. I do not believe it would be particularly helpful to, in a news conference, to negotiate with regard to what we are going to talk about at the conference. That is a matter that we will negotiate with the enemy.

As far as a coalition government is concerned, no. We will not negotiate with the enemy for accomplishing what they cannot accomplish themselves and that is to impose against their will on the people of South Vietnam a coalition government with the Communists.

However, we will be constructive, we will be forthcoming. An internationally supervised cease-fire, a total withdrawal of all Americans within four months, a total cessation of all bombing, these, we think, are very reasonable offers and we believe the enemy should very seriously consider them.

Q: Mr. President, hardly had you signed the Arms Control Agreements in Moscow, then your Administration asked for new money for new strategic weapons. Some of your critics are saying this is almost a deception giving the Pentagon what it wants, namely concentration on developing quality weapons. Will you try to dispel this grim prediction?

THE PRESIDENT: Mr. Morgan, the problem with regard to arms control is that we do not deal with it in a vacuum. We have to deal with the problem as it affects the security of the United States. Now, first, let me say that if we had not had an arms control agreement, a limitation of ABMs and a temporary limitation for five years on certain classifications of offensive weapons, I would—and I am saying this conservatively—have had to ask the Congress of the United States to approve an increase in the defense budget for nuclear strategic weapons of at least $15 billion a year on a crash program. Reason: Had there been no arms control agreement, the Soviet Union's plans called for an increase of their ABMs to 1,000 over the next five years. The Arms Control Agreement limits them to 200 as it does us. Had there been no Arms Control Agreement, the Soviet Union had a program under way in the field of submarines which would have brought them up to over 90.

The Agreement limits them to 62. And, had there been no Arms Control Agreement—and this is the most important point—in the terms of offensive strategic weapons, the Soviet Union has now passed us in offensive strategic weapons. They have 1,600, we have roughly 1,000. They would have built 1,000 more over the next five years. Now, under those circumstances, any President of the United States could see that in five years the United States would be hopelessly behind; our security would be threatened, our allies would be terrified, particularly in those areas, and our friends, like the Mid-East, where the possibility of Soviet adventurism is considered to be rather great.

Therefore, the Arms Control Agreement at least put a brake on new weapons. Now, with regard to the new weapons that you refer to, however, let me point out they are not for the next five year period. We are really talking about the period after that. And they are absolutely essential for the security of the United States for another reason—because looking at this not in a vacuum but in terms of what the other side is doing, Mr. Brezhnev made it very clear that he intended to go forward in those categories that were not limited.

Now, in fairness to him, he also said, and made it very clear—he made it perfectly clear, I should say—he said that he expected that we would go forward. Now, under these circumstances, then, for the United States not to go forward in those areas that were not controlled would mean that at the end of the 70s we would be in an inferior position and no President of the United States can take the responsibility of allowing the United States to be the second most powerful nation in the world, not because of any jingoistic idea, but because if we are in that position, our foreign policy, our commitments around the world would be very, very seriously jeopardized.

Now the important point I have saved for the last and that is this: I think these agreements are in the interest of the United States. I think that they are very much in the interest of arms control and therefore in the interest of world peace. But, they are only a beginning; they are only the foundation. Now, what we have to do is to really go forward with the second step. That is what the Phase 2 of the Arms Control Limitation, which we hope will begin in October, provided the Congress approves the ones we have before them at the present time—Phase 2, which will be a permanent arms control agreement on all offensive nuclear weapons—this is the one that we think can have an even far greater significance than Phase 1.

Phase 1 is the breakthrough and Phase 2 is the culmination. And Phase 2, if we can reach agreement with the Soviets—and it will take long and hard bargaining—but if we can reach it, it will mean, then, that we not only hold our arms budgets where they are, but that in these new programs instead of going forward with them on the basis presently projected we will be able to cut them back.

That is our goal and I think we can achieve it provided we approve Phase 1, and provided we continue a credible arms program, because, believe me, the Soviets are not going to agree to limit their future programs unless they have something to get from us.

Q: Mr. President, in consideration of your argument on our need for offensive weapons, why, then, do you insist on developments of the costly B-1 bomber when in fact the Soviet Union has shown little interest in the bomber course in recent years and as far as we know have no new bomber course on the drawing boards at this time?

THE PRESIDENT: Each power, the Soviet Union and the United States, must have those forces that are needed for its own security. We basically are not only a land power but a land and sea power. The Soviet Union is primarily a land power with certain definite requirements having that in mind. We believe that the B-1 bomber is, for our security interest, necessary.

As far as the Soviet Union is concerned, the fact that they are not developing bombers does not mean that they do not respect ours. And I would say, too, that had we not had our present advantage in bombers we could not then stand by and allow the Soviets to have a 1,600 to 1,000 advantage in terms of missiles that are land based. So, our bombers are an offset for that.

Q: It was made perfectly clear to us this week that you would be less than overjoyed if the Senate should attach a 20 percent Social Security increase to the debt ceiling extension bill which expires tomorrow night. It looks like that might happen tomorrow. I wonder what you see as the consequences, and what you could do about it?

THE PRESIDENT: Well, there should be an increase in Social Security. There has been an increase in the cost of living, and I have favored an increase in Social Security. The problem with the 20 percent increase which the Senate will consider is that it does

to the Social Security System, and also what it does to the cost of living and to future taxes in this country.

We must realize that if a 20 percent Social Security (increase) is passed by the Senate and by the Congress, the increased payroll tax to pay for it will completely wipe out the tax reduction that was given to middle-income and low middle-income wage earners in 1969. That is a question that the Congress has got to address itself to.

If, on the other hand, the Congress passes the 20 percent increase in Social Security and does not finance it adequately, it will seriously jeopardize the integrity of the Social Security Trust Fund, and it could be highly inflationary which, of course, will hurt most the Social Security people, the retired people.

So these are considerations that have motivated me in expressing concern. It is not that we do not want an increase in Social Security. It isn't that we do not want as high an increase as possible. But the increase must be a responsible one. It should be funded. And the Congress, if it does not fund it, would be doing something that would not be in the interest of retired people, who would be faced with an increase in the cost of living.

Q: I know you have said you don't care to discuss politics until after the Republican Convention, which has to make you kind of an unusual man in Washington, but in your answer a while ago regarding Vice President Agnew, I gained the impression that he may be a one-term Vice President. Am I correct in that?

THE PRESIDENT: Certainly not, no. As I said to Mr. Rather—I cannot reconstruct it exactly; he probably can—but in any event, as I said to him on that program, Mr. Agnew had conducted himself, I thought, with great dignity, with great courage, some controversy—which is inevitable when you have courage—and that under these circumstances, since he was a member of a winning team, I did not believe breaking up a winning team was a good idea.

That was my view then and that is my view now. However, the final decision, as I indicated in my answer a few moments ago, will be deferred until before the Republican Convention, and I will make it in time for the delegates to know what my views are.

Mr. President, with all the shifts in the economy, unemployment seems to be stalled at just under six percent. What plans do you have to do something about that?

THE PRESIDENT: We have been making great strides on the employment side, as you know, Mr. Theiss: 2,300,000 new jobs since the new economic policy was announced on August 15. We expect that the rapid expansion of the economy, which most economists agree is taking place, is going to reflect itself in reducing unemployment rolls, not as far as we would like, but in reducing them, through the fall and winter months.

As far as additional actions are concerned, we do not contemplate any at this time, except that we are going to continue those policies that have resulted in the economy growing at a rate of 5½ percent in real growth, and that have resulted—and this is perhaps the most important number to those who are employed, the 80 million or so—have resulted in the wage earners of this country getting off the treadmill.

For five years before we arrived here in 1969 the wages had gone up but the wage increases had been almost entirely eaten up by price increases. The most significant thing that has happened since the new economic policy is that we have cut the rate of inflation down so that it is half of what it was in 1970, from 6 to 3 percent. Wages have continued to go up, even though at a lower rate, but real, spendable earnings of 80 million wage earners have gone up 5 percent. That is as compared with going up at the rate of only one percent a year in the 60s. It is this kind of progress that is good.

On the other hand, I am not a bit satisfied with the fact that unemployment is at 5.9 percent, and we are continuing to explore other means of trying to bring it down faster.

Mr. Lisagor.

Q: Mr. President, a clarifying question on the bombing, please. You have said that the sole purpose of your bombing and your mining, in your May 8th speech, was to protect the 60,000 American troops there. Did I understand you to say, in answer to an earlier question, that that bombing is now contingent upon the release of the prisoners? And I would like to ask an additional question that is slightly related: Were there any conditions attached by each side to the return to the Paris peace talks?

THE PRESIDENT: No, there are no conditions attached to either side. We are going back to the talks prepared to negotiate wothout conditions, which we think is the most constructive way to obtain results. For example, the condition—I assume this is the implication of your question—there was no condition that if we would go back to the talks we would stop the bombing. We do not intend to. We will stop the bombing when the conditions are met that I laid out in my May 8th speech.

In my May 8th speech, Mr. Lisagor, as you recall, I laid down three conditions: I said that we were bombing military targets in the North, that we were mining the harbor and that we were doing so for three purposes: to prevent the imposition of a Communist government in South Vietnam, to protect our remaining forces in South Vietnam, which were then 60,000 and, in addition, for the purpose of obtaining the release of our POWs.

Those are the three conditions that we have as far as the bombing is concerned.

But we are prepared to negotiate on those points with the enemy. We have no desire to continue the bombing for one moment longer than necessary to accomplish what we consider to be these very minimal objectives.

Q: Mr. President, do you regard capital punishment as cruel and unusual, and do you think steps should be taken to reinstate it?

THE PRESIDENT: I was expecting that question tonight, but as you know, the court just handed down its decision and I immediately got hold of Mr. Dean, Counsel to the President, and I said, "Send it over to me." He said, "There are nine opinions."

Now I try to read fast, but I couldn't get through all nine opinions. But I did get through the Chief Justice's.

As I understand it, the holding of the court must not be taken at this time to rule out capital punishment in all kinds of crime. This had dealt apparently with crimes at the state level and will apply to 35 states in which we do have the situation where capital punishment does apply.

Now, it is my view that as far as cruel and inhumane punishment is concerned, any punishment is cruel and inhuman which takes the life of a man, or woman, for that matter.

But, on the other hand, the point I wish to emphasize is this: In the case of kidnapping and in the case of hijacking, federal crimes, what we are trying to do is to prevent the loss of lives.

I recall the situation at the time of the Lindbergh kidnapping. I recall that kidnappings were sort of par for the course then. Any wealthy family was a possible subject for kidnapping.

Kidnapping has been substantially reduced. Now some experts will say that the deterrent of the Lindbergh Law was not what did it. Something had to have that effect. Therefore, I have said in the past and I do not retreat from that now, I believe that capital punishment is a necessary deterrent for capital crimes of that type as far as the federal jurisdiction is concerned—kidnapping and hijacking.

Now, as far as the court's decision is concerned, except for three of the judges who based their decision on the Eighth Amendment, which rules out cruel and inhumane punishment and as far as the court's decision is concerned, I do not understand it necessarily to apply to these federal crimes. I would hope that it would not.

I have expressed my views and I will also say, of course, that we will carry out whatever the court finally determines to be the law of the land. But I would hope that the court's decision does not go so far as to rule out capital punishment for kidnapping and hijacking.

Q: Mr. President, in light of the attempted assassination of Governor Wallace, have you changed your thinking at all on the need for federal laws controlling the sale of hand guns?

THE PRESIDENT: Well, my thinking has not changed. I have always felt there should be a federal law for the control of hand guns, as you will note, Mr. Kleindienst testified to that effect earlier today and he did testify to that effect after checking my own position on it.

The problem there is to write the law, the legislation, in such a way that it is precise and deals with that kind of hand gun which ought to be controlled. And I am referring now to the Saturday night specials. These are ones where you would have federal jurisdiction because many of them come in from abroad and, being imported from abroad, it would be particularly a matter for federal control.

I believe, however, that the legislation, if it is therefore precisely written—and we have been cooperating with the Senate committee, particularly with Senator Hruska in attempting to work out the proper language—that the Congress should pass such a law and I will sign it, ruling out Saturday night specials, which I think is the major source of this kind of crime you speak about.

Q: Mr. President, do you consider the Supreme Court now to be in balance or do you think it needs another dose of strict constructionism if that occasion should arise.

THE PRESIDENT: I have expressed myself with regard to the court on previous occasions, but I feel at the present time, that the court is as balanced as I have had an opportunity to make it. (Laughter)

I have been interested to note that there have been several five-to-four decisions, but let me also say—and the Chief Justice was in to see me the other day and we talked about a number of things—let me also say that of the people I have appointed to that court— and each one of them will bear this out—I have never talked to them directly or indirectly about a matter before the court.

I had a pretty good idea before they went on how I thought they might think, but sometimes they have ruled differently, because lawyers never agree.

Q: Mr. President, sir, since you have taken care of many of the problems with Peking and Moscow and had some agreements and now you seem to have made great progress with the war, I wonder what areas of the world you would like to work on next?

THE PRESIDENT: Well, I don't want to go to the moon. (Laughter).

Q: Mr. President, the history of American bombing of North Vietnam indicates that it has served to hinder negotiations rather than stimulate negotiations. Why do you think it is going to work now in view of that history?

THE PRESIDENT: I am not sure that my evaluation of the history is the same as yours. My own view is that we have tried every device possible over the past three years to get negotiations going. We have withdrawn forces, we have made very forthcoming offers, we have wound down combat activity on our part and the result has been simply an ever increasing intransigence on the part of the enemy.

Believe me, it was only as a last resort that I made the very difficult decision, but having made that decision, I think it was the right decision and I think the fact that our summit meetings went ahead despite that decision, the fact that we are going back to the negotiating table despite that decision, indicates that it may be that those who feel that a strong hand at the negotiating table is one that results in no negotiation, may be wrong.

It has always been my theory that in dealing with these very pragmatic men—and we must respect them for their strengths and their pragmatism—who led the Communist nations, that they respect strength—not belligerence but strength—and at least that is the way I am always going to approach it, and I think it is going to be successful.

Q: Mr. President, in the middle of May, Vice President Agnew told a number of reporters that he thought it was totally unrealistic for anyone to imagine a Republican convention nominating a Democrat like John Connally.

Can you tell us if you discussed that statement with him and if you knew he was going to make it?

Finally, if the answer to that question was no, can you give us your reaction to it?

THE PRESIDENT: I did not discuss it with Vice President Agnew. I almost said "Vice President Connally," But, I did not discuss it with the Vice President. I would say in terms of political evaluation, he, of course, is correct. A Republican convention or a Democratic convention tends to nominate members of their own party to their high offices.

Now, as far as Secretary Connally is concerned, however, I think we can only say that he is a man who has served his country extremely well in national office, as Governor of his state, and then as Secretary of the Treasury. I certainly hope that in the future he will serve his country in some capacity.

I am not going to go further, though, on the Vice Presidency. I have expressed my views with regard to Vice President Agnew and I will at the proper time inform the delegates of my views.

Q: Mr. President, this is kind of an in-house question, but I think it is of interest.

THE PRESIDENT: You would not ask an "outhouse" question, would you? (Laughter)

Q: I am not sure what an outhouse question is.

THE PRESIDENT: I know.

Q: Nevertheless, I think this is of interest to our viewers and listeners and readers and that is that you seem to have done very well tonight, you are certainly in command of this situation, and yet this is the first time in a year that you have been willing to meet with us in this kind of forum.

What is your feeling about these types of press conferences?

THE PRESIDENT: It is not that I am afraid to do it. I have to determine the best way of communication and also, and this will sound self-serving and is intended to be: I have to use the press conference—I don't mean use the reporters but use the press conference when I believe that is the best way to communicate or inform the people.

Now, for example, I had to make a decision—it may have been wrong—but I concluded that in the very sensitive period leading up to the Peking trip and the period thereafter and in the even more sensitive period, as it turned out to be, leading up to the Moscow trip and the period immediately thereafter, that the press conference, even "no-commenting" questions was not a useful thing for the President of the United States to engage in.

I felt I was, of course, on television enough in that period anyway, if that was the problem. As you know, I have met with the press, not perhaps as often as some members of the press would like, or maybe as often as I would like, but I have met them in other formats than the televised conference.

The other point that I should like to make is this: I know that many members of the press have been discussing the press conference and they feel that perhaps the President is tempted to downgrade the press or downgrade the press conference. I am not trying to do that. It is useful and it is important. It requires hard work in preparing for it, I can assure you. But I think I can best put it this way: Every President has to make a decision when he enters the office about his relations with the press and about his job. I am as human as anybody else. I like to get a good press but on the other hand I had to determine, as I am sure most Presidents do, that what was most important at this time was for me to do a good job because the stakes were so high, particularly in foreign policy, and also in some areas of domestic policy.

Now, if I do a good job, the fact that I get bad press isn't going to matter; if I do a bad job, a good press isn't going to help. When November comes, the people will decide whether I have done a good job or not and whether I have had so many press conferences is probably not going to make a lot of difference.

I trust I can do both because it is essential for a President to communicate with the people, to inform the press who, of course, do talk to the people, either on television or radio or through what they write.

I hope perhaps in the future we can avoid the feeling on the part of the press that the President is antagonistic to them. I can't say whether the President thinks the press is antagonistic to him, but that is another matter.

THE PRESS: Thank you, Mr. President.

JULY 27

Following is the text, as made available by the White House, of President Nixon's July 27 news conference.

THE PRESIDENT: We will go ahead with some questions if you like.

Q: Mr. President, you have said that it is against U.S. policy to bomb the dikes and dams in North Vietnam. Yesterday, the State Department acknowledged there had been incidental and inadvertent damage from the bombing nearby.

My question is: Is it worth the risk of possible flooding and having world opinion turned against us as a result of bombing dams?

THE PRESIDENT: I think your question would be better answered by my discussing the policy toward bombing of civilian installations of North Vietnam generally, and then coming down to the specifics of your question, in giving a general answer.

Some of you who were in Texas with me will recall that that question was raised on the Connally Ranch, and it was raised, actually, by an advocate of bombing dikes as to why we did not bomb dikes. I said it had not been U.S. policy even before the bombing halt of 1968 to bomb the dikes; that it was not our policy now, and it would not be in the future, because it is the policy of the United States in all of its activities in North Vietnam to direct its attacks against military targets only.

This was the policy in the 60s and it is now the policy since we have had to resume the bombing for the reasons that I mentioned in my speech of May 8th.

With regard to the situation on the dikes, let us understand what we are confronted with here. This is approximately a 2,700-mile chain of installations, including perhaps a half-dozen major dams which are the heart of the system, and then peripheral areas getting down to mounds, which have, of course, the purpose of controlling the floodwaters in that particular area.

If it were the policy of the United States to bomb the dikes, we could take them out, the significant part of them out, in a week. We don't do so for the reasons that I have mentioned, because we are trying to avoid civilian casualties, not cause them.

Now, with regard to the reports that have come from Hanoi that there had been some damage to some parts of the dike system, I think it is important to note two things: One, there has been no report of any flooding and second, there has been no report of any strikes on the major dike areas.

What I am referring to is the big dams which are the heart of the system. There have been reports of incidental damage to some of the peripheral installations in this 2700-mile system which covers the country of North Vietnam.

Now, under these circumstances, I think that it is well to keep in context first what our policy is, and second, what its effect has been. Our policy is not to bomb civilian installations and second, our restraint, it seems to me, rather than being subject to criticisms, should be subject to objective analysis and, it seems to me, a considerable amount of support.

As far as this matter is concerned, I think, too, it is time to strip away the double standard. I noted with interest that the Secretary General of the U.N., just like his predecessor, seized upon this enemy-inspired propaganda, which has taken in many well-intentioned and naive people to attack the American bombing of civilian installations and risking civilian lives, and yet not raising one word against deliberate bombing of civilian installations in South Vietnam.

Just so the record will be kept straight—and it should be stated at this point—all of you ladies and gentlemen are aware of it, of course; you have printed it, and perhaps you will see fit to again in this context:

I just got a cable from Ambassador Bunker. I had asked him what had happened to civilians in the new offensive. You recall

in my speech of May 8th, I said 20,000 civilian casualties, including women and children, have resulted because of the deliberate shelling of the cities and the slaughtering of refugees indiscriminately by the North Vietnamese.

The number is now 45,000, including women and children, of which 15,000 are dead.

I asked him for the number of refugees. It is higher than I had thought. There have been 860,000 made homeless by the North Vietnamese invasion of South Vietnam, this newest invasion to date, 600,000 of them are still in refugee camps, away from their homes.

Looking back over the period of this very difficult war, we find that since 1965 there have been 600,000 civilian casualties in South Vietnam as a result of deliberate policies of the North Vietnamese Communists, not accidental, but deliberate.

In North Vietnam, in the period from 1954 to 1956, in their so-called land reform program, a minimum of 50,000 were murdered, assassinated, and according to the Catholic Bishop of Danang, whom I talked to when I was there in 1956, in South Vietnam, in addition to the 800,000 refugees who came south, there were at least a half million who died in slave labor camps in North Vietnam.

Now, I did not relate this series of incidents for the purpose of saying, because they did something bad, we can do something bad.

What I am simply saying is, let's not have a hypocritical double standard. The United States has been restrained, greater restraint than any great power has ever shown in handling this war. We will continue to be restrained. We have to bomb military targets in order to accomplish the objectives I have described in my goal, in my speech of May 8th.

On the other hand, as far as this particular matter is concerned, I can only say that if damage did occur that we are making every possible effort to see that it will not occur again, which gets to your question. Military commanders, aircraft commanders and so forth, in terms of where military targets are, are instructed to avoid civilian damage where they can.

That is why some targets in the heart of Hanoi, for example, major power installations, fuel installations, in the heart of Hanoi have not been hit, because I have not wanted to have civilian casualties if we could possibly avoid it.

I will simply close by saying that this is a major propaganda campaign, it is one that does concern us. But let us keep the record straight. In the event that the United States followed the course of action recommended by some of those who have voted for the so-called End The War Resolution in the Senate of the United States, it would mean that there would be visited upon South Vietnam the same atrocities that were visited upon North Vietnam, with perhaps at least one million marked for assassination because they had fought against the North Vietnamese attempts to conquer South Vietnam.

I will add one other thing. As far as the negotiations are concerned, we are negotiating. We have negotiated in public. We have had one private conference a week ago, lasting approximately six hours. We hope to continue to negotiate.

We have made fair offers on withdrawal, on a cease-fire, on political settlement. We have not made them on a take-it or leave-it basis.

We made fair offers on exchange of prisoners of war and unaccounted missing in action.

Having done this, there is one thing we have not offered and this is one hang-up in the settlement today. That is the demands of the enemy directly or indirectly to do what they cannot accomplish themselves, impose a Communist Government in South Vietnam. That would be the height of immorality to impose on the 17 million people of South Vietnam a Communist Government with the blood bath that would follow.

Q: Mr. President, you mentioned the political settlement. What do you foresee as a possibility without necessarily elections—do you see the two factions in South Vietnam coming together in some kind of an agreement without an election as one possible solution in the Paris talks?

THE PRESIDENT: That is a very perceptive question, but it is one that I think any of you here would agree that I should not comment upon for the reason that negotiations are now under way. I have read these long negotiating sessions—the public ones, of course, and even more important, the private ones—in great detail. At a time that matters are being discussed, it is not well for me to state anything with regard to what is happening in the negotiations.

I will only say that we are negotiating with the desire of ending this war as soon as possible. The fastest way to end the war and the best way to end it is through negotiation. We would hope that public figures in their comments will not do anything to undercut the negotiations, that Congress, in its actions, will not in effect give a message to the enemy, "Don't negotiate with the present Administration; wait for us and we will give you what you want in South Vietnam."

Q: Mr. President, to follow up the first question, if I may, there had been reports that SAM sites have been put on top of some of those dikes or dams. Does your policy rule out the bombing of that particular area where there are SAM sites?

THE PRESIDENT: I have seen those reports, Mr. Lisagor. As you know, the Secretary of Defense has made some indirect comments about it. The situation there is one that we would lean against taking out SAM sites on targets that would result in civilian casualties of a substantial amount.

However, I have not seen in recent days any reports indicating that any such SAM sites will be hit and in view of the present debate, I think we are going to be very careful with regard to hitting them. We would do so only if we had to do so in order to protect American fliers who otherwise would be hit down by the SAMs.

Q: Mr. President, do you think that anyone with a history of mental illness should run for high office?

THE PRESIDENT: Well, Miss Thomas, the question that you ask, of course, is related to some of the conjecture with regard to the ticket on the other side. Mr. Ziegler has correctly reported to all of you ladies and gentlemen of the press that I have given the strictest instructions that there are to be no comments directly, or, in the case of your question, indirectly, on this subject. This is a personal matter.

The question of the selection of a Vice Presidential candidate is one which is a matter for the Presidential candidate to decide, with, of course, the advice and consent of his convention. I am not going to interject myself into that problem except to say that since it is a personal matter, it does give me an opportunity to say that not now on this matter, nor in this campaign in the future, are we going to campaign on personalities or on party labels.

The issues that divide the opposite side and this Administration are so wide—in fact, the clearest choice in this century—that we must campaign on issues. There is an honest difference of opinion on foreign policy, an honest difference of opinion on domestic policy, and an honest difference of opinion on most major defense issues.

Under these circumstances, this is a campaign which I think should be waged—I think all should, but this one particularly should—be waged on the issues so that the American people can make their choice between the two: the present President and the challenger, who honestly so basically disagree on fundamental ends and goals for the American people.

Q: Mr. President, are we to understand that now that stop bombing the dikes has been made a political slogan this year, perhaps those who have gotten behind it have not thoroughly checked the background of those accusations?

THE PRESIDENT: I did not use the word "naive" unintentionally. The North Vietnamese are very skillful at propaganda. They have, of course, brought those who have been invited into the country to the areas where they have found bomb damage. They have not gone to any great pains to fill those holes, which they would naturally want to do before the possibility of rain and flood again comes to the North.

In my view, this is a deliberate attempt on the part of the North Vietnamese to create an extraneous issue, to divert attention from one of the most barbaric invasions in history, compounded by a violation of all concepts of international law in handling the prisoners of war. For them, with their policy of deliberate murder, and assassination, and otherwise attacks on civilians for the purpose of killing civilians, for them to try to seize on this and divert attention from that, first, is a patent propaganda effort, and it is one that I think needs to be answered.

We have to, of course, be responsible for what we do. But it is time that in this terribly difficult war some Americans, or that most of us, should perhaps realize that when we talk about morality, that it is never an easy question.

If I can digress for a moment, and then I will come to your follow-up question on the other matter, I remember one of the first conversations I had with President Eisenhower about war. We were riding back from Quantico. You may remember it. Charlie Wilson used to have those meetings in Quantico of the Defense Establishment people. He asked me to ride back with him. It was very early in the Administration, the first year.

He was talking a little about the decisions he had to make in World War II. One of the questions I raised with him was: Here, on our part, the deliberate bombing of German cities, the tragedy of Dresden, of Essen, of Hamburg, not to mention Berlin. General Eisenhower said that was a terribly difficult decision for us, the strategic bombing of civilians in Germany. But he said, "On the moral question, we had to answer to ourselves this fundamental problem." He said, "The height of immorality would be to allow Hitler to rule Europe."

Now, in our case we have not gone that far. We are not going to bomb civilian targets in the North. We are not using the great power that could finish off North Vietnam in an afternoon, and we will not. But it would be the height of immorality for the United States at this point to leave Vietnam, and in leaving, to turn over to the North Vietnamese the fate of 17 million South Vietnamese who do not want a Communist Government, to turn it over to them.

That is what this is about. That is the only issue that is left. Those who say "End the war" really should name their resolution "Prolong the war." They should name it "Prolong the war" not because they deliberately want to. They want to end the war just as I do, but we have to face this fact: We have only one President at a time, as I said in 1968. At that time, as you may recall, I was pressed quite often by you ladies and gentlemen, "What do you think we ought to do about negotiation?" I didn't think there was much chance for successful negotiation then.

But I said, correctly, we had only one President, and I didn't want to destroy any chance he might have to end this war. At this point, the chance for a negotiated settlement is better now than it has ever been. It is not sure, and I am not going to raise any false hopes, but the enemy is failing in its military offensive, although there is still some hard fighting to take place in the Quangtri-Hue area, but the enemy is also, of course, suffering the consequences of mining and cutting the roads and other systems that would bring in supplies to North Vietnam.

Under these circumstances, the enemy—because also we have made a very fair offer—has every incentive to negotiate. But when you put yourself in the position of the enemy, and they hear that the Congress of the United States says, in effect, "We will give you what you want regardless of what the President has offered," why not wait? This is the problem, and I would hope that as Senators and Congressmen consult their consciences, they would realize that we have just three months left before the election. In those three months we hope to do everything we can to bring this war to an end, and they should take no action which would jeopardize those negotiations. I can only say that the resolutions to this point cannot help. They can only confuse the enemy, at best; and at the worst, they will prolong the war.

Q: The Vice Presidential nominee often is chosen under great pressure. This means often that the Vice President eventually is under great pressure of time and circumstance. Sometimes this turns out all right and sometimes it doesn't. Do you think that that method could be improved?

THE PRESIDENT: I was a Vice President once, too. (Laughter)

I will answer. I can only give my own experience and I know this was the experience of President Eisenhower. When an individual feels that he is quite, shall we say, has a better than even chance or an even chance to be President, he does a lot of thinking about who should be the Vice Presidential candidate, both because of his potentialities as a candidate and in terms of could he fill the office of Vice President, and in the case of an accident, the President.

I can assure you that naturally I went through that process making my decision and I would think that any candidate would do that. I don't think it is quite as, shall we say, off-the-top of your head as you would indicate, because most of us, when we are seeking the Presidency, long before the convention, have a pretty good idea as to whether we have a good shot at it and we do a lot of thinking about the Vice Presidential nomination.

Q: Mr. President, given the continuing demands for revealing the financial backgrounds of candidates and office holders, what is your reaction to the suggestion that medical records of candidates and office holders be revealed and, as a corollary to that, which you will understand, have you ever felt yourself in more danger of being over-confident? (Laughter)

THE PRESIDENT: Is that something for medical records?

Q: It is a bridge, but it is not direct.

THE PRESIDENT: Well, let me say that for me to answer that question is really so self-serving that I hesitate to do so. My medical records, of course, like my financial records, are already on the books, open to the press.

You will recall in 1968, the question was raised about my medical history and Mr. Ziegler, at that time, put out the medical history, including the examinations, some of the examinations, what the yearly examinations that we all have were, going back to the time that I came to Washington in 1946.

So, as far as my financial records are concerned, they also have been made public and then every year my medical record is made public by Dr. Tkach in briefings which seem to create some interest. I don't know why.

I would also suggest in my case, too, it was somewhat of a self-serving record, because Dr. Tkach was pointing out to me a few days ago that according to his computations, and I will not vouch for his figures, that I have been in this office 3½ years and have never missed an appointment because of health.

Considering what I have been through, some fairly stern crises and rather extensive travel, I don't think anybody would question the state of my health.

I think that in answer to your question, that that is a matter that will inevitably be a subject that will be raised and in which the candidates, each of them, will have to make his own determination. I made mine. I don't suggest that others should do likewise.

As far as over-confident—about what, my health?

Q: No, sir, in terms of the circumstances and the situation, given your position today as an incumbent President running for re-election, you are the favorite. Events in the past two or three weeks, let alone the last two or three days, have enhanced that. That is what I was talking about.

THE PRESIDENT: Well, I recall historically, an incident, and you were covering us at that time. We both go back 25 years. I recall in 1952 when another Vice Presidential candidate was urged to get off the ticket and there were many who thought that the fact that he was urged to get off it, whether he stayed on or got off, that it was going to sink the Presidential candidate. It did not.

So, I would say that that incident certainly would not enter into my predictions at this time. As far as making a prediction is concerned, I will give it more thought and will be glad to

respond to it when I have what I call a political press conference, which I will have immediately after the Republican Convention at the Western White House in San Clemente.

As far as what the situation is now, though, looking at the facts, the Democratic Party has a much higher registration than the Republican Party. Looking at the volatile mix of the American voting public, it is my belief—and I have told all of my associates this—that regardless of what the polls show, whether we are ahead or behind, this will be a close, hard-fought election right down to the wire.

People who make predictions now could look very, very bad later. We are going to assume throughout this election that we have a very hard fight on our hands. We think that is is a good thing that it is going to be a fight on the issues, a good hard clean fight on the issues before the American people. We think it will be close and we hope to win.

Q: What impact on the American policy in the Middle East is the withdrawal of Soviet personnel likely to have?

THE PRESIDENT: This question I noticed has been reflected on by some lower level officials in the Government, but not because Secretary Rogers and I have talked about this matter and Dr. Kissinger and I, not by us. For this reason, our goal, as you know, is a just settlement in the Middle East. The situation there is still one that is not clear and any comment upon it, first, might possibly be erroneous, and second, could very well be harmful to our goal of a just settlement.

So I am not trying to dodge your question, but I don't think it would be helpful to our goal of a just settlement in the Middle East. It might exacerbate the problem by trying to evaluate what happened between Sadat and the Soviet leaders.

Q: On the subject of your selection of the Vice President, of your selection of Mr. Agnew, could you tell us if you considered anybody else for the job and who they were?

THE PRESIDENT: No. My thoughts with regard to Vice President Agnew were expressed at rather great length in this very room in an interview with one of the other networks. I think it was CBS.

On that occasion, I expressed my confidence in the Vice President. I wouldn't go over those matters that I covered at considerable length then now, except to say that I reaffirm that confidence as expressed then.

Under the circumstances, I believe that the choice I made four years ago is one that should now be reaffirmed by asking him to run for the office again.

Now, there has been speculation, I would hasten to say, about other people for the Vice Presidency. That is inevitable. The Vice President could get sick or the Vice President might decide not to run, all of these things. I don't think he is going to get sick. He is also in excellent health, better than I. He plays tennis. But, in any event, there has been a lot of speculation. Secretary Connally's name comes to mind.

I should point out that a really great injustice was done to Secretary Connally in the suggestion, I think, on one of the news reports to the effect that I gave Secretary Connally the bad news that he was not going to be the Vice Presidential candidate when I saw him Friday night.

This was not bad news to him. As a matter of fact, it was not news at all. He and I had discussed this problem when he came to California after his world trip. At that time, I discussed the Vice Presidency. After all, not only from the standpoint of ability to hold the office of Vice President, but from the standpoint of ability to win the election, Secretary Connally, whose political judgment I respect very much, strongly urged that Vice President Agnew be continued on the ticket.

Q: Mr. President, on the bombing of the dikes and dams, would you say that you have been resisting pressure from the military to bomb such installations?

THE PRESIDENT: No. The pressure does not come from the military. I have talked this over with Admiral Moorer and naturally General Abrams. As a matter of fact, let me just say one thing about our military, because somebody ought to speak up for it now and then.

We get the idea they are a bunch of savage fly-boys and they love to get down and machine gun all the innocent little civilians and all the rest.

We can be very proud of our military, not only the men who are flying, they are brave and courageous, but also the men on the ground. We can be very proud of the Marines, all of them have gone now, for what they have done—the Marines, the Army, and the ground soldiers—for the civilians and refugees there. It is a story of generosity in a country that has never been equalled by American fighting men or anybody else.

As far as our military commanders are concerned, while they do give me their judgment as to what will affect the military outcome in Vietnam, they have never recommended, for example, bombing Hanoi. You have seen some of these signs "Bomb Hanoi," in fact, they were around in '68 even, a few, as well as '64.

Our military doesn't want to do that. They believe it would be counter-productive; and secondly, they believe it is not necessary. It might shorten the war, but it would leave the legacy of hatred throughout that part of the world from which we might never recover. So our military have not advocated bombing the dikes; they have not advocated bombing civilian centers. They are doing their best in carrying out the policy we want of hitting military targets only.

When, as a result of what will often happen, a bomb is dropped, if it is in an area of injury to civilians, it is not by intent, and there is a very great difference.

Q: Sir, a similar question was asked another President in your experience. Would you please tell us what policy decisions Vice President Agnew has contributed to in your Administration?

THE PRESIDENT: Well, I only need a couple of minutes. (Laughter)

Miss McClendon, as a matter of fact, one of the considerations that motivates a President when he selects a Vice President for running again is: How does he handle himself with the tough decisions? Now, the Vice President does not make decisions. I learned that, and Vice President Agnew knows that. Decisions with regard to his schedule, yes; advice, and so forth; but not decisions. The President only makes them.

But in the Cabinet Room, and sometimes in this office, we have had some pretty hard ones—the May 8th decision; the Cambodian decision was not easy, the November 3rd decision that I made on that occasion; the decision with regard to the SALT agreements, which involved a fight between the hawks and doves, was not an easy one.

I don't mean to indicate that Vice President Agnew just sat there as a yes man. He is very outspoken—very quiet but very outspoken—and articulate. What has impressed me in those meetings is that he is a man of poise, calm, and judgment. When it gets down to the final tough decision, he is, from my evaluation, always cool and poised, and is one who therefore could be expected to make decisions in the future in a calm, cool, judicial way.

Now, that does not mean that all of his decisions will be good because calm, cool, judicial men make bad decisions just as emotional men sometimes make good decisions, but my point is that in his case, in all of the so-called mini-crises and major crises we have had in the Administration, he has been strong, courageous and loyal. Those are attributes that are interesting to come by.

Let me say one other thing since you are talking about the Vice Presidency. I think we who have been Vice Presidents ought to form a little club. It is the most maligned office, you know. The reason is that we tend not to look at the records of Vice Presidents who have become President. Now that did not happen to me so this is not a self-serving statement in this case. I mean became President as a result of being Vice President.

But look at this Century: Two striking examples. Around the turn of the Century, Theodore Roosevelt—and some of you remember Mark Hanna, a great McKinley man. McKinley was in marvelous health and he was shot. Theodore Roosevelt came in to the presidency and Mark Hanna, who did not care much for Theodore Roosevelt, said, "Now we have this fanatic in the White House" and yet Theodore Roosevelt became a great President.

Perhaps that is not the best analogy because Theodore Roosevelt added, they thought, a great deal to the ticket.

Let's look at Harry Truman a moment—and I must say I was in the group at that time, being in the other Party—but here is Harry Truman succeeding the towering figure of his time, Franklin Roosevelt. I remember the editorials: "Harry Truman, the man from Independence"—the very question somebody asked here a few moments ago, "Shouldn't we have a better method of selecting Vice Presidents?" They said, "How in the world? Now we have this little man from Missouri in the Presidency." You all know Harry Truman and I have had our differences. You will also remember that on public occasions I have praised him for three very tough decisions he made.

I was reading Winston Churchill the other night, about the first meeting with Truman at Potsdam where Truman took him over in a corner and told him about the use of the bomb. This was a terribly difficult decision. But he thought, probably correctly—and President Eisenhower agreed with this—that it would save a million American lives, as probably it did, and that is why he used the bomb in ending the war with Japan.

The second decision, which I had the opportunity to support, was the Greek-Turkish aid program. That was a tough one. It split his Party. It split it into the Henry Wallace wing and his wing. Byrnes and Wallace, remember, had their fight. It was a good decision and I supported it in the Congress of the United States.

Incidentally, I still support aid to Greece and Turkey. It is just as necessary today as it was then, for most of the same reasons, now particularly added because of the fact that without aid to Greece and aid to Turkey you have no viable policy to save Israel.

Finally, there were, of course, decisions that Mr. Truman made on the Korean War. I criticized the conduct of the war as did many of us who were out. But his decision to go into Korea was right; it was necessary, and it was tough.

Just before Dean Acheson died I was in his office and we talked about how Truman had made that decision. I have talked too long on that but what I am simply saying is this: Here was the little man from Missouri. He was the Vice President. People said, "Why did not Roosevelt pick some of the others, the towering figures in his cabinet or the Senate, or the rest, rather than the little man from Missouri?"

But the little man from Missouri had that indefinable quality, as did the big man from New York, Theodore Roosevelt, of character, that made him a man capable of making tough decisions and that is the most important thing that a Vice President needs.

THE PRESS: Thank you.

AUGUST 29

Following is the text, as made available by the White House, of President Nixon's news conference Aug. 29 at San Clemente, Calif.

THE PRESIDENT: We will go right ahead with our questions, because I know you want to cover perhaps some international as well as domestic matters, including, I understand, for the first time, political matters.

Q: Mr. President, are you personally investigating the mishandling of some of your campaign funds, and do you agree with former Secretary Connally that these changes are harmful to your re-election?

THE PRESIDENT: Well, I commented upon this on other occasions, and I will repeat my position now.

With regard to the matter of the handling of campaign funds, we have a new law here in which technical violations have occurred and are occurring, apparently, on both sides. As far as we are concerned, we have in charge, in Secretary Stans, a man who is an honest man and one who is very meticulous—as I have learned from having him as my treasurer and finance chairman in two previous campaigns—in the handling of matters of this sort.

Whatever technical violations have occurred, certainly he will correct them and will thoroughly comply with the law. He is conducting an investigation on this matter, and conducting it very, very thoroughly, because he doesn't want any evidence at all to be outstanding, indicating that we have not complied with the law.

Several Inquiries

Q: Mr. President, wouldn't it be a good idea for a special prosecutor, even from your standpoint, to be appointed to investigate the contribution situation and also the Watergate case?

THE PRESIDENT: With regard to who is investigating it now, I think it would be well to notice that the FBI is conducting a full field investigation. The Department of Justice, of course, is in charge of the prosecution and presenting the matter to the grand jury. The Senate Banking and Currency Committee is conducting an investigation. The Government Accounting Office, an independent agency, is conducting an investigation of those aspects which involve the campaign spending law.

Now, with all of these investigations that are being conducted, I don't believe that adding another special prosecutor would serve any useful purpose.

The other point that I should make is that these investigations—the investigation by the GAO, the investigation by the FBI, by the Department of Justice—have, at my direction, had the total cooperation of the-not only the White House but also of all agencies of Government.

In addition to that, within our own staff, under my direction, counsel to the President, Mr. Dean, has conducted a complete investigation of all leads which might involve any present members of the White House staff or anybody in the Government. I can say categorically that his investigation indicates that no one in the White House staff, no one in this Administration, presently employed, was involved in this very bizarre incident.

At the same time, the committee itself is conducting its own investigation, independent of the rest, because the committee desires to clear the air and to be sure that, as far as any people who have responsibility for this campaign are concerned, that there is nothing that hangs over them. Before Mr. Mitchell left as campaign chairman he had employed a very good law firm with investigatory experience to look into the matter. Mr. MacGregor has continued that investigation and is continuing it now.

I will say in that respect that anyone on the campaign committee, Mr. MacGregor has assured me, who does not cooperate with the investigation or anyone against whom charges are leveled where there is a prima facie case where those charges might indicate involvement, will be discharged immediately. That, also, is true of anybody in the Government. I think under these circumstances we are doing everything we can to take this incident and to investigate it and not to cover it up.

What really hurts in matters of this sort is not the fact that they occur, because overzealous people in campaigns do things that are wrong. What really hurts is if you try to cover it up. I would say that here we are, with control of the agencies of the Government and presumably with control of the investigatory agencies of the Government with the exception of GAO, which is independent. We have cooperated completely. We have indicated that we want all the facts brought out and as far as any people who are guilty are concerned, they should be prosecuted.

This kind of activity, as I have often indicated, has no place whatever in our political process. We want the air cleared. We want it cleared as soon as possible.

Peace in Vietnam

Q: Mr. President, in your last news conference, on July 27th, you said the chances for a settlement have never been better. Mr. Rogers in late August forecast early settlement and you were quoted by Stewart Alsop—you were quoted saying the war won't be hanging over us the second term. I want to know whether this is politics or is there any substance, any movement in negotiations or any other track toward peace?

THE PRESIDENT: Mr. Potter, as I also told Mr. Alsop in that interview, I did not indicate to him that any breakthrough had occurred in the negotiations that have been taking place between Dr. Kissinger and Mr. Le Duc Tho at this point. Now, let me divide the answer into its component parts, if I may.

First, with regard to negotiations, I will not comment on past negotiations. I will not comment upon any negotiations that may take place in the future. By agreement of both sides we are not going to comment, either the other side or we, on our part, on the substance of negotiations or whether or when or what will happen in the future. All that we will do is announce, after negotiations do take place, if they do—and I do not suggest that more will take place—announce the fact that those have taken place.

Secondly, with regard to what the prospects are, I think what we are all referring to is that this long and difficult war—long and difficult and costly for both sides—has reached a point where it should be brought to an end. We are being very reasonable in the proposals that we have made in our various discussions with the other side. Also, with regard to the battlefront, it is significant to note that the South Vietnamese, by heroic efforts, have stopped the invasion from the north on the ground and they have done that without our assistance on the ground.

It is also significant to note that the enemy at this point, while it is able to launch a spurt here and there, does not have the capability to overrun South Vietnam.

Now, under these circumstances, we believe that this is the time for a negotiated settlement. If the enemy does not feel that way, then we are prepared to go on as we have indicated, to continue the training of the South Vietnamese. We have completed virtually the ground training because they are undertaking the ground fighting entirely themselves, but we will continue the training in the air and on the sea so that they, by themselves, can defend their country against the Communist invaders from the north.

Q: Mr. President, you announced today another reduction in the force levels in Vietnam, and it was unclear from the announcement whether this your last announcement. Do you see this residual force in Vietnam as a necessary bargaining lever?

THE PRESIDENT: I can't imagine that Mr. Ziegler didn't make everything perfectly clear. But I shall try to, under those circumstances.

The announcement of 27,500 (27,000) does not indicate that 27,500 (27,000) is the force that is going to remain in South Vietnam indefinitely. We are going to look at the situation again before the first of December—after the election, incidentally—because we are not going to play election politics with this next withdrawal—or announcement, I should say—because I am not suggesting that there will be another withdrawal.

We will look at the sitatuion and the three principles I have always applied with regard to withdrawals will in this case control it: the status of our POW and MIA situations; the status with regard to negotiations, and the status of enemy activity. At that time we will determine what the American force level should be. It should be noted that the present force level of 39,000, and the level that we will reach of 27,500 (27,000) involves no ground combat personnel. It involves only advisory and training personnel and, of course, air support personnel. It is entirely a volunteer force.

I will add something that perhaps everyone here is quite aware of: That as far as any so-called residual force is concerned, our offer is for a total withdrawal. We want to withdraw all American forces, but that offer is conditioned on what I laid down on May 8th, and one of those conditions is the situation with regard to our POW's and MIA's. As long as there is one POW in North Vietnam, or one missing in action not accounted for, there will be an American volunteer force in South Vietnam.

Bombing Halt

Q: Mr. President, how do you reconcile your 1968 campaign promise to end the war with the massive bombing of North Vietnam that is now going on?

THE PRESIDENT: Well, in terms of what I said in 1968, all you who were following me will remember that I said that we would seek an honorable end to the war. We have come a long way in reaching that. We have reduced our casualties by 98 per cent; we have withdrawn over half a million men from the forces that we found that were there; we have completely finished the American ground combat role.

Only volunteers will be serving in Vietnam in the future. What is left now simply is to complete the long-term involvement of the United States in a way that does not destroy respect, trust and, if I may use the term, honor for the United States around the world. I think that we may have come—it seems to me made very significant progress in this respect and we expect to make more.

On the negotiating front, we have gone very far, as far as any reasonable person, I think, would suggest, and under the circumstances I believe the record is good.

As far as what can happen in the future, I know that there are those who believe—I noted some report out of the Air Force to the effect that we probably would be bombing in North Vietnam two or three years from now. That, of course, is quite ridiculous.

As far as the future is concerned, we believe that our training program for the South Vietnamese not only on the ground but in the air, has gone forward so successfully that if the enemy still refuses to negotiate, as we have asked them to negotiate, then the South Vietnamese will be able to undertake the total defense of their country.

At the present time, let the record show that while we hear a lot about what the Americans are doing in terms of undertaking bombing activities, that now approximately 50 per cent of all ground support air sorties are being made by the South Vietnamese air force, which is a good air force and which is growing in strength.

Q: Is there a possiblity that you would call off the bombing or slacken it even if there is no all-inclusive agreement on Indochina?

THE PRESIDENT: Absolutely not, I have noted some press speculation to the effect that since 1968, the bombing halt seemed to have a rather dramatic effect on the election chances of Senator Humphrey—Vice President Humphrey, now a Senator—that people have suggested that as a gimmick, or more or less as an election eve tactic that we would call a bombing halt even though our prisoners of war are not accounted for. No progress has been made there, and even though the enemy continued its activities and was still stonewalling us in the negotiations, unless there is progress on the negotiating front, which is substantial, there will be no reduction of the bombing of North Vietnam and there will be no lifting of the mining.

Asian Policy

Q: Mr. President, I would like to ask about a 1968 statement you made and find out whether you still agree with it. It is: "Those who have had a chance for four years and could not produce peace should not be given another chance."

THE PRESIDENT: I think that the answer I gave to the other question is as responsive as I can make it. We always, of course, set our goals high. We do our very best to reach those goals. I think there are those who have faulted this Administration on its efforts to seek peace, but those who fault it, I would respectfully suggest, are ones that would have the United States seek peace at the cost of surrender, dishonor and the destruction of the ability of the United States to conduct foreign policy in a responsible way.

That I did not pledge in 1968. I do not pledge it now. We will seek peace. We will seek better relations with our adversaries, but we are going to keep the United States strong. We are going to resist the efforts of those who would cut our defense budget to make us second to any power in the world, and second particularly to the Soviet Union, and in order to do that, it means that we have to continue the responsible policy that we have carried out.

Q: Mr. President, if it is, as you say, "quite ridiculous" that we will be bombing two or three years from now—by the way, I don't know if you mean North Vietnam or all of Vietnam—then how about a year from now? Is it likely that bombing would no longer be necessary in present plan or thinking?

THE PRESIDENT: No. I would not comment on what the situation will will be a year from now because, with the fact that we have had negotiating proposals made—I am not indicating progress; I am simply indicating they have been made—and with also the progress that is being made by the South Vietnamese, the very outstanding progress in their ability to defend themselves, and also to undertake the air effort as well as the ground effort, I am not going to put any limitation on when the U.S. activities in the air would stop.

Also, I am not going to indicate they are going to continue for any length of time. We are going to continue to watch the situation month by month. We will do what is necessary to protect our interests. We will do what is necessary to assure the return of our POW's and accounting for our missing in action. We will do what is necessary to prevent the imposition, against their will, of a Communist government on the people of South Vietnam.

All this we will do, but on the other hand, we are not there for the purpose of staying any moment that is longer than is necessary.

Will Run Hard

Q: Mr. President, the confidence expressed at the Republican convention suggested that many Republicans, perhaps yourself included, consider the election a mere formality. Yet you have said at your last press conference that you expected this election to be a close one that goes right down to the wire. Do you still feel that way?

THE PRESIDENT: Yes, I do. That has always been my theory. I recall the year I ran for the first time for Congress in 1946. I was somewhat of a neophyte, never having run for public office before.

I talked to someone who had had great experience in running for office. He gave me very good advice that has been my guiding principle in campaigns since. He said, "Pay no attention to the polls. Pay no attention to what your friends say about your chances, or your opponents." He said, "Always run as if you are one million votes behind, and then you might win by one vote."

In 1960 I learned what he meant because elections can be very, very close in this country.

I am conducting this campaign, and I have urged on my colleagues in the campaign to conduct it without regard to the polls. I am not going to comment on the polls one way or the other, when they are good or bad. We are running on the basis of the great issues before the country.

We are presenting, I think, a very clear choice before the country. We are seeking in this election something that no President has had since 1956, with the exception of President Johnson in '64 after his landslide, and that is a majority, because there was none in 1960 and there was none in 1968 because of third party candidates.

I think what we need now is clear majority of the American people. That means a clear mandate, mandate for what I have described as change that works, for progress. Because, when I see what has happened to, for example, revenue sharing, Government reorganization, our health plan, our welfare reform, and all of our programs—there are 12 different bills on the environment that are still stuck in the mud of Senate and House controversy—when I see that, I think that the country needs to speak out.

I would also suggest, Mr. Lisagor, because I know that you, like myself, have sort of followed campaigns over the years, and we go back this far, at least I do—I believe that if we can get a clear majority, if we can get a new majority at the Presidential level in this country, and crossing all the lines of various age groups and religious groups and ethnic groups, et cetera, that we could have a legislative record in the first six months in the next Congress which could equal in excitement, in reform, the 100 days of 1933. It will be very different from the 100 days but we have it all there, and my State of the Union Message summed it up early this year.

What we are not only seeking here is a majority for the President but we are seeking a new majority, of course, in the House and Senate which will support the President in terms of his domestic policies, and we trust continue to support us on national defense and foreign policy.

Q: Mr. President, how are you going to conduct the campaign personally in terms of your travel plans, and would you be willing to debate with Senator McGovern over national television?

THE PRESIDENT: Mr. Schecter, let me turn to the debate question first, because it is one which I know many of you have speculated about, and we might as well set the speculation to rest.

Mr. MacGregor, and before him Mr. Mitchell, both indicated it would be not in the national interest for the President to debate. I did not share that view in 1964. Quite candidly, you may remember when Senator Goldwater was a candidate I said that having been Vice President and having debated and knowing all of the information that the President debated, I saw no reason why the President shouldn't debate.

Frankly, I think I was wrong. I was wrong, in that President Johnson was right, Senator Mansfield was right, and even Senator Pastore, who support Amendment 315 but who said that even in supporting the 315 amendment he said he had serious doubt about whether a President of the United States should debate.

Now just to say why. The reason does not have so much to do with confidential information that a President has, because such information can be made available to the other candidate, if he desires to obtain it. What really is involved is that when a President speaks, as distinguished from a Vice President, even, he makes policy every time he opens his mouth. For example, just as I spoke a moment ago with regard to our plans in Vietnam, what is going to happen, that is policy.

Now, when we are involved—even though it is the concluding phase—but when we are involved in a war, for a President in the heat of partisan debate to make policy would not be in the national interest. So I have decided there will be no debates between the President and the challenger in this year, 1972.

Now, with regard to my own plans. You have often heard me describe that a President wears two hats. Well, he wears three, actually, but we put the commander-in-chief off here. We have already discussed those questions. The other two hats that he wears are that as President of the United States and as leader of his party, and as candidate after the nomination.

Now, I am a candidate in the one sense and the President in the other. What comes first? Putting priorities where they belong. I shall always have to put my responsibilities to conduct the Presidency first. I had hoped that the Congress would be

out of here with a record, which they have not yet made. Incidentally, this Congress, in order to avoid being called a very inept Congress, one that never talked as much and did less— to avoid that, is going to have to do four months work in four weeks and it will be a real issue in this campaign, the fact that the Congress has not acted on revenue sharing and on Government reorganization and on health and on welfare.

But, since the Congress is going to be in, I understand, until Oct. 10th, or the 15th, or maybe the 1st, or whatever it is, as long as the Congress is there, my responsibilities as President will require that I stay in Washington except for perhaps an occasional trip through the country, but only for a day. I could perhaps over a weekend, I haven't figured it out yet, but we will, of course, inform you so you can pack your bags. None of these will be overnight trips, you will be glad to know.

After the Congress adjourns, I still, of course, have my responsibility as President, and I cannot go out and spend six to seven days a week. I realize that some Presidents have done that. Harry Truman did in 1948. But the problems that we had then, great as they were, are not as great as those we have now.

It will be necessary for me to continue to spend a great deal of time in Washington, but I don't want to leave the impression that one-day trips that I will make between now and the time Congress adjourns, and then the time I will be able to devote to campaigning in the last three weeks, means that it will be leisurely, complacent, take-it-easy campaign.

As I have indicated in my answer to Mr. Lisagor, I consider this campaign enormously important. It provides the clearest choice that certainly I have seen in my political lifetime. I believe we have to hit hard on the issues; in other words, hit hard on the problems, and not on the personalities. And we are going to do that, and I would assume that the other side would do likewise.

In order to do that, we are going to cover the whole country. We are not going to take any state for grented. We are not going to concede any state, and more than that, we are going to cover all groups.

One thing I should mention when I speak of the new majority, I reject the idea of a new coalition. A coalition is not a healthy thing in a free society. Coalition automatically adds up the young against the old, the black against the whites, the Catholic against the Protestants, the city people against the country people, et cetera, et cetera.

What we are doing is to make our appeal across the board and try to build a new majority on the basis of people from all the groups supporting us on the basis of what we believe.

Q: Mr. President, you have objected and given your reasons for not entering a debate with your opponent. Would you entertain the possiblity of a debate on a lower level, between the Vice-Presidential candidates?

THE PRESIDENT: I would be very confident as to the results on that, because I think Vice President Agnew's four years of experience, his coolness, his lawyer's background, would serve him in good stead in a debate. I do not believe, however, that a debate at the Vice-Presidential level would serve any useful purpose, but I don't rule it out. I don't think it would serve any useful purpose.

Meeting With Japanese

Q: Mr. President, may I ask a question concerning your meeting with Mr. Tanaka?

THE PRESIDENT: Sure.

Q: Mr. Tanaka has made his intention clear, that he would like to discuss further with you China and discuss less economic problems. But I am also told that the United States wants to discuss the economic problems as widely and deeply as the other issues, and it can be said that it is an open secret that the United States is asking Japan for another revaluation of the yen in the near future. Could you tell me to what extent are you going to discuss with Tanaka the economic issues?

THE PRESIDENT: Our meeting with Mr. Tanaka is, first, very important because it is the first chance I will have to meet him as Prime Minister, although I did meet him here, you will recall, when he came with Premier Sato, and I have known him for many years and have great respect for him as one of the new leaders of Japan. So it will first provide an opportunity for establishing a dialogue between these two countries, both of whom are economic superpowers.

Second, we will naturally cover the whole range of problems of the Pacific. Both Japan and the United States are tremendously interested in peace in the Pacific.

On the economic side, I think both sides will be prepared to discuss the fact that there is now an unfavorable balance of trade between Japan and the United States of three and four-tenths billion dollars a year. Naturally, that is not healthy for the United States, but responsible Japanese leaders do not believe it is healthy for Japan, because what will happen if that kind of imbalance continues? It will inevitably feed the fire of those in this country who would want to set up quotas and other restrictions, and the interest of Japan and the United States will better be served by freer trade rather than more restrictive trade.

I believe that out of this meeting will come some progress in trying to reduce that unfavorable balance between Japan and the United States.

Now, with regard to the devaluation of the yen and that sort of thing, I won't comment on that. I have no expectation that that kind of technical international monetary matter will be one that we will discuss.

I say that for the reason that saying anything else is likely to have the stock markets in Tokyo and New York go up and down, so I will categorically say that revaluation of the yen is not on the agenda, but the other matters of how we can adjust this trade balance so that it is less unfavorable to the United States is, of course, in order.

One final thing that I would say from a symbolic standpoint: Since World War II, Presidents of the United States have welcomed Prime Ministers of Japan to Washington on several occasions. I welcomed, as you know, the Emperor in the United States, in Anchorage, and we have met here with Prime Minister Sato.

It seems to me that we could have no better proof of the fact that the war is over, not only the shooting, but also the emnity, than the fact that we are having this meeting between the leader of Japan and the leader of the United States in Hawaii, where the war began, and I am very glad that the Prime Minister and I mutually agreed that we should have it in Hawaii because we talk about the initiatives towards the People's Republic of China and towards the Soviet Union and the rest. As I have often said, and I repeat again, Japan being an economic giant with great potentials for political and other leadership in the Pacific plays an indispensable role if we are going to have peace in the Pacific.

As I have said, Japanese-American friendship and cooperation is the linchpin of peace in the Pacific and we are going to try to strengthen that linchpin in these meetings.

Q: Mr. President, back to the campaign fiancing. You said that there had been technical violations of the law on both sides. I was just wondering what Democratic violations you had in mind.

THE PRESIDENT. I think that will come out in the balance of this week. I will let the political people talk about that, but I understand there have been on both sides.

Draft Evaders

Q: Mr. President, you have touched on the question of amnesty before, but since it is obviously a campaign issue, I wonder if you could spell out what you perceive to be the differences between your thoughts on amnesty and those of your opponent.

THE PRESIDENT: Mr. Semple, the Vice President made a very responsible statement on that and I read it before he made it. That statement totally reflects my views and I back it, in other words, the speech he made just a few days ago. Insofar as my own views are concerned, without going into that statement, because as you know it involves legal matters and a lot of other things, it is my view, and I hold it very strongly, that those who chose to desert the United States or to break the law by dodging the draft have to pay the penalty for breaking the law and deserting the United States before they can obtain amnesty and pardon, or whatever you want to call it. Where we disagree, apparently, is that the other side does not share my view. I say: Pay a penalty; other paid with their lives.

Politics

Q: Mr. President, the majority you talked about a minute ago, what kind of majority will it be, a Nixon majority or a Republican majority, and will it bring a Congress along with it?

THE PRESIDENT: First, with regard to the majority, the thrust of our campaign, I have tried to emphasize to our campaign people to make it a positive majority rather than a negative majority. There has been a great deal of talk with regard to why people should be against the challenger in this respect, mainly because his views, as I pointed out in the acceptance speech, departed from their economic philosophy and some of their basic views.

Now, what we want, however, is a positive mandate; in other words, what we are for, not simply what we might be against or what the country is against. Now that means that this majority will be one that we would hope would send us in with a clear mandate to keep the United States strong and not to go along with a $30-billion defense cut which would make the United States second in the air, the second strongest navy, the second strongest missiles, as well as the second on the ground, which we already are with the Soviet Union, and completely destroy the chance for arms limitation and completely, in my view, destroy the ability of the United States to be a peacemaker of the world as the major free world power.

At home—and here are the areas we don't often get into in these conferences—that we could have at home the kind of a mandate where the country would say we want change, but we want change that works. It is not a question of whether it is radical or not. My trip to China was radical; it was bold, radical and different. What really matters is: Does it work, or has it been thought through or is it a half-baked scheme where you have one today and one tomorrow and then you check the P.M.'s to see whether or not there is a new one?

As far as we are concerned, what we are saying is that we need a mandate for revenue sharing, we need a mandate for welfare reform, we need a mandate for our programs in the environment, for our new health programs, a mandate to continue progress without raising taxes, a mandate to continue to help those who are poor, without having an enormous increase in the welfare rolls.

Finally, we believe that we need support in this country—and this is something that is rather hard to put your finger on, it is an intangible attitude—there has been a subtle shift over the last four years. Some may not have seen it. I think I have. Four years ago the country was torn apart, torn apart physically and torn apart inside. It has changed very subtly, but very definitely. What we need in this country is a new sense of mission, a new sense of confidence, a new sense of purpose as to where we are going.

The fact is that abroad this country does not follow Hitlerite policies; the President of the United States is not the number one war-maker of the world, but as a matter of fact, the United States with its great power, is using it well and the world is fortunate to have the United States as the most powerful of the free world nations.

At home, the United States is not a country where we are repressive to the poor and play always to the rich; pointing out the fact, for example, that when we look at our tax laws that we provided the biggest individual tax reduction in history in 1969 and at the same time increased the burden for corporations by $4-billion; that we moved against the auto companies, for example, to have them roll back a price increase; that we moved against the other companies that have been polluting. In other words, this is not a pro-business or pro-labor Administration. It is an Administration that calls it right down the middle. When labor is wrong we say so, as I did when I was in Miami with Mr. Meany. When business is wrong we say so.

Now I have digressed a bit, but let me come back to the point. We need a mandate, therefore, in which the President receives a clear majority. We are going to work for a clear majority and as big a one as we can get. Although, as I say, we don't assume that it is going to be big but it will be clear because there is not a third-party candidate of significance.

Secondly, we need a new Congress. Now, on the Congress, I am as sophisticated enough, as all of you are because I have read some of your columns, to know that in both the House and Senate it is tough for us to elect a Republican majority. Also, I am honest enough to say that there are enough Democrats in the House and several Senators without whose support I could not have conducted the foreign policy of the United States over these past four years.

When I speak of a new Congress, I mean a Congress—and I would hope it would be a Republican Congress because then at least we could have responsibility for leadership—but if it is not, I hope there is a new majority in Congress made up of Republicans and Democrats who support what the President believes in. Then we can get action on some of these things rather than being stuck in the mud as we have been these past three years, particularly since we have offered our new initiatives.

Q: Thank you, Mr. President.

OCTOBER 5

Following is the text, as made available by the White House, of President Nixon's Oct. 5 news conference.

THE PRESIDENT: Go ahead.

Q: Mr. President, what are you planning to do to defend yourself against the charges of corruption in your Administration?

THE PRESIDENT: Well, I have noted such charges; as a matter of fact, I have noted that this Administration has been charged with being the most corrupt in history, and I have been charged with being the most deceitful President in history.

The President of the United States has been compared in his policies with Adolph Hitler. The policies of the U.S. Government to prevent a Communist takeover by force in South Vietnam have been called the worst crime since the Nazi extermination of the Jews in Germany. And the President who went to China and to Moscow, and who has brought 500,000 home from Vietnam, has been called the Number One warmaker in the world.

Needless to say, some of my more partisan advisers feel that I should respond in kind. I shall not do so; not now, not throughout this campaign. I am not going to dignify such comments.

In view of the fact that one of the very few Members of the Congress who is publicly and actively supporting the opposition ticket in this campaign has very vigorously, yesterday, criticized this kind of tactics, it seems to me it makes it not necessary for me to respond.

I think the responsible members of the Democratic Party will be turned off by this kind of campaigning, and I would suggest that responsible members of the press, following the single

standard to which they are deeply devoted, will also be turned off by it.

Q: Mr. President, do you feel that, as Vice President Agnew said the other day, that Senator McGovern is waging a smear campaign against you, would you characterize it as that?

THE PRESIDENT: I am not going to characterize the Senator's campaign. As a matter of fact, I don't question his motives. I think he deeply believes in a number of actions that he believes that this Government should take that I think would be very disastrous for this Nation, as I pointed out in my acceptance speech. Consequently, as far as I am concerned, I will discuss those issues, but I am not going to raise my doubts about his motives. Incidentally, I have no complaint with his doubts about mine. That is his choice.

Vietnam Settlement

Q: Mr. President, do you see any possibility of a negotiated settlement in Vietnam before the election?

THE PRESIDENT: The settlement will come just as soon as we can possibly get a settlement which is right, right for the South Vietnamese, the North Vietnamese, and for us, one that will have in mind our goals of preventing the imposition by force of a Communist Government in South Vietnam and, of course, a goal that is particularly close to our hearts, in a humanitarian sense, the return of our prisoners of war.

I should emphasize, however, that under no circumstances will the timing of a settlement, for example, the possible negotiation of a cease-fire, the possible negotiation of, or unilateral action with regard to a bombing halt, under no circumstances will such action be affected by the fact that there is going to be an election November 7th.

If we can make the right kind of a settlement before the election, we will make it. If we cannot, we are not going to make the wrong kind of a settlement before the election. We were around that track in 1968 when well-intentioned men made a very, very great mistake in stopping the bombing without adequate agreements from the other side.

I do not criticize them for that, of course, as far as their motives are concerned. I simply said, having seen what happened then, we are not going to make that mistake now.

The election, I repeat, will not in any way influence what we do at the negotiating table.

Secondly, because I know this subject has been discussed by a number of you, as it should be, in your commentaries and in your reports, the negotiations at this time, as you know, have been in the private channel, very extensive. We have agreed that neither side will discuss the content of those negotiations. I will not discuss them one way or another.

I will only say that the negotiations are in a sensitive state. I cannot predict and will not predict that they will or will not succeed. I cannot and will not predict when they will succeed.

But I will say that any comment on my part with regard to how the negotiations are going could only have a detrimental effect on the goal that we are seeking, and that is as early as possible a negotiated settlement of this long and difficult war.

Q: Mr. President, it has been said that Hanoi may be waiting until after the election to make a settlement on the theory that if they got a Democrat elected they would get better terms for them. How do you answer that?

THE PRESIDENT: They could be motivated by that. There are those who believe that they were motivated to an extent in 1968 by political considerations in agreeing to a bombing halt before the election with the thought that defeating me was more in their interest than electing my opponent.

I do not claim that that was the case. I must say that both Senator Humphrey and I, I think, were quite responsible in that election campaign in refusing to comment on what were then only preliminary negotiations, recognizing that any comment by one who might be President might jeopardize the success of the negotiations.

Now, as far as Hanoi's putting their eggs in that basket, that only indicates that the American political scene is one that no one can predict. Despite what the polls say, and despite some indications on our side that we believe we have a good chance to win, there are many in this country and many abroad who think that there is a chance the other side might win.

Under those circumstances, they obviously could conclude, with some justification, that my insistence that we will never agree to a settlement which would impose a Communist Government directly or indirectly on the people of South Vietnam, as compared with the statements of our opponents to the contrary on this particular point, might be influencing them.

On the other hand, we are talking. If we have the opportunity, we will continue to talk before this election and we will try to convince them that waiting until after the election is not good strategy.

Purpose of Bombing

Q: Mr. President, there are those of your critics who say that the bombing is really serving no useful purpose and it is needless. What purpose is the bombing now serving in view of the fact that the negotiations have not resulted in a settlement and in view of the fact that there still seems to be a good deal of military activity in the south?

THE PRESIDENT: Well, I think, Mr. Lisagor, you could really go further. There are those who say that the bombing and mining serve no useful purpose and are serving no useful purpose. Those same critics, as I pointed out in San Clemente, and have since had an opportunity to review, on May 1st, that weekend, all had reached the conclusion that South Vietnam was down the tube. Time, Newsweek, the New York Times, the Washington Post, the three television network commentators—I am not referring to you, ladies and gentlemen, who are reporters— all in varying degrees wrote and spoke of the specter of defeat and the hopelessness of the South Vietnamese cause.

On May 8th, I acted to prevent that Communist takeover, which all of these same critics then predicted. After I took that action of mining and bombing, the same critics predicted that the summit was torpedoed. Some even went so far as to say we were risking World War III.

Those predictions proved to be wrong. Now these same critics say the bombing and mining was not necessary, it has accomplished no purpose and is not necessary for the future. Well, I would say, based on their track record, I would not give much credence to what the critics have said in any respect.

I will only say that the bombing and mining was essential to turn around what was a potentially disastrous situation in South Vietnam. The back of the enemy offensive has been broken. They hold no provincial capitals now at all.

This could not have been accomplished without the mining and the bombing, and the mining and the bombing will continue, of course, until we get some agreements on the negotiating front.

Wheat Agreement

Q: Mr. President, what is your reply to the critics who charge that scandal was involved in your Russian wheat agreement?

THE PRESIDENT: My reply is to have such allegations investigated; incidentally, with the thorough and complete agreement of Secretary Butz. Secretary Butz and the House Committee on Agriculture both looked into these charges that some of the big grain dealers, the so-called Big Six, got advance information and made a lot of money; and that particularly some of the wheat growers in the Southwestern part of the country who sell their wheat early, usually, in order to get a premium, were left holding the bag when, if they had the advance information that there was going to be a deal, they could have made some more money.

Now, if there was any impropriety, if there was any illegality, we want to know it. The way to find out is to put the best

investigative agency in the world to work at finding out. As soon as their investigation is completed, and we want it just as quickly as we can, it will be made available to the Secretary and he will take whatever action is needed if there is an illegality or impropriety.

Let me turn, if I could, on the wheat deal, however, to another side of it that has also come to my attention. I have been rather amused by some of the comments to the effect that the wheat deal was really a bad one for the United States; that we got schnookered by the Russians. When I used that term with Mr. Gromyko he asked for a translation, but in any event—and I said, "Well, you acted like capitalists,"—but in any event—"because you didn't tell us that your grain failure was as great as it was."

Of course, his response was, "Well, what could you have done?" He said, "We knew we had to buy a lot of wheat and we didn't want to push the price up as fast."

But in any event, let me take very briefly a moment of your time to point out what was in it for us and what was in it for them. First, the wheat deal cost us $120 million in, as you know, payments, farm payments. But this is what we got from it: The farmers got $1 billion in more farm income. There were thousands of jobs created, including jobs in the American merchant marine as well as on the farm and in the processing areas as a result of the wheat deal.

The taxpayers were saved $200 million in farm payments that would otherwise have had to be made if we kept the wheat in storage and had not sold it.

Now, in addition, the wheat deal, this one, the one we have made with the Chinese, the one we have made with the Japanese for grain, and so forth, and so on have had a very significant effect in moving our balance of trade and balance of payments position.

As far as the terms were concerned, when we went in I negotiated this directly after a lot of preliminary work had been done, and very good preliminary work, by Secretary Peterson and, of course Secretary Butz. They wanted 10 years at 2 percent credit and they finally took three years at over 6 percent.

Now they got something they needed. They have a short wheat crop and they needed this wheat in order to feed their people, but it was also good for us. Despite that, however, we certainly want no one to have gotten any inside information to make a profit out of it which was illegal or improper. If that did happen, we are going to find out, and we will take action against it.

Q: Mr. President, do you agree with Secretary Butz that if he had known that one of his aides was going to join a grain dealer that he would not have taken him along in negotiating the Russian deal?

THE PRESIDENT: I have very great respect for Secretary Butz's judgment in this matter. The only addition I would make to it is that when we announced the grain deal on July 8 in San Clemente, if you recall, it was only then that we were sure—and incidentally many are now wondering what is going to happen to the trade agreement.

I can't tell you whether there will be one or when. I think there will be one, but my point is that when we negotiated in this economic field as is the case when we negotiated in the field of arms control, it is tough bargaining up and down the line, and until we get it nailed down we are not sure that we are going to get it. In this instance, while Mr. Butz's assistant did take a trip to the Soviet Union, he certainly, I think, would have been very unwise to rely on the possibility that there was going to be a deal until one was made.

If he did rely on it, he probably in this instance, came out well. He could have come out the other way.

Property Taxes

Q: Mr. President, on the question of property taxes Mr. Ehrlichman has said that the Administration can reduce property taxes 50 percent which will mean about $16 billion from the

Federal Government presumably to states to make up for the property tax loss. How will you find that $16 billion without having to increase Federal taxes?

THE PRESIDENT: We can't do it all in one bite. We have to begin with that, as Mr. Ehrlichman has indicated. That is why we have set as a goal a 50 percent reduction.

Now, let me indicate to you the priorities that I see developing with regard to property tax relief. We have to start first with the elderly. When I met with Mr. Merriam, who, as you know, is the professional working with the Advisory Committee on Intergovernmental Relations, he gave me some statistics, which to me were terribly depressing. There are one million retired people in this country who have incomes of less than $2,000 a year, and, who, on the average pay a property tax of 33-1/3 percent of that income.*

Now that is fiscally wrong, morally wrong, and certainly tax wrong. We must begin by lifting that burden from those people who have worked all their lives, are now retired on what is basically an inadequate amount and are paying one-third of their taxes (incomes) for property taxes to send, basically, children to school.

I have discussed this matter not only with Mr. Merriam, but Mr. Shultz and I have had, as you have noted, a number of meetings on this in the past few weeks. We hope to have a plan which we can present at an early date. I cannot indicate to you what that date will be, but I will say this: One, we are going to propose to the next Congress a plan that will relieve, what will start down the road of reducing the burden of property taxes.

The first priority will be to reduce the burden of property taxes on the elderly and second, whatever step we take, one condition is, it must not require any increase in other taxes. We think we have found a formula to do that.

Watergate Affair

Q: Mr. President, don't you think that your administration and the public would be served considerably and that the men under indictment would be treated better, if you people would come through and make a clean breast about what you were trying to get done at the Watergate?

THE PRESIDENT: One thing that has always puzzled me about it is why anybody would have tried to get anything out of the Watergate. Be that as it may, that decision having been made at a lower level, with which I had no knowledge, and, as I pointed out—

Q: Surely you know now, sir.

THE PRESIDENT: I certainly feel that under the circumstances that we have to look at what has happened and to put the matter into perspective.

Now when we talk about a clean breast, let's look at what has happened. The FBI has assigned 133 agents to this investigation. It followed out 1,800 leads. It conducted 1,500 interviews.

Incidentally, I conducted the investigation of the Hiss case. I know that is a very unpopular subject to raise in some quarters, but I conducted it. It was successful. The FBI did a magnificent job, but that investigation involving the security of this country, was basically a Sunday school exercise compared to the amount of effort that was put into this.

I agree with the amount of effort that was put into it. I wanted every lead carried out to the end because I wanted to be sure that no member of the White House staff and no man or woman in a position of major responsibility in the Committee for Re-election had anything to do with this kind of reprehensible activity.

Now, the grand jury has handed down indictments. It has indicted incidentally two who were with the Committee for Re-election and one who refused to cooperate and another who was apprehended. Under these circumstances, the grand jury now

having acted, it is now time to have the judicial process go forward and for the evidence to be presented.

I would say finally with regard to commenting on any of those who have been indicted, with regard to saying anything about the judicial process, I am going to follow the good advice, which I appreciate, of the members of the press corps, my constant, and I trust will always continue to be, very responsible critics.

I stepped into one on that when you recall I made inadvertently a comment in Denver about an individual who had been indicted in California, the Manson case. I was vigorously criticized for making any comment about the case, so of course, I know you would want me to follow the same single standard by not commenting on this case.

Campaign Tactics

Q: Mr. President, when are you going to begin intensive campaigning, and are you going to begin intensive campaigning?

THE PRESIDENT: I repeat, Mr. Warren, what I have said previously in San Clemente and at San Francisco. Until the Congress adjourns, my primary responsibility is to stay here and particularly to stay here to fight the battle against bigger spending that would lead to bigger taxes.

I have made a commitment, and I make it here again today. There will be no tax increase in 1973. However, there is one problem with that commitment. There will be no presidential tax increase. Now, we need the cooperation of the Congress, and there could be a congressional tax increase. If the Congress, for example, does not approve the $250-billion ceiling that we have requested, that is going to make the chances of avoiding a tax increase more difficult.

It does not make it impossible, however, because we have a second line of defense. If the Congress, as appears likely, continues to pass bills that substantially exceed the budget, which already is at the highest limits that our tax income will pay for, if the Congress continues to pass bills and send them to the President's desk that exceed that budget, the Congress will have voted for a tax increase. However, I still have one weapon left, that is the veto.

My own prediction is that after talking to our own leaders and after hearing from some responsible Democrats in the House and Senate, that even though the Congress will probably send to my desk in the next two or three weeks a number of bills that will substantially exceed the budget, and that would result in a congressional tax increase, I think my vetoes of those bills will be sustained and that will make it possible for me to keep my commitment for no tax increase.

That shows one of the reasons why it is important for me to stay on the job here in Washington until the Congress adjourns and until that very great danger of a tax increase caused by congressional overspending is met and defeated.

Now, once the Congress leaves, or once I see that danger passing, then I can make plans to go into various parts of the country. In the meantime, I am going to have to limit my travel, as I have indicated, to perhaps once a week, on a day that I see no significant problems that I need to attend to here, but I will not do more than that.

If I have to choose between engaging in all of the spectaculars of a campaign, which I have been doing virtually all my life, every two years for 25 years—if I have to choose between that and staying on the job and doing something that would result in avoiding a tax increase for the American people, I am going to stay right here on the job.

Q: Mr. President, to follow that up, if you can be a prognosticator, in 1968 you received 301 electoral votes. What do you see for yourself in 1972?

THE PRESIDENT: 301 was enough, wasn't it?

Q: True.

THE PRESIDENT: Our goal is to get as many as we can, electoral votes, and as many popular votes as we can. I know that the political questions have been discussed very broadly. I would

---

The 33-1/3 percent figure refers to low income retired persons in the Northeast. Nationwide, the average is about 16 percent of retiree's income.

take a moment on that and might refer to your question, too, but then you follow up if I don't answer.

The problem with a candidate who is ahead in the polls—of course, I like this kind of a problem better than being behind—but the problem of a candidate who is ahead in the polls, and his organization, is a very significant one in this respect: It is the problem of getting his vote out. What we need above everything else is a big vote. In order to get a big vote, it means that people have to be stimulated to vote. That is one of the reasons that going to the country and participating will help get that big vote out, and when the time permits, I will go to the country in order to get the vote out, among other things.

With the candidate who is behind substantially in the polls, he doesn't have that problem. With all the pollsters—and the pollsters always remember when they predicted right, but never when they predicted wrong—this doesn't prove anything necessarily, because when the margins are up in the 60-40 range, on the fringes it is always quite soft either way.

But in 1964 I was interested to find that Gallup never had Goldwater with more than 32 percent against Johnson. In fact, Gallup's poll, taken one week before the election, showed Goldwater at 32 percent. He got 39 percent. Why? The Goldwater people voted and many of the Johnson people thought they had it made.

We, of course, have the same problem. Of course, Johnson still won. Maybe we will. What I am simply suggesting is that as far as predictions are concerned, I have told all of our people, "Don't rely on the polls."

"Remember that the candidate who is behind will tend to get his vote out. Ours will tend not to get out. Get our vote out and try to win as big a popular vote as we can and as big an electoral vote as we can."

The purpose: Not to make the other candidates look bad, but the purpose is to get what I have described as the new American majority in which Republicans, Democrats, and Independents, join together in supporting not a party, or not an individual, but supporting the record of the past four years, the positions which are very clear-cut that I have taken on the great issues, and thereby giving us the opportunity to continue in those four years.

Press Conferences

Q: Mr. President, as election day comes closer, you have also been criticized for isolating yourself, not making yourself available for questioning.

Q: Hiding.

Q: Apart from going out and hitting the hustings, do you plan to have more press conferences between now and election day?

THE PRESIDENT: Well, I would plan to try to find ways to be available for purposes of presenting my position as I can. For example, on the matter of taxes, how we avoid a tax increase, I know that Mr. Ehrlichman has represented my views and Mr. Shultz, as have a number of others. I have tried to cover it here briefly this morning.

But at Camp David yesterday, I completed a speech that I had made on the subject and while I cannot get away this weekend, I am going to deliver it by nation-wide radio on Saturday night. So for the writing press, you will have time for the Sunday papers. That is only coincidental, of course.

Q: In light of the fact that because Congress has not adjourned, you cannot get out, why can't you accept us as a surrogate for the people you can't see and have more press conferences between now and November 7th?

THE PRESIDENT: If you would like to be a surrogate, we have plenty—

Q: We can ask the questions the public is asking.

THE PRESIDENT: Well, Mr. Potter, the press conference, to me is not basically a chore. When I say "a chore," it is always a challenge, and it is one that requires hard work. I recall, incidentally, in that connection, speaking of the press conference,

I think I have told you once when we were riding in the back of the plane, it was not as good as the one we have now, but you remember those days, we had very few good planes, a DC3. But I recall that we were talking about speech writing and how I hated to write speeches and I talked to Foster Dulles about it, after he returned from one of his many trips abroad and he always made a speech and I said, "Don't you hate to write speeches?"

He said, "Yes I used to. But," he said, "now I do it, I consider it necessary to go through the torture, because the writing of the speech disciplines my mind and makes me think through the issue."

I must say that preparation for the press conference helps to discipline my mind to talk about the issues. To come precisely now to your question, I think that the format of questions and answers, for members of the press, can be useful. Certainly I will consider the possibility of using that format. Maybe not just here, maybe in other places as well. But we wouldn't stack the questions.

Welfare Reform

Q: Mr. President, now that welfare reform appears to be dead, or at least going, on Capitol Hill, I am wondering, if after all this, you still support the principle implicit in HR 1 of the minimum income assistance for poor families and whether you would push for those principles in a second term?

THE PRESIDENT: The answer is yes to both questions. As far as welfare reform generally is concerned, the Senate has not completed its actions, its consideration. The problem with the Roth amendment, of the test, is that it lacks the trigger device and it means you would start all over again.

The one point I want to emphasize with regard to welfare reform, the program that we have presented for welfare reform, with its strong work requirements and with its assistance to the working poor, with the purpose of providing a bridge and an incentive for them to get off of welfare and to work, from a fiscal standpoint, stretches the budget as far as it can be stretched. We can't add anything to it.

And, from the standpoint of the amount to be provided, it goes as far as it should go, and I would oppose any program that would add more people to the welfare rolls, millions more, as would all three of the programs advocated by our opponents, whichever one you want to pick. I would oppose any program that would add more to the welfare rolls than HR 1.

What we need are programs that will move toward moving people off of welfare and not raising the ante so that people are encouraged to go on it.

So, I would take HR 1. I would very greatly strengthen the work requirements in it. If the Senate and the House, as appears possible now, not certain, I hope not certain, fail to act, we will grapple with it in the new term and try to get the support for it.

Anti-Busing Bill

Q: Mr. President, there is an anti-busing bill on the Senate calendar that I believe you support. Its passage is problematical, as I understand it. If it is not passed, I wonder if you would support the constitutional amendment?

THE PRESIDENT: I have indicated that, first, I am against busing. This is, of course, one of those clear-cut issues in this campaign. When people want to know what they are, I am against amnesty, I am against busing, I am against massive increases in spending that would require a tax increase. I am against cutting our defenses by $30-billion, which would make us second to the Soviet Union.

I am for the domestic proposals that I set forth in such great detail in the '72 State of the Union, and that, incidentally, Mr. Semple, was in it. I endorsed all of those. Those are part of the program for the future, health, government reorganization, welfare reform and the rest and we hope to have a Congress that will be more responsive in getting them through.

Now, the question of what to do about busing is now right in the Congress' lap. If the Congress fails to act in a way that provides some relief from these excessive busing orders that have caused racial strife, and primarily in northern cities as distinguished from southern cities, then I intend to find another way.

There are two ways we can go: With a new Congress, which might be very much more responsive on this issue after they have found out what people think in the hustings, with a new Congress we might get very quick action on the legislative front. That I would prefer.

If we cannot get Congress to act on the legislation front, then we would have to move on the constitutional amendment front.

I would point out that, however, the legislative front is preferable and also easier, and quicker, because it requires only a majority and not two-thirds and also can move quickly on the issue.

So, if we don't get it now, we will go for it as a matter of the highest priority in the First Session of the next Congress.

THE PRESS: Thank you, sir.

(Nixon Acceptance continued from p. 105-A)

the cemetery I saw the picture of a 12-year-old girl. She was a beautiful child. Her name was Tanya. I read her diary. It tells the terrible story of war. In the simple words of a child, she wrote of the deaths of the members of her family—Senya in December, Granny in January, then Yenka, then Uncle Basha, then Uncle Leosha, then Mama in May.

And finally these were the last words in her diary: "All are dead, only Tanya is left."

Let us think of Tanya and of the other Tanyas and their brothers and sisters everywhere in Russia and in China and in America as we proudly meet our responsibilities for leadership in the world in a way worthy of a great people.

I ask you, my fellow Americans, to join our new majority not just in the cause of winning an election but in achieving a hope that mankind has had since the beginning of civilization.

Let us build a peace that our children and all the children of the world can enjoy for generations to come.

INDEX TO PRESIDENTIAL TEXTS